Thomas Moran

The Field Sketches, 1856–1923

Thomas Moran

The Field Sketches, 1856–1923

By Anne Morand

With an Introduction by
Joan Carpenter Troccoli

Published by the
University of Oklahoma Press : Norman and London
for the Thomas Gilcrease Institute
of American History and Art : Tulsa

This project was made possible in part by grants from the National Endowment for the Arts, The Thomas Gilcrease Museum Association, the State Arts Council of Oklahoma, and the Maxine and Jack Zarrow Foundation.

Library of Congress Cataloging-in-Publication Data

Moran, Thomas, 1837–1926.
    Thomas Moran, the field sketches, 1856–1923 / Anne Morand ; introduction by Joan Carpenter Troccoli.
        p.   cm.
    Includes bibliographical references (p.   –   ) and index.
        ISBN 0-8061-2704-X
    1. Moran, Thomas, 1837–1926—Themes, motives—Catalogs.
N6537.M6443A4
I. Morand, Anne, 1951–   .   II. Title.
759.13—dc20   94-49719
                                    CIP

Text design by Cathy Carney Imboden. Text typeface is Old Style 7.

Thomas Moran: The Field Sketches, 1856–1923 is Volume 4 in The Gilcrease-Oklahoma Series on Western Art and Artists.

The paper in this book meets the guidelines for permanence and durability of the Committee on Production Guidelines for Book Longevity of the Council on Library Resources, Inc.

1 2 3 4 5 6 7 8 9 10

Contents

vii   List of Illustrations

xi   Preface
        By Anne Morand

3   Introduction
        By Joan Carpenter Troccoli

11   "The Artistic Side of the Trip":
        The Travels and Field Sketches of Thomas Moran
            By Anne Morand

101   Checklist of Field Sketches of Thomas Moran
        By Anne Morand and Norma Ewing

303   Bibliography

307   Index

Illustrations

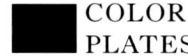

COLOR
PLATES

Following page 100

Plate 1. William Merritt Chase, *Portrait of Thomas Moran* (Gilcrease Institute, 0126.2338)

Plate 2. No. 1, *Bridge over the Schuylkill, Philadelphia* (Gilcrease Institute, 0226.798)

Plate 3. Thomas Moran, *Summer on the Susquehanna at Catawissa* (Gilcrease Institute, 0126.2335)

Plate 4. No. 64, *Hastings* (Gilcrease Institute, 0276.839)

Plate 5. No. 60, *Bexhill* (Gilcrease Institute, 0276.933)

Plate 6. No. 63, *Hastings* (Gilcrease Institute, 0276.838)

Plate 7. No. 61, *Hastings* (Gilcrease Institute, 0276.841)

Plate 8. No. 65, *Hastings* (Gilcrease Institute, 0276.935)

Plate 9. Thomas Moran, *The Yellowstone Range from near Fort Ellis* (Gilcrease Institute, 0226.1358)

Plate 10. No. 81, *Johnstown* (Gilcrease Institute, 0226.795)

Plate 11. No. 85, *Conemaugh at Bolivar* (Gilcrease Institute, 0226.794)

Plate 12. No. 93, *Spruce Creek, Pennsylvania* (Gilcrease Institute, 0226.942)

Plate 13. Thomas Moran, *Upper Falls of the Yellowstone* (Gilcrease Institute, 0226.1451)

Plate 14. No. 154, *Colosseum, Rome* (Gilcrease Institute, 0276.863)

Plate 15. No. 155, *Ruins of the Palace of the Caesars, Rome* (Gilcrease Institute, 0276.864)

Plate 16. No. 156, *Palace of the Caesars, Rome* (Gilcrease Institute, 0276.941)

Plate 17. No. 202, *First Sketch Made in the West at Green River, Wyoming* (Gilcrease Institute, 0236.882)

Plate 18. No. 230, *In Lower Madison Canyon* (Gilcrease Institute, 0236.1576)

Plate 19. No. 274, *In the Narrows, Zion Valley, the Gate Keeper* (Gilcrease Institute, 0236.878)

Plate 20. No. 304, *Third Lake, Madison, Wisconsin* (Gilcrease Institute, 0226.939)

Plate 21. No. 336, *Fort George Island* (Gilcrease Institute, 0226.792)

Plate 22. No. 349, *Near Feltville, New Jersey* (Gilcrease Institute, 0226.789)

Plate 23. No. 392, *Tahoe* (Gilcrease Institute, 0236.886)

Plate 24. No. 393, *Lake Tahoe* (Gilcrease Institute, 0236.881)

Plate 25. No. 407, *Near the Summit of Cottonwood Canyon* (Gilcrease Institute, 0236.890)

Plate 26. No. 403, *In Little Cottonwood Canyon* (Gilcrease Institute, 0236.887)

Plate 27. No. 411, *American Fork Canyon* (Gilcrease Institute, 0236.888)

Plate 28. No. 406, *Upper End of Cottonwood Canyon* (Gilcrease Institute, 0236.884)

Plate 29. No. 408, *Toledo Mine, Cottonwood Canyon, Utah* (Gilcrease Institute, 0236.889)

Plate 30. No. 412, *Portneuf Canyon, Idaho* (Gilcrease Institute, 0236.855)

Plate 31. No. 415, *Iowa Gulch, Idaho* (Gilcrease Institute, 0236.892)

Plate 32. No. 436, *Green River Buttes, Wyoming* (Gilcrease Institute, 0236.885)

Plate 33. No. 439, *Cliffs of Green River, Wyoming* (Gilcrease Institute, 0236.930)

Plate 34. No. 431, *Green River* (Gilcrease Institute, 0236.891)

Plate 35. No. 568, *Garden of the Gods* (Gilcrease Institute, 0236.844)

Plate 36. No. 573, *San Juan, New Mexico* (Gilcrease Institute, 0236.843)

Plate 37. No. 572, *Ojo Caliente* (Gilcrease Institute, 0236.845)

Plate 38. No. 570, *Heywood Hot Springs* (Gilcrease Institute, 0236.846)

Plate 39. No. 569, *Glen Eyrie* (Gilcrease Institute, 0236.781)

Plate 40. No. 586, *Green River* (Gilcrease Institute, 0236.898)

Plate 41. Thomas Moran, *Pass at Glencoe, Scotland* (Gilcrease Institute, 0226.1636)

Plate 42. No. 604, *Conway, North Wales* (Gilcrease Institute, 0276.803)

Plate 43. No. 606, *Conway Castle* (Gilcrease Institute, 0276.804)

Plate 44. No. 618, *Harlech Castle, North Wales* (Gilcrease Institute, 0276.938)

Plate 45. No. 611, *Afon Wen, North Wales, Cardigan Bay* (Gilcrease Institute, 0276.805)

Plate 46. No. 612, *Criccieth Castle, Cardigan Bay, North Wales* (Gilcrease Institute, 0276.806)

Plate 47. No. 627, *Havana* (Gilcrease Institute, 0296.825)

Plate 48. No. 629, *Havana* (Gilcrease Institute, 0296.807)

Plate 49. No. 630, *Sunset, Gulf of Mexico* (Gilcrease Institute, 0296.814)

Plate 50. No. 632, *San Juan d'Ulloa, Vera Cruz* (Gilcrease Institute, 0246.826)

Plate 51. No. 631, *Vera Cruz* (Gilcrease Institute, 0246.815)

Plate 52. No. 644, *The Peak of Orizaba from Esperanza* (Gilcrease Institute, 0246.827)

Plate 53. No. 649, *Mexico* (Gilcrease Institute, 0246.813)

Plate 54. No. 653, *Maravatio* (Gilcrease Institute, 0246.809)

Plate 55. No. 654, *Sunday Morning, Maravatio* (Gilcrease Institute, 0246.812)

Plate 56. No. 663, *Maravatio* (Gilcrease Institute, 0246.811)

Plate 57. No. 655, *From Acambaro, West* (Gilcrease Institute, 0246.821)

Plate 58. No. 642, *Near Vera Cruz* (Gilcrease Institute, 0246.810)

Plate 59. No. 665, *San José, Beyond Maravatio* (Gilcrease Institute, 0246.822)

Plate 60. No. 667, *Morelia, Mexico* (Gilcrease Institute, 0246.824)

Plate 61. No. 674, *Ravine near the Trojes Mine, Mexico* (Gilcrease Institute, 0246.823)

Plate 62. No. 683, *On the Plateau above Dolores* (Gilcrease Institute, 0246.816)

Plate 63. No. 680, *Calderon, Mexico* (Gilcrease Institute, 0246.808)

Plate 64. No. 691, *Ojo de Agua, Saltillo* (Gilcrease Institute, 0246.818)

Plate 65. No. 699, *Monterrey, from the Hotel Roof* (Gilcrease Institute, 0246.819)

Plate 66. Thomas Moran, *Vera Cruz* (Gilcrease Institute, 0126.1109)

Plate 67. Thomas Moran, *Fiesta at Cuernavaca* (Gilcrease Institute, 0127.1110)

Plate 68. No. 704, *Gardiner Bay* (Gilcrease Institute, 0226.936)

Plate 69. Thomas Moran, *Spectres from the North* (Gilcrease Institute, 0126.2340)

Plate 70. No. 793, *Picture of Sails from Chioggia* (Gilcrease Institute, 0276.832)

Plate 71. No. 777, *Murano* (Gilcrease Institute, 0276.766)

Plate 72. No. 790, *Venice* (Gilcrease Institute, 0276.765)

Plate 73. No. 791, *Venice from Malamocco* (Gilcrease Institute, 0276.833)

Plate 74. No. 800, *The Grand Canyon of the Colorado* (Gilcrease Institute, 0236.931)

Plate 75. No. 836, *Index Peak* (Gilcrease Institute, 0236.850)

Plate 76. No. 837, *Index Peak* (Gilcrease Institute, 0236.849)

Plate 77. No. 845, *Upper Basins* (Gilcrease Institute, 0236.831)

Plate 78. No. 877, *Lower Geyser Basin* (Gilcrease Institute, 0236.829)

Plate 79. No. 898, *Moran Point, Yellowstone Canyon* (Gilcrease Institute, 0236.830)

Plate 80. No. 928, *Blue Lakes, Idaho* (Gilcrease Institute, 0237.1578)

Plate 81. Louis Prang after Thomas Moran, *The Great Falls of Snake River, Idaho Territory* (Gilcrease Institute, 2426.47.13)

Plate 82. Thomas Moran, *Shoshone Falls on the Snake River* (Gilcrease Institute, 0126.2339)

■ BLACK-AND-WHITE ILLUSTRATIONS

Napoleon Sarony, *Portrait of Thomas Moran* (Gilcrease Institute, 4326.6126)   12

Thomas Moran, *Death of Pan-Puk-Keewis* (Gilcrease Institute, 0226.904)   14

John Moran after Thomas Moran, *The Wissahickon* (Gilcrease Institute, 4316.7845)   18

Thomas Moran, *The Mud Volcano* (Gilcrease Institute, 0226.1694)   36

William H. Jackson, *Mammoth Hot Springs* (Gilcrease Institute, 4536.84.9)   37

William H. Jackson, *Yellowstone Lake* (Gilcrease Institute, 4336.84.29)   37

William H. Jackson, *Minerva Terrace* (Gilcrease Institute, 4337.7913)   79

Note: In the Checklist of Field Sketches, an asterisk preceding an item indicates a sketch reproduced in color in the text; a dagger preceding an item indicates a sketch reproduced larger in black-and-white in the text.

Preface

This catalogue of the field sketches of Thomas Moran is the second volume to consider the artist's work represented in the collection of the Thomas Gilcrease Institute of American History and Art, following *The Prints of Thomas Moran.* It is, therefore, a handbook to the Gilcrease collection of sketches, which represents about 75 percent of Moran's extant fieldwork.

Most of the remainder of the fieldwork resides in several public collections, gifts of Moran and his younger daughter to the National Park Service, to departments of the Smithsonian Institution, and to the library in East Hampton, New York. Because these sketches record significant aspects of the artist's travel and work, the catalogue has been expanded to include them.

Although these 1,080 sketches, made between 1856 and 1923, provide the opportunity to examine the greater part of Moran's oeuvre in the field, this volume is not a catalogue raisonné. Most of these sketches, including all those in the Gilcrease collection, are illustrated in the checklist. Many, reproduced in color or in black-and-white, are used to illustrate the text.

With the exception of Thomas S. Fern's catalogue, *The Drawings and Watercolors of Thomas Moran, 1837–1926,* most past discussions of Moran's field sketches have been brief in studies dealing with the artist's entire career. This catalogue presents a chronological, illustrated checklist that will inform the art public of the significance and breadth of Moran's sketch production. It may also serve to inspire further research into Moran's immediate response to his surroundings. The essay accompanying the checklist illuminates the complexity and range of that response, with respect to both medium and execution.

Earlier works on Moran provide a great deal of information regarding his life and career in general, making it unnecessary to discuss such matters in detail in this study. Thurman Wilkins's enduring biography, *Thomas Moran: Artist of the Mountains,* originally published in 1966, and Joni L. Kinsey's *Thomas Moran and the Surveying of the American West,* published in 1992, represent perhaps the best early and recent scholarship on Moran.

———————◆———————

There are many people whose assistance enabled this project to come to fruition. First, I thank Norma Ewing, with whom I developed the catalogue. Her interest in Moran, insights into the artist and his work, superb organizational and photographic skills, and attention to detail contributed immeasurably to the success of the project.

As always, the Gilcrease staff have offered great support and assistance. Director Joan Troccoli, whose participation in this project began even before she became director, edited the manuscript and wrote the introduction. The curator of archival collections, Sarah Erwin, in whose happy charge the Moran archives rest, was endlessly resourceful in aiding the research. Museum photographer Shane Culpepper cheerfully took on the daunting job of making the Gilcrease images for this book, which he did with care and distinction.

The Gilcrease Institute is blessed with an active and able volunteer group, several members of which played important roles in the completion of this project. I am particularly grateful to several volunteers who came to love working with the Moran collection as much as I did: Nancy Apgar, Ursula Ekren, Betty Feldner, Hubert Noble, Pat Peters, Nieta Powell, Pam Proctor, and Shirley Schelper. Two college interns also were valuable assets, Adriane Bell and Michele Raine.

Thanks to the generosity of the National Endowment for the Arts, Norma Ewing and I were able to travel to several of the important collections of Moran material. I thank the staff members with whom we worked, for their courtesy in allowing us access to their information and objects: in St. Louis, at the Jefferson National Expansion Memorial, Kathryn Thomas, curator of cultural resources, and Kathleen Moenster, curatorial assistant; in Washington, at the National Museum of American Art, Abbey Terrones, collections manager for graphic arts, and Martina Norelli, associate curator for graphic arts; in Boston, at the Museum of Fine Arts, Clifford Ackley, curator of prints, drawings, and photographs, and Edith Schmidt; in Washington, at the Corcoran Gallery of Art, Linda Crocker Simmons, associate curator of collections for prints and drawings; at Yosemite National Park, David Forgang, curator, and Barbara Beroza, collections manager; at the East Hampton Library, Dorothy King; at the Guild Hall, East Hampton, Helen Harrison; in New York, at the Cooper-Hewitt Museum, Gayle Davidson, assistant curator for drawings and prints; at Grand Teton National Park, John Daugherty, supervisory park ranger, and C. J. Brafford, curator; and in Philadelphia, at the Library Company, Ken Finkel, curator of prints, drawings, and photographs.

Several people generously offered information useful in identifying sites: Carl Schrier, at Yellowstone National Park; James C. Woods, director of the Herrett Museum, College of Southern Idaho; Peter Boag, assistant professor of history, Idaho State University; Mark Nelson, curator of Sweetwater County Historical Museum, Green River, Wyoming; Earle G. Shettleworth, Jr., director, and Kirk F. Mohney, architectural historian, Maine Historical Preservation Commission, Augusta.

I would also like to thank several longtime Gilcrease advocates whose encouragement helped to make this project a reality: Nancy Friese, Mickey Mishne, Len and Alice Pakman, Mel and Betty Peterson, and Jack and Maxine Zarrow. Mildred Thompson Ladner graciously read this manuscript, and John Drayton, editor-in-chief of the University of Oklahoma Press, gave support and courtesy that have been much appreciated.

ANNE MORAND

Thomas Moran

The Field Sketches, 1856–1923

Introduction

Joan Carpenter Troccoli

Of the more than two thousand works by Thomas Moran purchased by Thomas Gilcrease from the artist's daughter Ruth in 1948, nearly seven hundred are field sketches. One of them is inscribed "First Sketch Made in the West at Green River, Wyoming": testimony to the fundamental importance of these drawings and watercolors, the largest single group of Moran's fieldworks. Every sketch technique Moran employed and virtually every subject he depicted are represented in this collection. No serious formal study of Moran's work can be made without reference to it.

Moran's sketches document the travels in Europe and North America that were essential to his development as an artist as well as the source of the subjects that ensured his ultimate success as a landscapist. The sketches provide important insights into his creative process and the variations it sustained over a career that spanned seventy years. And, in their own right, they appeal to the contemporary taste for pre-liminary and unfinished works, satisfying our fascination with the myriad forms an artist's preparatory material can take. Their range encompasses summary contour drawings of the spectacular topography of the American West, luminous watercolors that simultaneously fix local color and evoke the artist's rapturous response to the natural world, and fully realized works that nevertheless preserve the intensity of Moran's firsthand experience of his plein air subjects.

In view of its importance to Moran studies, this catalogue is long overdue. Its creation was no easy affair. In tackling the formidable task of identifying subjects and establishing chronologies, Anne Morand may have been less aided than obstructed by the artist himself. Moran inscribed dates and occasionally locations on many of his sketches years after their execution. Not surprisingly, his memory was sometimes inaccurate. Matters of chronology are further complicated by Moran's adherence to a personal version of artistic decorum, the venerable academic tradition of matching style to subject. In the field even more than in the studio, Moran used a variety of styles and techniques chosen to suit the landscape at hand. As the artist's many errors in dating confirm, this practice, which is at the heart of his personality as a painter, made ordering his work almost as difficult for him as it is for us.

Moran was protean in the field. Just as he was at his best when painting nature in states of change—the unstable volcanic landscapes of Yellowstone, for example—his image making is characterized by an almost metamorphic variability. Although Moran's steadily increasing mastery and consequent economy of technique is obvious, no simple linear account of stylistic development can be constructed from an examination of the mass of his field sketches. Moran could switch techniques almost from one moment to the next—or, to be more accurate, from one subject to the next. Pure contour drawings with a bare-bones, even crystalline, effect alternate in his oeuvre with sheets loaded with graphite. Compositions may be claustrophobic or cosmic, execution hasty or meticulous. Moran's use of colored papers and a variety of watercolor techniques adds yet another wide spectrum of effects to his sketches.

Like many other nineteenth-century American painters, Moran devised his own artistic education. His fieldworks throw valuable light on the eclectic curriculum he set himself. A great strength of the Gilcrease collection is the extensive chronicle in sketch form that it provides of the beginnings, progress, and maturity of one of the greatest autodidacts in the history of American art.

Moran's earliest works show signs of the reliance on a catalogue of artistic techniques that became so important to his later practice. He began his career in Philadelphia as a follower of the doctrine of "truth to nature" preached by the English critic John Ruskin and the American painter Asher Brown Durand. The discipline as a draftsman instilled in Moran during his apprenticeship to a wood engraver prepared him to follow their exacting lead. From the outset of his career, however, Moran's own, very Victorian

work ethic was oriented to overall productivity rather than to the laborious execution of individual works. The painstaking depiction of humble aspects of the landscape, as in *Crescentville* (No. 4), coexisted in his sketches of the 1850s with a more generalized approach to view making that he may have absorbed from drawing manuals as well as from the formulaic works of such early Philadelphia landscapists as Thomas Birch, Thomas Doughty, and Joshua Shaw. Moran's *Bridge over the Schuylkill, Philadelphia* (No. 1; see Plate 2), for example, with its picturesque deployment of the neoclassical structures in Fairmount Park, proves that the eighteenth-century British topographical tradition furnished a viable and elegant, if old-fashioned, mode of landscape depiction in America as late as 1856.

This alternation of the closely observed and the broadly conceived was also characteristic of the fieldwork Moran produced during his first wilderness trip to Lake Superior in 1860. In his initial encounter with an American landscape that qualifies as natural spectacle, Moran proved himself to be a conscientious, if tentative, artistic geologist in the Ruskinian mode. He executed *At Miners River, Pictured Rocks, Lake Superior* (No. 12), a busy patchwork of graphite, with the fastidiousness of the earnest beginner. Variations in tone among the trees and undergrowth on a rocky ledge are so carefully registered that the image seems to ripple; formal elements appear to project forward from the shallow space of the drawing as if it were a bas-relief. Moran's painstaking effort is less visible in other sketches of the scenery of Michigan's Upper Peninsula. Although his pencil marks in *Entrance to the Great Cave, Pictured Rocks* (No. 16) and *The Great Cave, Pictured Rocks from the East* (No. 17) lack assurance, they anticipate his future work in the American West. Moran's reduction of the rocky landscape to sometimes indecisive curved and jagged contours, his rejection of conventional means of representing space and volume, and his jotting of color notes forecast things to come. A decade later, Moran would be able to convey far more with just as little, or even less.

In the mid-1860s, Moran's picturesque approach persisted in such views as *The Juniata at Mill Creek* (No. 100) and the exquisite *On the Conemaugh below Lockport* (No. 83). But he simultaneously produced a far more modern series of drawings, works that are strongly reminiscent of Durand's closely observed paintings of rocks in forest settings. Like the other woodland interiors Moran sketched in rural Pennsylvania, *Sawkill* (No. 116) represents very few landscape elements whole, although the composition is worked out to the edges of the paper. Borrowing a printer's term, one might describe this dense image as a detail from a larger scene that bleeds off the page. Such sketches, with their multiple cutoffs, may at first seem to be casual, even random, glimpses of the forest, but they are anything but relaxed in feeling. In this series Moran consistently focused on the trunks of great canting trees, on extravagant patterns of arching branches and twisted roots, and on rugged boulders bordering flowing waters. These sketches of wilderness motifs possessed of distinctive, almost animate, character presage the energy of Moran's western paintings, different as they are in subject and style. At the same time, they inevitably bring to mind Thomas Cole's description in his "Essay on American Scenery" (1836) of the "green umbrageous masses—lofty and scathed trunks—contorted branches thrust athwart the sky—the mouldering dead below, shrouded in moss of every hue and texture" of the "primitive" American forest. Such trees, "wild and uncultivated, battling with the elements and with one another for the possession of a morsel of soil, or a favoring rock to which they may cling—they exhibit striking peculiarities, and sometimes grand originality."[1]

The Pennsylvania sketches mark a technical advance over Moran's Lake Superior work that must be credited in large part to his first journey abroad. His trips to England in 1862 and to Great Britain and the Continent in 1866–67 were crucial to his future course as an artist.

For those who equate Moran with the American West, his European sketches will be a revelation, both in quality and in stylistic range. Moran's copying sessions in museums and his pilgrimages to sites depicted by old and modern masters honed his representational skills and fueled his sometimes overwhelming eclecticism. The European field sketches document the flowering of Moran's lifelong habit of depicting—even, perhaps, seeing—landscapes in the manner of his predecessors. He pays homage to Turner, whose work he studied in the National Gallery before retracing his steps throughout southeastern England, in his sketches of Margate and Richmond as well as of St. Gotthard's Pass in the Alps. He later gave similar tribute to the English master in his finished pictures of the mountains and canyons of the West, not to mention his views of Venice and Vera Cruz. Moran's drawings and paintings of eastern Long Island's dunes and wooded marshlands, as well as his surprisingly bucolic sketches of industrial buildings set among the meadows of nineteenth-century Newark, look back to the work of the seventeenth-century Dutch landscapists he copied as well as to John Constable's depictions of his native Stour Valley.[2] Constable's spirit also inheres in Moran's oil pictures of sunny Mexican villages framed by verdant copses; when Moran painted the same villages enveloped in morning mists, he made near counterfeits of the late pastoral idylls of Jean-Baptiste Camille Corot. The eclecticism of Moran's field and studio work, along with the technical virtuosity that allowed him to achieve it, is perhaps the most salient aspect of his oeuvre. It can be attributed to the poverty of Moran's formal training and perhaps to a misunderstanding of the academy's encouragement to emulate past masters, but it is also true that the nineteenth century was an eclectic age. Moran's artistic hero J.M.W. Turner was himself a practitioner of several styles during the early decades of the century, the period of his career that Moran most admired.[3]

Moran's sketches of Rome and the Campagna of 1867 are perhaps the most remarkable of all his European works. Here, undoubtedly mindful of the precedents set by illustrious predecessors such as Claude, Turner, Corot, and Thomas Cole, Moran nevertheless achieved an original expression, precisely because he rejected their arcadian vision in favor of a brooding, vaguely disturbing view. Even one of the tiniest of Moran's watercolors of ancient Roman landmarks, *Colosseum, Rome* (No. 154; see Plate 14), is unsettling. Black-robed figures stroll among the ruins, rendered in a loose wet-on-wet technique that muddles architectural detail. Columns, arches, and friezes drift in and out of focus as if seen in a dream. This is not a city in decay, but one that literally dissolves before our eyes. Moran's two most elaborate Roman sketches, *Ruins of the Palace of the Caesars, Rome* (No. 155; see Plate 15) and *Palace of the Caesars, Rome* (No. 156; see Plate 16), have a haunted look. He rendered these great breathing masses of masonry, their strangely organic quality reinforced by the vegetation they support, in a combination of very free and precise graphite strokes. The golden light of Italy is entirely missing here, and Moran's red and green washes create little of the optical vitality to be expected from this alternation of complementaries because the color is muted by his heavy graphite underdrawing. These works are almost expressionistic, as if the artist had been emotionally affected by the gaping Piranesian ruins; the white gouache in the sky of *Palace of the Caesars, Rome* is more suggestive of ghostly emanations than of clouds.

In 1871 Moran made a trip to the Yellowstone country of Wyoming and Montana that became the turning point of his career. He was a restless seeker after fresh experience, and Yellowstone's startling landscapes gave him an untouched subject in which innovation could be married to eclecticism. Although one might discern a conceptual parallel between the Colosseum and the wilderness landmarks of the Far West, which America's cultural nationalists promoted as natural equivalents of Europe's historical monuments, Moran's depictions of them differ widely. In Moran's view, the Campagna is a spooky, depopulated landscape scattered with rather grotesque ruins. *First Sketch Made in the West at Green River, Wyoming* (No. 202; see Plate 17), although no less lonely and strange, is luminous rather than gloomy. Its high-keyed

color scheme of white, blue, warm tan, and rosy pink suggests the ecstasy of the explorer's first glimpse of an unexpected new world, rather than the melancholy of the tourist wandering among the broken remains of an extinct civilization. Like many of Moran's western field watercolors, the small *First Sketch Made in the West* is distinguished by a brilliant, buoyant sky. Moran's skies are often brightest at the point where they touch the horizon; they seem to billow up from the earth like great translucent balloons of silvery sunlight.

Moran is closely associated with America's first national parks, especially Yellowstone, and with the promotion of other tourist destinations in the West. This, along with his production of monumentally scaled canvases that are the apotheosis of the wilderness sublime, has engaged a late twentieth-century audience enamored of environmentalism and uneasy about the capitalist motives that drove western expansion.[4] At Yellowstone and Yosemite, and also in such less well-known locales as the Rangeley Lakes of southwestern Maine and the mining regions of south-central Mexico, Moran often worked hand in hand with the burgeoning nineteenth-century rail and tourist industries.

Considering their contribution to his commercial, popular, and critical success, Moran's field sketches of these landscapes are often surprisingly minimal. Nathaniel Langford, in an article illustrated by Moran, described Yellowstone as a region "illimitable in resource, grand in extent, wonderful in variety, in a climate favored of Heaven, and amid scenery the most stupendous on the continent."[5] Yet Moran rendered this landscape with a few lines of graphite and an occasional wash of color. An exception is *In Lower Madison Canyon* (No. 230; see Plate 18), a field watercolor of unusual delicacy. Moran detailed the rocky canyon walls with fine strokes and sharp-edged patches of wash in subtle tones of gray and gold and used white gouache sparingly for highlights. By and large, however, Moran's early interest in close, quasi-scientific investigation of nature, reflected in his Lake Superior and Pennsylvania woodland sketches of the 1860s, seems to have faded by the early 1870s. Perhaps the representational shortcuts and suavity of execution he had picked up from his studies in Europe had supplanted the self-taught artist's compulsion to set down every detail. At any rate, the awkward hesitation of Moran's pencil in his Lake Superior sketches was replaced by a breadth of conception and a confident sweep of hand completely in tune with the expansive prospects of the West.

Although some fine watercolors are among them, most of the Yellowstone sketches that Moran gave to the National Park Service and the Cooper Union (today the Cooper-Hewitt Museum, the Smithsonian Institution's National Museum of Design) are little more than concise topographical profiles. Such brevity probably is not just the result of the challenges to art making posed by travel through difficult territory. It may also stem in part from Moran's confidence that the photographs of William Henry Jackson, who accompanied the same 1871 expedition into Yellowstone, would provide him with detailed aides-mémoire. After all, Jackson set up his cumbersome equipment and carried out the arduous process of preparing, exposing, and developing his glass plates in vertiginous terrain— and Moran found time to help him.[6]

Moran undoubtedly appreciated the way the camera handily reduces to two dimensions the complications presented by the real, three-dimensional world. The camera, in fact, was part of his artistic kit almost from the beginning of his career; he explored the Pennsylvania countryside with his photographer brother John in the 1860s. The compositional naïveté of the camera's all-inclusive eye may have influenced the slice-of-life framing of his woodland interiors, at once so crowded and fragmented, as well as their organization into distinct areas of light and dark tone. Later, in the West, Moran used the photographs of Jackson, John K. Hillers, and Timothy O'Sullivan to relieve himself of the tedium of setting down the details as well as the overall disposition of the landscape. It is worth remarking that Moran's notations on his sketches are about color and fleeting meteorological conditions—exactly those things which the camera could not record.

From the early 1870s on, Moran's fieldwork became increasingly synoptic. A comparison of his drawing of rocky cliffs at Hastings of 1862 and some of his sketches of the Fontainebleau Forest from 1867, with their near photographic illusionism, to his western fieldwork of the succeeding decades shows how far Moran had traveled from his provincial Pre-Raphaelitism. Moran once declared that "[Emile] Zola's definition of art exactly fills my demands when he said, 'Art is nature seen through a temperament.'"[7] He thereby gave fervent voice to his belief in the supremacy of the artist as magisterial interpreter rather than patient recorder of nature—a sentiment that he may have originally absorbed from Ruskin, who always accorded imaginative expression first place among artistic ideals.[8] Moran imposed an artistic vision on almost every landscape he saw. At times one wonders if Moran's love of nature even came close to his love of making art, which he did almost without cease. His daughter Ruth reported, "From the beginning to the end of his long life, my father was a dreamer and a painter of dreams. He would forget everything except his painting."[9]

Moran's field sketches are a copious reminder that the successful exercise of his imagination required a consummate control of artistic technique. His mastery of atmospheric effect and seemingly easy command of the medium in his finished paintings and watercolors correspond to a brevity and fluency in his fieldwork that increased as he matured. Throughout his career, the prolific Moran was inclined to experiment with shortcuts to the development of effective imagery. His study of Constable, Corot, and above all Turner was not a deep exploration of the philosophies behind their painting but a search for helpful skills he could use to compress the interval between his visualization of a scene and its physical realization.

As Moran's field sketches became more summary, they became, in an equal measure, more evocative. They limpidly suggest the infinite spaces of the West by more direct, yet still poetic, means than many of his finished works, tricked out as they are with obscuring mists, splashes of brilliant white, and discrete patches of detail. His pencil strokes in panoramic views, such as *Cliffs of Green River, Wyoming* (No. 437) and *Blue Lakes, Idaho* (No. 928; see Plate 80), are as incisive as they are economical. In the latter work Moran honed in on a particularly engaging aspect of the landscape without concern for the overall cohesion of his composition. He layered blue, green, and rust watercolor over the radically foreshortened Alfius Creek, creating an ellipse of shimmering emerald that is not so much the focal point of the image as a stunning intruder in a matter-of-fact topographical account. Moran achieved a kind of apotheosis of economical expression in his sketches of the Grand Canyon of the Colorado of the early 1900s. A half-century of growth in his confidence and skill as a draftsman separates his Lake Superior sketches of 1860 from *Looking West, Bright Angel* (No. 1022) of 1905. The hesitant, stop-and-start draftsmanship of the young Moran's Lake Superior work contrasts almost painfully with the light, continuous flow of graphite across the pages of the Grand Canyon sketchbook he filled in his maturity. It is as if Moran drew this often recorded site less for documentary purposes than for the sheer joy of moving his hand over the sheet in a purposeful way. In *Looking West, Bright Angel,* as in *Hermit Chasm, Grand Canyon* (No. 1021) with its graphite smudges signifying mist clinging to the plateaus, the most powerful of nature's works are rendered in tracery of the sheerest fragility. In another sketch of the Grand Canyon (No. 1023), we may even discover a classic "old age" style. At first glance we see nothing but chaos; this is no aid for the explorer or evening's entertainment for the armchair tourist. Topography has been transformed into pure energy, and drawing has been reduced to its essentials. In his neglect of even the most rudimentary niceties of finish, we may detect a diminution of Moran's physical capacity, but his powers of expression were as strong as ever.

The virtuoso economy of Moran's field watercolors is at times breathtaking. As early as 1873, he used zigzags of wash to represent currents and reflections in *Eddy on Rangeley Stream* (No. 251), a sketch in which masterful abbreviation makes us see much more than is actually on the paper. Moran's seductive views of Mexico, such as *Morelia, Mexico* (No. 667; see Plate 60), do not descend from the "tinted drawings" of eighteenth-century British topographical artists. Rather, they fall into a grand colorist tradition of exotic landscape, more associated with the Orient than the American West, that includes Delacroix's watercolors of Morocco and Edward Lear's sketches of India. Wielding his brush with enviable dexterity, Moran divided *Morelia, Mexico* into bands of prismatic color: gold and tan across the foreground plain, green in the parklike town, and blue and lavender at the mountainous horizon. He integrated his gray paper flecked with blue into volumes and voids, enlivening the image's surface and unifying its three distinct zones of color and terrain.

If *Morelia, Mexico* recalls Delacroix, *Eddy on Rangeley Stream* brings to mind, in both its subject and its masterfully summary execution, Winslow Homer's watercolors of sportsmen in the Adirondacks. Moran's later field watercolors, in contrast to the works he carefully lined and stippled with gouache in his studio, approach Homer in their freedom of brushwork and transparency of medium. Although Moran's use of colored, rather than white, paper diminished the luminosity of his colors and forced him to resort to gouache for his highest lights, these sketches qualify him for membership in America's most progressive watercolor school of the late nineteenth century.

Like Homer, Moran achieved the effects possible in watercolor when the artist both liberates and imposes discipline on the capricious medium. He let blooms and plumes of liquid color form scrubby trees and their reflections in the foreground of *Portneuf Canyon, Idaho* (No. 412; see Plate 30). In the middle ground of this mysterious, enchanted scene is a butte washed in a narrow but rich spectrum of color that progresses from brown and blue to gold and brick red before modulating back to blue. Moran also shared with Homer a willingness to experiment with a variety of techniques. He dragged a nearly dry brush across the foreground of *San Juan, New Mexico* (No. 573; see Plate 36) to represent reeds and blades of tall grass. Elsewhere in the sketch, there is much pooling of color. Little drops of green deposited by the tip of the brush stand for the leaves of the tree in the upper right corner. The sky is defined not by conventional cloud forms but by variations in the amount of pigment used and the direction of the flow of color.

Such works are marvels of artistic practice. The aesthetic pleasure they give is due in large part to our admiration for Moran's subtle exploitation of his technical powers and his sure sense of design. In *Picture of Sails from Chioggia* (No. 793; see Plate 70), Moran superimposed studies of the heraldically decorated lateen sails of Venetian feluccas upon two fragmentary cityscapes and a sketch of a boat's prow. Boats skim across the lagoon in the lower image; the disconnected sails, banners of intoxicating color, float free above them. Like Moran's sketch of a very different subject, *Green River Buttes, Wyoming* (No. 436; see Plate 32), *Picture of Sails from Chioggia* is a composition of eccentric shapes and hot and cold colors—the hue Moran called "Salmon red" played off against icy blue and white—that can be appreciated for its purely pictorial qualities alone.

Moran seldom based a finished work directly on a field sketch. In this he differed from Albert Bierstadt, whose paintings represent a sorting and recombination of the motifs recorded in his plein air oil sketches. Moran instead used his work in the field to initiate a process of parallel creation in which invention and improvisation played an integral role. Moran's blot drawings in the tradition of Alexander Cozens and his later "metamorphoses"—the photographic reproductions that he cut from newspapers and transformed, with pencil and eraser and occasionally gouache, from, say, fashion plates to mountainscapes—epitomize his dedication to the free play of the imagination.

His devotion to imagination may have affected his decision to create increasingly elliptical, and therefore uninhibiting, fieldwork as well.

Many scholars have cited Moran's famous visual memory as an explanation for the abbreviation of his later fieldwork. The part it played in his work marks a significant point in American art history, where Cole's comment that "I must wait for Time to draw a veil over the common details, the unessential parts, which shall leave the great features [of the landscape] . . . dominant in the mind" intersects with Symbolism.[10] Moran's memory was geared not to topography but to emotional experience; in this he is close to George Inness. Moran's field sketches served to trigger his recall of his presence at a place rather than to record hard facts. Those who praise Moran's western work for its "accuracy"—or suggest that his adjustments of the landscape to fit his artistic vision were less than honest—misunderstand the artist's ambition.

In a famous statement of 1879, Moran declared, "I place no value upon literal transcripts from Nature. My general scope is not realistic; all my tendencies are toward idealization. Of course, all art must come through Nature; I do not mean to depreciate Nature or naturalism; but I believe that a place, as a place, has . . . value in itself for the artist only so far as it furnishes the material from which to construct a picture. Topography in art is valueless."[11]

Moran aspired to wed objective vision to imagination, a loftier goal than the mere accumulation of fact represented by cartographic or geological documentation. He would have agreed with Ruskin that "all mathematical, and arithmetical, and generally scientific truth, is . . . truth of the husk and surface, hard and shallow . . . only the imaginative truth is precious."[12]

Moran's field sketches, at their best, are more than records of scenery on the one hand or technical tours de force on the other. Like his greatest paintings, they penetrate the "husk and surface" of their landscape motifs to reveal the inner workings of the creative personality. We may come, indeed, to prefer Moran's sketches to his finished works for what they tell us about him and about our own willingness to surrender to imaginative reverie. As Ruskin so aptly put it, "imperfect sketches, . . . outlines, . . . and other forms of abstraction, possess a charm which the most finished picture frequently wants. For not only does the finished picture excite the imagination less, but like nature itself, it *taxes* it more. None of it can be enjoyed till the imagination is brought to bear upon it."[13]

NOTES

1. Cole, "Essay on American Scenery," pp. 106–7.

2. The Gilcrease collection includes copies by Moran after landscapes by Rembrandt and Herman Swanevelt.

3. Gaunt, *Concise History,* p. 155: "[Turner] seems on the whole to have been less influenced by his English predecessors than to have considered in turn the best examples he could find irrespective of country, sometimes with a suggestion of deliberate rivalry but no doubt as much in the creative spirit of adapting the suggestions they gave. This accounts for the many differences of style and effect in works executed between 1800 and 1820." Moran himself, it must be noted, would have vigorously resisted such an appraisal. In "Thomas Moran, N.A.," p. 210, Richard Ladegast quotes Moran's complaint that "the great trouble with many of our young students . . . is that they insist upon seeing art through the eyes of a teacher, or in accordance with the methods of a certain school. An artist comes into this world qualified with intuitions that enable him to acquire knowledge through his own struggles, mistakes, and successes. The regime of ordinary studio work, with its foolish hero-worship, is calculated to stifle the originality, and growth of even the most talented. The young artists of to-day should learn to study the old masters, and feel willing to work out their own salvation."

4. See, for example, Truettner, "'Scenes of Majesty and Enduring Interest': Thomas Moran Goes West," p. 251; and Anderson, "'The Kiss of Enterprise': The Western Landscape as Symbol and Resource," pp. 237–83, especially pp. 246–55.

5. Langford, "Wonders of Yellowstone," p. 128. Moran based his illustrations on the amateur sketches of two members of Langford's party, which was led by Henry Dana Washburn.

6. See Jackson, "With Moran in the Yellowstone," in Fryxell, *Thomas Moran: Explorer in Search of Beauty* (East Hampton, N.Y.: East Hampton Free Library, 1958), pp. 55–56.

7. Thomas Moran, "Knowledge a Prime Requisite in Art," p. 15.

8. Ruskin's celebration of the imagination runs through most of his criticism. In *The Eagle's Nest* (1872), for example, he informed artists that "having learned to represent actual appearances faithfully, if you have any human faculty of your own, visionary appearances will take place to you which will be nobler and more true than any actual or material appearances; and the realization of these is the function of every fine art, which is founded absolutely, therefore, in truth, and consists absolutely in imagination" (quoted by Robert Herbert in his introduction to *The Art Criticism of John Ruskin,* p. xx).

9. Quoted in Fryxell, *Thomas Moran: Explorer in Search of Beauty,* p. 18.

10. Quoted by Parry, *Art of Thomas Cole,* p. 201.

11. Sheldon, *American Painters,* p. 125.

12. *Modern Painters IV* [33–45], in Herbert, *The Art Criticism of John Ruskin,* p. 14.

13. *Modern Painters I* [176–77], in ibid., p. 69.

"The Artistic Side of the Trip":
The Travels and Field Sketches of Thomas Moran

Anne Morand

With his variety of themes, ranging from historical subjects to literary fantasies, Thomas Moran built a solid career as an American artist during the second half of the nineteenth century (Plate 1). His art appeared in many forms—paintings, watercolors, prints, and illustrations—and his output between the 1850s and 1920s was tremendous.[1] While landscape was his major subject, its diversity within his oeuvre was most remarkable. In addition to his well-known panoramic images of the West, Moran painted eastern scenery and views of Europe and Mexico. Extensive travel on his own initiative, as well as on government expeditions and for commercial commissions, resulted in a prodigious number of field sketches, the major resource Moran used in creating his finished works.[2]

A study of Moran's fieldwork yields many insights into the life and work of this peripatetic artist. Moran's sketches, which he made almost compulsively, form a diary of his travels and activities. Although the subjects of his fieldworks often parallel those of his studio works, they more often diverge and thus demonstrate his broad range of interests. Moran's fieldworks reveal the artistic forces that affected him, from specific artists to commercial trends, and measure his growth as an artist. More than one thousand field sketches exist today in public collections. Most of them remained in Moran's possession until his death, which clearly suggests their continued importance and value to him.

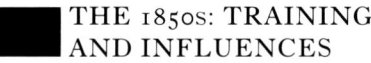

THE 1850s: TRAINING AND INFLUENCES

MORAN inaugurated his lifelong practice of sketching from nature in the 1850s, when he began to consider the feasibility of an artistic career. Not surprisingly, his initial field sketches depict familiar places in and around Philadelphia (*Crescentville,* No. 4), where he lived after emigrating to the United States from England with his family in 1844. Moran received his only

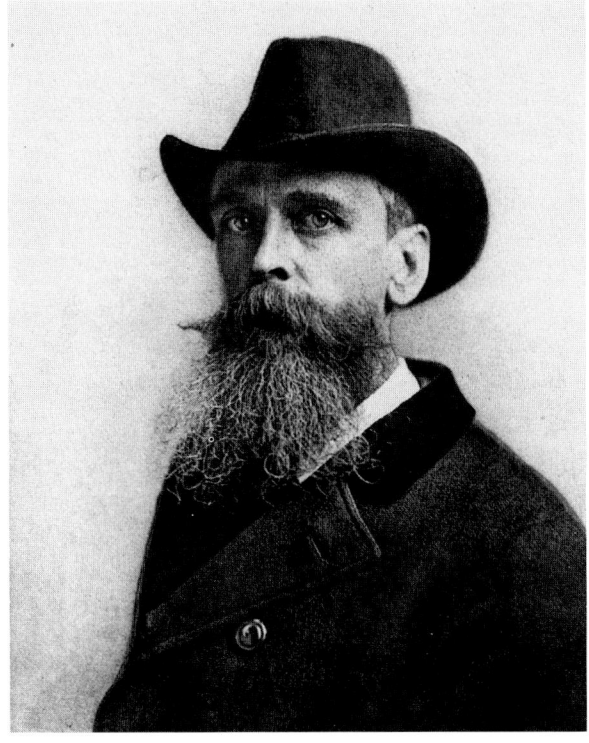

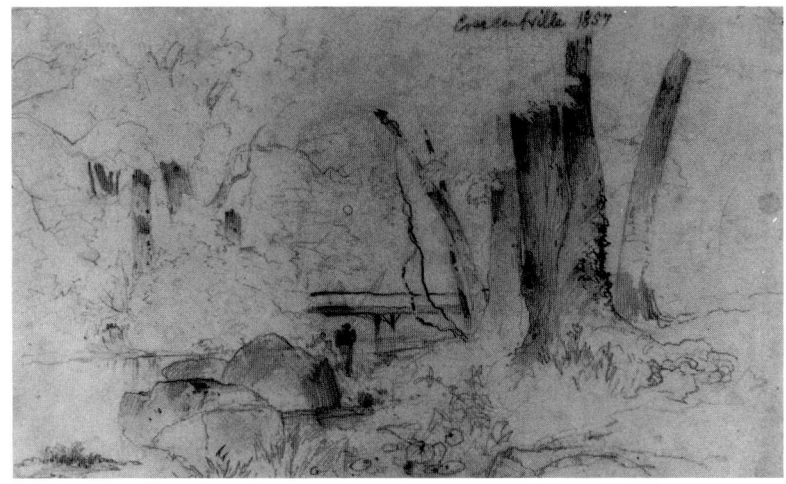

formal art training during an apprenticeship with the wood-engraving firm of Scattergood & Telfer, during which time he showed himself to be a competent draftsman. Although the apprenticeship was rather short, just three years, the experience benefited Moran in significant ways. It refined his skills as a draftsman, it reinforced the young artist's self-discipline, and it paved the way for a lucrative career in periodical illustration. Moran's fieldwork, which he began to make just after leaving the wood engravers' shop, is ample evidence of his youthful proficiency.

In 1856, when he made his first field sketches, Moran was nineteen years old. He had behind him his experience in wood engraving, which did not necessarily prepare him for work outdoors. He may have sought insights in the series of nine "Letters on Landscape Painting" written by America's leading landscape artist, Asher B. Durand (1796–1886). Published in the American art journal *The Crayon* in 1855,[3] these letters encouraged artists to observe and work from na-

ture and emphasized rigorous observation and detailed draftsmanship.

At this time Philadelphia was an advantageous place for an aspiring landscape painter to live. As a young man, Moran would have seen the landscapes of American as well as British artists exhibited at the Pennsylvania Academy of the Fine Arts. Two years after the publication of Durand's "Letters," John Ruskin's influential books *The Elements of Drawing* and *The Elements of Perspective* appeared in the United States, and both were reviewed in *The Crayon*.[4] Because there was little opportunity for academic training in the United States, American artists had long turned to manuals on drawing and painting for technical instruction; Moran may well have done so, too.

In America in the 1850s a younger generation of painters, still influenced by the philosophies that had shaped the Hudson River School in the 1820s and 1830s, was seeking innovation in landscape art. The U.S. publication of Ruskin's books coincided with an exhibition of English

Left: Napoleon Sarony, *Portrait of Thomas Moran* (c. 1870, Gilcrease Institute, 4326.6126), photogravure, 5 1/4 by 4 inches.

Right: No. 4. *Crescentville* (Gilcrease Institute, 1326.770), graphite on wove, 7 3/4 by 12 1/2 inches.

art shown in New York in 1857 and in Philadelphia and Boston in 1858.[5] The exhibition introduced American artists and the public to the work of the English Pre-Raphaelites, who painted in accordance with some of the principles set forth in Ruskin's writings. Ruskin's own *Fragment of the Alps* (c. 1854–56, Harvard University Art Museums, Cambridge) was included in the Philadelphia showing. *The Crayon* in its November 1857 issue praised it as "masterly . . . one of the most complete studies he has ever made."[6]

Moran's reading of Ruskin's books and of articles in the Ruskinian *Crayon,* as well as his familiarity with the work of such English-influenced American artists as James Hamilton (1819–78), prepared him to be receptive to the British exhibition. By the time the British exhibition opened in Philadelphia, Moran had been showing for two years pictures influenced by ideals similar to those held by the artists represented. The well-received exhibition enhanced public appreciation of his own work.

Coupled with Ruskin's writings, the exhibition also stimulated the American Pre-Raphaelite movement, which often followed to the extreme Ruskin's advocacy of truth to nature. Although he sympathized with the basic tenets of Pre-Raphaelitism, Moran never considered himself part of the movement. He later stated that his finished works were not "literal transcriptions of nature," but instead exemplified the French writer Emile Zola's assertion that "art is nature seen through a temperament."[7]

Other sources of artistic inspiration for Moran were J.M.W. Turner's (1775–1851) *Liber studiorum* and *The Rivers of France* and Claude Lorrain's (1600–1682) *Liber veritatis.*[8] These volumes of engravings offered Moran his initial exposure to the work of these great landscape painters, whose influence became evident even in his earliest works.

Moran joined his older brother Edward (1829–1901) in Edward's studio, which had been established in mid-1850s at the urging of James Hamilton. Edward Moran, who achieved a good measure of success as a marine painter, served as an encouraging model for both Thomas and another younger brother, Peter (1841–1914), who also eventually joined Edward's studio. Both young men profited from Edward's experience and informal instruction, as well as from the advice of his artist acquaintances.[9]

James Hamilton was at this time considered "the American Turner," an appellation that was later bestowed on Thomas Moran. Hamilton had spent a year in 1854/55 in London studying the work of Turner, and his example encouraged Thomas and Edward Moran to do the same. The brothers sojourned in London and the surrounding area in 1861 and 1862.

Moran was busy in the interval between the end of his apprenticeship in 1856 and his voyage to England. He recorded rural as well as urban scenery, making frequent day trips into the countryside around Philadelphia. He followed the standard seasonal schedule of nineteenth-century American landscape painters: sketching trips during the summer alternated with painting in the studio in the winter.

The Schuylkill River was Moran's first plein air subject. The Schuylkill is a source of much of Philadelphia's water as well as a picturesque addition to the cityscape. Several drawings, including *Bridge over the Schuylkill, Philadelphia* (No. 1; Plate 2), show Moran's earliest use of techniques he employed throughout his career. Moran typically began his field sketches with a contour drawing that established the major forms. To *Bridge over the Schuylkill, Philadelphia* he then added watercolor as well as white gouache to further define and color the landscape. Moran's great facility with water media, which later brought him acclaim, is apparent even in this early work.

Two sketches of the Philadelphia waterworks (*Fairmount Water Works, Philadelphia,* Nos. 6 and 7) are important documentary images. They are typical of Moran's depictions of American and European cities, in which he strove to secure the recognizable profile of an urban center. The waterworks were built on Fairmount Heights above Philadelphia in the early part of the nineteenth century to supply the city with water from the Schuylkill. By the 1860s

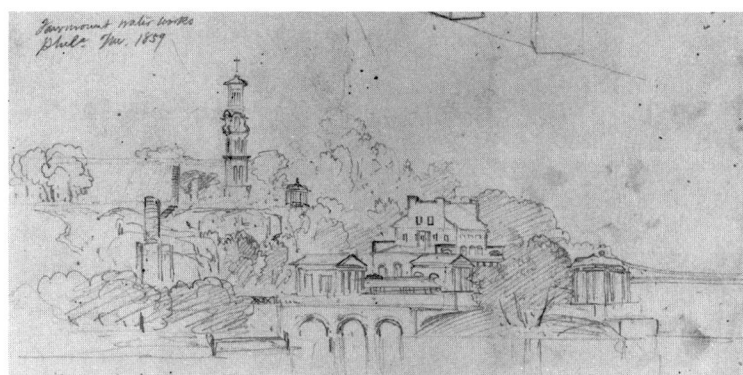

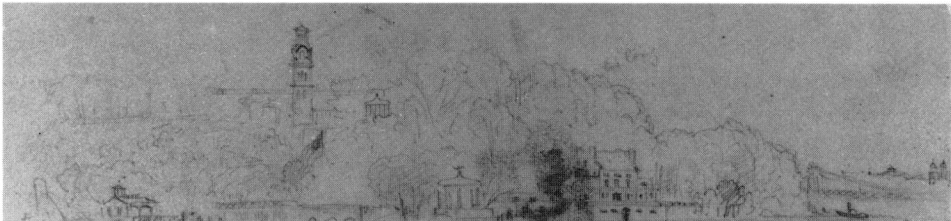

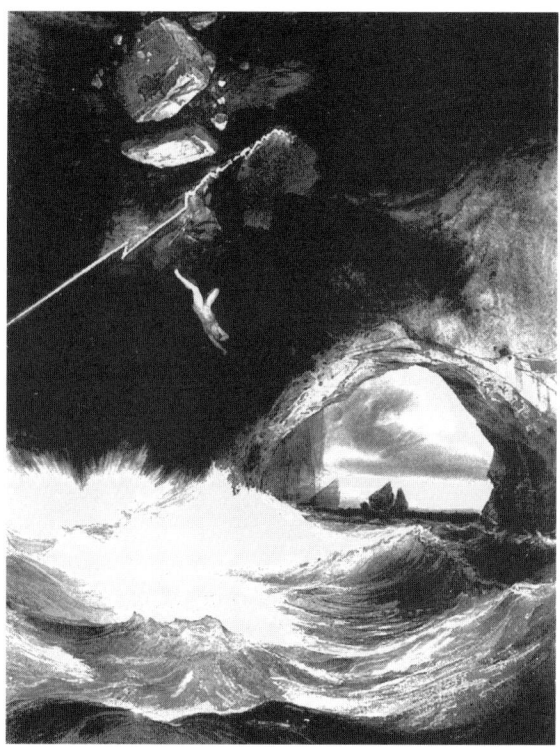

the demand for water had increased, and the City of Philadelphia annexed a tributary, Wissahickon Creek, also a subject of Moran's sketches, upriver from the waterworks. The entire area was made into a city park, today one of the largest in the United States. Moran sketched in Fairmount Park during its construction.[10] His documentation of public park lands thus began before his famous trip into the Yellowstone country with the U.S. Geological Survey in 1871.

THE 1850s: EASTERN AMERICA AND EUROPE

MORAN'S first extended sketching trip outside Philadelphia occurred during the summer of 1860 when he visited Michigan's remote Upper Peninsula, sketching the wilderness of the south shore of Lake Superior. Moran traveled with Isaac Williams (1819–95), a former portrait painter who had become interested in landscape. This trip marked the beginning of Moran's en-

gagement with America's natural wonders, an involvement that further shaped the course of his career when he traveled to the West in the 1870s. Michigan's Upper Peninsula had been surveyed for the first time about a decade earlier by geologists J. W. Foster and J. D. Whitney, who expressed surprise that no American artist of any stature had made use of the visual resources there.[11] Moran was the first artist to depict the rugged landscape of the Upper Peninsula, and his pictures stimulated interest in the region. Throughout his career Moran periodically incorporated the Lake Superior landscape into his paintings.[12]

This trip in 1860 may have been the result of a youthful desire to see scenery other than that of Pennsylvania, but the area as well as the idea of searching out new vistas must have appealed to Moran. He created his first large collection of field sketches in Michigan, and they proved valuable for a variety of projects. In 1873 his views of Lake Superior, translated into wood engravings, appeared in *The Aldine*.[13] Two years later,

Top left: No. 6. *Fairmount Water Works, Philadelphia* (Gilcrease Institute, 1326.769), graphite on wove, 5 3/4 by 11 inches.

Bottom left: No. 7. *Fairmount Water Works, Philadelphia* (Gilcrease Institute, 1326.541), graphite on wove, 2 3/4 by 9 1/2 inches.

Top right: Thomas Moran, *Death of Pan-Puk-Keewis* (1875, Gilcrease Institute, 0226.904), black ink wash on paper, 17 1/2 by 12 7/8 inches.

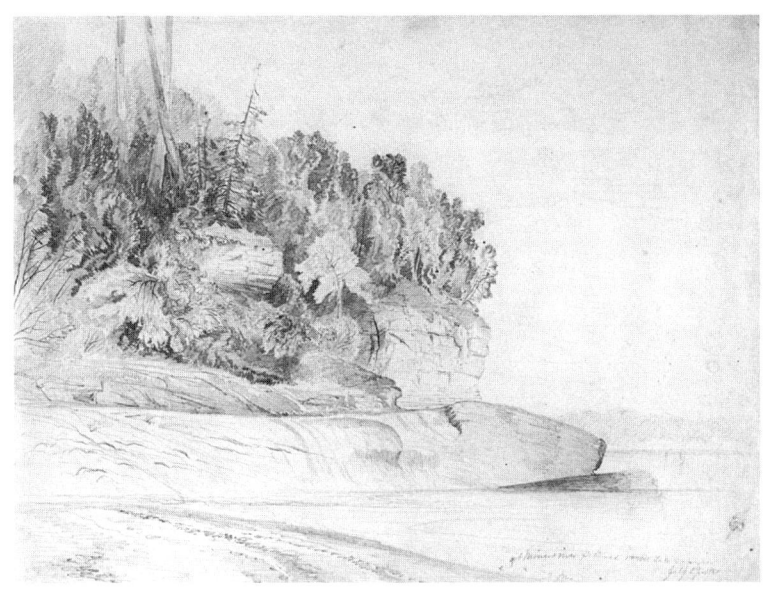 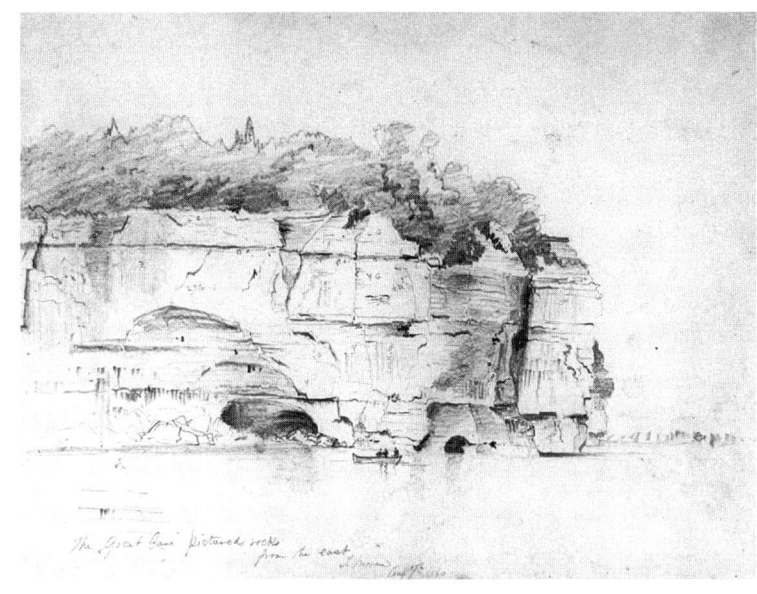

Left: No. 12. *At Miners River, Pictured Rocks, Lake Superior* (Gilcrease Institute, 1326.756), graphite on wove, 9¾ by 12⅝ inches.

Right: No. 17. *The Great Cave, Pictured Rocks from the East* (Gilcrease Institute, 1326.762), graphite on wove, 9¾ by 12½ inches.

in 1875, Moran prepared a series of illustrations for an edition of Henry Wadsworth Longfellow's *Song of Hiawatha* (first published in 1855).[14] His work for *Song of Hiawatha* inspired Moran to make numerous paintings of various episodes from the poem, including *Hiawatha and the Serpents of the Kenabeek* (1867, Baltimore Museum of Art) and *Fiercely the Red Sun Descending Burned His Way across the Heavens* (1875–76, North Carolina Museum of Art, Raleigh).

Moran began his Lake Superior sketches as contour drawings; he fleshed out some of them with hatch marks (*At Miners River, Pictured Rocks, Lake Superior,* No. 12). He rarely smudged his contours to indicate shade, preferring the more graphic solution of linear hachure. The sketches from the Michigan trip demonstrate his interest in landscape morphology and geological documentation. Many of them, especially the drawings of the Pictured Rocks, are careful delineations of rock forms. Moran sketched no large panoramas on the Upper Peninsula; instead he concentrated on details of the jutting

rock forms. He paid scant attention to foliage. Although *The Great Cave, Pictured Rocks from the East* (No. 17), includes human figures, it is evident that they were intended to serve as scale references rather than as sources of anecdotal interest.

While in Michigan Moran began to experiment with colored papers, a practice he continued for the rest of his life. About half of the thirteen sketches from the trip were executed on sheets from a pad of blue-gray paper, some of which, for economy, he tore into smaller pieces (*Looking from the South Entrance of the Great Cave, Pictured Rocks Lake Superior,* No. 14, and *Side of Entrance to the Great Cave, Pictured Rocks,* No. 15).

In the earliest sketches in the Lake Superior series, Moran's pencil touch was somewhat tentative, but it became more confident as his work progressed. Moran manipulated a combination of hard and soft leads to create marks to approximate a variety of surface textures. On some of the Lake Superior sketches, such as *Side of Entrance to the Great Cave, Pictured Rocks* (No.

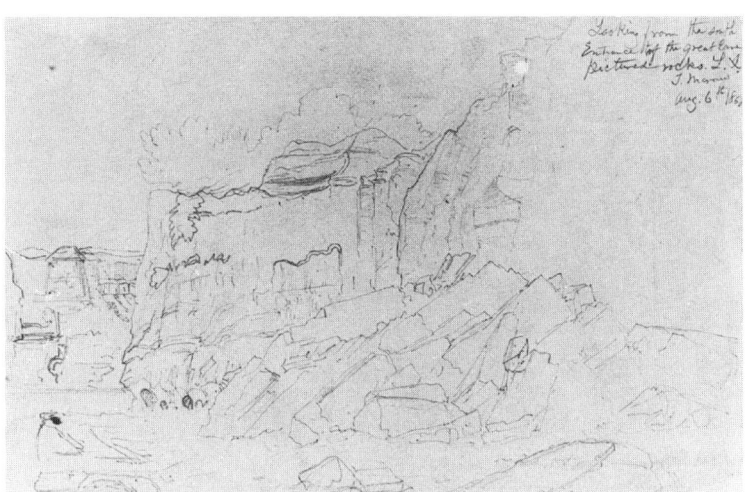

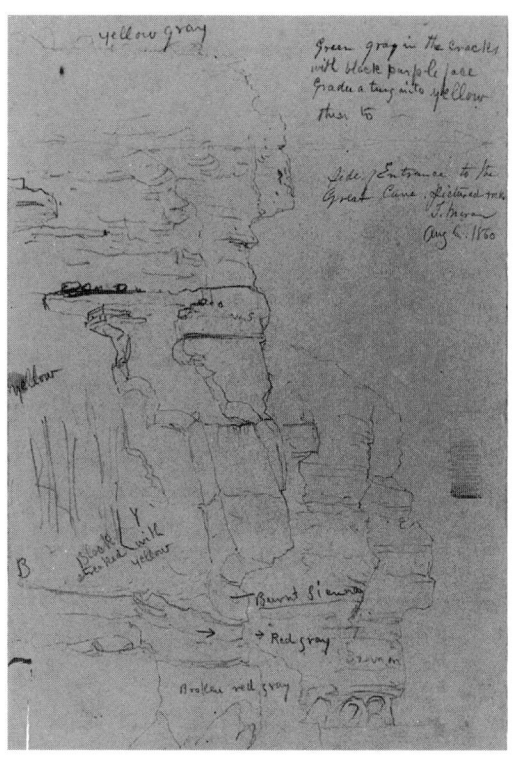

15) and *Entrance to the Great Cave, Pictured Rocks* (No. 16), Moran jotted down color notations for reference in the studio, a procedure he followed in much of his later fieldwork.

Moran sketched in the forest of nearby Munising (*In the Forest at Munising, Lake Superior,* No. 18). From there he wrote to his future wife, Mary Nimmo, "Since my last letter we have seen the great sight, the Pictured Rocks. They exceeded my expectations though in a manner different from what I supposed them. . . . I shall stay here about a week longer to finish my sketches."[15]

Outside Detroit, Moran drew *The St. Clair Flats* (No. 20). This sketch is evidence of his constant endeavor to capture the essence of a site, the *genius loci.* Since there were no major geological features to command his attention, Moran represented the flats in near panoramic proportions. The sketch is far more atmospheric than his earlier work, with uncharacteristic smudging employed to simulate the hazy, humid sky.

On his way home, Moran recorded the *Delaware Water Gap* (No. 22). His sketch of the folded strata and eroded layers of the cliffs lining the gap demonstrates his continuing fascination with unusual geological formations. In spite of the thrill of new scenery, views closer to home, such as *Crescentville* (No. 27) and *Bellews Rocks on the Tohickon* (No. 26) had not lost their appeal for Moran. The latter, portraying a spot in Bucks County, Pennsylvania, may be tied to work he did in the company of his brother John (1832–1903). Thomas visited and sketched Tohickon and Wissahickon Creeks with John, who was one of the earliest—if not the first—American artistic landscape photographers.[16] The documentary photographs and sketches they made served as the basis of such paintings as *A Scene on Tohickon Creek, Autumn* (1868, Minneapolis Institute of Arts) and *The Wissahickon* (painting not located; shown here is a photograph of the charcoal drawing).[17]

Three of the Moran brothers worked together in the spring of 1861, when Thomas, John, and Edward went to Catawissa, a small town on the Susquehanna River. A series of illustrations

Left: No. 14. *Looking from the South Entrance of the Great Cave, Pictured Rocks Lake Superior* (Gilcrease Institute, 1326.754), graphite on wove, 6 1/4 by 9 5/8 inches.

Right: No. 15. *Side of Entrance to the Great Cave, Pictured Rocks* (Gilcrease Institute, 1326.758), graphite on wove, 9 5/8 by 6 3/8 inches.

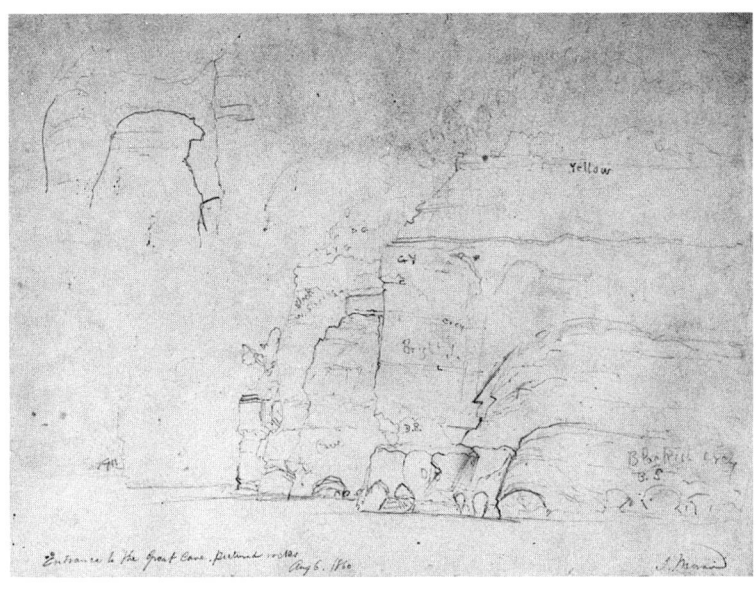

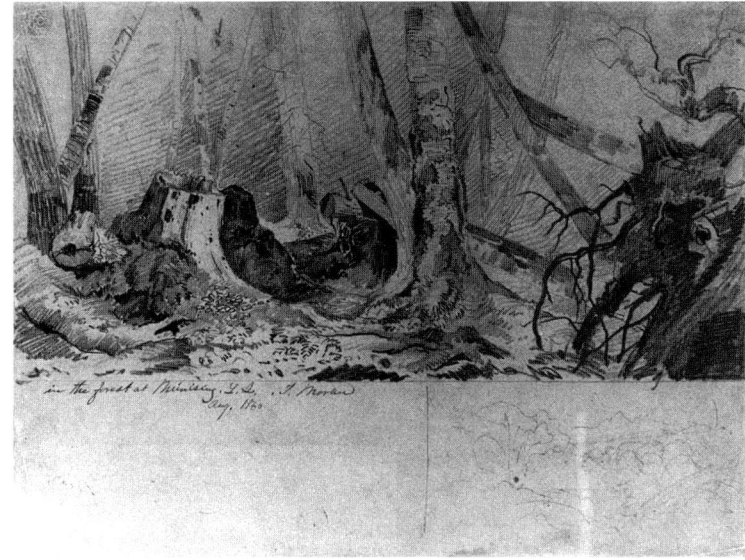

Top left: No. 16. *Entrance to the Great Cave, Pictured Rocks* (Gilcrease Institute, 1326.765), graphite on gray wove, 9¹/₂ by 12¹/₂ inches.

Top right: No. 18. *In the Forest at Munising, Lake Superior* (Gilcrease Institute, 1326.755), graphite on wove, 9¹/₂ by 12⁵/₈ inches.

Bottom right: No. 20. *The St. Clair Flats* (Gilcrease Institute, 1326.766), graphite on gray wove, 6¹/₄ by 9⁵/₈ inches.

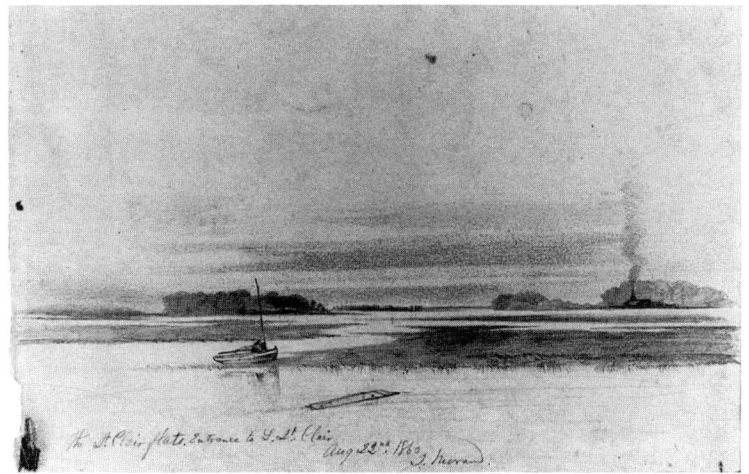

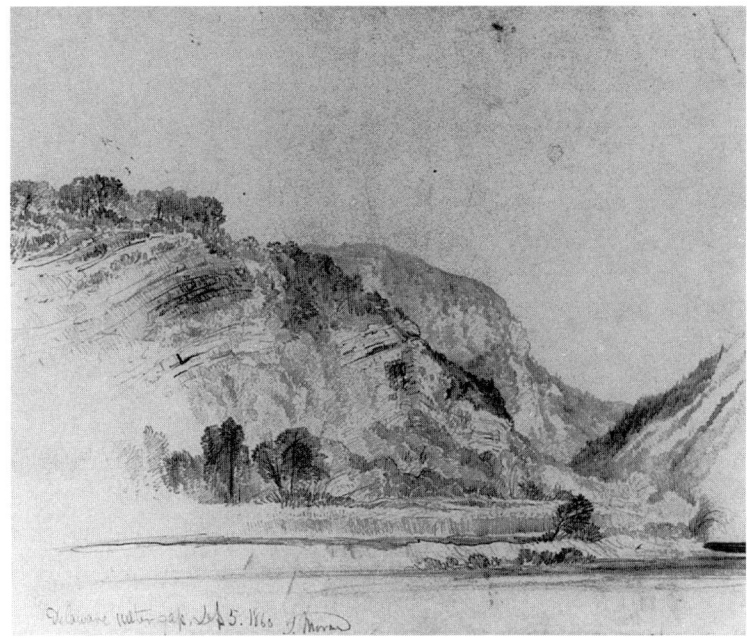

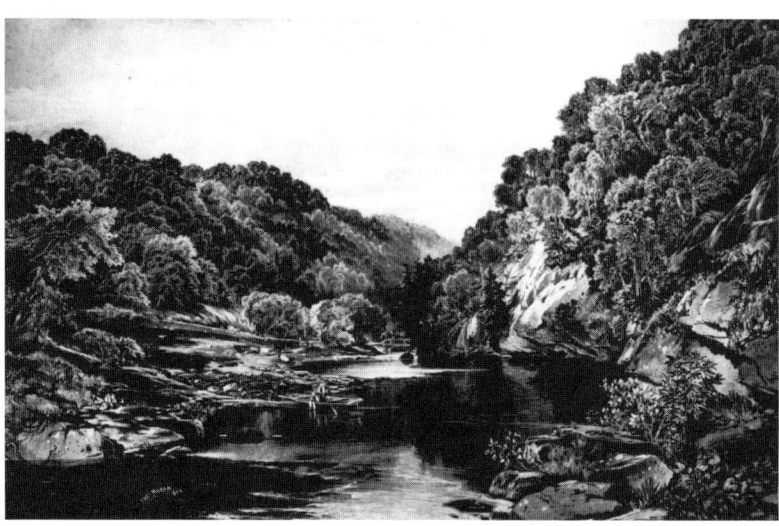

resulted from this trip, for "The Catawissa Railway," published in the June 1862 issue of *Harper's Monthly*. Although many of John Moran's photographs from this trip have been preserved, very few sketches by Thomas have been located. This may mean that he had already begun to rely on photographs as references in his studio work. One of the few known sketches is *At Port Clinton/From Barren Hill, Catawissa* (No. 37).[18] Thomas made several paintings of this scenery, such as *Summer on the Susquehanna at Catawissa* (1862, Gilcrease Institute; Plate 3).[19]

Sometime during the early months of 1861, Moran made sketches of Manayunk, an industrial town on the Schuylkill River west of Philadelphia. *Manayunk* (No. 30) illustrates the warehouses that lined the canal at that time. The incursions of industry on the landscape fascinated Moran, and indeed many nineteenth-century Americans, who even made pleasure tours to some industrial regions—much as those interested in industrial archaeology do today. Moran later made sketches, etchings, and paintings of

such industrial subjects as the sugar refineries at Communipaw, New Jersey, and the sawmills on the Wissahickon and at Feltville, New Jersey.[20]

By the summer of 1861, Thomas and Edward Moran were in London. While Edward attended the school of the Royal Academy of Arts, Thomas decided not to pursue formal training and instead spent several months studying Turner's work at the National Gallery.[21] He attempted to learn Turner's techniques in the time-tested manner—by copying his work. Available to him were Turner's paintings and also the drawings in the Turner Bequest, which had been carefully arranged and catalogued by Ruskin. While in London, Moran also copied the work of Claude Lorrain, Peter De Wint (1784–1849), and John Varley (1778–1842) at the British Museum,[22] as well as the sketches of John Constable (1776–1837) at the South Kensington Museum (later the Victoria and Albert Museum).

Moran was soon anxious to see the sites Turner had recorded. At the end of June 1862, he abandoned London's museums to embark upon

Left: No. 22. *Delaware Water Gap* (Gilcrease Institute, 1326.768), graphite on wove, 9¹/₂ by 11¹/₈ inches.

Right: John Moran after Thomas Moran, *The Wissahickon* (1864, Gilcrease Institute, 4316.7845), photograph of charcoal on canvas, 9¹/₂ by 14 inches.

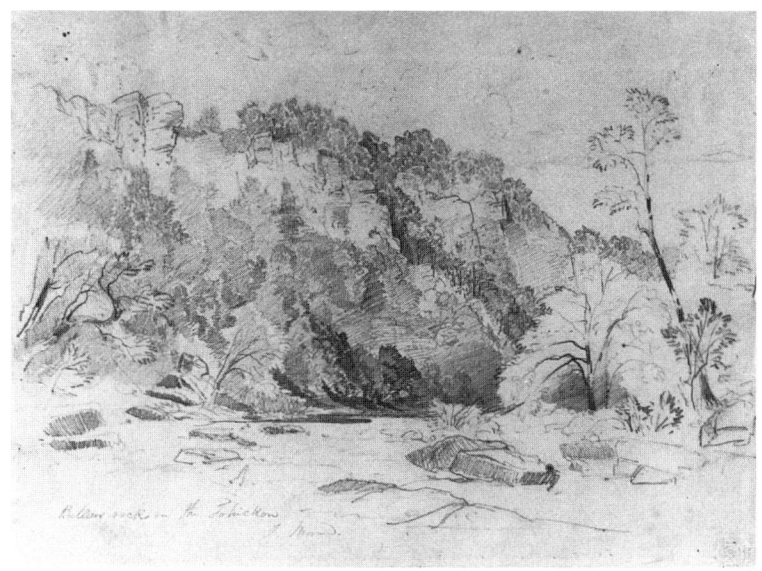

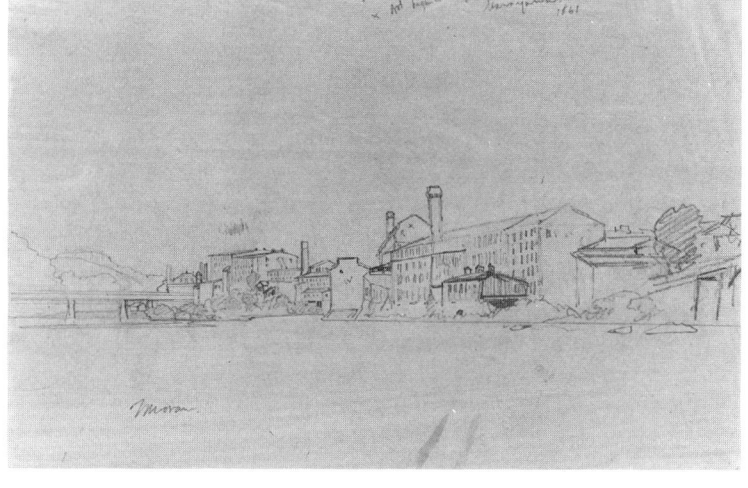

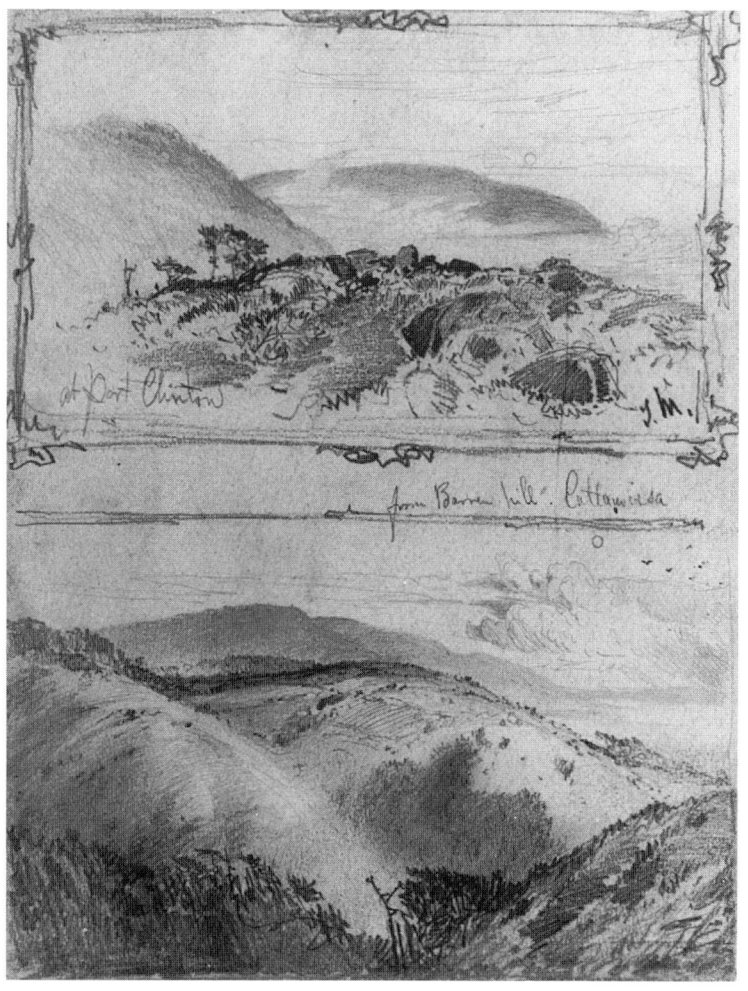

Top leftt: No. 26. *Bellews Rocks on the Tohickon* (Gilcrease Institute, 1326.706), graphite on gray wove, 9⅝ by 12⅝ inches.

Top right: No. 30. *Manayunk* (Gilcrease Institute, 1326.751), graphite on newsprint, 7⅝ by 11 inches.

Bottom right: No. 37a. *At Port Clinton* (Gilcrease Institute, 1326.707), graphite on wove, upper sketch 4 by 6½ inches, sheet 9¼ by 6⅞ inches.
No.37b. *From Barren Hill, Catawissa* (Gilcrease Institute, 1326.707), graphite on wove, lower sketch 4½ by 6⅞ inches, sheet 9¼ by 6⅞ inches.

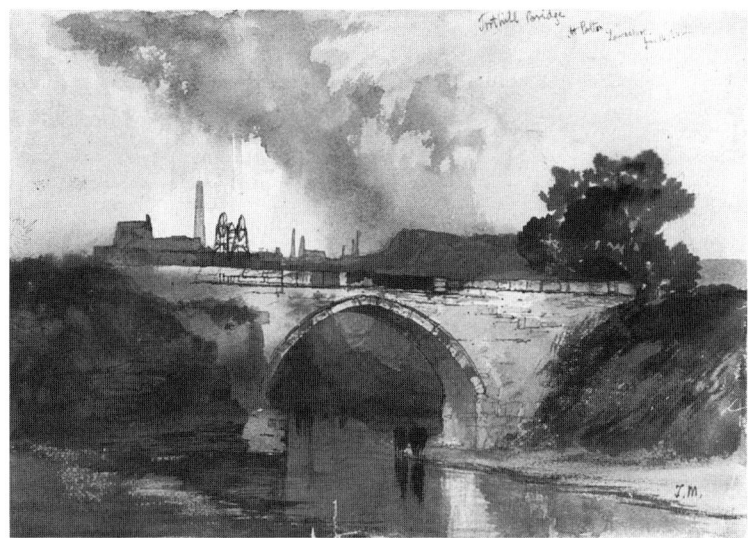 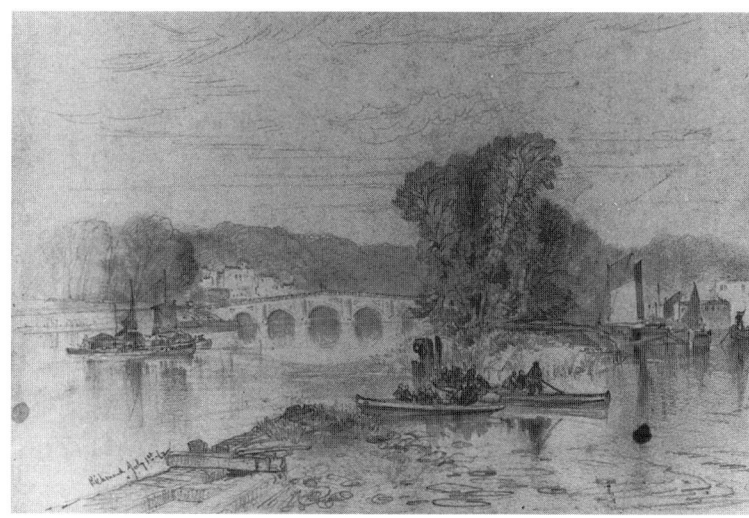

a series of sketching trips, traveling to Liverpool and visiting his birthplace of Bolton before returning to London to sketch Windsor Castle, the Houses of Parliament, St. Paul's Cathedral, and the suburbs of Richmond and Greenwich. Progressing to the southeastern coast, he followed a route derived from his study of Turner's sketches and *Rivers of England* (1823–25). He spent July recording his own observations of Margate, Ramsgate, Deal, Dover, Arundel, Hastings, Bexhill, Lewes, and Carisbrooke. He documented the distinctive skyline and prominent buildings, especially the castles, of each town he visited.

Moran used very little color in the sketches he made during June and July 1862; most are executed solely in graphite pencil. However, he applied sepia wash over the contour drawing of *Forthill Bridge at Bolton, Lancashire* (No. 39), *Margate* (No. 47), and *Richmond* (No. 46). He also added white gouache and touches of red conté crayon to a series of small sketches of Hastings, all on toned paper. He used gouache effectively to create the highlights on the waves and

the reflections on the slick surfaces of the boats in *Hastings* (No. 64; Plate 4) and *Bexhill* (No. 60; Plate 5) and to accent the crumpled white sail in *Hastings* (No. 63; Plate 6). Even the remarkable seaside cliffs—the subject of *Hastings* (No. 61; Plate 7) and seen in the backgrounds of *Bexhill* (No. 60) and *Hastings* (No. 65; Plate 8)—are touched with white. The white gouache appears particularly brilliant in contrast to the dull hues of the papers Moran used.

The remainder of the English sketches from 1862 make up a catalogue of Moran's pencil techniques. In the first of two views of Windsor created on the same day (*Windsor,* No. 40), Moran quickly sketched the contour of the castle, adding minimal architectural detail and roughing in foliage and other landscape elements. In the second sketch, *Windsor Castle* (No. 41), made from a slightly different viewpoint, Moran used a sharper pencil (his sharpening strokes are visible in the upper left corner of the sketch) to record more carefully the details of the architecture of the castle. When Moran wanted to elab-

Left: No. 39. *Forthill Bridge at Bolton, Lancashire* (Gilcrease Institute, 0276.801), graphite and sepia wash on wove, 10 by 14 inches.

Right: No. 46. *Richmond* (Gilcrease Institute, 0276.802), graphite and sepia wash on wove, 10^1/8 by 14^7/8 inches.

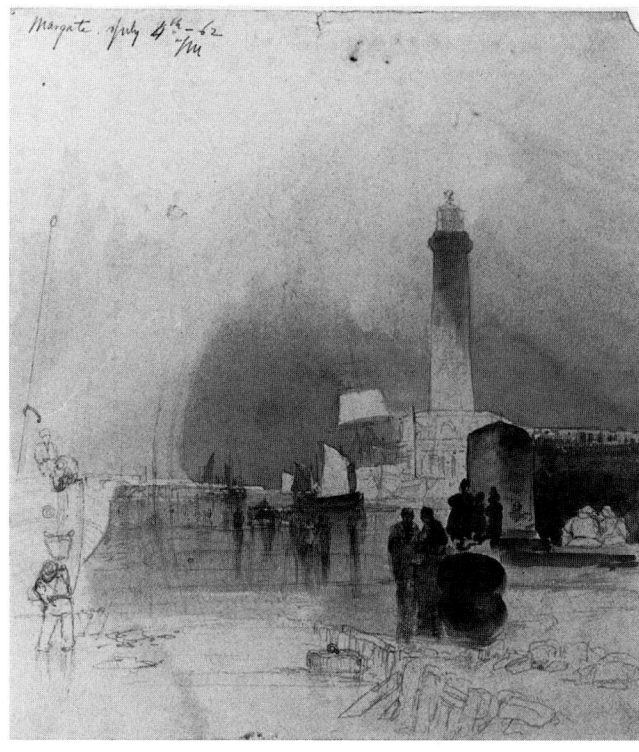

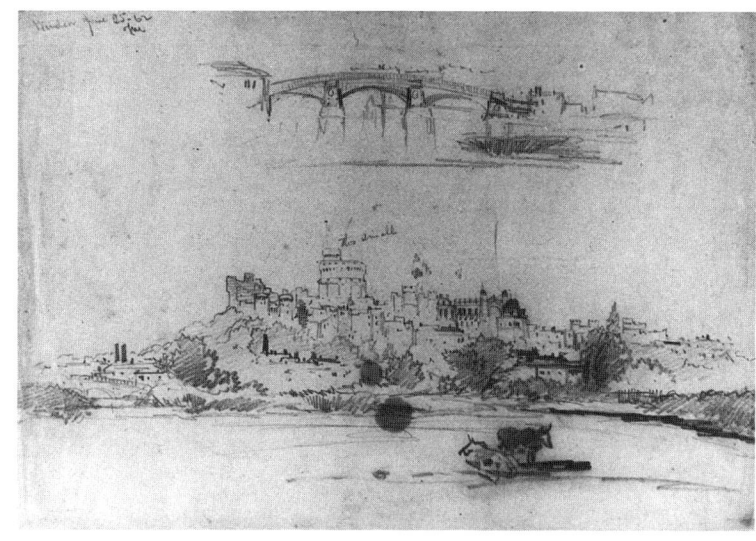

Left: No. 47. *Margate* (Gilcrease Institute, 0276.800), graphite and sepia wash on wove, 11³/₄ by 10¹/₈ inches.

Right: No. 40. *Windsor* (Gilcrease Institute, 1376.895), graphite on wove, 9³/₄ by 14 inches.

orate a specific aspect of a composition, he drew a more detailed sketch in a blank area of his sheet and marked its proper place in the larger scene with an *x*. An example of this practice is the vignette at the lower right of *Windsor Castle* (No. 41).

In Greenwich Park (No. 42) is one of the most highly finished drawings Moran completed in England. Instead of recording a cityscape or massive architecture, he focused on a close-up view of a fountain in the park. He held his pencil on its side, stroking broadly to build shapes and varying the direction of his strokes to create textural effects. This work contrasts with *Houses of Parliament from Hungerford Bridge* (No. 43), a quickly executed study of the seat of English government. It is evident that Moran felt neither the need nor the inclination to document every site carefully. Moreover, as he gained confidence in his sketching skills and in his memory, he developed a graphic shorthand. This can be seen, for example, in his rendering of the arch of the bridge in *Arundel Town and Castle* (No. 54). The

masonry is suggested by quickly jotted parallel lines. Trees and other vegetation are rarely particularized in Moran's sketches.

The use of such a shorthand method suggests that Moran often worked quickly. However, the refined execution of some sketches, such as *Richmond* (No. 46), indicates that at times he also traveled and drew at a more leisurely pace. *Richmond* is carefully detailed, including aspects of the landscape, such as the river and the bridge spanning it, and also boats and buildings. *Richmond,* like several other sketches Moran made in England, includes figures, as rare in Moran's fieldwork as in his paintings. *Richmond* resembles Turner's watercolor *Richmond Hill and Bridge, Surrey* (c. 1831, British Museum, London), which Moran saw in the British Museum. Moran chose a slightly different point of view, however, one that focuses attention on the river rather than on the bridge.

Moran's sketches of England are not just sentimental souvenirs of his native land. In England he had an opportunity to study and sketch

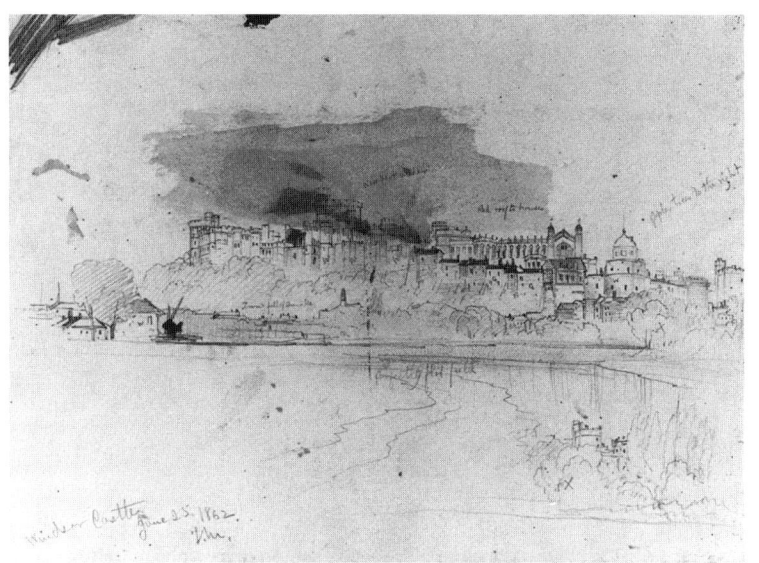

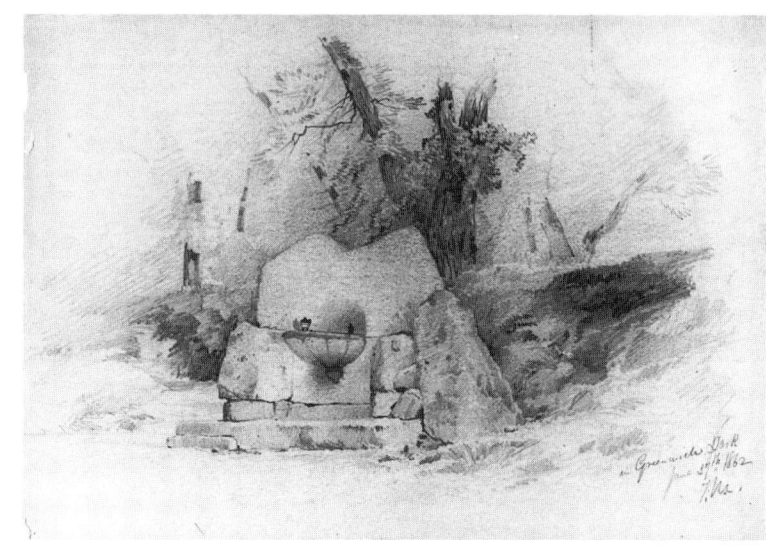

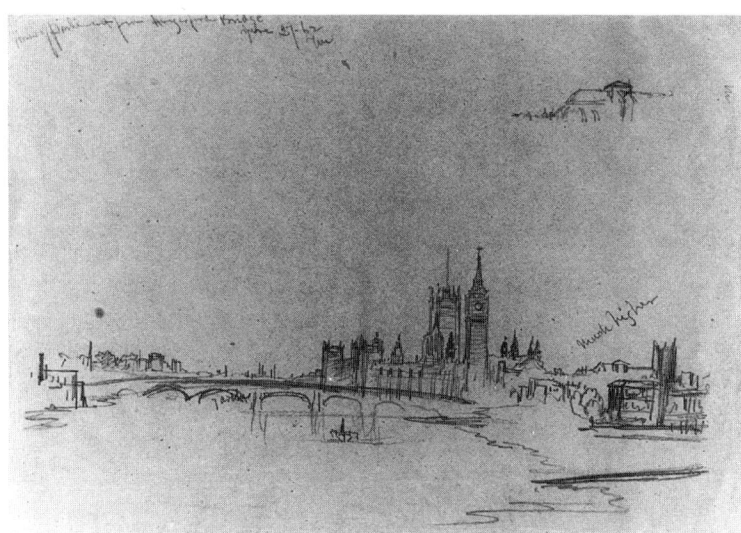

Top left: No. 41. *Windsor Castle* (Gilcrease Institute, 1376.896), graphite and sepia wash on wove, 9³/₄ by 13¹/₈ inches.

Top right: No. 42. *In Greenwich Park* (Gilcrease Institute, 1376.899), graphite on wove, 11 by 14⁷/₈ inches.

Bottom left: No. 43. *Houses of Parliament from Hungerford Bridge* (Gilcrease Institute, 1376.897), graphite on wove, 10 by 14 inches.

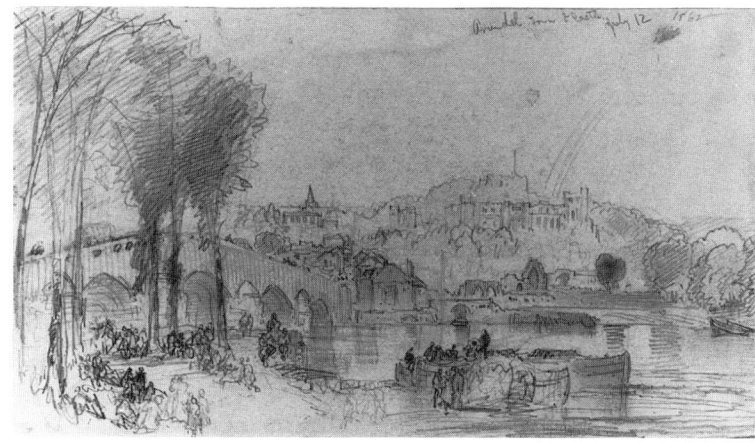

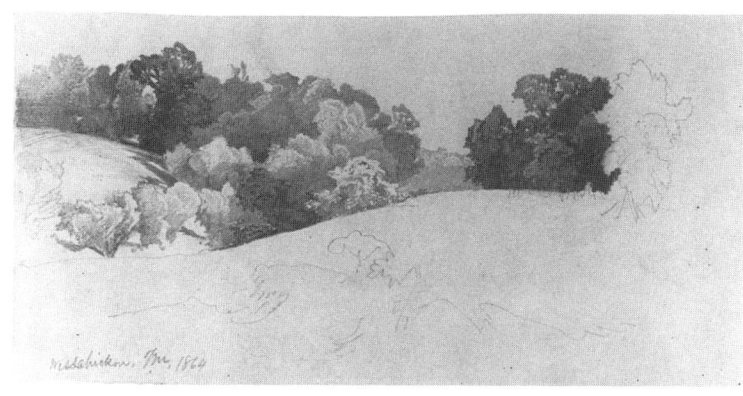

Left: No. 54. *Arundel Town and Castle* (Gilcrease Institute, 1376.902), graphite on wove, 8¼ by 14 inches.

Right: No. 73. *Wissahickon* (Gilcrease Institute, 1326.719), graphite on gray wove, 6⅝ by 12⅞ inches.

things that could not be found in America, such as medieval architecture, which he later incorporated into his fantasy and literary paintings. Most important, the sketches made in England document the development of his powers of observation and his remarkable technical facility.

The Moran brothers returned home to Philadelphia probably by autumn of 1862.[23] Moran's next journeys took him to other sections of Pennsylvania, prompting him to create two series of sketches of rivers in rural parts of the state. During the summer of 1864, he followed the course of the Upper Juniata River in the Alleghenies, and in the summer of 1865 he visited the Delaware River in scenic Pike County. Possibly Moran wished to create an American version of Turner's *Rivers of France* and *Rivers of England*.[24] Moran made some river landscapes immediately after his return from England in 1862, sketching the familiar Wissahickon Creek (*Wissahickon,* No. 73).

From late July through August of 1864 Moran traveled through central Pennsylvania, sketching along the Juniata and Conemaugh rivers near the towns of Huntingdon, Johnstown, Wilmore, Lockport, Gallitzin, Spruce Creek, and Mapleton. Frequent gaps, formed by Warriors Ridge and Tussey Mountain, occur in the Alleghenies east of Huntingdon. The scenery is as noteworthy as that of the better known Delaware Water Gap, and Moran made at least thirty sketches here.

Moran's route, when traced on a map, appears to have been an erratic course through central Pennsylvania, but it followed the tracks of the Pennsylvania Central Railroad.[25] As with his works created in England in the early 1860s and in the American West in the following decades, the Pennsylvania work reveals his lifelong affinity for railroads, which brought picturesque and sublime landscapes within relatively easy reach.

This region of central Pennsylvania, densely populated and home to many hydraulically powered mills, the symbols of progress and prosperity, began to attract tourists after the Civil War. Instead of focusing on the signs of commerce, as he had in sketches of the Manayunk warehouses

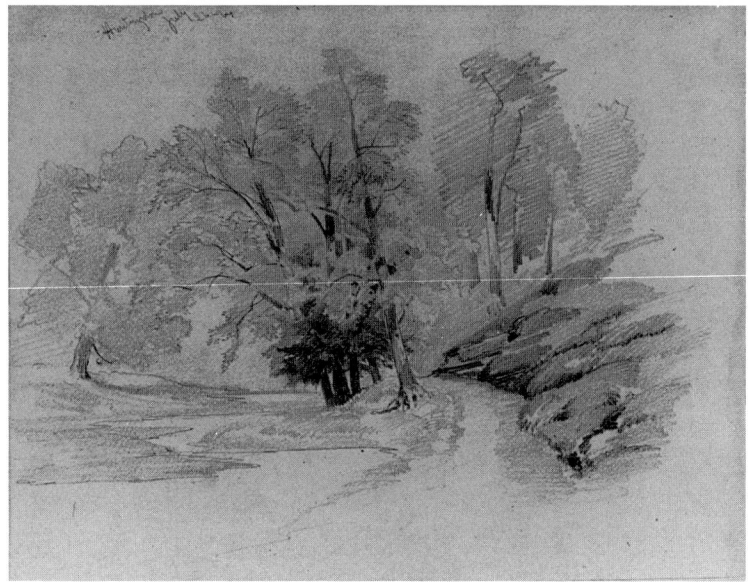

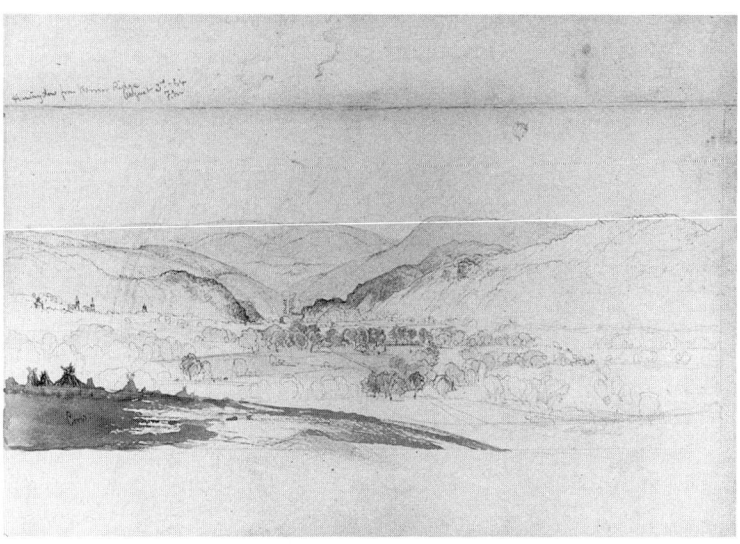

in 1861, this time Moran selected the scenic aspects of the sites he visited, rendering images of beauty and tranquility.

Moran's first sketch of this trip, *Huntingdon* (No. 76), is a simple study of trees, rocks, and a meandering watercourse. His economical use of line is evident in the subtle shading of the forms. A hike up to Warriors Ridge north of town provided the opportunity to make *Huntingdon from Warriors Ridge* (No. 77). To several of the sketches executed during this trip Moran applied a very light blue wash over the contour drawing, a practice he did not repeat until his visit to the Roman Campagna in 1867. The wash adds a sense of distance and represents Moran's initial experimentation with the atmospheric perspective that he later employed so effectively in his Yellowstone watercolors, such as *The Yellowstone Range from Near Fort Ellis* (1872, Gilcrease Institute; Plate 9). The composition of *Huntingdon from Warriors Ridge* is panoramic, with all aspects of the landscape reduced to tiny, repetitive forms.

Warriors Ridge, Huntingdon, Pennsylvania (No. 79) illustrates yet another approach, one that recalls Moran's investigations of rock formations at the Pictured Rocks, Lake Superior. In contrast to the artist's rather generalized examination of the valley below, the rocks in *Warriors Ridge, Huntingdon, Pennsylvania* are rendered with great care, the result of the artist's deliberate concentration on individual elements of the landscape.

Moran repeated the design of *Huntingdon from Warriors Ridge* (No. 77) in sketches such as *The Juniata below Huntingdon* (No. 80) and *Johnstown* (No. 81; Plate 10). He added substantially more blue wash to *Johnstown* than to the sketches executed previously, but applied none to *The Juniata below Huntingdon*. In these sketches, the receding hills overlap, forming diagonals that lead the eye to the river cutting through the hills. Scale relationships are established by the many trees and the few manmade structures that line the riverbanks.

Wilmore (No. 82a), another sketch from this

Left: No. 76. *Huntingdon* (Gilcrease Institute, 1326.716), graphite on wove, 7 1/2 by 9 3/4 inches.

Right: No. 77. *Huntingdon from Warriors Ridge* (Gilcrease Institute, 1326.715), graphite, blue and gray washes on wove, 9 3/4 by 13 3/8 inches.

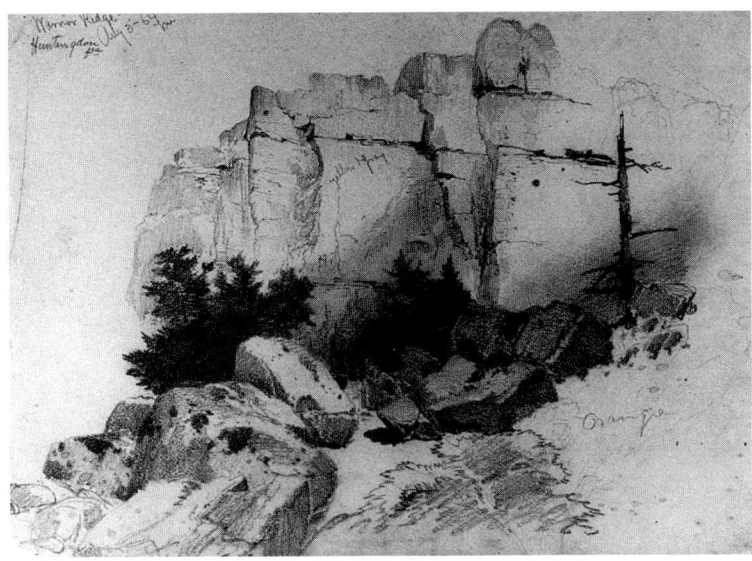 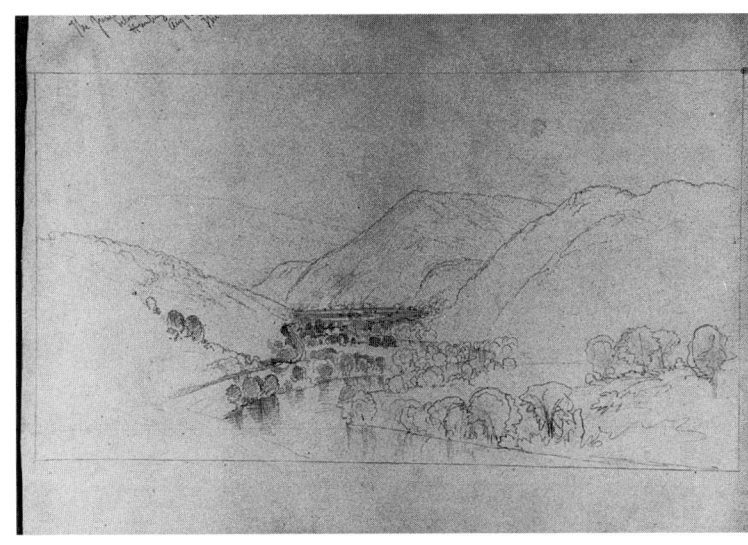

Left: No. 79. *Warriors Ridge, Huntingdon, Pennsylvania* (Gilcrease Institute, 1326.1028), graphite and black conté crayon on wove, 9⅝ by 13 inches.

Right: No. 80. *The Juniata below Huntingdon* (Gilcrease Institute, 1326.717), graphite on wove, 9¾ by 13¼ inches.

trip, is the first in a series of smaller, more intimate forest interior scenes. These illustrate Moran's fascination with convoluted natural forms, such as tree roots and branches and overlapping foliage.

At the Conemaugh River at Bolivar, his westernmost stop on this trip, Moran worked in a simpler wide-angle format to make *On the Conemaugh below Lockport* (No. 83) and *Conemaugh at Bolivar* (No. 85; Plate 11). In the latter he added a new element, the careful documentation of the sky, with cloud forms and colors conscientiously noted.

A group of sketches made at Gallitzin (*Gallitzin*, No. 88) echoes the earlier *Wilmore* (No. 82a); they are small, carefully drawn studies of rocks and foliage. The format of these works, often drawn two to the sheet and averaging four inches in height, suggests that Moran was considering the possibilities of reproduction. His execution—linear, bold, and very graphic—resembles wood engraving.

Moran sketched *Spruce Creek, Pennsylvania* (No. 93; Plate 12) using blue wash to define

rock forms and shadows. At Tussey Mountain, the ridge above Spruce Creek, he made a sketch of rocks (*Tussey Mountain, Spruce Creek*, No. 94) similar to that executed on Warriors Ridge. He returned to a more intimate rendering in two sketches of Spruce Creek (Nos. 95 and 96) and made distant views of Mill Creek (*Mill Creek* and *The Juniata at Mill Creek*, Nos. 98 and 100). Perhaps no group of works better demonstrates Moran's ability to adapt his execution to the site.

Moran may have made this trip with his brother John, who photographed the region. Thomas probably used John's photographs in his compositions, not as models to be copied but rather as aides-mémoire and as a creative stimulus in the compositional process—just as he used his own fieldworks.[26] Thomas, who would have been predisposed by his graphic training to appreciate the effectiveness of black-and-white photographic imagery, must have quickly grasped the possibilities the medium offered the painter. Certainly, he recognized that photography offered a quick and easy way to record detail.

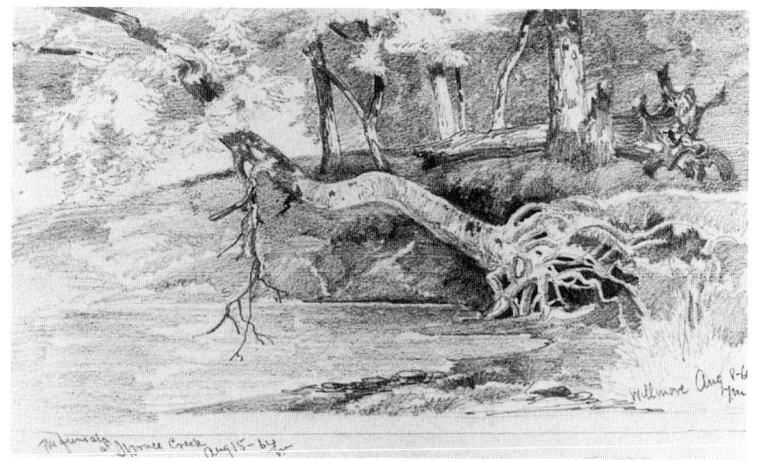

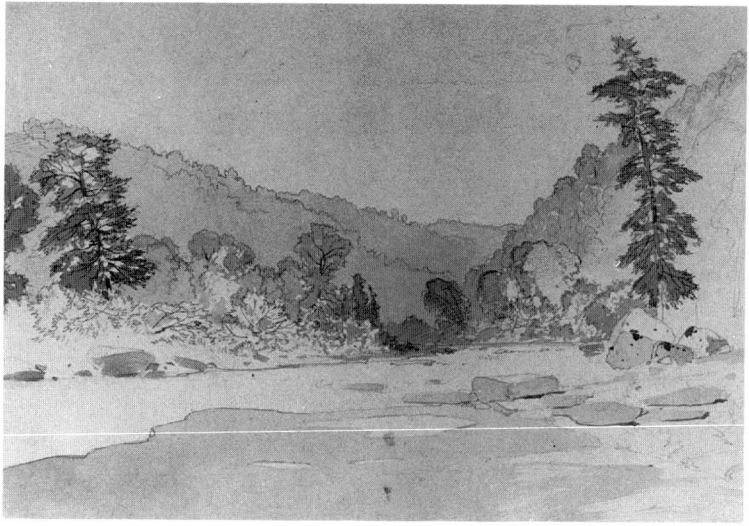

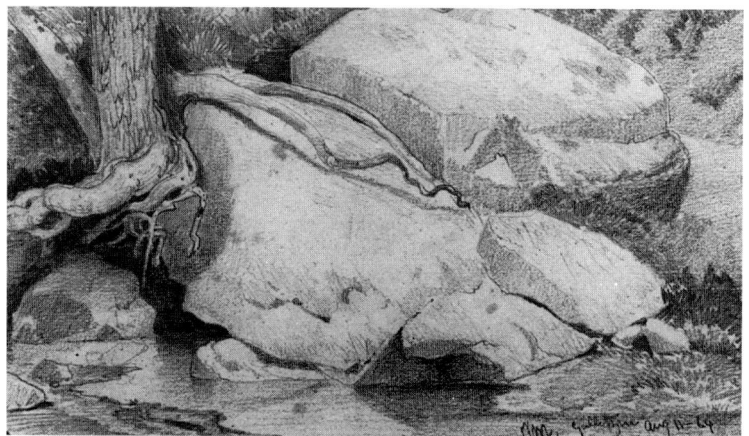

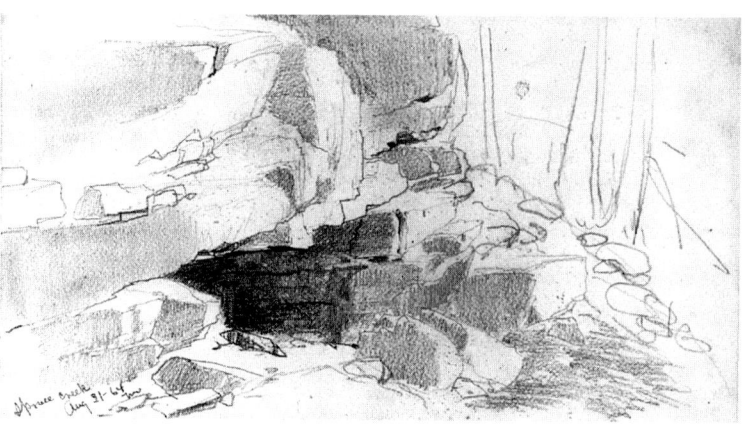

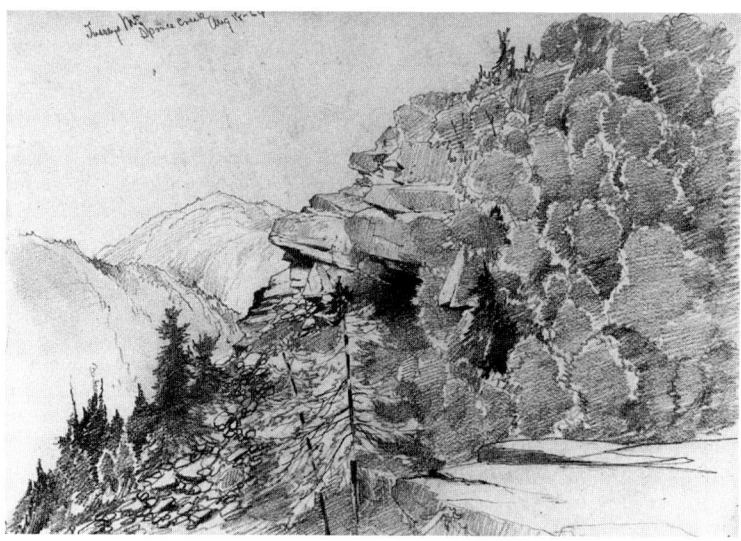

Top left: No. 82a. *Wilmore* (Gilcrease Institute, 1326.712), graphite on wove, upper sketch 4$\frac{1}{2}$ by 7$\frac{3}{4}$ inches, sheet 9$\frac{5}{8}$ by 7$\frac{3}{4}$ inches.

Top right: No. 83. *On the Conemaugh below Lockport* (Gilcrease Institute, 0226.796), graphite, blue and gray washes on wove, 9$\frac{3}{4}$ by 13$\frac{1}{2}$ inches.

Middle left: No. 88. *Gallitzin* (Gilcrease Institute, 1326.1021), graphite on wove, 4$\frac{7}{8}$ by 6$\frac{5}{8}$ inches.

Middle Right: No. 95. *Spruce Creek* (Gilcrease Institute, 1326.748), graphite on wove, 5$\frac{1}{2}$ by 9$\frac{5}{8}$ inches.

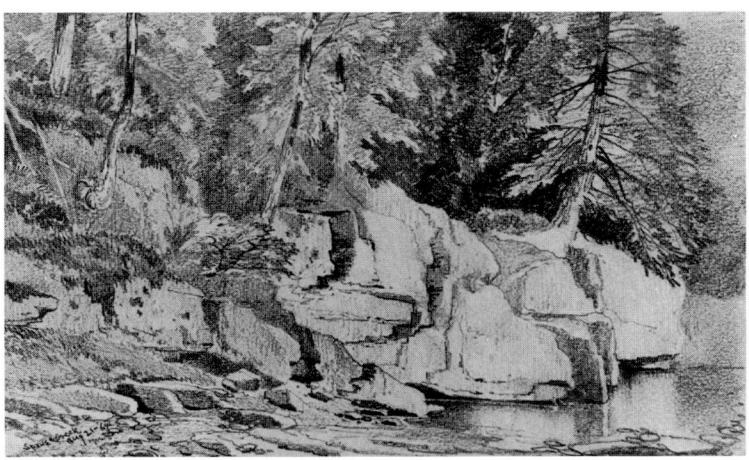

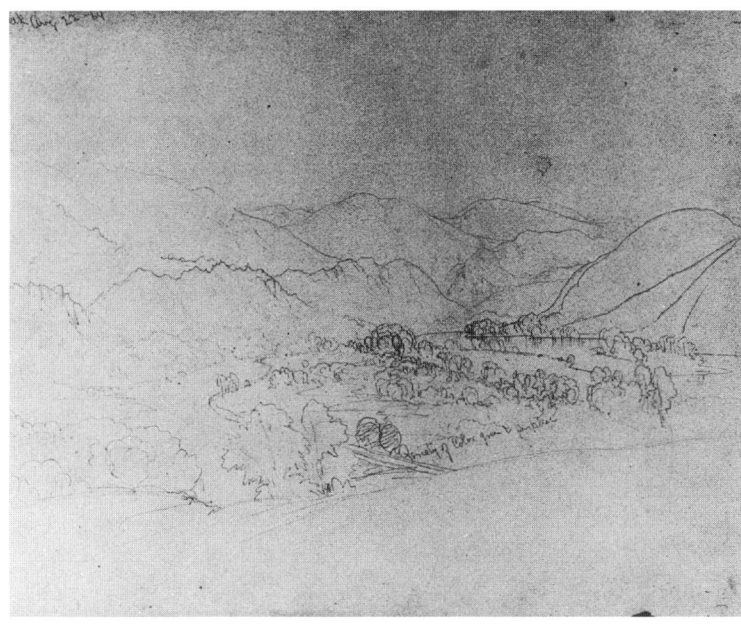

Moran's work with his photographer brother anticipates his relationship with survey photographers William Henry Jackson (1843–1942), who accompanied the government expedition to the Yellowstone in 1871, and John K. Hillers (1843–1925), who documented John Wesley Powell's exploration of the Grand Canyon of the Colorado in 1873.

In the summer of 1865, probably seeking relief from the oppressive heat in Philadelphia, Moran visited the Delaware River region of Pike County in the northeastern part of Pennsylvania, sketching Milford and Vandermark and the waterfalls at Raymondskill, Adams Creek, and Sawkill (*Sawkill Fall,* No. 116). He spent three weeks during July and August roaming the creeks and small waterfalls that feed a ten-mile stretch of the Delaware.

Moran sketched an area known as the Delaware Valley Resort Cataract Region, which became a haven for hunters and fishermen as well as health seekers fleeing the malarial lowlands. His later work with various rail companies was often used to promote tourism, so it is reasonable to speculate that he may have been involved in a small way with the development of this resort area. Illustrations based on his sketches appeared in such promotional guidebooks as *The Pennsylvania Railroad,* published in 1875, ten years after Moran's trek. That the region was already attracting tourists is suggested by the title of one of the Sawkill sketches, *Picnic Rock* (No. 124b).

Nearly all of the forty sketches associated with this excursion include water in some form, from still pool to dashing torrent. Moran had already proven himself capable of depicting water, and he rose to the pictorial challenge posed by the many small waterfalls along the course of the Delaware. Two sketches in particular, *Sawkill Fall* (No. 111) and *Sawkill* (No. 112), may be seen as precursors of western watercolors, such as *Upper Falls of the Yellowstone* (1872, Gilcrease Institute; Plate 13), not only in composition but also as exercises in the convincing portrayal of rushing water.

The sketches of 1865 are executed exclu-

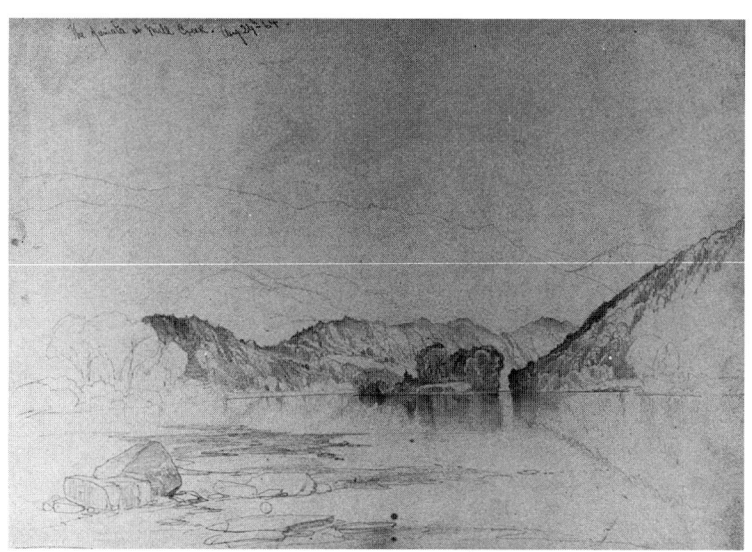

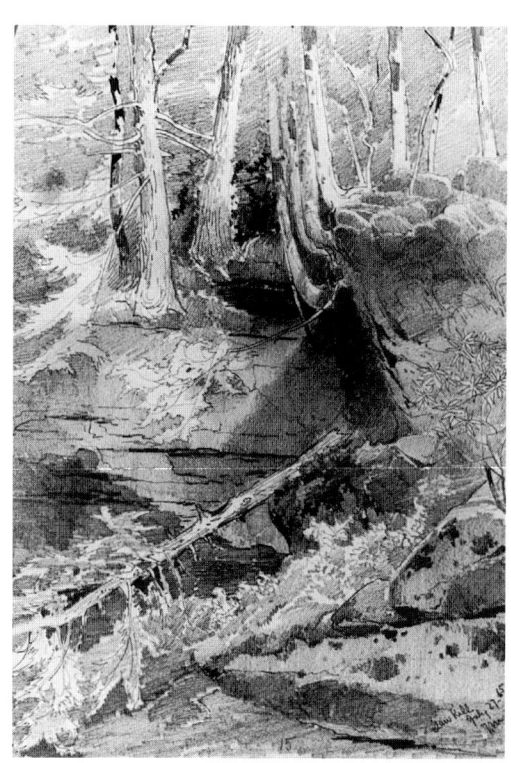

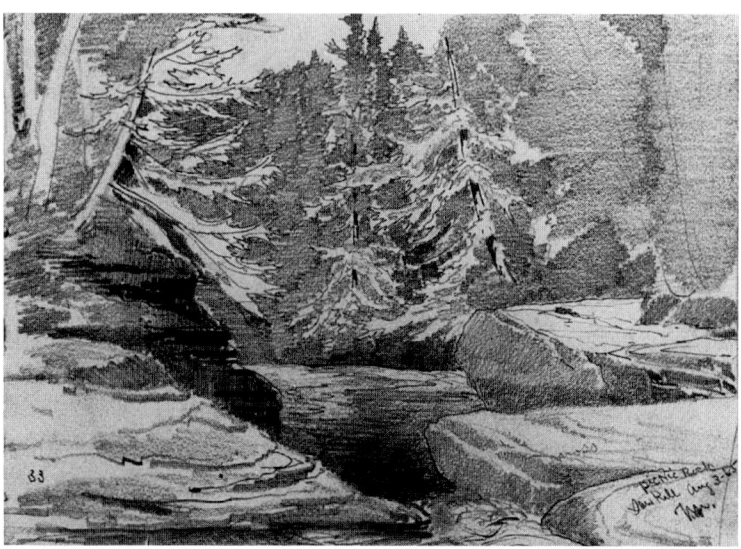

Top left: No. 100. *The Juniata at Mill Creek* (Gilcrease Institute, 1326. 718), graphite on wove, 9³/₄ by 13¹/₄ inches.

Top right: No. 116. *Sawkill Fall* (Gilcrease Institute, 1326.1019), graphite on wove, 9¹/₂ by 6³/₈ inches.

Bottom: No. 124b. *Picnic Rock, Sawkill* (Gilcrease Institute, 1326. 730), graphite on wove, lower sketch 4¹/₂ by 6¹/₈ inches, sheet 9¹/₂ by 6¹/₈ inches.

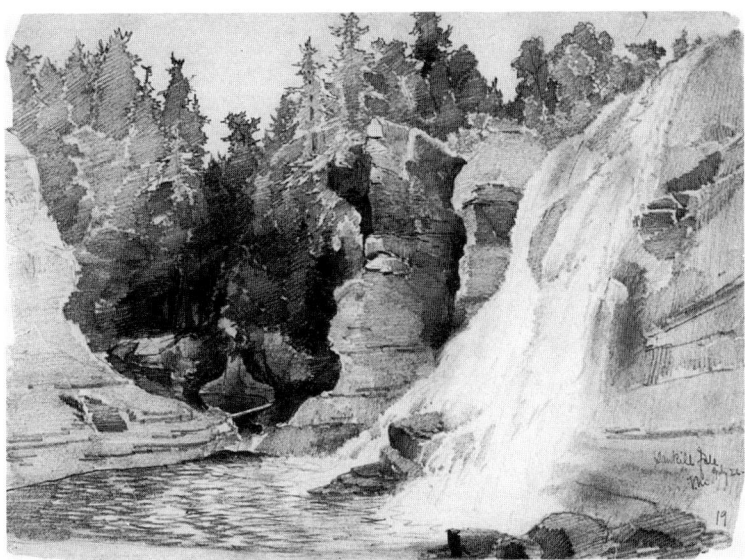

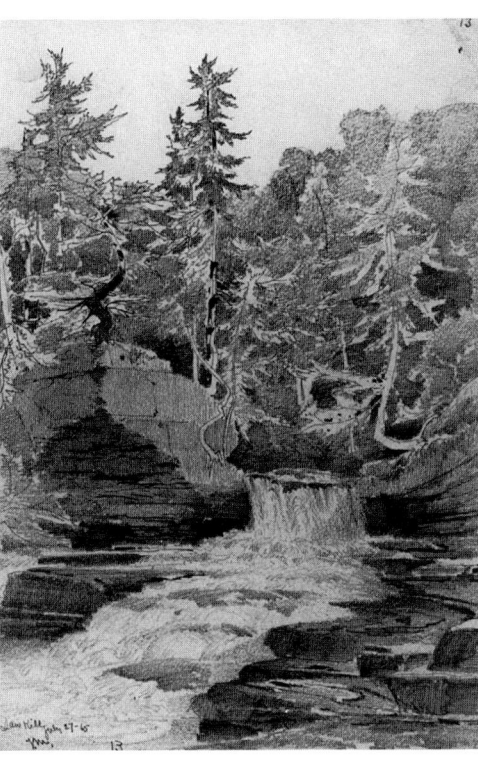

Left: No. 111. *Sawkill Fall* (Gilcrease Institute, 1326.1013), graphite on wove, 9³/₄ by 12³/₄ inches.

Right: No. 112. *Sawkill* (Gilcrease Institute, 1326.733), graphite on wove, 9³/₈ by 6¹/₄ inches.

sively in pencil. Some, such as *Vandermark* (No. 123), are tightly constructed, with lush undergrowth filling closed-in spaces. They are cloistered in feeling and intricate; their execution was unquestionably affected by Moran's background in wood engraving. He used hatching and cross-hatching for shading and used linear strokes to define planes, such as the facets of rocks in *Vandermark*. The legacy of the geologically minded Ruskin is quite evident in this work, as is the influence of such artists of the native plein air tradition as Durand and John Frederick Kensett (1816–72), who favored an almost photographic depiction of rocks.

Other sketches are less detailed but no less competent. The background and rock forms in *Hemlock, Sawkill Fall* (No. 130) and *Milford* (No. 122) are broadly rendered. Moran gave slightly more attention to the contours defining the tree trunks, reducing the foliage to a few scribbles. His careful observation of natural forms, as counseled by Durand in his "Letters," enabled Moran to render them effectively by the most minimal

means. The deployment of pencil marks in *Milford* (No. 104) evokes the light/dark, sun/shadow patterns of the forest. Moran handled trees, rocks, and creeks with great variety and subtlety.

The Delaware River sketches were executed on large sheets of paper, some of which Moran cut into halves and quarters. Certain techniques used in these sketches seem associated with his work in etching, with which he had been experimenting since the mid-1850s. For example, in the lower left and central sections of *Adams Creek* (No. 137) he laid down a heavy layer of graphite, then removed the excess by scraping with a sharp point, just as if he were working on an etching plate.

In the summer of 1866 Moran began a second year of foreign study, this one punctuated by his exhibition of two paintings at the Paris Universal Exposition of 1867. Accompanied by his wife and infant son, he returned briefly to England before setting up a studio in Paris. He later offhandedly acknowledged the significance for his artistic development of this time spent abroad. In his autobiographical essay, which he wrote in

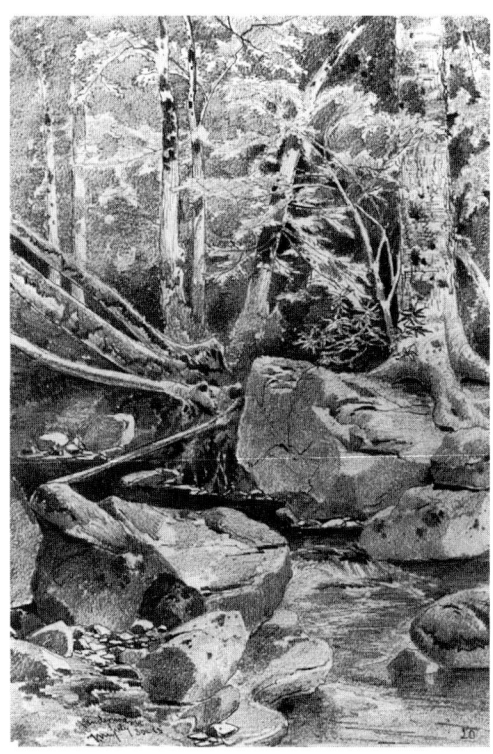

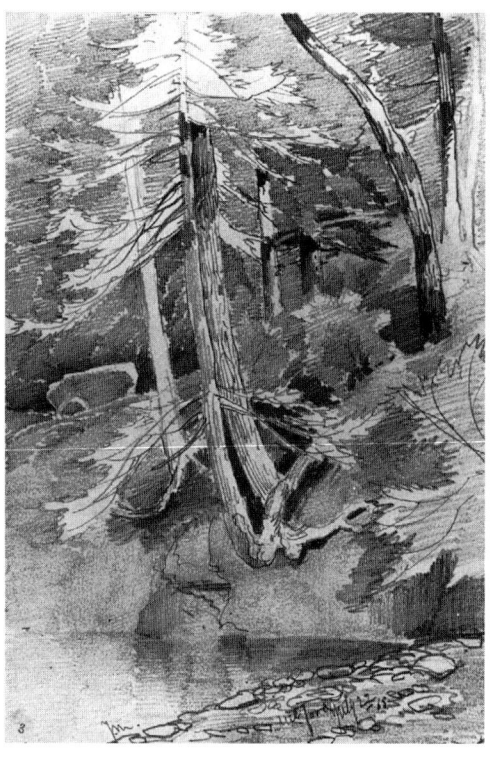

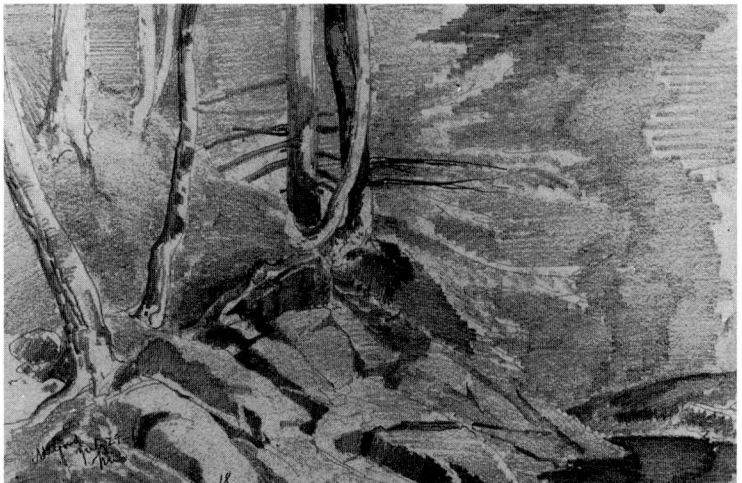

Top left: No. 123. *Vandermark* (Gilcrease Institute, 1326.721), graphite on wove, sketch 9¹/₂ by 6¹/₄ inches, mount 10³/₄ by 7¹/₈ inches.

Top right: No. 104. *Milford* (Gilcrease Institute, 1326.740), graphite on wove, 9³/₈ by 6³/₈ inches.

Bottom left: No. 122. *Milford* (Gilcrease Institute, 1326.1026), graphite on wove, 6¹/₂ by 9¹/₂ inches.

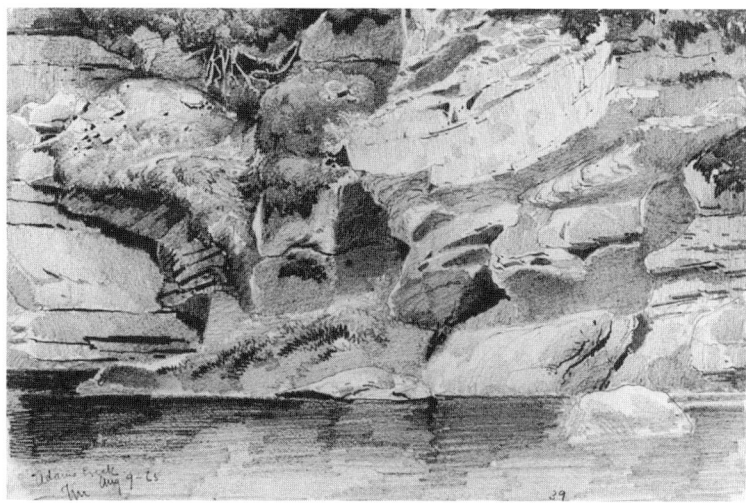

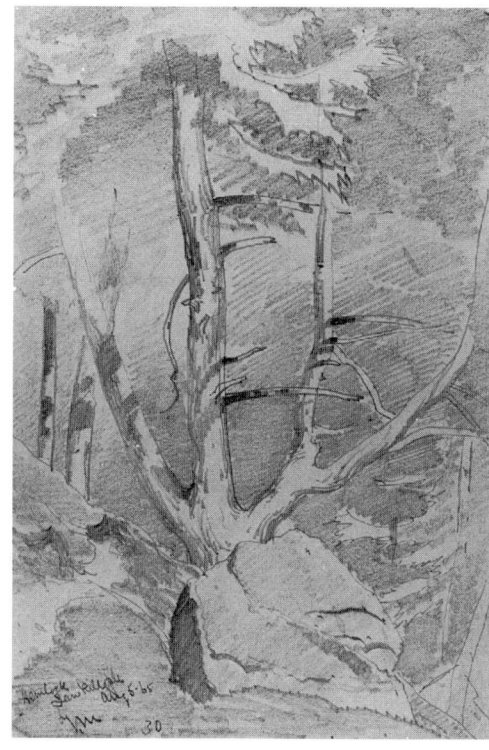

Left: No. 137. *Adams Creek* (Gilcrease Institute, 1326.734), graphite on wove, 6¹/₂ by 9³/₈ inches.

Right: No. 130. *Hemlock, Sawkill Fall* (Gilcrease Institute, 1326.723), graphite on wove, 9³/₈ by 6¹/₂ inches.

the third person, he noted: "In 1867 he visited England and the continent more particularly to study the work of the Old Masters. Although gaining most of his art knowledge abroad he remained an essentially American painter."[27]

Moran's daily routine in Paris is not documented, but presumably he did not pursue any formal art instruction. He probably sketched after the masterworks in the Musée du Louvre. Several undated sketches in the Gilcrease collection after artists such as Rembrandt (1606–69) and Herman Swanevelt (about 1600–1655) may have been made at this time. Moran was particularly drawn to the work of the great seventeenth-century Dutch landscapists.

Moran visited the aged French painter Jean-Baptiste Camille Corot (1796–1875) sometime during the five months he spent in Paris.[28] Edith Singleton reported his reaction to Corot in her authorized, though incomplete and unpublished, biography of Moran: "Among the many interesting artistic experiences of this year was an afternoon in Corot's studio. 'Corot was a most amiable old man' is Moran's recollection, 'always smiling and full of jokes.'"[29]

Perhaps at Corot's suggestion, Moran decided to sketch in the Forest of Fontainebleau about thirty miles from Paris. It had been Corot's practice to summer at Fontainebleau and winter in Paris, and he inspired several American painters to do the same. Moran followed his lead and at the same time yielded to his own taste for woodland subjects.

Although the length of Moran's sojourn at Fontainebleau is not documented, evidence provided by his sketches suggests that his stay was short. The trees are fully covered with foliage in all the sketches, implying that Moran was at Fontainebleau in the summer of 1866 or the spring of 1867.[30] Moran's five field sketches of the Forest of Fontainebleau in the Gilcrease collection are his only known drawings of the subject. All are identical in style and similar to his sketches of Pike County, Pennsylvania: both sets include contour drawings detailed with hatching and cross-hatching.[31]

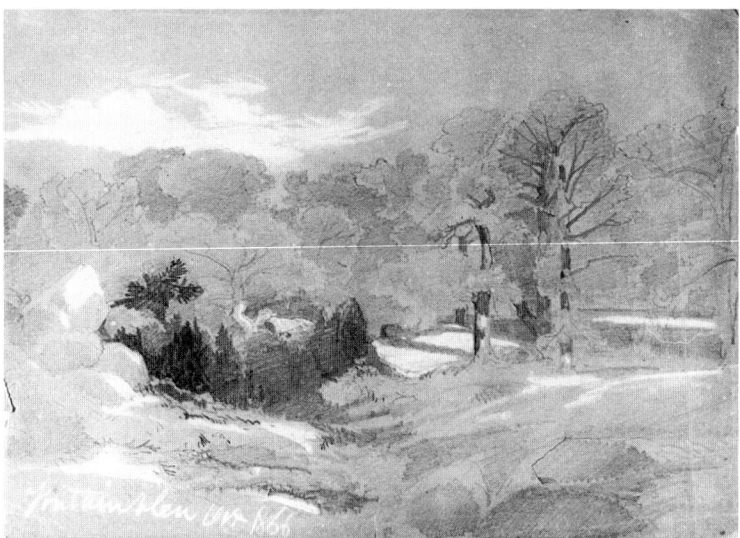

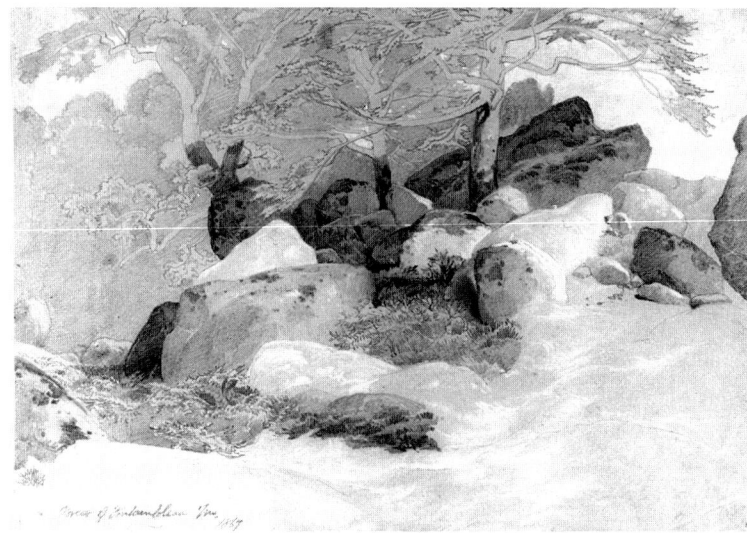

In France, Moran seems to have added a new technique to his repertoire. In *Forest of Fontainebleau* (No. 146) he applied white chalk over some of the pencil drawing to simulate dappled sunlight on rocks, trees, and earth and to indicate clouds. These white highlights are very subtle; the gray paper furnishes the middle tone. In one of the drawings, *Fontainebleau* (No. 144), Moran applied chalk, then used a moistened brush to soften the hard edges. This hybrid technique imparts an uncharacteristic fluidity to the dry medium.

Moran's visit with Corot may also have influenced his decision to go to Italy. Most of his artistic heroes—Poussin, Claude, Turner, and Hamilton, as well as Corot—were admirers of Italian landscape and Italian artists. The Morans spent a frenetic few months in Italy, traveling from Rome to Naples and then north to the Swiss Alps. The subjects of Moran's first field sketches in Italy were harbors (*Leghorn,* No. 149, and *Civitavecchia,* No. 150). *Civitavecchia* is reminiscent of Claude Lorrain's sketch of

that city, which Moran had probably seen in the British Museum in 1862 and perhaps again in 1866.[32]

The Italian trip is well documented in sketches, suggesting that Moran found Italy more inspiring than France. Although he sketched in Rome—rather cursorily, as in the view of the Colosseum (No. 154; Plate 14)—he was particularly captivated by the Campagna, the historic pastoral landscape south of the city. Here, in February and March of 1867, Moran's work underwent a dramatic change. Gone is the closed-in, claustrophobically detailed space of his sketches of Pike County, Pennsylvania, and the Forest of Fontainebleau. Instead, he sketched a sweeping vista sparsely populated with ruins.

Moran's work on the Campagna was panoramic, suggesting deep space and large scale in diminutive drawings. As he had done in his Pennsylvania river sketches, he used color washes to create atmospheric perspective, with which he was becoming increasingly adept. His use of atmospheric perspective reached its high point in

Left: No. 144. *Fontainebleau* (Gilcrease Institute, 1376.743), graphite and white chalk on wove, 9³/₄ by 13¹/₂ inches.

Right: No. 146. *Forest of Fontainebleau* (Gilcrease Institute, 1376.931), graphite and white chalk on gray wove, 9³/₄ by 13¹/₂ inches.

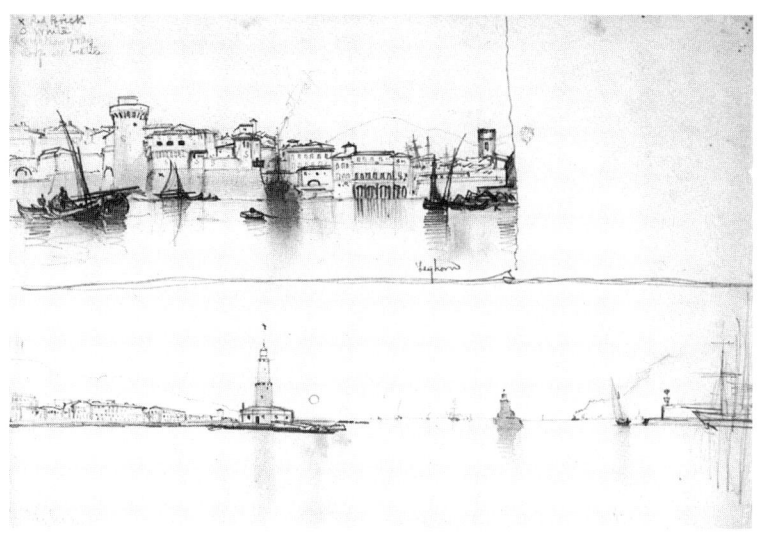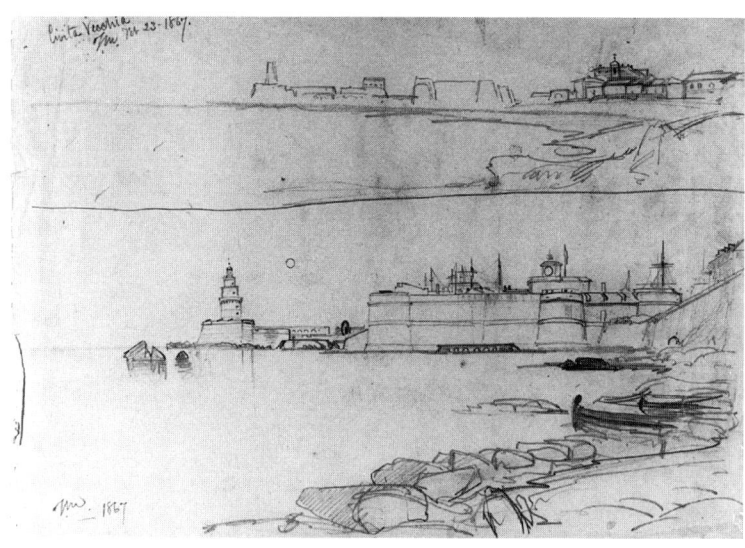

Left: No. 149a. *Leghorn* (Gilcrease Institute, 1376.595), graphite on wove, upper sketch 5 by 9¹/₂ inches, sheet 10 by 14 inches.
No. 149b. *Leghorn* (Gilcrease Institute, 1376.595), graphite on wove, lower sketch 5 by 14 inches, sheet 10 by 14 inches.

Right: No. 150a. *Civitavecchia* (Gilcrease Institute, 1376.935), graphite on gray wove, upper sketch 3⁷/₈ by 13⁵/₈ inches, sheet 9³/₄ by 13⁵/₈ inches.
No. 150b. *Civitavecchia* (Gilcrease Institute, 1376.935), graphite on gray wove, lower sketch 6¹/₈ by 13⁵/₈ inches, sheet 9³/₄ by 13⁵/₈ inches.

the American West, where he was challenged by the greatest distances and the widest vistas.

In *Ruins of the Palace of the Caesars, Rome* (No. 155; Plate 15), Moran used pencil hatching to indicate shadows, then laid washes of green, blue, and pink over the pencil. Here he employed a greater variety of color washes than in any work since his first field sketches of the 1850s. He applied the washes carefully, not allowing colors to overlap or bleed into one another.

Drawn on gray paper and enhanced by washes of color, *Palace of the Caesars, Rome* (No. 156; Plate 16) is the most ambitious of the Campagna sketches. Although most of the sketch is carefully rendered, Moran used his characteristic shorthand for the masonry, merely suggesting the bricks in the crumbling walls. In the sketches done in February, he brightened the clouds behind the ruins with opaque white. In those executed in March, he used gouache to represent the blazing white limestone of the ruins themselves.

The Great Aqueduct of the Campagna, Rome (No. 169) is one of the few sketches in which

Moran indicated the effect of direct sunlight, which is responsible for the long shadows cast by the ruins. The illumination in the wedge-shaped groups of ruins, and even the detail of the tiny shepherd and his flock in the middle ground, are reminiscent of Thomas Cole's *Roman Campagna* (1843, Wadsworth Atheneum, Hartford). One must wonder if Moran was acquainted with Cole's painting or, more likely, a reproduction of it.[33]

Moran sketched in the park of the Villa Borghese, where he studied umbrella pines and ancient oaks, such as *Oaks in the Villa Borghese, Rome* (No. 183). In contrast to the lack of detail with which Moran recorded the Campagna, *Oaks in the Villa Borghese, Rome* is distinguished by a notable refinement of drawing. These evocative tree forms found their way into some of Moran's later studio work, regardless of subject.

After his extensive work in Rome, Moran limited his documentation of his Italian travels to one or two representative sketches of each city

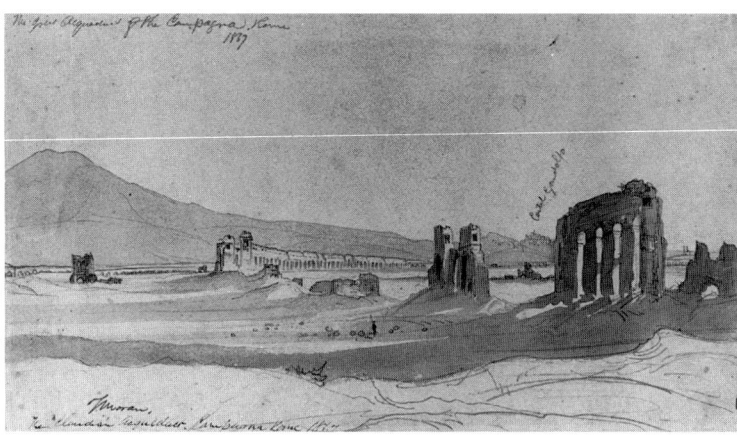

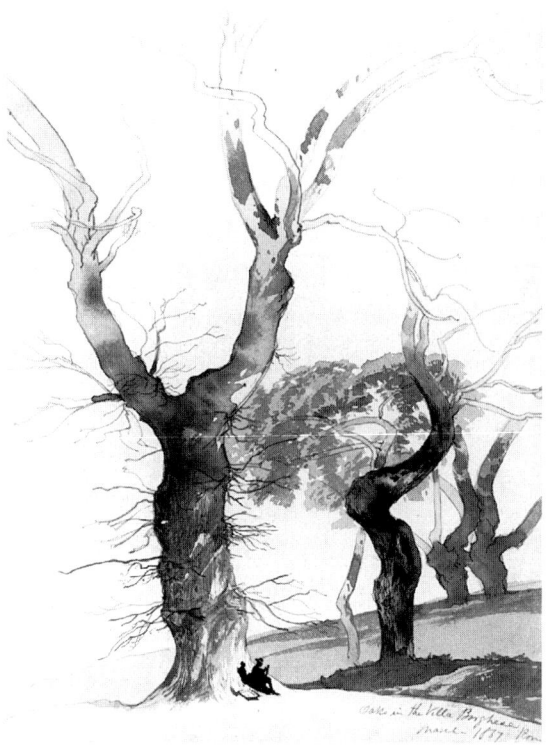

he visited. He was probably consciously follow-ing Turner's trail, as he had done in England in 1862. Moran, like Turner and many other artists, sketched Castel Gandolfo, Naples, the Bay of Baiae, Pozzuoli, Palestrina, Lake Nemi, and Ariccia in southern Italy before he traveled north to Florence (*Between Florence and Bologna,* No. 186), Lake Albano, and Lake Como.

The Morans left Italy in April by way of St. Gotthard Pass in the Swiss Alps and probably returned to Paris by rail. Moran remained there long enough to see his paintings *Children of the Mountain* (1866, Anschutz Collection, Denver) and *Autumn on the Conemaugh* (1865, location unknown) installed in the American section of the Universal Exposition, which opened April 1, 1867, before he returned to Philadelphia. Per-haps equal to the pleasure of being included in such an important international event was that of exhibiting in the company of the American artist he greatly admired, Frederic Church.[34] Church's *Niagara* (1857, Corcoran Gallery of Art, Washington, D.C.) received the silver medal, the

only American painting in the exposition to be singled out for an award.[35]

Moran devoted the next few years to work-ing in his studio on paintings of subjects drawn from his travels in Europe and America. He also became involved with painter-lithography,[36] an activity that occupied him until 1869. At this time he began a long, successful career as an illustrator for the newly established *Scribner's Monthly Magazine.* Apparently, he did not travel again until the summer of 1871. His few field sketches of this period demonstrate a renewed interest in a local site, Fairmount Park, perhaps prompted by a commission for illustrations for two articles for *Scribner's.*[37]

In June of 1870, Moran made a small series of cloud studies reminiscent of those of Consta-ble, Turner, Corot, and most especially Alexan-der Cozens (1700–1786), some of which he may have seen in England.[38] These sketches are quick and elemental, the loosest, most immediate works Moran had yet created. It is only from inscrip-tions (such as that on *Falls of Schuylkill,* No. 193)

Left: No. 169. *The Great Aqueduct of the Campagna, Rome* (Gilcrease Insti-tute, 0276.860), graphite, blue and gray washes on wove, sketch 7³/₄ by 13¹/₄ inches, mount 8¹/₈ by 13²/₄ inches.

Right: No. 183. *Oaks in the Villa Bor-ghese, Rome* (Gilcrease Institute, 0276. 869), graphite and sepia wash on wove, 15¹/₄ by 9¹/₄ inches.

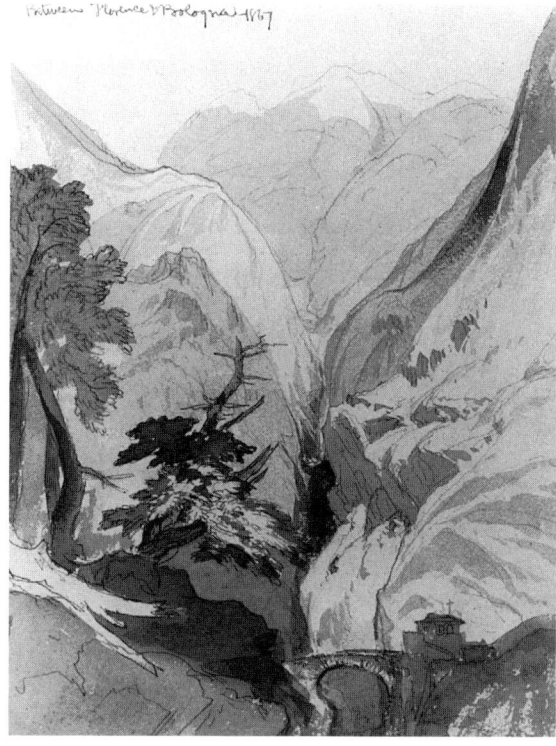

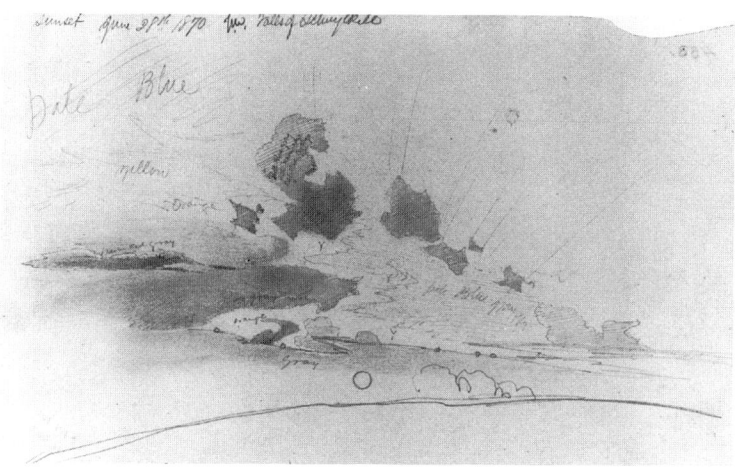

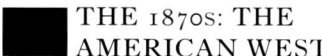

Left: No. 186. *Between Florence and Bologna* (Gilcrease Institute, 0276.865), graphite and sepia wash on wove, 10¹/8 by 7¹/2 inches.

Right: No. 193. *Falls of Schuylkill* (Gilcrease Institute, 1326.953), graphite on newsprint, 7³/4 by 12¹/8 inches.

that the site, the Falls of Schuylkill, can be determined, for Moran included no identifying landmarks. Another in this group of sketches, *Falls of Schuylkill* (No. 194), testifies strongly to Moran's interest in atmosphere. His concern with the accurate description of the form, color, shape, and type of clouds is manifested in the key to his marks and notes at the bottom of the sketch. Although Moran frequently wrote brief compositional and color notes on his sketches, he rarely did so in such detail.

◼ THE 1870s: THE AMERICAN WEST

THE YEAR 1871 marked the beginning of a new period in Moran's career. A decade of travel, study, and hard work had prepared Moran to capitalize on the good fortune of an invitation to accompany the U.S. Geological Survey to the Yellowstone during the summer of 1871.[39] Sketches he made during that summer provided the basis

of many of his paintings, watercolors, and prints for the next few decades. Views of Yellowstone's natural wonders proved to be one of Moran's most popular categories of work; he found it challenging to fulfill the demand for them.[40]

Moran's interest in the West began in his youth, perhaps as early as the 1850s, with exposure to James Hamilton's drawings to illustrate General John C. Frémont's memoirs.[41] Surely viewing such masterpieces as Albert Bierstadt's *The Rocky Mountains, Lander's Peak* (1863, Metropolitan Museum of Art, New York), exhibited at the Paris Universal Exposition in 1867, affected him as well.[42]

Moran's involvement with Yellowstone subject matter began a year before his visit, when he was asked to illustrate Nathaniel P. Langford's two-part article, "The Wonders of the Yellowstone," published in the May and June 1871 issues of *Scribner's*. Langford had been part of an expedition to the area in the summer of 1870. Moran based his illustrations on sketches produced by Walter Trumbull and

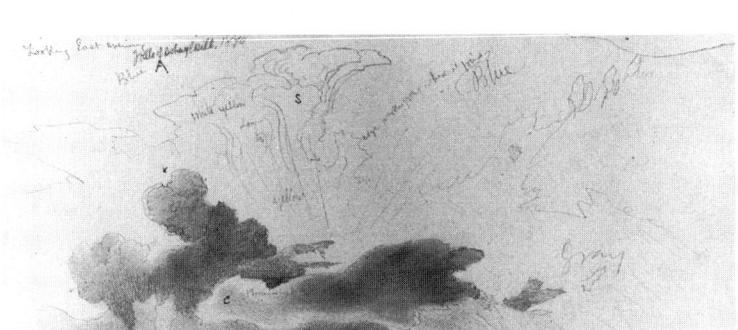

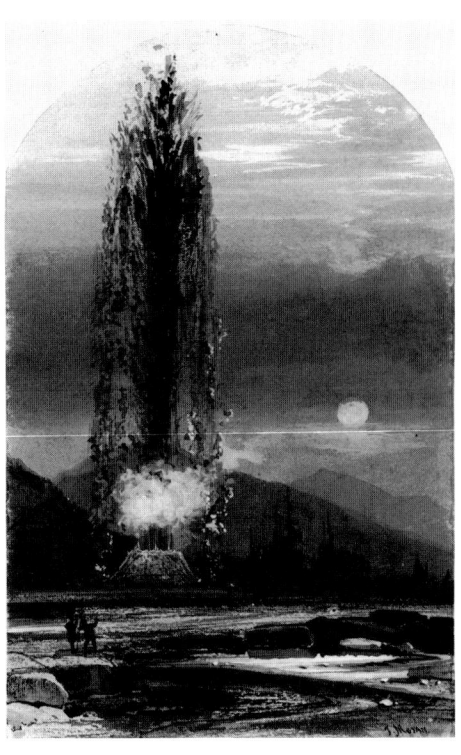

Charles Moore, members of Langford's party. The resulting images, such as *The Mud Volcano* (1870, Gilcrease Institute), were necessarily crude and inaccurate, but the experience of making them, along with reading Langford's rhetoric, certainly instilled in Moran a profound desire to see the real Yellowstone.

Moran secured letters of introduction to Dr. Ferdinand V. Hayden, head of the U.S. Geological and Geographical Survey of the Territories, who was planning to lead a party to the Yellowstone the following summer. Moran's petition was successful, and he left Philadelphia to join Hayden in late June as a welcome, if uncompensated, member of the expedition. The costs of his journey were offset by loans against existing and future work from Roswell Smith, one of the owners of *Scribner's,* and Jay Cooke, an official of the Northern Pacific Railroad.

Moran traveled the first leg of his journey in relative comfort on the Union Pacific Railroad, arriving in Green River, Wyoming, in late June. The founding of Green River in 1868 was di-

rectly linked to the extension of the rail lines, although Moran's sketches and paintings of the site never acknowledge the industrial presence recorded in the photographs of his contemporaries William Henry Jackson and Andrew J. Russell (1830–1902).[43] Here Moran made the work he inscribed *First Sketch Made in the West at Green River, Wyoming* (No. 202; Plate 17).

First Sketch Made in the West at Green River, Wyoming is the only known drawing from the trip that includes considerable color, in the form of washes of blue, pink, and brown and touches of white and gold gouache laid over Moran's usual base of contour drawing. In this first western landscape, as in the sketches of the Roman Campagna in 1867, Moran succeeded in creating an impression of breadth and depth in a small format. In fact, the configuration of the cliffs recalls the wedge-shaped ruins in his Campagna drawings. His manipulation of the paint to suggest the varying textures of rock, water, and clouds is impressive. The infinite skies of the West fascinated Moran, and he attempted to re-

Left: No. 194. *Falls of Schuylkill* (Gilcrease Institute, 1326.955), graphite on newsprint, sketch 7³/₄ by 12¹/₈ inches, mount 10³/₄ by 14³/₄ inches.

Right: Thomas Moran, *The Mud Volcano* (1870, Gilcrease Institute, 0226.1694), black ink wash on paper, 8¹/₂ by 5¹/₄ inches.

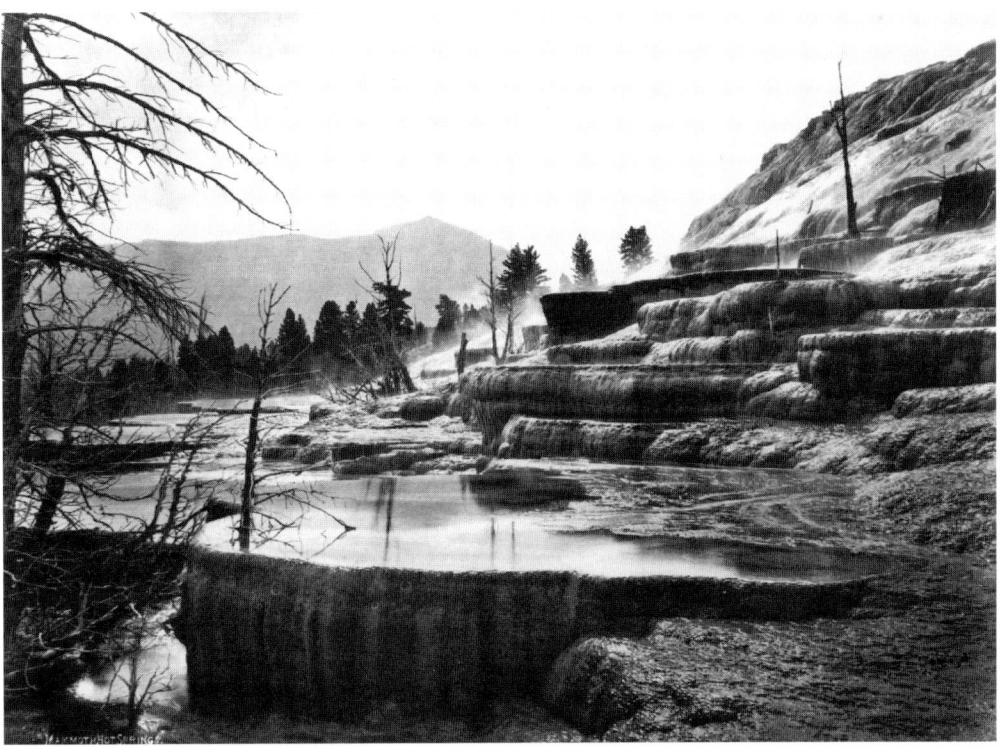

Above: William H. Jackson, *Mammoth Hot Springs* (1871, Gilcrease Institute, 4536.84.9), photograph, 9¹/₂ by 13 inches.

produce a range of atmospheric effects in this eight-inch-wide study.

Moran continued from Green River by rail to Corinne, Utah.[44] From Corinne a stagecoach took him to join Hayden's party at Virginia City, Montana. Hayden's plan was to acquire provisions at Fort Ellis, near Bozeman, and enter the Yellowstone region from the north. He established a base camp at Boettlers Ranch on the Yellowstone River, about thirty miles east of Fort Ellis.[45] The party followed a circuitous route to such natural spectacles as the Tower Fall, the Grand Canyon of the Yellowstone, the Upper and Lower Falls of the Yellowstone River, Yellowstone Lake, and finally the Upper and Lower Geyser Basins of the Firehole River.

Moran did not sketch as actively that summer as might have been expected, especially considering the unique qualities of the Yellowstone landscape. Also, none of his sketches is marked by the attention to detail he had shown in his previous American fieldwork. The decline in the quantity and detail of his sketches may be at-

tributed to Moran's association with the photographer William Henry Jackson, an official member of Hayden's party. Moran may have spent more time helping Jackson compose photographs than he did working on his own sketches.[46] Of course, Moran had produced numerous detailed sketches while working in the field with his photographer brother John, but in the Yellowstone conditions were more primitive, and he may have had less time to sketch.[47]

The sketches Moran made during the summer of 1871 indicate the hurried conditions under which he worked. In sketches such as *Bunsen Peak* (No. 212), he concentrated on topographical rather than geological features, relying on Jackson's photographs, such as *Mammoth Hot Springs* (1871, Gilcrease Institute), for information about the latter.

A comparison of Moran's sketch *Yellowstone Lake* (No. 227) and Jackson's photograph bearing the same title (1871, Gilcrease Institute) reveals the artistic collaboration between painter and photographer. The compositions are practi-

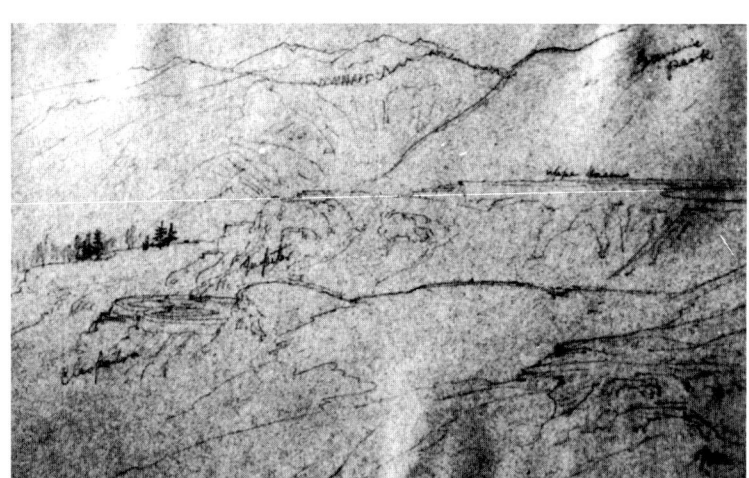

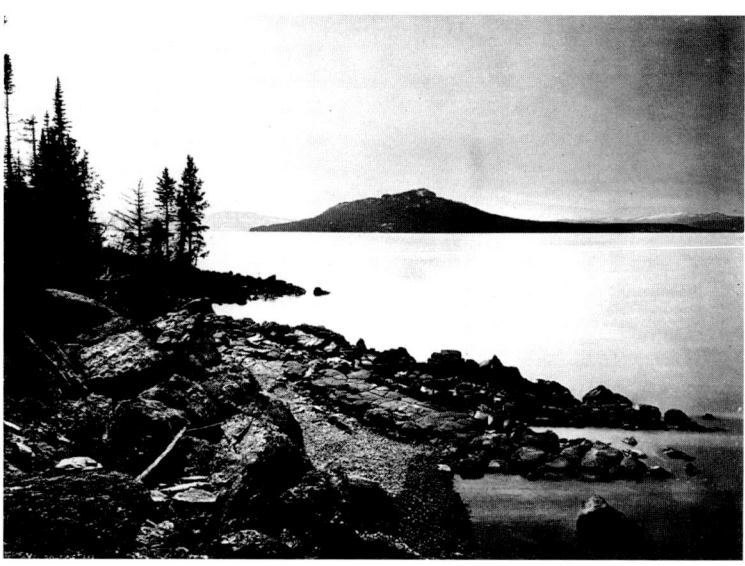

cally mirror images, both capturing the serene lake and a wedge of its rock-strewn shore. Both artists used a cluster of pines, offset, to provide a vertical accent to the dominant horizontality of the compositions. Moran made the trees his main focal point, while Jackson chose to emphasize the rugged foreground.

Most of the sketches made that summer are unadorned contour drawings, although some, such as *In Lower Madison Canyon* (No. 230; Plate 18), are enhanced with simple two-color washes. The color was probably added in camp rather than at the site.

Moran left Hayden's party in mid-August, before the completion of the survey. He made immediate use of his sketches and Jackson's photographs, spending the rest of 1871 and the early part of 1872 fulfilling commissions. He provided images to *Harper's Weekly, The Aldine,* and *Scribner's,* all of which carried articles on the most recent Yellowstone discoveries. The *Scribner's* article was written by Hayden, who also used Moran's images to illustrate his official re-

port.[48] Moran worked on two watercolor commissions, one for Jay Cooke and another for the British industrialist William Blackmore,[49] as well as an enormous canvas, *The Grand Canyon of the Yellowstone* (1872, U.S. Department of the Interior, Washington, D.C.).

Moran's Yellowstone paintings and watercolors won him his first real success and led to a great demand for his services from leaders of government expeditions in the West, magazine editors, and private collectors. Both Hayden, who had organized a return party to the Yellowstone, and John Wesley Powell, leader of the government survey of the Grand Canyon of the Colorado, asked Moran to accompany their 1872 expeditions. Moran declined both invitations, citing his obligation to complete commissioned work. In late August of that year, however, Moran made a western trip after all. He traveled with his wife Mary on the Central and Union Pacific Railroads, perhaps as far as San Francisco, before visiting and sketching sites in the Yosemite Valley on the western slope of the Sierra Nevada.[50]

Left: No. 212. *Bunsen Peak* (Jefferson National Expansion Memorial 5847), graphite on blue wove, 6¼ by 10 inches.

Right: William H. Jackson, *Yellowstone Lake* (1871, Gilcrease Institute, 4336.84.29), photograph, 9½ by 13 inches.

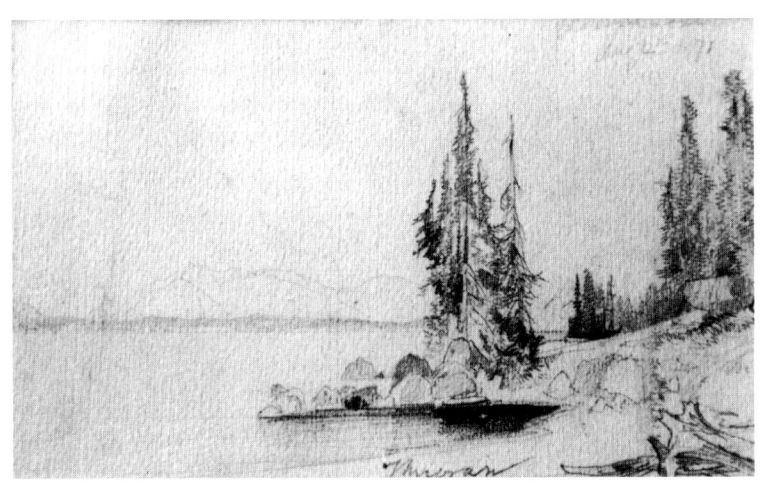 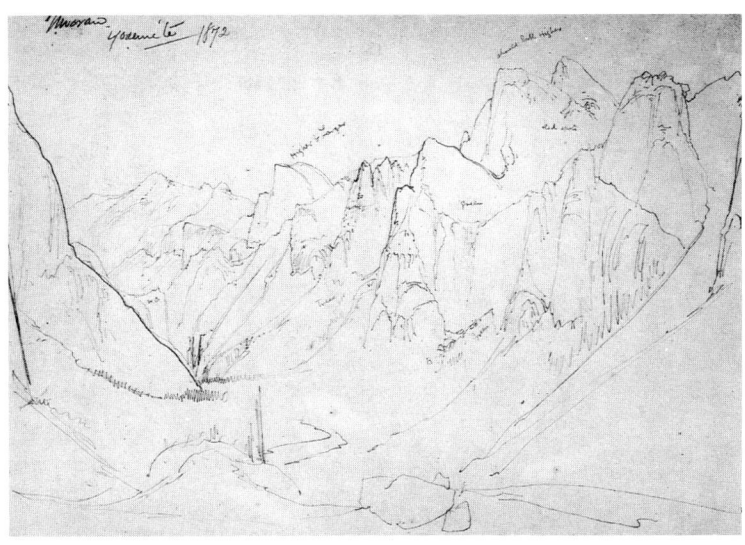

Left: No. 227. *Yellowstone Lake* (Jefferson National Expansion Memorial 4217), graphite on laid, 5 by 7 inches.

Right: No. 233. *Yosemite* (Yosemite National Park 57 778), graphite on wove, 10³/₄ by 14⁷/₈ inches.

The accessible area of Yosemite, the valley floor, was more contained than the area Moran had roamed in Yellowstone, but the journey in was far more difficult. It required a grueling ride on horseback, probably along the predecessor to Four Mile Trail, which was finished the year of Moran's trip. Sketching from the trail could not have been easy. After visiting in 1865, Frederick Law Olmsted wrote that tourists arrived "in the majority of cases quite overcome with the fatigue and unaccustomed hardship of the journey. Few persons, especially few women, are able to enjoy or profit by the scenery and air for days afterward . . . and many leave before they have recovered from their first exhaustion and return home jaded and ill."[51] During this trip, Mary suffered exhaustion to the extent that she never again accompanied her husband during his western journeys. Moran himself apparently sustained no lasting ill effects. Sketches such as *Yosemite* (No. 233) document his approach to the valley. Moran deftly employed his simple contour technique to set down all the prominent fea-

tures that rise from the valley floor and added compositional and color notes. To imply the great breadth of the valley, Moran composed the sketch in a horizontal format that is unusual for the sketches from this trip.

The Morans probably lodged at the hotel at Glacier Point. From there, Moran ventured out to sketch Yosemite's landmarks—South Dome (now called Half Dome), Sentinel and El Capitan, Cathedral Rock, and Vernal and Nevada Falls—in works such as *Glacier Point from Trail to Vernal Fall*·(No. 243).

Once again, Moran's artistic involvement with the location preceded his visit by many months. In January he had designed illustrations based on the photographs of Carleton E. Watkins (1829–1916)[52] for a *Scribner's* article.[53] Because Moran made few paintings of Yosemite after the 1872 visit, its importance to his career has generally been downplayed along with the artist's personal response to the region. Yet on this trip he completed about twenty pencil-and-wash studies of the sites he had earlier illustrated for "Won-

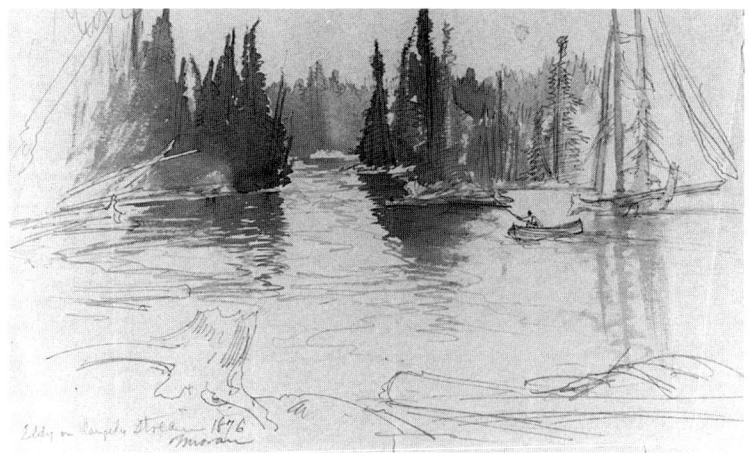

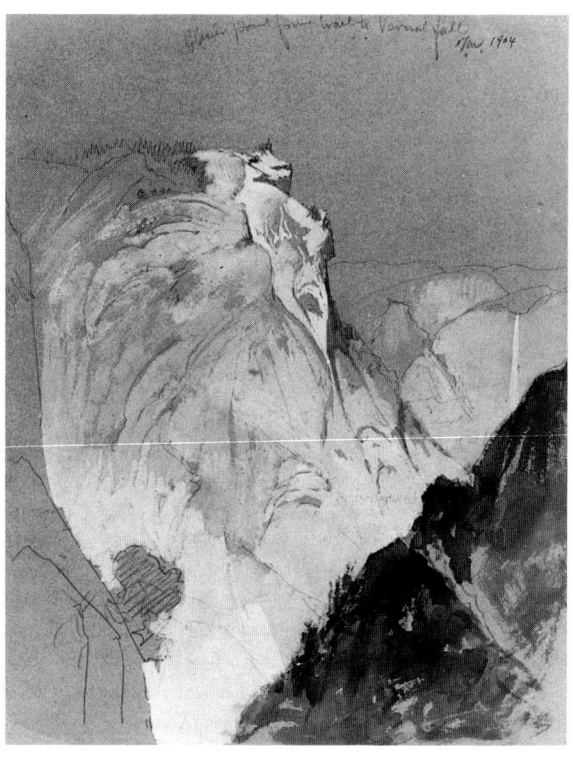

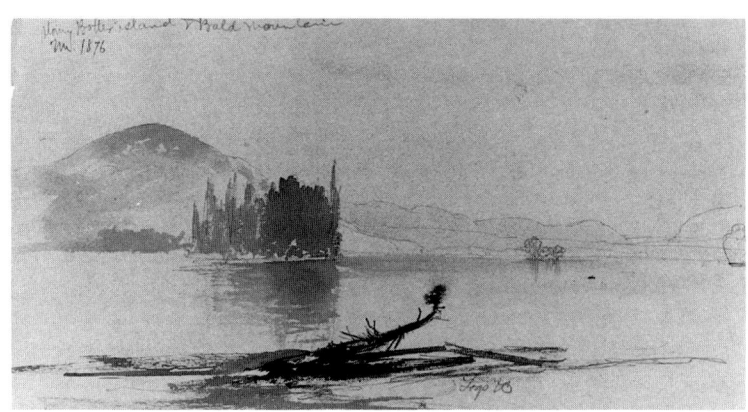

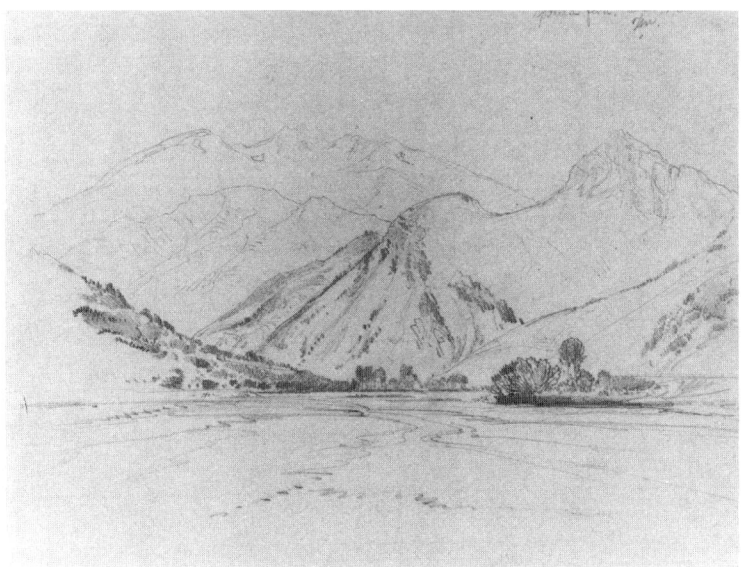

Top left: No. 251. *Eddy on Rangeley Stream* (Gilcrease Institute, 0226.877), graphite and wash on gray wove, 9³/₄ by 12⁵/₈ inches.

Top right: No. 243. *Glacier Point from Trail to Vernal Fall* (Gilcrease Institute, 0236.835), graphite, wash, and white gouache on gray wove, 12³/₄ by 9⁷/₈ inches.

Middle left: No. 253. *Stony Batter Island and Bald Mountain* (Gilcrease Institute, 0226.876), graphite and wash on gray wove, 7 by 12⁵/₈ inches.

Bottom left: No. 258. *Spanish Fork Canyon* (Gilcrease Institute, 1336.952), graphite on gray wove, 9⁷/₈ by 12³/₄ inches.

ders of the West" but had not seen for himself until now. Clearly, he responded to the unusual geology and landscape of Yosemite with all the interest he showed for any new territory. It should be noted, however, that Moran saw the Yosemite Valley in the autumn, when many of its breathtaking waterfalls, fed in springtime by snowmelt, were dry.

Sketches such as *Glacier Point from Trail to Vernal Fall* (No. 243) are vertical in format, in keeping with the dramatic height of the rock structures. Begun as a contour drawing, this sketch is enhanced by subtle black and gray washes that Moran used in half of his Yosemite work, most often to describe granite. The absence of color washes may indicate that he considered using this work as the basis of an illustration.

In Yosemite, Moran indulged his perennial love of rocks, which he sketched in detail. Other landscape elements, such as the trees that top the ridge, are reduced to scribbles, included only to indicate scale relationships. *Glacier Point from Trail to Vernal Fall* (No. 243) also represents a rare use of white gouache in Moran's Yosemite sketches. Here he used the dazzling white to set off the ridge from the darker formations nearby.

As a result of his other obligations as well as the volume of work based on his later trips to the Grand Canyon of the Colorado in 1873 and to the Mountain of the Holy Cross in 1874, Moran did not use his Yosemite sketches for several years.[54] His rare Yosemite paintings seem to have been inspired by a visit of 1904, although Moran probably also drew upon his stock of sketches from 1872 when he made them.

During the summer of 1873, Moran returned to the West as a member of Major John Wesley Powell's expedition through the canyons of the Colorado River. Once again, Moran had more invitations than he could accept and had to refuse another offer from Hayden. Before departing for the West, Moran left his new home in Newark, New Jersey, to make a brief excursion to a sportsman's haven, the Rangeley Lakes of southwestern Maine, where he fished and made sketches (*Eddy on Rangeley Stream*, No. 251).

Several, such as *Stony Batter Island and Bald Mountain* (No. 253), he used to illustrate another article for *Scribner's*.[55] Moran joined Powell in early July at Salt Lake City. From there the party proceeded through Lehi and Springville to Spanish Fork Canyon, about twenty miles south, where they camped and where Moran made his first sketches.

In his three pencil sketches of Spanish Fork Canyon, Moran concentrated on the canyon walls and cliffs that rise steeply above the riverbed. He made *Spanish Fork Canyon, Utah* (No. 259) from a point just above the river and contrasted the serpentine path of the water with the sharp, angular forms of the rocky cliffs. From a different perspective, Moran viewed the rock walls from the broad horizontal plane of the riverbed and drew *Spanish Fork Canyon* (No. 258). As was usually the case in his panoramic views of the West, he included details of trees and vegetation to indicate the vast scale of the terrain.

The expedition followed a generally southsouthwesterly route, arriving in late July at what is now Zion National Park in the Valley of the Rio Virgin. At this site, Moran made sketches that document his working relationship with this expedition's photographer, John K. Hillers.[56] In circumstances similar to those surrounding the creation of images of Yellowstone Lake by Moran and Jackson in 1871, Hillers and Moran may have collaborated on views of the Valley of the Rio Virgin. Moran's two-part sketch, *Valley of the Rio Virgin, South Utah* (No. 263) and *Valley of the Rio Virgin* (No. 264), closely resembles Hillers's photograph *Virgin River Valley, below Zion Canyon, Utah* (1873, National Archives photograph No. 57-PS-80, Geological Survey Collection).[57] That Moran was not simply copying Hillers's photograph is shown by variations in the compositions and also, more important, by details such as the tree at the right of Hillers's photograph and just to the left of center in Moran's sketch (No. 263). The tree became dominant when seen through the camera lens, while Moran deemphasized this distracting element.

In a letter to his wife written at Kanab, Utah, Moran commented on his fortuitous relationship

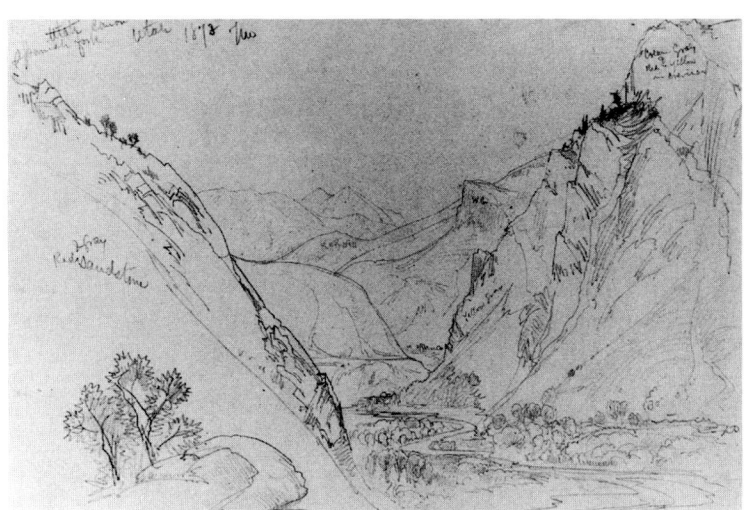

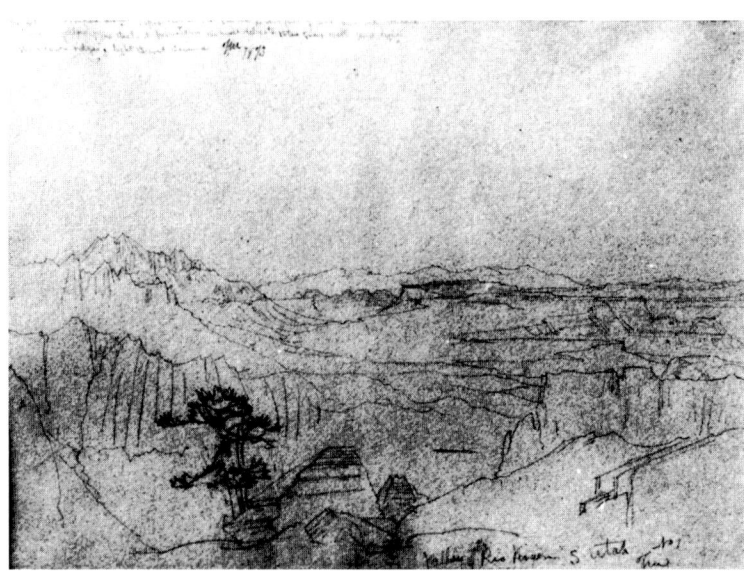

with Hillers: "I made an outline and did a little color work but had not time nor was it worth while to make a detailed study in color. We made several photos which will give me all the details I want if I conclude to paint the view."[58]

The Narrows, in the northeastern part of Zion, interested Moran. His deceptively simple sketch *In the Narrows, Zion Valley, The Gate Keeper* (No. 274; Plate 19), which he tinted with blue and brown watercolor and enhanced with white gouache and red conté crayon, reveals accurately the characteristic geology of the site. Soaring light and dark rock pinnacles crowd so closely in places that the passable course narrows to fifty feet. Moran recorded trees that cling to the steep slopes; the tiny scribbles emphasize the height and immensity of the formation.

By the first week of August, Powell's main party had entered present-day Arizona, arriving at the North Rim of the Grand Canyon, south of the Kaibab Plateau. Moran apparently had more time than usual to sketch here, and from this vantage point he created some of his most pain-stakingly delineated drawings of the canyon. *Grand Canyon* (No. 278) is typical of this group of very precise contour sketches of rock forma-tions and eroded strata. He did not, however, de-vote much time and energy to solidifying forms with shade and shadow. He made at least eight drawings,[59] all measuring 10 3/4 by 15 inches, from the rim as he looked out over the breadth of the canyon. When viewed together, they form a profile recording several miles of topography.

Powell's party ultimately descended into the canyon, but by then Moran had returned to Newark. There he began to work on a multitude of drawings, many of which enriched Powell's report, *Explorations of the Colorado of the West and Its Tributaries* (1875); Powell's two-part article for *Scribner's,* "The Cañons of the Col-orado" (February and March 1875); J. E. Col-burn's "The Canyons of the Colorado" (*Pic-turesque America,* vol. 2);[60] and Colburn's "Utah Scenery," published in *The Aldine* (January 1874). He also had commissions for watercolors and oils of the canyon.[61] Moran used his sketches

Top left: No. 259. *Spanish Fork Can-yon* (Gilcrease Institute, 1336.951), graphite on wove, 7 1/2 by 10 7/8 inches.

Top right: No. 263. *Valley of the Rio Vir-gin, South Utah* (Jefferson National Ex-pansion Memorial, 5852), graphite on blue wove, 10 3/4 by 15 inches.

as references, along with photographs by Hillers and E. O. Beaman and perhaps sketches by artists such as William Henry Holmes.[62] Moran was particularly reliant on Hillers's photographs in his work that autumn on *The Chasm of the Colorado* (1873, U.S. Department of the Interior, Washington, D.C.), the pendant to his monumental canvas of Yellowstone.[63]

Hayden continued to ask Moran to accompany his government expeditions. In 1874 he arranged for the artist to visit the legendary Mountain of the Holy Cross on a trip that was not part of the regular survey. Moran, who had based an illustration for *Picturesque America* on a photograph of the "sacred mountain" taken by William Henry Jackson during Hayden's survey the year before, was once again eager to see for himself another spectacular western site.

The first ascent of the peak, located about one hundred miles west of Denver in the Sawatch Range, had been made during the summer of 1873. The cruciform fissures on its face, filled year-round with snow, had long made the Mountain of the Holy Cross the subject of legend and an emblem of the West as the New Eden.

Hayden himself did not make the 1874 trip. He put Moran in the care of his assistant, James Stevenson, a friend of Moran's since the Yellowstone trip. Moran arrived at the survey headquarters near Denver in early August, where he joined a small party under Stevenson's command and started for the peak.

For a variety of reasons, Moran made very few sketches during this trip; only fourteen are the property of public institutions.[64] In a letter to his wife he noted his lack of time for sketching: "The scenery . . . was very beautiful as we are fairly into the Rocky Mountains. One view, [Pikes Peak] in particular, was magnificent . . . I did not make a sketch as we were on the march at the time, but I can remember it near enough."[65] In another letter, he complained about the quality of other scenery: "The main range of the Rockies is in full view, but the forms are very poor. Mount Lincoln, 14,000 feet high, looks like a big sand hill."[66] The paucity of sketches also reflects the difficulty of the journey: "We began the ascent of the inter-vening mountain between us and the *Roche Moutonnee* Valley, & of all the hard climbing that I have experienced, this beat it."[67]

Many of Moran's sketches from this trip record campsites. One site was poetically named Camp of the Evening Star, although the name of another, Camp Vexation, is probably a more accurate gauge of the hardships of camp life. The camp sketches are unique. In each of these Moran included evidence of human presence: tents, wagons, and sometimes figures. This is a rarity in his work. *Camp of the Evening Star, on the Platte* (No. 288) contains all three elements, set against the receding diagonals of the mountain forms and Moran's characteristic bottle-brush trees. Moran displayed an unusual interest in weather conditions in this sketch. Diagonal lines indicate wind direction, and a tiny circle represents the sun at the upper center. He sometimes used the sun-circle as a reminder of the time of day and to avoid taking the time to denote shadows, although in *Holy Cross Trip, Camp Vexation* (No. 289) shadows are very clearly indicated.

Moran's only sketch of the Mountain of the Holy Cross is one of the most detailed works from the trip. According to his letter, it was made from 800 feet below the peak.[68] *Mount Holy Cross* (No. 295) bears no resemblance to his major oil painting of the subject. Unlike the painting, the sketch is horizontal in format. In the painting the cross of snow is seen straight on; in the sketch the landmark, delineated by heavy pencil strokes, is viewed obliquely. Moran's compositional and geological notations on *Mount Holy Cross* and other sketches from the trip function as substitutes for the landscape details and effects he apparently lacked the time to draw.

Moran spent the next several years working primarily in the studio, completing his painting *The Mountain of the Holy Cross* (1875, Autry Museum of Western Heritage, Los Angeles) and several other canvases depicting the canyon country he had visited in 1873. His travel, limited to several short trips, included jaunts to the Bushkill River in Easton, Pennsylvania, and to Madison, Wisconsin, to sketch the lakes region in

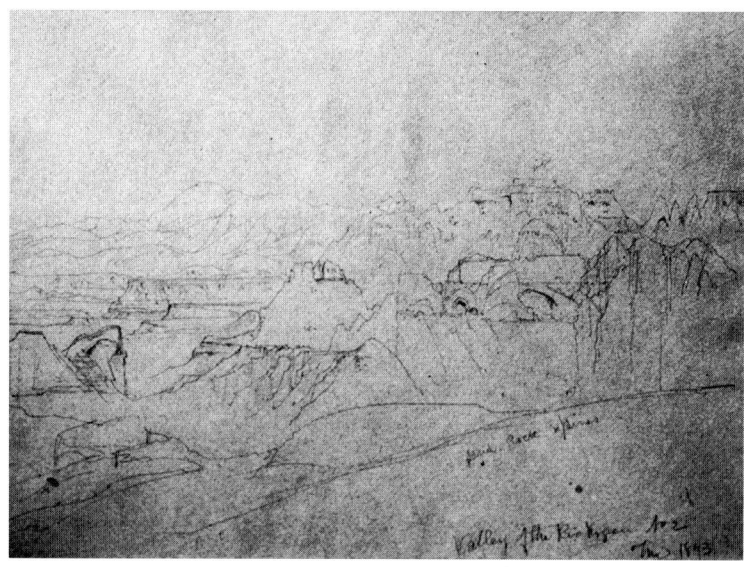

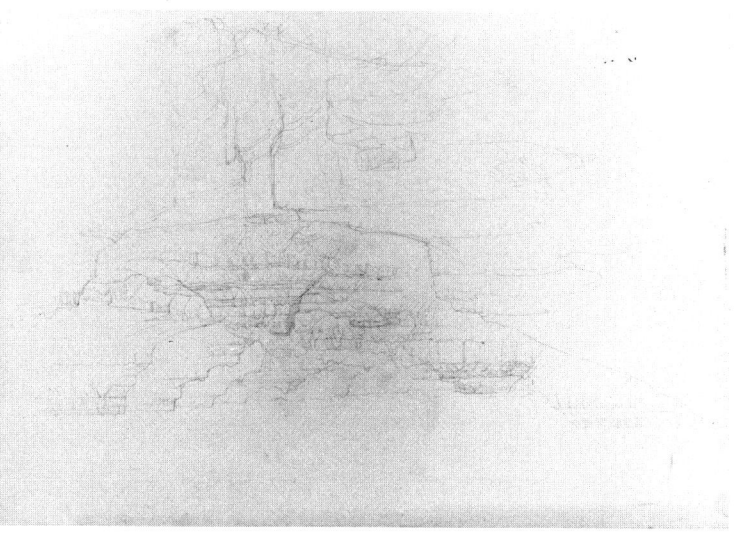

preparation for paintings commissioned by the Women's Centennial Committee of that state (No. 304; Plate 20).

During the late winter of 1877, Moran accepted a commission from *Scribner's* to illustrate an article about Fort George Island, Florida, located about twenty-five miles from Jacksonville. In an attempt to divert some of Jacksonville's burgeoning tourist business to Fort George Island, residents and developers were promoting the unspoiled beauty of the quaint and quiet island. After a four-day trip by steamship from New York, Moran and his wife landed at Jacksonville, then took a ferry to the island. By the 1880s a rail line had been constructed to handle the increased volume of tourism to Florida.

After devoting six years to sketching mountainous, often sparsely vegetated terrain, Moran discovered a new challenge in Florida's lush tropical landscape. He paid particular attention to the indigenous flora: palms, live oaks, pines. The Florida sketches, such as *Sand and Palmetto* (No. 312), contrast markedly with those he made in the West. They reveal Moran's fascination with any new stimulus, as seen, for example, in the intricate pattern of palm fronds in *Lake Isabel, Fort George Island, Florida* (No. 313).[69] The Florida sketches have a full-bodied character that distinguishes them from Moran's minimal drawings made in the West, and they also differ from his tightly constructed sketches of rural Pennsylvania. Like the western sketches, however, they show some spontaneity, as Moran applied the principle, if not the technique, of the rapid execution he had practiced in the West.

For about two weeks the Morans explored Fort George Island, seeking images for "An Island of the Sea," an article by Julia E. Dodge published in *Scribner's* in September 1877. *Sand and Palmetto* (No. 312) was the inspiration for *The Southern End of Fort George Island*,[70] one of the five illustrations that bear Moran's colophon. Although it was to be the basis of a black-and-white illustration, color notations along the top seem to indicate that he considered working it up as a painting or watercolor. He made at

Left: No. 264. *Valley of the Rio Virgin* (Jefferson National Expansion Memorial 5850), graphite on blue wove, 10³/₄ by 15 inches.

Right: No. 278. *Grand Canyon* (Gilcrease Institute, 1336.916), graphite on wove, 10⁷/₈ by 14¹/₂ inches.

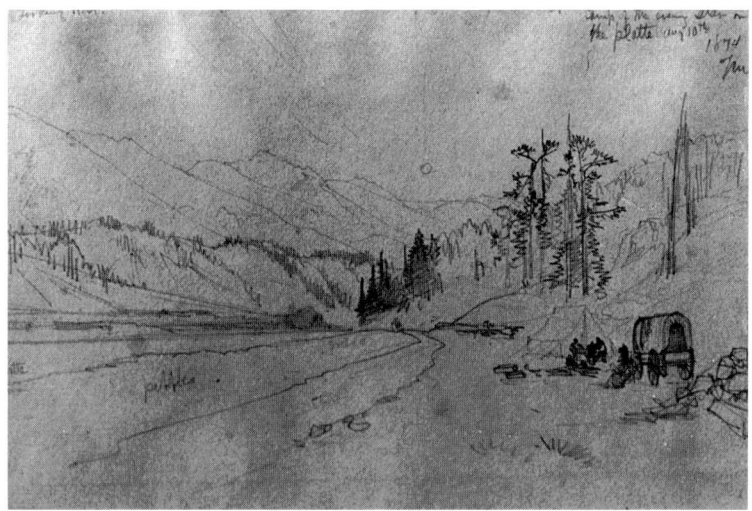

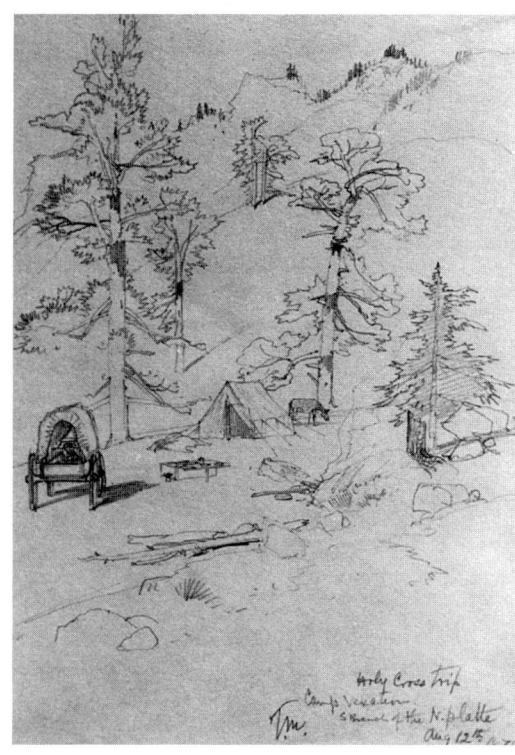

Left: No. 288. *Camp of the Evening Star on the Platte* (Jefferson National Expansion Memorial, 4249), graphite on wove, 7 1/2 by 10 3/4 inches.

Right: No. 289. *Holy Cross Trip, Camp Vexation* (Jefferson National Expansion Memorial 4245), graphite on wove, 7 1/4 by 10 3/4 inches.

least one watercolor-enhanced sketch, *Fort George Island* (No. 336; Plate 21). In it he expressively manipulated his color to imply a range of perceptions of an intensely sunlit, breezy, humid tropical day.

Moran made many more sketches than were used for the *Scribner's* article, as he sought out scenes that corresponded to the author's prose. *Old Slave Quarters, Fort George Island* (No. 328) is a very quickly executed design that was considered as an illustration of Dodge's description of "tabby" cabins, some of which were occupied, although most were in ruins.[71] (Compare Moran's shorthand treatment of the palms in *Old Slave Quarters* with the portrayal of those in *Sand and Palmetto* [No. 312].)

The curving road that originates in the foreground and disappears into the middle ground of *From Shell Hummocks, Fort George Island* (No. 308) became a recurrent motif in Moran's eastern work. Here it functions as a time-honored device to lead the viewer's eye into the composition. It also records a renowned network of paths paved

with oyster shells: "Miles of avenue have been cut with fine taste and discrimination in all directions through the woods, and connected with the drive upon the beach; a part of them are covered with the quickly crumbling oyster-shells, making the splendid 'shell road' so famous in the south."[72] These brilliant white paths were practical, easing access to terrain that could change from sandy to swampy within a few feet, and a visual treat as well.

From Shell Hummocks, Fort George Island (No. 308) is an intimate scene, reminiscent of Moran's early work in Pennsylvania and the Forest of Fontainebleau. In two sketches inscribed *Lake Isabel, Fort George Island, Florida* (Nos. 313 and 314), Moran suggested the expanse of this coastal area by including a gap in the foreground vegetation through which is seen the distant water.

These were not Moran's first sketches of coastal scenes; he had sketched the seaside in England in 1862 and in Italy in 1867. His earlier work had focused on the signs of human endeavor:

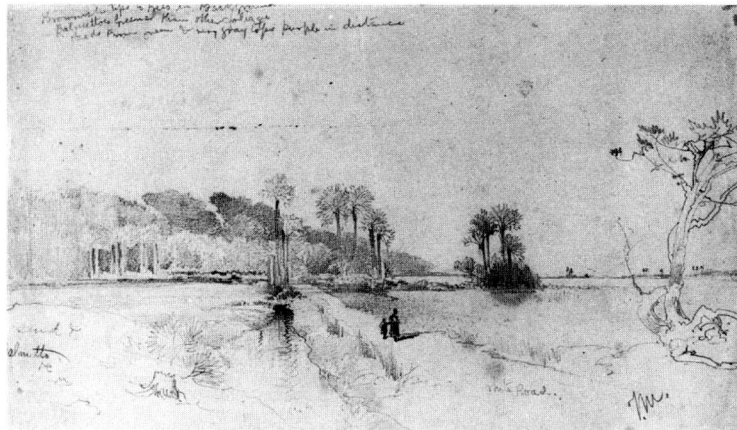

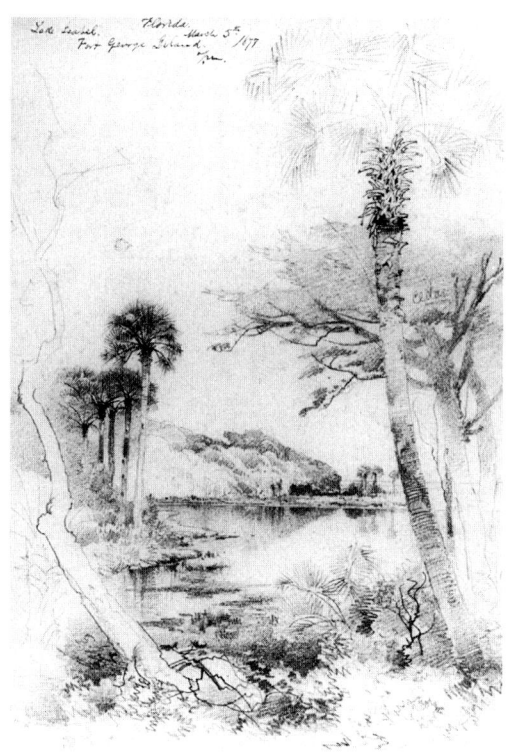

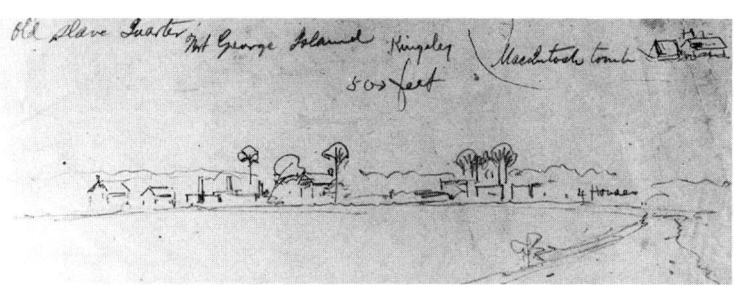

boats, docks, harbor scenes. In Florida he dealt almost exclusively with the natural environment in work that prepared him for a coastal region that became his greatest source of sketches and finished works: Long Island, New York.

By 1878 Moran was considering establishing a summer residence and studio.[73] During that summer, accompanied by his family, he made sketching trips to two possible sites, Feltville, New Jersey, and East Hampton, New York.

The Morans spent about two weeks in the abandoned mill town of Feltville a few miles southwest of Newark. Moran filled the first pages of a pocket sketchbook with scenes of the countryside and of the rustic remnants of water-powered mills. His fascination with the mills at Feltville recalls Frederic Church's engagement with the same subject at Mount Desert, Maine, during the 1850s.[74] Most of Moran's sketches were very quickly executed in graphite. He used black conté crayon, however, to produce several more elaborately detailed sketches (Nos. 342, 343, and 344). The grainy effect of the conté crayon sketches

recalls his lithographic work of the late 1860s, such as *In the Forest of the Wissahickon* (1868, Gilcrease Institute).[75] Although there is no proof that he was considering a return to lithography, in 1878 he began to etch again after an eighteen-year hiatus, so it is not inconceivable that he might have been investigating new possibilities for lithography as well. Some of these sketches, such as *Feltville* (No. 342), have been boxed in, which suggests that Moran may have intended to use them as the basis of some kind of finished work.[76]

Two larger, more detailed sketches, *Feltville* (No. 350) and *Near Feltville, New Jersey* (No. 349; Plate 22), both executed on blue paper, may have been plein air studies for finished works. *Near Feltville, New Jersey* was enhanced with black wash and an effective use of opaque white for highlights in the sky and reflections in the mill stream. On the verso of this drawing, Moran noted the colors he observed in the landscape, suggesting that he was planning to further develop this subject.

Top left: No. 312. *Sand and Palmetto* (Gilcrease Institute, 1326.659), graphite on wove, 7³/₈ by 12³/₈ inches.

Top right: No. 313. *Lake Isabel, Fort George Island, Florida* (Gilcrease Institute, 1326.1015), graphite on wove, 10³/₄ by 7³/₈ inches.

Bottom left: No. 328. *Old Slave Quarters, Fort George Island* (Gilcrease Institute, 1326.646), graphite and ink on wove, 3³/₄ by 9¹/₂ inches.

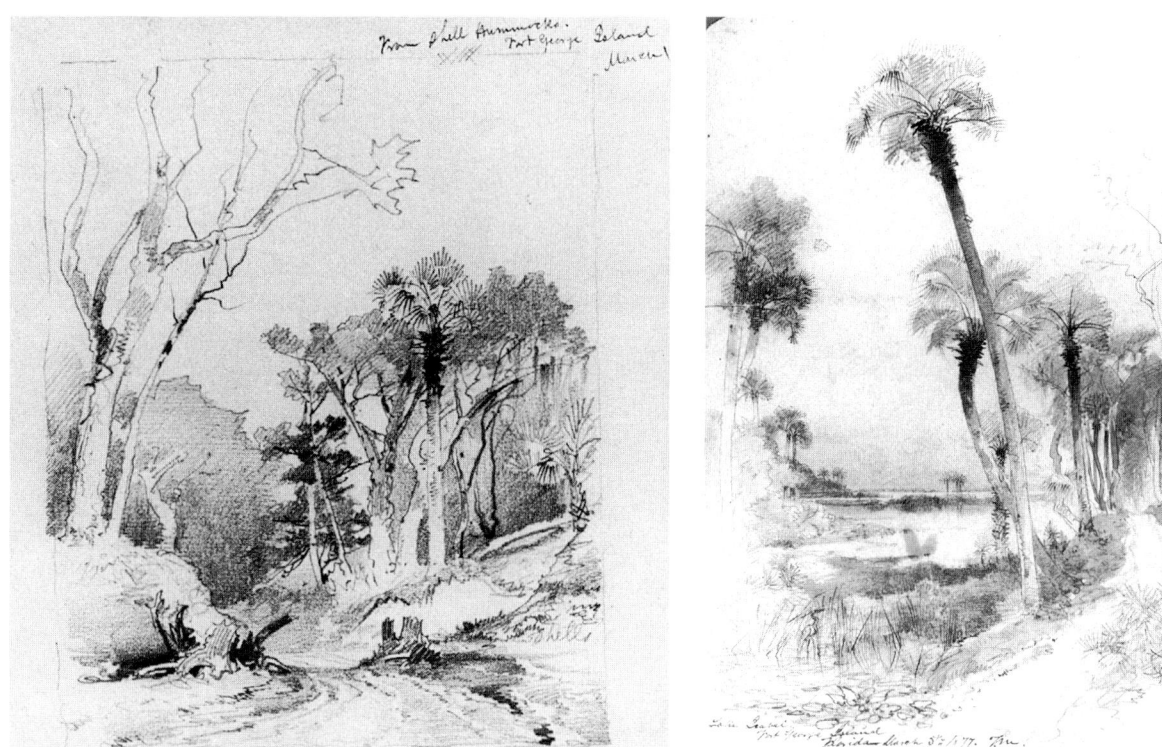

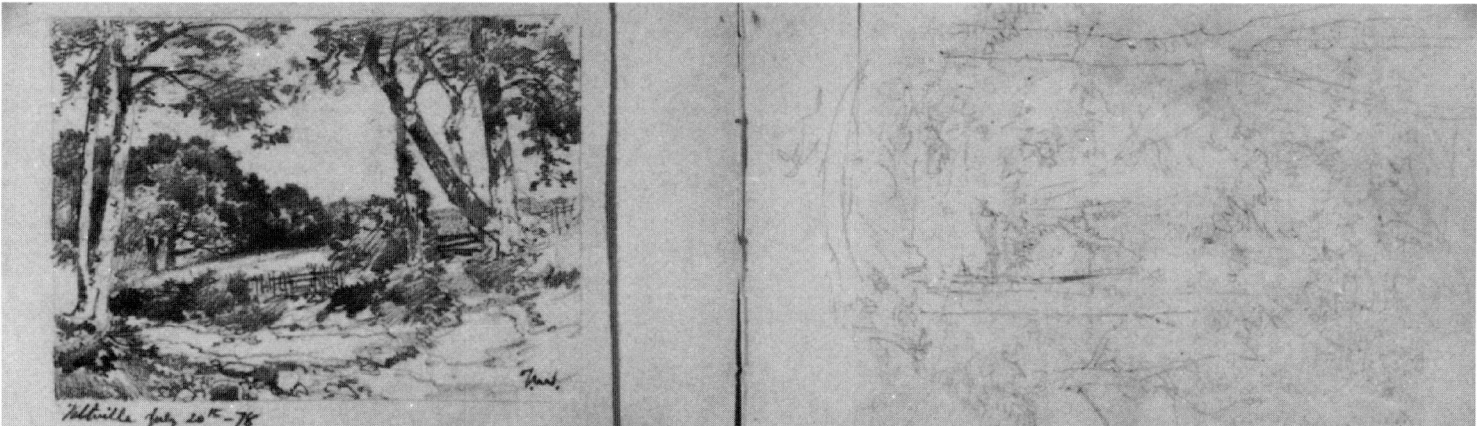

Top left: No. 308. *From the Shell Hummocks,*
Fort George Island (Gilcrease Institute, 1326.
1029), graphite on wove, 6⁷/₈ by 6³/₈ inches.

Top right: No. 314. *Lake Isabel, Fort George*
Island, Florida (Gilcrease Institute, 0226.873),
graphite and wash on wove, 11 by 7¹/₂ inches.

Bottom: No. 342. *Feltville* (Gilcrease Institute, 1826.16.5), graphite on wove, 8¹/₈ by 4⁷/₈
inches.

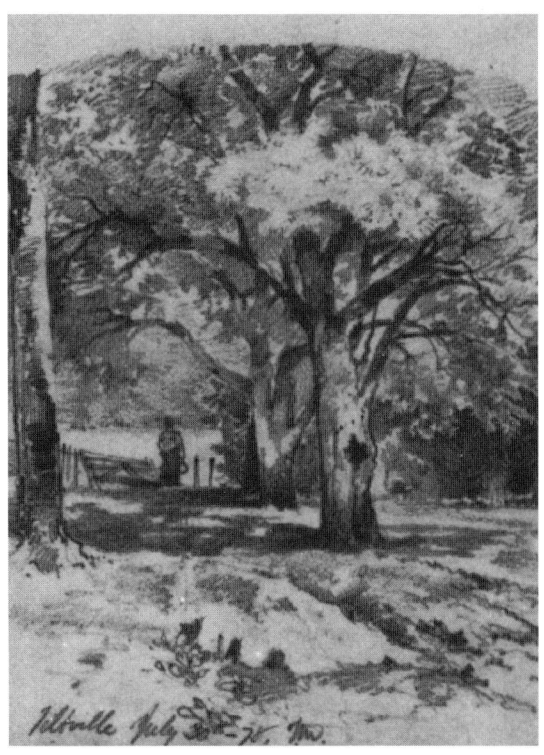

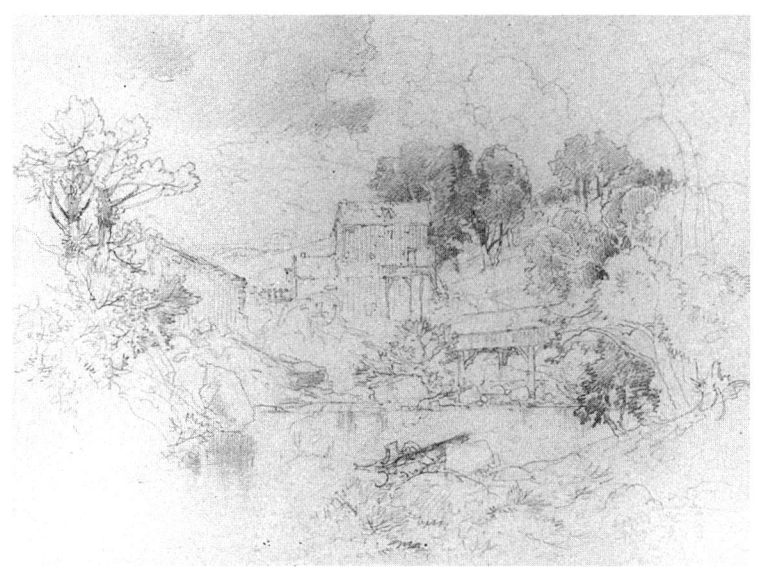

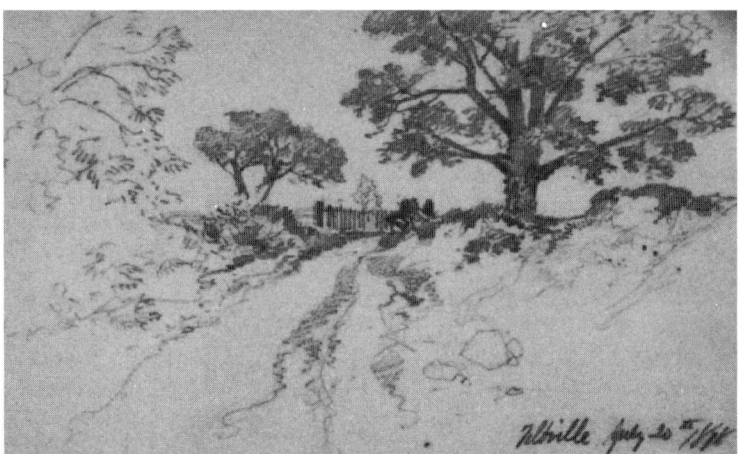

Left: No. 343. *Feltville* (Gilcrease Institute, 1826.16.6), graphite and black conté crayon on wove, 8¹/₈ by 4⁷/₈ inches.

Right: No. 350. *Feltville* (Gilcrease Institute, 1326.528), graphite on blue wove, 9³/₄ by 12⁵/₈ inches.

Bottom left: No. 344. *Feltville* (Gilcrease Institute, 1826.16.7), graphite and black conté crayon on wove, 4⁷/₈ by 8¹/₈ inches.

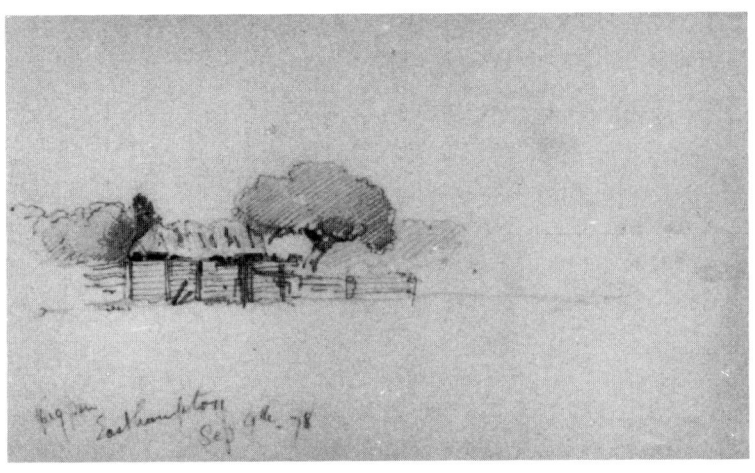

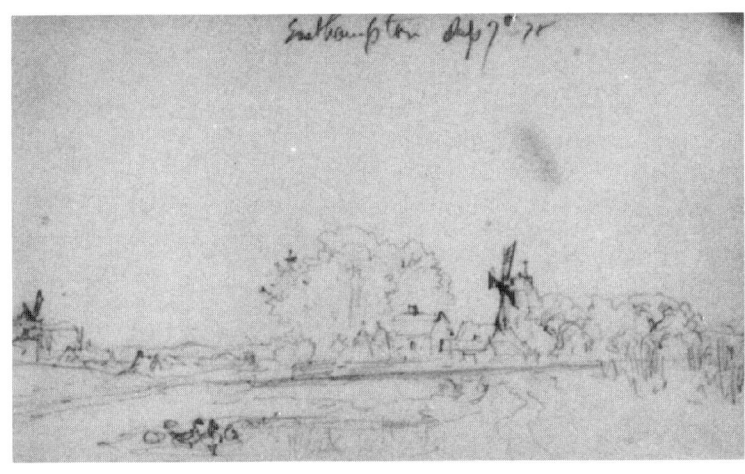

Left: No. 356. *Pig-Pen, East Hampton* (Gilcrease Institute, 1826. 16.12), graphite on wove, 4⁷/₈ by 8¹/₈ inches.

Right: No. 357. *East Hampton* (Gilcrease Institute, 1826.16.13), graphite on wove, 4⁷/₈ by 8¹/₈ inches.

Later that summer Moran visited Long Island in the company of members of the Tile Club. He was so taken with the picturesque setting that he and his family returned each summer for many years. By 1884 he had built a permanent home and studio there. East Hampton, and indeed much of the eastern tip of Long Island, was rich in scenery suitable for sketching. Here, Moran was at ease. Pressured neither by time nor by the necessity of fulfilling commissions, he could sketch what appealed to him. Florida had given him an appetite for the seashore, and Pennsylvania had fueled his love of rural countryside. Moran could satisfy both tastes on Long Island.

During the summer of 1878 Moran filled the remainder of the pocket sketchbook he had begun at Feltville with views of Long Island. Over the next two decades, he sketched there extensively, producing fluent pencil drawings characterized by minimal detail and a compelling sense of place. East Hampton, Moran's home base, was the subject of the majority of his sketches, and he suc-

ceeded in capturing its varied character. Long stretches of seemingly isolated shoreline (No. 363) were within walking distance of the town (No. 357), whose windmills with sails (No. 366) were a continuing attraction for a man whose own quixotic nature surfaced from time to time. Even the humblest of subjects—*Pig-Pen, East Hampton* (No. 356)—rated notice.

The Tile Club extended its peregrinations that summer to Long Island's most easterly point, Montauk, and Moran joined them in that trek. The picturesque lighthouse (*Montauk,* No. 377) perched on the rocky point became another recurring motif in his Long Island sketches and paintings.

Late the next summer Moran returned to the West, this time with his brother Peter. Moran had hoped for several years to accompany Major Powell on a return trip to the western canyonlands, but it was not to be. Instead, in 1879 Moran traveled without government support, collecting images for a commission from the Union Pacific Railroad. Evidence provided by the sketches in-

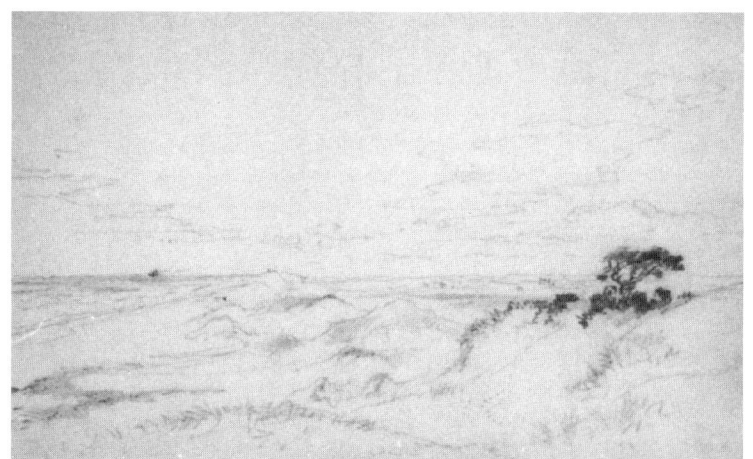

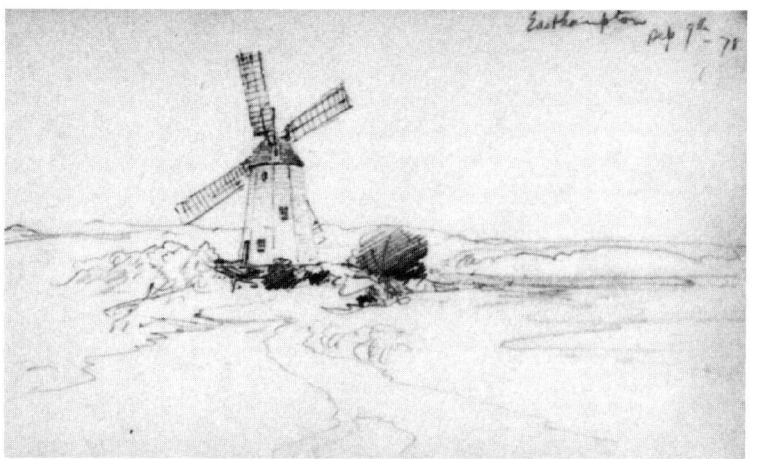

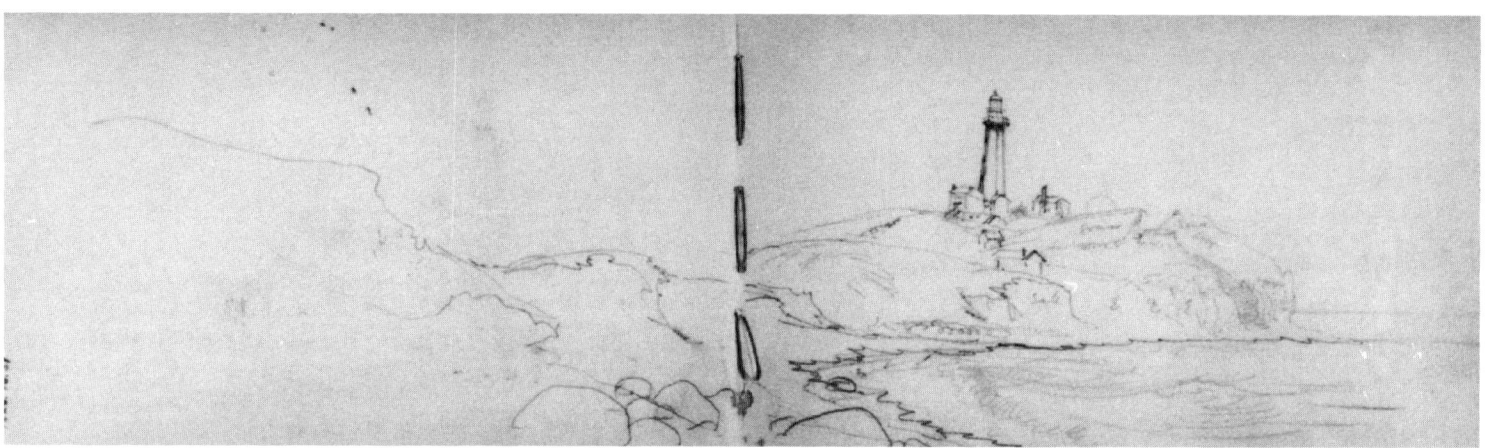

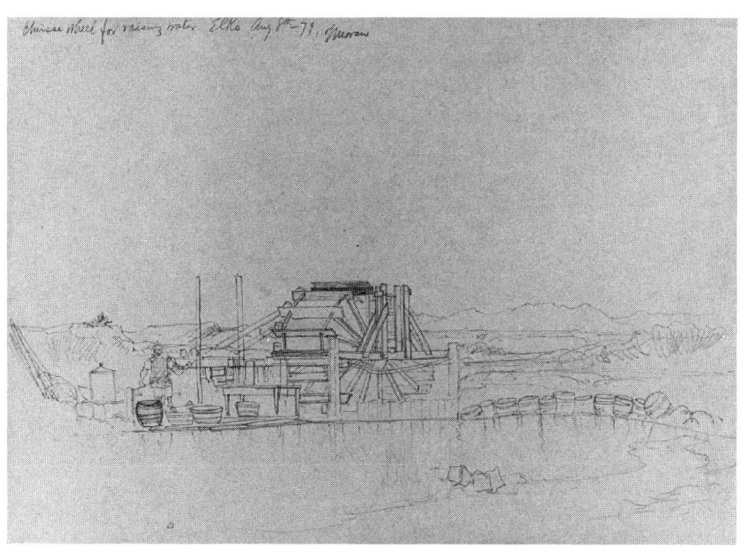

Top left: No. 363. *East Hampton* (Gilcrease Institute, 1826.16.19), graphite on wove, 4⁷/₈ by 8¹/₈ inches.

Top right: No. 366. *East Hampton* (Gilcrease Institute, 1826.16.22), graphite on wove, 4⁷/₈ by 8¹/₈ inches.

Middle: No. 377. *Montauk* (Gilcrease Institute, 1826.16.32), graphite on wove, 4⁷/₈ by 16¹/₄ inches.

Bottom left: No. 394. *Chinese Wheel for Raising Water, Elko* (Gilcrease Institute, 1336.965), graphite on pink wove, 10³/₄ by 14¹/₂ inches.

dicates that the brothers rode the train at least as far as Lake Tahoe before retracing their route back to Salt Lake City. From Salt Lake City they trekked east into Cottonwood and American Fork Canyons. Another arduous side trip took them north into Idaho, where Moran saw the Tetons for the first time. After returning to the Union Pacific route, they lingered for several days at Green River, Wyoming, before returning home in mid-September.

Although Moran was in the West that summer to help promote tourist travel over the extended rail lines, his work seldom acknowledged human presence and settlement. Rare in his work is the appearance of an established mechanism of tourism. *Tahoe* (No. 392; Plate 23) is uncommonly candid in this respect. On the elevated shore of the lake are hotels and summer cabins and on the lake are boats designed for pleasure cruising. Moran incorporated these commercial elements into a landscape that is at once inviting and seemingly immune to the changes posed by tourism. The still, clear, glassy surface of the lake reflects not only the limitless sky but also the boats and buildings. Even the sketch *Lake Tahoe* (No. 393; Plate 24), although less obvious, concedes the necessity of vacation comforts with its boat dock and deck chair.

Like these two sketches of Tahoe, Moran's other sketches of the summer of 1879 are among the most colorful works he made in the field. Cottonwood Canyon, a silver-mining region promoted by the railroad, particularly engaged Moran's color sense; he applied watercolor over the contour drawing of half of the twelve known sketches he made there. Subtle washes of color enliven the desolate cliffs represented in *Near the Summit of Cottonwood Canyon* (No. 407; Plate 25) and *In Little Cottonwood Canyon* (No. 403; Plate 26), as well as those of *American Fork Canyon* (No. 411; Plate 27). Additionally, gleaming white gouache defines enormous boulders that dwarf two tiny figures in *Upper End of Cottonwood Canyon* (No. 406; Plate 28).

In sketches such as *Toledo Mine, Cottonwood Canyon, Utah* (No. 408; Plate 29), Moran integrated manmade structures with natural elements. These structures seem to function as secondary topographical details indicating the vast scale of the landscape rather than as commentary on human encroachment on the unsullied wilderness.

Two rather schematic drawings, *Railroad and Taylor's Bridge, Snake River* (No. 417) and *Chinese Wheel for Raising Water, Elko* (No. 394), are notable exceptions to Moran's usual practice of subordinating the work of man to that of nature. He was clearly intrigued by the exotically contrived Chinese wheel.

Few known sketches document Moran's introduction to the Tetons. Weather conditions and the smoke from the many forest fires that raged that summer obscured Moran's view, and it must have been difficult to work during the strenuous journey on horseback from Fort Hall, Idaho.[77] Only four sketches show the three peaks.[78] *The Tetons* (No. 422) features their famous silhouette and records the rugged terrain over which Moran labored in order to see them.

Not all the Idaho sites noted during the trip were so difficult to reach. Sketches of *Portneuf Canyon* (No. 412; Plate 30) and *Iowa Gulch* (No. 415; Plate 31) represent two sites near Fort Hall that appealed to Moran for their beauty as well as for their relative ease of access.

Of the nearly fifty sketches he made during the summer of 1879, seventeen represent the brilliantly hued cliffs that line the riverbank at Green River, Wyoming.[79] The cliffs were an ideal subject for Moran, satisfying his taste for unusual geological formations and glorious natural color.

Many of these sketches are small; a few, such as *Green River Buttes, Wyoming* (No. 436; Plate 32), focus on individual formations. At the same time, Moran also developed more expansive compositions that correspond in their panoramic format to the wedge-shaped expanse of the cliffs. *Cliffs of Green River, Wyoming* (No. 439; Plate 33), for example, is spread over two sheets, which Moran later mounted together.

Cliffs of Green River, Wyoming (Nos. 437 and 438) is also the title of another two-piece panorama. Moran concentrated here on defining carefully in pencil the stratification of the cliffs.

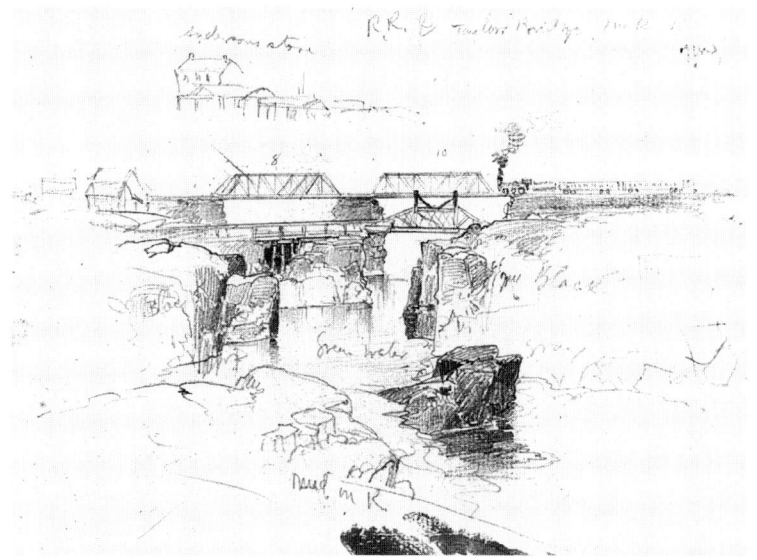

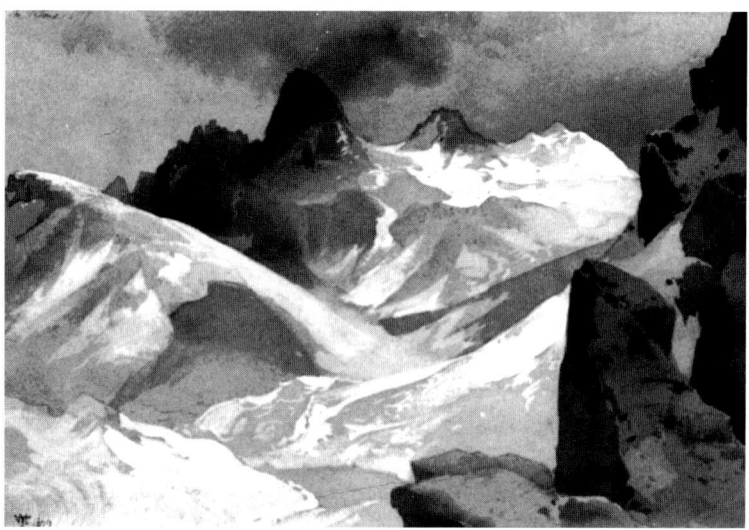

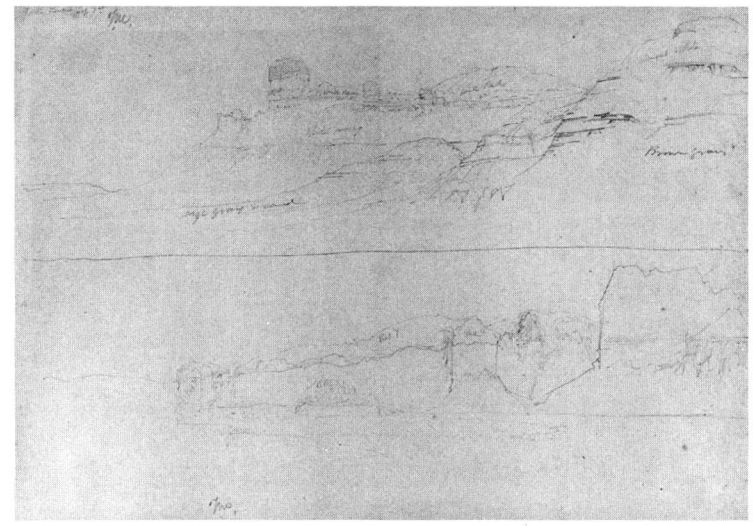

Left: No. 417. *Railroad and Taylor's Bridge, Snake River* (Gilcrease Institute, 1336.918), graphite on laid, 6¹/₄ by 8¹/₄ inches.

Right: No. 422. *The Tetons* (Yellowstone National Park 8530), graphite and watercolor on wove, 9³/₄ by 13⁷/₈ inches.

Bottom: No. 423a. *Green River* (Gilcrease Institute, 1336.907), graphite on wove, upper sketch 4⁷/₈ by 14 5/8 inches, sheet 10³/₈ by 14⁵/₈ inches.
No. 423b. *Green River* (Gilcrease Institute, 1336.907), graphite on wove, lower sketch 5¹/₂ by 14 5/8 inches, sheet 10³/₈ by 14⁵/₈ inches.

He made several more topographical sketches of the site, such as *Green River* (No. 423), on which he wrote color notes. A quick sketch, *Back of the Castle Rock, Green River, Wyoming* (No. 424), shows another aspect of this spectacular landscape. *Green River* (No. 431; Plate 34) exhibits Moran's masterly use of white gouache. With deft manipulation he used it to represent the mirrorlike surface of the river, reflecting the cloud-filled sky.

The Green River, which he began to paint at least as early as 1879, became a perennially popular subject for Moran. The variety of field sketches he made provided him with almost endless compositional possibilities, although the paintings he created became something of a cliché. Typically, the arrangements are characterized by a dominant cliff form, spectacular color, and oddly exotic Indian riders in the foreground who resemble Arab horsemen. The Tetons also became a popular subject over the next twenty years, although Moran's field sketches of them are few.

■ THE 1880s: EASTERN AMERICA, GREAT BRITAIN, MEXICO, ITALY

IN THE 1880s Moran traveled less than he had during the two preceding decades. He devoted more time to painting in the studio, etching, and investigating landscapes closer to home. When he did travel, however, his destinations were far afield. He returned once to the West and once to Great Britain, and he made his first trips to Mexico and Venice. All of these trips resulted in a prodigious amount of fieldwork.

Moran's sketching in Feltville had inspired him to explore more of the countryside around Newark. One spot that remained surprisingly attractive to him was the industrial harbor at Communipaw. He had earlier responded to the signs of technology at Manayunk and Feltville, but those were antiquated, even ruined remnants of industrial enterprise. The Communipaw sketches of 1880 are the first indication that Moran's interest extended to active modern industry. Images of sugar refineries, their chim-

neys belching smoke, form an iconographic counterpoint to the pristine wilderness to which Moran had devoted so much energy in the 1870s. Several small studies of the refineries, including *Communipaw* (No. 449), are unprecedented in Moran's work both in their subject matter and also in their medium, pen and ink. Moran very rarely used this medium for sketching in the field; fewer than ten pen-and-ink sketches have been located.[80] Moran's ink sketches are wonderfully spontaneous and fluid. The strokes are bold and expressive; he used gray and black ink washes to enhance the effect of recession into depth.

Moran also sketched views of Communipaw in his more accustomed medium of pencil, views that anticipated paintings such as *Lower Manhattan from Communipaw* (1880, Washington County Museum of Fine Arts, Hagerstown, Maryland). In sketched compositions, such as *Communipaw* (No. 446) and *Newark* (No. 445), Moran placed the refinery buildings and freighters along a horizon line that bisects each page. Buildings are drawn very precisely, in contrast to the sketchier rendering of the pier and rowboats in the foreground of the views. The Communipaw sketches contain expanses of water that distance the signs of industry from the viewer. Rural foreground details act as a psychological barrier as well; one observes but is separated from the industrial activity.

Moran sketched other scenes near Newark that included signs of industrialization. In *Newark Meadows* (No. 441) and *Newark* (No. 442), however, industry is less central to the image than in the Communipaw views. Trees placed along the same horizon line as the buildings in *Newark* are larger than the smoking chimneys in the distance and divert one's attention from them.

Extensive sketching on Long Island also occupied Moran during the summer of 1880, when he broadened his range beyond East Hampton to include vignettes of nearby Sag Harbor, Amagansett, Three Mile Harbor, and Montauk. In these and later sketches on Long Island, he repeatedly turned to a handful of motifs. Two drawings of stretches of undulating beach dunes near

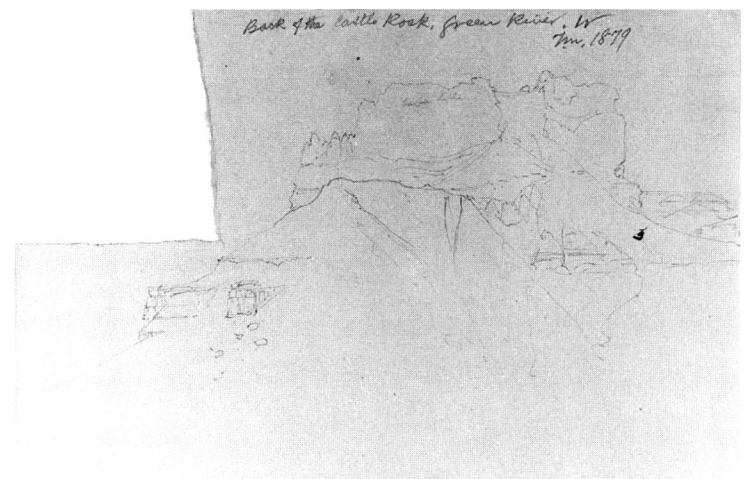

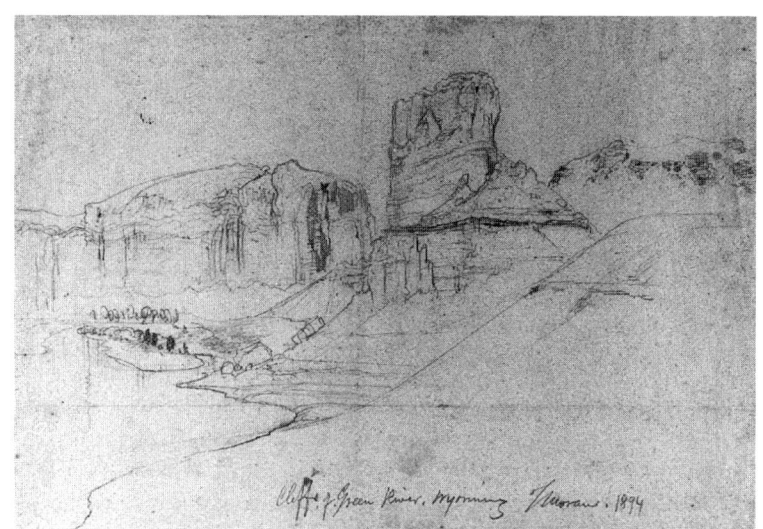

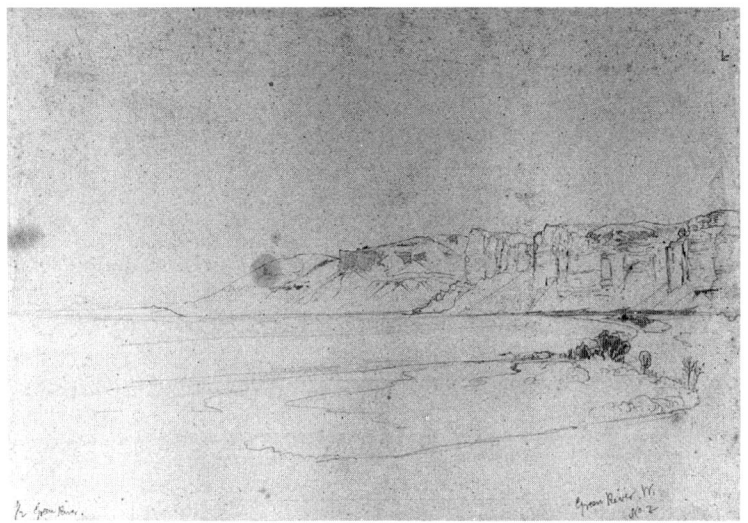

Top left: No. 424. *Back of the Castle Rock, Green River, Wyoming* (Gilcrease Institute, 1336.964), graphite on wove, 7 1/2 by 10 3/4 inches (irregular).

Top right: No. 437. *Cliffs of Green River, Wyoming* (Gilcrease Institute, 1336.849), graphite on watermarked gray laid, 10 1/2 by 14 3/4 inches.

Bottom left: No. 438. *Green River, Wyoming* (Gilcrease Institute, 1336. 911), graphite on watermarked laid, 10 1/2 by 14 3/4 inches.

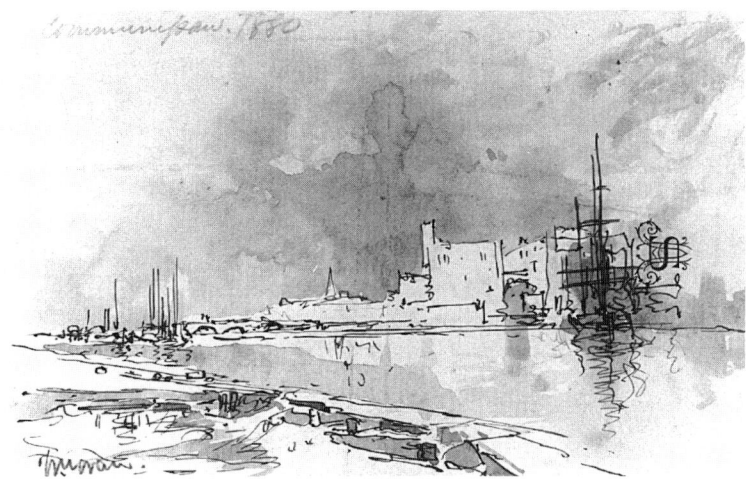

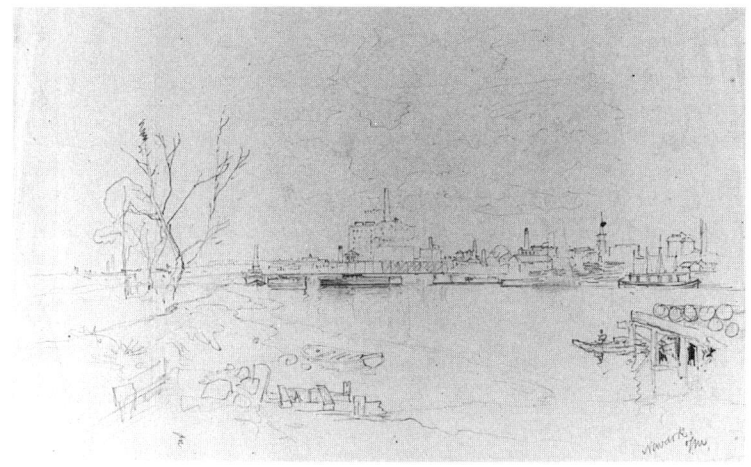

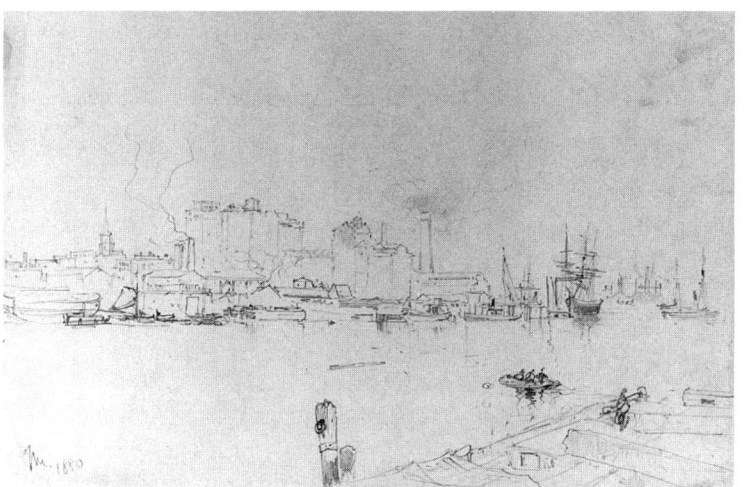

Top right: No. 449. *Communipaw* (Gilcrease Institute, 1326.989), graphite, pen and ink, and gray wash on laid embossed with *AS* conjoined, 4½ by 6⅞ inches.

Top left: No. 445. *Newark* (Gilcrease Institute, 1326.680), graphite on wove, 9½ by 15 inches.

Middle right: No. 446. *Communipaw* (Gilcrease Institute, 1326.981), graphite on wove, 9 by 13⅝ inches.

Bottom right: No. 441. *Newark Meadows* (Gilcrease Institute, 0226.790), graphite and gray wash on wove, 5¼ by 12⅛ inches.

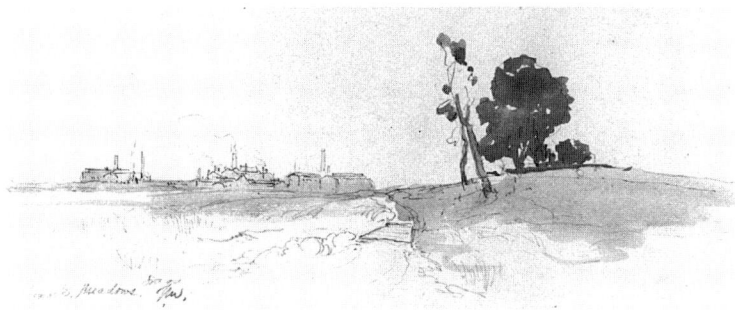

East Hampton (Nos. 497 and 498) illustrate his continuing engagement with the shoreline. Moran sketched stands of contorted sassafras trees (Nos. 525 and 526) with a dynamism that contrasts with the stately but static palms of Florida and the majestic pines of the West. Another favorite subject was freshwater ponds, especially Georgica Pond (*Georgica Pond, East Hampton,* No. 493), located near Moran's home.

Long Island, especially East Hampton, was a haven for Moran, and that tranquility is reflected in sketches such as *Evening, East Hampton* (No. 495). Moran spent much of his professional life dealing with new and challenging motifs. The scenery of Long Island was a comfortable and consistent subject to which he could return often, and it became the subject of numerous paintings and prints.

In contrast to the peaceful summer of 1880, the summer of 1881 was hectic for Moran. Three commissions for illustrations resulted in three excursions. In late June he visited Niagara Falls, during August he traveled the route of the Baltimore & Ohio Railroad between Baltimore and Pittsburgh, and in September he journeyed to Colorado, New Mexico, and Utah.

Moran's work at Niagara Falls was commissioned by the publishing company of Schell & Hogan. His three known sketches of Niagara are executed on deep gray paper in pencil, black wash, and white gouache. Although they are complex drawings, they seem less controlled than even the sketchiest of his previous works. The wash applied over faint contour work in *The Rapids below Lower Suspension Bridge, Niagara* (No. 537) seems careless, but it imparts vitality to the scene, suggesting natural forces in rapid motion: dark, lowering storm clouds, wind whipping through trees and undergrowth, churning water, rising foam and mist. Moran attempted to translate these forces into a wood engraving based on the sketch, but the hard-edged precision of that medium robbed the image of its vigor.[81]

The Rapids below Lower Suspension Bridge, Niagara (No. 537) and another sketch, *Under the American Fall from Goat Island* (No. 539), were both made at the water's edge; the spray is almost tangible.[82] *The Niagara River, from Brock Monument* (No. 538), by contrast, is a full panoramic view made from a point high above the water. In this sketch, Moran relied less on black wash and more on crystalline white gouache than he had done in the previous ones made near the falls. He still managed to create an impressive array of atmospheric effects, from the storm in the middle distance to the sliver of sunlight illuminating the distant horizon line.

This visit encouraged Moran to paint views of Niagara, which he had not previously felt compelled to do, in spite of his admiration for Church's *Niagara* during the Paris Universal Exposition in 1867. His *Rainbow over Niagara Falls* (1885, location unknown) frankly emulates Church's earlier version.[83]

During the summer of 1881 the publicity department of the Baltimore & Ohio Railroad hired Moran to collect images for J. G. Pangborn's *Picturesque B. & O. Historical and Descriptive,* published in 1882. Most of the sketches Moran completed along the B & O route between Baltimore and Pittsburgh are his typical quick contour drawings, which were later fleshed out in the illustrations. They are less ambitious than the few surviving Niagara drawings, reflecting once again the time constraints under which Moran worked when in company other than family. On this trip, Moran traveled with Pangborn, John Karst, who would engrave many of the images Moran provided, and an official of the railroad.

Images such as *Allegheny Mountains, Tunnel near the Source of the Potomac* (No. 558) relate directly to Pangborn's text[84] and often include notations about page size, indicating that Moran was sketching to the publication's format. It is even possible that Moran and Pangborn were developing text and illustrations simultaneously. *Allegheny Mountains, Tunnel near the Source of the Potomac* was squared and washed with ink, probably to aid the wood engraver, John Karst, who used it as the basis of *Near the Source of the Potomac.*[85]

Although *View in the Narrows, Cumberland* (No. 559) is probably a documentary sketch, it is undeniable evidence of Moran's aestheticism.

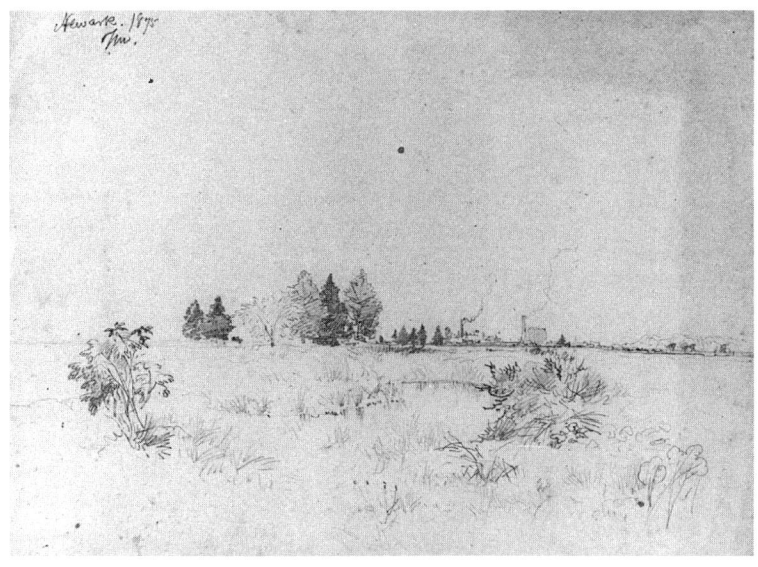 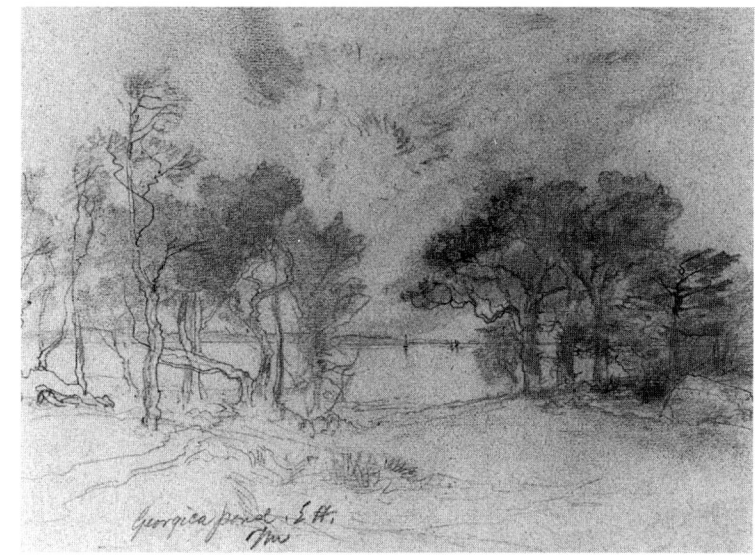

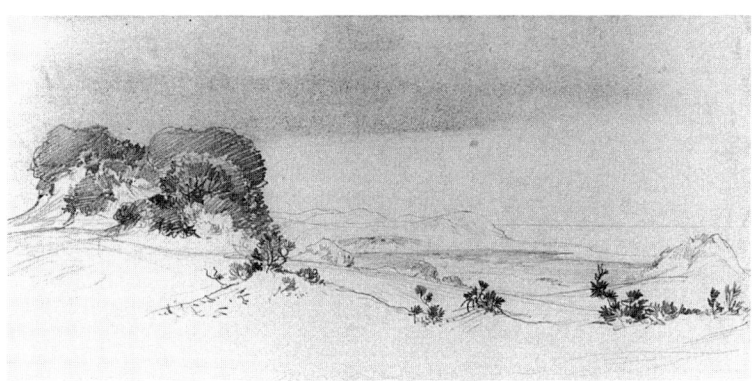 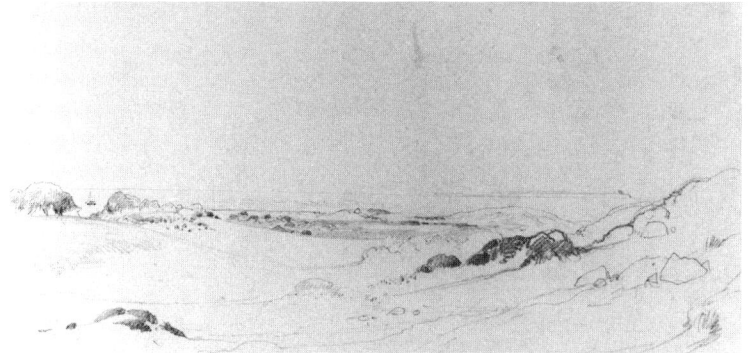

Top left: No. 442. *Newark* (Gilcrease Institute, 1326.946), graphite on wove, 9⅝ by 12⅞ inches.

Top right: No. 493. *Georgica Pond, East Hampton* (Gilcrease Institute, 1326.700), graphite on green wove, 8⅞ by 11½ inches.

Middle left: No. 497. *East Hampton* (Gilcrease Institute, 1326.550), graphite on wove, 6¼ by 12½ inches.

Middle right: No. 498. *East Hampton* (Gilcrease Institute, 1326.564), graphite on wove, 6½ by 12½ inches.

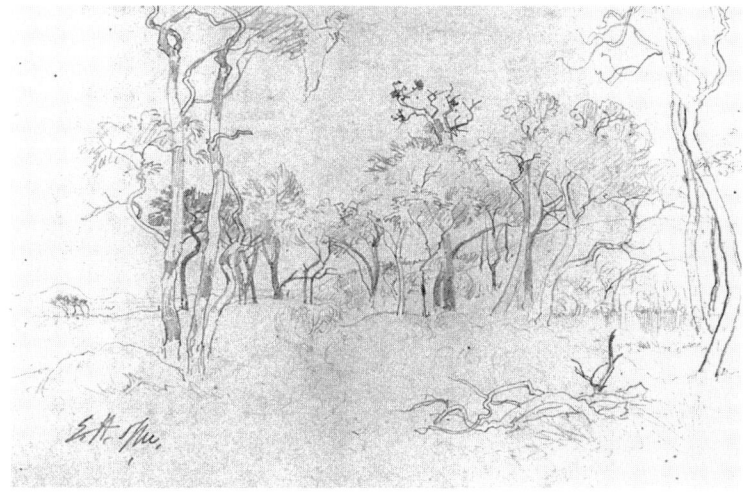

Bottom right: No. 525. *East Hampton* (Gilcrease Institute, 1326.691), graphite on wove, 6¾ by 9¾ inches.

His quickly executed but superb composition focuses on a quaint arched bridge. Details are few but significant to the beauty of the scene: reflections in the water, foreground rocks and foliage, and puffy clouds, all rendered in luminous white gouache. *Cumberland, from Rose Hills Cemetery* (No. 560), *Hillside, Pittsburgh* (No. 565), and *Harpers Ferry* (No. 546) are examples of one of Moran's favorite compositions: a town set into a river valley viewed from a hillside. He had used this arrangement as early as 1864. In each of the 1881 sketches, the river enters the composition from the lower left corner and disappears among hills when it reaches the center. Signs of human habitation are present in most of these sketches. The purpose of this work was to advertise the beauties of regional scenery to promote tourism, so Moran made sure the viewer understood that the area was easily accessible and furnished with amenities for the traveler.

Moran's illustrations of the wondrous Luray Cave in Virginia include the guard rails (*Luray Cave,* No. 556) and surfaced pathways (*Angel Wing Fallen Column and Saracen Den, Luray Cave,* No. 555) installed for tourists. These and two other sketches of Luray Cave represent the only works Moran is known to have executed underground. Aided by electric light, he struggled to illustrate the vast subterranean chasm. The effect of artificial illumination is most dramatic in the wood engraving Karst based on Moran's sketches, *Luray Cave, Virginia.*[86] The disorienting lack of customary motifs such as trees necessitated the rare inclusion of a human figure in *In Luray Cave* (No. 557) to demonstrate the immensity of a columnar formation.

At one point during this trip, Moran was drawn to a picturesque ruin, as he had been earlier at Feltville, New Jersey. Leaving the train at Ohiopyle, Pennsylvania, he and his three traveling companions hiked into the hills. In his narrative, Pangborn related that Moran "dallied to sketch [*Ohiopyle,* No. 562] a rustic structure bridging the rivulet that danced its way to the Youghiogheny, and just above this the old tannery long since passed into decay. The bridge, the dilapidated buildings, the narrow gorge, and the woods, made a study for a sketch not to be passed over by the artistic eye."[87]

The group arrived in Pittsburgh at the end of August. Moran and Karst continued on by rail, reaching Denver by the first week of September. They were joined there by William Henry Jackson and the author Ernest Ingersoll. Moran and Karst collaborated on sketches and wood engravings illustrating Ingersoll's *Crest of the Continent,* published in 1885. Moran's images were also featured in *Colorado Tourist,* a publication devoted to rail travel, and in an article Ingersoll wrote for *Harper's Monthly,* "Silver San Juan."[88]

The group traveled on the Denver & Rio Grande Railroad from Denver as far as Española, New Mexico, the railroad's southern terminus at that time. Backtracking to Antonito, Colorado, they headed west to the silver-mining region in the San Juan Mountains. From there, Moran continued on alone to the northwest as far as the Wasatch Mountains in north-central Utah.

Considering the vast amount of scenic territory covered, very few sketches exist, perhaps due once again to Jackson's camera. Charming watercolor-enhanced sketches of *Garden of the Gods* (No. 568; Plate 35), *San Juan, New Mexico* (No. 573; Plate 36), and *Ojo Caliente* (No. 572; Plate 37) prove that Moran found these places suitable subjects. His views of New Mexican pueblos are among the earliest images of southwestern Indian habitations.

Moran's handling of watercolor during this trip was unusually varied both in color range and technique. Most remarkable is his wet-on-wet watercolor application, in which very liquid color is applied to wet paper—a technique he rarely used in his earlier fieldwork. The effect, seen clearly in the foreground foliage and the upper left portion of the sky of *Garden of the Gods* (No. 568), is soft and blurred; the paint was absorbed into the moist paper. Normally, Moran painted wet-on-dry, which held the brushstroke intact and permitted him to crisply define the edges of forms. This same wet-on-wet technique can be seen in *Heywood Hot Springs* (No. 570; Plate 38). Moran's combination of the two techniques in these works may have been an experi-

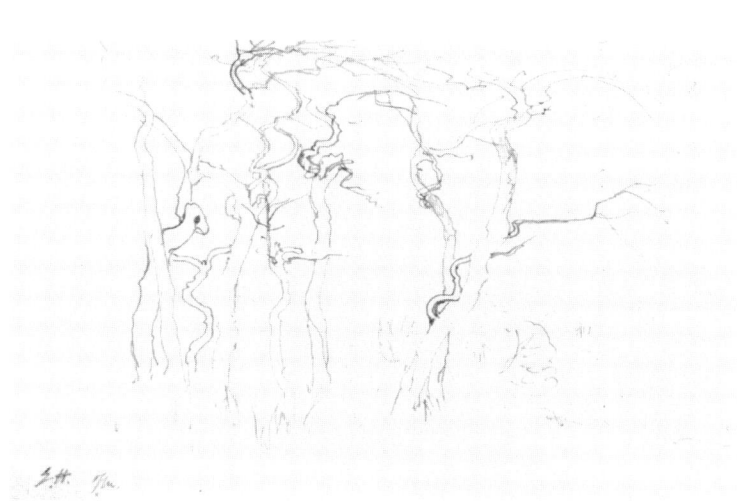

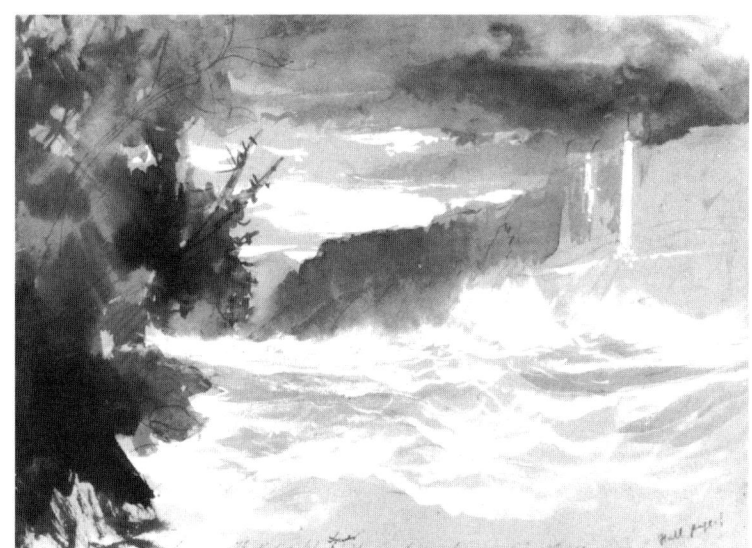

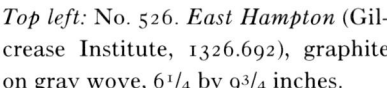

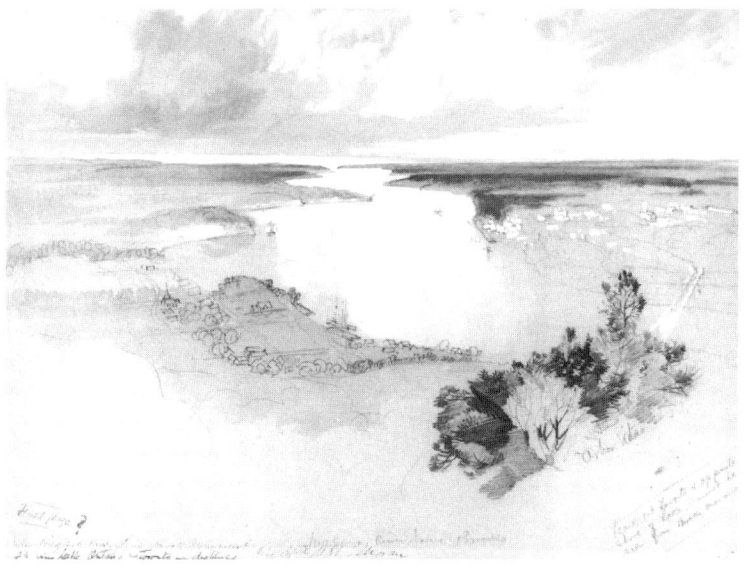

Top left: No. 526. *East Hampton* (Gilcrease Institute, 1326.692), graphite on gray wove, 6¼ by 9¾ inches.

Top right: No. 537. *Rapids below Lower Suspension Bridge, Niagara* (Gilcrease Institute, 0226.901), graphite, gray wash, and white gouache on gray wove, 10⅞ by 14¼ inches.

Bottom left: No. 495. *Evening, East Hampton* (Gilcrease Institute, 1326.987), graphite on green wove, 4½ by 10¼ inches.

Bottom right: No. 538. *Niagara River, from Brock Monument* (Gilcrease Institute, 0226.900), graphite, gray wash, and white gouache on gray wove, 11 by 14⅜ inches.

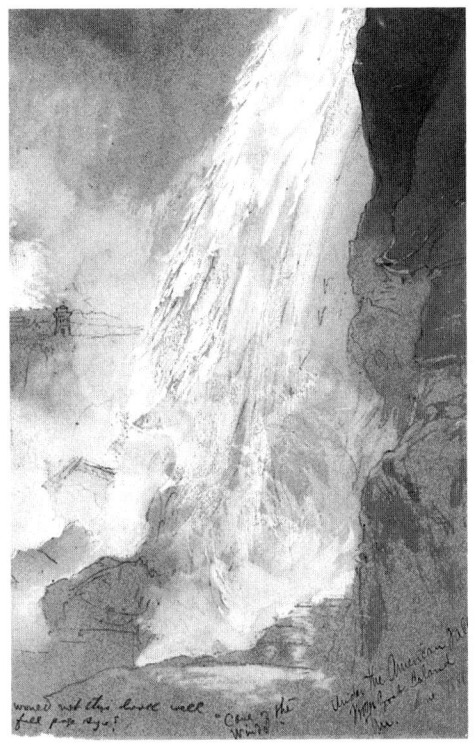

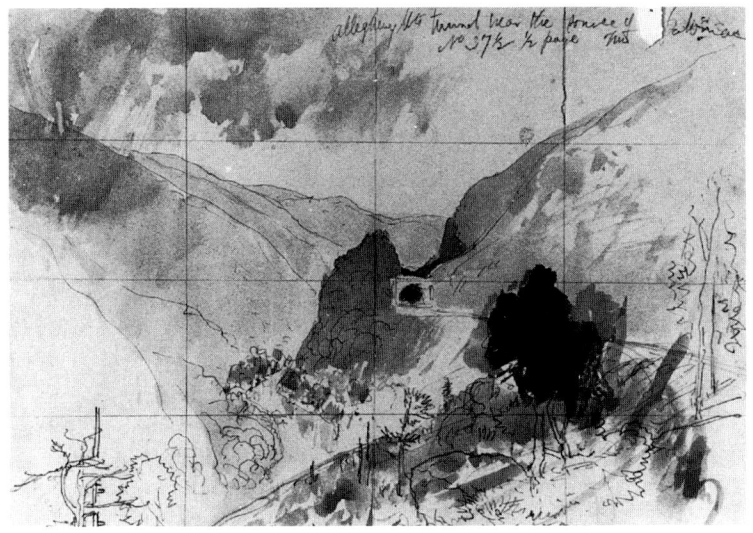

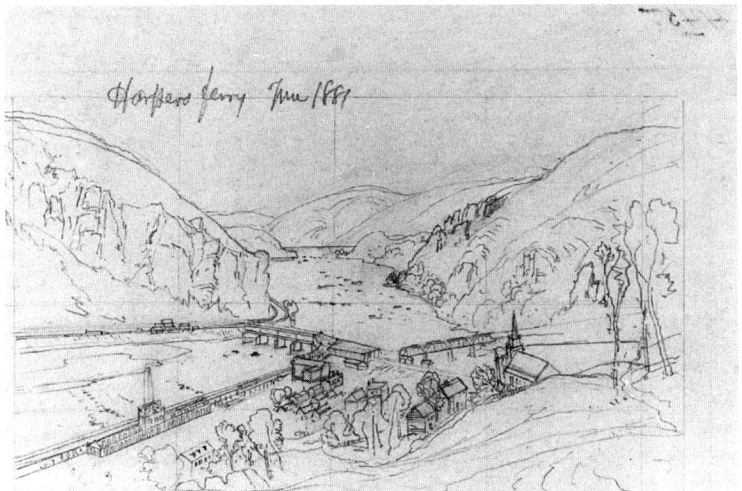

Top left: No. 539. *Under the American Fall from Goat Island* (Gilcrease Institute, 0226.899), graphite, gray wash, and white gouache on gray wove, 11 by 7 1/8 inches.

Top right: No. 558. *Allegheny Mountains, Tunnel near the Source of the Potomac* (Gilcrease Institute, 0226.791), graphite and wash on wove, 8 5/8 by 11 7/8 inches.

Bottom left: No. 546. *Harpers Ferry* (Gilcrease Institute, 1326.1002), graphite on wove, 4 1/4 by 6 7/8 inches.

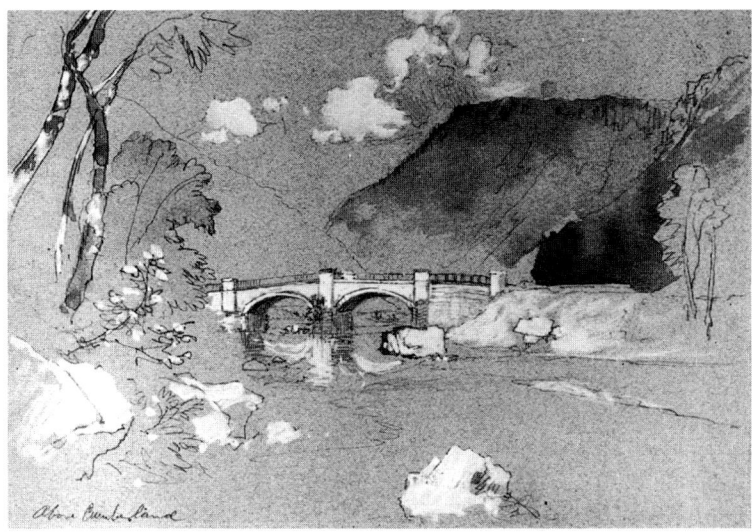

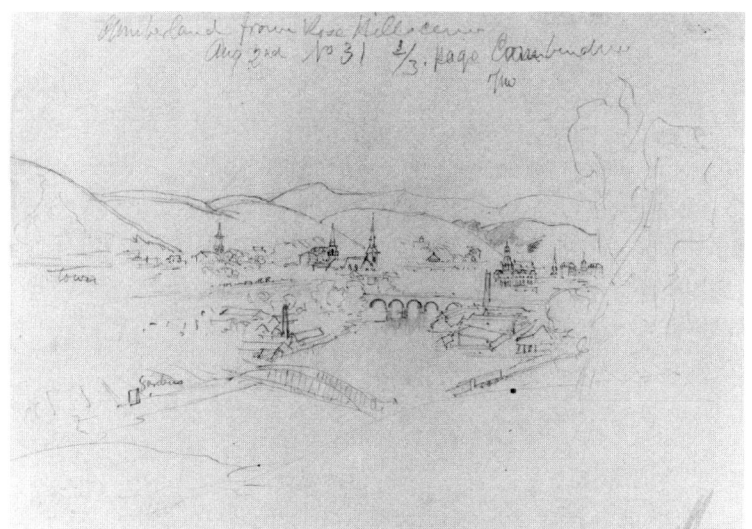

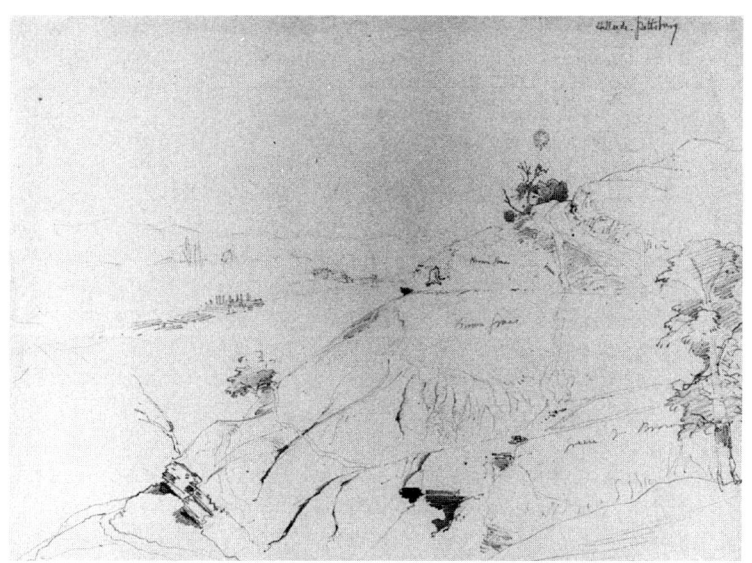

Top left: No. 559. *View in the Nar-rows, Cumberland, B & O* (Gilcrease Institute, 0226.896), graphite, gray and blue washes, and white gouache on green wove, 9⅞ by 12⅞ inches.

Top right: No. 560. *Cumberland, from Rose Hills Cemetary* (Gilcrease Insti-tute, 1326.709), graphite on wove, 8⅝ by 8⅞ inches.

Middle right: No. 565: *Hillside, Pitts-burgh* (Gilcrease Institute, 1326.642), graphite on wove, 9⅝ by 12⅞ inches.

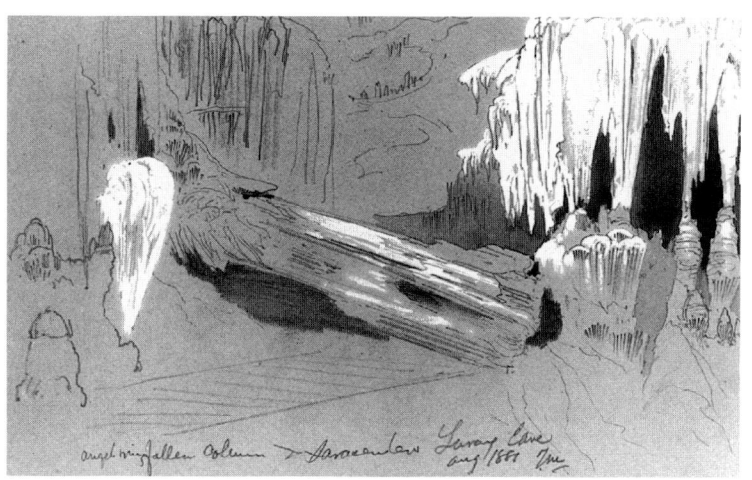

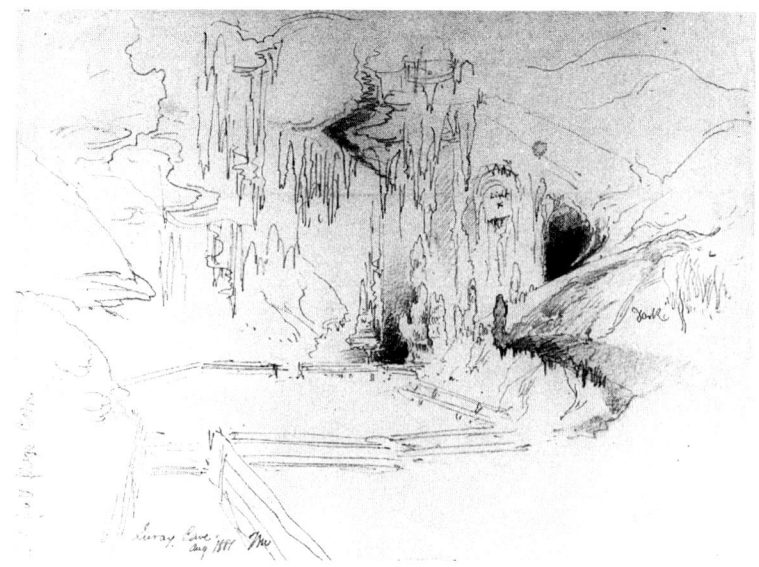

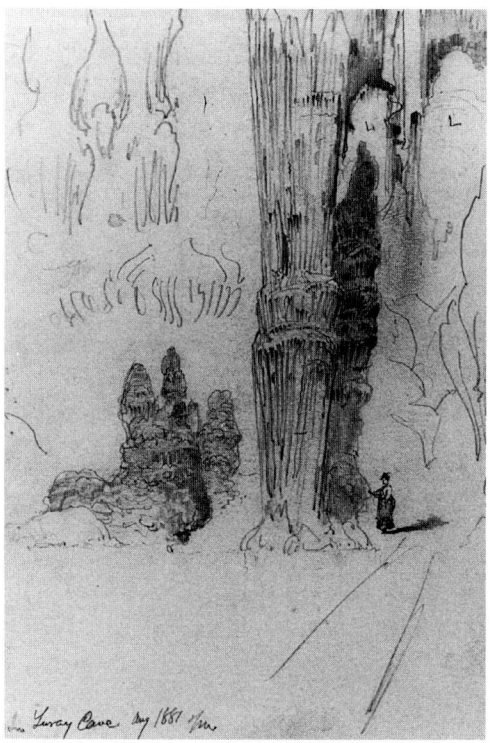

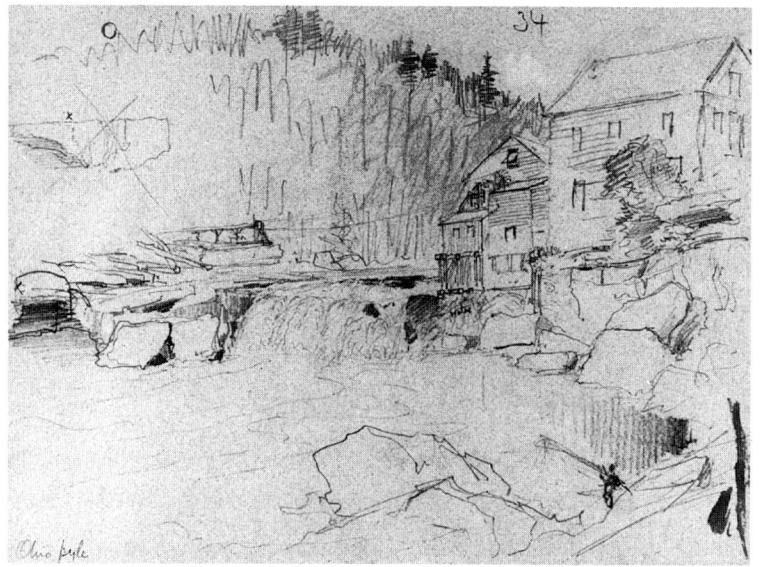

Top left: No. 555. *Angel Wing Fallen Column and Saracen Den, Luray Cave* (Gilcrease Institute, 0226.897), graphite, wash, and white gouache on gray wove, 6 1/2 by 9 7/8 inches.

Top right: No. 556. *Luray Cave* (Gilcrease Institute, 1326.995), graphite on gray wove, 11 by 14 3/8 inches.

Bottom left: No. 557. *In Luray Cave* (Gilcrease Institute, 1326.1006), graphite on wove, 10 7/8 by 7 1/4 inches.

Bottom right: No. 562. *Ohiopyle* (Gilcrease Institute, 1326.656), graphite on blue wove, 9 3/4 by 12 7/8 inches.

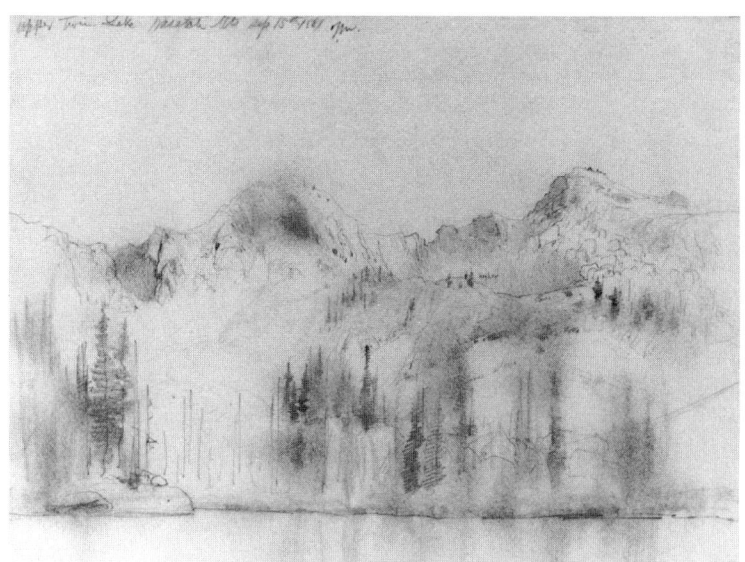

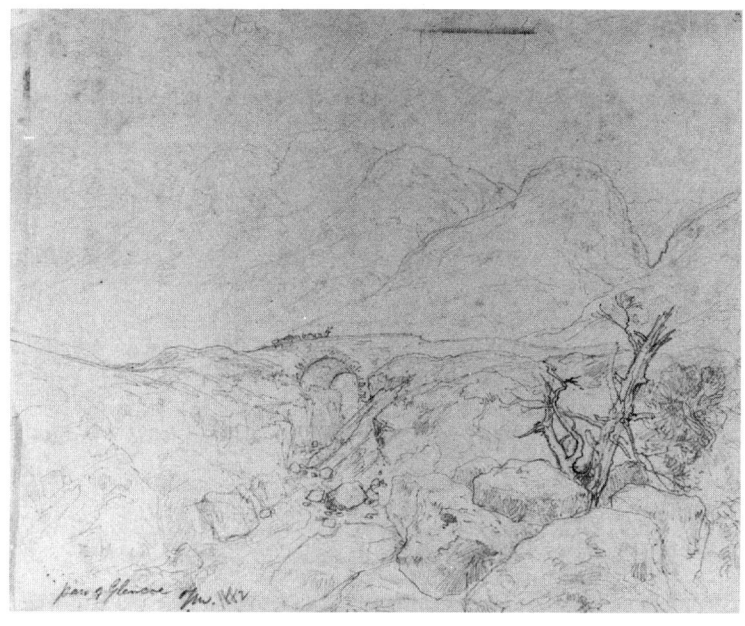

Left: No. 582. *Upper Twin Lake, Wasatch Mountains* (Gilcrease Institute, 1336.996), graphite on wove, 10¹/₂ by 14 inches.

Right: No. 593. *Pass of Glencoe* (Gilcrease Institute, 1376.782), graphite on newsprint, 12¹/₂ by 10 inches.

ment in more effectively replicating various textures and surfaces.

Another sketch that includes watercolor was probably made at this time. Moran added washes of pink, salmon, and olive green to his pencil rendering of *Glen Eyrie* (No. 569; Plate 39). The rocky, barren acclivity becomes slightly less inhospitable with the addition of the delicate tints.

By mid-September Moran was sketching lakes in Utah's Wasatch Mountains. *Upper Twin Lake, Wasatch Mountains* (No. 582) is another departure from his usual contour work. His smudging of graphite over the contour outline to suggest mist is unusual.[89]

According to the drawings, Moran visited Green River, Utah, on September 20, 1881, before returning home to New York.[90] This was his first visit to the spectacular cliffs that border this section of the river. *Green River* (No. 586; Plate 40) differs from the sketches made at Green River, Wyoming, in which he concentrated on the panorama. Here he focused on the individual formations, using one of his standard paper-

saving devices: he drew additional forms in the empty sky area at the upper right. In doing this, he produced a wonderfully ambiguous spatial relationship.

With his wife and children, Moran returned to England perhaps as early as November 1881.[91] This trip, prompted by exhibitions of his work in his hometown of Bolton and in London, was quite different from the brief visit the Morans had made fifteen years before. This time their stay was lengthy and extended by trips to Scotland and Wales. They had a memorable encounter with the now aged critic John Ruskin and met Francis Seymour Haden, a leader of the London Society of Painter-Etchers. Perhaps motivated by their recent election to membership in this newly formed organization, the Morans based a group of etchings on sketches made in Britain in 1882, Thomas producing six and Mary three.[92]

A highlight of the Morans' trip to Scotland was a visit to the Pass of Glencoe in the Highlands. Moran reproduced his sketch *Pass of Glencoe* (No. 593) in an etching, *Bridge in the Pass of Glen-*

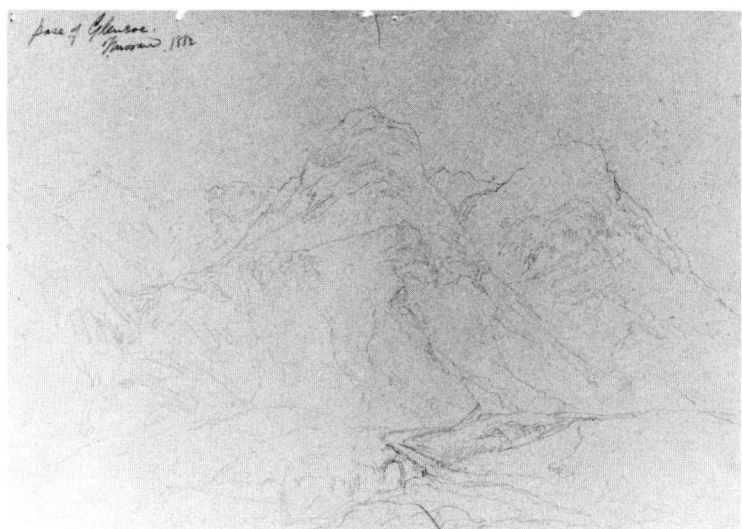

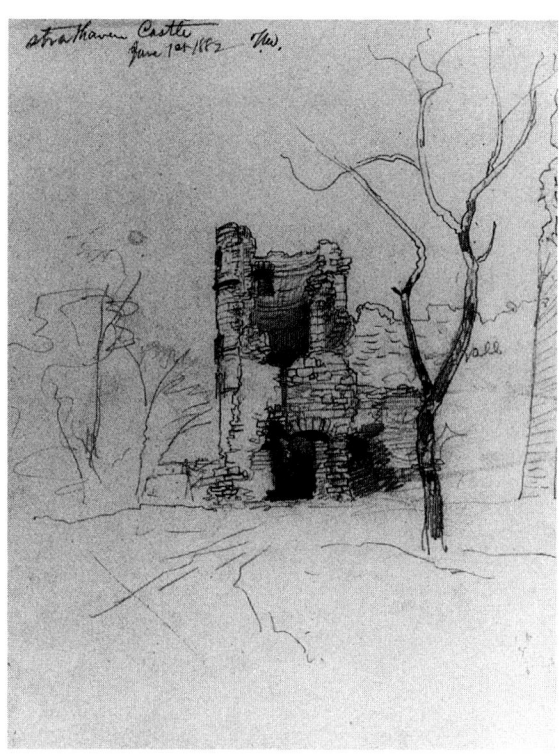

coe—*Scotland,* as well as in an extraordinary studio watercolor, *Pass at Glencoe, Scotland* (1882, Gilcrease Institute; Plate 41).[93] Another sketch, *Pass of Glencoe* (No. 592), is related to the etching *The Pass of Glencoe.*[94] At this place, the scene of a terrible massacre in 1692, Moran found a quintessentially Romantic landscape of craggy, barren hills, blasted trees amid tumbled boulders, and an ancient stone bridge traversing a steep declivity.

Only one other Scottish site, Mary Moran's birthplace, Strathaven, seems to have appealed artistically to Moran. He made two sketches of the ruins of Strathaven castle (Nos. 588 and 589). The latter sketch inspired his etching *Strathaven Castle—Scotland.*[95] The etching exactly duplicates the composition of the sketch, a testament to Moran's ability to block out compositions suitable for finished work even while working outdoors.

Moran was still attracted by castles, just as he had been in his earlier British trip of 1862. He particularly appreciated the Welsh strongholds of Harlech and Conway, devoting more sketches to them than to any other subject during the 1882 trip. As in 1862, his itinerary may have been inspired by the work of Turner, who had sketched and painted both sites, but Moran probably recalled John Varley's paintings of Harlech as well.[96]

Moran dashed off sketches like *Conway Castle* (No. 599), deftly recording the distinctive profile of the fortress. He sketched the castle from nearly every angle and from vantage points near and far, producing panoramic views as well as tiny vignettes. His point of view in *Conway Castle from the Walls* (No. 603), for example, endows the sketch with a sense of vertiginous immediacy. The small male figure at the top of the stairway at the upper right is perhaps a self-portrait.

The castle's environs also commanded Moran's attention. *Near Conway* (No. 609) is a mellow pastoral study reminiscent of his sketches of the Long Island shore. Several other sketches, such as *Conway, North Wales* (No. 604; Plate 42) and *Conway from across the River, near Turner's Point of View* (No. 605), show the castle and

Left: No. 592. *Pass of Glencoe* (Gilcrease Institute, 1376.783), graphite on blue wove, 10¼ by 14⅝ inches.

Right: No. 588. *Strathaven Castle* (Gilcrease Institute, 1376.774), graphite on wove, 12¾ by 10 inches.

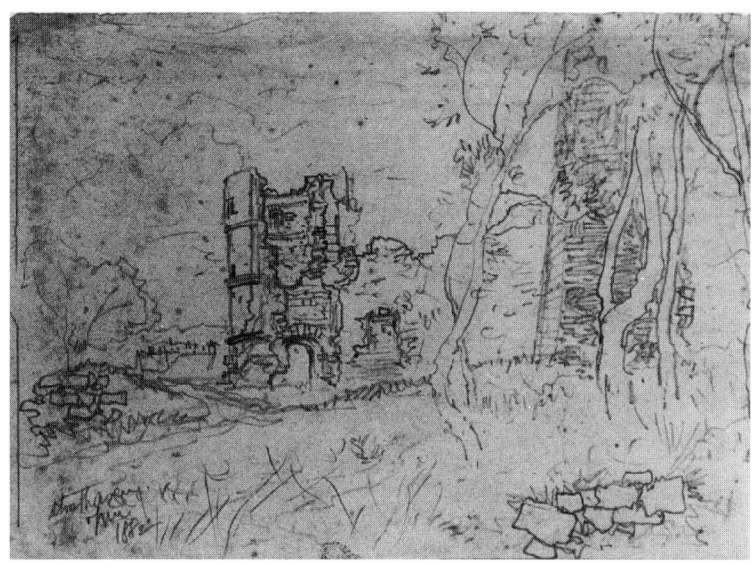 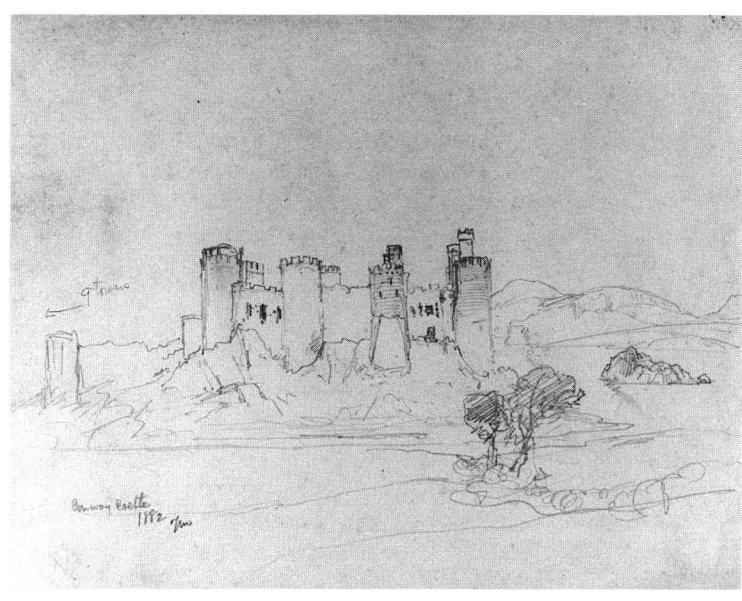

Left: No. 589. *Strathaven* (East Hampton Library), graphite on wove, 6¹/₂ by 8⁷/₈ inches.

Right: No. 599. *Conway Castle* (Gilcrease Institute, 1376.771), graphite on newsprint, 10 by 12¹/₂ inches.

town in their valley setting. The latter sketch is almost identical to Moran's 1879 etching, *Conway Castle,* which reproduces an alleged Turner painting Moran bought in 1878.[97] Notations establish that this is a site sketch made in 1882 rather than a study for the etching.

Moran seldom used watercolor in the field that year. Only six of the thirty-seven sketches made in 1882, including two of Conway, are embellished with watercolor. *Conway Castle* (No. 606; Plate 43), brushed with the most preliminary of wet-on-wet washes, was perhaps a field experiment with color. It is rather muddy and uninspired, especially when compared to Moran's other watercolor work in the field.

Moran's sketches of Harlech Castle also record a variety of views. The most interesting is *Harlech* (No. 620), in which the castle is partially obscured by trees and the town walls. This effective composition inspired the etching *Harlech Castle—Wales,* in which the figures in the sketch (perhaps Moran's wife and one of his children) do not appear.[98]

Moran added watercolor to *Harlech Castle, North Wales* (No. 618; Plate 44), a sketch that is smaller and less detailed than the comparable wash drawing of Conway (*Conway Castle,* No. 606). The application of color washes is quick, fresh, and immediate, not labored as in the larger work. This sketch, like most of Moran's views that year, was taken from a point above and to the right of the castle. In these sketches, he usually filled the lower right quadrant of the composition with a large mass, which anchors the composition and contrasts with an airy open space in the upper left.

At Cardigan Bay, Wales, Moran made two shore views of an elegant simplicity. The windswept *Afon Wen, North Wales, Cardigan Bay* (No. 611; Plate 45) and the desolate *Criccieth Castle, Cardigan Bay, North Wales* (No. 612; Plate 46), populated by a few lonely boats, represent rare occasions when Moran sketched the British landscape in its purest, most unadorned state. Moran colored the sea and shore in these sketches with broad washes of blue and green.

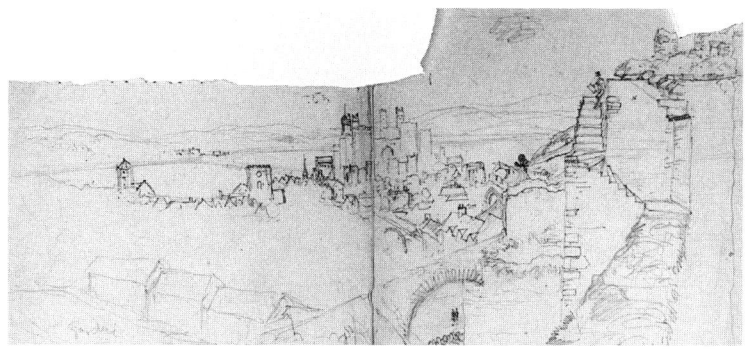

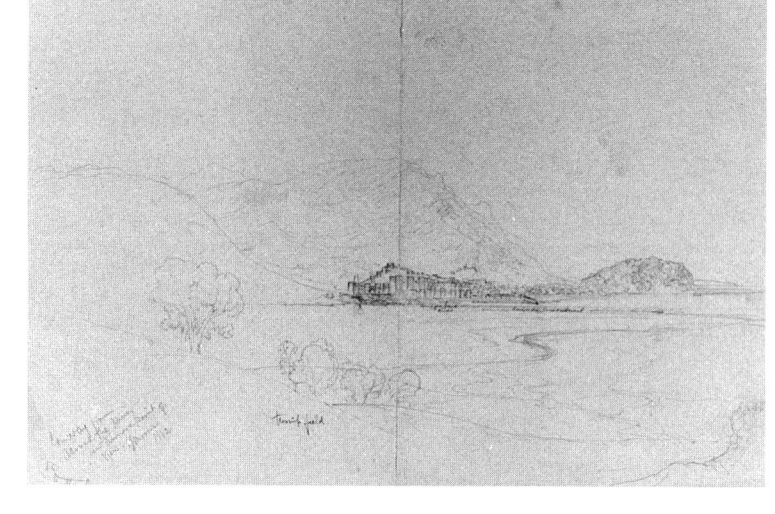

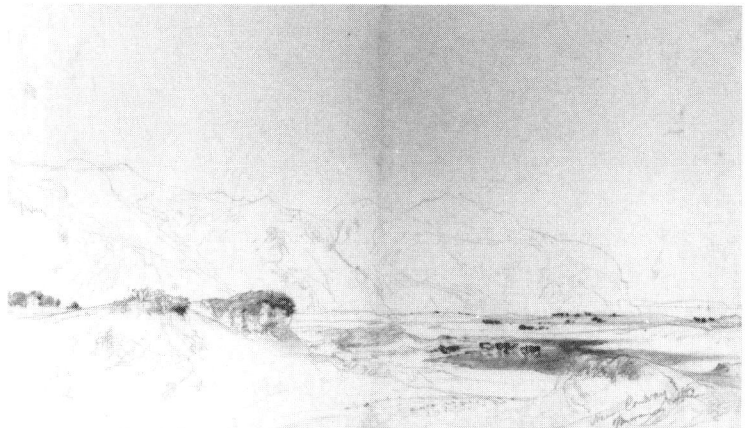

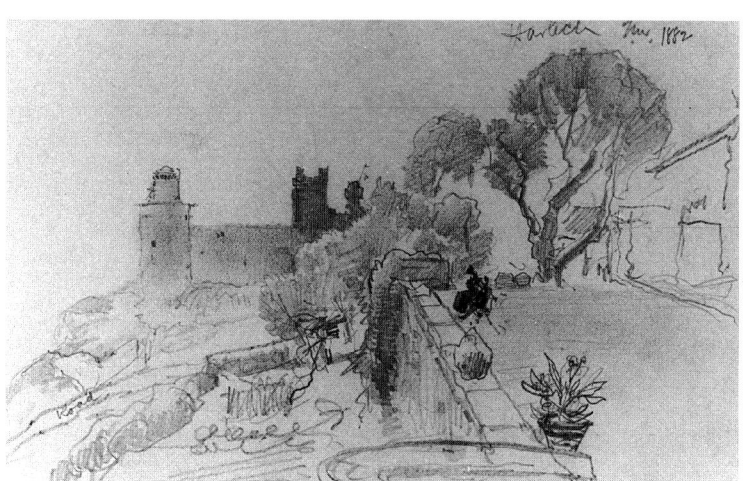

Top left: No. 603. *Conway Castle from the Walls* (Gilcrease Institute, 1376. 788), graphite on wove, 11 5/8 by 20 inches (irregularly torn edges and two pieces joined).

Top right: No. 605. *Conway from across the River, near Turner's Point of View* (Gilcrease Institute, 1376.793), graphite on blue wove (two pieces joined), 15 by 21 1/2 inches.

Middle left: No. 609. *Near Conway* (Gilcrease Institute, 1376.787), graphite on wove, 12 7/8 by 20 inches.

Bottom left: No. 620. *Harlech* (Gilcrease Institute, 1376.775), graphite on wove, 6 1/2 by 10 inches.

After his return to New York in late September 1882, Moran began to work on paintings and etchings inspired by the trip. His usual routine of spending the winter months in the studio was interrupted by a journey to Mexico between late January and mid-March 1883, probably connected with the promotion of the Mexican National Railroad.[99] Moran's Mexican sketches form the largest group of his fieldworks produced during a single trip.[100] These sketches, along with a brief journal account and letters to his wife, establish Moran's itinerary from Vera Cruz to Laredo.

The exact circumstances leading to Moran's trip through Mexico are unknown; it may have resulted from his acquaintance with William J. Palmer, a cofounder of the Denver & Rio Grande Railroad, who was the concessionaire and builder of the Mexican National Railroad.[101] Moran may have known Palmer because of his commercial relationships with William Blackmore (principal financier of the Denver & Rio Grande) and William A. Bell (the other cofounder), who had purchased his celebrated painting *The Mount of The Holy Cross* in 1880.[102]

In his desire to promote the Mexican rail line, Palmer may have hired Moran to create idealized views of the countryside, as the artist had done for the Denver & Rio Grande in the western United States.[103] Palmer's plans would have had less to do with promoting tourism than with encouraging commercial use of the railroads in the mining areas of Mexico. Still, he, like many frontier entrepreneurs, may have wished to promote the beauty as well as the natural resources of this unsettled country as reason for its economic development. The precedent was established with books such as *History of the Mexican Railway: Wealth of Mexico,* by Gustavo Baz and E. L. Gallo.[104] High-quality lithographs illustrate bird's-eye views of towns, details of railroad engineering, and scenic points, while the text extols the underexploited resources and pleasant climate of the country.

Moran sailed from New York with a British representative of the Mexican National Railroad, Arthur G. Renshaw, and a mining engineer identified only as Mr. Hahn. Renshaw and Moran had become acquainted at least the year before; Moran recorded in one of his ledgers that together they presented Moran's watercolor *Hot Springs of Gardiner's River, Yellowstone National Park, Wyoming Territory* (1872) to the Geological Society of London. The three men left New York in late January, taking the traditional water route to Vera Cruz by way of Cuba.[105] Moran wrote his wife about his brief visit to Havana: "We went ashore and spent the day in the city which is I think the most picturesque place I ever saw. Everywhere is a picture. The color is something indescribably beautiful. . . . I made some sketches from the vessel which are quite good. I would have liked to have made some sketches in the city but had no time. I have made six sketches in color so far all of them good and useful."[106]

Two sketches of Havana show the city from the water. *Havana* (No. 627; Plate 47) is a typical Moran harbor view, with buildings arrayed along a perfectly straight horizon line drawn one-third of the way up from the bottom edge of the paper. A very quick and immediate contour drawing, it contrasts with his usual more careful work. Applying very wet paint to dry paper, Moran added hints of blue wash to the sky and touches of color to the buildings to articulate windows. Moran's second sketch, *Havana* (No. 629; Plate 48), and *Sunset, Gulf of Mexico* (No. 630; Plate 49) are unusual in their lack of underdrawing. The result is much more impressionistic than most of Moran's watercolor sketch work. *Sunset, Gulf of Mexico* illustrates the spectacular fiery skies that Moran saw while on board ship. It is one of the few sketches Moran made that exclude geological reference.

On February 3 Moran arrived at Vera Cruz, the site of the beginning of the Mexican National Railroad.[107] In a letter to Mary he remarked on the "quiet smooth sea reflecting the castle and buildings."[108] He detailed the architecture of the picturesque castle of San Juan d'Ulloa in sketches (*San Juan d'Ulloa, Vera Cruz,* No. 632; Plate 50) that provided the inspiration for paintings and an etching. In *Vera Cruz* (No. 631; Plate 51) he

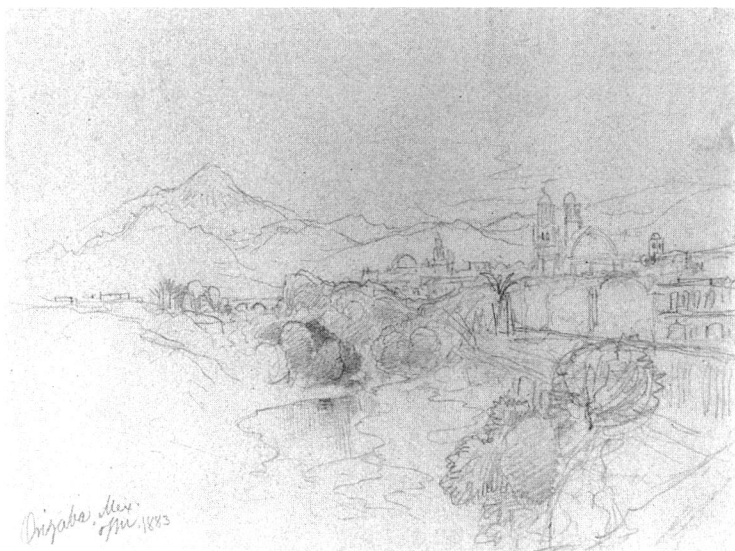 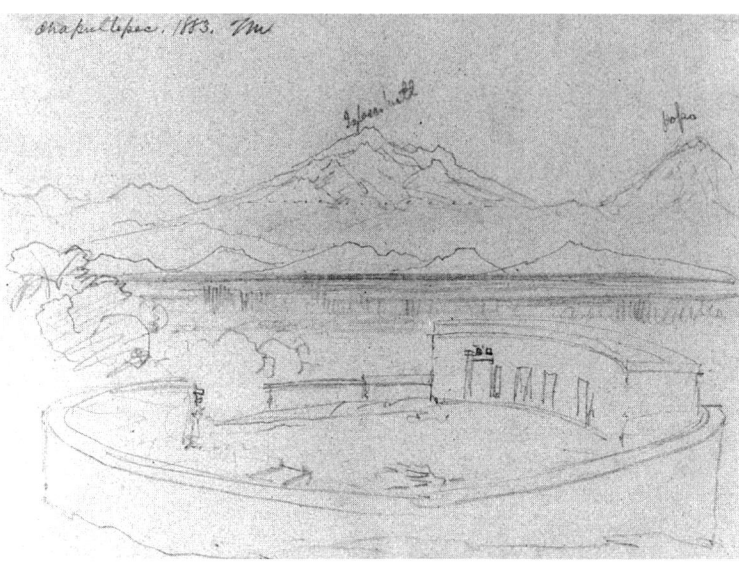

delineated the city's profile as seen from the bay. All the elements of this serene composition are arrayed across a narrow horizontal strip in the lower middle portion of the paper and delicately accented with pastel hues.

Moran, Renshaw, and Hahn prepared to travel through the interior of Mexico. From Vera Cruz they went west about a hundred miles to Orizaba, long a haven for travelers. Moran described Orizaba, beautifully situated at the foot of Citlaltépetl, Mexico's tallest mountain, as "the most pictorial town I ever saw. I will not attempt to describe it as only a picture could give any idea of its beauty."[109] He made several sketches, most of which, like *Orizaba, Mexico* (No. 640), show the town against its backdrop of volcanic peaks. Of *The Peak of Orizaba from Esperanza* (No. 644; Plate 52), Moran wrote: "We reached Esperanza [just outside Orizaba] at two o'clock . . . and here we had a fine view of the snow covered peak . . . I made a sketch while the train was waiting."[110] He made sparing but effective use of watercolor in this sketch, in which pure white

gouache on the snow-covered summit contrasts vividly with the pale blue sky.

The 200-mile journey on to Mexico City bored Moran. He remarked, "Between Esperanza and the City of Mexico I saw nothing that was particularly striking as the country seems very barren and we passed no towns of any consequence."[111] His arrival in the capital was a relief: "I wandered about the town and found it very interesting and pictorial."[112] He sketched the interior of the town, its skyline, and also the two volcanoes, Popocatépetl and Ixtacihuatl, which tower above it. Labeled, they are shown in the background of *Chapultepec* (No. 646). On a tiny strip of paper Moran sketched their profiles (*Ixtacihuatl and Popocatépetl,* No. 648), highlighting their snowy tops with opaque white. About them, he remarked: "From the outskirts this morning I had a fine view of the two great mountains snow covered and rising into the clear sky nearly 18,000 feet, two of the finest mountains I have ever seen. I have made some sketches about the city that I think I can make

Left: No. 640. *Orizaba, Mexico* (Gilcrease Institute, 1346.808), graphite on blue laid, 8⅝ by 11⅝ inches.

Right: No. 646. *Chapultepec* (Gilcrease Institute, 1346.799), graphite on blue laid, 8⅝ by 11⅝ inches.

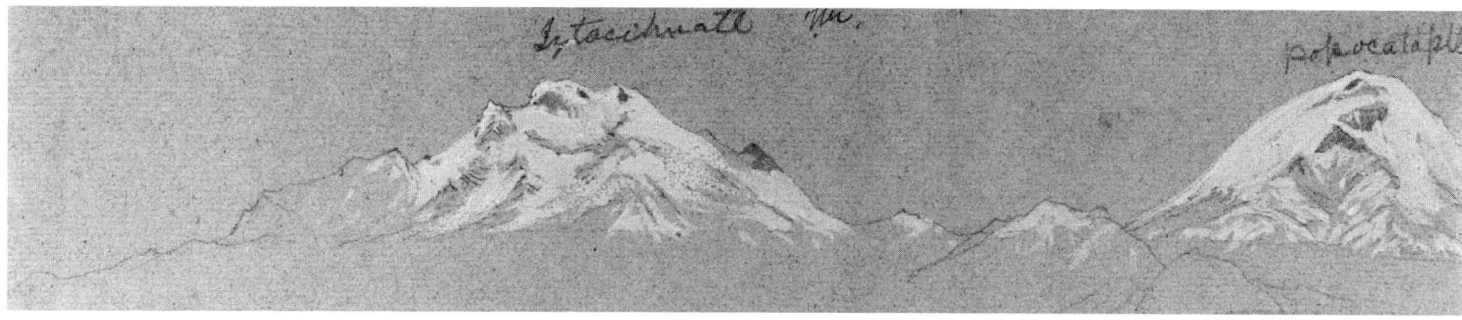

Top: No. 648. *Ixtacihuatl and Popocatépetl* (Gilcrease Institute, 1346.628), graphite and white gouache on blue laid, 2⁷/₈ by 11⁵/₈ inches.

good use of and Mexico has furnished me with lots of suggestions."[113]

In Mexico City Moran found more than majestic mountains and impressive architecture. *Mexico* (No. 649; Plate 53) is a beautiful color study of a modest dwelling that includes several small figures. More figures appear in Moran's Mexican sketches than in any other body of his fieldwork, a characteristic of his studio paintings of Mexican subjects as well. The Mexican peasant as a motif may have appealed to his sense of the picturesque.

Moran next sketched a few miles west of Mexico City, at Maravatio, which he seems to have found extremely inviting. He produced more sketches here than in any other town in Mexico, and many of his finished Mexican paintings depict Maravatio. The composition of *Maravatio* (No. 653; Plate 54) is typical of Moran's views of Mexican towns: buildings are profiled against mountains. He added broad washes of color to the landscape in the middle distance and background of this drawing, rendering the town

in rather skeletal fashion. By contrast, he fully developed a detail of Spanish colonial architecture in *Sunday Morning, Maravatio* (No. 654; Plate 55). In this work he executed the cathedral entrance with extraordinary panache. His rendering of the robed, kneeling worshippers gathered in front of the cathedral is also remarkable for its painterly economy of means. He deftly captured the demeanor of the figures with a minimum of strokes.[114]

In one simple yet fascinating small sketch, *Payday, beyond Maravatio* (No. 657), Moran brought together all the elements of his Mexican sketches. Mountains, town view, and figures are here reduced to their most basic forms. The only use of color is brilliant touches of red added to several of the figures, particularly the one in the foreground who faces the viewer. The placement of this odd figure enhances the spontaneous effect of the work; she appears to have popped up in front of Moran while he was sketching.

Payday, beyond Maravatio (No. 657) is exe-

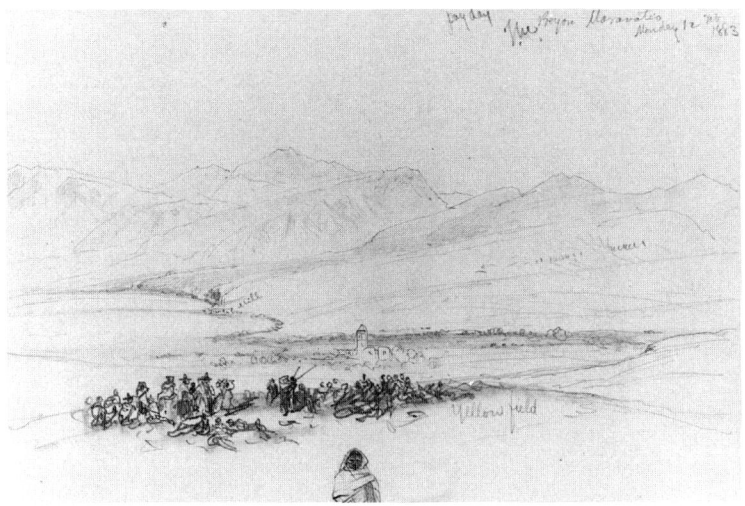 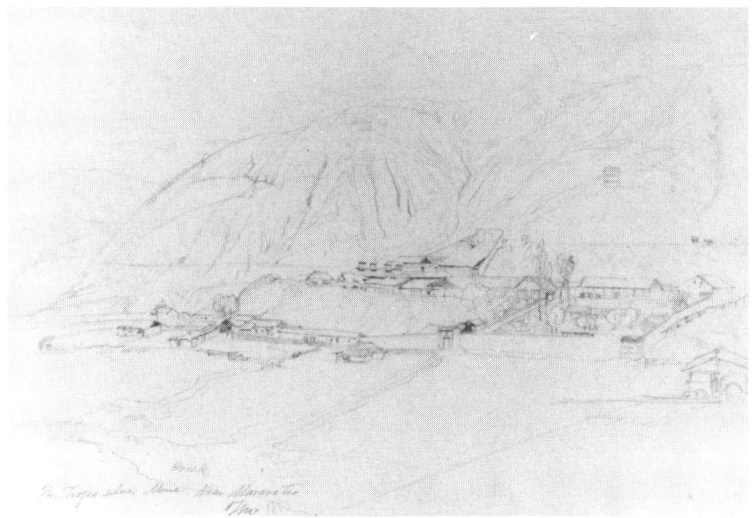

cuted on newsprint, a seldom used support for Moran's field sketches. Three other newsprint sketches of Mexican subjects—*Maravatio* (No. 663; Plate 56), *From Acambaro, West* (No. 655; Plate 57), and *Near Vera Cruz* (No. 642; Plate 58)—are tinted with watercolor, which is even more unusual because newsprint is not a particularly substantial support. For *San José beyond Maravatio* (No. 665; Plate 59) and *Morelia, Mexico* (No. 667; Plate 60), Moran returned to the stouter, colored wove paper on which he sketched much of his Mexican work.

Toward the end of February, Moran's party traveled about fifty miles on the Mexican National Railroad to the Trojes silver mine near Angangueo, south-southeast of Maravatio. In the late nineteenth century, Mexican mines produced nearly one-seventh of the world's silver; the metal was the country's principal export. Access to the silver mines was the main objective of the railroad builders, and in sketches such as *Ravine near the Trojes Mine, Mexico* (No. 674; Plate 61), Moran showed how the scenic possi-

bilities of the area could be exploited to generate public interest.

Moran made two minutely detailed sketches of the Trojes mine. *The Trojes Silver Mine, near Maravatio* (No. 675) shows the mining works and the outlying buildings, which hugged the side of a mountain. *The Trojes Mine, Mexico* (No. 676) is a closer view of the uppermost buildings, taken from a different vantage point. In both of these complex sketches, Moran precisely delineated the buildings with an extremely sharp pencil. More characteristic of his work are the freely rendered trees, clouds, and mountains.[115]

Eventually the railroad was to extend north to Laredo and connect with rail lines in the United States. In 1883, however, the completed track of this leg reached just beyond Maravatio, so Moran traveled 400 miles to Saltillo by wagon. The central part of Mexico, with its flat plains bounded by the ancient remnants of volcanic peaks, appealed to him, and he made some remarkable sketches of villages and their environs. A great cloud-filled expanse of sky occupies the

Left: No. 657. *Payday, Beyond Maravatio* (Gilcrease Institute, 1346. 806), graphite and red watercolor on newsprint, 5⅞ by 8⅜ inches.

Right: No. 675. *The Trojes Silver Mine, near Maravatio* (Gilcrease Institute, 1346.1033), graphite on wove, 10 by 14¼ inches.

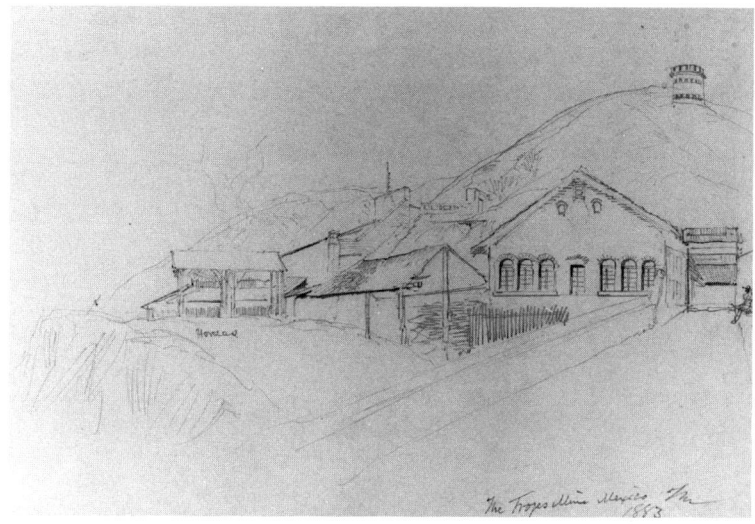 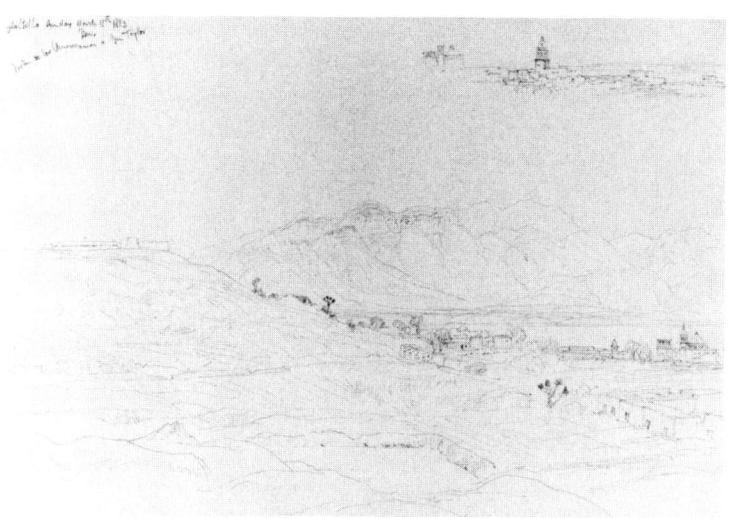

Left: No. 676. *The Trojes Mine, Mexico* (Gilcrease Institute, 1346.830), graphite on wove, 10 by 14¼ inches.

Right: No. 694. *Saltillo* (Gilcrease Institute, 1346.823), graphite on blue wove, 10 by 14¼ inches.

upper half of *On the Plateau above Dolores* (No. 683; Plate 62), contrasting with the nearly empty terrain in the foreground. In *Calderon, Mexico* (No. 680; Plate 63) Moran compressed the broad sweep of plain in the middle ground and placed a tiny village on a rise in the foreground, thus mitigating the sense of desolation.

In the second week in March Moran reached Saltillo, about fifty miles southwest of Monterrey. Here he sketched actively, making a series of drawings on the blue-fibered paper that he used extensively in Mexico. These sketches reveal that he had time to familiarize himself with the particular features of this town, located near the site of the Battle of Buena Vista (1847). He even recorded the ruins of General Zachary Taylor's stronghold on a hill overlooking the town, sketching them in a vignette in the upper lefthand corner of *Saltillo* (No. 694).

The composition of *Saltillo, Mexico* (No. 693) is similar to that of many of Moran's village profiles, but instead of leaving his foreground empty as usual, he described a large,

eroded cutbank in the arroyo, which recalls in miniature his drawings of the Grand Canyon of the Colorado. The conjunction of the cutbank and the mountains in the background creates an interesting interplay of negative and positive space.

Moran investigated more eroded topography in *The Arroyo at Saltillo* (No. 692), again recalling earlier work. As he had done at Spanish Fork Canyon in Utah, he positioned himself in the depths of a ravine to sketch the rugged, convoluted terrain cut by the forces of wind and water. He made his usual color notes, such as "tops warm gray to pink gray, rocks at the bottom a yellow gray green," on the Saltillo sketches, and he added color to at least one of the drawings, *Ojo de Agua, Saltillo* (No. 691; Plate 64). In Mexico Moran made much greater use of opaque color—pinks and yellows, as well as white—than he had in earlier fieldworks. He may have used these brilliant colors to suggest the unrelenting strength of the desert sun. These touches of gouache contrast with the soft blue of the paper

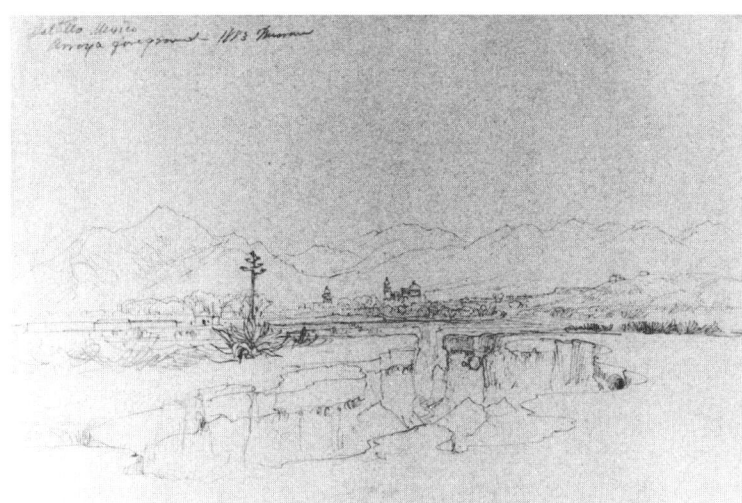 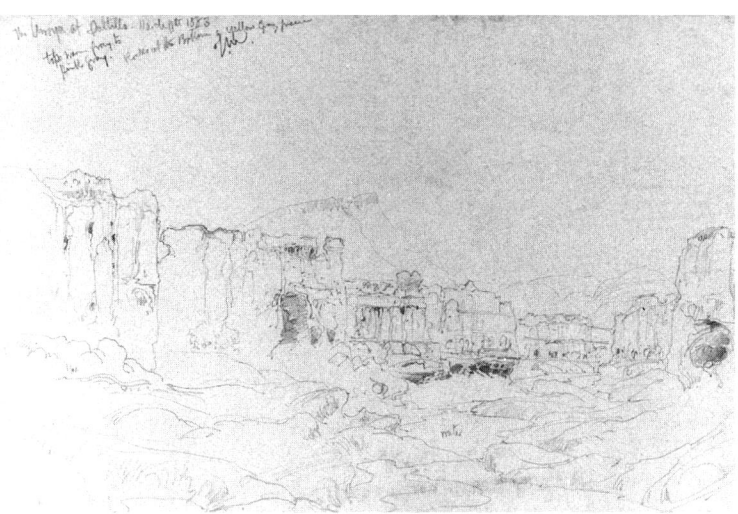

as well as with the transparent color he continued to use. He often applied gouache to adobe and stone buildings; perhaps he felt its opacity imparted a greater feeling of density and weight to these earthbound structures.

Moran made his final Mexican sketches of 1883 in Monterrey. The frieze of buildings disposed across the middle ground of *Monterrey, from the Hotel Roof* (No. 699; Plate 65) is resplendent in its dazzling pastel hues. Foreground elements are indifferently sketched; some are hastily washed with earth colors. In this composition, Moran seems to mimic human vision, in which the eye focuses on one portion of a scene while elements at the periphery remain indistinct.

Moran returned to his New York studio to create Mexican harbor scenes, such as *Vera Cruz* (1885, Gilcrease Institute; Plate 66), strongly reminiscent of Turner. Mexico also later prompted him to try his hand at misty pastorals, such as *Fiesta at Cuernavaca* (1913, Gilcrease Institute; Plate 67), in the style of Corot, complete with Corot's dancing peasant motif.

Moran passed the summer of 1883 at East Hampton. Perhaps pleased with the effects produced by his use of gouache in the Mexican sketches, he added it to several shore scenes made in late August 1883. White gouache on gray-green paper impressively defines the high-blown clouds and crystalline sand in *Gardiner Bay* (No. 704; Plate 68). Moran's adroit handling of gouache, ranging from full-bodied to delicate, is eloquent testimony to his ability to express subtle atmospheric variations.

Three years passed before Moran's next major voyage. He returned to Italy in April 1886, visiting Venice for the first time. One of many Americans drawn to the island city during the 1880s, he again followed in the footsteps of Turner, who had sketched there as early as 1819.

Moran's first stay in Venice was productive, resulting in at least thirty sketches,[116] but his spirits were dampened by the fact that he traveled alone. The gregarious artist was happiest in the company of friends or family. The single extant letter of that year to his wife reflects this:

Left: No. 693. *Saltillo* (Gilcrease Institute, 1346.829), graphite on blue wove, 10 by 14¹/₄ inches.

Right: No. 692. *The Arroyo at Saltillo* (Gilcrease Institute, 1346.814), graphite on blue wove, 10 by 14¹/₄ inches.

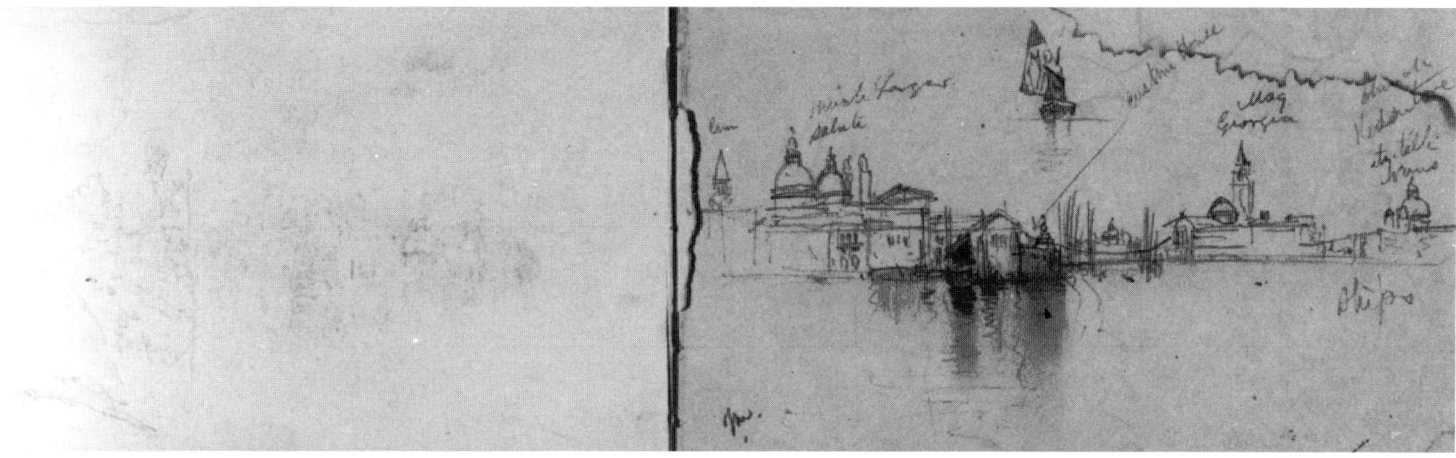

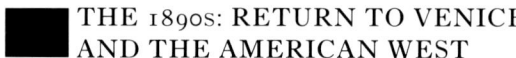

Above: No. 730. *Customs House* (Gilcrease Institute, 1876.17.4), graphite on wove, 5½ by 9⅛ inches.

"Venice is all & more, than travellers have reported of it. It is wonderful. . . . But in spite of all its grandeur & magnificence I can not say that I enjoy it: *because you are not here.*"[117]

Moran spent nearly six weeks in Venice, returning to New York in late June. One wonders what occupied his time there, considering that, in contrast to most of his previous excursions, he covered very little territory. His sketches appear to have been executed hastily. Many of the drawings in his pocket sketchbook, such as *Customs House* (No. 730) and *St. Michael in Campo Santo* (No. 733), depict buildings bordering the canals. Moran sometimes hurriedly sketched individual landmarks, as in *The Tutella* (No. 737), and rarely took time to add much detail.

Even the sketch *Venice* (No. 745), which inspired Moran's critically acclaimed painting *The Gate of Venice* (1887; location unknown), is quite minimal. Like his Yellowstone sketches, it provides little intimation of the glories of the subject's incarnation on canvas. When he painted *The Gate of Venice,* Moran may have turned for

details to Turner's work and to A. F. Bunner's painting *Venice,* which he had reproduced as an etching in 1887.[118] Moran's *Gate of Venice* heralded his most ambitious etching, completed in 1888. Both the painting and the etching are impressive results of the 1886 trip, but Moran produced far more works from his later visit in 1890, made with his wife.

Between the two trips, Moran did little sketching. He occupied himself with studio work, including the production of twenty new etchings; made a return trip to Fort George Island in 1887; and participated with his wife in a joint print exhibition in 1889 that commemorated their first decade as painter-etchers.

■ THE 1890s: RETURN TO VENICE AND THE AMERICAN WEST

MORAN'S second journey to Venice was eventful from the start. On the way to Antwerp in late April, the Morans' ship passed an iceberg. This

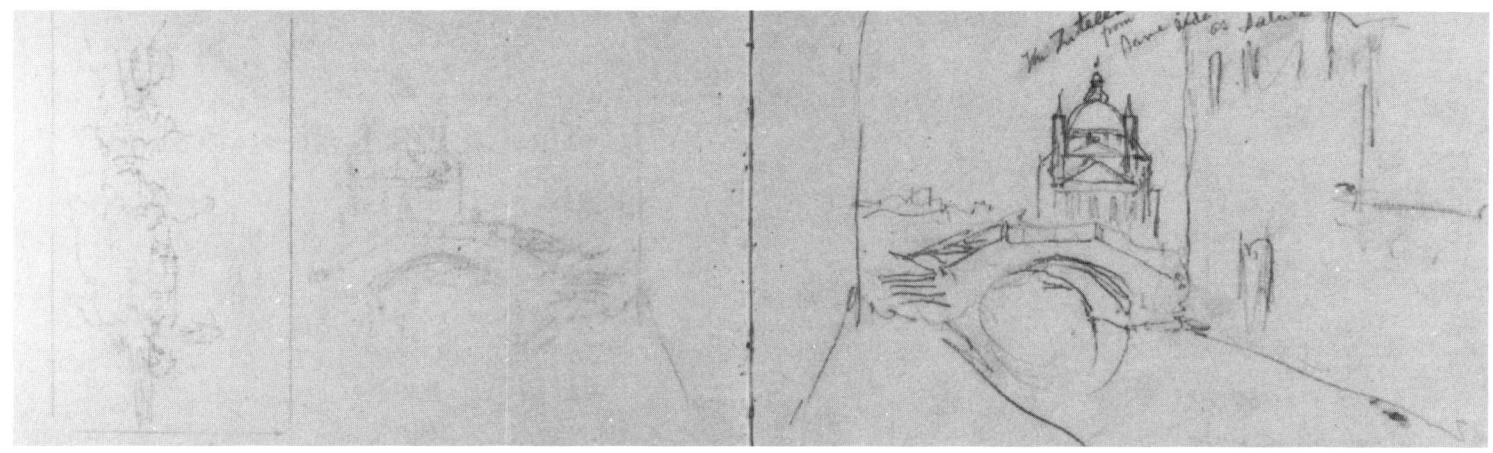

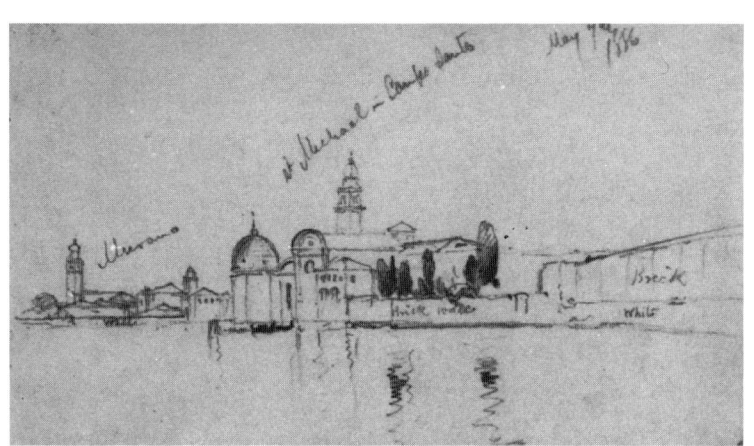
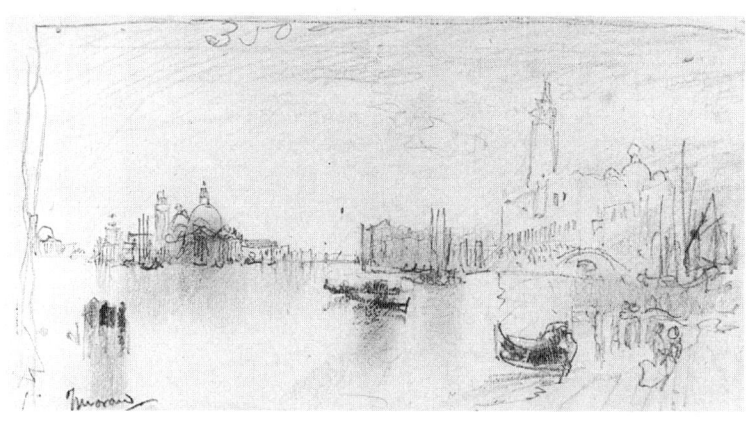

Top: No. 737. *The Tutella* (Gilcrease Institute, 1876.17.11), graphite on wove, 5¹/₂ by 9⁷/₈ inches.

Middle left: No. 733. *St. Michael in Campo Santo* (Gilcrease Institute, 1876.17.7), graphite on wove, 5¹/₂ by 9¹/₈ inches.

Middle right: No. 745. *Venice* (Gilcrease Institute, 1376.580), graphite on wove, 4¹/₂ by 7³/₄ inches.

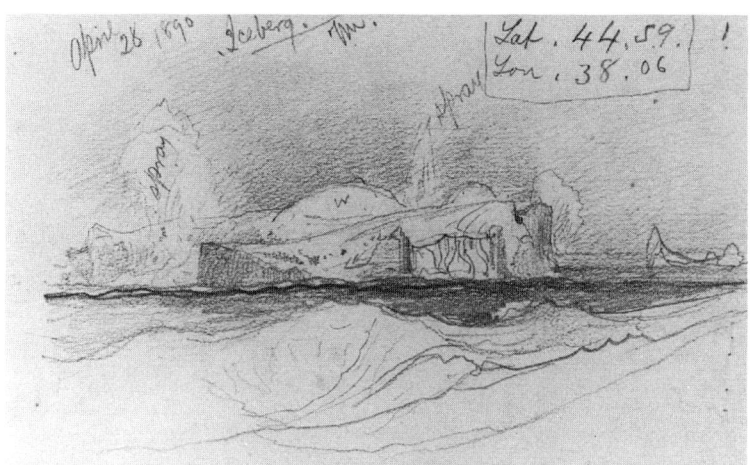 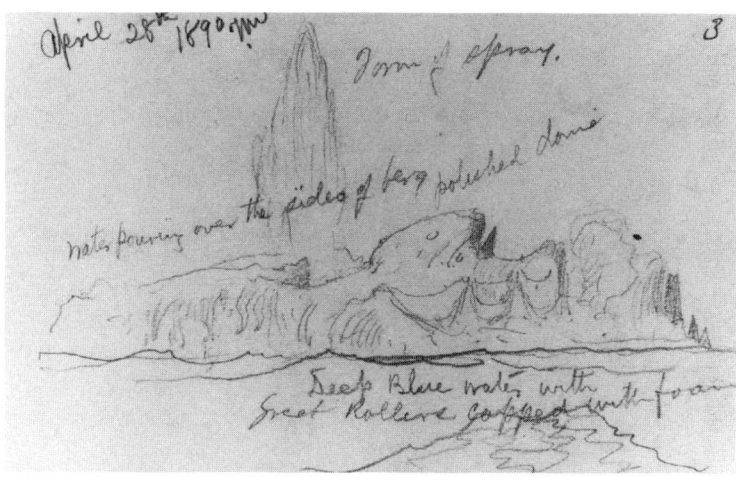

Left: No. 759. *Iceberg* (Gilcrease Institute, 1396.1236), graphite on wove, 4¹/₂ by 7 inches.

Right: No. 761. *Tower of Spray* (Gilcrease Institute, 1396.1239), graphite on wove, 4¹/₂ by 7 inches.

sublime spectacle soon provided Moran another opportunity to emulate Church, after whom Moran seems to have patterned his own career and whose enormous painting *The Icebergs* (1861, Dallas Museum of Art) he must have known.[119] Moran made rapid pencil drawings in a pocket sketchbook, recording the contour of the ice formation and such data as its longitude and latitude, seen in the upper right corner of *Iceberg* (No. 759). Details he could not set down quickly in the drawing, he described verbally: "water pouring over the sides of berg . . . Deep Blue water with great Rollers capped with foam" (*Tower of Spray,* No. 761). Moran's swift, vigorous execution in *Iceberg* (No. 762) captures the dynamic energy of the waves crashing against the berg. Immediately upon his return from Europe, he developed a painting, *Spectres from the North* (1890, Gilcrease Institute; Plate 69), that realizes all the potential inherent in the sketches and honors Church as well.[120]

By the second week of May, the Morans were in Cologne, and Moran added a sketch of St.

Mark's Cathedral (*St. Mark, Cologne,* No. 769) to his pocket sketchbook. On May 17 he sketched *Verona, from the Bridge of St. Peter* (No. 770), augmenting the pencil drawing with pale gray wash. The simple addition of wash to differentiate the sky and water and to create shadows on buildings adds remarkable depth to this tiny cityscape.

Moran reached Venice the next day. His pencil sketch *Venice* (No. 773), executed soon after his arrival, records details of the colorful lateen sails of the boats in the lagoon. He was so taken with the nautical spectacle that two weeks later he created the colorful *Picture of Sails from Chioggia* (No. 793; Plate 70).

Moran catalogued some of the significant structures that lined the Grand Canal, revisiting those that particularly interested him. *San Giorgio Maggiore from the Giudecca* (No. 776) and *San Giorgio Maggiore* (No. 774), for example, were made two days apart from different points of view.

The tiny islands Burano and Murano and a small town on the Lido, Malamocco, also drew

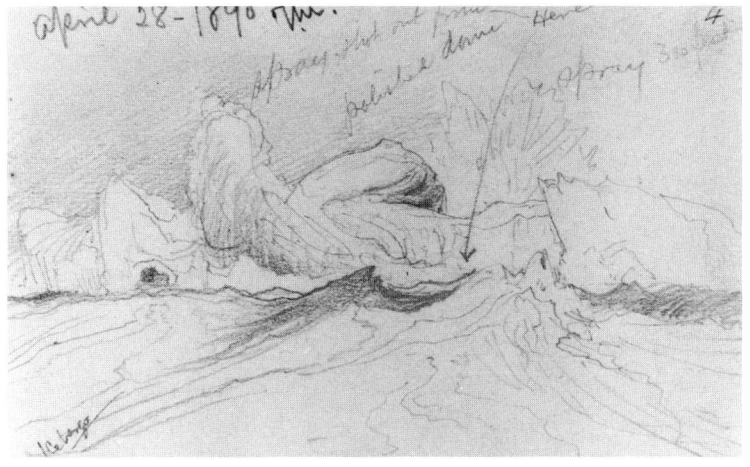

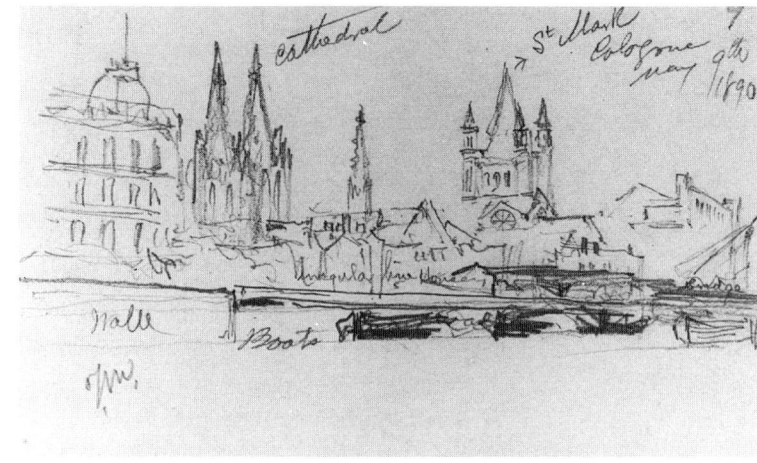

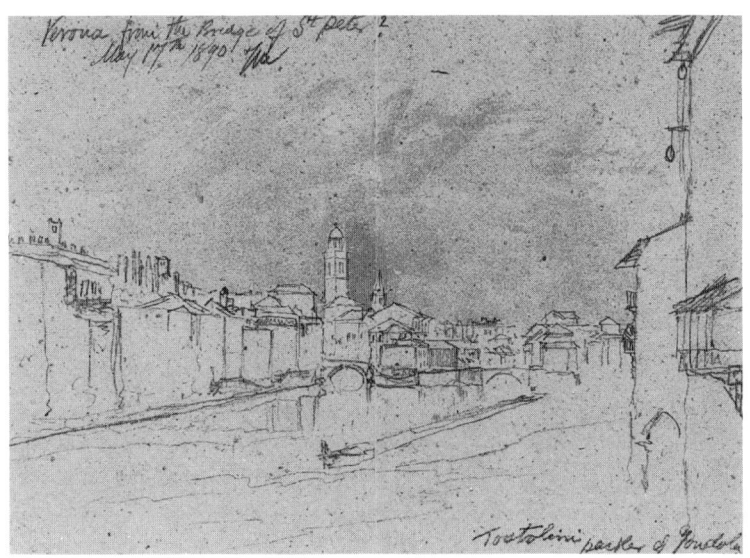

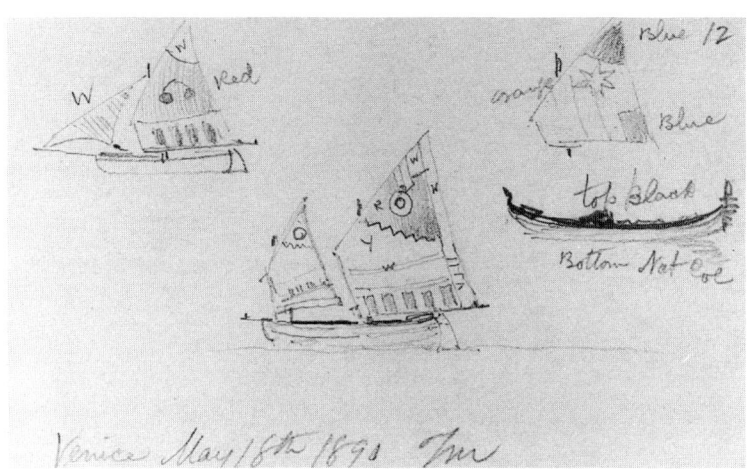

Top left: No. 762. *Iceberg* (Gilcrease Institute, 1396.1240), graphite on wove, 4½ by 7 inches.

Top right: No. 769. *St. Mark, Cologne* (Gilcrease Institute, 1376.837), graphite on wove, 4½ by 7 inches.

Bottom left: No. 770. *Verona from the Bridge of St. Peter* (Gilcrease Institute, 1376.834), graphite and blue wash on gold wove, 8⅝ by 11¾ inches.

Bottom right: No. 773. *Venice* (Gilcrease Institute, 1376.838), graphite on wove, 4½ by 7 inches.

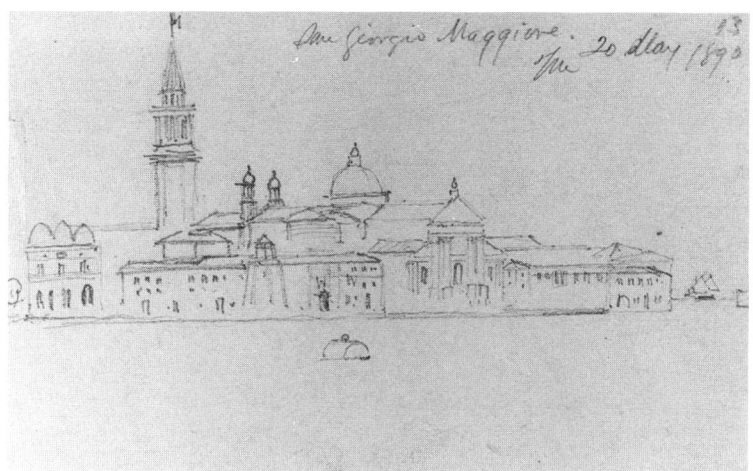 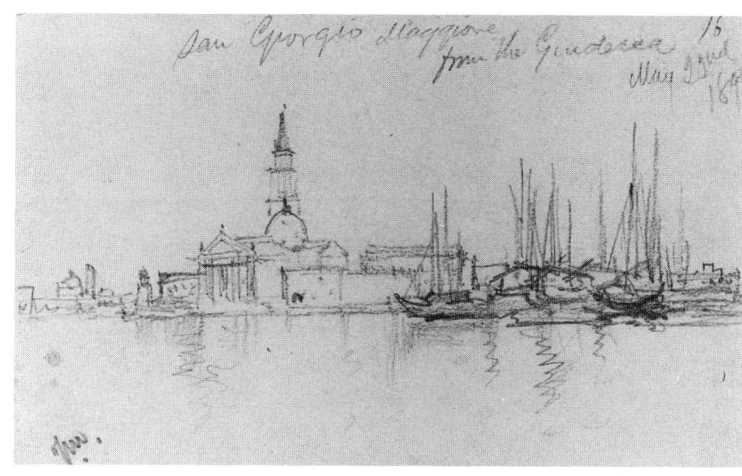

Left: No. 774. *San Giorgio Maggiore* (Gilcrease Institute, 1376. 839), graphite on wove, 4¹/₂ by 7 inches.

Right: No. 776. *San Giorgio Maggiore from the Giudecca* (Gilcrease Institute, 1376.832), graphite on wove, 4¹/₂ by 7 inches.

Moran's attention. Sometimes he visited these sites for their own sake, as he did to make a small sketch, *Murano* (No. 777; Plate 71), embellished with washes of soft pink and blue. More often, he used the islands as vantage points from which to make panoramic views, such as *Venice* (No. 790; Plate 72). Moran set the horizon line of this cityscape very low; the upper two-thirds of his sheet is given over to a nearly empty sky. This sketch, with its narrow horizontal band of buildings strung across a seemingly infinite expanse of water and sky, recalls the format of his views of Vera Cruz and Havana.

Moran employed a similar spacious composition in *Venice from Malamocco* (No. 791; Plate 73). He further enhanced the depth of the view by placing a series of rotting pilings in diminishing perspective along a subtle diagonal that connects the structures in the middle ground to the tiny cityscape at the horizon. Just to the right of center, he detailed a little votive shrine that stands out in sharp contrast to the distant buildings of Venice. As in *Venice* (No. 790), subtle

washes of blue above and below the horizon signify lagoon and sky.

Moran's paintings of Venice eventually surpassed in popularity his depictions of the American West, as American travelers rediscovered the visual riches of the jewel of the Adriatic. In Venice Moran had hit upon a subject that was commercially rewarding and aesthetically congenial, suiting his taste for the Turneresque.

The next year, 1891, Moran returned to Florida, a visit documented by paintings such as *San Pablo Beach Florida* (1891, destroyed)[121] as well as by etchings by Mary Moran. Only one sketch, however, is extant: *Villa Alexandria* (No. 796). He made only one other lengthy trip in the 1890s, a return to the West to revisit the Grand Canyon and Yellowstone. In the late spring of 1892, Moran and his son Paul left New York for Arizona under the auspices of the Santa Fe Railroad, which gave them passage in return for the reproduction rights to a painting of the Grand Canyon. At that time the Santa Fe reached only to Flagstaff, nearly one hundred miles from the

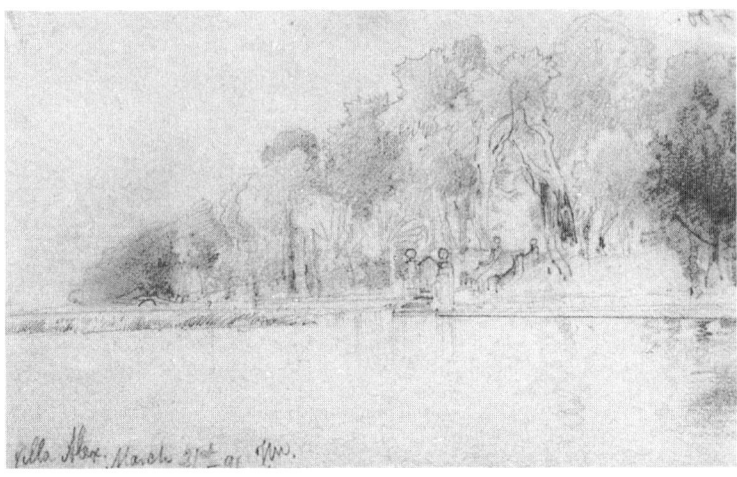

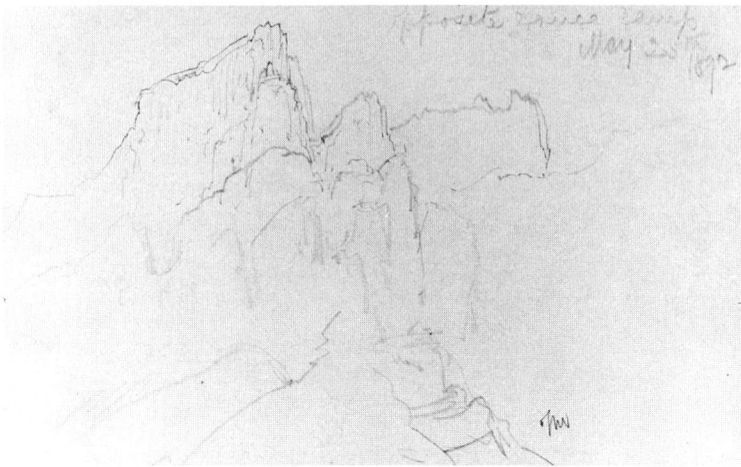

Grand Canyon. There, during the last week of May, the Morans were joined by William Henry Jackson; together they traveled on to the Grand Canyon by coach.

The 1892 trip was far easier than the journey of nineteen years before. Moran viewed the canyon from its more accessible south rim, and now his "base camp" was located at a hotel rather than in the open air. His 1892 sketches of the canyon differ significantly from those of 1873. Although he retained an interest in the geology and topography of the region, his execution of the later sketches was far more cursory; compare, for example, *Grand Canyon* (No. 278) of 1873 to *Opposite Hance Camp* (No. 798). He recorded various aspects of the canyon in pocket sketchbooks. Many of these drawings, such as *Shiva Temple* (No. 806), are executed in pencil and lightly washed with color. Their small size, around 4 by 8 inches, encouraged Moran to concentrate on individual formations rather than panoramic views. A remarkable exception is *The Grand Canyon of the Colorado* (No. 800; Plate 74), a large-format sketch that encompasses miles of terrain. He rather carefully distinguished the varying strata, not with pencil line as in earlier work, but with watercolor.

After a week at the Grand Canyon, Moran sent his son home to New York and continued with Jackson to Denver and then to the Yellowstone country at the invitation of Wyoming state officials. Moran had been commissioned to make a painting representing the newly admitted state for the World's Columbian Exposition in Chicago.

Moran was anxious to see Yellowstone again after twenty-one years, but the journey was long, tedious, and filled with delays. Moran and Jackson traveled by train from Denver to the frontier town of Gillette, Wyoming, arriving in late June. More delays, plus a wearying trip by stage, postponed their arrival by another month. Moran used the time to sketch possible subjects for future paintings of Wyoming's novel scenery, such as two colorful but hasty studies of Index Peak (Nos. 836 and 837; Plates 75 and 76). The two men finally reached Hot Springs of Gardner

Left: No. 796. *Villa Alexandria* (East Hampton Library), graphite on green wove, 4¹/₂ by 7 inches.

Right: No. 798. *Opposite Hance Camp* (Gilcrease Institute, 1336.843), graphite on wove, 5 by 7⁷/₈ inches.

River where, as at the Grand Canyon, they enjoyed the luxury of hotel accommodations.

During their two weeks in Yellowstone, Moran and Jackson ranged widely, revisiting familiar places, such as Mammoth Hot Springs, where Jackson photographed the stunning *Minerva Terrace* (1892, Gilcrease Institute) and Moran made the sketch he later inscribed *Upper Basins* (No. 845; Plate 77).[122] Until this point in the trip, Moran's work this time had consisted primarily of small, quick pencil sketches, such as *Stream from Faithful* (No. 871). A few sketches have faint color washes. Although he continued this practice in Yellowstone, he also developed larger images, especially in areas of thermal activity, such as *Upper Basins,* to which he added opaque as well as transparent color. In their brilliance, these works recall his studio watercolors of the 1870s and even the chromolithographs based on them, published by Louis Prang in 1876.

The following week, Moran sketched another familiar site, the lower geyser basin on the Firehole River. Moran used a white laid paper— it may have been his personal stationery—as the support for his sketch *Lower Geyser Basin* (No. 877; Plate 78). The use of white paper is unusual for Moran, who tended to use tan, green, or blue wove papers for his sketches as well as for his studio watercolors. Both transparent and opaque paints are very effective on papers of these colors; the paper functions as a mid-range tone. Most of the papers Moran used are wove, a type that furnishes a smooth, even surface. Laid paper, especially of the kind used for *Lower Geyser Basin,* in which the chain-and-laid pattern creates an independent texture, can interfere with the success of a watercolor. The liquid color pools in gullies between the chain lines, forming a pattern that can be distracting. In *Lower Geyser Basin* this effect, most obvious in the flat pools of water, may have been accidental, but its simulation of reflections on the water is serendipitous.

The Grand Canyon of the Yellowstone commanded most of Moran's attention. He spent several days sketching there, climbing to various vantage points to depict formations that appealed to him. *Moran Point, Yellowstone Canyon* (No. 898; Plate 79) is one of the more elaborate drawings he made that summer, although by the 1890s his work was liberated from the niggling detail of his youthful work of the 1860s. The complexity of *Moran Point, Yellowstone Canyon* is due not to the minute reproduction of every rock and leaf but to its elegant composition and the expressive integration of the graphic and water media.

Moran and Jackson left the park the first week of August; Moran returned to New York, and Jackson went on to the Tetons. Although Moran continued to travel in the West, returning often to the Grand Canyon in Arizona, he never again visited Yellowstone. The reason may have been the difficulty of getting there; the Grand Canyon was far more accessible. Rail service was extended to Grand Canyon Village during the early twentieth century, and Moran made nearly annual pilgrimages.

Moran spent a busy winter in the studio. Large paintings of the Grand Canyon and of the Yellowstone were the immediate results of the summer's sketching. He also went to Denver for a retrospective exhibition arranged by Jackson at the Denver Art League. It was the first display of Moran's work to include a large group of his field sketches, along with paintings, studio watercolors, and prints.[123]

Ever curious, Moran, perhaps with Jackson, also sketched in the vicinity, making *Pikes Peak from the Bluffs East of Colorado Springs* (No. 920) and a series of drawings of the massive rock formations at Glen Eyrie.[124] These drawings are larger than most of Moran's later western fieldwork. *Glen Eyrie, Colorado* (No. 916) is one of his last detailed western sketches. Its composition encompasses great space, although the panorama is cut off by the foreground elements that he uncharacteristically placed at the left edge of the paper.

Moran was tied to the studio for remainder of the decade. He created new compositions and revisited old subjects, imaginary and real, all influenced by his travels of recent years.[125] Scenes of Long Island, particularly East Hampton, were perennial favorites.

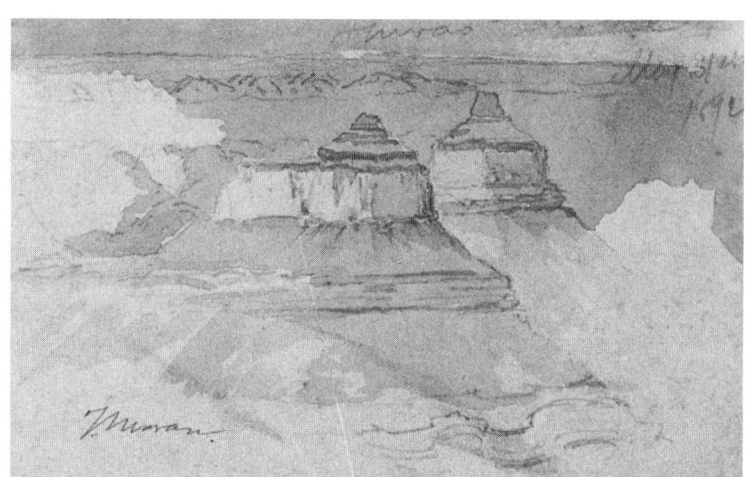

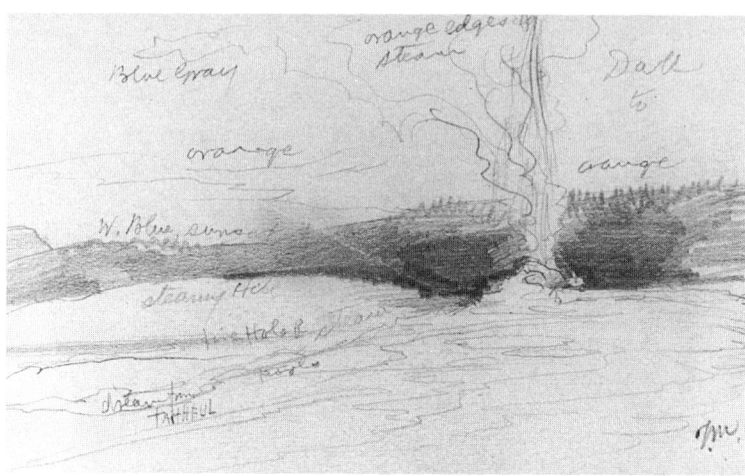

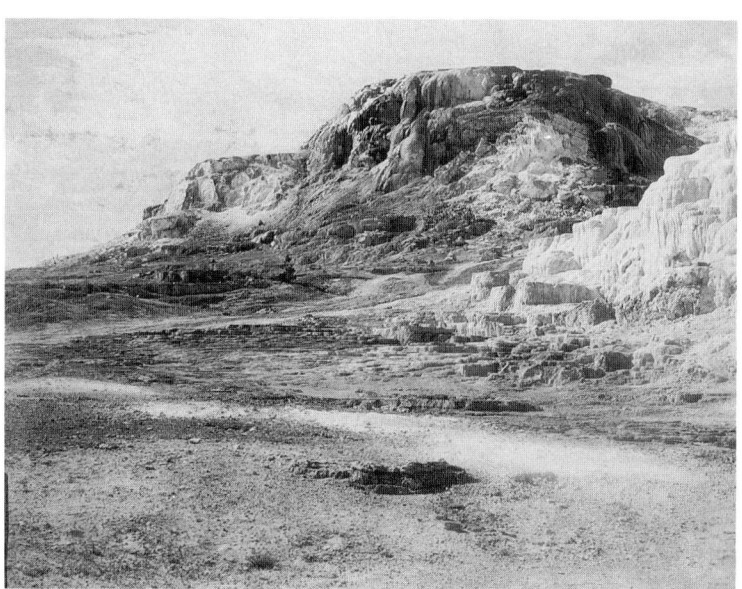

Top left: No. 806. *Shiva Temple* (East Hampton Library), graphite and watercolor on wove, 4³/₈ by 6³/₈ inches.

Top right: No. 871. *Stream from Faithful* (Gilcrease Institute, 1336. 1016), graphite on wove, 4¹/₂ by 7 inches.

Bottom left: William H. Jackson, *Minerva Terrace* (1892, Gilcrease Institute, 4337.7913), photograph, 15³/₄ by 18¹/₂ inches.

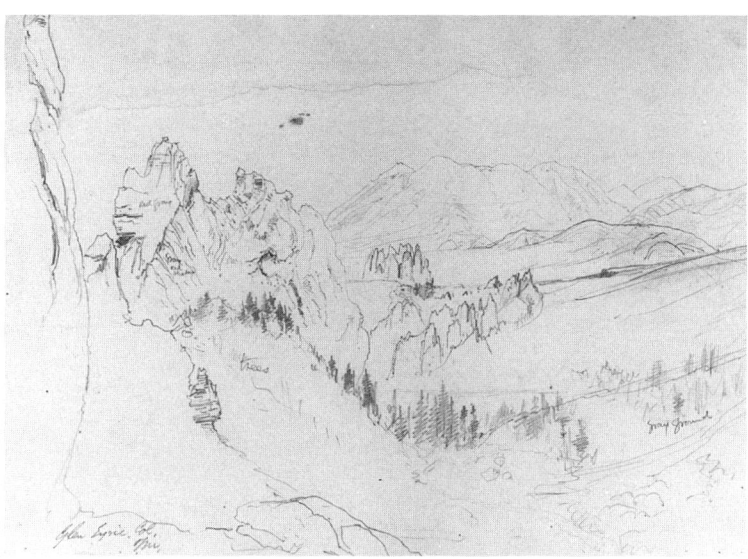

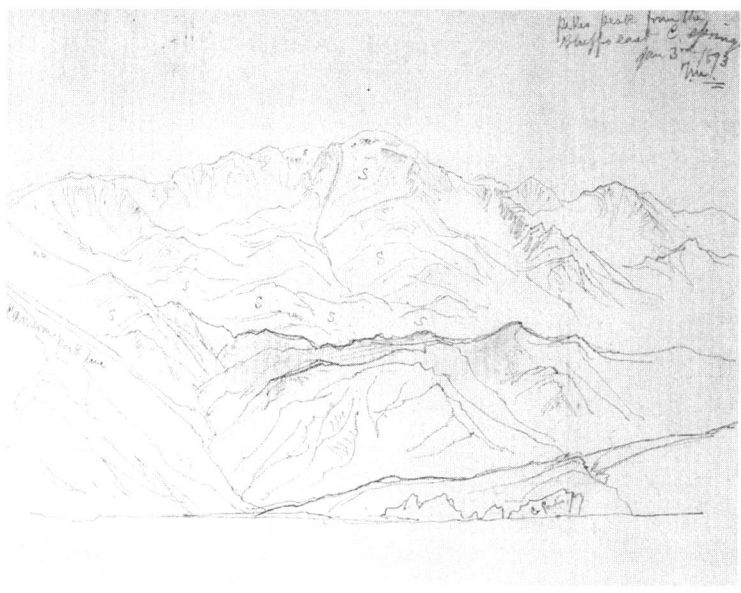

Left: No. 916. *Glen Eyrie, Colorado* (Gilcrease Institute, 1336.666), graphite on wove, 10¹/₂ by 13⁷/₈ inches.

Right: No. 920. *Pikes Peak from the Bluffs East of Colorado Springs* (Gilcrease Institute, 1336.848), graphite on wove, 8 by 10 inches.

■ THE 1900s: IDAHO, MEXICO AND GREAT BRITAIN

IN THE autumn of 1899, Moran's beloved wife died of enteric fever. Her death profoundly affected him, and the following spring he made a voyage of consolation to the West. His itinerary included the pueblos of Laguna and Acoma in New Mexico and culminated in a visit to the "Western Niagara," Shoshone Falls on the Snake River in Idaho.

Moran had illustrated the imposing falls in an article entitled "Idaho Scenery" that appeared in *The Aldine* in 1876.[126] A chromolithograph based on Moran's studio watercolor was among Louis Prang's illustrations for Ferdinand Hayden's *Yellowstone National Park and the Mountain Ranges of Portions of Idaho, Nevada, Colorado and Utah,* also published in 1876 (Plate 81). These images, however, were based on Timothy O'Sullivan's (1840–82) photographs, made in 1874, rather than on Moran's personal observations.[127]

Perhaps because of his earlier, though secondhand, familiarity, Moran made just a few sketches at Shoshone Falls. The known sketches are all large, about 10 by 15 inches, and executed on blue paper. These drawings epitomize his mature approach to sketching new territory, in which he recorded the essential data by the most economical means possible. In *Shoshone Falls* (No. 930), for example, he used a few quick, curving lines to establish the positions of the bluffs and terraces that gird the river until it flows over the brink. In the distance, he hinted at the palisades of volcanic rock that gave the falls its distinctive character and made it far superior, in his view, to Niagara Falls.[128]

Moran added color to only one of the Idaho sketches, *Blue Lakes, Idaho* (No. 928; Plate 80). A beautiful blue-green swath of paint defines the flowing water. Like some of Moran's earlier works, these sketches bear scant witness to the power of the finished work with which they are associated, the painting *Shoshone Falls on the Snake River* (1900, Gilcrease Institute; Plate 82),

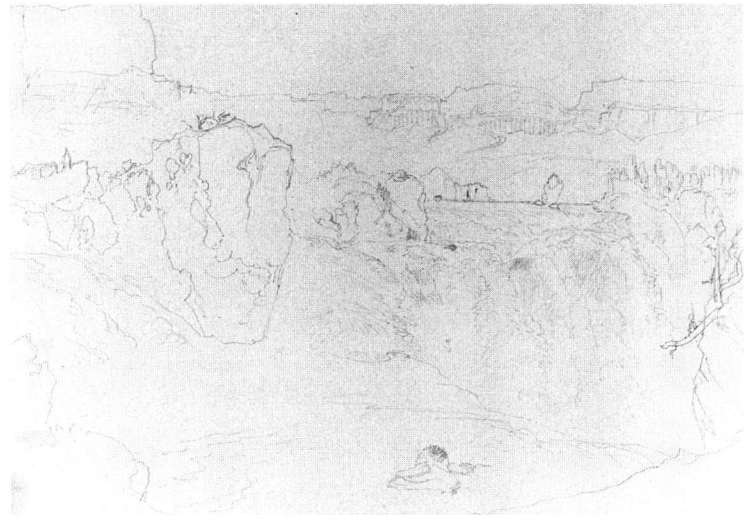 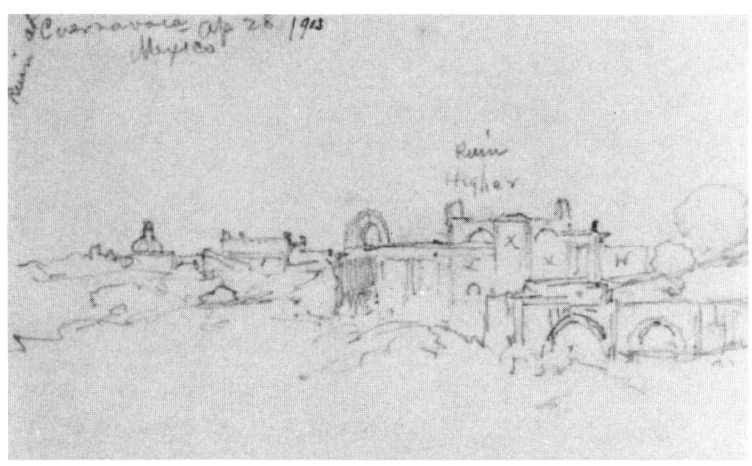

which Moran began immediately upon his return to New York. They are, however, continuing evidence of Moran's ability to translate the most minimal and literal fieldwork into sublime Romantic visions. He may have intended *Shoshone Falls on the Snake River* to be a response to Church's masterpiece, *Niagara*. The obvious comparisons in composition and contrasts in the waterfalls themselves lend eloquent support to the idea. Even though much earlier in his career Moran himself had proposed his *Mountain of the Holy Cross* as *Niagara*'s western pendant, *Shoshone Falls* could conceivably have superseded his earlier choice.

Moran continued to travel during the first decades of the twentieth century, renewing his acquaintance with familiar places and also visiting some new ones. When he returned to Mexico in 1903, he went to Cuernavaca, about forty miles south of Mexico City, which he had not visited in 1883. He was now sketching so little that he recorded views such as *Ruin at Cuernavaca, Mexico* (No. 957) in sketchbooks al-

ready partially filled with drawings made at other sites.

In the fall of 1906 Moran returned to Great Britain and repeated his pilgrimage through the castle country of North Wales, revisiting Conway and Harlech. In contrast to the productivity of his visit of twenty-four years before, he made only a handful of drawings in one of his many pocket sketchbooks.[129] He sketched Conway in a rather unorthodox medium, a purple pencil; his ordinarily bold execution is robbed of its vitality by the faintness of his stroke. *Conway from the Mountain* (No. 1001) echoes his earlier compositions, such as *Conway, North Wales* (No. 604). One sketch, *A Lighter at Conway* (No. 1003), recalls his 1862 drawings of boats at Hastings (No. 63) in even more evanescent fashion.

By the time Moran reached Harlech Castle, he had obtained an ordinary graphite pencil, which he used to make several conventional views of the stronghold perched on its rocky promontory, including *Harlech Castle from the North* (No. 1007). Here, another motif captured his at-

Left: No. 930. *Shoshone Falls* (Gilcrease Institute, 1337.851), graphite on blue wove, $10^{3}/_{4}$ by 15 inches.

Right: No. 957. *Ruin at Cuernavaca, Mexico* (Gilcrease Institute, 1847.18.6), graphite on wove, $4^{3}/_{8}$ by $7^{1}/_{4}$ inches.

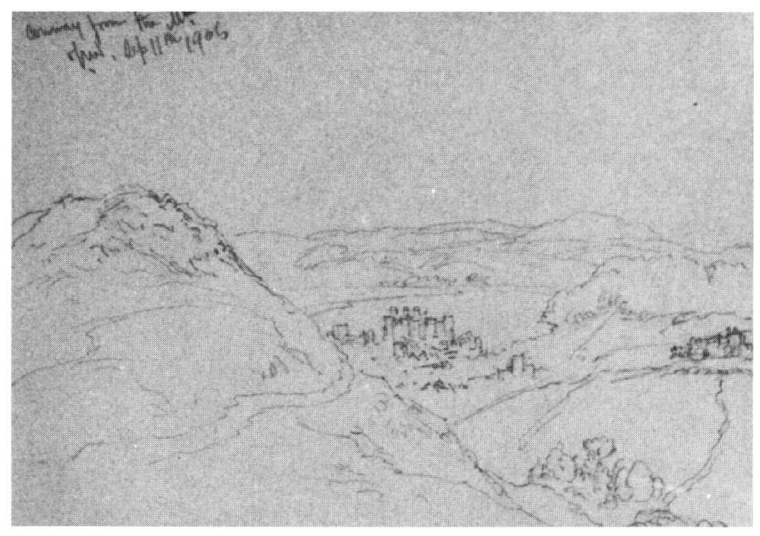 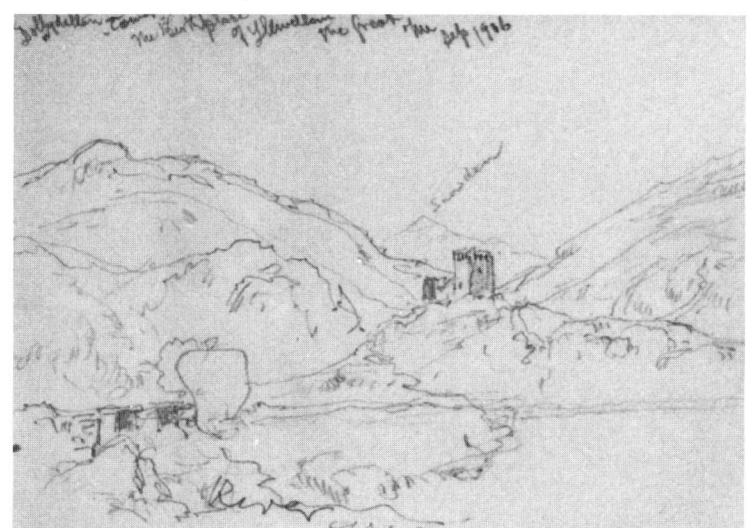

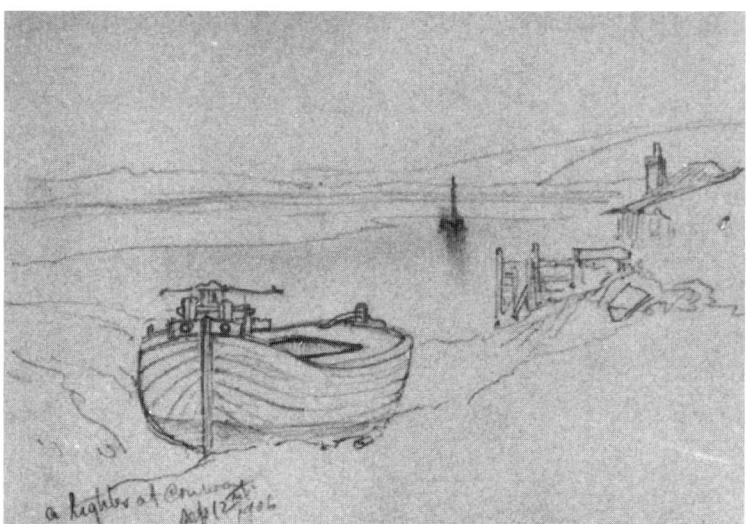 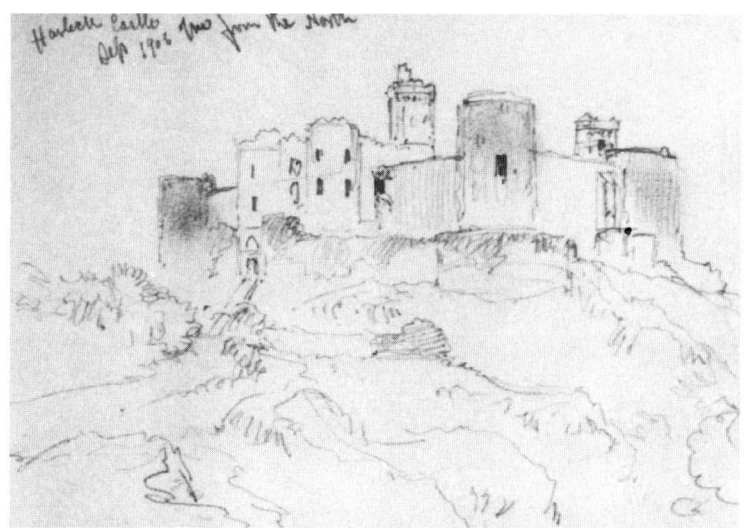

Top left: No. 1001. *Conway from the Mountain* (Gilcrease Institute, 1877.20.6), purple pencil on wove, 5 by 7 inches.

Top right: No. 1006. *Dollwydellan Tower* (Gilcrease Institute, 1877.20.11), graphite on wove, 5 by 7 inches.

Bottom left: No. 1003. *A Lighter at Conway* (Gilcrease Institute, 1877. 20.8), purple pencil on wove, 5 by 7 inches.

Bottom right: No. 1007. *Harlech Castle from the North* (Gilcrease Institute, 1877.20.12), graphite on wove, 5 by 7 inches.

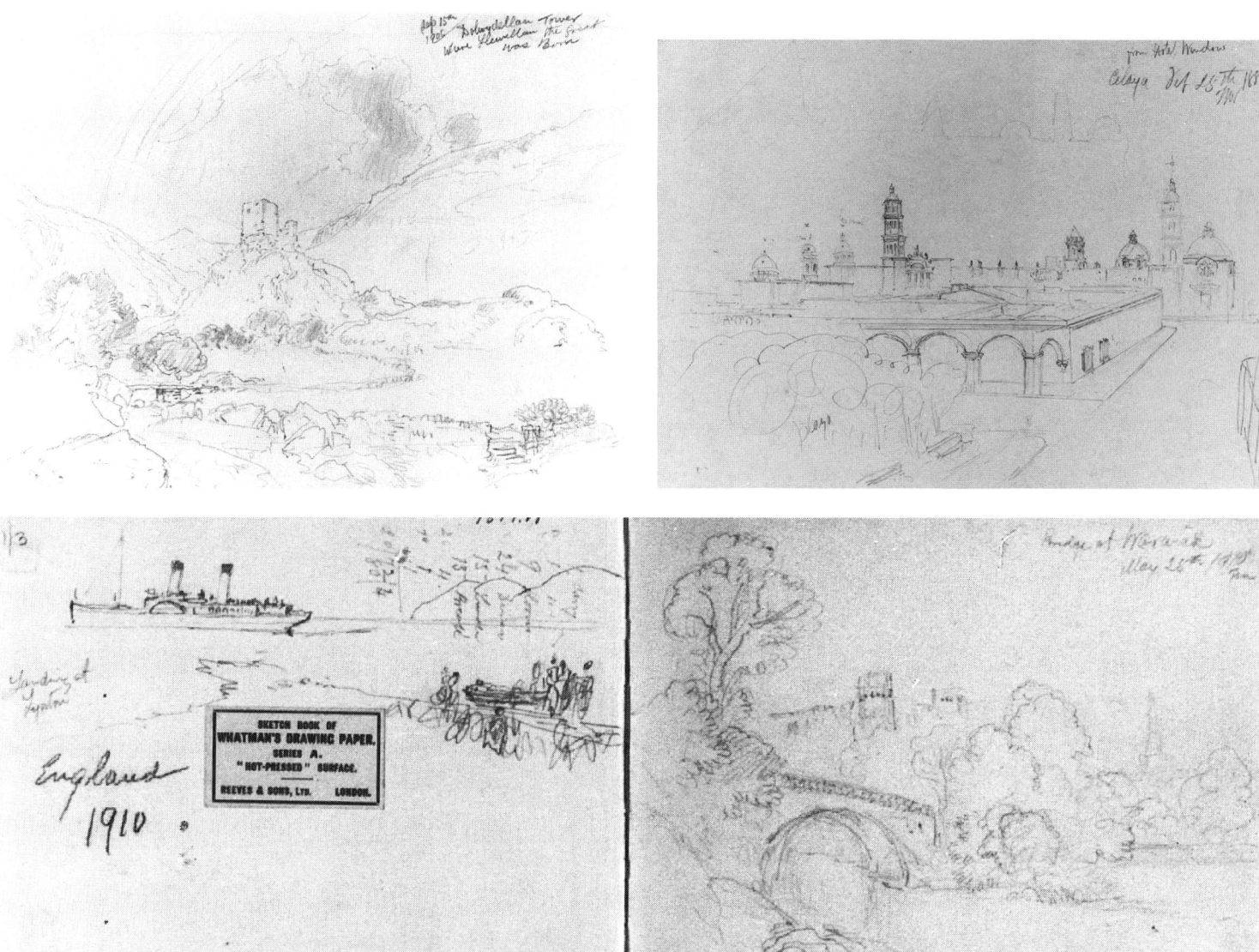

Top left: No. 1011. *Dollwydellan Tower* (Gilcrease Institute, 1377.862), graphite on ruled wove, 8 by 10 1/4 inches.

Top right: No. 679. *From Hotel Window, Celaya* (Gilcrease Institute, 1346.778), graphite on wove, 10 by 14 1/4 inches.

Bottom: No. 1034. *Bridge at Warwick* (Gilcrease Institute, 1877.19.1), graphite on wove, 5 by 6 3/4 inches.

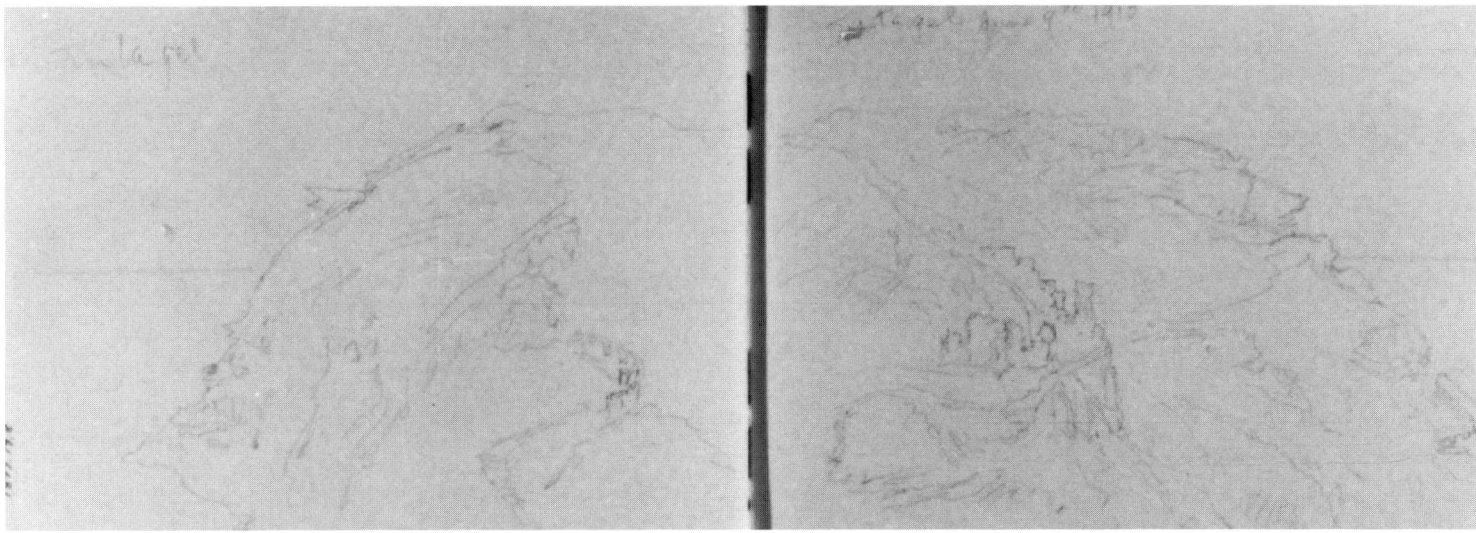

Top: No. 1045. *Tintagel* (Gilcrease Institute, 1877.19.9), graphite on wove, 5 by 13 1/2 inches.

tention. He jotted down a view of Dollwydellan Tower, the birthplace of Llewellyn the Great, in his small sketchbook (*Dollwydellan Tower,* No. 1006), which he later worked up into a more complex study (No. 1011). For the most part, however, he added little to the record of Wales he had produced in 1882.

The situation changed in 1910, when Moran traveled through parts of England and Scotland he had not seen before. Toward the end of May, he made his first sketch, *Bridge at Warwick* (No. 1034), in central Warwickshire. He confined his fieldwork that spring and summer almost exclusively to the pages of another little pocket sketchbook, recording impressions of cities along the coasts of Devon, Cornwall, and Somerset. The execution of these sketches corresponds to the quick gesture drawings he had been making since the turn of the century at such sites as the Grand Canyon. They are ordered chronologically and geographically, so Moran may have considered his sketchbook a sort of visual diary.

England offered a theme the American

West could not provide, the rocky sea coast, seen in *Anstey Cove* (No. 1036) and *Ilfracombe* (No. 1052). Of course, Moran frequently sketched the sea at home in East Hampton, but the less rugged shore of eastern America presented few such dramatic opportunities.[130] These sketches, and others such as *Tintagel* (No. 1045), differ from those of his earlier trips to Britain, when castles often commanded his attention. Instead, he focused almost entirely on nature, ignoring the many signs of habitation that must have been present in this much visited tourist haven. In a few sketches he included manmade structures, such as the walled walkway descending from the cliffside to the strand in *Clovelly* (No. 1050). Here, he chose to sketch a very close view, as he had done in other British and Mexican sketches, such as *Harlech* (No. 620) and *From Hotel Window, Celaya* (No. 679). The walkway is cut off, seeming to disappear into the foreground as if the viewer were standing at the curve.

Not all of Moran's sketches of that summer

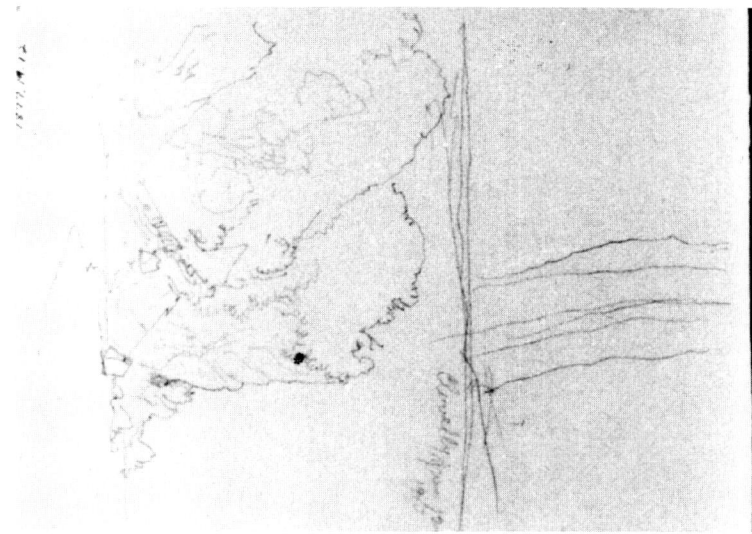

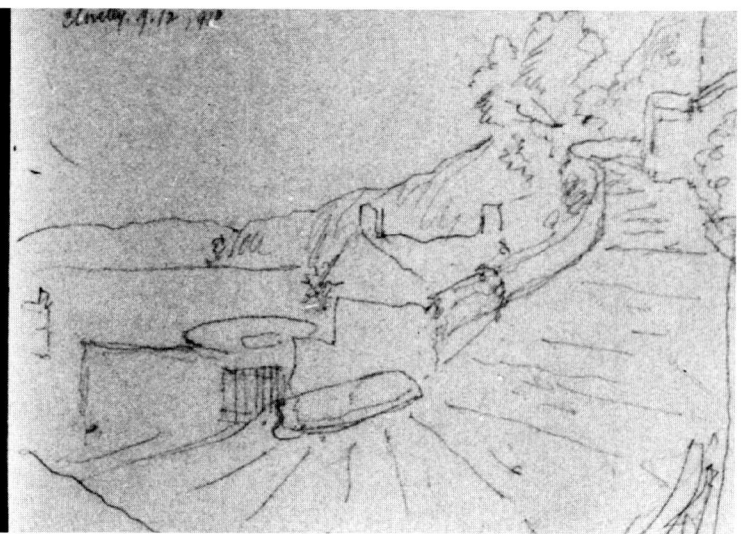

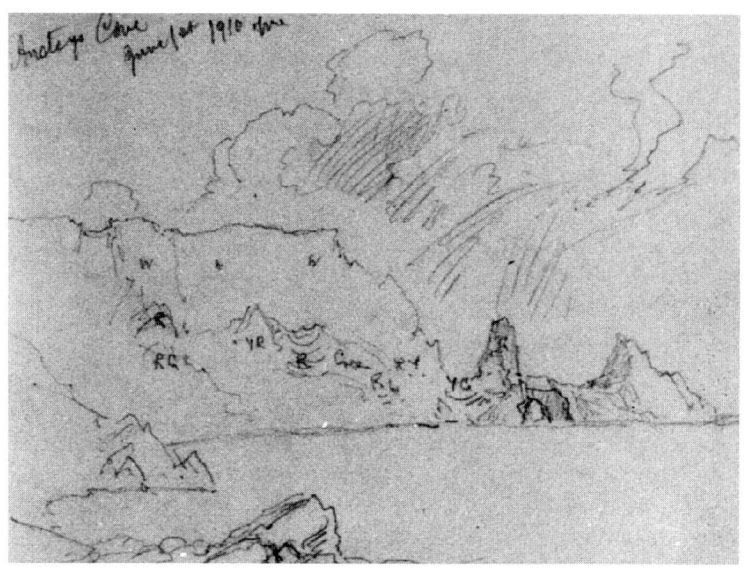

Top: No. 1050. *Clovelly* (Gilcrease Institute, 1877.19.13), graphite on wove, 5 by 6¾ inches.

Bottom: No. 1036. Anstey Cove (Gilcrease Institute, 1877.19.3), graphite on wove, 5 by 6¾ inches.

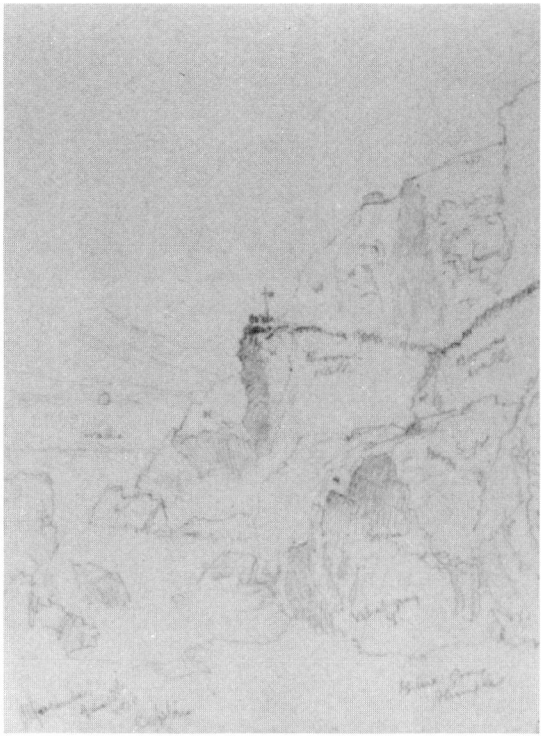

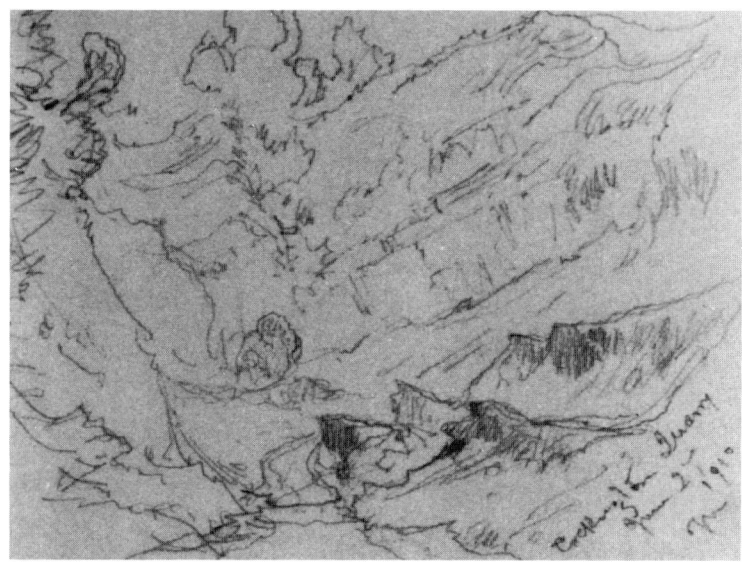

Left: No. 1052. *Ilfracombe* (Gilcrease Institute, 1877.19.15), graphite on wove, 6³/₄ by 5 inches.

Right: No. 1038. *Cockington Quarry* (Gilcrease Institute, 1877.19.5), graphite on wove, 5 by 6³/₄ inches.

describe the coastline. Scenes of the interior, such as *Cockington Quarry* (No. 1038), are peculiarly chaotic scribbles that leave the viewer disoriented. When compared with *Cockington Quarry,* a sketch like *Ilfracombe* (No. 1052) seems almost precise. Moran was taken with Cockington and painted *Cockington Lane* (1910) after his return to New York.[131]

Sketches of Scotland—made at Trossachs, Bass Rock, and Lake Katrine—filled out the sketchbook and marked the end of his trip. Moran never again traveled outside the United States, and he limited his American travel to repeat visits to the Southwest. His journeys over the Santa Fe Railroad often included the pueblos of New Mexico, although his ultimate destination was frequently the Grand Canyon. While his paintings of the Grand Canyon from this period are elaborate and repetitive, his sketches are limited to a few minimal but elegant and impressionistic notations of a well-loved site (Nos. 1021–1023).

A small series of quickly executed sketches made at Laguna Pueblo, possibly in 1907 or 1908,[132] formed the basis for paintings such as *Indian Pueblo, Laguna, New Mexico* (1908, Anschutz Collection, Denver). Although Moran drew *Rain Pool in Rocks, Laguna* (No. 1027) so hastily that it resembles a collection of child's blocks more than an Indian village, he added tiny vertical lines to the elliptical form in the left foreground to detail reflections in a pool of water.

Moran never again produced large bodies of sketches during his trips, but he usually recorded his current perceptions of the Grand Canyon. Sketches such as *Grand Canyon* (No. 1012) proclaim his persistent love of topography. By contrast, *Grand Canyon* (No. 1015) is a hastily dashed-off gesture drawing that is impressionistic in its immediacy.

Moran's last known sketches of the canyon were made at the scenic overlook at Desert View in May 1920, when he was eight-three. They are also the last sketches of any complexity that the aged artist composed. *Desert View* (No. 1073) is

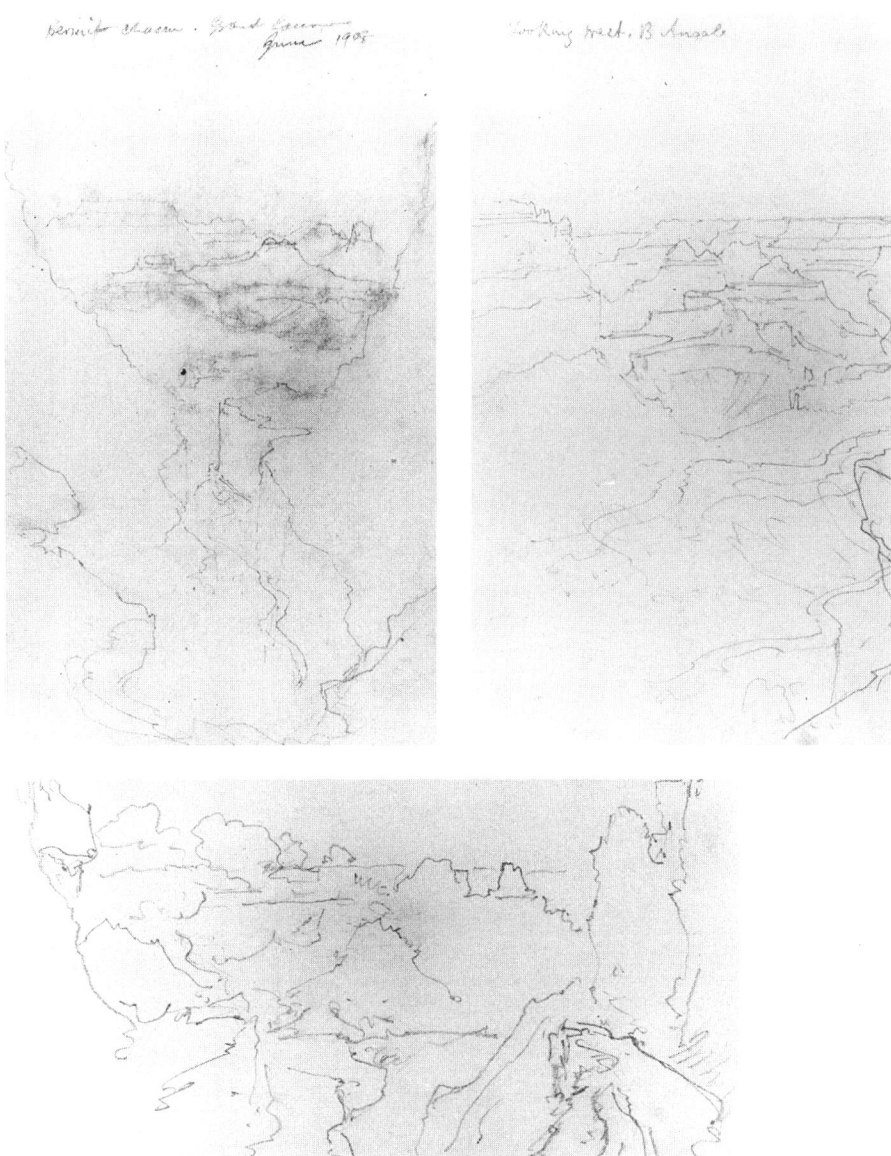

Top left: No. 1021. *Hermit Chasm, Grand Canyon* (Gilcrease Institute, 1337.864), graphite on wove, 8 1/8 by 4 7/8 inches.

Top right: No. 1022. *Looking West, Bright Angel* (Gilcrease Institute, 1337.861), graphite on wove, 8 1/8 by 4 7/8 inches.

Bottom left: No. 1023. *Grand Canyon* (Gilcrease Institute, 1337.623), graphite on wove, 4 7/8 by 8 1/8 inches.

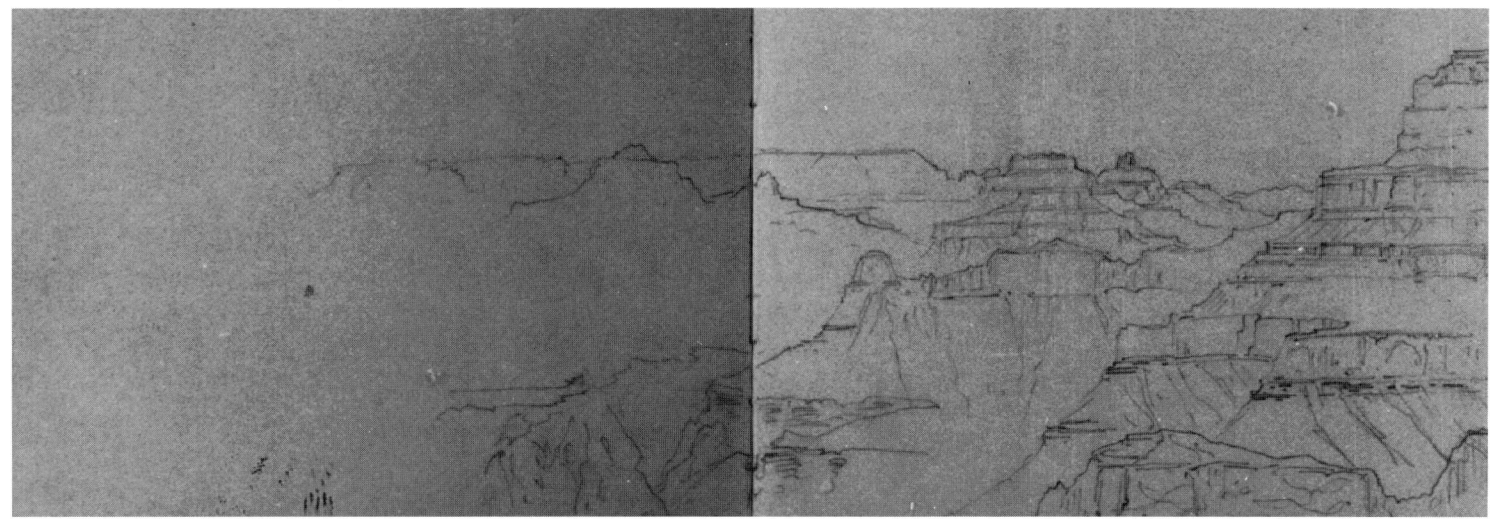

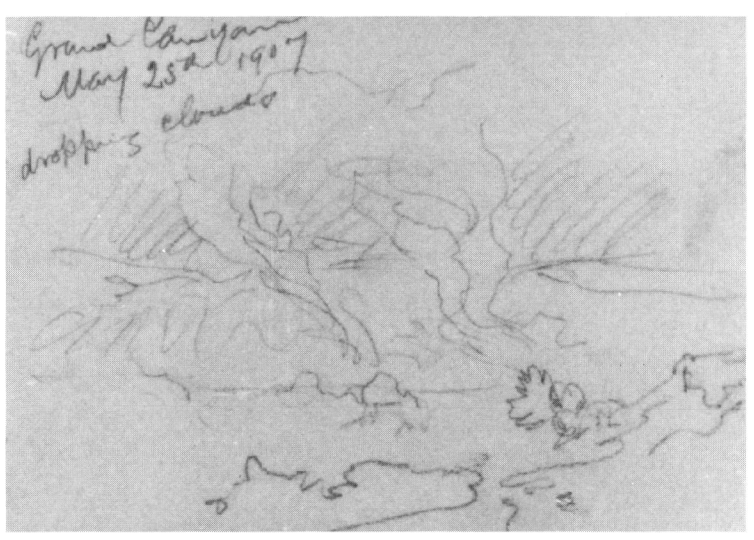

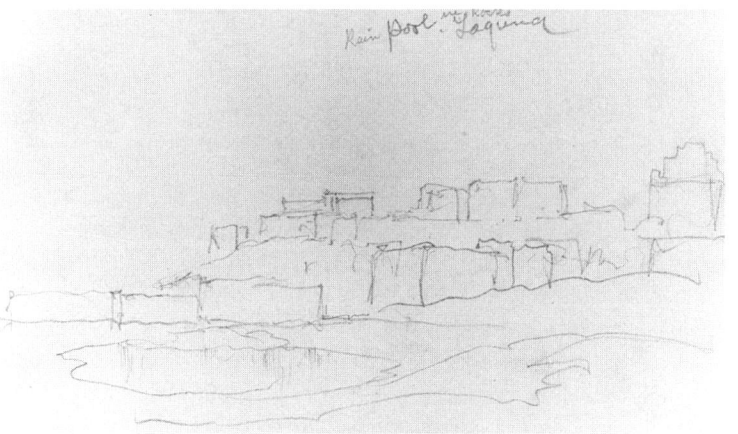

Top: No. 1012. *Grand Canyon* (Gilcrease Institute, 1837.20.16), graphite on wove, 5 by 14 inches.

Left: No. 1015. *Grand Canyon* (Gilcrease Institute, 1837.20.19), graphite on wove, 5 by 7 inches.

Right: No. 1027. *Rain Pool in Rocks, Laguna* (Gilcrease Institute, 1337.866), graphite on wove, 4⁷/₈ by 8¹/₈ inches.

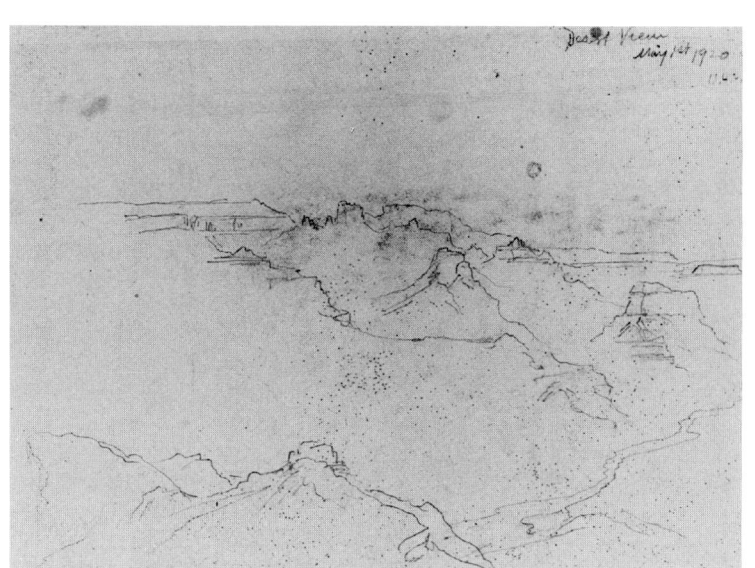

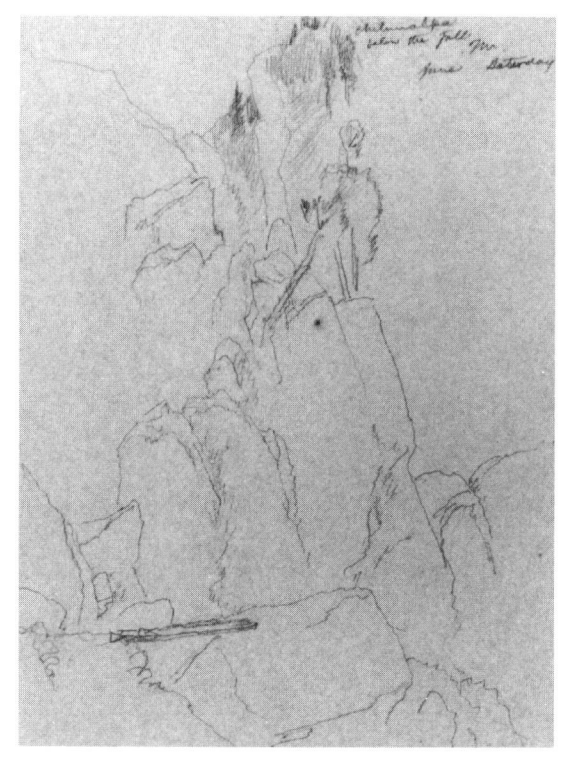

Left: No. 1073. *Desert View* (Gilcrease Institute, 1337.873), graphite on wove, 8¼ by 10⅞ inches.

Right: No. 1075. *Chilnualna, below the Fall* (Gilcrease Institute, 1337. 649), graphite on green wove, 18 by 9½ inches.

Bottom: No. 1076. *Chilnualna Fall* (Gilcrease Institute, 1337.539), graphite on green wove, 17 by 9⅜ inches.

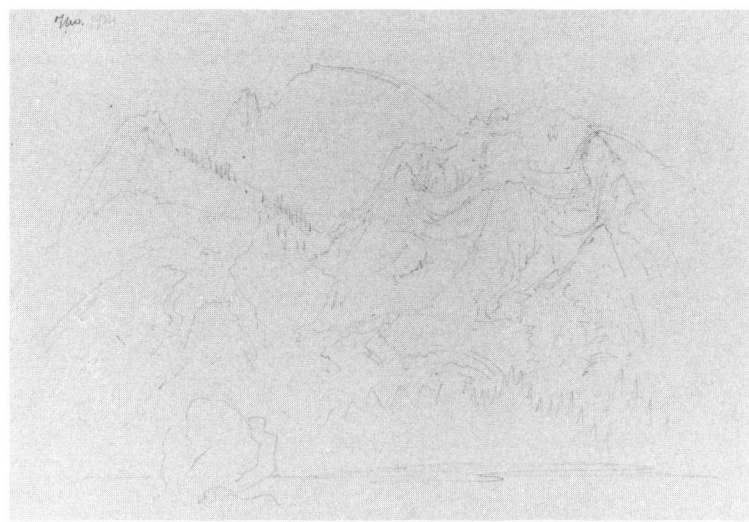 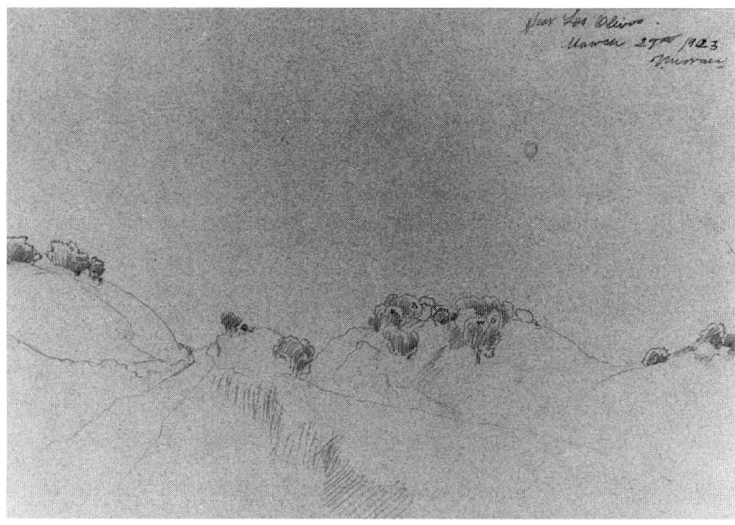

Left: No. 1077. *Yosemite* (Gilcrease Institute, 1337.859), graphite on blue wove, 10¾ by 15 inches.

Right: No. 1078. *Near Los Olivos* (Gilcrease Institute, 1337.874), graphite on wove, 10¾ by 15 inches.

panoramic, encompassing both rims and the Colorado River below.

In 1916, Moran moved from his longtime home in East Hampton to Santa Barbara, California, to take advantage of the climate. He moved his studio as well and continued to paint. His final sketches in the field were of California sites. One last trip to Yosemite in 1922, made in comfort by automobile, yielded three known sketches. Two are unusually long vertical renderings of Chilnualna Fall (Nos. 1075 and 1076). The third features a briskly drawn Half Dome (No. 1077). Moran ended an enviable sixty-seven-year career of sketching outdoors on March 29, 1923, with three drawings of Los Olivos, California (Nos. 1078–80), located just outside Santa Barbara. Although he painted for at least another year, he never again ventured out of the studio in search of inspiration.

Moran valued and used his fieldworks throughout his life, taking them with him in 1916 when he moved to California. His sketches prove

that he was endlessly innovative in his responses to new stimuli. He adapted his methods according to such criteria as time constraints and ease of execution in the field as well as the desires of patrons, especially in his work in the American West. Many of his fresh, elemental sketches that served him as visual memoranda appeal to a contemporary interest in immediacy. Others, such as those composed in Europe in the company of the specters of past masters, show his ability to blend other artists' influences with his own vision into sketches of, for example, the Roman Campagna.

Even as Moran matured and made recurring visits to accustomed places—the Grand Canyon, East Hampton—the resulting sketches do not suffer from overfamiliarity. Each visit, each sketch offered new possibilities for interpretation. Moran remarked, "I have hundreds of sketches of the Rockies and the Sierra Nevadas, for I have been making them for years, but I want still more."[133] As familiarity increased, he was less burdened by the recording of fact and

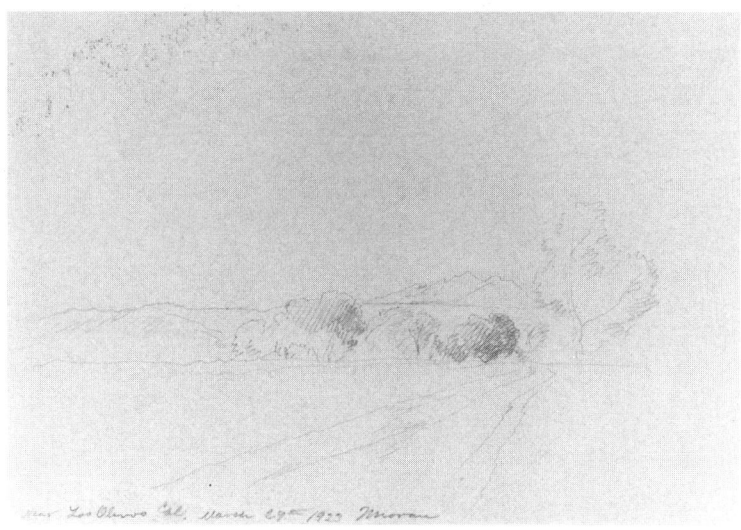

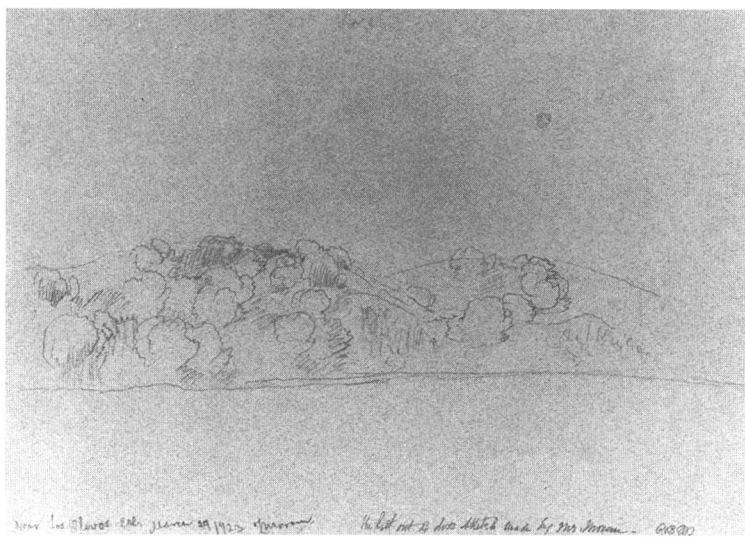

was free to redefine the environs. In his youth, sketching outdoors had been almost an obsession. Sketches made in his final years indicate that it continued to be a pleasant habit. The late sketches retain a certain vigor in their brevity and provide no suggestion that his powers were diminishing. Examination of the full spectrum of Moran's sketches reveals a familiar, uninhibited side of this diverse artist, whose paintings may be considered an embodiment of the nineteenth-century Romantic tradition.

Left: No. 1079. *Near Los Olivos, California* (Gilcrease Institute, 1337. 875), graphite on blue wove, 10³/₄ by 15 inches.

Right: No. 1080. *Near Los Olivos, California* (Gilcrease Institute, 1337. 876), graphite on blue wove, 10³/₄ by 15 inches.

NOTES

1. Moran made at least two thousand paintings during his career, and probably more. Moran's ledgers are helpful in establishing his output, but far more paintings exist than are accounted for in his records.

2. The title of this essay has been taken from a letter Moran wrote to his wife from the Yellowstone, July 26, 1892: "I am very well satisfied with the artistic side of the trip so far and I think the financial part will pan out all right when I get some work out" (Bassford and Fryxell, eds., *Home Thoughts from Afar*, p. 121).

3. *The Crayon* 1 (1855): 34–35, 97–98. *The Crayon* was founded in 1855 by William James Still-man and John Durand (son of Asher B. Durand), who were both enamored of the ideas of the English art critic, John Ruskin (1819–1900). Ruskin was an accomplished amateur draftsman and watercolorist as well as an articulate proponent of "truth to nature" who sought to do away with reliance on conventional visual formulae in painting. Articles in *The Crayon* often echoed Ruskin's emphasis on fidelity to natural appearances in drawing and painting.

4. Review of *The Elements of Drawing, The Crayon* 4 (1857): 288. For a discussion of the impact of *The Elements of Drawing,* see pp. 86–92 of Kathleen A. Foster's essay "The Pre-Raphaelite Medium: Ruskin,

Turner, and American Watercolor," in Ferber and Gerdts, eds., *The New Path,* pp. 79–102.

5. The exhibition opened in New York at the National Academy of Design on November 20, 1857, and closed in early December. It ran in Philadelphia at the Pennsylvania Academy of the Fine Arts February 3–March 20, 1858, and in Boston at the Boston Atheneum April 5–June 19, 1858. For a discussion of the evolution and promotion of the exhibition, see Susan P. Casteras, "The 1857–58 Exhibition of English Art in America," in Ferber and Gerdts, eds., *The New Path,* pp. 109–33.

6. *The Crayon* 4 (November 1857): 343.

7. Thomas Moran, "Knowledge a Prime Requisite in Art," p. 15.

8. A passage in one of the biographical manuscripts in the Gilcrease Institute Archives (4027.3925–72) indicates that Moran traded his watercolors for these books.

9. Wilkins, *Thomas Moran: Artist of the Mountains,* pp. 22–24, discusses Hamilton's impact on the Moran brothers.

10. *A View of Fairmount Waterworks, Philadelphia* (oil on canvas, illustrated in Christie's catalogue, May 25, 1989, lot no. 45) indicates that Moran also found this aspect of the park suitable for painting.

11. *Report on the Geology of the Lake Superior District,* Part 2, Senate Executive Document No. 4, Special Session, March 1851, p. 124. See also Sweeney, *Artists of Michigan,* p. 34. Although George Catlin (1796–1872) passed through this area before Moran, Catlin's work related to the Indians instead of the landscape.

12. Moran created at least two major paintings, *The Pictured Rocks from Miners River* and *The Grand Portal of the Pictured Rocks,* based on scenery that impressed him during this trip. He exhibited both at the Pennsylvania Academy of the Fine Arts in 1861; their present whereabouts are unknown.

13. "The Pictured Rocks of Lake Superior," *The Aldine* 5–6 (January 1873): 14–15.

14. A set of black-and-white ink wash studio drawings illustrating the poem is in the Gilcrease collection.

15. Bassford and Fryxell, eds., *Home Thoughts from Afar,* p. 23. Moran rarely verbalized his thoughts and reactions. When he did so, it was most often in letters to his wife.

16. The *Monthly Illustrator Magazine* reported in January 1893 that "John Moran was the first and for many years the only artistic landscape photographer in America" (p. 81). I thank Mary Panzer for calling this information to my attention.

17. An oil of the Wissahickon has not been located. However, John Moran's photograph of Thomas's charcoal version is preserved in the Gilcrease Institute Archives (4316.7845).

18. John Moran's photographs of Pennsylvania river scenes are included in the collections of the Library Company, Philadelphia, and George Eastman House, Rochester.

19. According to the *Record of Exhibition Catalogues* for the Pennsylvania Academy of the Fine Arts, Moran exhibited five paintings depicting landscapes viewed during this trip in 1862.

20. The Gilcrease Thomas Moran collection includes an etching of Communipaw, a photograph by John Moran of Thomas's charcoal drawing on canvas of sawmills on the Wissahickon, and a series of sketches of mills at Feltville, New Jersey. Guild Hall in East Hampton, New York, owns a watercolor of Communipaw.

21. Moran's handwritten autobiographical notes— couched in the third person—in the Gilcrease Institute Archives (4017.4012).

22. The Gilcrease collection includes sketches Moran made after some of these painters.

23. Wilkins (*Thomas Moran: Artist of the Mountains,* p. 43), relying on the misinformation provided in some of Ruth Bedford Moran's jotted notes, reports that Moran returned to Philadelphia at that time to marry Mary Nimmo. The date of the marriage was February 9, 1863, verified by the records of marriages in the archives of the Assumption B.V.M. Church in Philadelphia. I wish to thank Nancy Apgar and John F. Murphy, Jr., for locating this information, and Father Francis McDermott for allowing Apgar access to his records.

24. Illustrations based on the 1864 trip appeared in "The River Scenery of Pennsylvania" (*The Aldine* 9 [May 1878]: 156–61), but it is unlikely that the commission for such images originated fourteen years before publication.

25. Modelski, *Railroad Maps of North America,* p. 57, illustrates G. Woolworth Colton's *Series of Rail-*

road Maps, No. 3: New York, New Jersey, Pennsylvania, Delaware, Maryland and Canada (1860).

26. John Moran's photographs, such as *Sand Ridge at Mapleton, Foot of Jack's Mountain* and *Old Bed of the Conemaugh River* (Library Company, Philadelphia), support the idea that he accompanied his brother. Of course, John could have taken these photographs at other times. But in light of the documented trip they made together to Catawissa, it is tempting to suppose that they traveled together again in 1864.

27. Autobiographical manuscript, Gilcrease Institute Archives (4026.3920.1–6).

28. An article in the *Brooklyn Daily Eagle,* August 18, 1889, recounts Moran's visit with Corot in Paris.

29. Edith Singleton, unpublished biography of Thomas Moran, East Hampton Library, New York. These pages were read, corrected, and approved by Thomas Moran.

30. The Morans must have left Paris by May 1867, as their second child, Mary Tassin, was born in Philadelphia in July.

31. Four of the sketches are dated 1867, and one is marked 1866. However, the date on the odd one was added later.

32. *Claude Lorrain: Dessins du British Museum,* p. 38, No. 23 (*Vue de Civitavecchia,* 1638, from the *Livre de la Campagna*). The Louvre also has four of Claude's sketches of Civitavecchia, which Moran may have seen.

33. At this time Cole's painting was in private hands. It had been shown at the National Academy of Design during the 1843–44 season, on loan from a Miss Hicks, but Moran, still a child, could not have seen it then. According to Parry (*The Art of Thomas Cole,* p. 294), it was reproduced in Cole's "Sicilian Scenery and Antiquities" (part 1) (*The Knickerbocker* 23 [February 1844]: 113).

34. Twice in the same interview, Moran lauds Church: "Perhaps Church was the greatest landscape-painter we have ever produced. . . . I have already named the three leading artists, in my humble opinion, this country has produced, and the greatest, perhaps, of these men was F. E. Church" ("Knowledge a Prime Requisite in Art," p. 15).

35. Troyen, "Innocents Abroad," p. 4.

36. The term *painter-lithography* refers to lithography used to create original prints rather than to make commercial reproductions. For information concerning Moran's work in lithography, see Morand and Friese, *Prints of Thomas Moran,* pp. 16–17, 42–43, 62–73.

37. Crane, "Fairmount Park"; and Headley, "Philadelphia."

38. *Studies of Clouds, Nos. 1–7,* by John Constable after Alexander Cozens, Courtauld Institute Galleries, London (illustrated in Sloan, *Alexander and John Robert Cozens,* p. 86). Although there is no manuscript evidence that Moran studied either these sketches or Cozens's originals, the similarity is striking.

39. This trip is chronicled in several sources. Wilkins, *Thomas Moran: Artist of the Mountains,* pp. 57–71, furnishes an excellent overview. Kinsey, "Creating a Sense of Place," pp. 96–261, provides an extensive examination of the motivation, itinerary, and results of Moran's Yellowstone experience, as well as an investigation of his relationship with principal figures.

40. Moran related his brisk activity in at least two letters to F. V. Hayden. On March 11, 1872, he wrote, "I have been intending to write to you for some months past but I have been so *very* busy with Yellowstone drawings, & so absorbed in designing & painting my picture of the *Great Cañon* that I could not find the time to write to anybody." On November 24, 1872, he noted that "I am overrun with work on the Yellowstone & the interest in them seems to increase." Both letters are in National Archives, Records of the Territorial Surveys, Record Group 57 (Hayden Survey: Letters Received).

41. Wilkins (*Thomas Moran: Artist of the Mountains,* p. 27) notes that in 1857, perhaps after scrutinizing Hamilton's western illustrations, Moran painted "an imagined 'western' scene."

42. This may have been Moran's initial view of any of Bierstadt's western paintings. Apparently, none was exhibited in Philadelphia until December 1866, months after Moran had left for Europe. Anderson and Ferber (*Albert Bierstadt: Art and Enterprise,* chronology, p. 183) indicate that *The Yosemite Valley (Looking Down Yosemite Valley, California)* (1865, Birmingham Museum of Art) was exhibited there on December 19, 1866. Moran would have been aware of

Bierstadt's western travels and flourishing reputation. Notice of Bierstadt's initial journey with Colonel Lander appeared in various popular media as well as in *The Crayon* ([May 1859]: 161–62). Reviews and notices of Bierstadt's western paintings began to appear in *The Crayon* in February 1860.

43. Russell's photograph *Temporary and Permanent Bridges and Citadel Rock, Green River (Wyoming)* (1867–68, Yale University, New Haven) shows the signs of commerce set against the rock formations. Jackson's photograph *Green River Butte* (Denver Public Library, Western History Collection) also illustrates the railroad's presence. Anderson ("'The Kiss of Enterprise'") elaborates on the commercial growth of Green River and on Jackson's and Russell's attraction to the area's technological achievements. As Anderson points out, comparison of the photographs to Moran's field sketches of Green River indicates a conscious decision on Moran's part to delete the signs of industry and feature instead the sublime beauty of the geological formations (pp. 245–48). This erasure echoes that which Moran contrived in his 1864 fieldwork along the route of the Pennsylvania Railroad.

44. The Union Pacific Railroad began at Omaha and ended at Ogden, Utah, where the Central Pacific commenced. Corinne was the first stop beyond Ogden.

45. No attempt is made in this study to establish a definitive route for Moran's movements during the summer. The movements of the party in general are recorded in Hayden, *Preliminary Report,* but it is widely believed that Moran and other members deviated occasionally from this route.

46. Moran's own collection of Jackson's photographs is in the Gilcrease Institute Archives. On many, Moran made identifying notes, and they attest to the value he placed on photography as an aid to the artist. Jackson was the first photographer to explore Yellowstone, but amateur artists Walter Trumbull and Charles Moore preceded Moran, in the company of the Washburn-Doane expedition in 1869.

47. Also Moran may have been made aware of Corot's interest in landscape photography during his visit with the French artist in 1867. Corot, like some other Barbizon painters, used photographs in connection with sketches as preparatory works. For a discussion, see Scharf, "Camille Corot and Landscape Photography."

48. Hayden, "The Wonders of the West—II: More about the Yellowstone"; and Hayden, *Preliminary Report.*

49. The Blackmore series is in the Gilcrease Institute collection; see Plates 9 and 13.

50. It has been thought that the main impetus for this trip was a commission from the Appleton Company to provide illustrations for the chapter in *Picturesque America* titled "The Plains and the Sierras." This may well be true, but no specific documentation (letters, contracts, notations in Moran's business papers) supports it, and no fieldwork from 1872 corresponds to the images Moran provided the publication for sites along the Union and Central Pacific Railroads. Kinsey ("Creating a Sense of Place," p. 359) states that for this commission, Moran worked from shots taken by various government survey photographers. Moran's trip in late summer of 1872 was probably too hurried for him to have done more than familiarize himself with the areas proposed for illustration, even if O. E. Bunce, the de facto editor of *Picturesque America,* knew by then which images he wished to use in the volume that appeared in 1874. A letter from Bunce to Hayden dated January 31, 1873 (quoted in Kinsey, "Creating a Sense of Place," p. 359), states that "Mr. Moran is now making drawings of scenes along the Union and Pacific roads." Moran illustrated two other chapters in the 1874 volume: "The Rocky Mountains" and "The Cañons of the Colorado." The images for these chapters also do not correspond with extant fieldwork. Bunce's letter to Hayden continues, "Shall then want scenes in Colorado and Nevada, etc; I am extremely grateful to you for your offer to give him the use of your photographs." I believe the reason for the trip may have been as simple as a desire to visit Yosemite after having illustrated it unseen for *Scribner's,* probably in hopes of obtaining additional work and commissions. For Appleton, Moran followed his previously established practice of providing illustrations for publications of sites he had not visited, this time relying on the work of photographers, such as Andrew J. Russell (1830–1902) who worked for the Union Pacific Railroad between 1868 and 1870 and documented the same sites. Moran then used the illustrations again, providing them to Henry T. Williams for *The Pacific Tourist,* first published in 1876 (Moran's notebook in the Gil-

crease archives, 3624.145, 40–4, *Receipts for Draw-ings* to March 13, 1876).

51. Quoted in Pomeroy, *In Search of the Golden West,* p. xlvi.

52. Watkins made the first of many treks into Yosemite in 1861. Moran must have been aware of his work even earlier than the *Scribner's* commission. In 1866 Watkins's work was featured in the *Philadelphia Photographer* (a periodical with which John Moran was involved) in E. L. Wilson's "Views in the Yosemite Valley." The next year Charles R. Savage was quoted in the same periodical, commending Watkins's work. Yosemite enticed several photographers very early. Besides Watkins, Charles C. Weed was there in 1859 and Eadweard Muybridge in 1867 and 1872. Other artists, such as Thomas A. Ayres as early as 1855, had preceded Moran as well.

53. Bromley, "Wonders of the West: The Big Trees and Yosemite."

54. Mary Moran made at least one watercolor of the spectacular three-tiered Yosemite Falls (National Park Service collection at Yosemite National Park).

55. Seymour, "Trout-Fishing in the Rangeley Lakes." Two of the four extant sketches are dated 1876, but the date was added later. It is possible that Moran made a second trip to Rangeley in 1876, but no documentation has been found to support this.

56. Hillers was returning to the Grand Canyon, again in Powell's employ, but his early visit in 1871 had not been as the expedition photographer, a job held by O. E. Beaman. Hillers had spent considerable time assisting Beaman (and later James Fennemore who replaced Beaman as the survey photographer) and learning all he could about wilderness photography, so that by 1872 Powell retained him as his survey photographer.

Timothy O'Sullivan, who traveled with Lieutenant George M. Wheeler's survey in 1871, is considered the first photographer to have worked in the Grand Canyon. William A. Bell replaced O'Sullivan as Wheeler's photographer during his second Grand Canyon survey in 1872.

57. This photograph (illustrated in Fowler, *Western Photographs of John K. Hillers,* pp. 38–39) may have been cropped for the book. If not, Moran's sketches record a broader panorama than the photograph.

58. Bassford and Fryxell, eds., *Home Thoughts from Afar,* p. 40.

59. Nos. 275–80 and 284–85 in the checklist.

60. As previously stated, Moran's illustrations of the canyon lands for *Picturesque America* were derived from others' photographs.

61. Bassford and Fryxell, eds., *Home Thoughts from Afar,* pp. 41–42.

62. Holmes accompanied Powell's expeditions between 1872 and 1877, beginning as a topographer on his trip to the Grand Canyon in 1872. Although Holmes and Moran later became good friends—Moran gave Holmes a large group of western sketches now in the National Museum of American Art—it is not known whether Moran could have seen Holmes's sketches of the canyon from 1872. In 1880 Holmes accompanied Clarence Dutton on his expedition to the Grand Canyon, again sketching in preparation for nine double-sheet lithographs that illustrated Dutton's *Tertiary History,* for which Moran also made illustrations. Moran's work appeared in the form of nine wood engravings and one lithograph; the lithograph duplicated a Holmes sketch, *The Transept.* Earlier, in 1871, Frederick Dellenbaugh had accompanied Powell to the Grand Canyon as artist and topographer.

63. *The Chasm of the Colorado,* like *Grand Canyon of the Yellowstone,* was purchased by the Department of the Interior just after it was painted.

64. The Gilcrease Institute collection includes one; that of the Cooper-Hewitt, three; and the National Parks collection, ten.

65. Bassford and Fryxell, eds. *Home Thoughts from Afar,* p. 47.

66. Ibid., p. 49.

67. Ibid., p. 53.

68. Ibid., p. 55.

69. Gustave Buek, a colleague of Moran's in East Hampton, remarked that the "scenery of Florida did not especially appeal to him" (typescript of Buek's notes, Gilcrease Institute Archives, 5117.235), commenting perhaps on the few paintings Moran made of Florida subjects. Another explanation may be that Moran became disenchanted following the critical rejection of two Florida paintings, *Ponce de Leon in Florida, 1513* (1877, National Cowboy Hall of Fame and Western Heritage Center, Oklahoma City)

and *Bringing Home the Cattle, Coast of Florida* (1879, Albright-Knox Art Gallery, Buffalo). The reception of both works is discussed in Wilkins, *Thomas Moran: Artist of the Mountains,* pp. 110–12 and 117–18.

70. Dodge, "Island of the Sea," p. 652.

71. Ibid., pp. 658–59.

72. Ibid., p. 655.

73. The Gilcrease Institute Archives (4027.3939) include brief statements about the summer residence and (4027.3970.3) his trip to Feltville.

74. A passage in O. B. Bunce's chapter in the first volume of *Picturesque America,* "Scenes along the Brandywine," sheds light on America's fascination with mills: "Was there ever an artist who could resist the desire to add a new sketch of a subject of this kind [old mills nesting quaintly among summer foliage] to his portfolio?" (p. 222).

75. Illustrated in Morand and Friese, *Prints of Thomas Moran,* p. 66.

76. Wilkins (*Thomas Moran: Artist of the Mountains,* p. 121) says the painting *The Watering Place* was inspired by the scenery of Feltville and nearby Scotch Plains. Moran illustrated an article of the same name in *The Aldine* (9 [1879]: 242).

77. The journey to the Tetons was recorded in a small diary now at Grand Teton National Park. It is published in its entirety in Fryxell, "Thomas Moran's Journey to the Tetons in 1879."

78. Nos. 419–22 in the checklist.

79. I wish to thank Mark Nelson, curator of the Sweetwater County Historical Museum, Green River, Wyoming, who verified that the sketches of Green River were made in Wyoming and not Utah.

80. There are three of Communipaw, two of Venice, and one of Florida.

81. Illustrated in Morand and Friese, *Prints of Thomas Moran,* p. 203.

82. *Under the American Fall from Goat Island* probably anticipated Moran's painting *Cave of the Winds, Niagara* (c. 1881, illustrated in Adamson, *Niagara: Two Centuries of Changing Attitudes,* p. 149).

83. This painting is illustrated in Hults, "Thomas Moran's *Shoshone Falls,*" p. 93, along with the similar etching also produced in 1885.

84. This illustration appeared in Pangborn, *Picturesque B & O,* p. 123.

85. Illustrated in Morand and Friese, *Prints of Thomas Moran,* p. 207.

86. Ibid., p. 209.

87. Pangborn, *Picturesque B & O,* p. 130.

88. *Harper's Monthly Magazine* 64 (April 1882): 689–704.

89. That this was not due to a later mishandling of the unprotected surface of this drawing is proven by an unsmudged sketch, *Lake, Wasatch Mts* (No. 584), executed on the same paper and stored in the same manner. The sketches are technically identical, except for the smudging.

90. Moran had moved his studio to Manhattan in 1880 and established a residence in the city in 1881 before leaving for the West.

91. Norma Ewing, who assisted greatly with the research for this study, offers evidence that Moran may have been in England as early as November 1881 (personal communication): "In the East Hampton Library Archives, a note states, 'In 1881–2 Moran again went to Europe and on this trip gave a successful exhibition of his pictures.' On November 21, 1881, a letter was written to Moran at a London address, 45 Margaret Street, Cavendish Square, from P. G. Hamerton of Autun, France (Gilcrease Institute Archives, 3876. 797). It is well established that while the Morans were in England in 1882, they stayed at the above address. These two references suggest the Morans may have sailed to England long before May 1882, which is generally cited as their date of departure. Perhaps they wished to attend the annual meeting of the London Society of Painter Etchers, held in January of each year. If the Morans were not already in London by the time Hamerton sent the letter, or very soon afterwards, it seems unlikely that Hamerton would have known where to send a letter to reach them seven months in the future in London. Also, if the Morans had not already gone to London and were still in the United States, it would be illogical that Hamerton would send the letter elsewhere. To add to the possibility of the earlier departure, the last commercial account in Moran's ledgers for 1881 was posted November 14, and the first one posted for 1882 was November."

92. British subjects are second in number only to Long Island scenes in Moran's etching oeuvre. For further information concerning Mary Moran's career

as an artist, see Nancy Friese, *Prints of Nature: Poetic Etchings of Mary Nimmo Moran* (Tulsa: University of Tulsa, 1984).

93. Etching illustrated in Morand and Friese, *Prints of Thomas Moran,* p. 112.

94. Ibid., p. 142.

95. Ibid., p. 114.

96. Moran had sketched after Varley during his first visit to England and certainly must have seen his oils as well.

97. Illustrated in Morand and Friese, *Prints of Thomas Moran,* p. 88.

98. Ibid., p. 118.

99. There is speculation that William Henry Jackson may have accompanied Moran. Jackson did visit Mexico; various references (particularly Hales, *William Henry Jackson and the Transformation of the American Landscape,* pp. 173–75, 319–20) record several trips the photographer made to Mexico, the first in 1883 at the request of the Mexican National Railroad. Moran, however, makes no mention of Jackson in his letters.

100. There are so many Mexican sketches that Moran listed ninety-three of them under a separate rubric in his 1916 ledger of sketches. Two other separate categories were "Western" and "Miscellaneous."

101. Initial plans for the Denver & Rio Grande included a southern terminus at Mexico City, which was never realized. See Kinsey, "Creating a Sense of Place," pp. 420–23, for information about the development of the business and market of the D & RG.

102. Palmer and Bell had become acquainted in 1867 when they both accompanied the Kansas Pacific Railroad Survey, Palmer as the general in charge of the army escort, and Bell as an amateur photographer.

103. Wilkins (*Thomas Moran: Artist of the Mountains,* p. 166) also mentions such possible motivations for the journey as a *Harper's Monthly Magazine* commission for a Mexican subject and Mary Hallock Foote's three articles published in *Century* between 1881 and 1882 about her trip between Mexico City and Morelia (Foote was an amateur artist and friend of Moran). Moran visited some of the same towns during his tour, due to shared interests. Foote's husband was involved in business relating to the silver mines near Morelia, and her trip grew out of his need to visit the region.

104. Published in Mexico by Gallo & Co. Editors, 1876.

105. Moran viewed, but probably did not visit, the Bahamas during his voyage. On January 29, 1883, he sketched *Bahama Island Light* (illustrated in Christie's catalogue, September 27, 1990, lot no. 89) and *Off the Bahamas* (illustrated in Sotheby's catalogue, December 18, 1991, lot no. 42a).

106. Bassford and Fryxell, eds., *Home Thoughts from Afar,* p. 61.

107. By 1837 plans existed for a national network of Mexican rail lines that would connect the Pacific with the Gulf of Mexico and the Atlantic trade routes, as well as provide links to cities in the United States. Over the next twenty years, however, only three miles of track were built between Vera Cruz and Mexico City. Diverse financial problems necessitated the introduction of foreign, mostly English, investors. Work began in earnest in 1876 when English capitalists acquired the concession for the Mexican National Railroad. By 1880 more than 400 miles of track had been laid; a main line, fed by numerous short feeder lines, connected Vera Cruz and Mexico City. After Palmer became involved in 1880, a 700-mile route between Saltillo and Laredo was completed. The central part linking the two sections was completed in 1884. See Cumberland, *Mexico: The Struggle for Modernity,* pp. 162, 211–13.

108. Bassford and Fryxell, eds., *Home Thoughts from Afar,* p. 62.

109. Ibid., p. 64.

110. Ibid., pp. 64–65.

111. Ibid., p. 65.

112. Ibid.

113. Ibid., p. 66.

114. This sketch bears an ink colophon that appears on many of Moran's studio works. However, No. 658 is most likely a field sketch. It bears penciled notations of site and date; Moran usually did not mar the face of finished works with such notes. He also listed it in his ledger of sketches, which does not include finished works. Moran frequently added signatures to fieldworks, particularly sketches lent for exhibitions or other purposes.

115. These sketches are reminiscent of one by John Russell Bartlett: *Ascent to the Quicksilver Mines, New Almaden, California* (c. 1851, The John

Carter Brown Library, Providence). Bartlett was commissioner of the United States/Mexico Boundary Survey between 1849 and 1853. He made a series of sketches, including this one, during a visit to the mines in 1851. It was illustrated in his *Personal Narrative of Explorations and Incidents* ([New York: D. Appleton, 1854], vol. 2, p. 62). Also, Mary Hallock Foote discussed this mine in her article "A California Mining Camp," *Scribner's Monthly* 15 (February 1878): 480–93.

116. Exactly how many sketches Moran made on this trip is unknown. The sketches he produced during his visits of 1886 and 1890 are quite similar in style, and only a few are securely dated. More than sixty Venetian sketches have been located.

117. Bassford and Fryxell, eds., *Home Thoughts from Afar,* p. 77.

118. Illustrated in Morand and Friese, *Prints of Thomas Moran,* p. 158.

119. One difference, of course, is that Church sought out his icebergs, while Moran happened on his. Church's painting disappeared after 1863, so it is unknown when Moran might have seen it. *Icebergs* was a highly publicized work, which Church premiered in New York during the spring of 1861, before Moran left for England. Perhaps later Moran saw the chromolithograph produced in England during the exhibition of the painting in 1863. James Hamilton's work of icebergs, done from Elisha Kent Kane's illustrations from Henry Grinnell's expedition, for Kane's *Arctic Explorations in the Years 1853, '54, '55* (Philadelphia, 1856), provided an even earlier model.

120. Carr (*The Icebergs,* p. 103) sees the title of Moran's painting *Spectres of the North* as a "belated but deliberate homage to Church's masterpiece." When Church's painting was first presented in 1861, it was often referred to as *The North,* a pointed reference to Church's pro-Union sympathies.

121. Although Moran destroyed the painting, a photograph of it exists (Gilcrease Institute Archives 4316.5695).

122. The inscription is on the mounting. The formation depicted is one of the hot springs at Mammoth.

123. *Catalogue of Pictures of Thomas Moran, N.A.: exhibited under the auspices of the Denver Art League* (Denver, 1892).

124. Jackson's photographs of Glen Eyrie and another formation Moran sketched that winter, Lizard Head (illustrated in Jackson, *Picture Maker of the Old West,* p. 294), offer evidence that they may have worked together.

125. Wilkins, *Thomas Moran: Artist of the Mountains,* pp. 208–9.

126. *The Aldine* 8 (June 1876): 194–96.

127. Moran may have known O'Sullivan, who had been the survey photographer for Thomas O. Selfridge's expedition to Panama in 1870. He served only briefly and was relieved by John Moran. O'Sullivan also met William Henry Jackson when both were in the Colorado mountains in 1874, O'Sullivan with Wheeler and Jackson with Hayden.

Another, earlier image of Shoshone Falls may also have been known to Moran. John Henry Hill (1839–1922) made a watercolor sketch during the summer of 1868 when he accompanied Clarence King's survey of the fortieth parallel. The party reached Shoshone Falls in September. Hill used the sketch as a model for other watercolors and oils. The sketch, in a private collection, is illustrated and discussed in Ferber and Gerdts, eds., *The New Path,* pp. 174–75.

128. James C. Woods, director of the Herrett Museum, College of Southern Idaho, described the vantage points from which Moran recorded the terrain (personal communication, June 29, 1988): "The two 'Blue Lakes' sketches are drawn from the headwaters of Alfius Creek which is located on the north side of the Snake River in Jerome County, Idaho. . . . I can even tell where Moran was positioned when the two sketches were produced. [*Blue Lakes, Idaho*] was drawn on a small, flat terrace looking south by southwest at the Blue Lakes. [*Blue Lakes Snake River*] was drawn from a large boulder above the terrace where the first sketch was produced. The Blue Lakes locale is . . . almost four miles below the Shoshone Falls. [*Shoshone Falls*] was drawn from the Jerome County side looking almost due south at the falls. It was drawn from a flat terrace above the falls."

129. The only located sketches made by Moran in Wales in 1906 are part of a small sketchbook in the Gilcrease collection. One sketch, *Conway,* in the East Hampton Library collection was torn from that sketchbook by Moran.

130. An exception was the rock promontory at Montauk, which Moran sketched and painted often, rarely varying the composition. Moran never visited eastern coastal regions, such as Maine, that would have provided a more rugged landscape, and he did not visit and sketch such California coastal scenes as Cyprus Point until several years later.

131. Gilcrease Institute Archives photograph (4317.5694); also illustrated in Wilkins, *Thomas Moran: Artist of the Mountains,* opposite p. 177.

132. Checklist Nos. 1026–33.

133. New York *Evening World,* June 12, 1911.

Color Plates

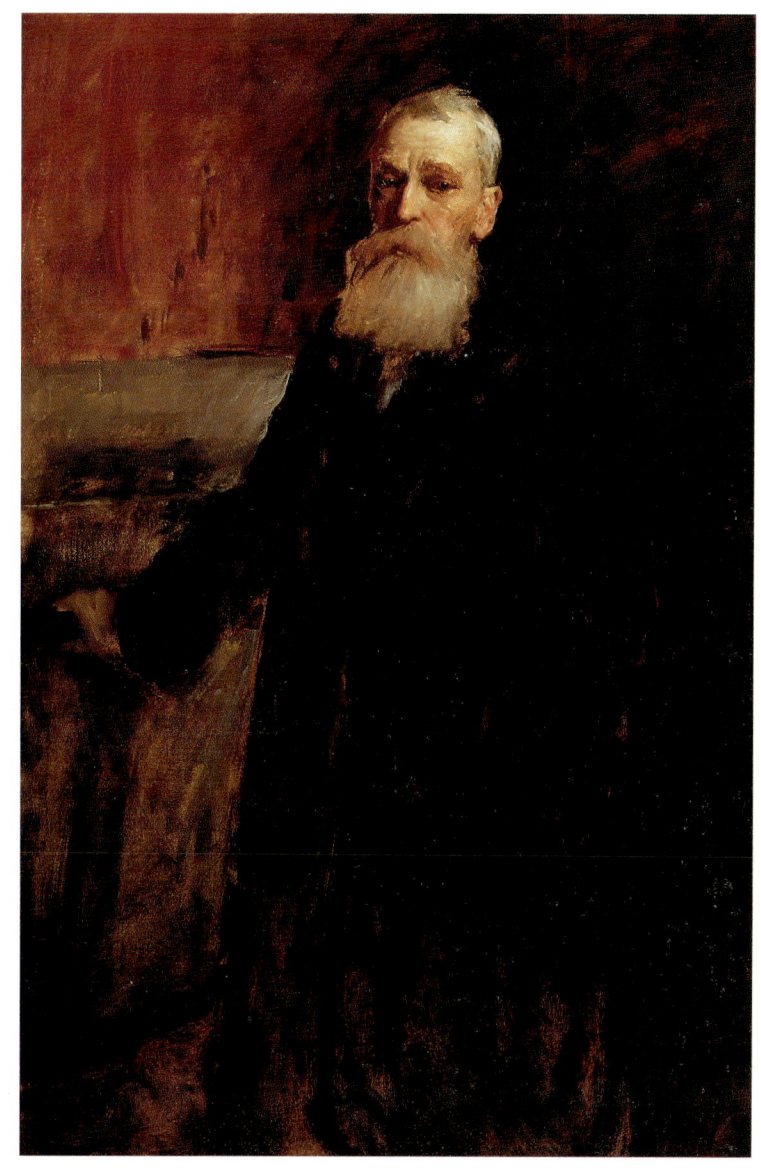

Plate 1. William Merritt Chase, *Portrait of Thomas Moran* (Gilcrease Institute, 0126.2338), oil on canvas, 36 by 55 inches.

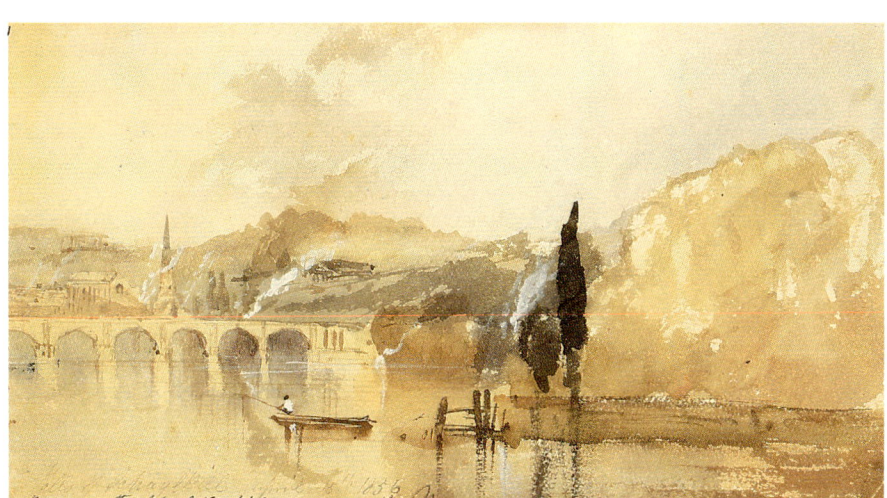

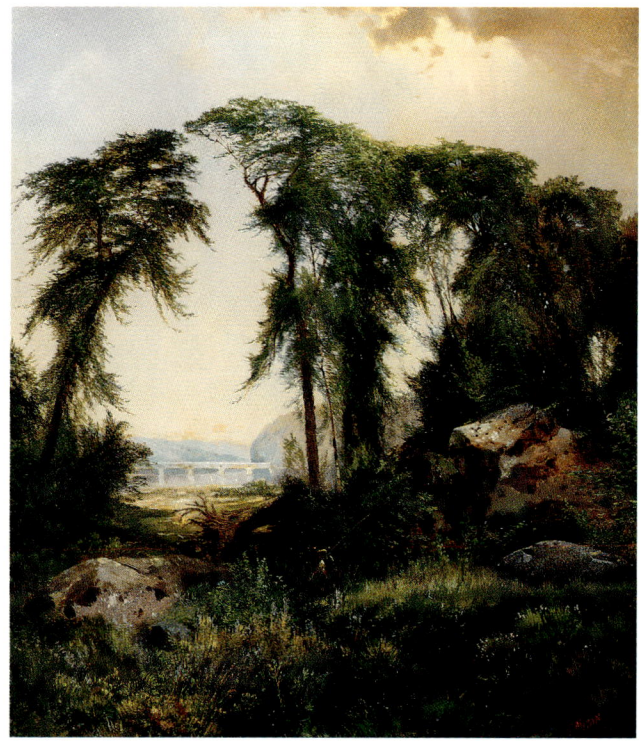

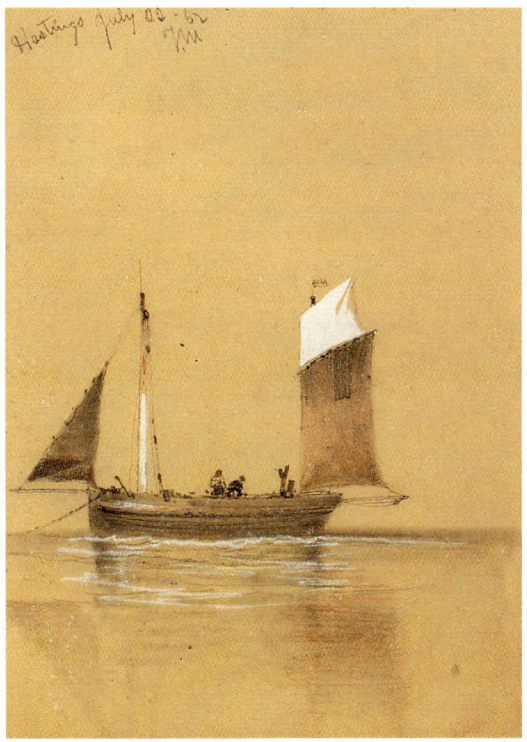

On the facing page

Top left: Plate 5. No. 60, *Bexhill* (Gilcrease Institute, 0276.933), graphite, red conté crayon, and white gouache on green wove, 5 by 7 inches.

Top left: Plate 2. No. 1, *Bridge over the Schuylkill, Philadelphia* (Gilcrease Institute, 0226.798), graphite, watercolor, and white gouache on wove, 6¹/₂ by 11⁵/₈ inches.

Top right: Plate 6. No. 63, *Hastings* (Gilcrease Institute, 0276.838), graphite, red conté crayon, and white gouache on wove, 5 by 7 inches.

Top right: Plate 3. Thomas Moran, *Summer on the Susquehanna at Catawissa* (1862, Gilcrease Institute, 0126.2335), oil on canvas, 24 by 20¹/₄ inches.

Bottom left: Plate 7. No. 61, *Hastings* (Gilcrease Institute, 0276.841), graphite and white gouache on wove, 5 by 7 inches.

Bottom: Plate 4. No. 64, *Hastings* (Gilcrease Institute, 0276.839), graphite, red conté crayon, and white gouache on wove, 7 by 5 inches.

Bottom right: Plate 8. No. 65, *Hastings* (Gilcrease Institute, 0276.935), graphite, red conté crayon, and white gouache on green wove, 5 by 7 inches.

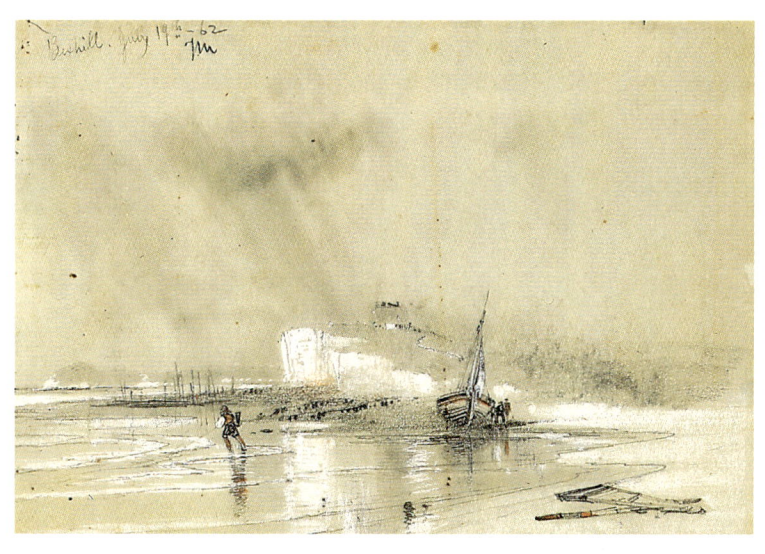

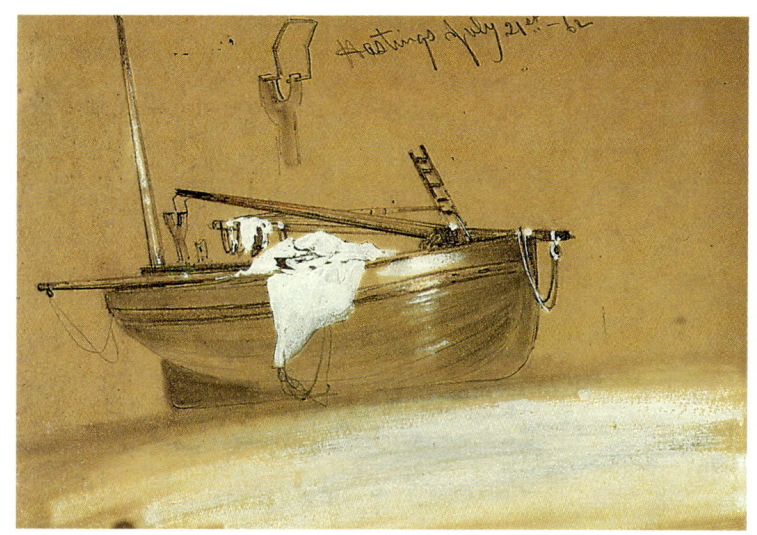

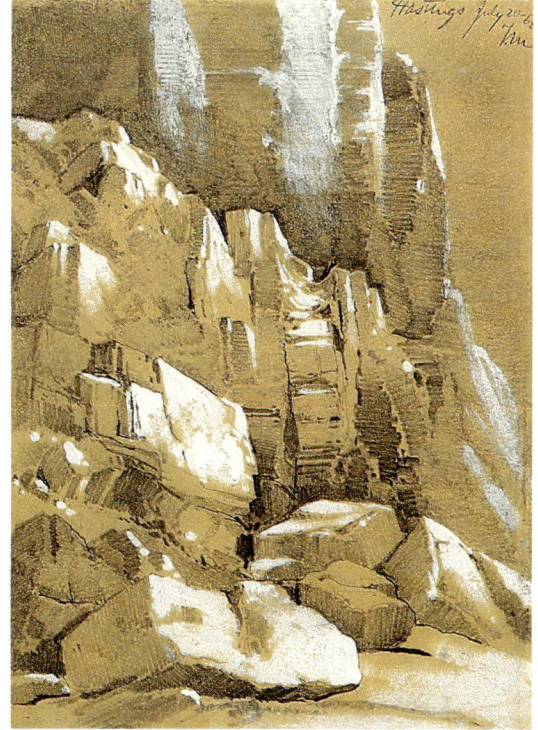

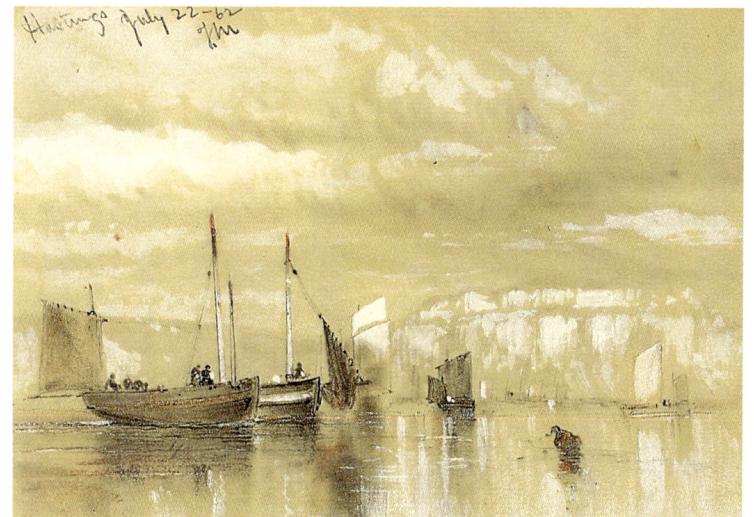

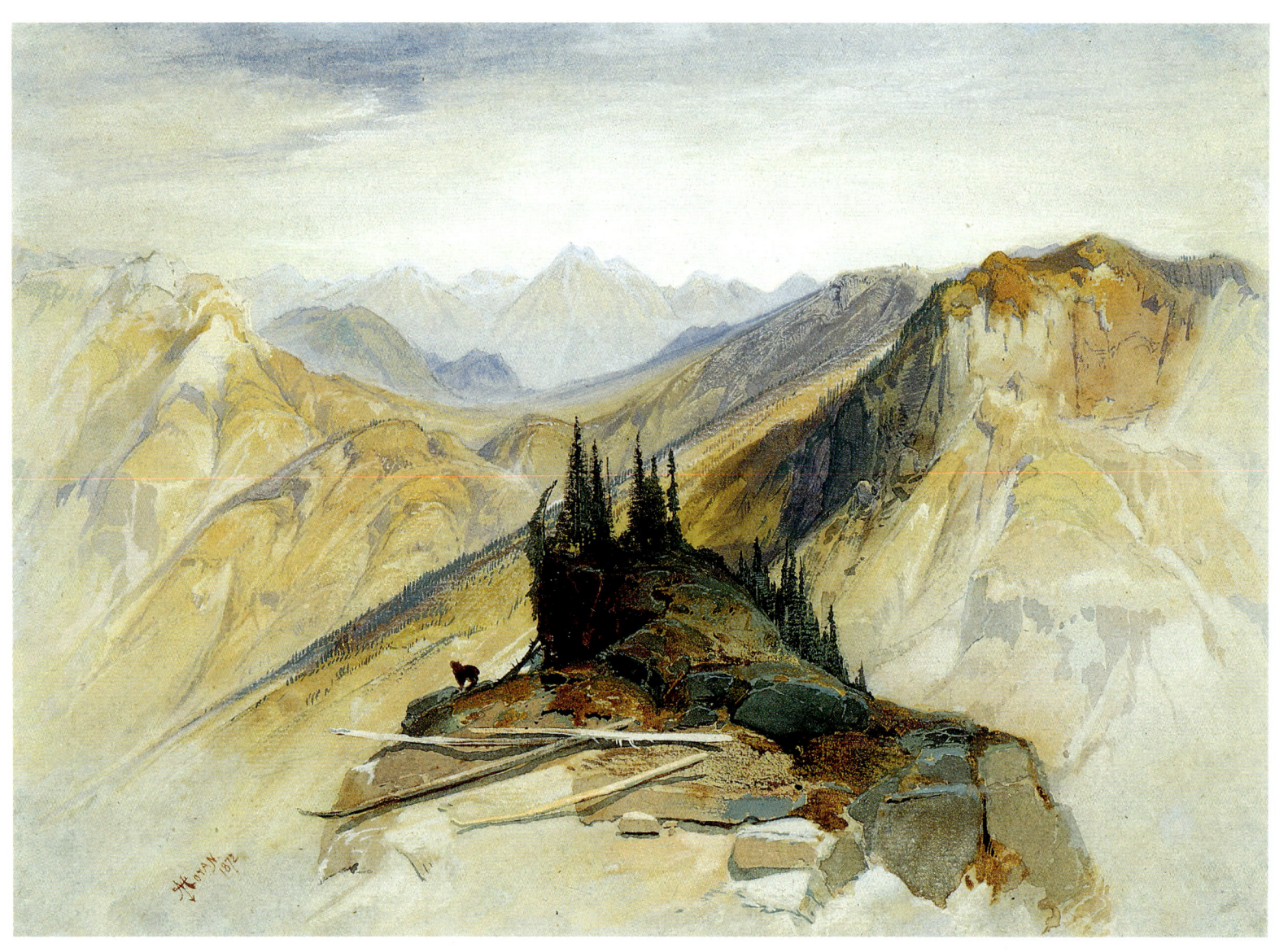

Plate 9. Thomas Moran, *The Yellowstone Range from near Fort Ellis* (1872, Gilcrease Institute, 0226.1358), watercolor on paper, 8 by 11 inches.

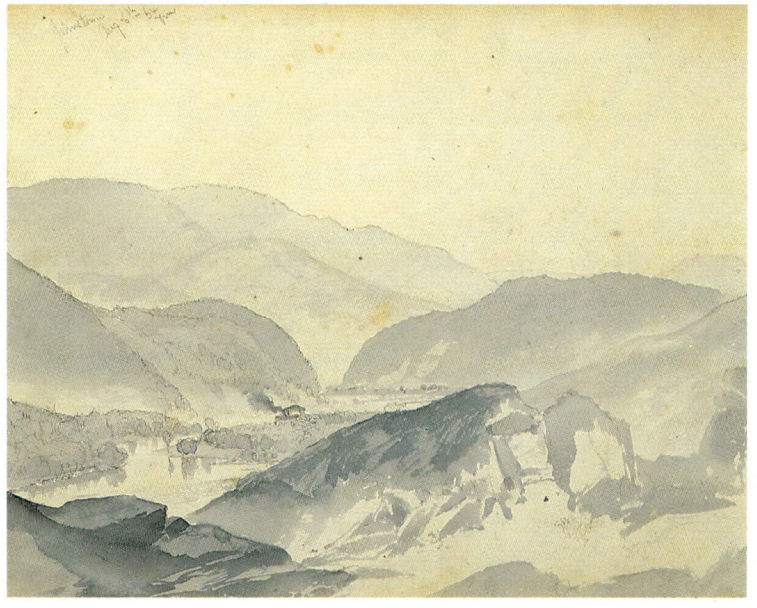

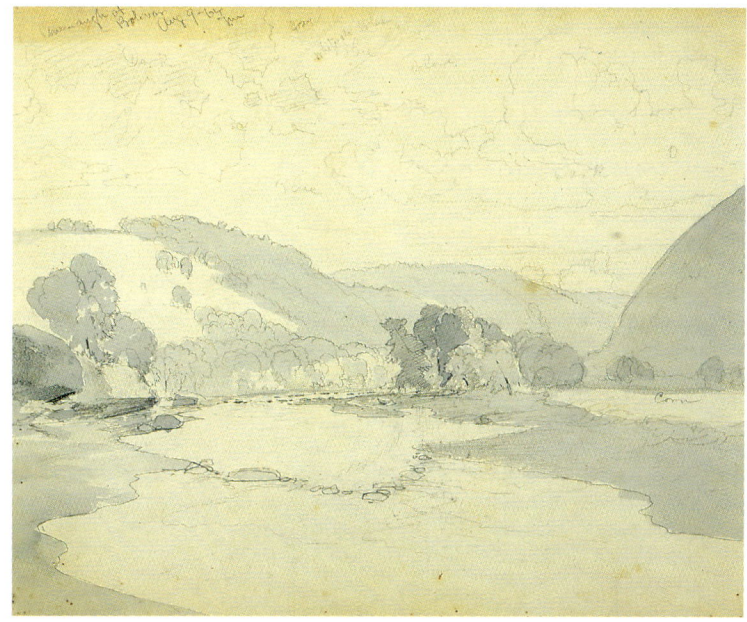

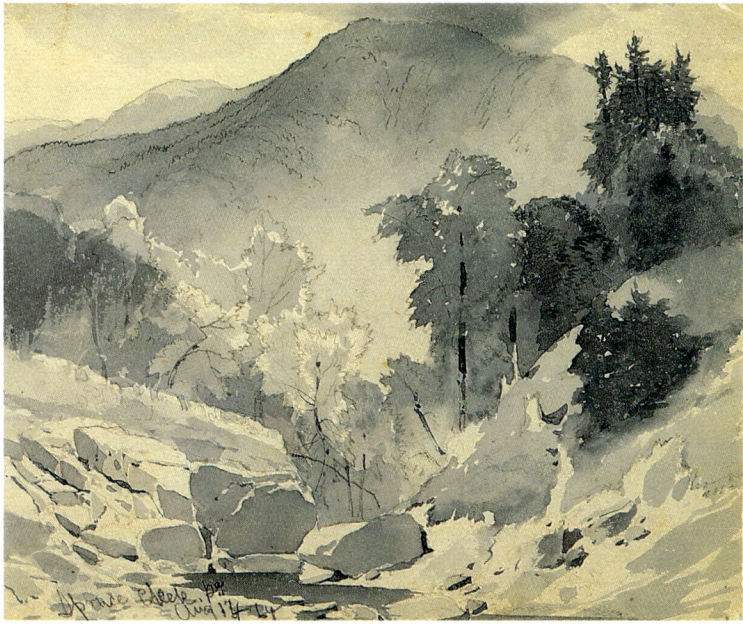

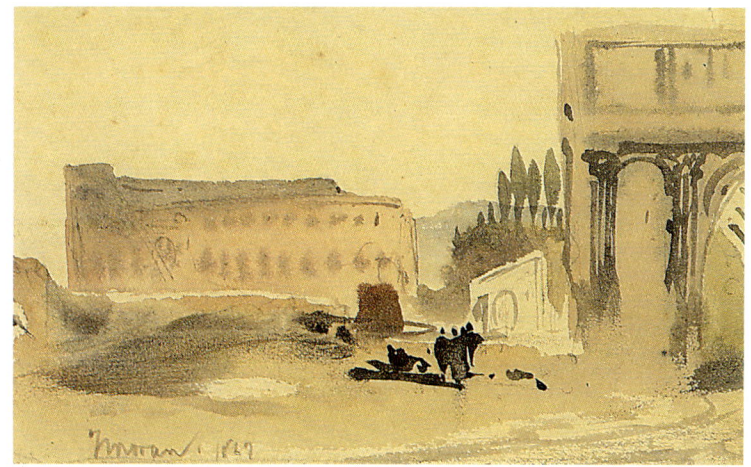

Bottom left: Plate 12. No. 93, *Spruce Creek, Pennsylvania* (Gilcrease Institute, 0226.942), graphite, blue and gray washes on wove, 5½ by 6⅜ inches.

Bottom right: Plate 14. No. 154, *Colosseum, Rome* (Gilcrease Institute, 0276.863), graphite and watercolor on wove, 3⅞ by 6⅛ inches.

Top left: Plate 10. No. 81, *Johnstown* (Gilcrease Institute, 0226.795), graphite, blue and gray washes on wove, 9¾ by 11⅝ inches.

Top right: Plate 11. No. 85, *Conemaugh at Bolivar* (Gilcrease Institute, 0226.794), graphite, blue and gray washes on wove, sketch ¾ by 11½ inches.

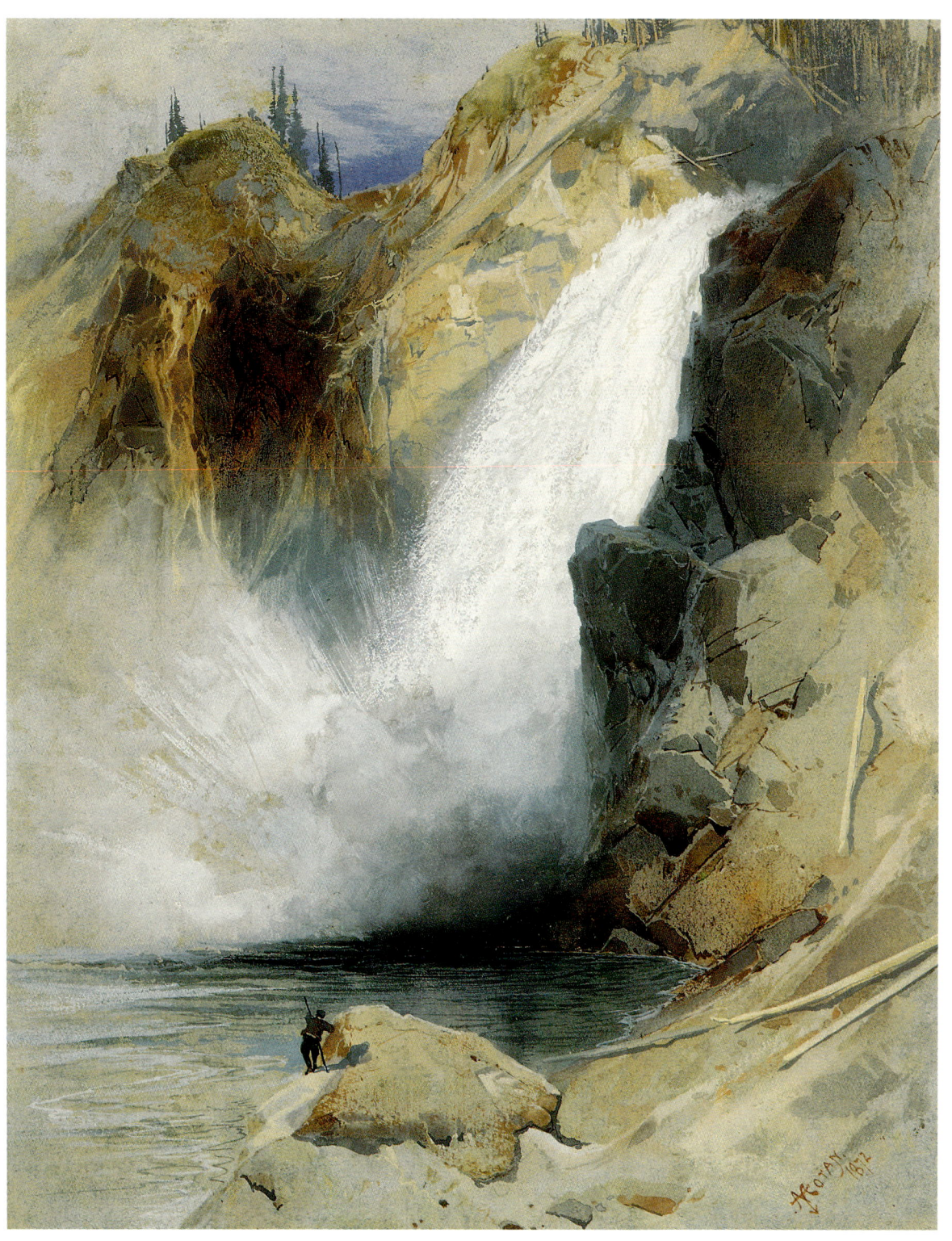

Plate 13. Thomas Moran, *Upper Falls of the Yellowstone* (1872, Gilcrease Institute, 0226.1451), watercolor on paper, 10 by 8 inches.

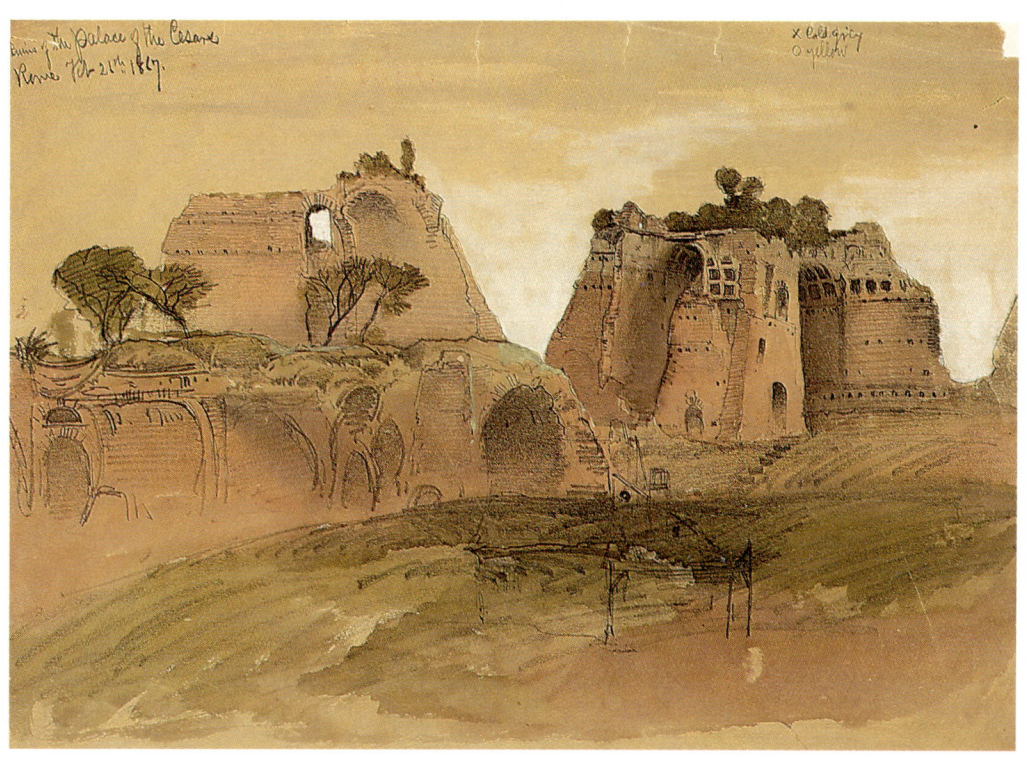

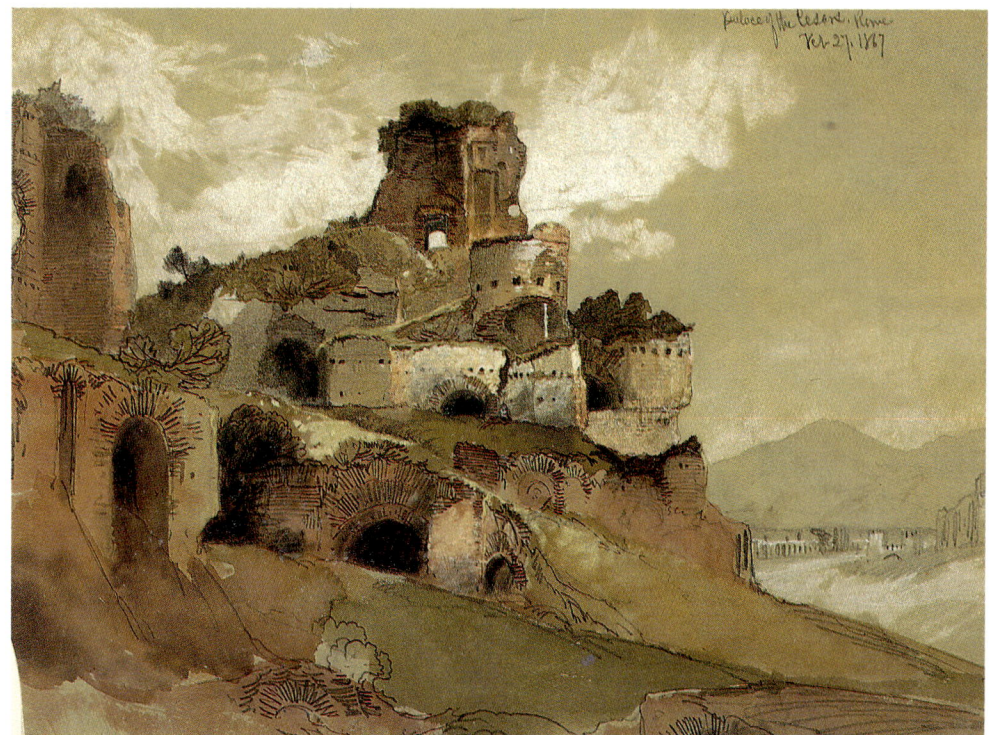

Top: Plate 15. No. 155, *Ruins of the Palace of the Caesars, Rome* (Gilcrease Institute, 0276.864), graphite, watercolor, and white gouache on wove, 9³/₄ by 13¹/₂ inches.

Bottom: Plate 16. No. 156, *Palace of the Caesars, Rome* (Gilcrease Institute, 0276.941), graphite, watercolor, and white gouache on gray wove, 9⁵/₈ by 13 inches.

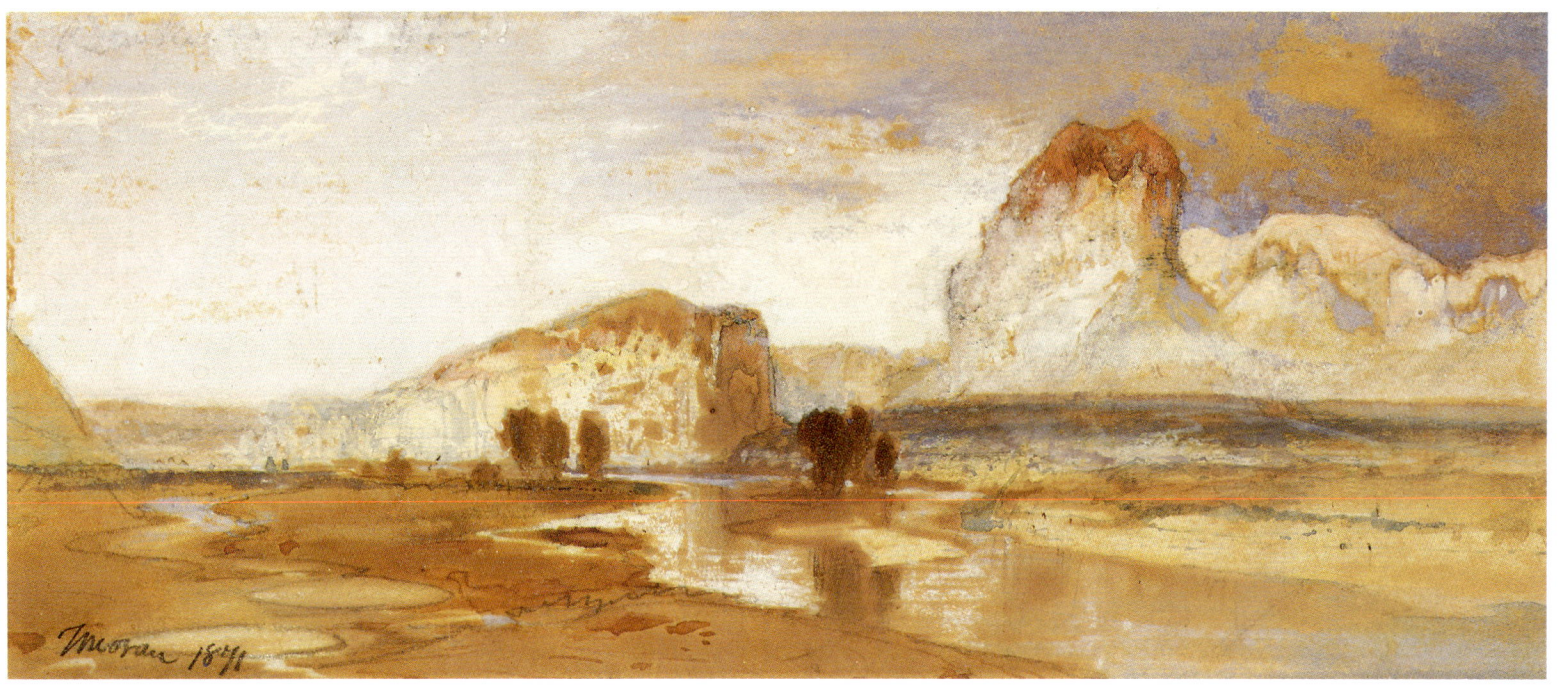

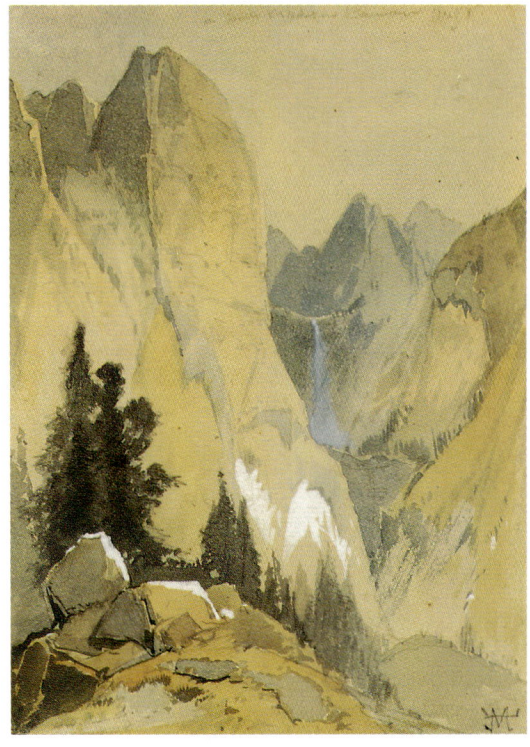

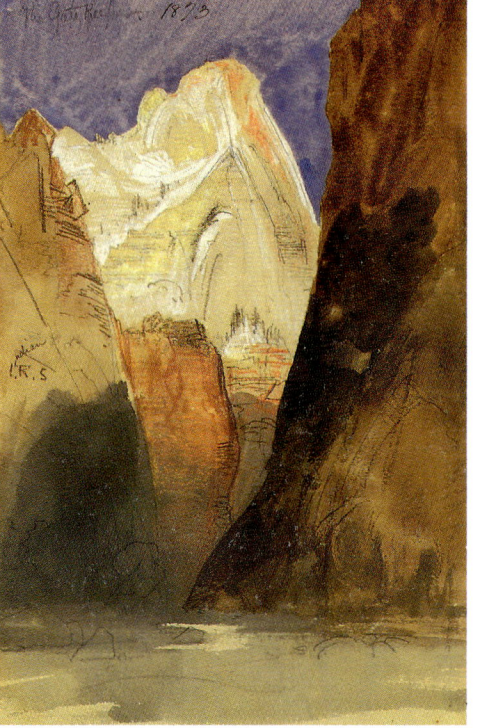

Top: Plate 17. No. 202, *First Sketch Made in the West at Green River, Wyoming* (Gilcrease Institute, 0236.882), graphite, watercolor, and white gouache on wove, 3³/₄ by 8¹/₈ inches.

Bottom left: Plate 18. No. 230, *In Lower Madison Canyon* (Gilcrease Institute, 0236.1576), graphite, watercolor, and white gouache on wove, 8¹/₈ by 5³/₄ inches.

Bottom right: Plate 19. No. 274, *In the Narrows, Zion Valley, the Gate Keeper* (Gilcrease Institute, 0236.878), graphite, watercolor, and white gouache on wove, sketch 9³/₄ by 6³/₈ inches, mount 15¹/₂ by 11³/₈ inches.

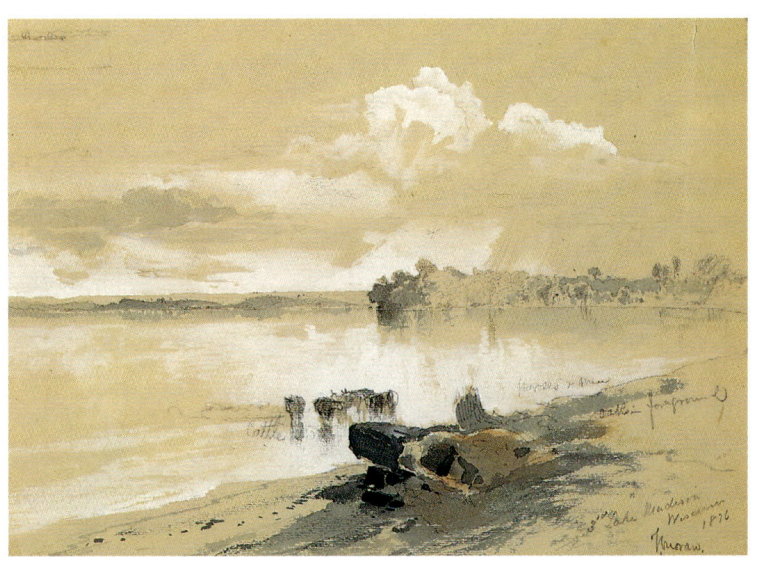

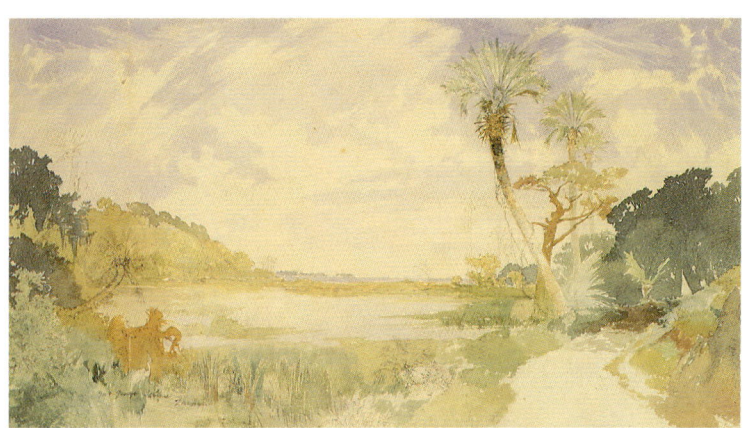

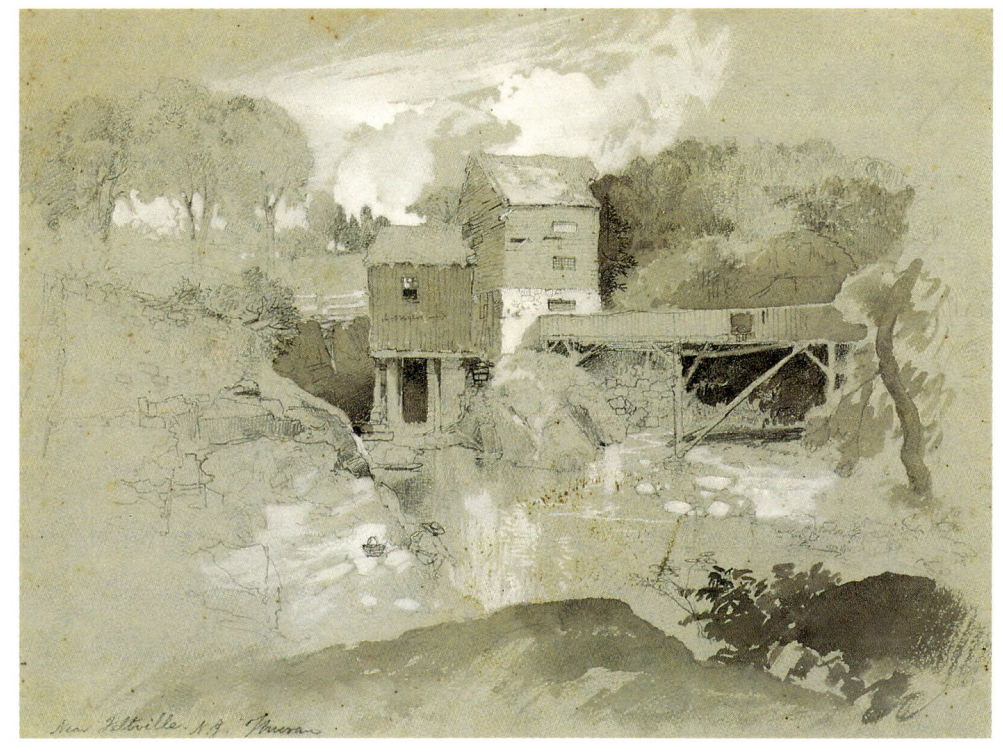

Top left: No. 304, *Third Lake, Madison, Wisconsin* (Gilcrease Institute, 0226.939), graphite, watercolor, and white gouache on wove, 9³/₄ by 13¹/₈ inches.

Top right: Plate 21. No. 336, *Fort George Island* (Gilcrease Institute, 0226.792), graphite and watercolor on wove, 10¹/₂ by 18⁵/₈ inches.

Bottom: Plate 22. No. 349, *Near Feltville, New Jersey* (Gilcrease Institute, 0226.789), graphite, wash, and white gouache on blue wove, 9⁵/₈ by 12⁵/₈ inches.

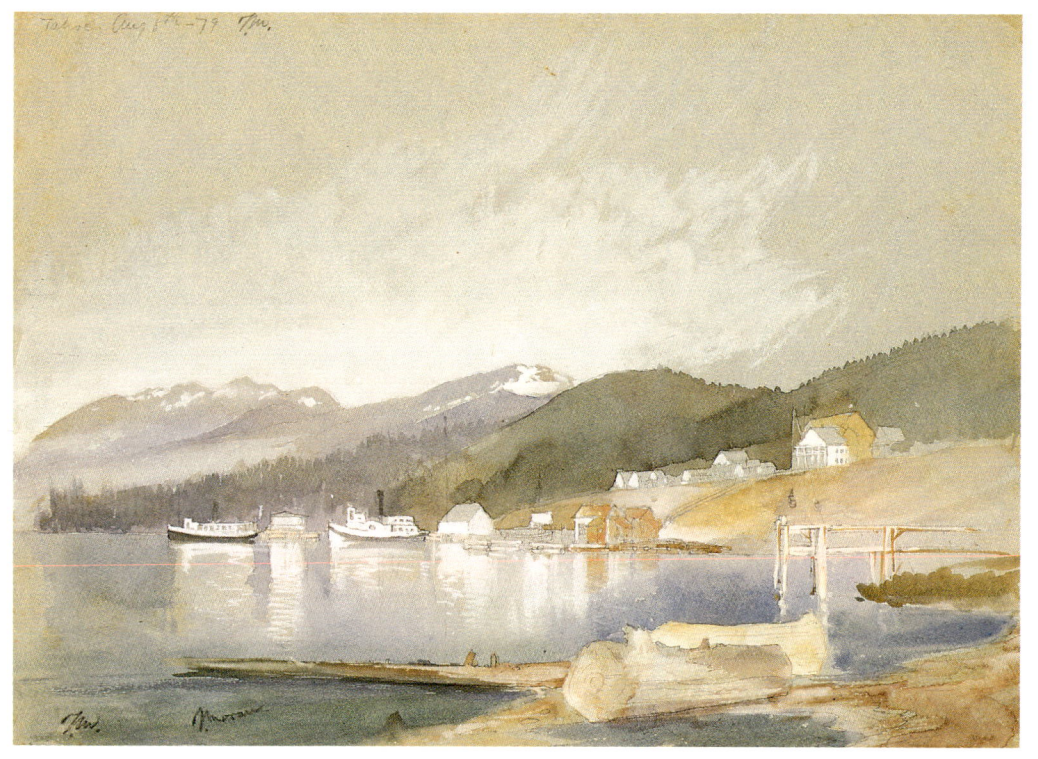

Top: Plate 23. No. 392, *Tahoe* (Gilcrease Institute, 0236.886), graphite, watercolor, and white gouache on blue wove, sketch 10⁷/₈ by 14³/₄ inches, mount 15¹/₂ by 19³/₄ inches.

Bottom left: Plate 24. No. 393, *Lake Tahoe* (Gilcrease Institute, 0236.881), graphite and watercolor on watermarked laid, 9¹/₂ by 12³/₈ inches.

Bottom right: Plate 26. No. 403, *In Little Cottonwood Canyon* (Gilcrease Institute, 0236.887), graphite and watercolor on watermarked gray laid, 10 by 14³/₄ inches.

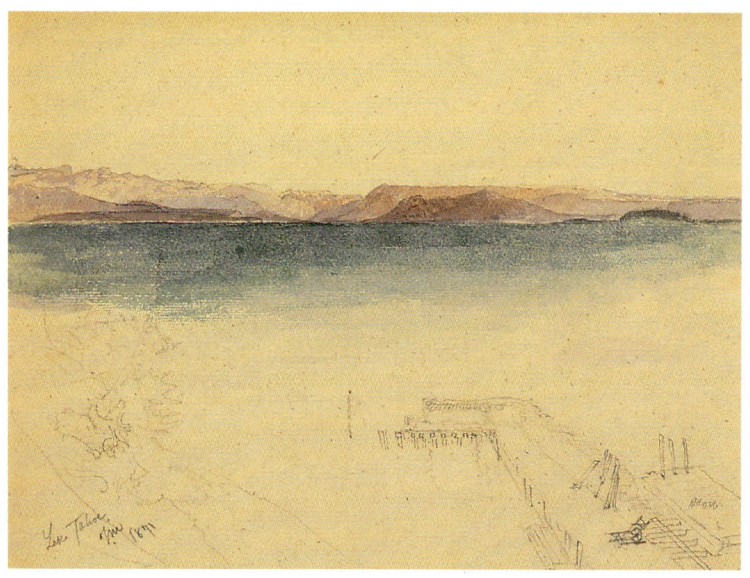

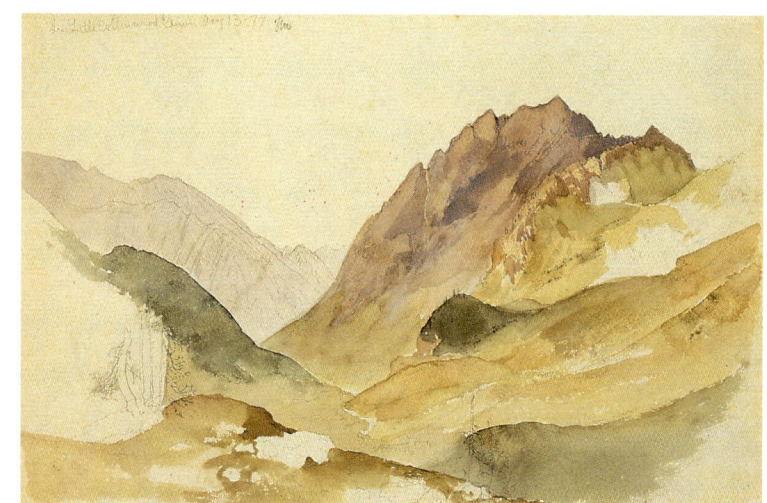

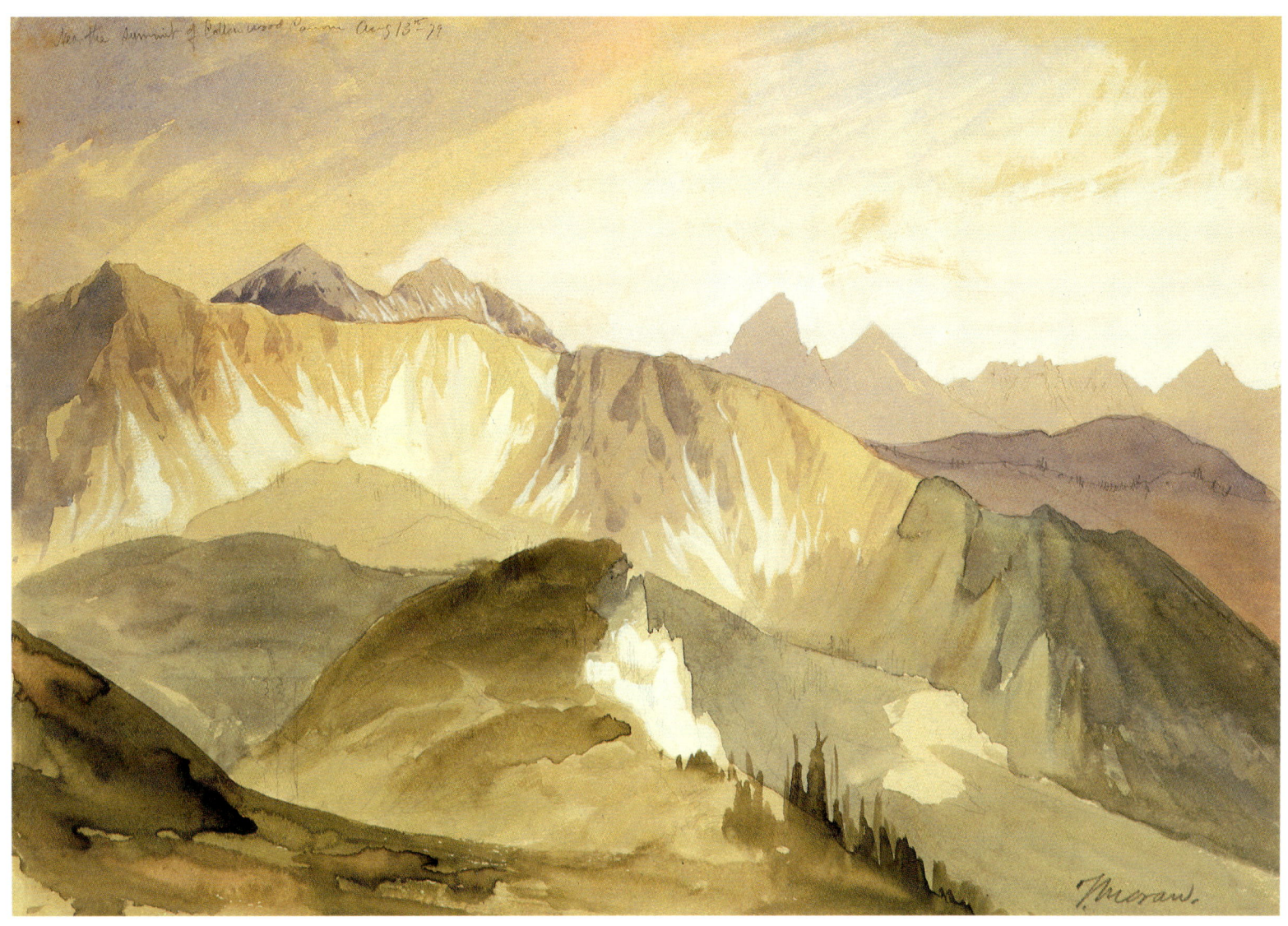

Plate 25. No. 407, *Near the Summit
of Cottonwood Canyon* (Gilcrease Institute, 0236.890), graphite, watercolor, and white gouache on pink
wove, 10½ by 14½ inches.

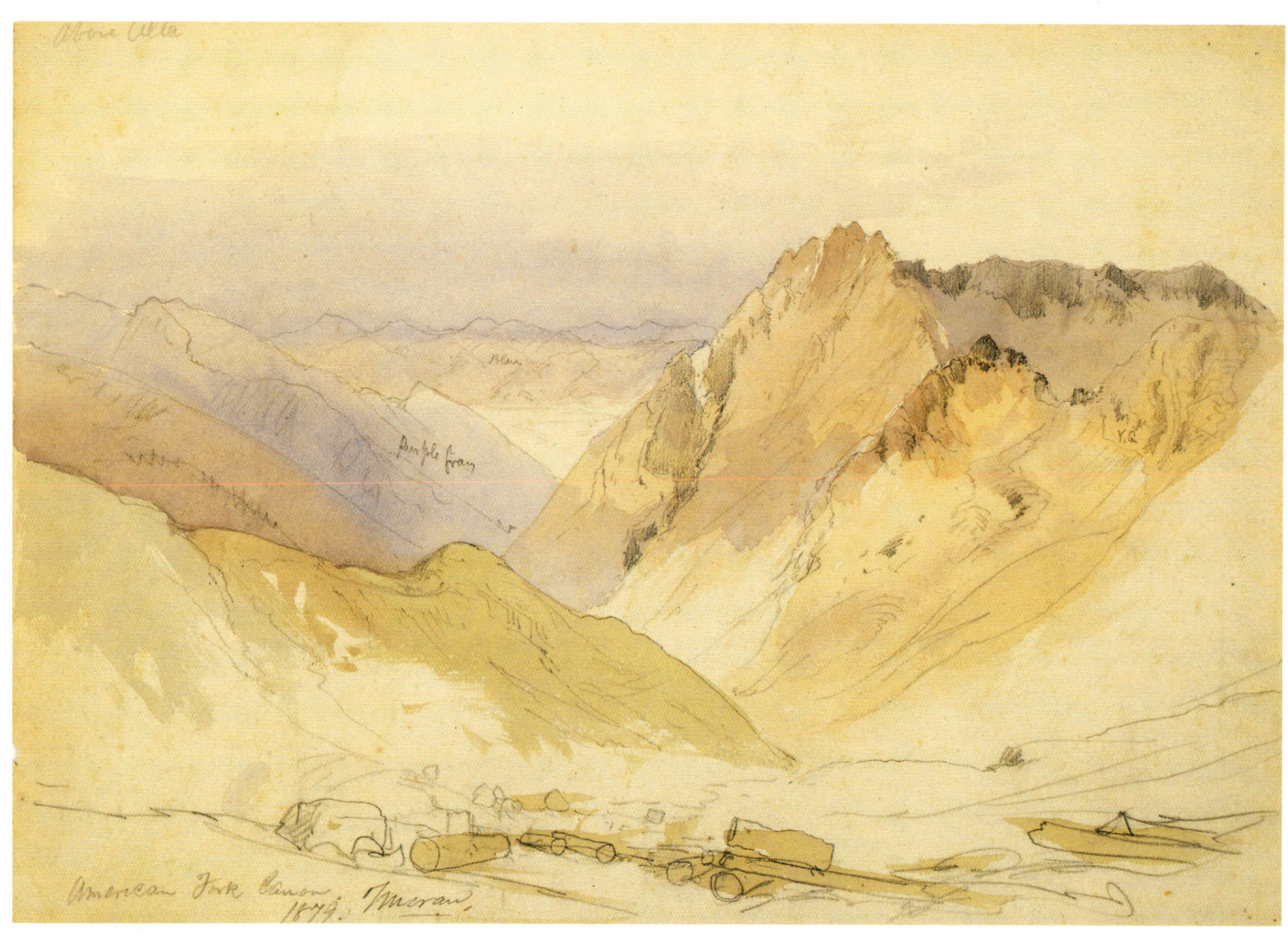

Plate 27. No. 411, *American Fork Canyon* (Gilcrease Institute, 0236.888), graphite and watercolor on wove, 10 by 13⁷/₈ inches.

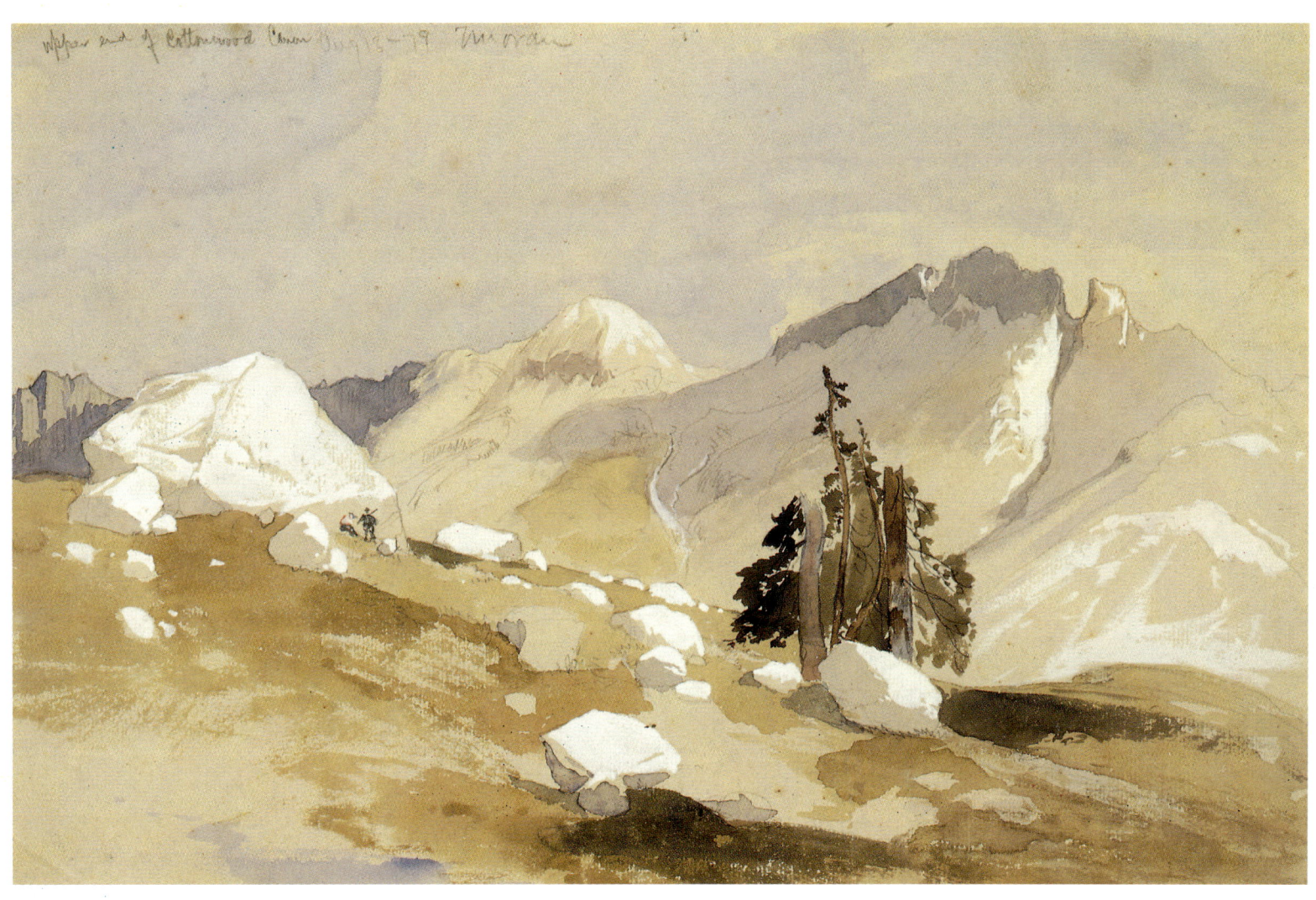

Plate 28. No. 406, *Upper End of Cottonwood Canyon* (Gilcrease Institute, 0236.884), graphite, watercolor, and white gouache on watermarked gray laid, 11 by 14⁵/₈ inches.

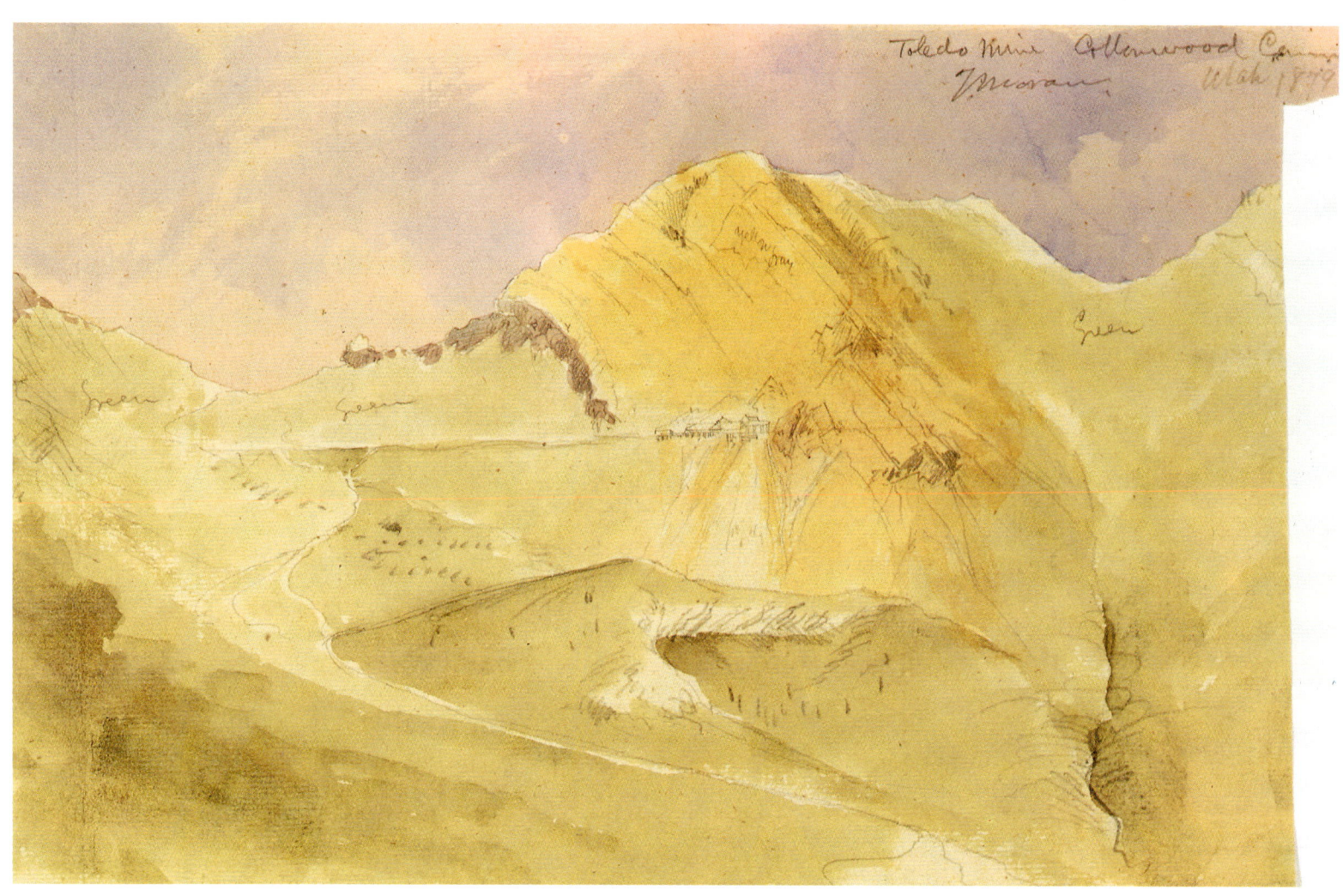

Plate 29. No. 408, *Toledo Mine, Cottonwood Canyon, Utah* (Gilcrease Institute, 0236.889), graphite and watercolor on laid, 8½ by 11¾ inches.

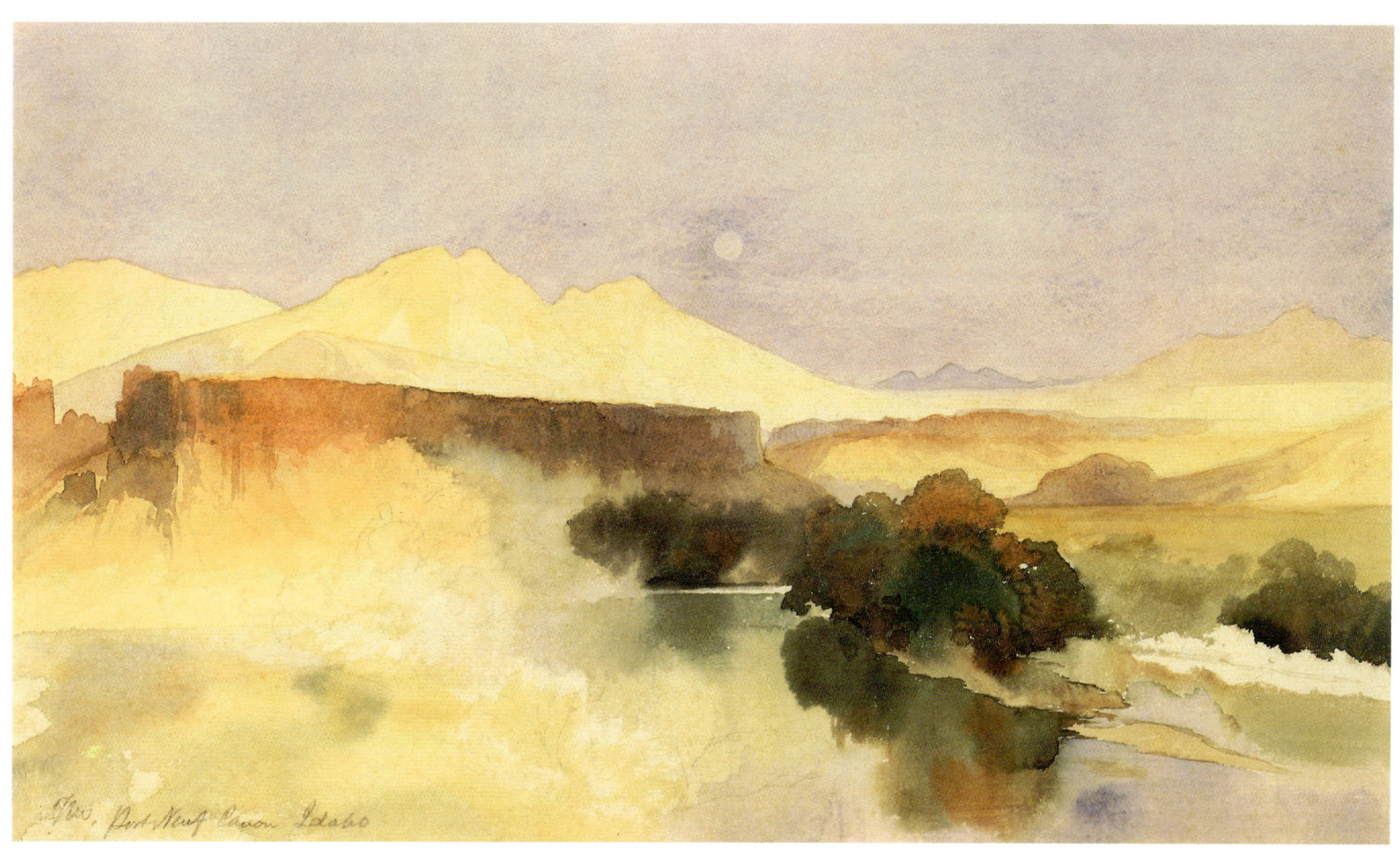

Plate 30. No. 412, *Portneuf Canyon,
Idaho* (Gilcrease Institute, 0236.855),
graphite and watercolor on wove, 12
by 19³/₄ inches.

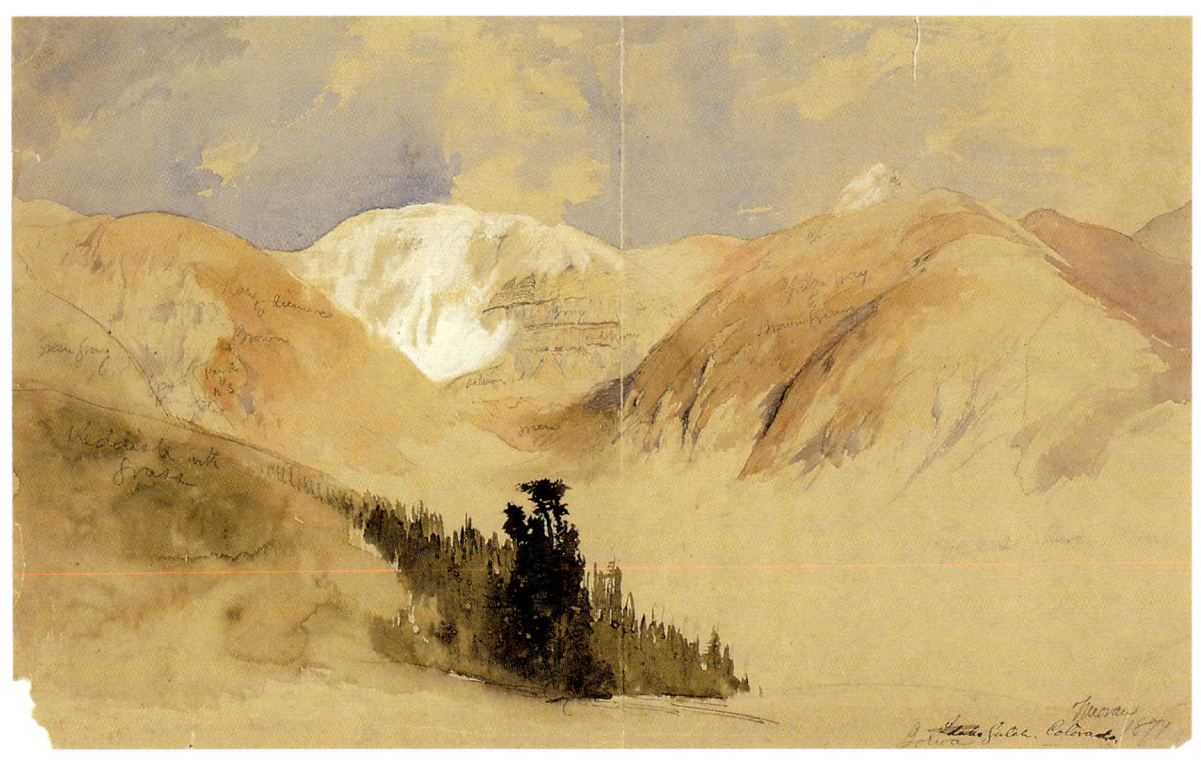

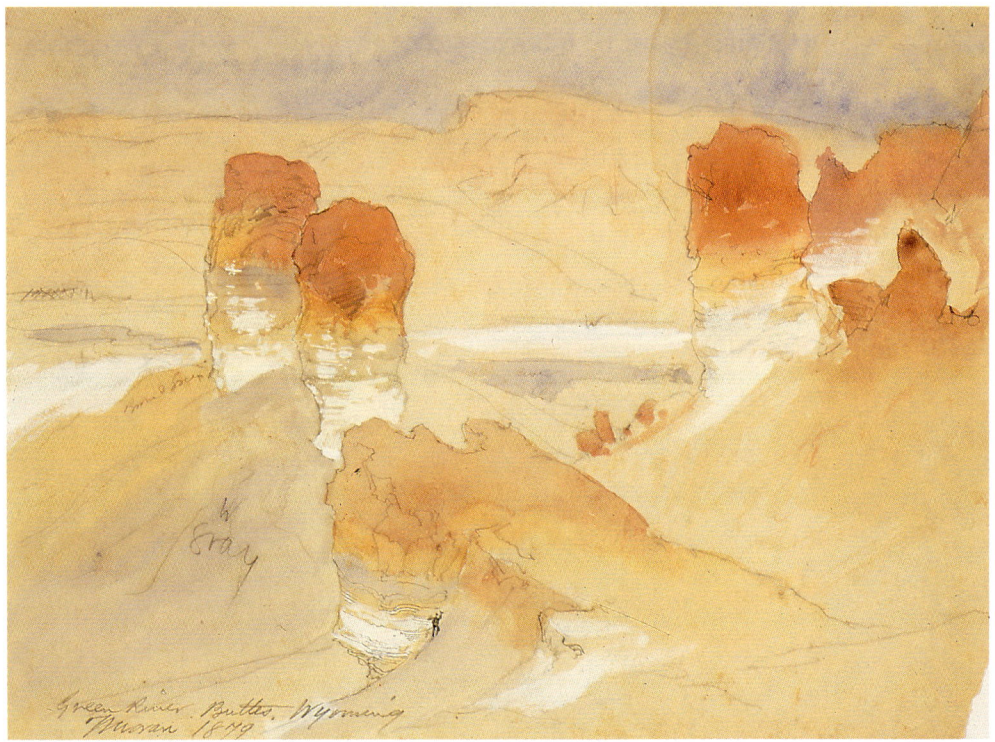

Top: Plate 31. No. 415, *Iowa Gulch, Idaho* (Gilcrease Institute, 0236.892), graphite, watercolor, and white gouache on wove, 11⅞ by 19⅜ inches.

Bottom: Plate 32. No. 436, *Green River Buttes, Wyoming* (Gilcrease Institute, 0236.885), graphite, watercolor, and white gouache on wove, 10¼ by 13⅞ inches.

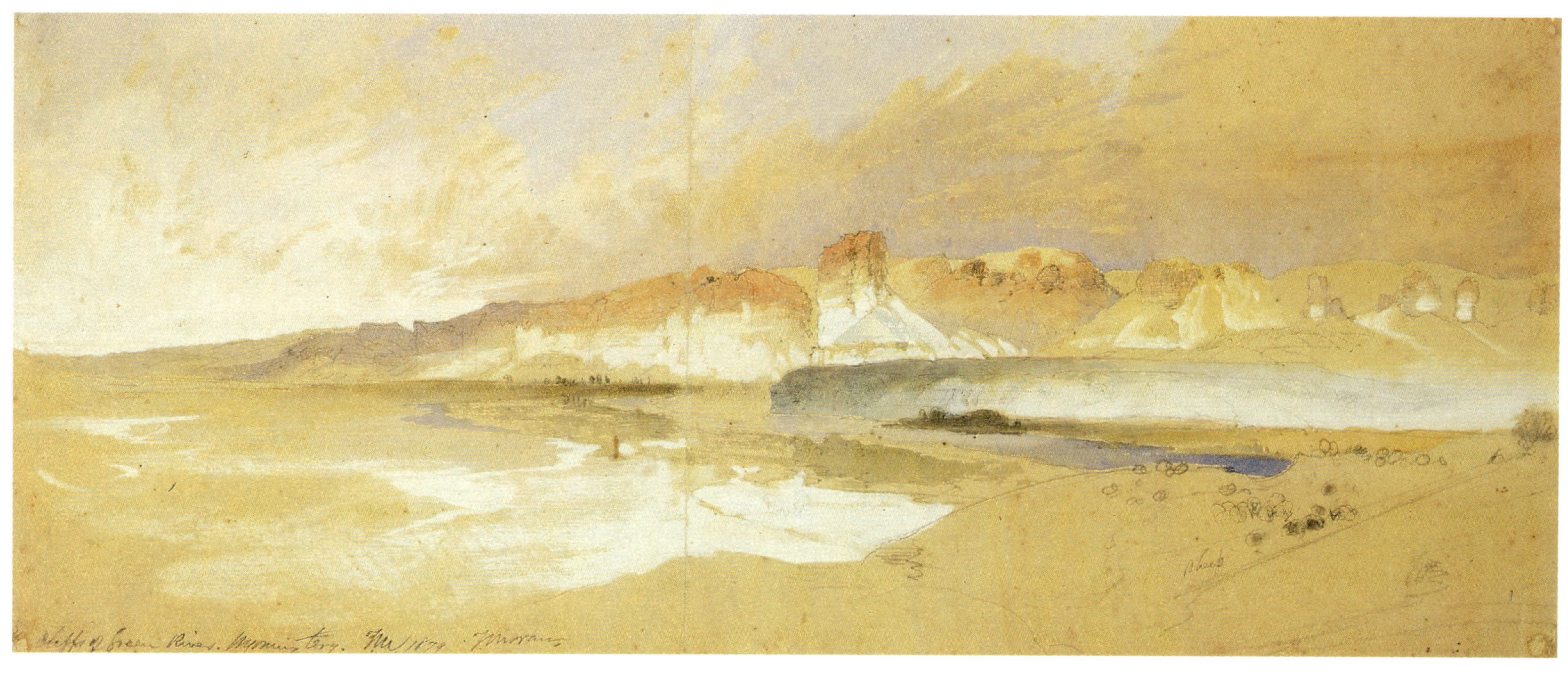

Plate 33. No. 439, *The Cliffs of Green River, Wyoming* (Gilcrease Institute, 0236.930), graphite, watercolor, and white gouache on laid, sketch 9³/₄ by 23 inches, mount 15¹/₂ by 25⁵/₈ inches.

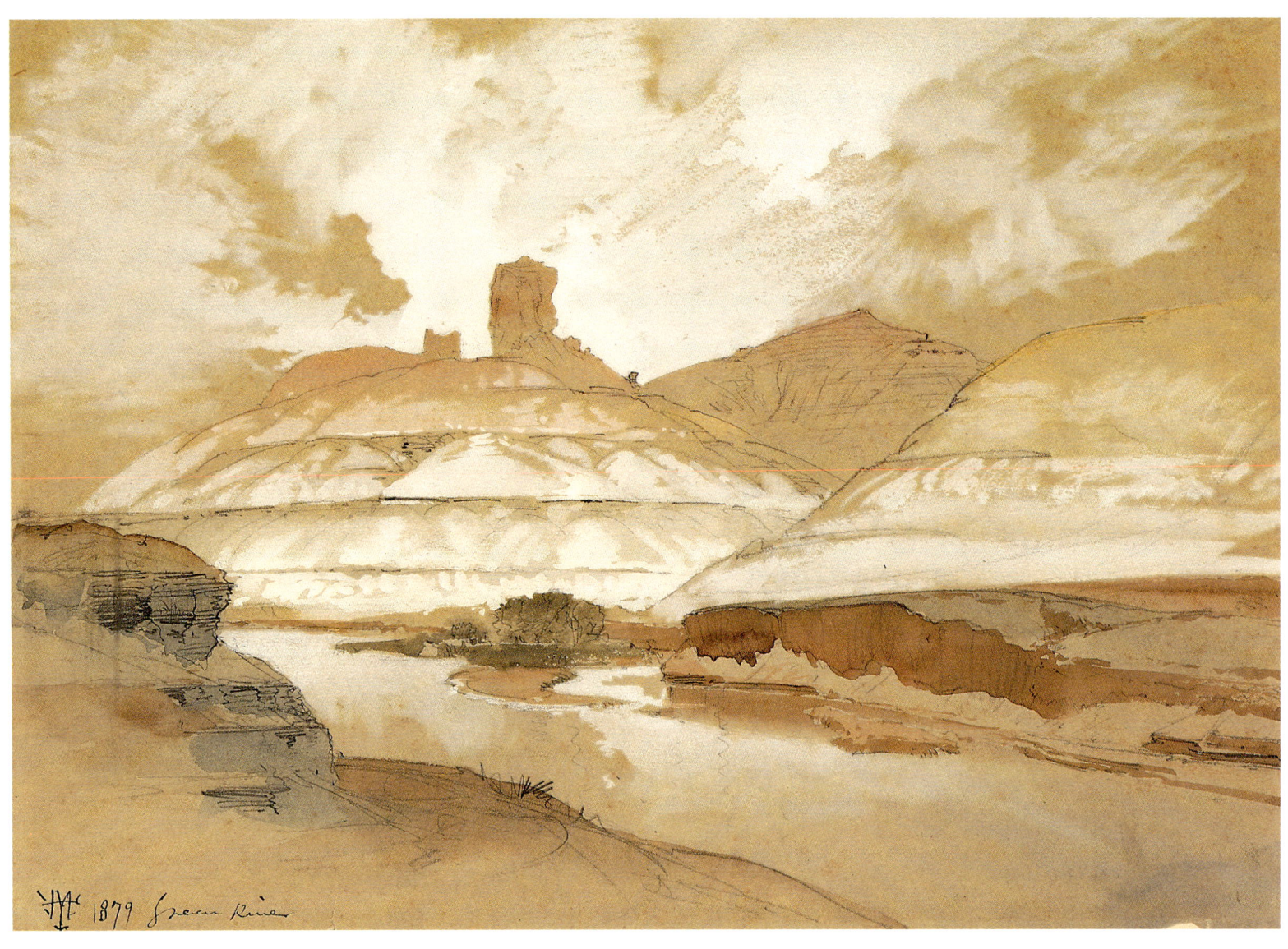

Plate 34. No. 431, *Green River* (Gilcrease Institute, 0236.891), graphite, watercolor, and white gouache on gray wove, sketch 9³/8 by 12³/4 inches, mount 12¹/8 by 15¹/8 inches.

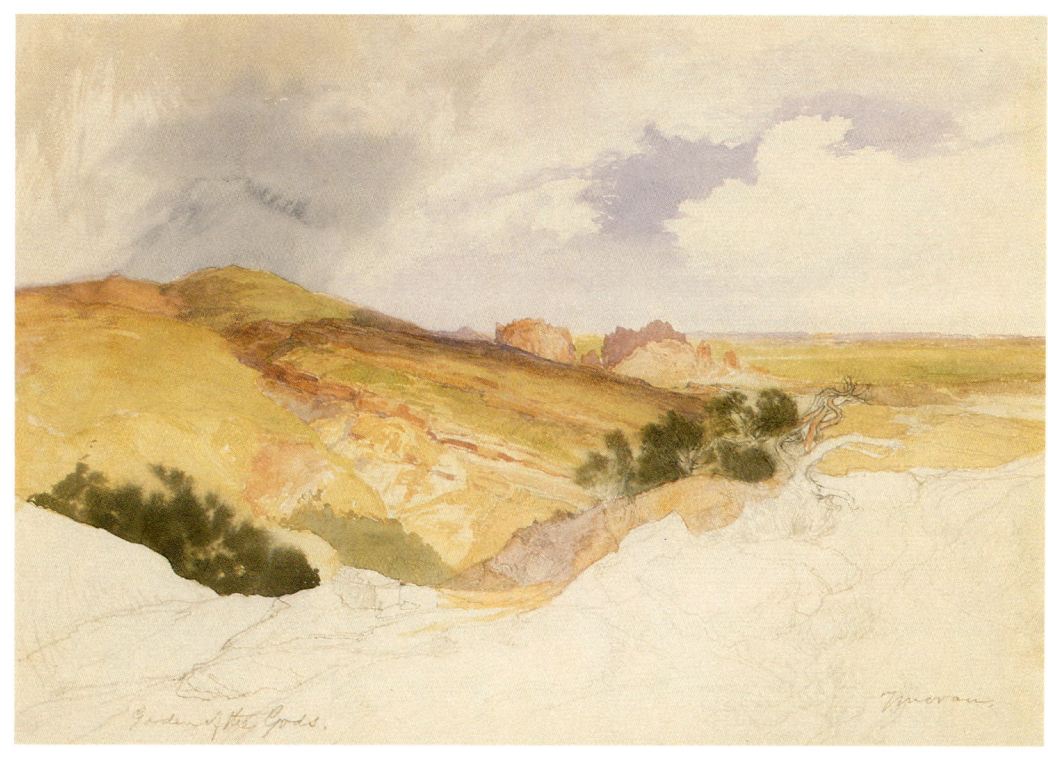

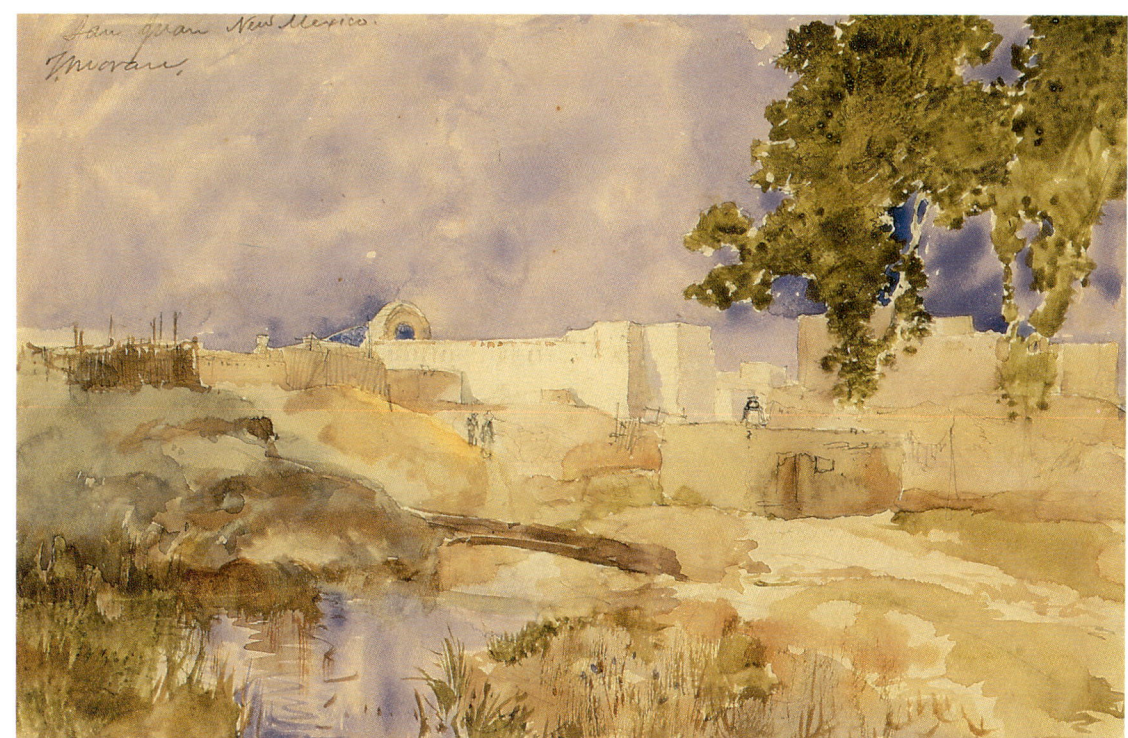

Top: Plate 35. No. 568, *Garden of the Gods* (Gilcrease Institute, 0236.844), graphite and watercolor on wove, sketch 10 by 13⁷/₈ inches, mount 15 by 19 inches.

Bottom: Plate 36. No. 573, *San Juan, New Mexico* (Gilcrease Institute, 0236.843), graphite and watercolor on wove, sketch 7¹/₄ by 10⁷/₈ inches, mount 11³/₄ by 16¹/₄ inches.

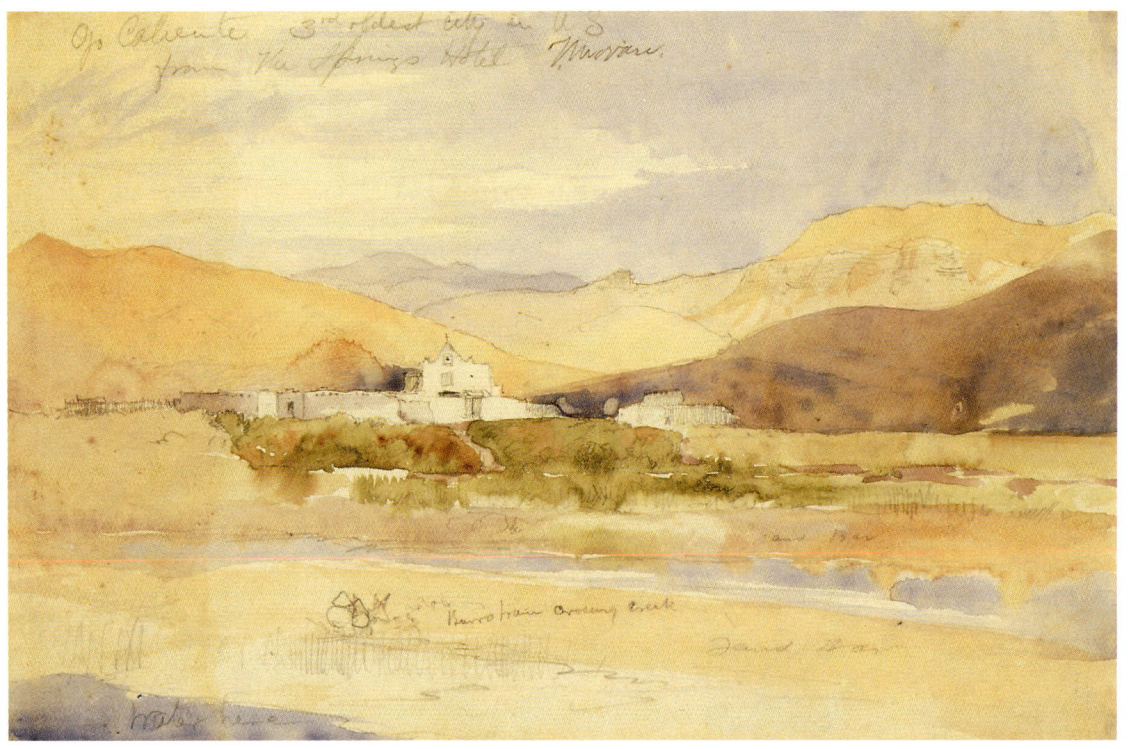

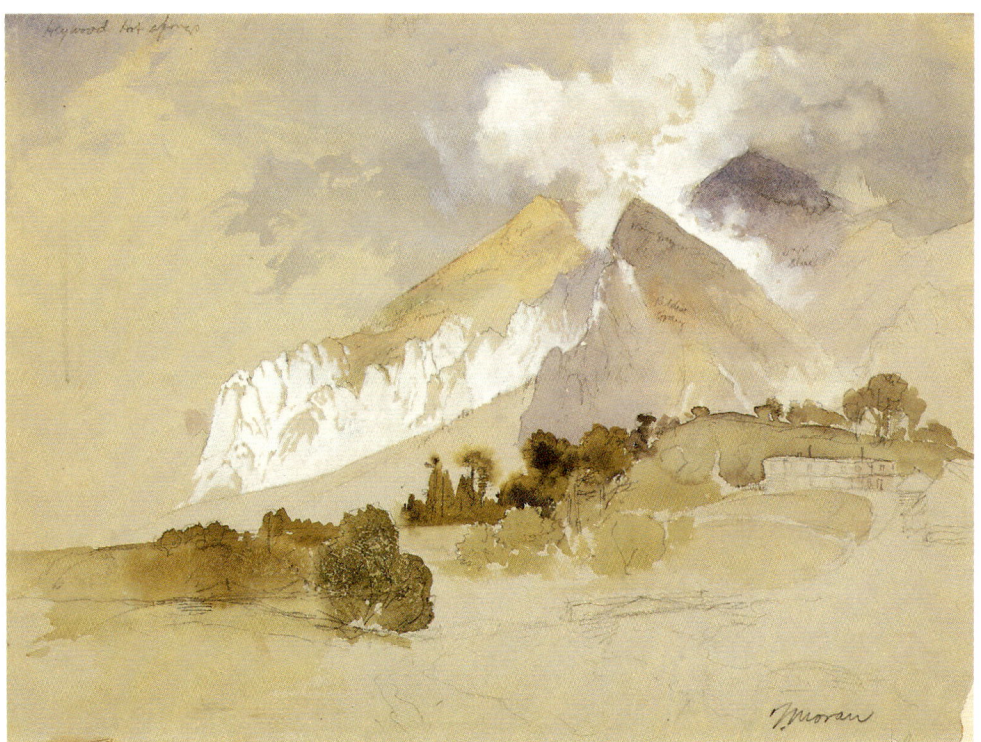

Top: Plate 37. No. 572, *Ojo Caliente* (Gilcrease Institute, 0236.845), graphite and watercolor on wove, sketch 7¼ by 10⅞ inches, mount 12¾ by 16 inches.

Bottom: Plate 38. No. 570, *Heywood Hot Springs* (Gilcrease Institute, 0236.846), graphite, watercolor, and white gouache on gray wove, sketch 9½ by 12½ inches, mount 12½ by 19 inches.

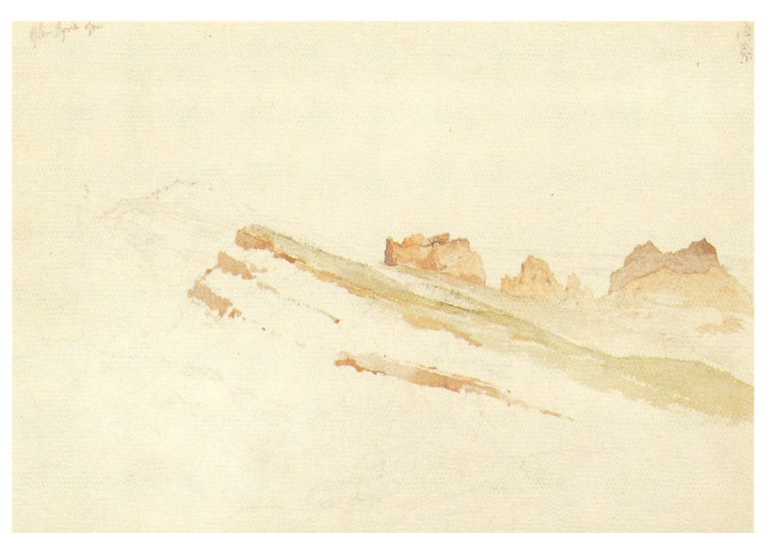

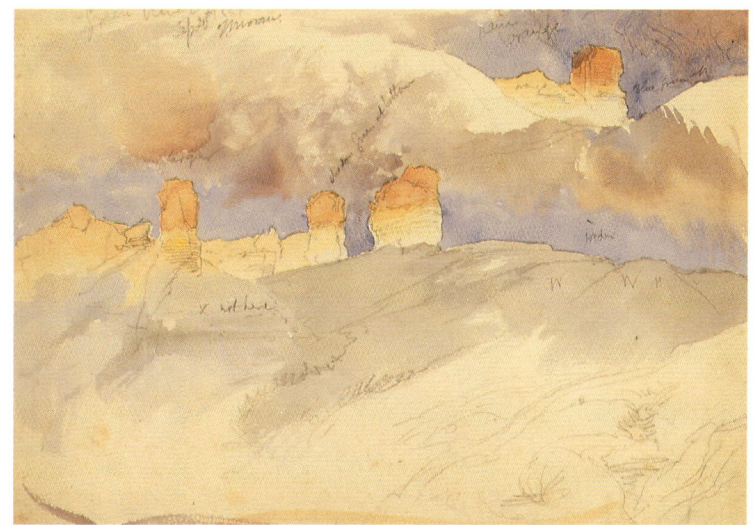

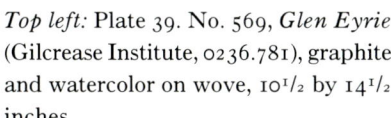

Top left: Plate 39. No. 569, *Glen Eyrie* (Gilcrease Institute, 0236.781), graphite and watercolor on wove, 10¹/₂ by 14¹/₂ inches.

Top right: Plate 40. No. 586, *Green River* (Gilcrease Institute, 0236.898), graphite and watercolor on wove, 9⁷/₈ by 13⁷/₈ inches.

Bottom: Plate 41. Thomas Moran, *Pass at Glencoe, Scotland* (1882, Gilcrease Institute, 0226.1636), watercolor, 20 by 30 inches.

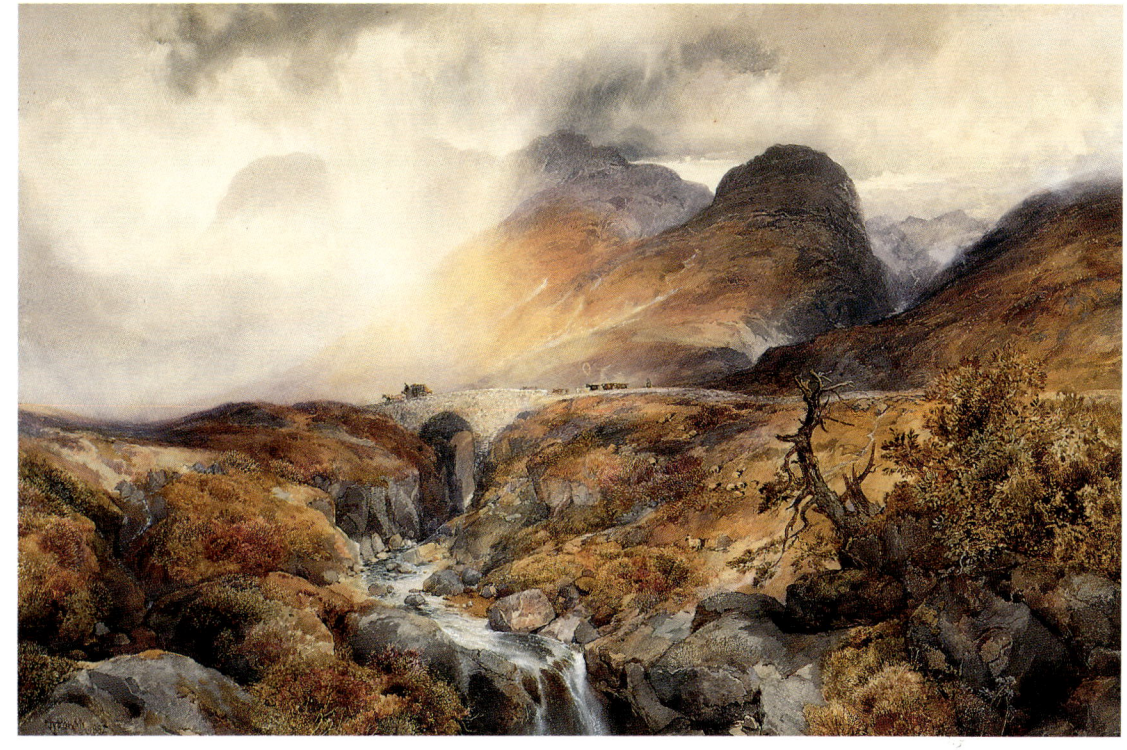

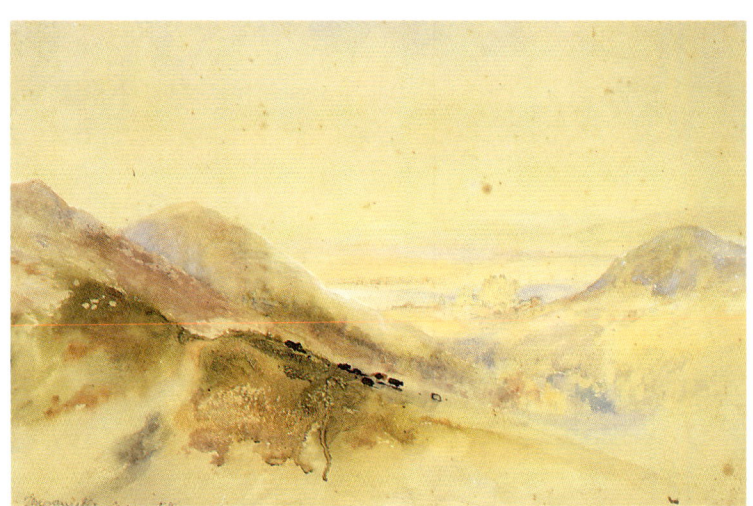

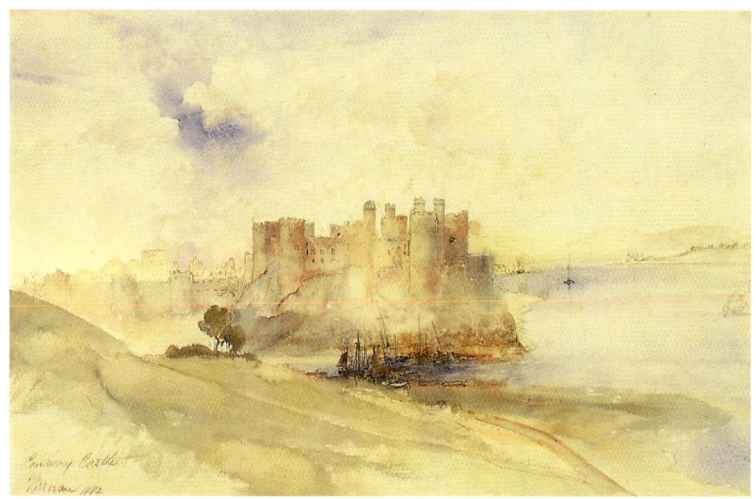

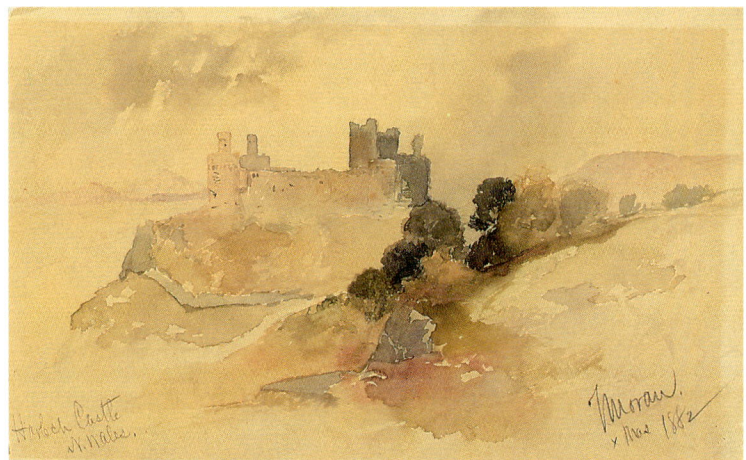

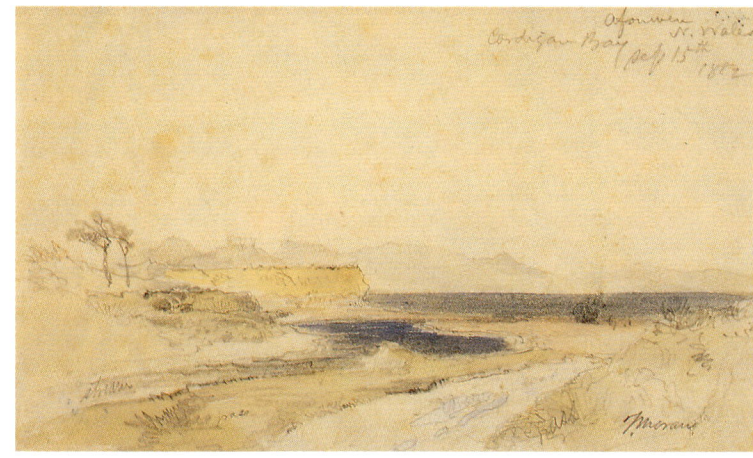

Top left: Plate 42. No. 604, *Conway, North Wales* (Gilcrease Institute, 0276.803), graphite and watercolor on wove, 12¹/8 by 17³/4 inches.

Top right: Plate 43. No. 606, *Conway Castle* (Gilcrease Institute, 0276.804), graphite and watercolor on wove, sketch 12 by 18 inches, mount 15³/4 by 22 inches.

Bottom left: Plate 44. No. 618, *Harlech Castle, North Wales* (Gilcrease Institute, 0276.938), graphite and watercolor on wove, 5³/4 by 9¹/4 inches.

Bottom right: Plate 45. No. 611, *Afon Wen, North Wales, Cardigan Bay* (Gilcrease Institute, 0276.805), graphite and watercolor on newsprint, 6¹/8 by 10 inches.

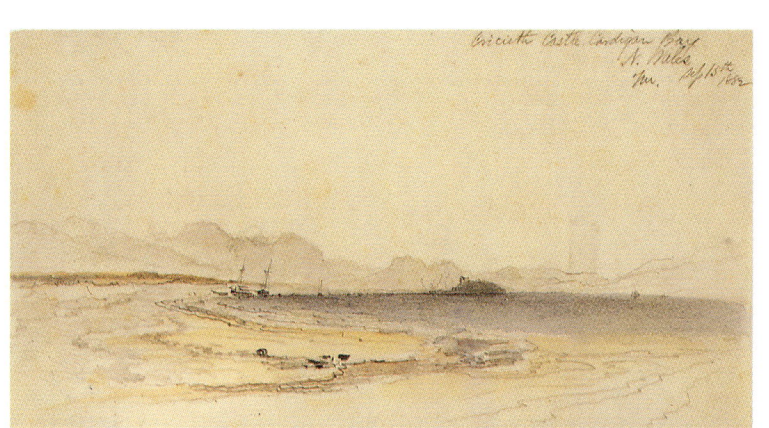

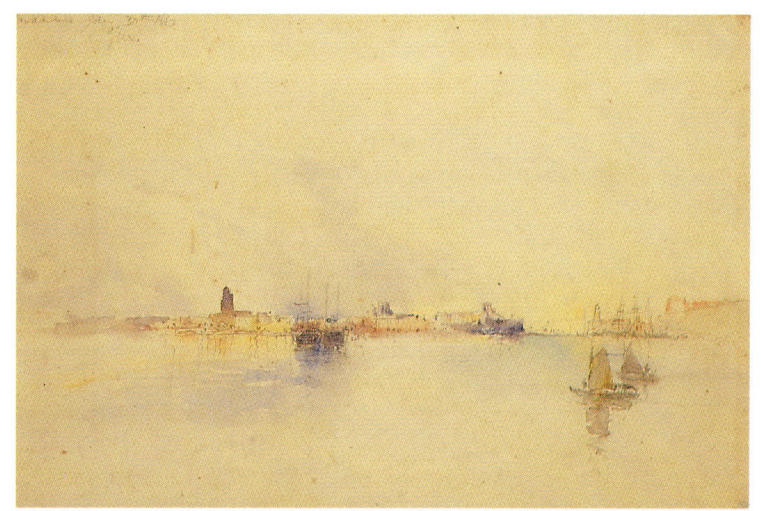

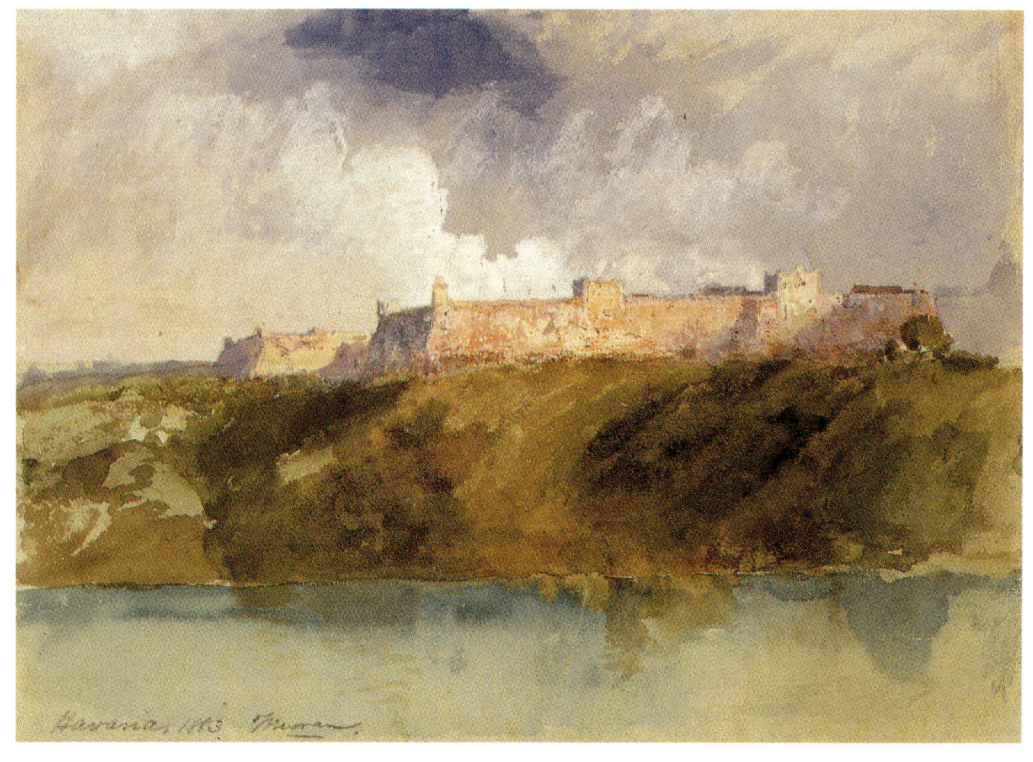

Top left: Plate 46. No. 612, *Criccieth Castle, Cardigan Bay, North Wales* (Gilcrease Institute, 0276.806), graphite and watercolor on newsprint, 5^1/$_2$ by 10 inches.

Top right: Plate 47. No. 627, *Havana* (Gilcrease Institute, 0296.825), graphite and watercolor on wove, sketch 9^1/$_2$ by 13^3/$_4$ inches, mount 15 by 18^3/$_4$ inches.

Bottom: Plate 48. No. 629, *Havana* (Gilcrease Institute, 0296.807), water-color and white gouache on blue laid, 8^5/$_8$ by 11^5/$_8$ inches.

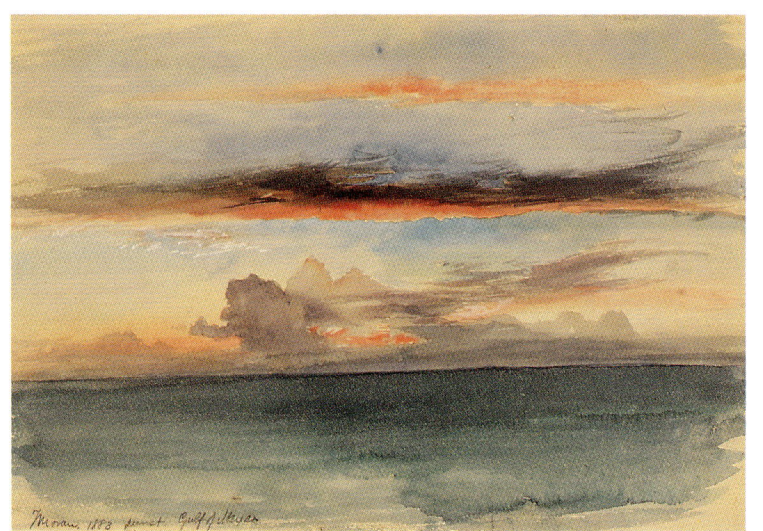

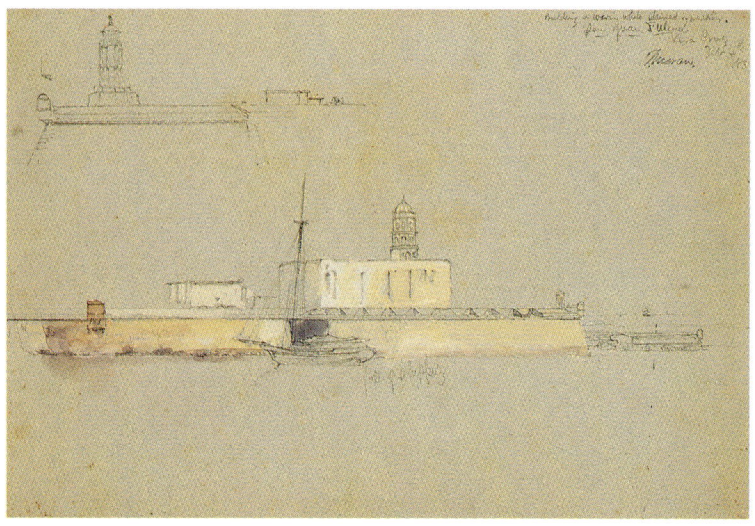

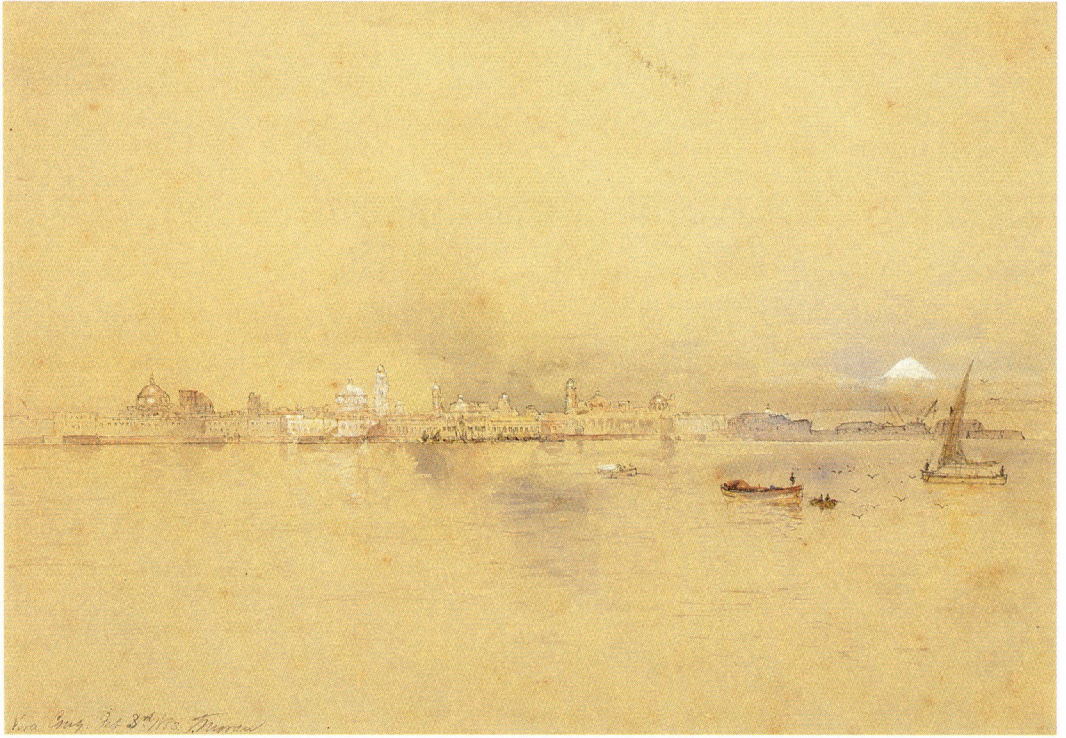

Top left: Plate 49. No. 630, *Sunset, Gulf of Mexico* (Gilcrease Institute, 0296.814), watercolor on wove, 10 by 14¹/₄ inches.

Top right: Plate 50. No. 632, *San Juan d'Ulloa, Vera Cruz* (Gilcrease Institute, 0246.826), graphite, watercolor, white and yellow gouache on blue wove, 10 by 14¹/₄ inches.

Bottom: Plate 51. No. 631, *Vera Cruz* (Gilcrease Institute, 0246.815), graphite, watercolor, and white gouache on wove, sketch 10 by 14¹/₄ inches, mount 14 by 19¹/₂ inches.

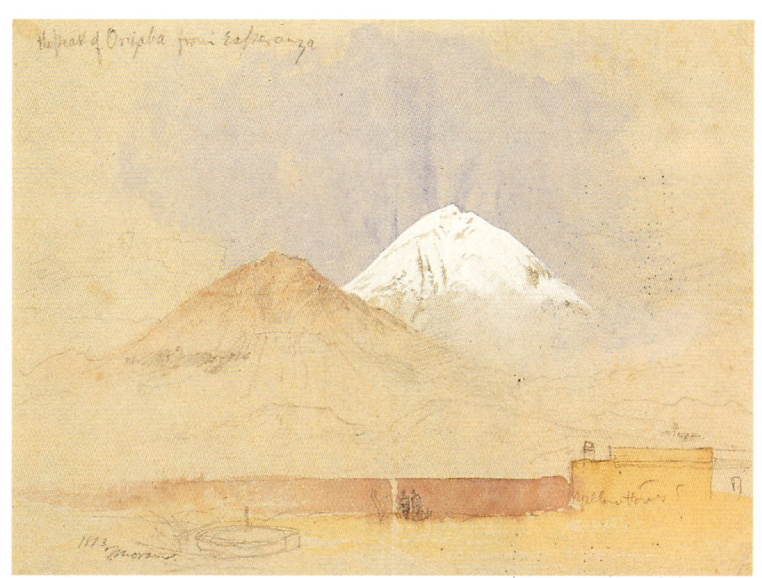

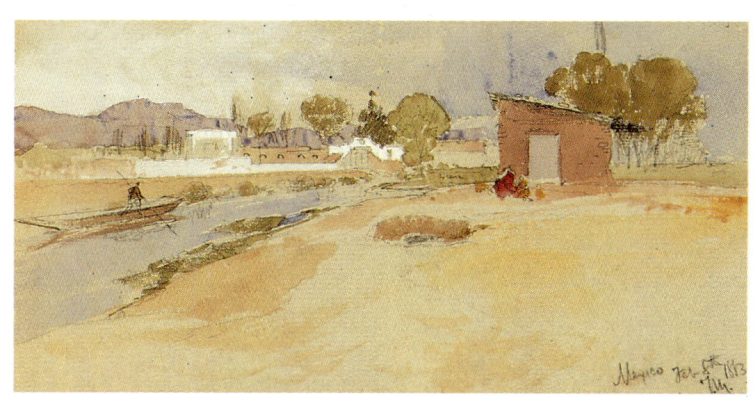

Top left: Plate 52. No. 644, *The Peak of Orizaba from Esperanza* (Gilcrease Institute, 0246.827), graphite, watercolor, and white gouache on blue laid, sketch 8⁵/₈ by 11⁵/₈ inches, mount 9¹/₄ by 12¹/₄ inches.

Top right: Plate 53. No. 649, *Mexico* (Gilcrease Institute, 0246.813), graphite, watercolor, and white gouache on blue laid, 6¹/₈ by 11⁵/₈ inches, mount 16⁵/₈ by 11⁵/₈ inches.

Bottom: Plate 54. No. 653, *Maravatio* (Gilcrease Institute, 0246.809), graphite and watercolor on wove, 10 by 14¹/₄ inches.

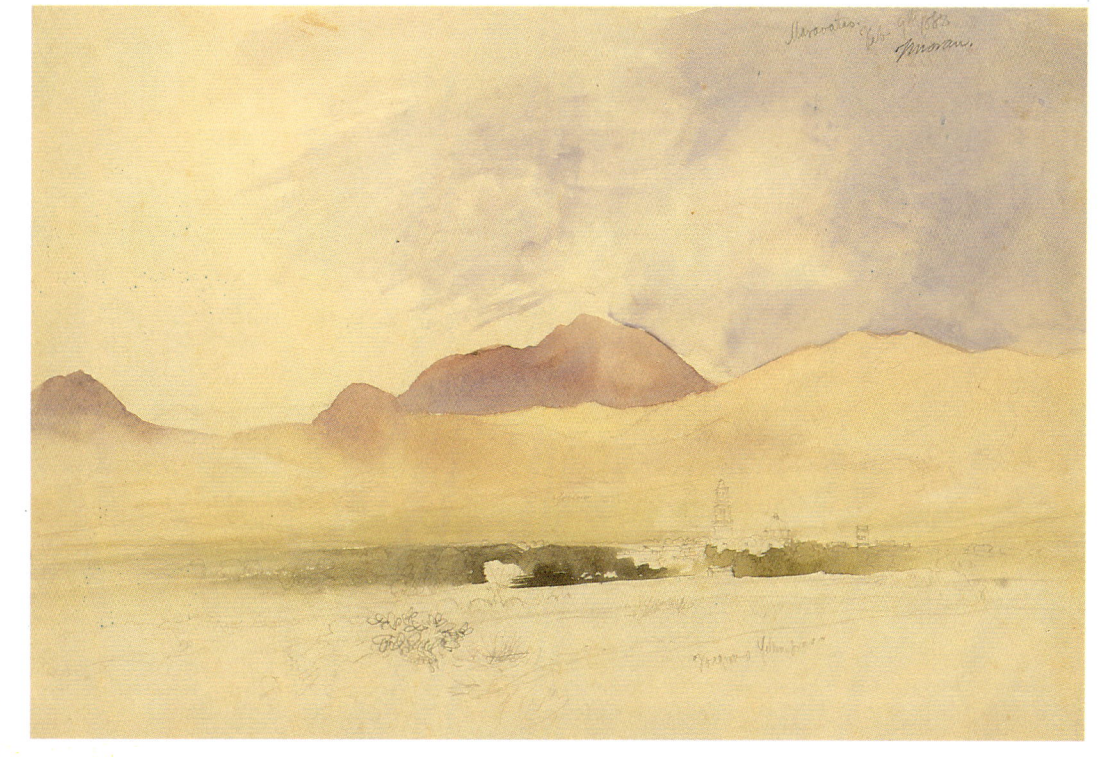

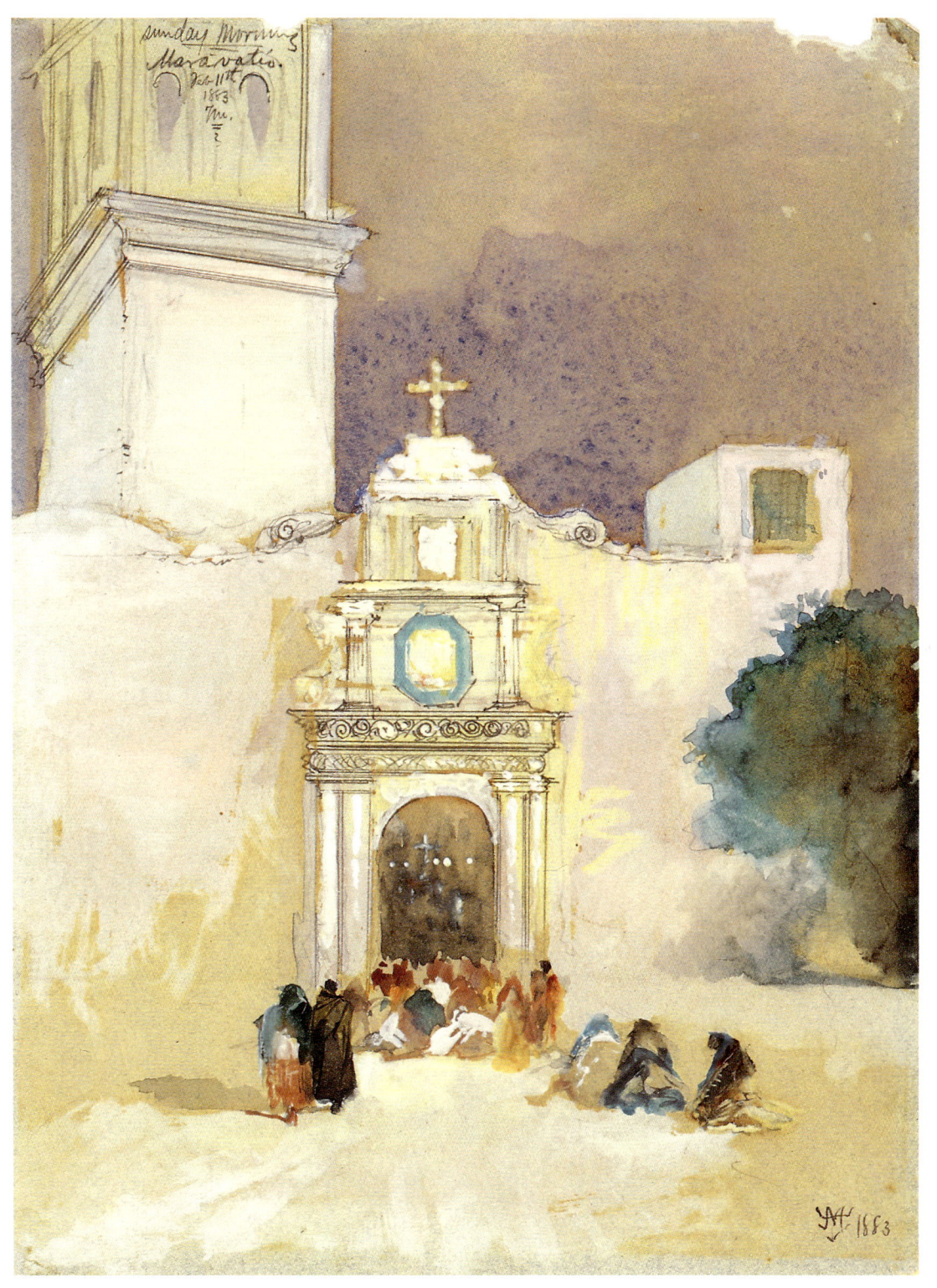

Plate 55. No. 654, *Sunday Morning, Maravatio* (Gilcrease Institute, 0246. 812), graphite, watercolor, and white gouache on blue wove, 10 by 7 3/8 inches.

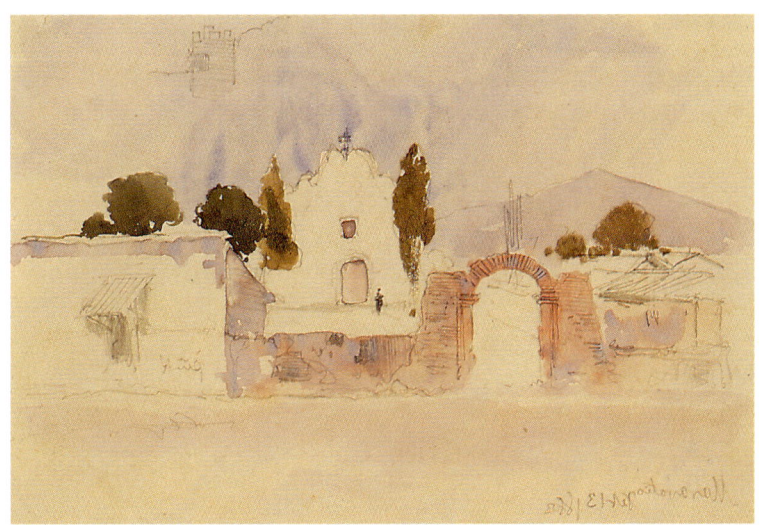

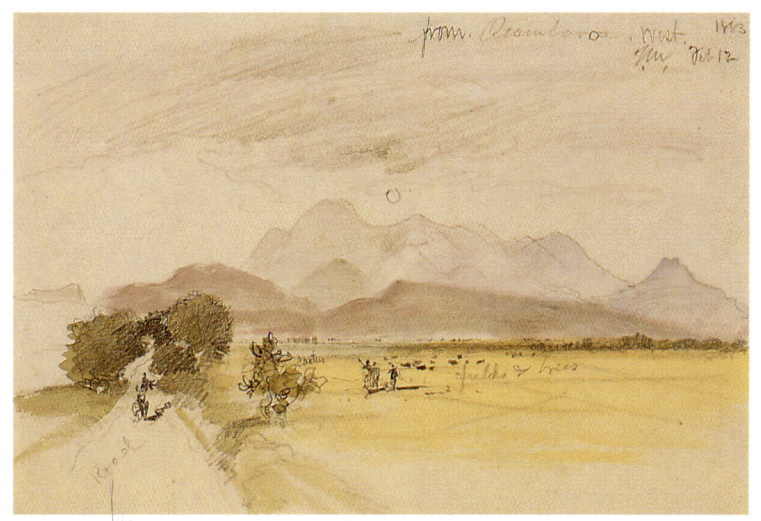

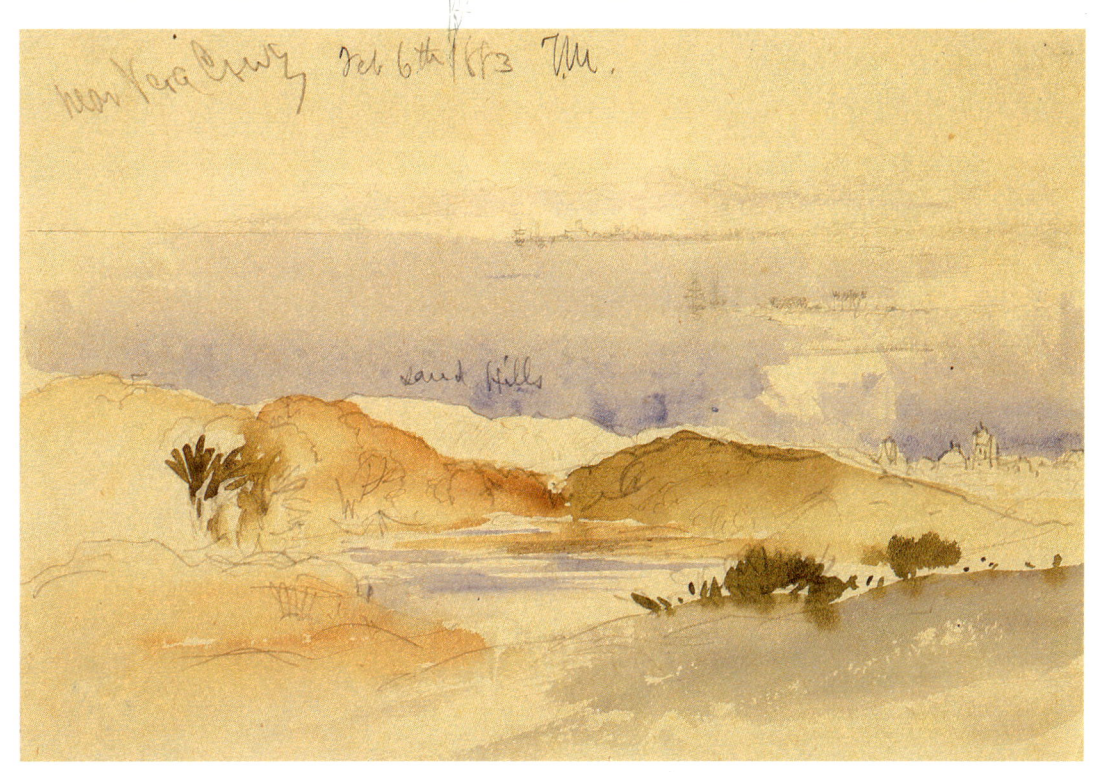

Top left: Plate 56. No. 663, *Maravatio* (Gilcrease Institute, 0246.811), graphite and watercolor on newsprint, 5⁷/₈ by 8³/₈ inches.

Top right: Plate 57. No. 655, *From Acambaro, West* (Gilcrease Institute, 0246.821), graphite and watercolor on newsprint, 5³/₈ by 8⁷/₈ inches.

Bottom: Plate 58. No. 642, *Near Vera Cruz* (Gilcrease Institute, 0246.810), graphite and watercolor on newsprint, 5⁷/₈ by 8³/₈ inches.

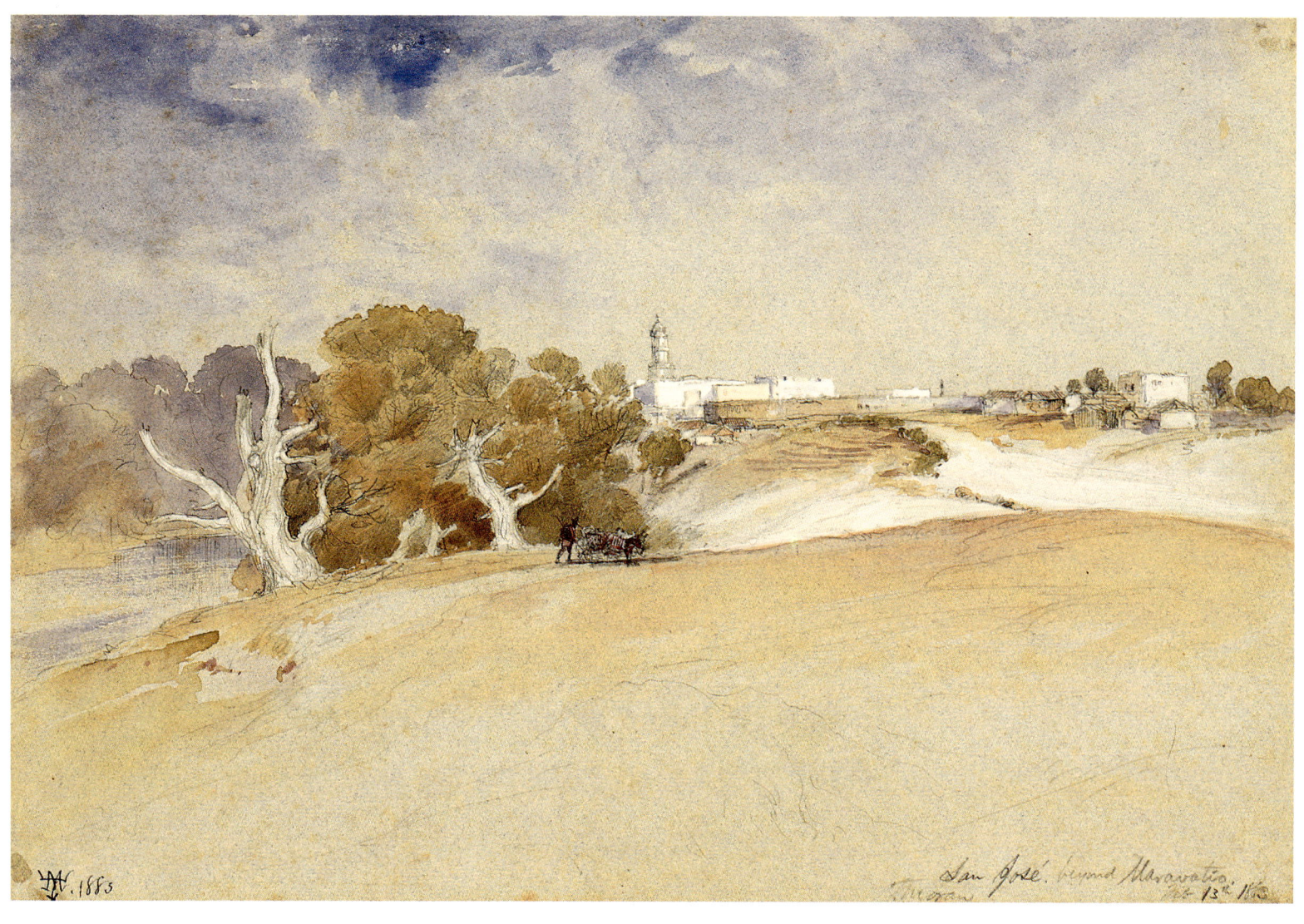

Plate 59. No. 665, *San José, beyond Maravatio* (Gilcrease Institute, 0246. 822), graphite, watercolor, and white gouache on blue wove, sketch 10 by 14¹/₄ inches, mount 15 by 19¹/₈ inches.

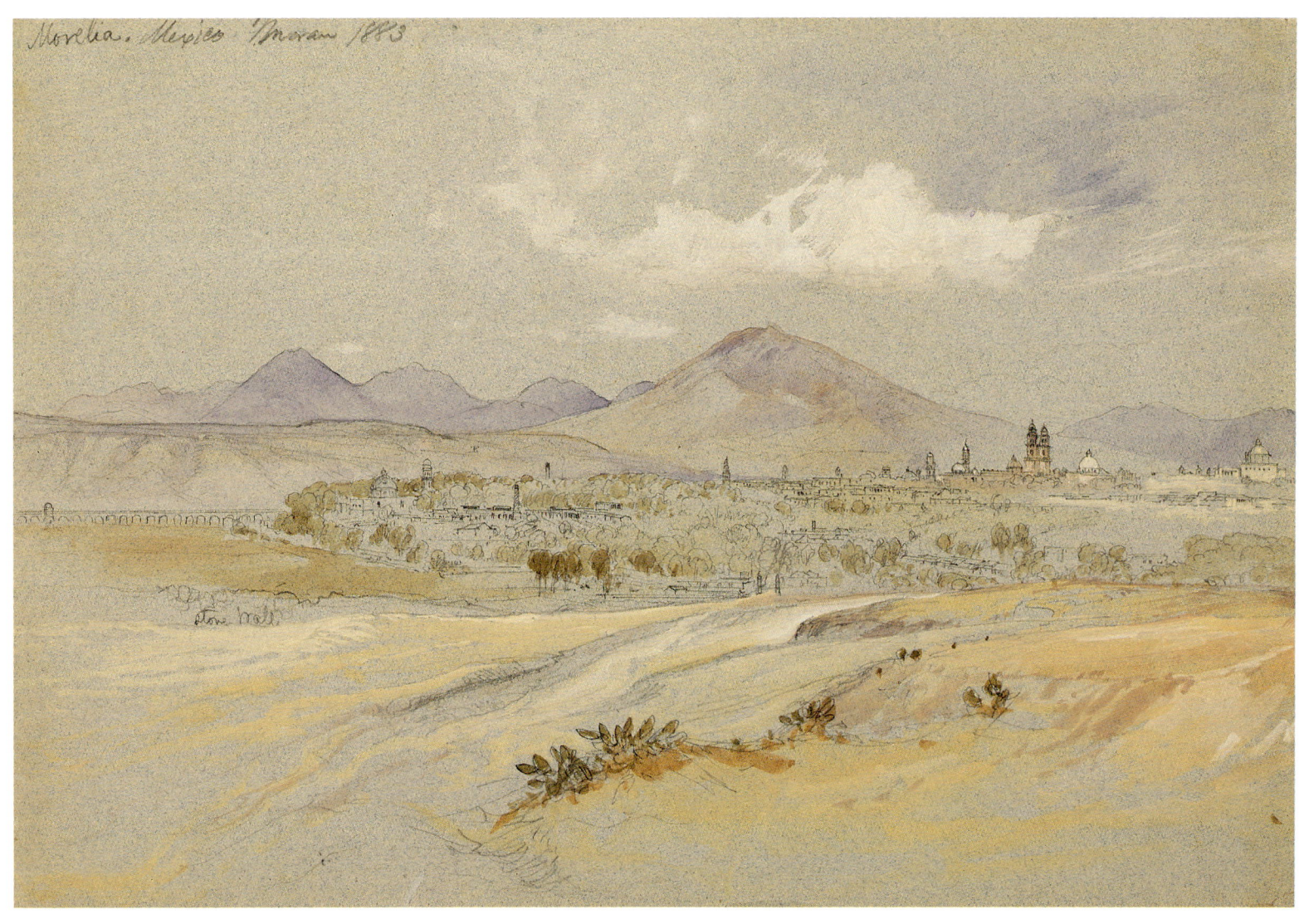

Plate 60. No. 667, *Morelia, Mexico*
(Gilcrease Institute, 0246.824), graphite,
watercolor, and white gouache on blue
wove, 10 by 14^1/$_4$ inches.

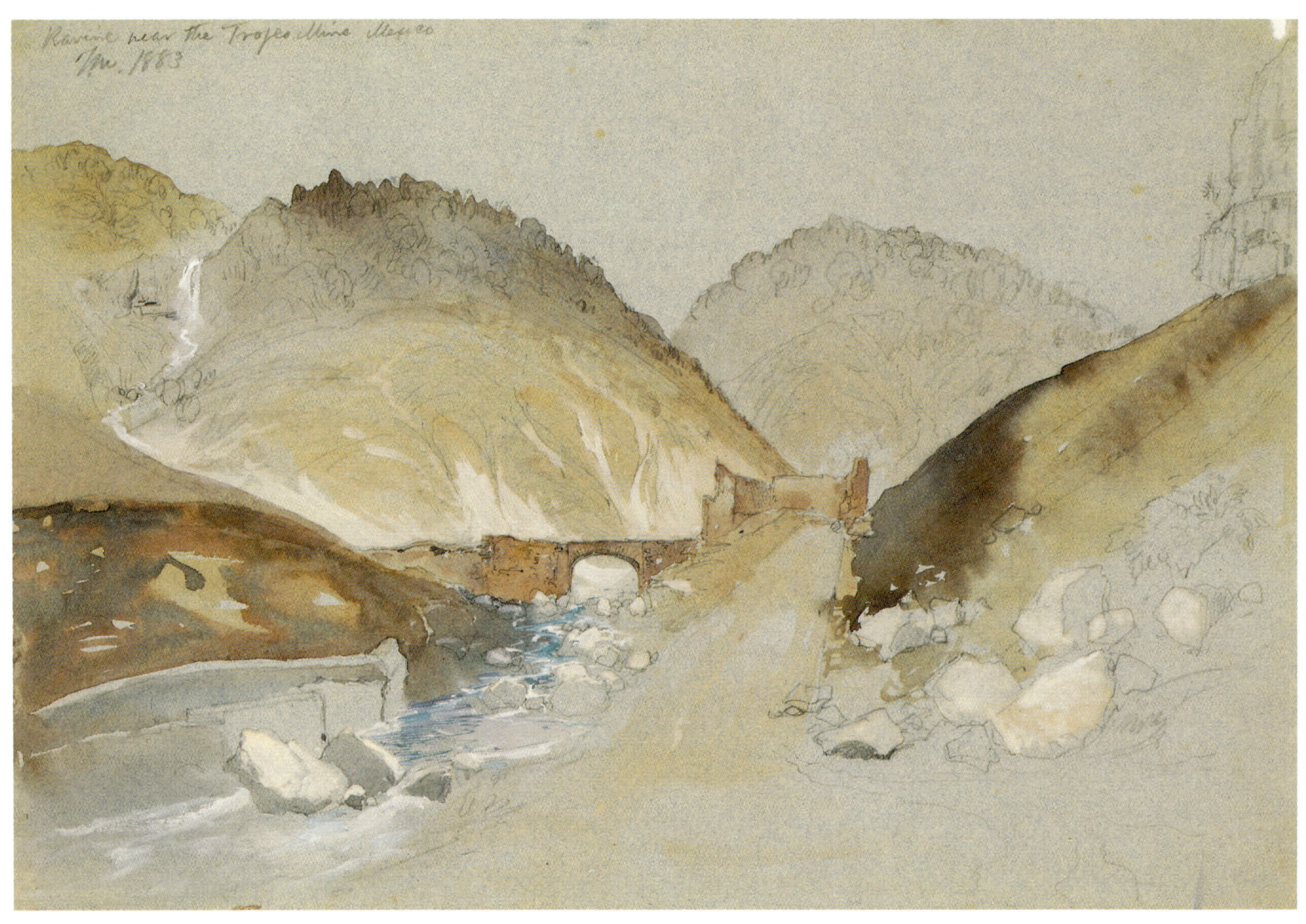

Ravine near the Trojes Mine Mexico
Jan. 1883

Plate 61. No. 674, *Ravine near the Trojes Mine, Mexico* (Gilcrease Institute, 0246.823), graphite, watercolor, and white gouache on blue wove, 10 by 14 1/4 inches.

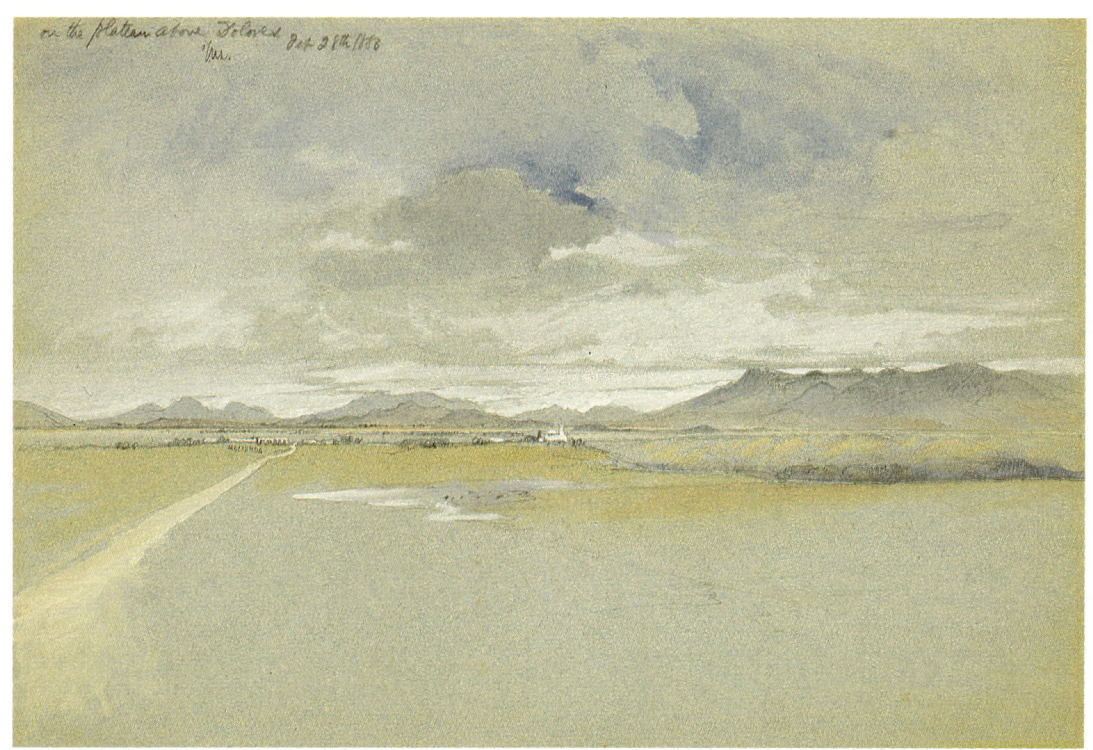

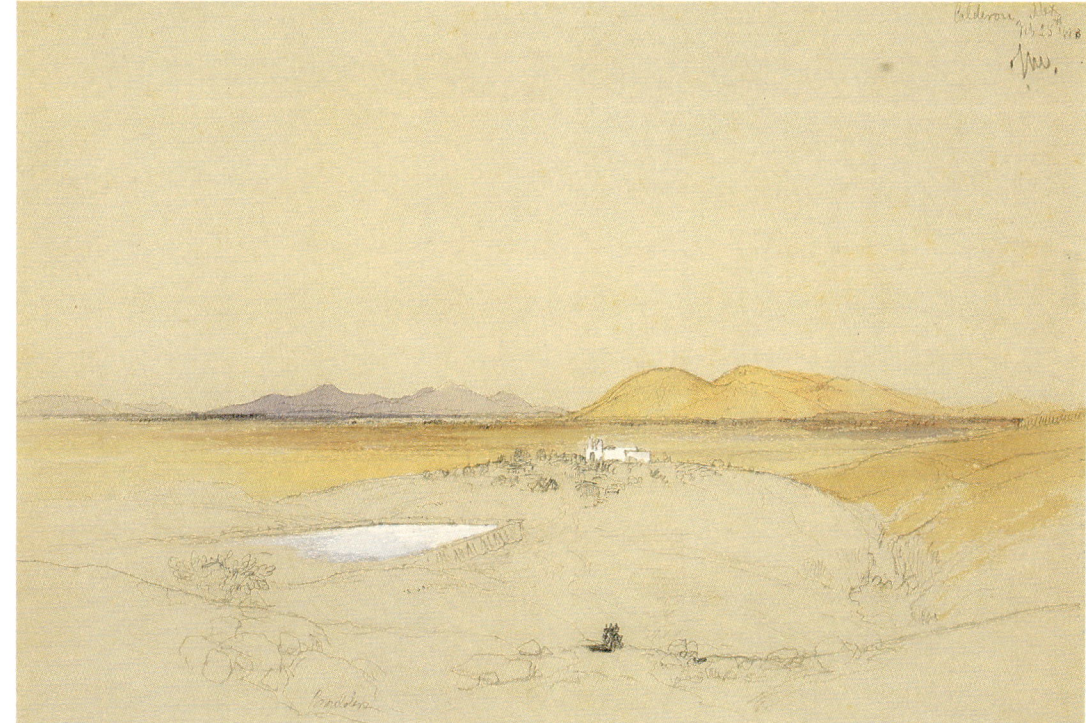

Top: Plate 62. No. 683, *On the Plateau above Dolores* (Gilcrease Institute, 0246.816), graphite, watercolor, and white gouache on blue wove, 10 by 14¹/₄ inches.

Bottom: Plate 63. No. 680, *Calderon, Mexico* (Gilcrease Institute, 0246.808), graphite, watercolor, and white gouache on wove, 10 by 14¹/₄ inches.

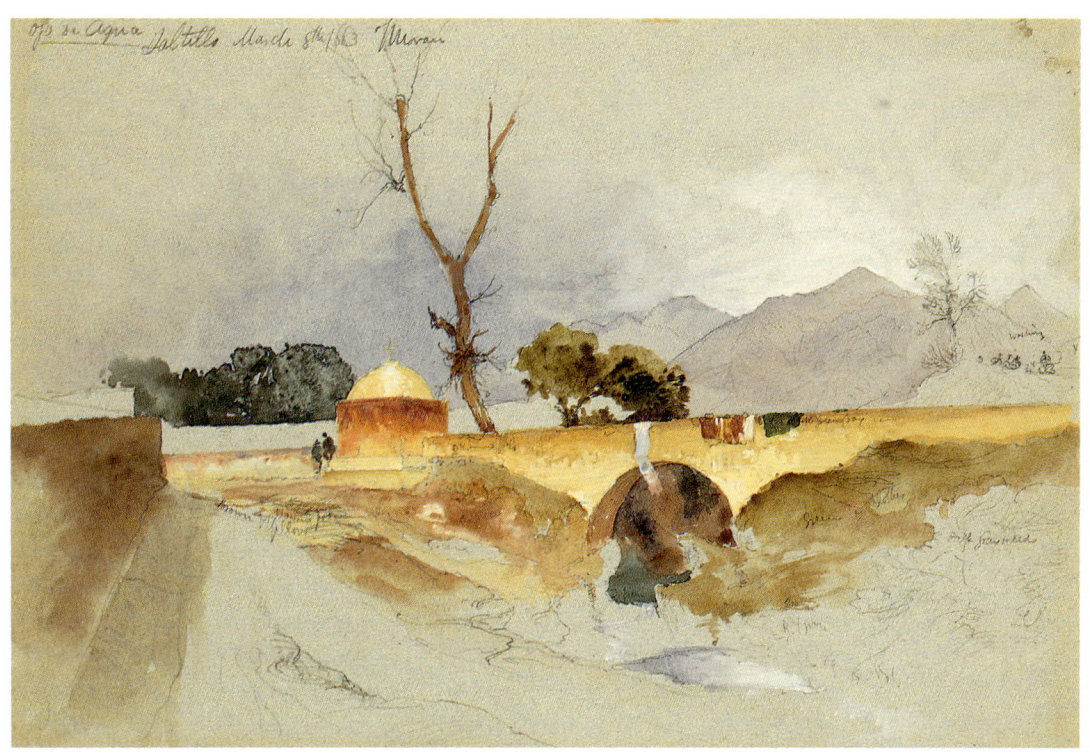

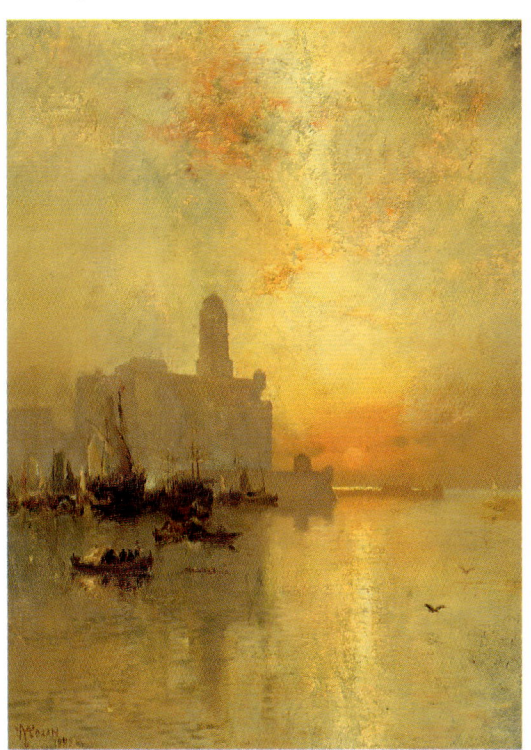

Top: Plate 64. No. 691, *Ojo de Agua, Saltillo* (Gilcrease Institute, 0246.818), graphite, watercolor, and white gouache on blue wove, 10 by 14¹/₄ inches.

Bottom: Plate 66. Thomas Moran, *Vera Cruz* (1885, Gilcrease Institute, 0126.1109), oil on canvas, 20¹/₈ by 14¹/₈ inches.

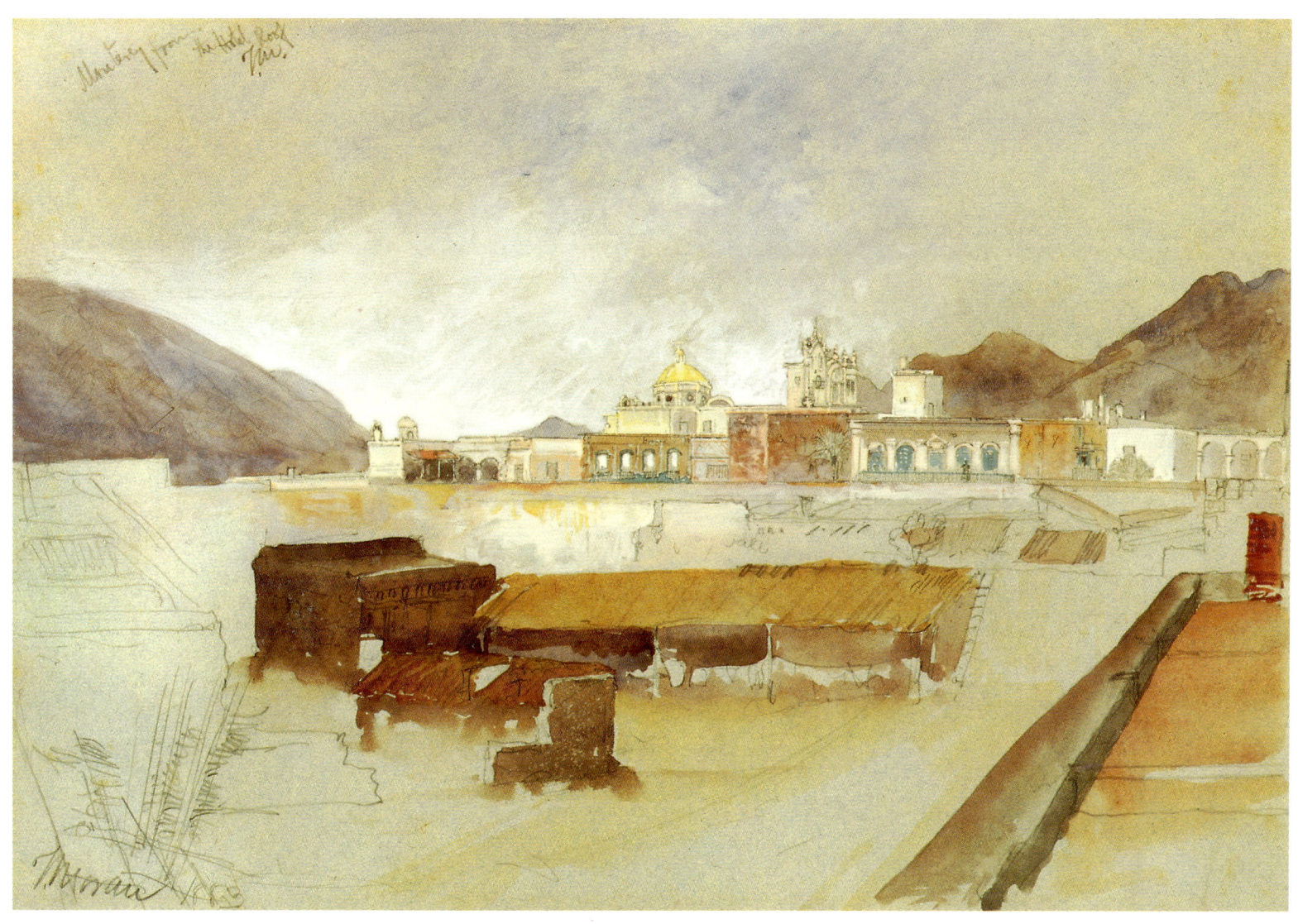

Plate 65. No. 699, *Monterrey, from the Hotel Roof* (Gilcrease Institute, 0246. 819), graphite, watercolor, and white gouache on blue wove, 10 by 14¹/₂ inches.

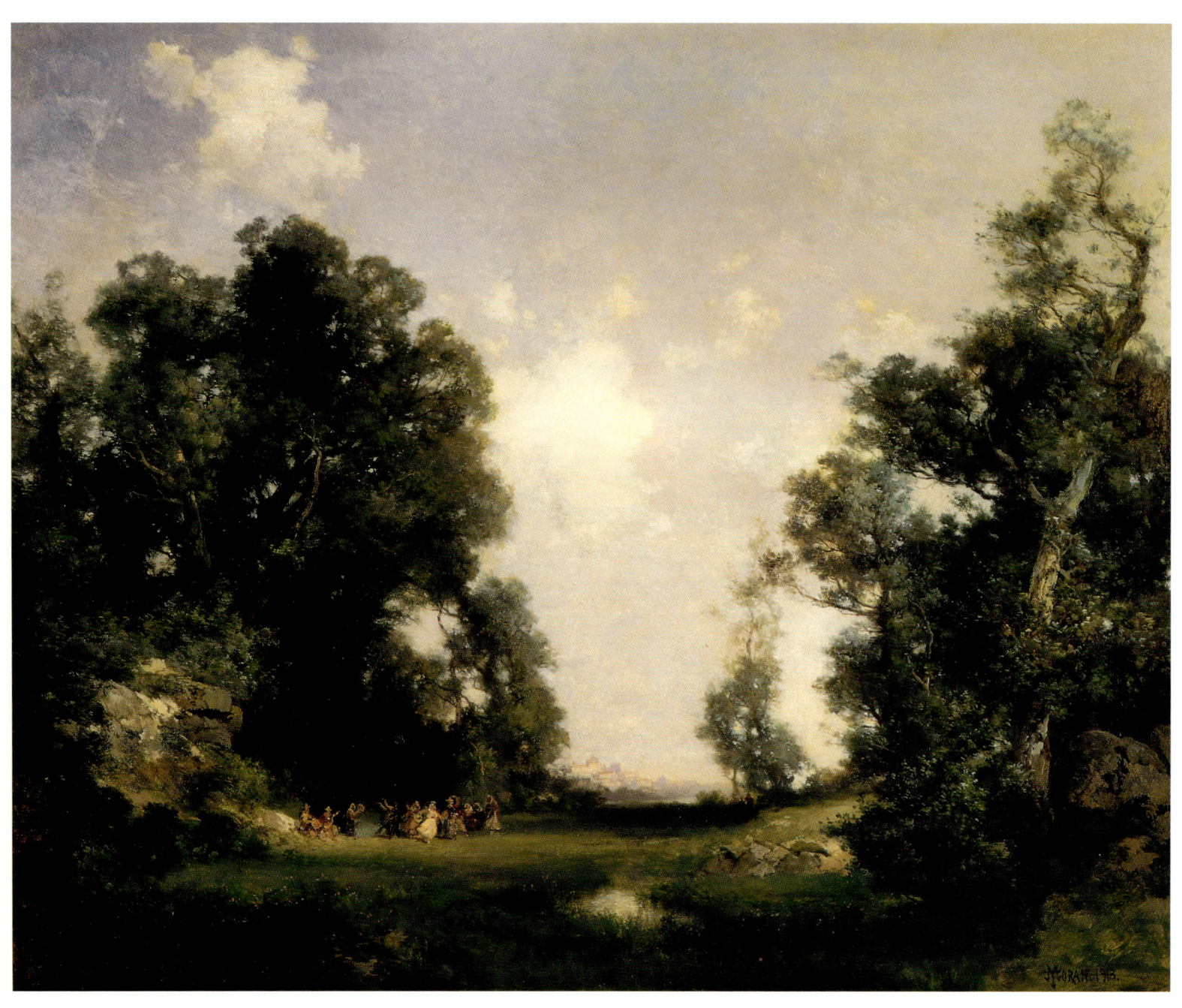

Plate 67. Thomas Moran, *Fiesta at Cuernavaca* (1913, Gilcrease Institute, 0127.1110), oil on canvas, 25 by 30 inches.

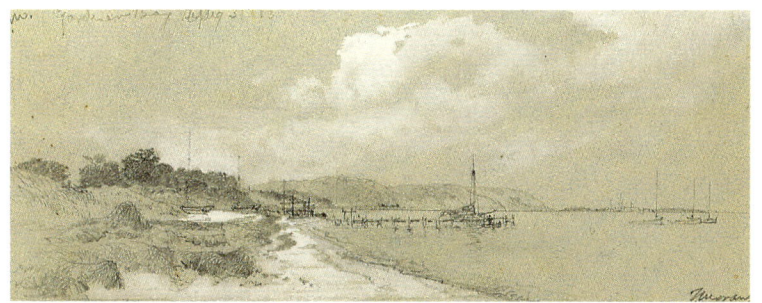

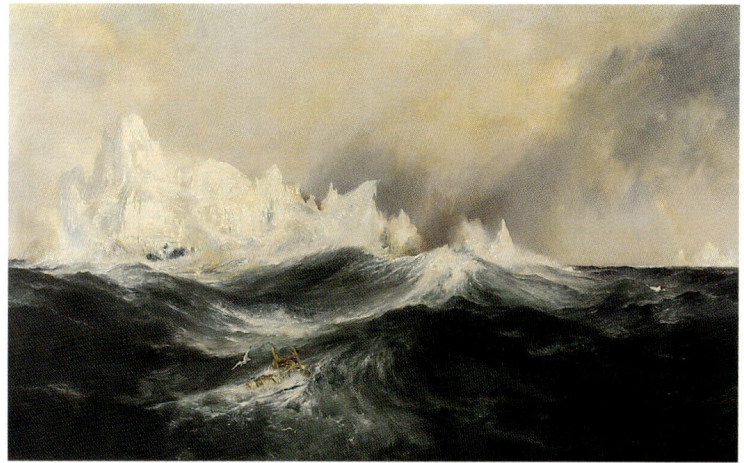

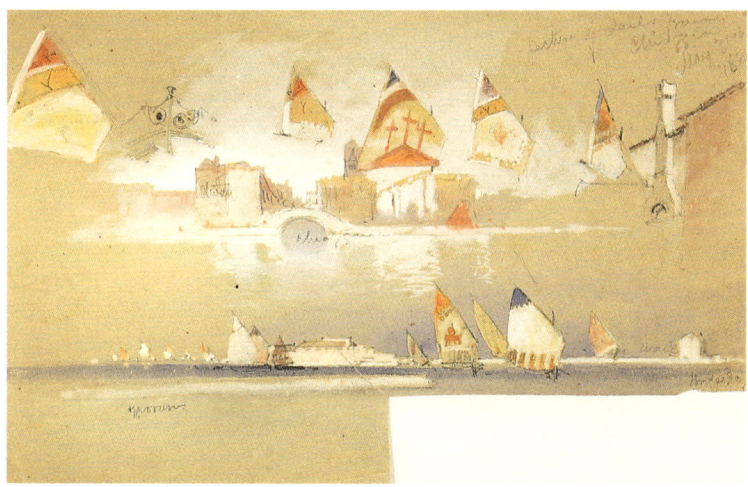

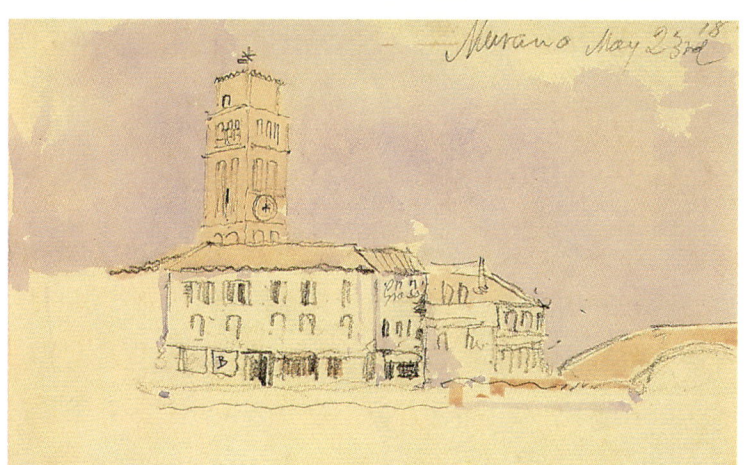

Top left: Plate 68. No. 704, *Gardiner Bay* (Gilcrease Institute, 0226.936), graphite and white gouache on blue wove, 4 by 10 inches.

Top right: Plate 69. Thomas Moran, *Spectres from the North* (1891, Gilcrease Institute, 0126.2340), oil on canvas, 74$\frac{1}{2}$ by 118$\frac{1}{4}$ inches.

Bottom left: Plate 70. No. 793, *Picture of Sails from Chioggia* (Gilcrease Institute, 0276.832), graphite, watercolor, and white gouache on green wove, 8$\frac{3}{8}$ by 12$\frac{3}{4}$ inches.

Bottom right: Plate 71. No. 777 *Murano* (Gilcrease Institute, 0276.766), graphite and watercolor on wove, 4$\frac{3}{8}$ by 6$\frac{7}{8}$ inches.

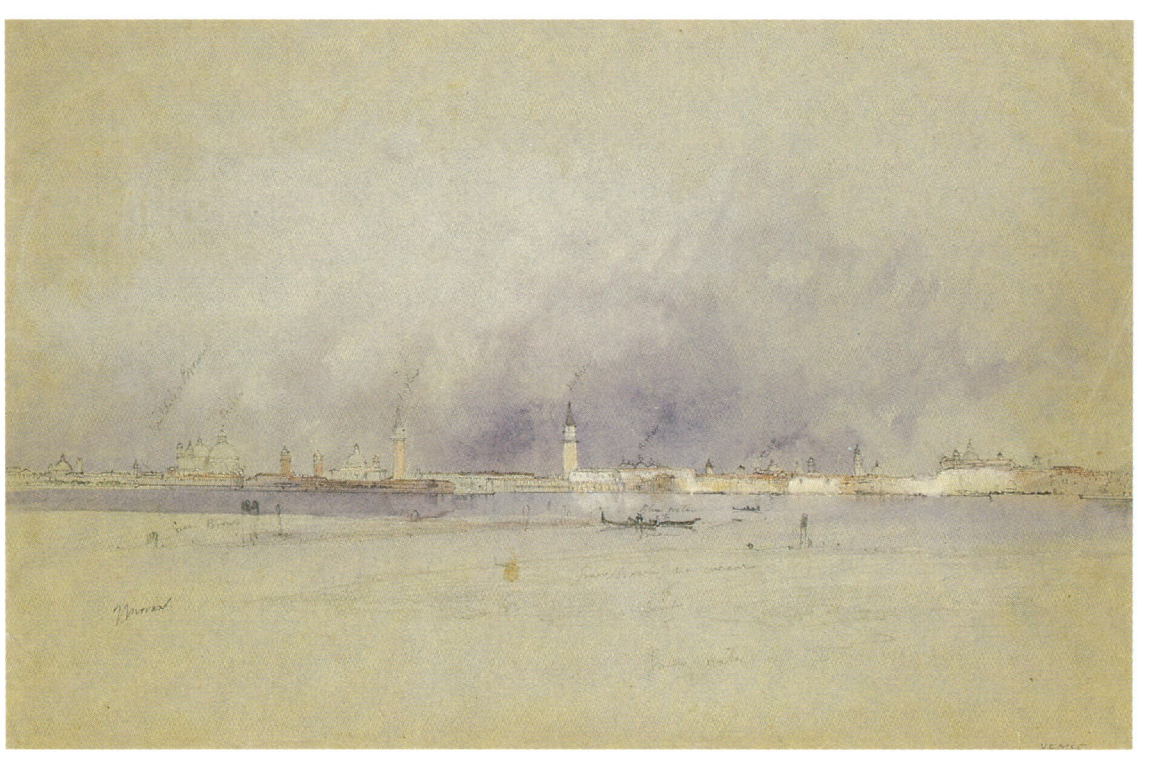

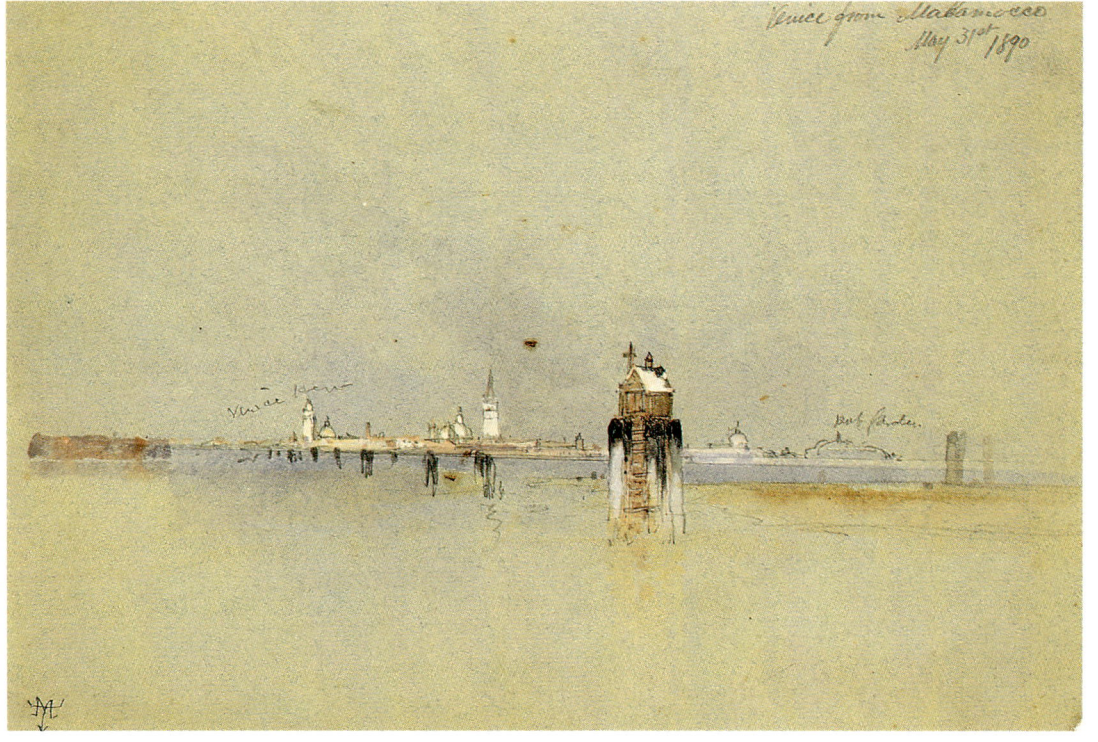

Top: Plate 72. No. 790, *Venice* (Gilcrease Institute, 0276.765), graphite, watercolor, and white gouache on green wove, 12³/₄ by 19¹/₂ inches.

Bottom: Plate 73. No. 791, *Venice from Malamocco* (Gilcrease Institute, 0276. 833), graphite and watercolor on green wove, 8³/₄ by 12³/₄ inches.

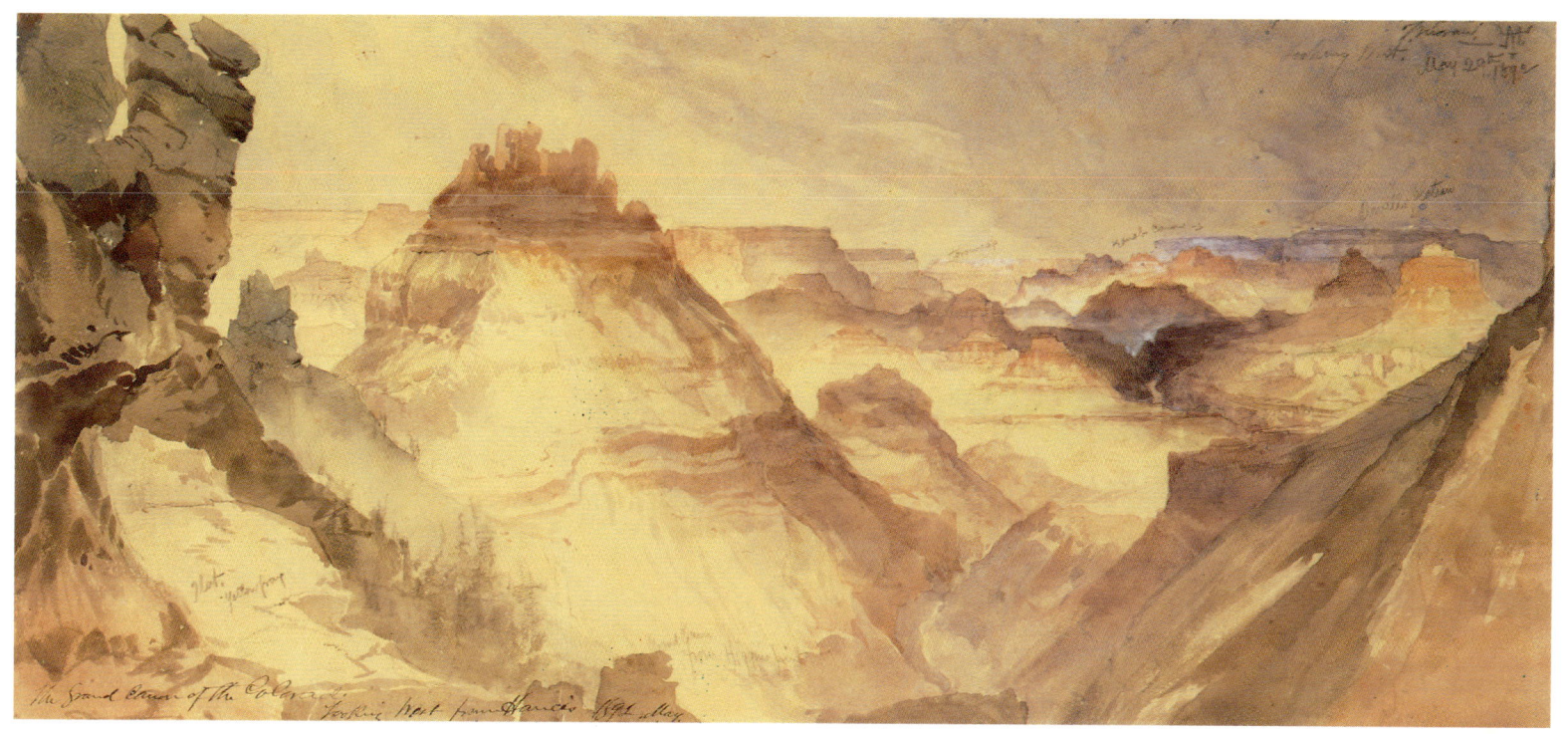

Plate 74. No. 800, *The Grand Canyon of the Colorado* (Gilcrease Institute, 0236.931), graphite and watercolor on wove, sketch $11^1/_2$ by $24^1/_2$ inches, mount $15^3/_4$ by $25^1/_4$ inches.

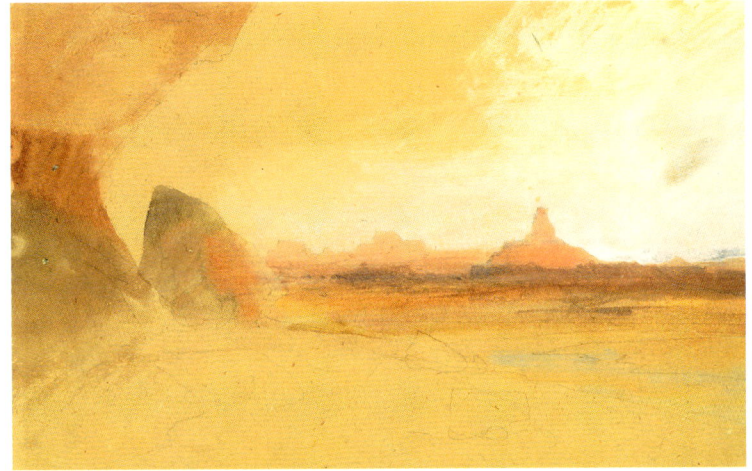

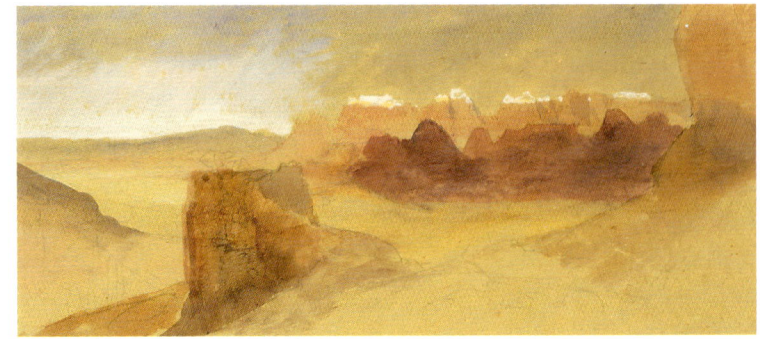

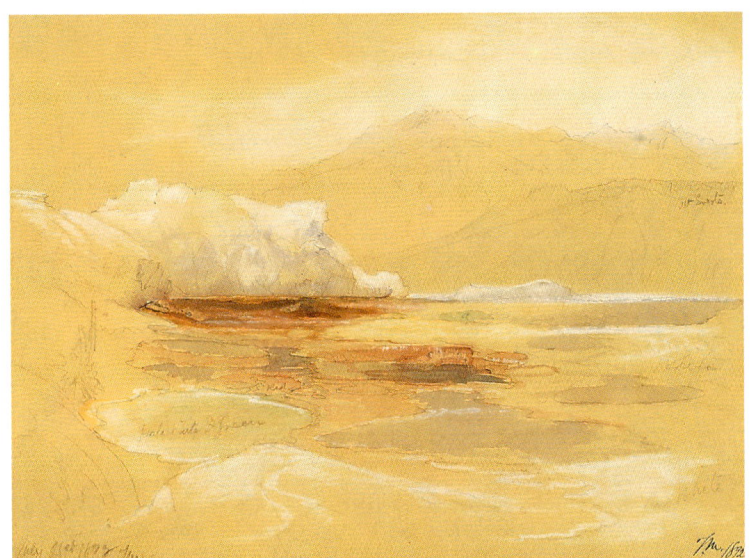

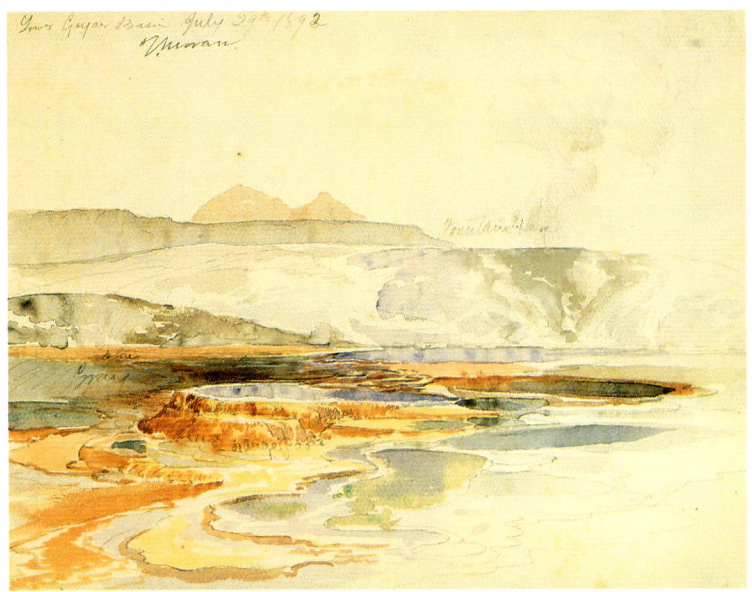

Top left: Plate 75. No. 836, *Index Peak* (Gilcrease Institute, 0236.850), graphite, watercolor, and white gouache on wove, 7^1/$_8$ by 11^1/$_8$ inches.

Top right: Plate 76. No. 837, *Index Peak* (Gilcrease Institute, 0236.849), graphite, watercolor, and white gouache on wove, 5^1/$_8$ by 11^1/$_4$ inches.

Bottom left: Plate 77. No. 845, *Upper Basins* (Gilcrease Institute, 0236.831), graphite, watercolor, and white chalk on wove, sketch 9^1/$_2$ by 12^5/$_8$ inches, mount 11 by 14^1/$_2$ inches.

Bottom right: Plate 78. No. 877, *Lower Geyser Basin* (Gilcrease Institute, 0236.829), graphite and watercolor on laid, sketch 7^7/$_8$ by 9^7/$_8$ inches, mount 9^5/$_8$ by 11^3/$_4$ inches.

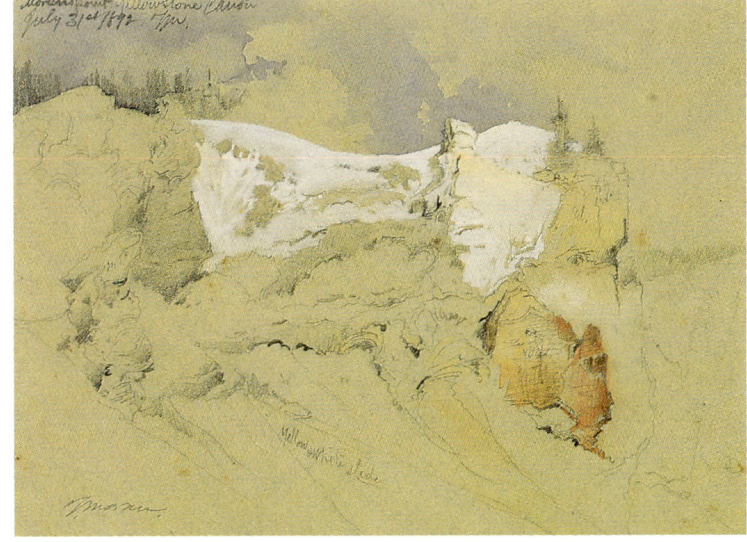

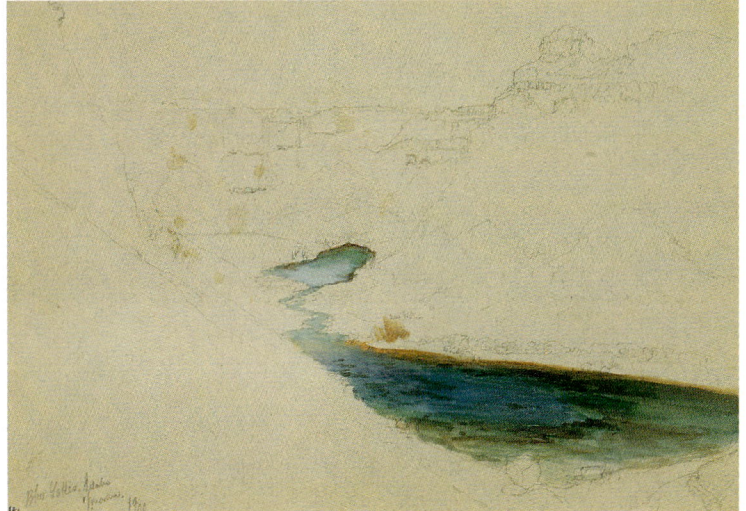

Top: Plate 79. No. 898, *Moran Point, Yellowstone Canyon* (Gilcrease Institute, 0236.830), graphite, watercolor, and white gouache on green wove, sketch 9$^1/_2$ by 12$^1/_2$ inches, mount 10$^1/_2$ by 13 inches.

Bottom: Plate 80. No. 928. *Blue Lakes, Idaho* (Gilcrease Institute, 0237.1578), graphite and watercolor on blue wove, 10$^3/_4$ by 15 inches.

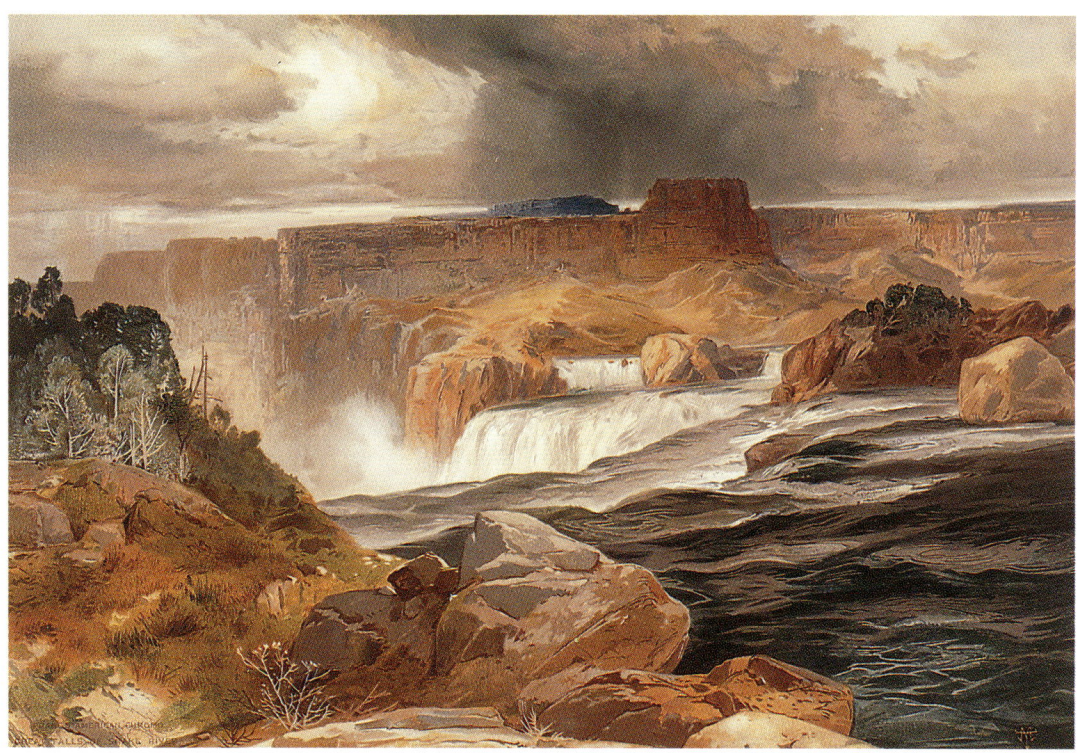

Top: Plate 81. Louis Prang after Thomas Moran, *The Great Falls of Snake River, Idaho* Territory (1876, Gilcrease Institute, 2426.47.13), chromolithograph, 19 by 27 ½ inches.

Bottom: Plate 82. Thomas Moran, *Shoshone Falls on the Snake River* (1900, Gilcrease Institute, 0126.2339), oil on canvas, 71 by 132 inches.

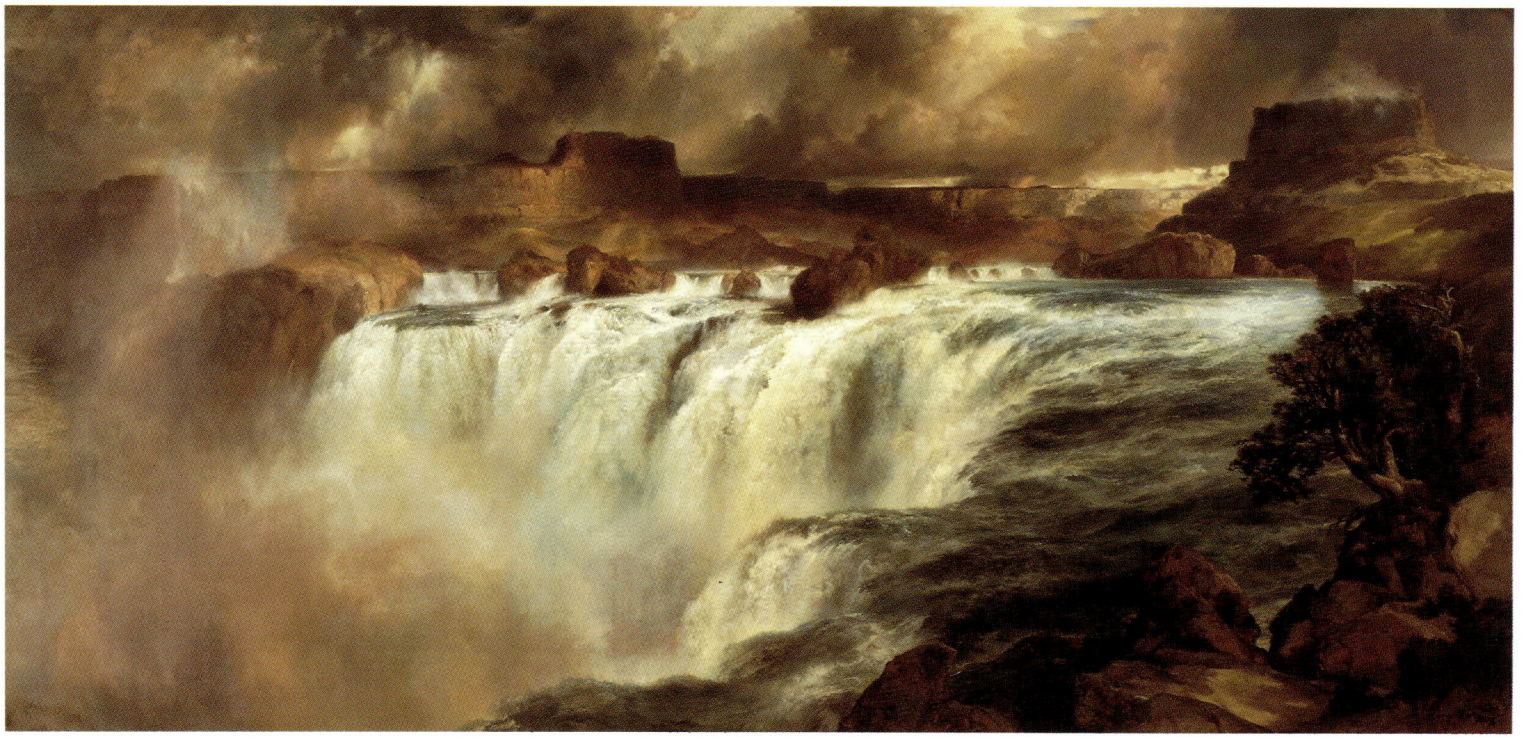

Checklist of Field Sketches of Thomas Moran

Anne Morand and Norma Ewing

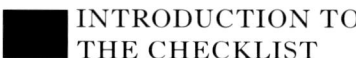 INTRODUCTION TO
THE CHECKLIST

This checklist is a complete inventory of Thomas Moran's field sketches owned by the Thomas Gilcrease Institute of American History and Art. To this list have been added sketches in several public collections. The sketches chronicle Moran's work outdoors between 1856 and 1923. The list is arranged chronologically, using Moran's inscriptive dates, stylistic analysis, and research. It constitutes an in-depth examination of Thomas Moran's travels and offers a chance to see his technical development as a documentary artist.

Included are sketches from the following collections (the number of sketches from each collection is given in parentheses): The Thomas Gilcrease Institute of American History and Art, Tulsa (684); East Hampton Library, East Hampton, New York (144); Cooper-Hewitt Museum, the Smithsonian Institution's National Museum of Design, New York (62); Jefferson National Ex-

pansion Memorial, St. Louis (57); National Museum of American Art, Smithsonian Institution, Washington, D.C. (55); Museum of Fine Arts, Boston (22); Yellowstone National Park, Wyoming (22); Yosemite National Park, California (17); Stark Museum of Art, Orange, Texas (4); Grand Tetons National Park, Wyoming (3); Corcoran Gallery of Art, Washington, D.C. (2); Cleveland Museum of Art (2); Guild Hall, East Hampton, New York (1); Amon Carter Museum of Art, Fort Worth, Texas (1); Parrish Art Museum, Southampton, New York (1); Washington County Museum of Fine Arts, Hagerstown, Maryland (1); Addison Gallery of American Art, Andover, Massachusetts (1); and Austin Arts Center, Trinity College, Hartford (1). Omission from this list does not imply doubt about attribution.

PROVENANCE

THOMAS MORAN maintained his studio collection, which included most of his field sketches, until his death. There are two notable exceptions. In 1917 he made a gift to the Cooper Union (now the Cooper-Hewitt Museum). The gift was acknowledged in the minutes of a reception given for the Council of the Cooper-Union to showcase recent acquisitions, on April 26, 1917, at the home of the Misses Hewitt (Gilcrease Moran Archives, 5127.254). According to the minutes, among the gifts was "a series of sketches selected personally by the dean of American painters, Thomas Moran, from his own life work, intended to express it fully for the benefit of our students and such others as care to familiarize themselves with the methods of perhaps the only American painter eulogized by John Ruskin."

Probably about the same time, Moran gave William H. Holmes, who had been working to develop the collections of the National Gallery, a selection of sketches from his trip to Yellowstone in 1892. A handwritten list made by Ruth Bedford Moran, titled "Gave to Dr. Holmes for Museum Yellowstone Studies," is stapled to the inside cover of Moran's sketch ledger of 1916 (described below). The sketches now reside at the National Museum of American Art, Washington, D.C.

At Moran's death in 1926, the remaining studio collection became the property of his younger daughter, Ruth. With the exception of gifts of sketches to the library in East Hampton, New York, and to the National Park Service, she kept most of the material intact. When she died in 1948, Thomas Gilcrease purchased most of her estate through M. Knoedler & Co.

Ruth Moran had hoped that her gifts would form the basis of special collections commemorating her father's accomplishments and role in the exploration of the West. The Thomas Moran Biographical Art Collection at East Hampton Library was accordingly created; it primarily holds materials associated with Moran's life in East Hampton, such as family and business papers, and sketches made on Long Island. Although the intention of the National Park Service was good, and Ruth Moran worked for the rest of her life to bring about the creation of a Moran National Parks collection, no such collection was ever established. The original gift was housed for some time at Yosemite National Park, where Ruth Moran hoped a museum would be dedicated to her father's work. However, the collection was eventually divided among several park sites. Jefferson National Expansion Memorial in St. Louis maintains much of the work devoted to the Grand Canyon. Yosemite and Grand Tetons National Parks house sketches specific to their location.

The provenances of the sketches are abbreviated as follows in the checklist:

EH   The artist; to Ruth Bedford Moran, East Hampton, N.Y., 1926; to East Hampton Library Thomas Moran Biographical Art Collection 1948.

GH   The artist; to Ruth Bedford Moran, East Hampton, N.Y., 1926; to Guild Hall, East Hampton, N.Y.

GP   The artist; to Ruth Bedford Moran, East Hampton, N.Y., 1926; Gift of George D. Pratt, Mrs. Henry Strong, Mr. John D. Rockefeller, Jr., Col. Herbert J. Slocum to Yellowstone National Park.

GT   The artist; to Ruth Bedford Moran, East Hampton, N.Y., 1926; to the National Park Service, Yosemite National Park; to Grand Tetons National Park.

JNEM   The artist; to Ruth Bedford Moran, East Hampton, N.Y., 1926; to the National Park Service, Yosemite National Park; to the Jefferson National Expansion Memorial, St. Louis, Mo.

MK   The artist; to Ruth Bedford Moran, East Hampton, N.Y., 1926; to Maxim Karolik; gift to the Museum of Fine Arts, Boston.

TG   The artist; to Ruth Bedford Moran, East Hampton, N.Y., 1926; to the Thomas Gilcrease Foundation, Tulsa, Okla., through M. Knoedler & Co., New York, 1948; to The Thomas Gilcrease Institute of American History and Art, Tulsa, Okla., 1955.

TM   The artist; to the Cooper Union, New York, now the Cooper-Hewitt Museum, 1917.

WH   The artist; Dr. William Henry Holmes, Washington, D.C.; to the National Gallery of Art, now the national Museum of American Art, Washington, D.C.

YOS   The artist; to Ruth Bedford Moran, East Hampton, N.Y., 1926; The National Park Service, Yosemite National Park.

This catalogue includes some sketches held in other public collections, and the provenances for those works are listed. No attempt has been made to locate sketches in private hands, or to provide a catalogue raisonné.

TITLES

THOMAS MORAN often made notations on his sketches, denoting place, date, and other technical information. The inscription that best identifies the subject or location is used as the title. His ledger of 1916—an inventory of sketches made that year when Moran moved from his long-time home and studio in East Hampton to Santa Barbara, California, and which is now part of the Moran Archives at Gilcrease—follows this practice. Where an inscriptive title is lacking, a simple descriptive title has been assigned, using comparisons with related works or recognition of a location, or else, when one exists, the title given in Moran's 1916 ledger is used. Descriptive titles and ledger titles are indicated as such. Spellings have been corrected or modernized.

DATING

DATING of Moran's fieldwork proves difficult, even though he provided inscriptive dates for many of his sketches. The problem is that Moran often added dates to his sketches years later. Occasionally he dated sketches incorrectly, since his dates sometimes do not correlate with documented visits to particular sites. Clues to the later addition of dates are that the handwriting is not contemporary and that other writing instruments are used. Therefore, liberty has been taken to re-date a few to fit within the known framework of Moran's work and travels, supported again by stylistic analysis and research in the Gilcrease Moran Archives and other sources. The undated sketches have been placed within the chronological framework using the same rationale.

MEASUREMENTS

ALL MEASUREMENTS in the checklist are given in inches, with height preceding width. The measurements have been taken to the nearest one-eighth of an inch.

MEDIA

THE PREVALENT media are graphite and watercolor on paper. Moran also used other media for variety and textural interest or for expediency. White gouache, lithographic crayon, colored pencil, pen and ink, and chalk appear infrequently. He used an assortment of papers as support, from high-quality watercolor paper to cheap newsprint, and from ruled tablet paper to letterhead stationery. Clearly, he often took whatever was handy when he was ready to sketch. He most often employed medium-weight, off-white, wove sketch paper, used full size or cut or torn as needed, although laid paper appears infrequently. He also preferred small, paged sketchbooks. Moran used colored paper on occasion. For watercolors he preferred to allow the paper color lightest tone. In the checklist, only paper colors such as blue, green, or gray are noted.

SIGNATURE AND INSCRIPTIONS

THE LOCATIONS of signatures and inscriptions are abbreviated as follows in the checklist:

u. l.   upper left
u. r.   upper right
u. c.   upper center
l. l.   lower left
l. r.   lower right
l. c.   lower center

Inscriptions are given as written by the artist. Moran also made brief notes on many of his sketches, referring to color and other technical information. Only longer notes are recorded as inscriptions. The others are indicated as color notes or miscellaneous notes. Moran most often signed his sketches "TM" or "TMoran," sometimes with punctuation, but often without. After 1872, he added his colophon, the *T* and *M* conjoined, to a few sketches.

Most of his signatures and inscriptions are written in graphite; special note is made only when they are written in ink or other media. In quotations of the inscriptions, Moran's spelling has not been corrected.

1916 LEDGER

MORAN'S sketches proved valuable to him throughout his career. In 1916, at the time of his move to California, Moran, with the help of his daughters Mary Moran Tassin and Ruth Bedford Moran, catalogued his field sketches in a three-part ledger. Most of his sketches to that date appear on the ledger. Moran made only a handful of sketches in the field after his move to Santa Barbara.

Mary Moran Tassin inscribed the ledger number for most of the sketches on the verso of each, in the upper lefthand corner, in ink. The 1916 ledger number, when it appears on a sketch, is recorded in the checklist.

NOTES

COMMENTS and miscellaneous information concerning a sketch are given in note form at the end of an entry. Full citations for references cited in short form can be found in the bibliography.

CHECKLIST OF FIELD SKETCHES OF THOMAS MORAN

Note. An asterisk preceding the checklist number refers to a color plate. A dagger preceding the number refers to a larger black-and-white illustration in the text. An alphabetical listing of places in the sketches can be found in the index.

*1

BRIDGE OVER THE SCHUYLKILL, PHILADELPHIA
Graphite, watercolor, and white gouache on wove
6¹/₂ by 11⁵/₈
0226.798 Gilcrease
Dated: "April 15th 1856" l.l.; "1856" l.l. in ink
Signed: "TM" l.c.
Inscribed: "Bridge over the Schuylkill. Phila" l.l. in ink; "Falls of Schuylkill" l.l.; "1" u.l. in ink
Provenance: TG
1916 ledger: 6

2

NEAR HUNTINGTON, PENNSYLVANIA
Graphite and wash on wove
7¹/₂ by 11¹/₂
56.375 Museum of Fine Arts, Boston
Dated: "1856" l.r.
Signed: "TMoran" l.r. in ink
Inscribed: "Near Huntington Penn" l.l. on attached mount
Provenance: MK
Note: This sketch has been placed here only by virtue of date. The inscriptive title appears on the mounting and may not reflect the true subject. The date 1856 was added later to the sketch. Huntington Mills is a Pennsylvania town located about twenty-five miles northeast of Catawissa, where Moran traveled in 1861. Huntingdon (alternate spelling) is among the towns he visited in 1864. This sketch, however, is dissimilar to works from both venues.

3

FALLS OF THE SCHUYLKILL
Graphite and wash on wove
8³/₈ by 12³/₈
57.271 Museum of Fine Arts, Boston
Dated: "27th 1857" l.r.; "Oct 27th 1857" on verso
Signed: "TMoran" l.l.
Inscribed: "Falls of the Schuylkill" l.r.; "A true perspective view of Reading R.R. Bridge at the Falls of the Schuylkill." on verso
Provenance: MK
1916 ledger: 101

†4

CRESCENTVILLE
Graphite on wove
7³/₄ by 12¹/₂
1326.770 Gilcrease
Dated: "1857" u.r. in conté crayon
Inscribed: "Crescentville" u.r. in conté crayon
Provenance: TG
Note: Sketches on verso

5

WILMINGTON
Graphite on wove
9⁵/₈ by 12¹/₄
56.376 Museum of Fine Arts, Boston
Dated: "1858" u.l.
Inscribed: "Wilmington" u.l.
Provenance: MK
1916 ledger: 85

†6

FAIRMOUNT WATER WORKS, PHILADELPHIA
Graphite on wove
5³/₄ by 11
1326.769 Gilcrease
Dated: "1859" u.l.
Signed: "TM" u.l.
Inscribed: "Fairmount Water Works Phila" u.l.
Provenance: TG
Note: Sketch on verso

†7

FAIRMOUNT WATER WORKS, PHILADELPHIA [descriptive]
Graphite on wove
2³/₄ by 9¹/₂
1326.541 Gilcrease
Provenance: TG
Note: Sketch on verso

8

MOORE'S COTTAGE
Graphite on wove
10^{1}/$_{8}$ by 12^{5}/$_{8}$
1326.532 Gilcrease
Inscribed: "Moores Cottage" u.l.
Provenance: TG
Note: This structure stands in Fairmount Park in Philadelphia. It was once the residence of poet Thomas Moore.

9

TREE STUMP [descriptive]
Graphite and white gouache on wove
9^{1}/$_{2}$ by 10^{7}/$_{8}$
50.3966 Museum of Fine Arts, Boston
Dated: "1859 Sep 9" l.r.
Signed: "TMoran" l.r.
Provenance: MK

10

AN OLD MILL WHEEL AT MARQUETTE, LAKE SUPERIOR
Graphite and white gouache on wove
9^{5}/$_{8}$ by 12^{3}/$_{4}$
1973.370 Museum of Fine Arts, Boston
Dated: "July 23 1860" u.c.; "July 24 1860" l.l.
Signed: "TMoran" l.l.
Inscribed: "An Old Mill Wheel at Marquette, Lake Superior" u.l.
Provenance: MK
1916 ledger: 40

11

THE MINERS CASTLE, PICTURED ROCKS, LAKE SUPERIOR
Graphite on gray wove
9^{5}/$_{8}$ by 12^{3}/$_{4}$
1326.757 Gilcrease
Dated: "July 26, 1860" u.c.
Signed: "TMoran" u.c.
Inscribed: "The Miners Castle Pictured Rocks Lake Superior" u.l.
Provenance: TG
Note: Sketch on verso

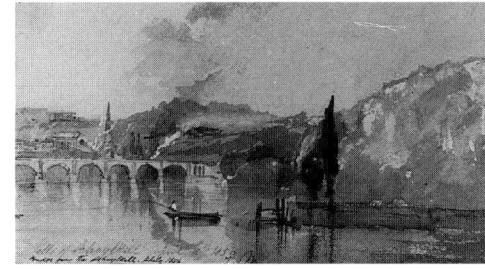

1

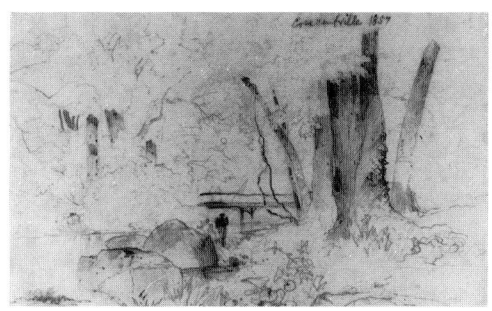

4

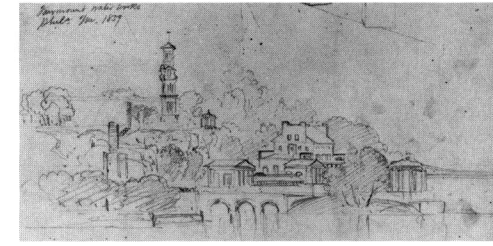

6

7

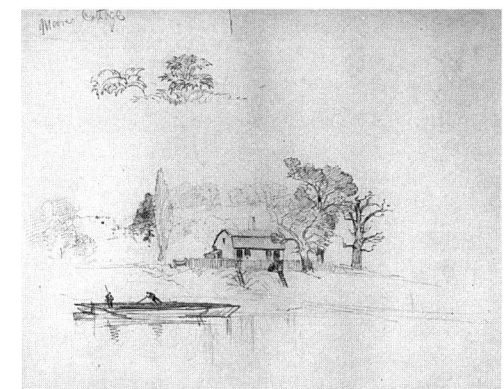

8

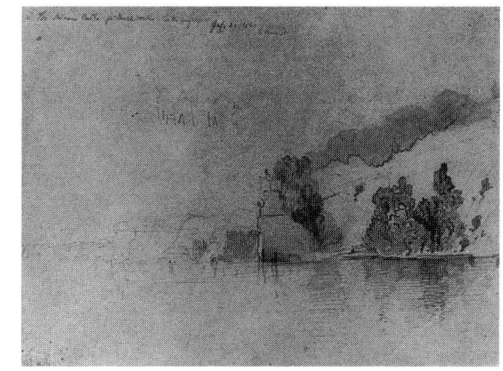

11

†12

AT MINERS RIVER, PICTURED ROCKS,
LAKE SUPERIOR
Graphite on wove
9³/₄ by 12⁵/₈
1326.756 Gilcrease
Dated: "July 29–1860" l.r.
Signed: "TM" l.r.
Inscribed: "At Miners river pictured rocks Lake
Superior" l.r.
Provenance: TG
1916 ledger: 80
Note: Sketches on verso

13

OUR CAMP AT THE PICTURED ROCKS,
LAKE SUPERIOR
Graphite and white gouache on wove
9⁵/₈ by 12¹/₂
50.3962 Museum of Fine Arts, Boston
Dated: "Aug 6th 1860" l.r.
Signed: "TMoran" l.c.
Inscribed: "Our Camp at the Pictured Rocks,
L.S." l.r.
Provenance: MK
1916 ledger: 250
Note: The campsites illustrated on this sketch
and the verso of No. 20 challenge the notion
perpetuated by Ruth Moran that her father's
first experience of camping in the open was dur-
ing his Yellowstone trip in 1871.

†14

LOOKING FROM THE SOUTH
ENTRANCE OF THE GREAT CAVE,
PICTURED ROCKS, LAKE SUPERIOR
Graphite on wove
6¹/₄ by 9⁵/₈
1326.754 Gilcrease
Dated: "Aug. 6th 1860" u.r.
Signed: "TMoran" u.r.
Inscribed: "Looking from the south Entrance of
the great Cave pictured rocks. L.S." u.r.
Provenance: TG
Note: Sketch on verso

†15

SIDE OF ENTRANCE TO THE GREAT
CAVE, PICTURED ROCKS
Graphite on wove

9⁵/₈ by 6³/₈
1326.758 Gilcrease
Dated: "Aug 6. 1860" u.r.
Signed: "TMoran" u.r.
Inscribed: "Side of Entrance to the Great Cave
pictured rocks" u.r.; color notes
Provenance: TG
Note: Sketch on verso

†16

ENTRANCE TO THE GREAT CAVE,
PICTURED ROCKS
Graphite on gray wove
9¹/₂ by 12¹/₂
1326.765 Gilcrease
Dated: "Aug 6, 1860" l.c.
Signed: "TMoran" l.r.
Inscribed: "Entrance to the Great Cave pictured
rocks" l.l.; color notes
Provenance: TG
Note: Sketch on verso

†17

THE GREAT CAVE, PICTURED ROCKS
FROM THE EAST
Graphite on wove
9³/₄ by 12¹/₂
1326.762 Gilcrease
Dated: "Aug 7th 1860" l.c.
Signed: "TMoran" l.c.
Inscribed: "The Great Cave Pictured Rocks from
the east" l.l.; color notes
Provenance: TG
Note: Sketch on verso

†18

IN THE FOREST AT MUNISING, LAKE
SUPERIOR
Graphite on wove
9¹/₂ by 12⁵/₈
1326.755 Gilcrease
Dated: "Aug. 1860" l.c.
Signed: "TMoran" l.c.
Inscribed: "in the forest at Munising. L.S." l.l.;
color notes
Provenance: TG
1916 ledger: 41
Note: Sketch on verso

19

A MILL AT NEWPORT RIVER, ST.
CLAIR, MICHIGAN
Graphite on gray wove
6¹/₄ by 9³/₄
60.432 Museum of Fine Arts, Boston
Dated: "Aug 22nd 1860" u.r.
Signed: "TMoran" u.r.
Inscribed: "A Mill at Newport River St. Clair
Michigan" u.r.
Provenance: MK
1916 ledger: 210

†20

THE ST. CLAIR FLATS
Graphite on gray wove
6¹/₄ by 9⁵/₈
1326.766 Gilcrease
Dated: "Aug 22nd, 1860" l.c.
Signed: "TMoran" l.c.
Inscribed: "The St. Clair flats. Entrance to
L. St. Clair" l.l.
Provenance: TG
Note: Sketch of a campsite on verso

21

SENECA LAKE FROM WATKINS
Graphite on wove
7³/₈ by 11¹/₄
1326.767 Gilcrease
Dated: "1860" l.l.
Signed: "TMoran" l.l.
Inscribed: "Seneca Lake from Watkins" u.l.
Provenance: TG
Note: Sketch on verso

†22

DELAWARE WATER GAP
Graphite on wove
9¹/₂ by 11¹/₈
1326.768 Gilcrease
Dated: "Sep 5, 1860" l.l.
Signed: "TMoran" l.c.
Inscribed: "Delaware Water Gap" l.l.
Provenance: TG
Note: Sketch on verso

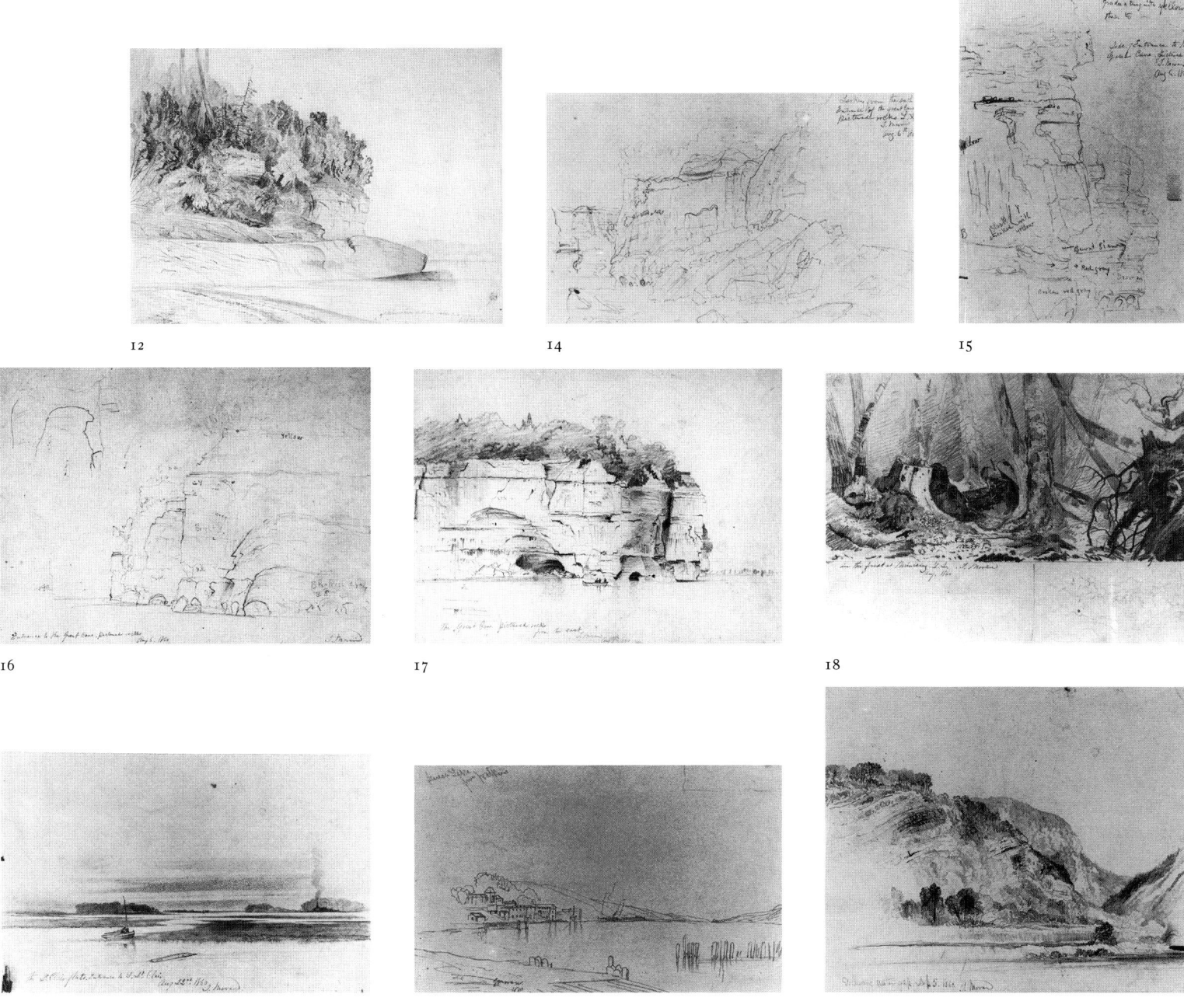

12

14

15

16

17

18

20

21

22

23
PASSAIC FALLS
Graphite on wove
11$\frac{1}{2}$ by 19$\frac{3}{8}$
1326.763 Gilcrease
Dated: "1860" l.r.
Signed: "Thomas Moran" l.r.
Inscribed: "passaic falls" l.c.
Provenance: TG

24
PASSAIC FALLS [descriptive]
Graphite on wove
12$\frac{3}{4}$ by 19$\frac{3}{8}$
1326.563 Gilcrease
Provenance: TG

25
PASSAIC FALLS [descriptive]
Graphite on wove
12$\frac{1}{2}$ by 19$\frac{1}{2}$
1326.558 Gilcrease
Provenance: TG
Note: Sketch on verso

†26
BELLEWS ROCKS ON THE TOHICKON
Graphite on gray wove
9$\frac{5}{8}$ by 12$\frac{5}{8}$
1326.706 Gilcrease
Signed: "TMoran" l.c.
Inscribed: "Bellews rocks on the Tohickon" l.l.
Provenance: TG

†27
CRESCENTVILLE
Graphite on wove
6$\frac{1}{4}$ by 9$\frac{1}{2}$
1326.761 Gilcrease
Dated: "Nov 1st 1860" u.r.
Signed: "TMoran" u.r.
Inscribed: "Crescentville" u.r.
Provenance: TG

28
FROM NATURE, GREEN LANE
Graphite on wove
9$\frac{5}{8}$ by 6$\frac{1}{4}$
1326.760 Gilcrease
Dated: "Nov 1st 1860" u.r.
Signed: "TMoran" u.r.
Inscribed: "from Nature Green Lane" u.c.
Provenance: TG
1916 ledger: 335

29
CRESCENTVILLE [descriptive]
Graphite on wove
11$\frac{5}{8}$ by 10
1326.759 Gilcrease
Dated: "1860" l.c.
Signed: "TMoran" l.c.
Provenance: TG

†30
MANAYUNK
Graphite on newsprint
7$\frac{5}{8}$ by 11
1326.751 Gilcrease
Dated: "1861" u.r.
Signed: "TMoran" l.l.
Inscribed: "Manayunk" u.r.; miscellaneous notes
Provenance: TG
Note: Sketch on verso

31
MANAYUNK [descriptive]
Graphite on newsprint
8 by 12$\frac{1}{2}$
1326.603 Gilcrease
Provenance: TG
Note: Sketch on verso

32
BRIDGE [descriptive]
Graphite on wove
6$\frac{1}{8}$ by 8$\frac{3}{4}$
27 East Hampton Library
Provenance: EH

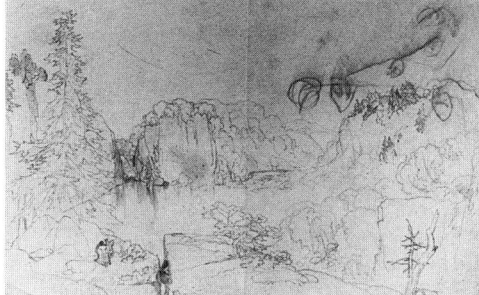

23

24

33
BRIDGE OVER THE CADORUS CREEK
AT YORK
Graphite on wove
5$\frac{5}{8}$ by 7$\frac{7}{8}$
1326.549 Gilcrease
Inscribed: "Bridge over the Cadorus Creek at
York" u.r.
Provenance: TG
Note: Sketch and inscription on verso: "Mills on
the Cadorus Creek at York"

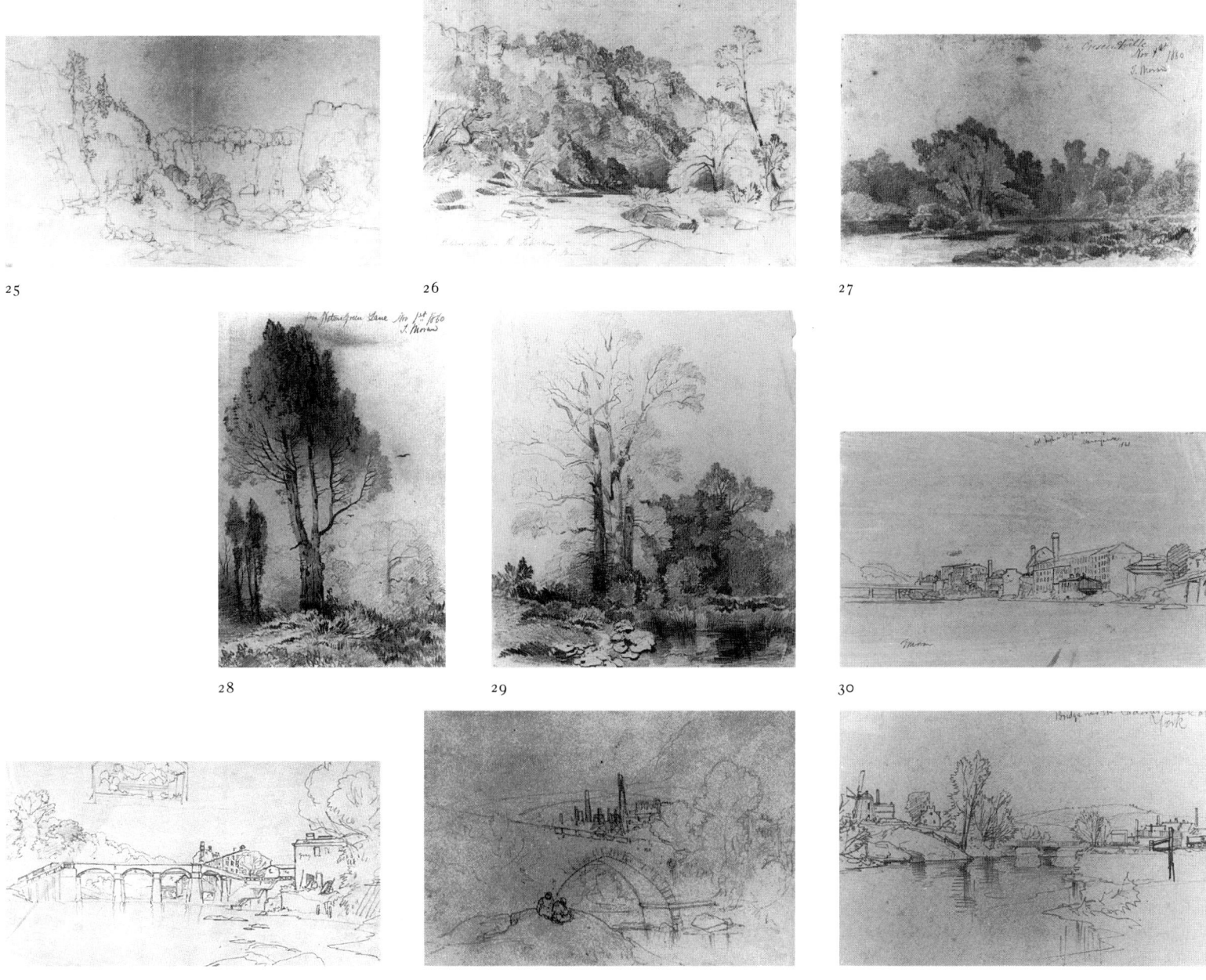

25

26

27

28

29

30

31

32

33

34
WISSAHICKON [descriptive]
Graphite on newsprint
7 by 10¹/₂
1326.606 Gilcrease
Provenance: TG

35
WISSAHICKON [descriptive]
Graphite on newsprint
7¹/₄ by 6
102 East Hampton Library
Provenance: EH

36
THE SUSQUEHANNA AT CATAWISSA
[descriptive]
Graphite and sepia wash on wove
10⁵/₈ by 8
56.374 Museum of Fine Arts, Boston
Provenance: MK
Note: Sketch on verso

†37a
AT PORT CLINTON
Graphite on wove
Upper sketch 4 by 6¹/₂, sheet 9¹/₄ by 6⁷/₈
1326.707 Gilcrease
Signed: "TM" l.r.
Inscribed: "at Port Clinton" l.l.
Provenance: TG

†37b
FROM BARREN HILL CATAWISSA
Graphite on wove
Lower sketch 4¹/₂ by 6⁷/₈, sheet 9¹/₄ by 6⁷/₈
1326.707 Gilcrease
Inscribed: "From Barren hill Cattawissa" u.r. in
margin
Provenance: TG

38
LIVERPOOL
Graphite on wove
9³/₄ by 14
1376.890 Gilcrease
Dated: "June 14th–62" u.l.
Signed: "TM" u.l.
Inscribed: "Liverpool" u.l.
Provenance: TG
1916 ledger: 242

†39
FORTHILL BRIDGE AT BOLTON,
LANCASHIRE
Graphite and sepia wash on wove
10 by 14
0276.801 Gilcrease
Dated: "June 16, 1862" u.r. in sepia ink
Signed: "TM" l.r. in sepia ink
Inscribed: "Forthill Bridge" u.r.; "At Bolton Lan-
cashire" u.r. in sepia ink
Provenance: TG
1916 ledger: 77

†40
WINDSOR
Graphite on wove
9³/₄ by 14
1376.895 Gilcrease
Dated: "June 25–62" u.l.
Signed: "TM" u.l.
Inscribed: "Windsor" u.l.; miscellaneous notes
Provenance: TG
Note: Sketch on verso; small sketch of bridge u.c.
on recto

†41
WINDSOR CASTLE
Graphite and sepia wash on wove
9³/₄ by 13¹/₈
1376.896 Gilcrease
Dated: "June 25 1862" l.l.
Signed: "TM" l.l.
Inscribed: "Windsor Castle" l.l.; miscellaneous notes
Provenance: TG

†42
IN GREENWICH PARK
Graphite on wove
11 by 14⁷/₈
1376.899 Gilcrease
Dated: "June 27th 1862" l.r.
Signed: "TM" l.r.
Inscribed: "in Greenwich Park" l.r.
Provenance: TG

†43
HOUSES OF PARLIAMENT FROM
HUNGERFORD BRIDGE
Graphite on wove
10 by 14

34

1376.897 Gilcrease
Dated: "June 27–62" u.l.
Signed: "TM" u.l.
Inscribed: "Houses of Parliament from Hunger-
ford Bridge" u.l.; miscellaneous notes and small
sketch u.c.
Provenance: TG

44
ST. PAUL'S FROM UNDER WATERLOO
BRIDGE
Graphite on wove
8¹/₄ by 11³/₈
49.42 Corcoran Gallery of Art
Dated: "June 27–62" u.r.
Signed: "TM" u.r.; "Thomas Moran" l.l.
Inscribed: "St Pauls from under Waterloo Bridge
Low tide" l.r.
Provenance: Milch Galleries, New York

45
FROM WATERLOO BRIDGE
Graphite on wove
8 by 13¹/₈
1376.893 Gilcrease
Dated: "July 1st–62" u.l.
Signed: "TM" u.l.
Inscribed: "from Waterloo Bridge" u.l.
Provenance: TG

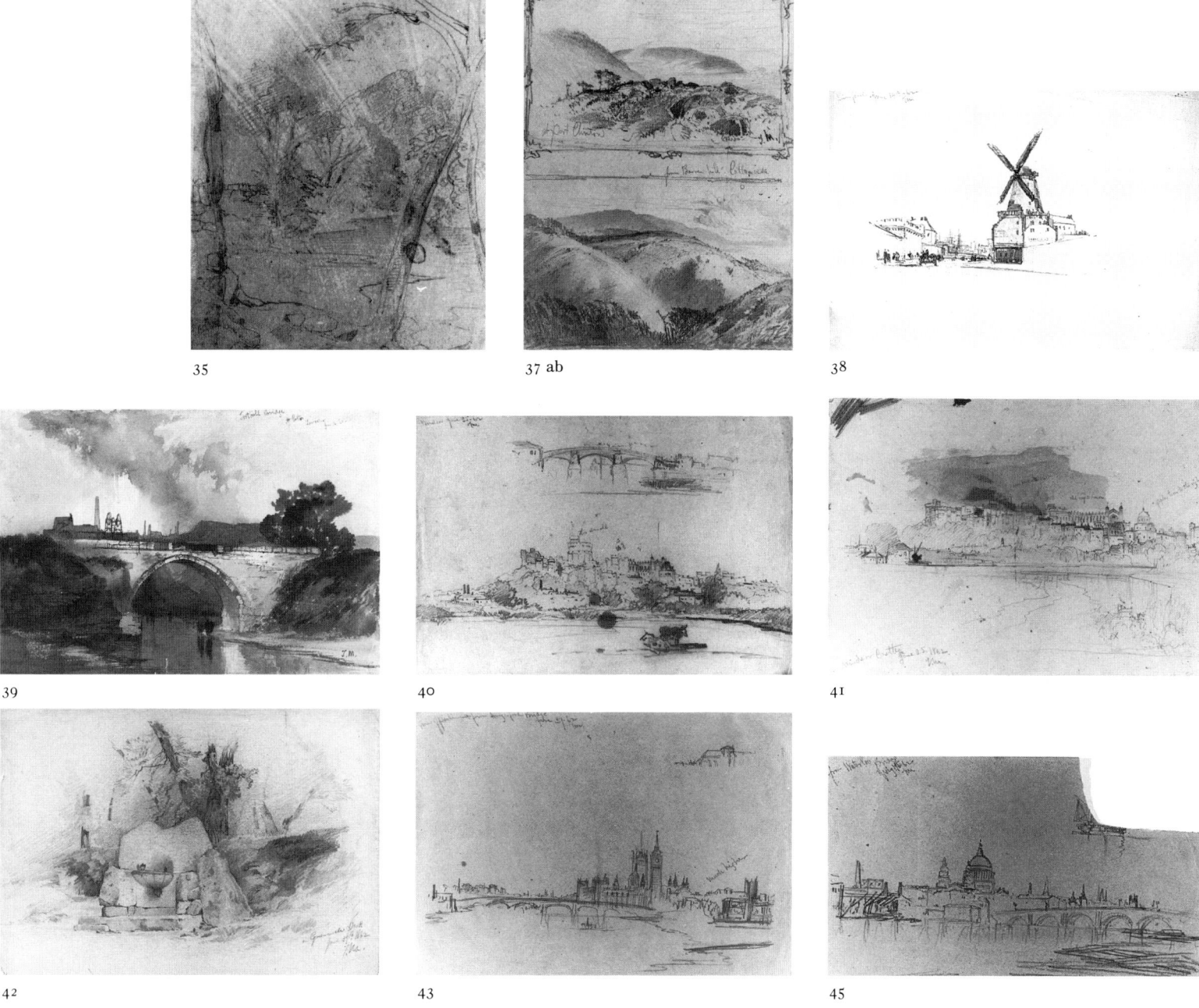

35

37 ab

38

39

40

41

42

43

45

†46
RICHMOND
Graphite and sepia wash on wove
10¹/₈ by 14⁷/₈
0276.802 Gilcrease
Dated: "July 1st–62" l.l.
Inscribed: "Richmond" l.l.
Provenance: TG

†47
MARGATE
Graphite and sepia wash on wove
11³/₄ by 10¹/₈
0276.800 Gilcrease
Dated: "July 4th–62" u.l.
Signed: "TM" u.l.
Inscribed: "Margate" u.l.
Provenance: TG

48
RAMSGATE
Graphite on wove
9⁷/₈ by 13³/₄
1376.904 Gilcrease
Dated: "July 5th 62" u.l.
Signed: "TMoran" l.r.; "TM" u.l.
Inscribed: "Ramsgate" u.l.
Provenance: TG
Note: Sketch on verso and small sketch on recto u.r

49
SANDOWN CASTLE
Graphite on wove
4¹/₂ by 10
1376.903 Gilcrease
Dated: "July 7–62" l.r.
Signed: "TM" l.r.
Inscribed: "Sandown Castle" and "Deal" l.r.;
"Sandown" u.l.
Provenance: TG

50
SANDOWN CASTLE, DEAL
Graphite on wove
6 by 9⁵/₈
1376.894 Gilcrease
Dated: "July 8. 62" u.l.
Signed: "TM" u.l.
Inscribed: "Sandown Castle. Deal." u.l.
Provenance: TG

51
DOVER
Graphite on wove
11 by 15
1376.905 Gilcrease
Dated: "July 8th–62" u.l.
Signed: "TM" u.l.
Inscribed: "Dover" u.l.
Provenance: TG
1916 ledger: 384

52
AT DOVER
Graphite on wove
3³/₄ by 11
15 East Hampton Library
Dated: "July 8–62" u.r.; "1862" l.l.
Signed: "TM" u.r.
Inscribed: "at Dover" u.r.; "Dover" l.l.
Provenance: EH
1916 ledger: 368

53
MARGATE
Graphite on wove
10³/₄ by 15
1376.898 Gilcrease
Dated: "July 8th–62" u.l.
Signed: "TM" u.l.
Inscribed: "Margate" u.l.
Provenance: TG
Note: Sketch and inscription on verso: "Margate July 4th–62 TM"

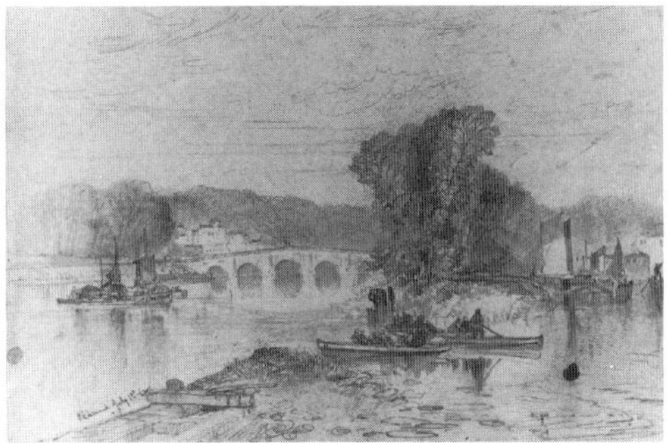

46

†54
ARUNDEL TOWN AND CASTLE
Graphite on wove
8¹/₄ by 14
1376.902 Gilcrease
Dated: "July 12 1862" u.r.
Inscribed: "Arundel Town & Castle" u.r.
Provenance: TG
Note: Sketch on verso

55
HASTINGS
Graphite on wove
9 by 15
1376.900 Gilcrease
Dated: "July 12–62" u.l.
Signed: "TM" u.l.
Inscribed: "Hastings" u.l.; miscellaneous notes
Provenance: TG
Note: Sketch on verso

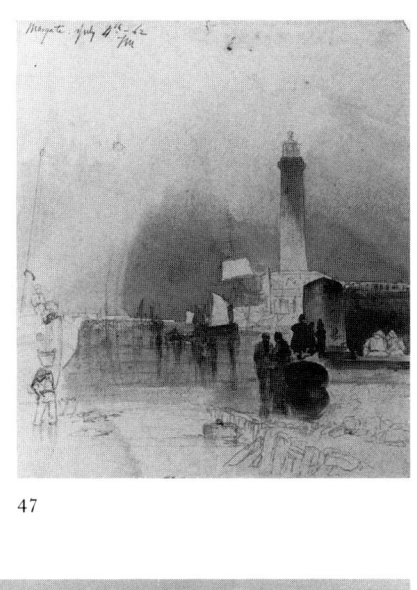

47

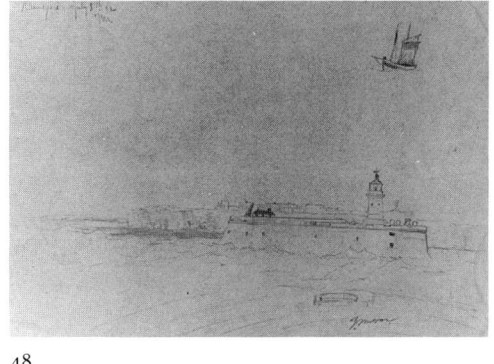

48

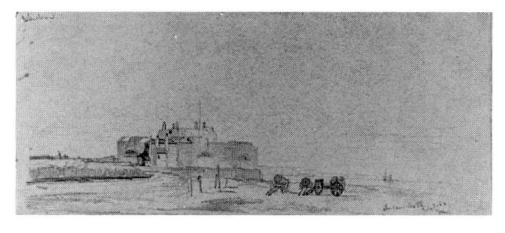

49

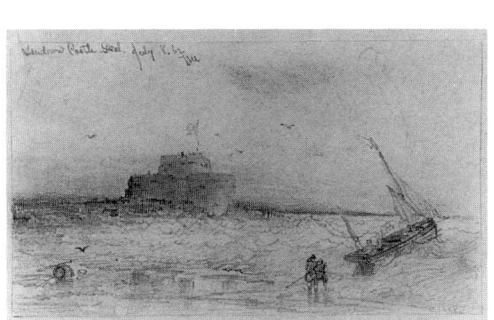

50

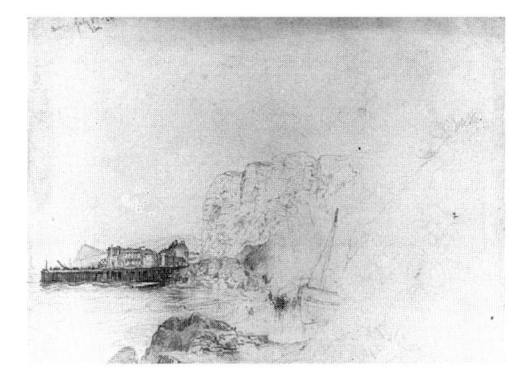

51

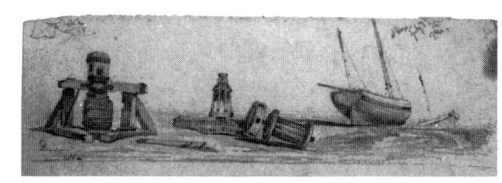

52

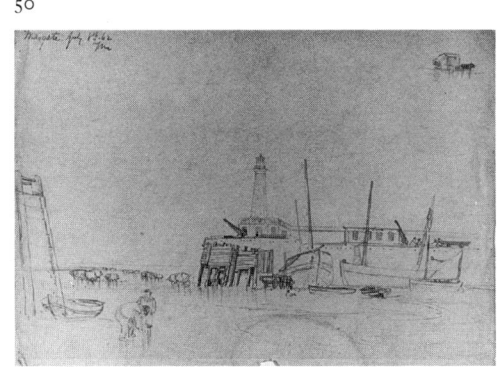

53

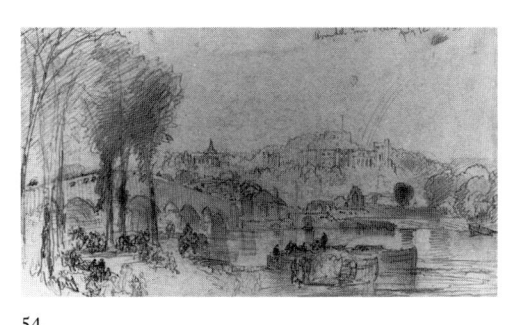

54

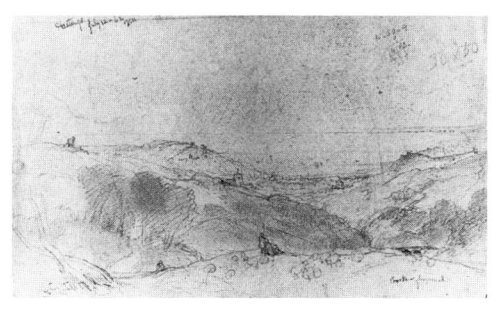

55

56
CLIFFS OF ECCLESBORNE, NEAR
HASTINGS
Graphite, wash, and white gouache on green
wove
85/8 by 101/2
49.43 Corcoran Gallery of Art, Washington,
D.C.
Dated: "July 13–62" l.r.
Signed: "TM" l.r.
Inscribed: "Cliffs of Ecclesborne Near Hastings" l.r.
Provenance: James Parmelee

57
EAST CLIFF, HASTINGS
Graphite on wove
121/2 by 93/4
1376.892 Gilcrease
Dated: "July 14th–62" u.l.
Signed: "TM" u.l.
Inscribed: "East Cliff Hastings" u.l.
Provenance: TG
Note: Sketch on verso

58
HASTINGS [descriptive]
Graphite on wove
93/4 by 121/2
1376.560 Gilcrease
Provenance: TG

59
PORTCHESTER
Graphite on wove
107/8 by 147/8
1376.891 Gilcrease
Dated: "July 15th–62"–l.l.
Signed: "TM" l.l.
Inscribed: "Portchester" l.l.
Provenance: TG

*60
BEXHILL
Graphite, red conté crayon, and white gouache
on green wove
5 by 7
0276.933 Gilcrease
Dated: "July 19th–62" u.l.
Signed: "TM" u.l.
Inscribed: "Bexhill" u.l.
Provenance: W. F. Davidson at M. Knoedler &

Co., New York; 1964 Thomas Gilcrease Foundation, Tulsa, Okla.; 1969 The Thomas Gilcrease Institute of American History and Art, Tulsa, Okla.

*61
HASTINGS
Graphite and white gouache on wove
5 by 7
0276.841 Gilcrease
Dated: "July 20–62" u.r.
Signed: "TM" u.r.
Inscribed: "Hastings" u.r.
Provenance: TG

62
ON THE BEACH, HASTINGS
Graphite, watercolor, and white gouache on gray
wove
7 by 5
60.431 Museum of Fine Arts, Boston
Dated: "July 20–62" u.c.
Signed: "TM" u.c.
Inscribed: "On the Beach Hastings" u.l.
Provenance: MK
1916 ledger: 117

*63
HASTINGS
Graphite, red conté crayon, and white gouache
on wove
5 by 7
0276.838 Gilcrease
Dated: "July 21st–62" u.c.
Inscribed: "Hastings" u.c.; sketch of oarlock u.l.
Provenance: TG
1916 ledger: 71

*64
HASTINGS
Graphite, red conté crayon, and white gouache
on wove
7 by 5
0276.839 Gilcrease
Dated: "July 22–62" u.l.
Signed: "TM" u.l.
Inscribed: "Hastings" u.l.
Provenance: TG
Note: Sketch on verso

57

*65
HASTINGS
Graphite, red conté crayon, and white gouache
on green wove
5 by 7
0276.935 Gilcrease
Dated: "July 22–62" u.l.
Signed: "TM" u.l.
Inscribed: "Hastings" u.l.
Provenance: Carmen H. Messmore, New York;
1964 Thomas Gilcrease Foundation; 1969 The
Thomas Gilcrease Institute of American History and Art, Tulsa, Okla.
1916 ledger: 387
Note: Sketch on verso

66
THE TOWN AND CASTLE OF LEWES
Graphite on wove
101/2 by 151/2
1376.901 Gilcrease
Dated: "July 24–62" u.l.
Signed: "TM" u.l.
Inscribed: "The town & Castle of Lewes" u.l.
Provenance: TG
1916 ledger: 241
Note: Sketch on verso

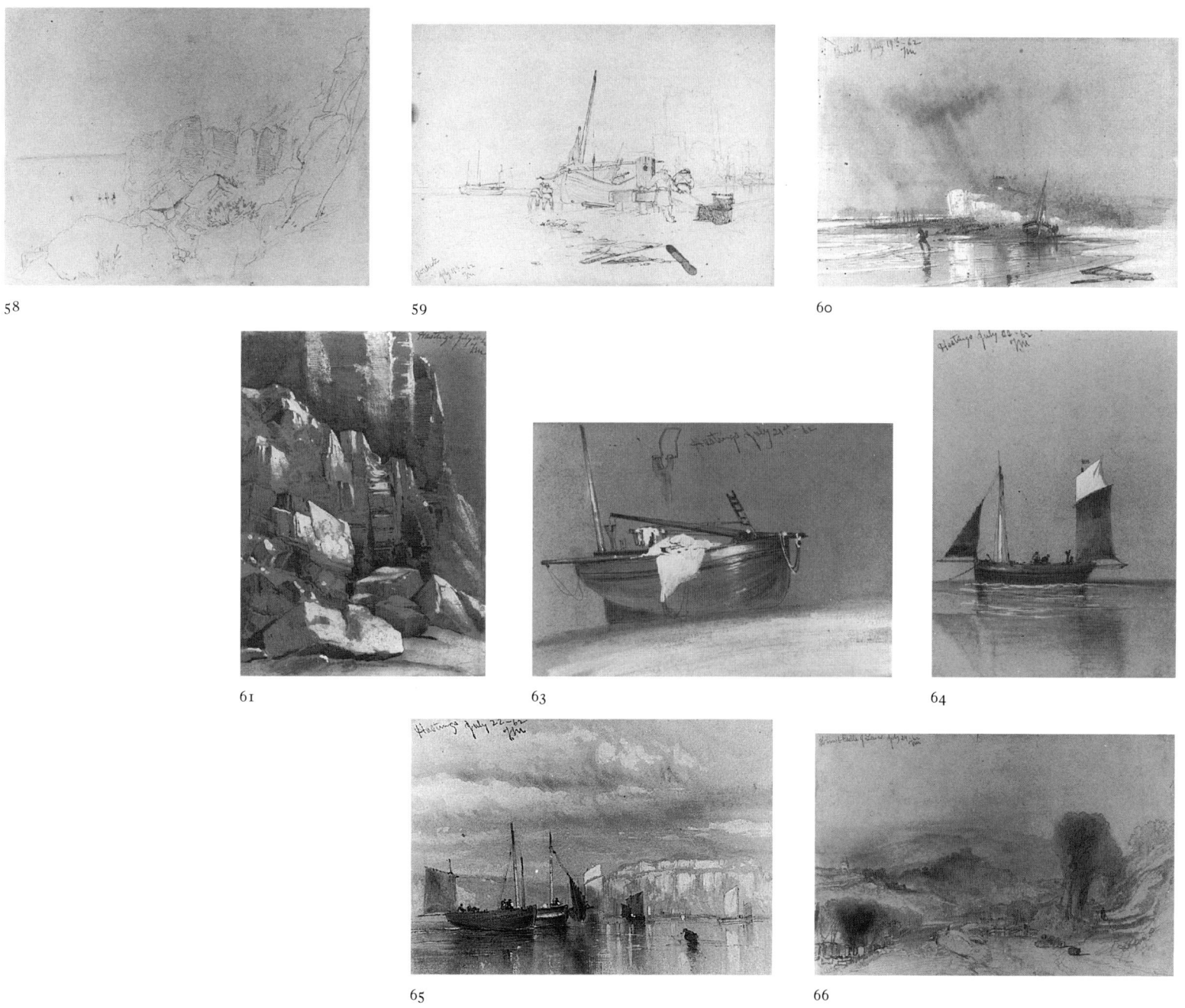

58

59

60

61

63

64

65

66

67
ARUNDEL TOWN AND CASTLE
Graphite on wove
9¹/₂ by 13¹/₈
1376.906 Gilcrease
Dated: "July 26th–1861" l.l. [see note]
Signed: "TM" l.l.
Inscribed: "Arundel Town & Castle" l.l.
Provenance: TG
1916 ledger: 349
Note: Although the inscribed date was changed by Moran from 1862 to 1861, it is catalogued with the 1862 sketches. The sketch relates in all ways to dated work from July 1862. Sketch and inscription on verso: "Arundel Castle from the Lake TM 26-July-62."

68
ARUNDEL TOWN AND CASTLE
[descriptive]
Graphite on wove
10¹/₂ by 15
1376.548 Gilcrease
Provenance: TG
Note: Sketches on verso

69
CARISBROOKE CASTLE, ISLE OF WIGHT
Graphite on wove
10⁷/₈ by 14⁷/₈
1376.752 Gilcrease
Dated: "July 29–61" u.l.
Signed: "TM" u.l.
Inscribed: "Carisbrook Castle. Isle of Wight." u.l.
Provenance: TG
1916 ledger: 333
Note: Although the inscribed date was changed by Moran from 1862 to 1861, this work is catalogued with the 1862 sketches. It relates in all ways to the dated work from July 1862. Sketch on verso.

70
THE OLD WALL OF SOUTHAMPTON
Graphite on wove
6⁵/₈ by 10¹/₄
1376.753 Gilcrease
Dated: "1861" u.c.
Signed: "TM" u.c.

Inscribed: "The old wall of Southampton" u.c.; "Southampt" on verso u.l. in ink
Provenance: TG
1916 ledger: 185
Note: Although the inscribed date was changed by Moran from 1862 to 1861, this work is catalogued with the 1862 sketches. It relates in all ways to the dated work from July 1862.

71
WISSAHICKON
Graphite on wove
7 by 5
1326.750 Gilcrease
Dated: "Sep./63" l.l.
Inscribed: "Wissahickon" l.l.
Provenance: TG
Note: Sketch on verso

72
THE WISSAHICKON
Graphite on wove
4³/₄ by 8⁷/₈
1326.887 Gilcrease
Dated: "1863" l.r.
Signed: "TM" l.r.
Inscribed: "The Wissahicon" l.r.; miscellaneous notes
Provenance: TG
Note: Sketch on verso

†73
WISSAHICKON
Graphite on gray wove
6⁵/₈ by 12⁷/₈
1326.719 Gilcrease
Dated: "1864" l.l.
Signed: "TM" l.l.
Inscribed: "Wissahickon" l.l.
Provenance: TG
1916 ledger: 394

74
THE WISSAHICKON
Graphite and white gouache on gray wove
12³/₈ by 9³/₈
1973.369 Museum of Fine Arts, Boston
Dated: "1864" l.l.

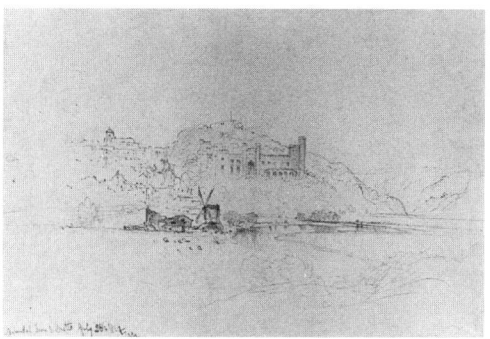

67

Signed: "TM" l.l.
Inscribed: "The Wissahicon" l.l.
Provenance: MK
1916 ledger: 60

75
A GLIMPSE OF THE WISSAHICKON
Graphite and conté crayon on wove
6¹/₄ by 4¹/₂
1326.1014 Gilcrease
Dated: "1864" l.r.
Inscribed: "A Glimpse of the Wissahickon" l.r. in conté crayon
Provenance: Carmen H. Messmore, New York; 1964 Thomas Gilcrease Foundation, Tulsa, Okla.; 1969 The Thomas Gilcrease Institute of American History and Art, Tulsa, Okla.
1916 ledger: 51
Note: This sketch relates to Moran's engraving with the same title, which illustrated the Fairmount Park Commission's Annual Report of 1878, opposite p. 24.

†76
HUNTINGDON
Graphite on wove
7¹/₂ by 9³/₄
1326.716 Gilcrease
Dated: "July 26–64" u.l.
Inscribed: "Huntingdon" u.l.
Provenance: TG
Note: Sketch on verso

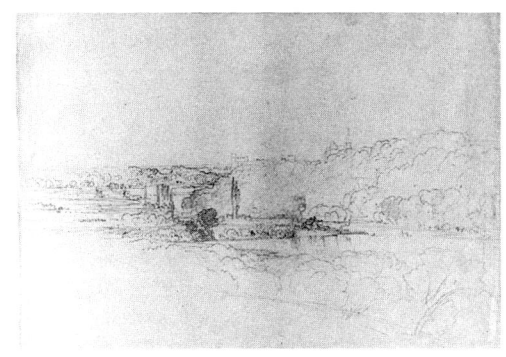

68

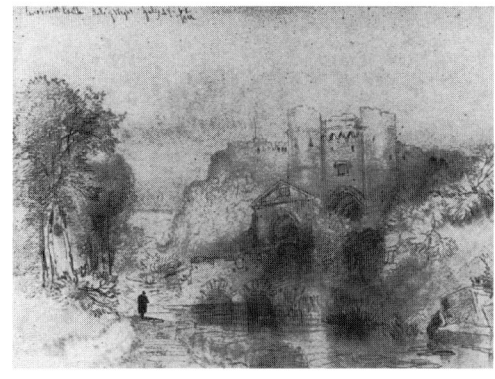

69

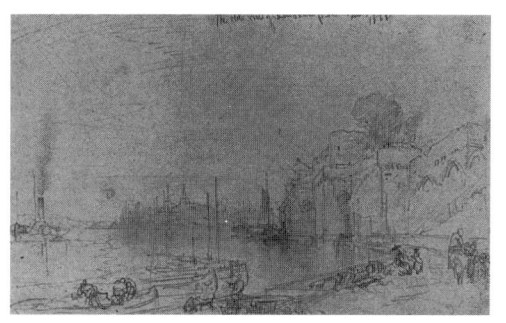

70

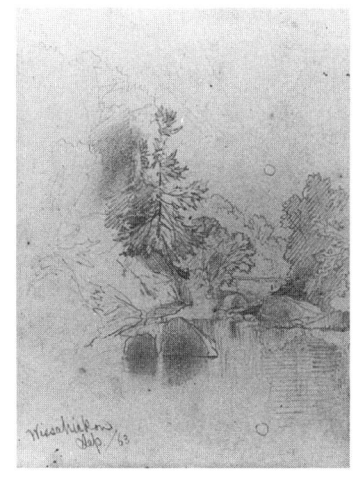

71

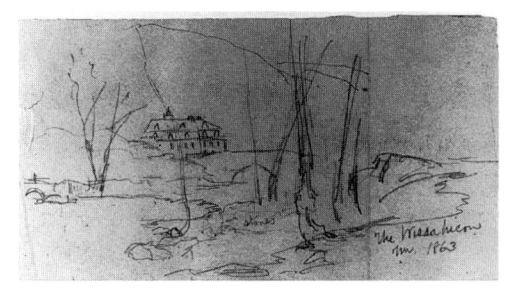

72

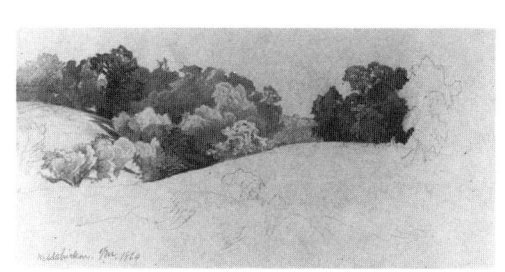

73

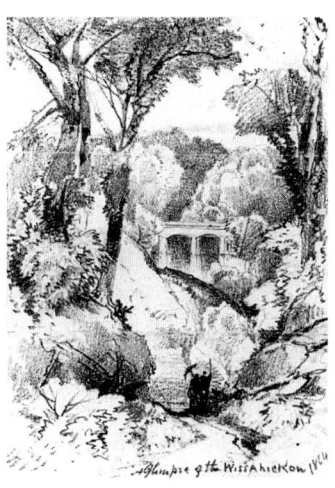

75

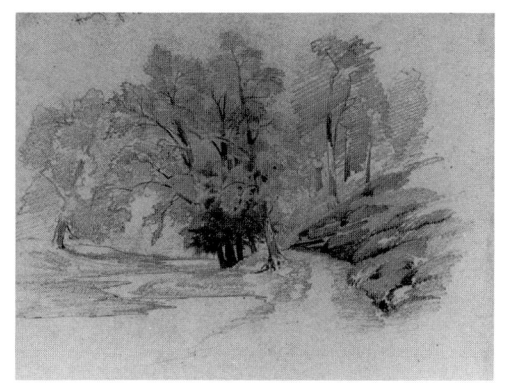

76

†77
HUNTINGDON FROM WARRIORS
RIDGE
Graphite, blue and gray washes on wove
9³/₄ by 13³/₈
1326.715 Gilcrease
Dated: "August 3rd-64" u.l.
Signed: "TM" u.l.
Inscribed: "Huntingdon from Warrior Ridge" u.l.;
miscellaneous notes
Provenance: TG

78
HUNTINGDON
Graphite on wove
10³/₈ by 9⁵/₈
50.3960 Museum of Fine Arts, Boston
Dated: "Aug 4th 1864" u.c.
Signed: "TM" u.c.
Inscribed: "Huntingdon" u.c.
Provenance: MK

†79
WARRIORS RIDGE, HUNTINGDON,
PENNSYLVANIA
Graphite and black conté crayon on wove
9⁵/₈ by 13
1326.1028 Gilcrease
Dated: "Aug 5–64" u.l.
Signed: "TM" u.l.
Inscribed: "Warrior Ridge Huntingdon Pa" u.l.;
color and miscellaneous notes
Provenance: Ruth K. Henschel, New York; 1964
Thomas Gilcrease Foundation, Tulsa, Okla.;
1970 The Thomas Gilcrease Institute of Ameri-
can History and Art, Tulsa, Okla.
1916 ledger: 62

†80
THE JUNIATA BELOW HUNTINGDON
Graphite on wove
9³/₄ by 13¹/₄
1326.717 Gilcrease
Dated: "Aug 6th–64" u.l.
Signed: "TM" u.l.
Inscribed: "The Juniata below Huntingdon" u.l.
Provenance: TG

*81
JOHNSTOWN
Graphite, blue and gray washes on wove
9³/₄ by 11⁵/₈
0226.795 Gilcrease
Dated: "Aug 6th–64" u.l.
Signed: "TM" u.l.
Inscribed: "Johnstown" u.l.
Provenance: TG

†82a
WILMORE
Graphite on wove
Upper sketch 4¹/₂ by 7³/₄, sheet 9⁵/₈ by 7³/₄
1326.712 Gilcrease
Dated: "Aug 8–64" l.r.
Signed: "TM" l.r.
Inscribed: "Willmore" l.r.
Provenance: TG
Note: Sketch on verso

82b
THE JUNIATA AT SPRUCE CREEK
Graphite on wove
Lower sketch 5¹/₈ by 7³/₄, sheet 9⁵/₈ by 7³/₄
1326.712 Gilcrease
Dated: "Aug 15–64" u.l.
Signed: "TM" u.l.
Inscribed: "The Juniata at Spruce Creek" u.l.
Provenance: TG

†83
ON THE CONEMAUGH BELOW
LOCKPORT
Graphite, blue and gray washes on wove
9³/₄ by 13¹/₂
0226.796 Gilcrease
Dated: "Aug 9th–64" u.l.
Signed: "TM" u.l.
Inscribed: "on the Conemaugh below Lockport"
u.l.
Provenance: TG

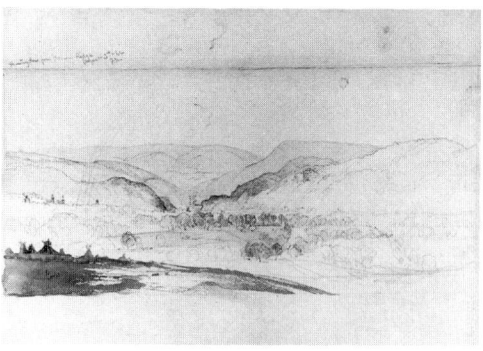

77

84
THE CONEMAUGH AT LOCKPORT
Graphite on wove
Sketch 8¹/₂ by 12³/₈, sheet 9³/₄ by 13¹/₄
1326.745 Gilcrease
Dated: "Aug 9th–64" u.l.
Signed: "TM" u.l.
Inscribed: "The Conemaugh at Lockport" u.l.;
color notes
Provenance: TG
1916 ledger: 313

*85
CONEMAUGH AT BOLIVAR
Graphite, blue and gray washes on wove
Sketch 9³/₄ by 11¹/₂, sheet 9³/₄ by 13¹/₄
0226.794 Gilcrease
Dated: "Aug 9–64" u.l.
Signed: "TM" u.l.
Inscribed: "Conemaugh at Bolivar" u.l.; color
notes
Provenance: TG

86
CONEMAUGH BELOW JOHNSTOWN
Graphite, blue and gray washes on wove
3⁷/₈ by 5³/₄
0226.793 Gilcrease
Dated: "Aug 11–64" u.c.
Inscribed: "Conemaugh below Johnstown" u.l.;
color notes
Provenance: TG

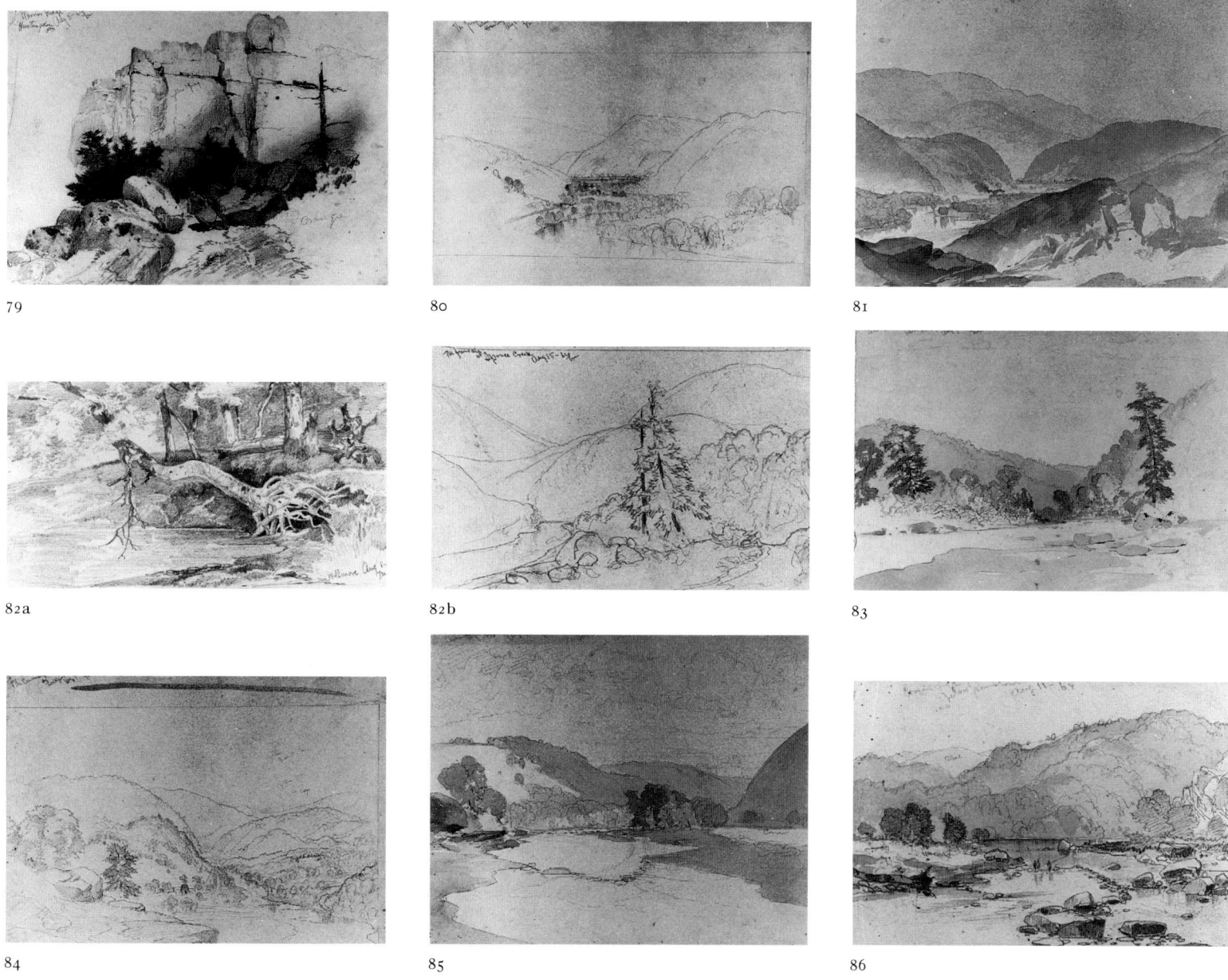

79

80

81

82a

82b

83

84

85

86

87a
WILMORE
Graphite on wove
Left sketch 5³/₈ by 4⁷/₈, sheet 5³/₈ by 9⁵/₈
1326.713 Gilcrease
Dated: "Aug 11–64" l.l.
Signed: "TM" l.l.
Inscribed: "Willmore" l.l.
Provenance: TG

87b
GALLITZIN
Graphite on wove
Right sketch 5³/₈ by 4³/₄, sheet 5³/₈ by 9⁵/₈
1326.713 Gilcrease
Dated: "Aug 12–64" l.r.
Inscribed: "Gallitzin" l.r.
Provenance: TG

†88
GALLITZIN
Graphite on wove
4⁷/₈ by 6⁵/₈
1326.1021 Gilcrease
Dated: "Aug 11–64" l.r.
Signed: "TM" l.r.
Inscribed: "Gallitzin" l.r.
Provenance: TG
1916 ledger: 14

89
GALLITZIN
Graphite on wove
5¹/₂ by 5⁷/₈
1326.1032 Gilcrease
Dated: "Aug 11–64" l.l.
Inscribed: "Gallitzin" l.l.
Provenance: Carmen H. Messmore, New York;
1964 Thomas Gilcrease Foundation, Tulsa, Okla.;
1970 The Thomas Gilcrease Institute of American History and Art, Tulsa, Okla.
1916 ledger: 135

90
GALLITZIN
Graphite on wove
5¹/₈ by 7³/₈
51 East Hampton Library
Dated: "Aug 11–64" l.l.
Signed: "TM" l.l.
Inscribed: "Gallitzin" l.l.
Provenance: EH
1916 ledger: 138

91
SPRUCE CREEK [descriptive]
Graphite on wove
4¹/₂ by 7
1326.614 Gilcrease
Provenance: TG
Note: Sketch and inscription on verso "Iti Sapis Potitis Hoss"

92
SPRUCE CREEK
Graphite on wove
4¹/₄ by 6³/₈
1326.749 Gilcrease
Dated: "Aug 14. 64" u.l.
Signed: "TM" u.l.
Inscribed: "Spruce Creek" u.l.
Provenance: TG

*93
SPRUCE CREEK, PENNSYLVANIA
Graphite, blue and gray washes on wove
5¹/₂ by 6³/₈
0226.942 Gilcrease
Dated: "Aug 14–64" l.l.
Inscribed: "Spruce Creek Pa" l.l.
Provenance: W. F. Davidson at M. Knoedler & Co., New York; 1964 Thomas Gilcrease Foundation, Tulsa, Okla.; 1970 The Thomas Gilcrease Institute of American History and Art, Tulsa, Okla.
1916 ledger: 69

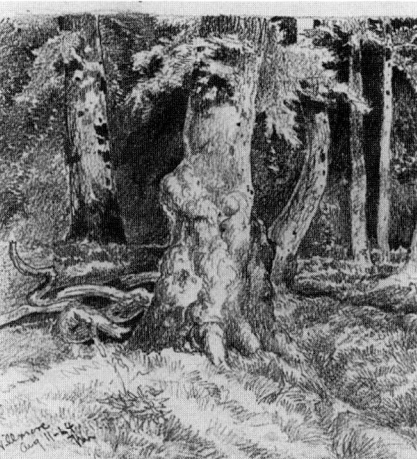

87a

†94
TUSSEY MOUNTAIN, SPRUCE CREEK
Graphite on wove
9³/₄ by 13¹/₂
1326.747 Gilcrease
Dated: "Aug 18–64" u.l.
Inscribed: "Tusseys Mt. Spruce Creek" u.l.
Provenance: TG
1916 ledger: 83
Note: Sketches and inscriptions on verso: "The Juniata from Warrior Ridge Aug 3–64 TM" and "Warrior R. Aug. 3–64 TM"

†95
SPRUCE CREEK
Graphite on wove
5¹/₂ by 9⁵/₈
1326.748 Gilcrease
Dated: "Aug 21–64" l.l.
Signed: "TM" l.l.
Inscribed: "Spruce Creek" l.l.
Provenance: TG
Note: Sketch on verso

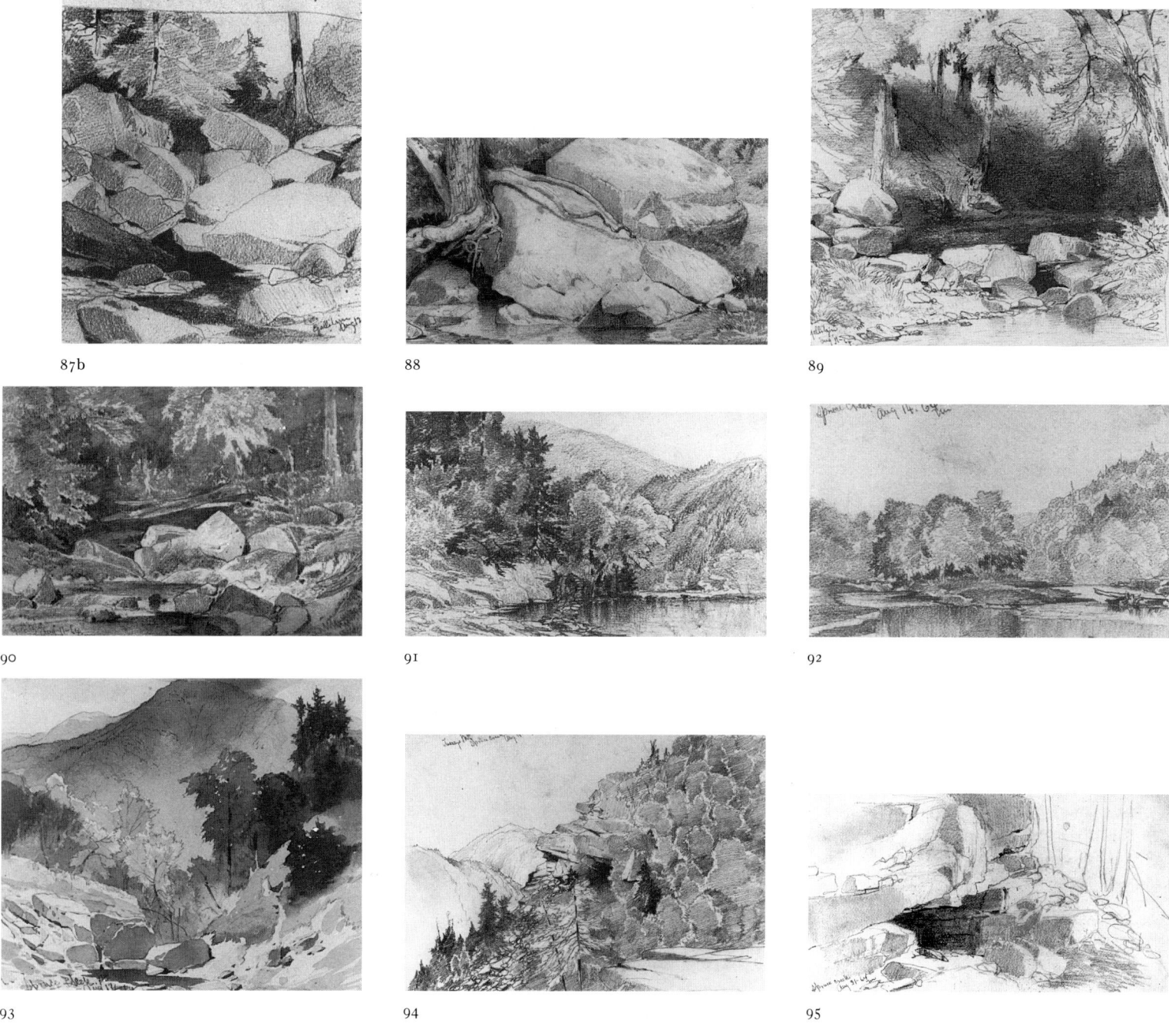

87b

88

89

90

91

92

93

94

95

†96
SPRUCE CREEK
Graphite on wove
4¹/₂ by 7³/₈
1326.744 Gilcrease
Dated: "Aug 21–64" l.l.
Signed: "TM" l.l.
Inscribed: "Spruce Creek" l.l.
Provenance: TG
1916 ledger: 130
Note: Sketch and inscription on verso: "dripping S. B&O TM"

97
WATER STREET
Graphite on wove
4³/₈ by 6¹/₂
4 East Hampton Library
Dated: "Aug-14–64" u.l.
Signed: "TM" l.l. and u.l.
Inscribed: "Water Street" u.l.
Provenance: EH

†98
MILL CREEK [descriptive]
Graphite on wove
9³/₄ by 11³/₄
1326.714 Gilcrease
Dated: "Aug 22–64" u.l.
Inscribed: "eek" u.l. [inscription cut off]; color notes
Provenance: TG
Note: Sketch on verso

99
NEAR MAPLETON
Graphite on wove
Sketch 4¹/₂ by 7¹/₄, sheet 5¹/₄ by 7¹/₂
1326.746 Gilcrease
Dated: "Aug 23–64" u.l.
Inscribed: "Near Mapleton" u.l.
Provenance: TG
Note: Sketch on verso

†100
THE JUNIATA AT MILL CREEK
Graphite on wove
9³/₄ by 13¹/₄
1326.718 Gilcrease
Dated: "Aug 24th–64" u.l.
Inscribed: "The Juniata at Mill Creek" u.l.
Provenance: TG
Note: Sketch on verso

101
MILL CREEK
Graphite on wove
7³/₄ by 4³/₄
25 East Hampton Library
Dated: "Aug-25–64" u.r.; "1864" l.l.
Signed: "TM" l.l.
Inscribed: "Mill Creek" u.r.; miscellaneous notes
Provenance: EH
1916 ledger: 198

102
ALONG THE JUNIATA [descriptive]
Graphite on wove
9³/₄ by 12¹/₂
1326.559 Gilcrease
Provenance: TG

103
ALLEGHENY MOUNTAINS
Graphite on wove
9³/₄ by 12⁷/₈
1326.1011 Gilcrease
Dated: "1862" l.l. [see note]
Signed: "TMoran" l.l.
Inscribed: "Allegheny Mts" l.l.
Provenance: TG
Note: Although Moran dated this sketch earlier than 1864, the drawing style and the type of paper strongly resemble the sketches of the later period. Also, the geographic location is more logical for 1864.

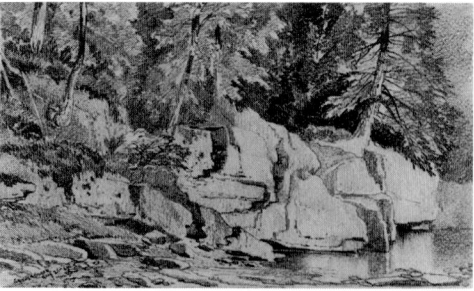

96

†104
MILFORD
Graphite on wove
9³/₈ by 6³/₈
1326.740 Gilcrease
Dated: "July 22–65" l.r.
Signed: "TM" l.l.
Inscribed: "Milford" l.c.; "3" l.l.
Provenance: TG
1916 ledger: 66

105
MILFORD
Graphite on wove
6³/₈ by 8¹/₂
50.3961 Museum of Fine Arts, Boston
Dated: "July 22–65" l.l.
Signed: "TM" l.l.
Inscribed: "Milford" l.l.; "4" l.r.
Provenance: MK

106
RAYMONDSKILL
Graphite on wove
9¹/₂ by 12¹/₂
13 East Hampton Library
Dated: "July 23–65" l.r.
Signed: "TM" l.r.
Inscribed: "Raymondskill" l.r.; "6" l.l.
Provenance: EH
1916 ledger: 81

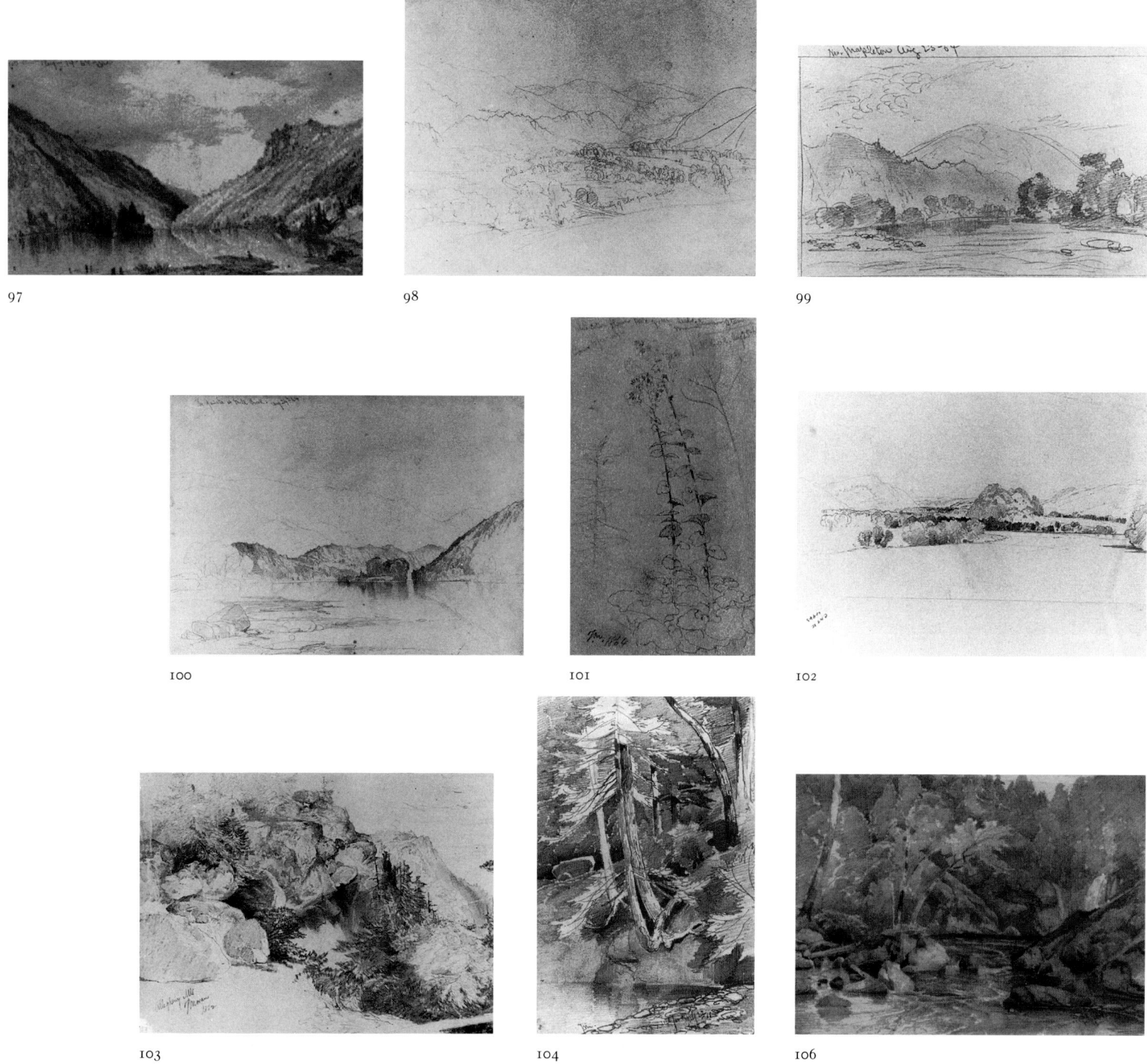

97

98

99

100

101

102

103

104

106

107
RAYMONDSKILL
Graphite on wove
9³/₈ by 12⁷/₈
50.3963 Museum of Fine Arts, Boston
Dated: "July 24–65" l.l.
Signed: "TM" l.l.
Inscribed: "Raymondskill" l.l.; "5" l.r.
Provenance: MK

108
SAWKILL
Graphite on wove
9¹/₂ by 6
1326.731 Gilcrease
Dated: "July 25–65" l.l.
Signed: "TM" l.l.
Inscribed: "Saw Kill" l.l.; "12" l.r.
Provenance: TG

109
SAWKILL FALLS
Graphite on wove
9¹/₂ by 6¹/₂
50.3965 Museum of Fine Arts, Boston
Dated: "July 25–65" l.r.
Signed: "TM" l.r.
Inscribed: "Saw Kill Falls" l.r.; "8" l.l.
Provenance: MK

110
SAWKILL FALLS
Graphite on wove
9¹/₂ by 13
14 East Hampton Library
Dated: "July 25–65" l.r.
Signed: "TM" l.r.
Inscribed: "Saw Kill Falls" l.r.; "5" l.r.
Provenance: EH
1916 ledger: 44

†111
SAWKILL FALL
Graphite on wove
9³/₄ by 12³/₄
1326.1013 Gilcrease
Dated: "July 26" l.r.
Signed: "TM" l.r.
Inscribed: "Sawkill fall" l.r.; "19" l.r.; color notes
Provenance: Carmen H. Messmore, New York;
1964 Thomas Gilcrease Foundation, Tulsa, Okla.;
1969 The Thomas Gilcrease Institute of American History and Art, Tulsa, Okla.

†112
SAWKILL
Graphite on wove
9³/₈ by 6¹/₄
1326.733 Gilcrease
Dated: "July 27–65" l.l.
Signed: "TM" l.l.
Inscribed: "Saw Kill" l.l.; "13" u.r. and l.l.
Provenance: TG

113
SAWKILL
Graphite on wove
6³/₈ by 9³/₈
1326.1022 Gilcrease
Dated: "July 27–65" l.l.
Signed: "TM" l.l.
Inscribed: "Sawkill" l.l.; "14" l.r.
Provenance: TG

114
SAWKILL [descriptive]
Graphite on wove
7 by 5¹/₈
1326.1017 Gilcrease
Dated: "1865" l.l.
Signed: "TM" l.l.
Provenance: TG

115
SAWKILL
Graphite on wove
6¹/₂ by 9¹/₂
50.3964 Museum of Fine Arts, Boston

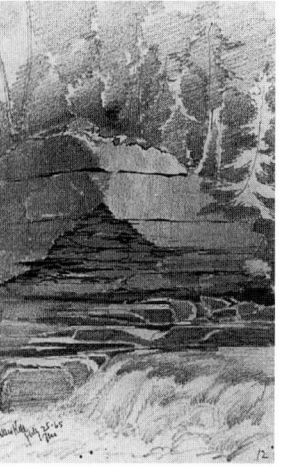

108

Dated: "1865" l.l.
Signed: "TM" l.l.
Inscribed: "Sawkill" l.l.; "46" l.r.
Provenance: MK
1916 ledger: 128

†116
SAWKILL
Graphite on wove
9¹/₂ by 6³/₈
1326.1019 Gilcrease
Dated: "July 27–65" l.r.
Signed: "TM" l.r.
Inscribed: "Saw Kill" l.r.; "15" l.c.
Provenance: Ruth K. Henschel, New York; 1964 Thomas Gilcrease Foundation, Tulsa, Okla.; 1971 The Thomas Gilcrease Institute of American History and Art, Tulsa, Okla.
1916 ledger: 82

117
SAWKILL
Graphite on wove
5 by 7¹/₄
1326.738 Gilcrease
Dated: "July 27–65" l.l.
Signed: "TM" l.l.
Inscribed: "Saw Kill" l.l.; "16" l.r.
Provenance: TG

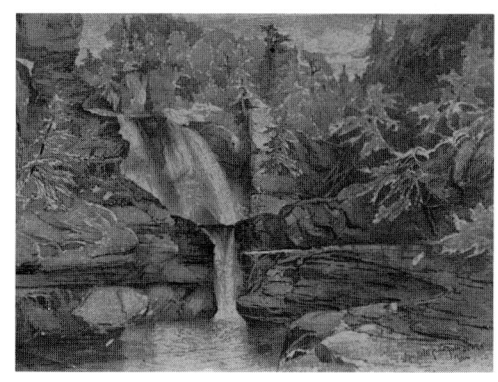

110

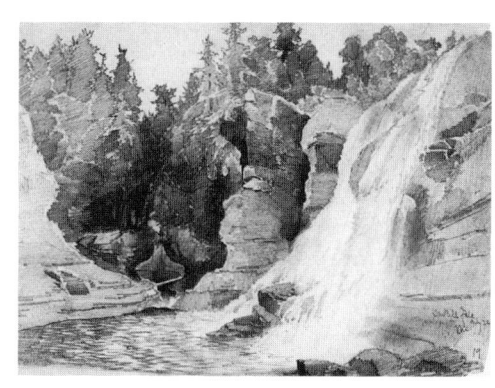

111

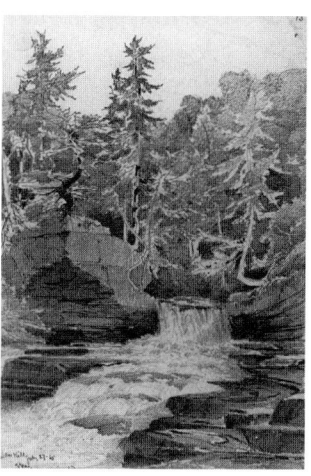

112

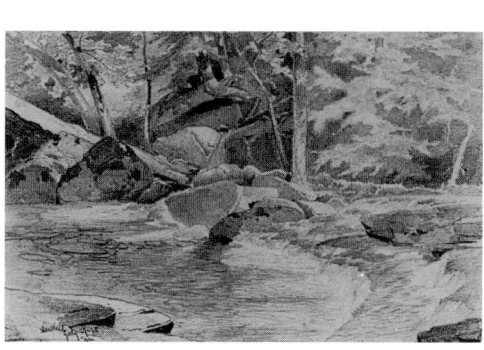

113

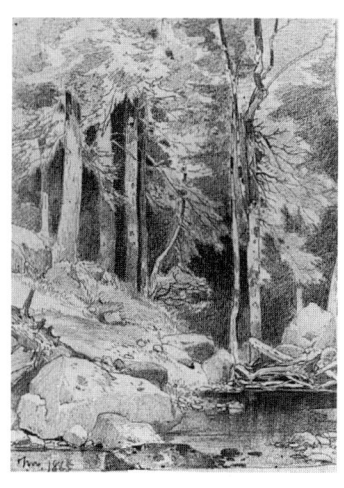

114

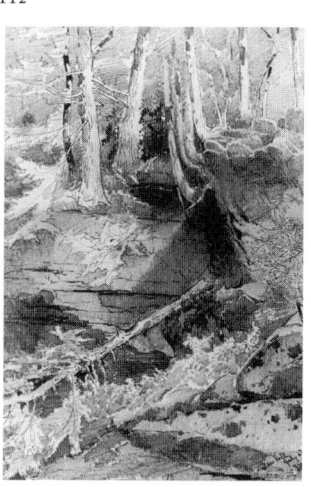

116

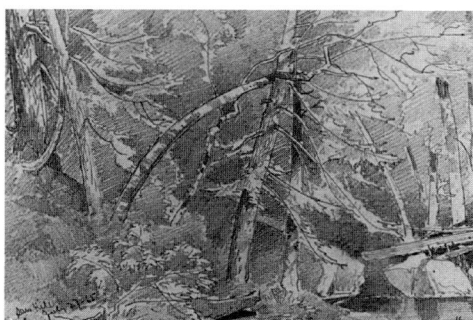

117

118
SAWKILL FALLS
Graphite on wove
9³/8 by 6⁷/8
1326.1018 Gilcrease
Dated: "July 27–65" l.l.
Signed: "TM" l.l.
Inscribed: "Saw-Kill falls" l.l.; "9" l.r.
Provenance: Ruth K. Henschel, New York; 1964
Thomas Gilcrease Foundation, Tulsa, Okla.;
1971 The Thomas Gilcrease Institute of American History and Art, Tulsa, Okla.

119
MILFORD
Graphite on wove
9³/8 by 6¹/2
Dated: "July 28–65" l.l.
1326.729 Gilcrease
Signed: "TM" l.l.
Inscribed: "Milford" l.l.; "17" l.r.
Provenance: TG
1916 ledger: 43

120
VANDERMARK
Graphite on wove
7¹/8 by 4¹/2
15 East Hampton Library
Dated: "July 29–65" l.r.
Signed: "TM" l.r.
Inscribed: "Vandermark" l.r.; "26" l.l.
Provenance: EH
1916 ledger: 60

121
HEMLOCK ROOT, VANDERMARK
Graphite on wove
4³/4 by 6¹/8
1326.728 Gilcrease
Dated: "July 29–65" l.l.
Signed: "TM" l.l.
Inscribed: "Hemlock Root Vandermark" l.l.; "22"
l.r.
Provenance: TG

†122
MILFORD
Graphite on wove
6¹/2 by 9¹/2
1326.1026 Gilcrease
Dated: "July 29–65" l.l.
Signed: "TM" l.l.
Inscribed: "Milford" l.l.; "18" l.c.
Provenance: Ruth K. Henschel, New York; 1964
Thomas Gilcrease Foundation, Tulsa, Okla.;
1971 The Thomas Gilcrease Institute of American History and Art, Tulsa, Okla.

†123
VANDERMARK
Graphite on wove
Sketch 9¹/2 by 6¹/4, mount 10³/4 by 7¹/8
1326.721 Gilcrease
Dated: "July 30–65" l.l.
Signed: "TM" l.l.
Inscribed: "Vandermark" l.l.; "20" l.r.; "Study
from Nature 1865. TMoran." l.l. in ink on mount;
"6. Graphite." u.l. in ink on mount
Provenance: TG
1916 ledger: 146

124a
SAWKILL
Graphite on wove
Upper sketch 4⁷/8 by 6¹/8, sheet 9¹/2 by 6¹/8
1326.730 Gilcrease
Dated: "Aug 3–65" l.r.
Signed: "TM" l.r.
Inscribed: "Saw Kill" l.r.; "34" l.r.
Provenance: TG

†124b
PICNIC ROCK, SAWKILL
Graphite on wove
Lower sketch 4¹/2 by 6¹/8, sheet 9¹/2 by 6¹/8
1326.730 Gilcrease
Dated: "Aug 3–65" l.r.
Signed: "TM" l.r.
Inscribed: "Picnic Rock Saw Kill" l.r.; "33" l.l.
Provenance: TG

118

125
SAWKILL FALL
Graphite on wove
4⁵/8 by 5³/8
1326.1150 Gilcrease
Dated: "Aug–65" l.r.
Signed: "TM" l.r.
Inscribed: "Saw Kill fall" l.r.; "25" l.r.
Provenance: TG

126a
SAWKILL
Graphite on wove
Upper sketch 4³/4 by 5⁷/8, sheet 9¹/2 by 5⁷/8
1326.732 Gilcrease
Dated: "Aug 3–65" l.l.
Signed: "TM" l.l.
Inscribed: "Sawkill" l.l.; "31" u.r.
Provenance: TG
1916 ledger: 127

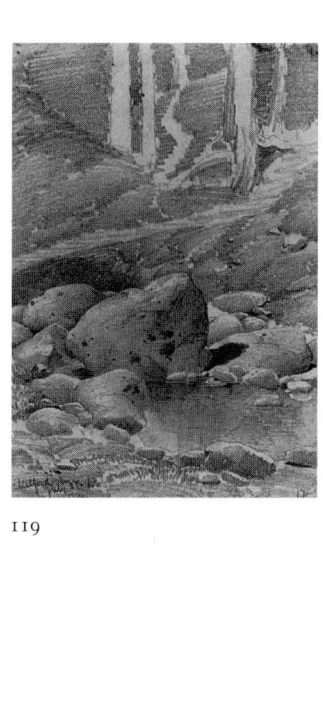

119

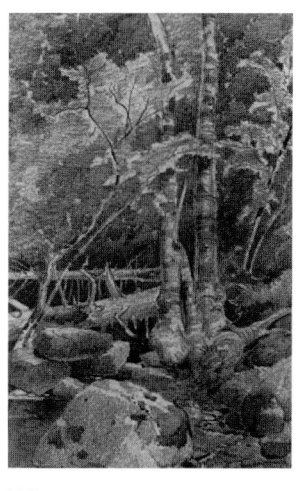

120

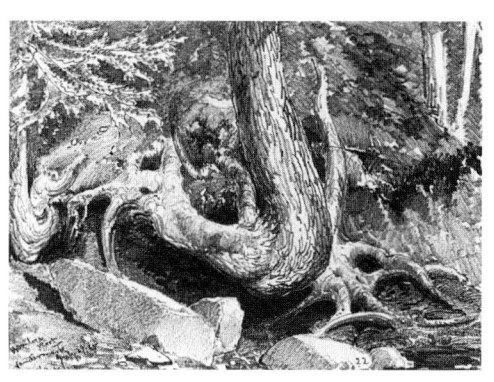

121

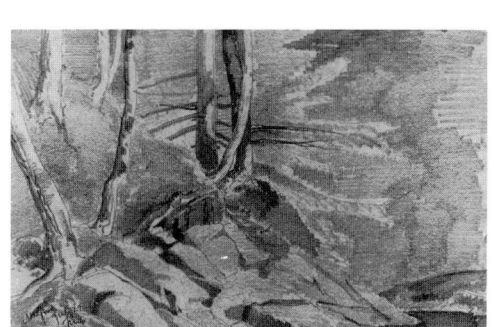

122

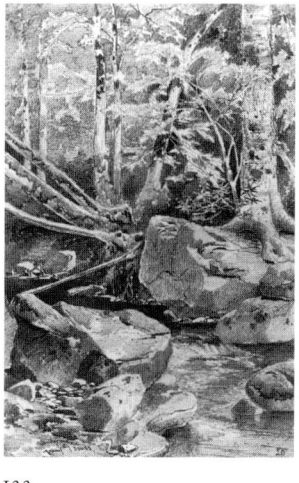

123

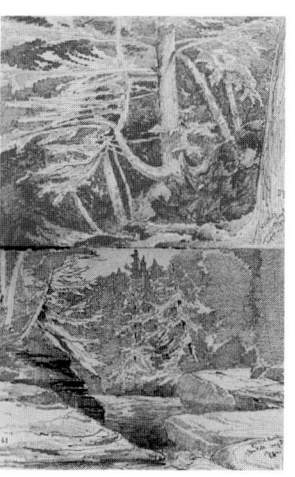

124 ab

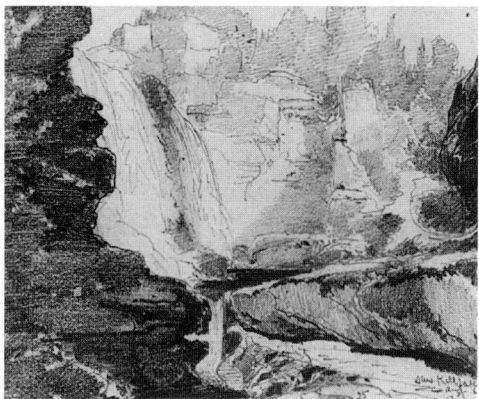

125

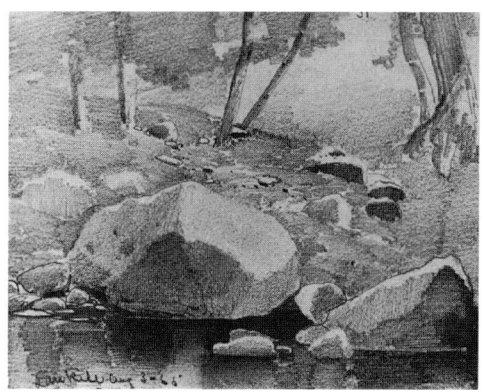

126a

126b
SAWKILL
Graphite on wove
Lower sketch 4³/₄ by 5⁷/₈, sheet 9¹/₂ by 5⁷/₈
1326.732 Gilcrease
Dated: "Aug 5–65" l.l.
Signed: "TM" l.l.
Inscribed: "Sawkill" l.l.; "32" u.r.
Provenance: TG

127
VANDERMARK
Graphite on wove
9¹/₂ by 6⁷/₈
1326.737 Gilcrease
Dated: "Aug 4th–65" l.l.
Signed: "TM" l.l.
Inscribed: "Vandermark" l.l.; "27" l.r.
Provenance: TG

128
SAWKILL FALL
Graphite on wove
9³/₈ by 7¹/₂
1326.735 Gilcrease
Dated: "Aug 5–65" l.r.
Signed: "TM" l.r.
Inscribed: "Sawkill fall" l.r.; "40" u.r.
Provenance: W. F. Davidson at M. Knoedler &
Co., New York; 1964 Thomas Gilcrease Founda-
tion, Tulsa, Okla.; 1974 The Thomas Gilcrease
Institute of American History and Art, Tulsa,
Okla.

129
SAWKILL
Graphite on wove
9¹/₂ by 6⁷/₈
1326.722 Gilcrease
Dated: "Aug 5–65" l.l.
Signed: "TM" l.l.
Inscribed: "Sawkill" l.l.; "28" l.l.
Provenance: TG

†130
HEMLOCK, SAWKILL FALL
Graphite on wove
9³/₈ by 6¹/₂
1326.723 Gilcrease
Dated: "Aug 5–65" l.l.
Signed: "TM" l.l.
Inscribed: "Hemlock Saw Kill fall" l.l.; "30" l.l.
Provenance: TG

131
SAWKILL [descriptive]
Graphite on wove
7⁷/₈ by 6¹/₂
1326.555 Gilcrease
Inscribed with color notes
Provenance: TG

132
ADAMS CREEK
Graphite on wove
9¹/₂ by 12⁷/₈
50.3958 Museum of Fine Arts, Boston
Dated: "Aug 5–65" l.l.
Signed: "TM" l.l.
Inscribed: "Adams Creek" l.l.; "36" l.l.
Provenance: MK
1916 ledger: 59

133
LOWER FALL OF ADAMS CREEK
Graphite on wove
9¹/₂ by 6¹/₄
1326.720 Gilcrease
Dated: "Aug 7th–65" l.l.
Signed: "TM" l.l.
Inscribed: "Lower fall of Adams Creek" l.l.; "35"
u.l.
Provenance: TG
1916 ledger: 41

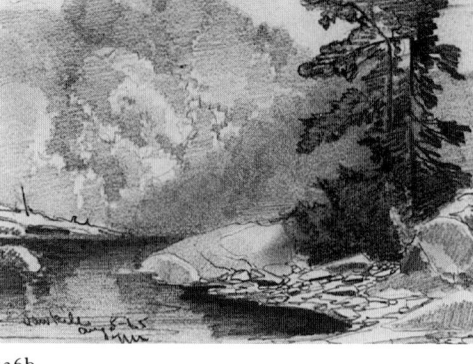

126b.

134
SAWKILL
Graphite on wove
9¹/₂ by 6¹/₂
1326.727 Gilcrease
Dated: "Aug 8–65" l.r.
Signed: "TM" l.r.
Inscribed: "Saw Kill" l.r.; "29" u.r.
Provenance: TG

135
SAWKILL
Graphite on wove
6³/₄ by 9³/₈
1326.742 Gilcrease
Dated: "Aug 9–65" l.l.
Signed: "TM" l.l.
Inscribed: "Saw Kill" and "42" l.l.
Provenance: TG

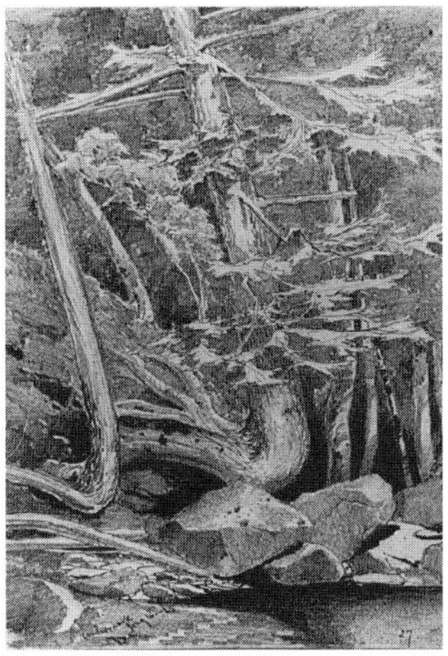

127

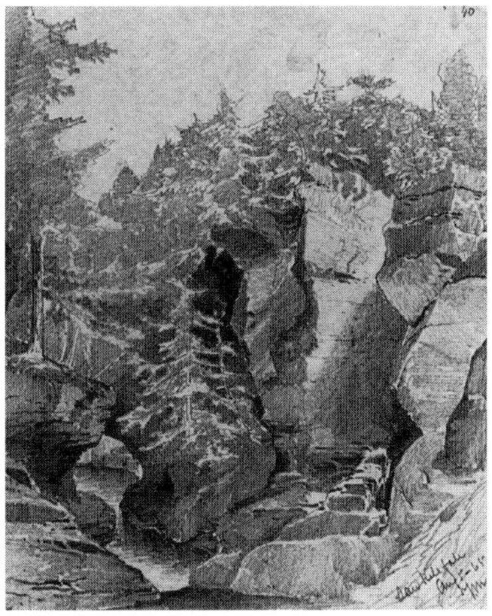

128

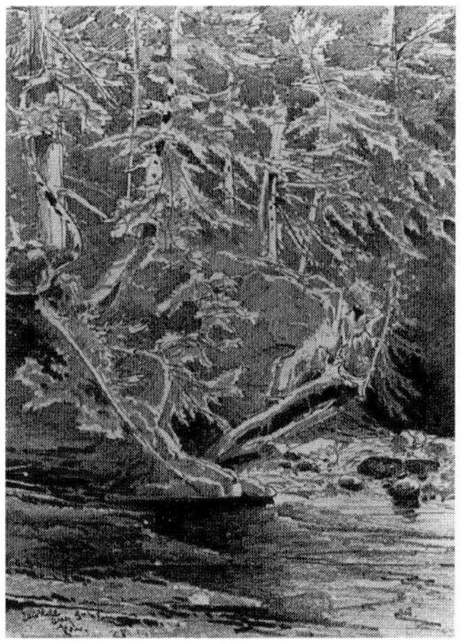

129

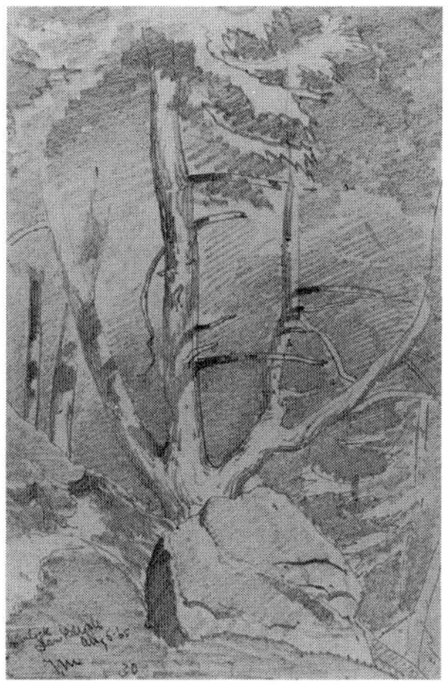

130

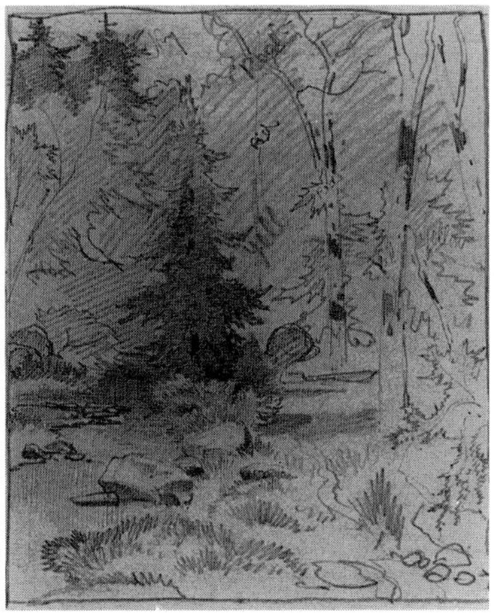

131

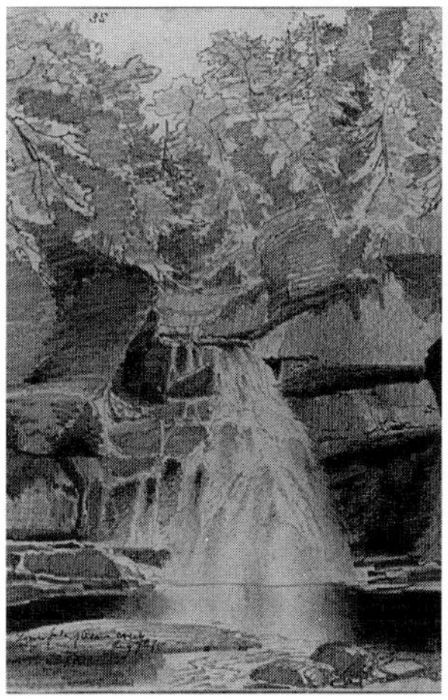

133

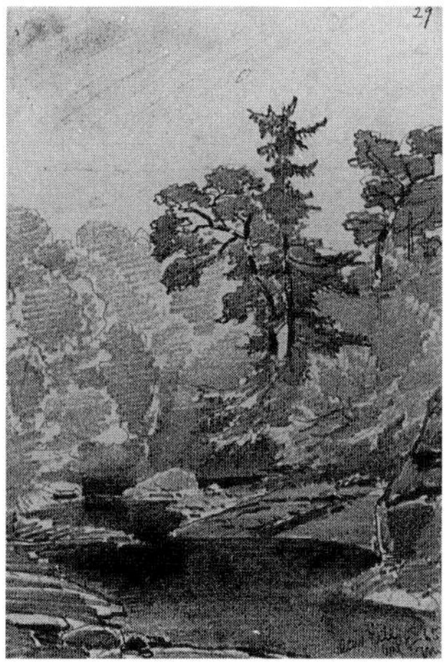

134

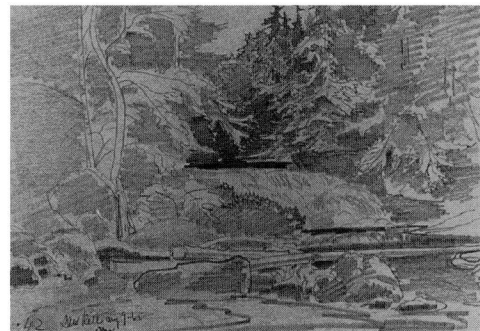

135

136
RAYMONDSKILL FALL
Graphite on wove
9¹/₂ by 6¹/₂
1326.1031 Gilcrease
Dated: "Aug–65" l.l.
Signed: "TM" l.l.
Inscribed: "Raymondskill fall" l.l.; "43" l.l.
Provenance: W. F. Davidson at M. Knoedler &
Co., New York; 1964 Thomas Gilcrease Founda-
tion, Tulsa, Okla.; 1970 The Thomas Gilcrease
Institute of American History and Art, Tulsa,
Okla.

†137
ADAMS CREEK
Graphite on wove
6¹/₂ by 9³/₈
1326.734 Gilcrease
Dated: "Aug 9–65" l.l.
Signed: "TM" l.l.
Inscribed: "Adams Creek" l.l.; "39" l.r.
Provenance: TG
1916 ledger: 35
Note: Sketch on verso

138
ADAMS CREEK
Graphite on wove
4³/₄ by 6¹/₈
1326.724 Gilcrease
Dated: "Aug–65" l.r.
Signed: "TM" l.r.
Inscribed: "Adams Creek" l.r.; "37" l.l.
Provenance: TG

139
ADAMS CREEK
Graphite on wove
4³/₄ by 6¹/₈
1326.725 Gilcrease
Dated: "Aug 9–65" l.l.
Signed: "TM" l.l.
Inscribed: "Adams Creek" l.l.; "38" l.r.
Provenance: TG

140
BULL RUN, MILFORD
Graphite on wove
9³/₈ by 6⁵/₈
1326.726 Gilcrease

Dated: "Aug 9–65" l.r.
Signed: "TM" l.r.
Inscribed: "Bull Run Milford" l.r.; "45" l.r.
Provenance: TG

141
SAWKILL
Graphite on wove
6¹/₂ by 9¹/₂
1326.739 Gilcrease
Dated: "Aug 12–65" u.l.
Signed: "TM" u.l.
Inscribed: "Sawkill" u.l.; "47" l.l.
Provenance: TG
1916 ledger: 74
Note: Sketch on verso

142
WILMINGTON, DELAWARE
Graphite on watermarked laid
10⁵/₈ by 8¹/₂
60.429 Museum of Fine Arts, Boston
Dated: "1865" l.l.
Inscribed: "Wilmington Del" l.l.
Provenance: MK
1916 ledger: 418

143
SHAKESPEARE CLIFF, DOVER
Graphite and chalk on gray wove, mounted on
wove
Sketch 7 by 9¹/₄, mount 10³/₄ by 15³/₄
0276.840 Gilcrease
Dated: "1862" l.l. of sketch; "1862" l.l. of mount
in ink [see note]
Signed: "TM" l.l. of sketch; "TMoran" l.l. of
mount in ink
Inscribed: "Shakespeare Cliff. Dover" l.l.; "5.
Pencil & Chalk" u.l. of mount in ink
Provenance: TG
1916 ledger: 141
Note: Stylistically this sketch resembles the work
done in Fontainebleau—the paper type, the use
of chalk—rather than the work in England in
1862.

†144
FONTAINEBLEAU
Graphite and white chalk on wove
9³/₄ by 13¹/₂
1376.743 Gilcrease

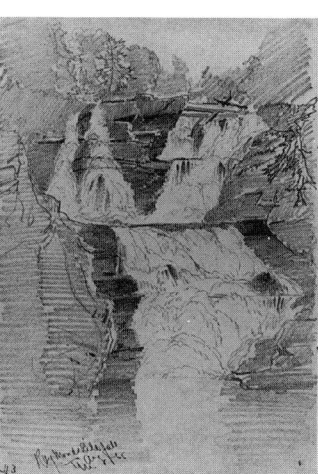

136

Dated: "Oct 1866" l.l. in chalk
Inscribed: "Fontainbleu" l.l. in white chalk
Provenance: TG
Note: Sketch on verso

145
FOREST OF FONTAINEBLEAU
Graphite and white chalk on gray wove
9³/₄ by 13¹/₂
1376.932 Gilcrease
Dated: "1867" u.r.
Inscribed: "Forest of Fontainbleu" u.r.
Provenance: TG
1916 ledger: 64

†146
FOREST OF FONTAINEBLEAU
Graphite and white chalk on gray wove
9³/₄ by 13¹/₂
1376.931 Gilcrease
Dated: "1867" l.l.
Signed: "TM" l.l.
Inscribed: "Forest of Fontainbleau" l.l.; "No. 2.
Pencil & Chalk" and "Study of Rocks. Fontain-
bleau TMoran 1867" in ink, removed from old
mounting and retained
Provenance: TG

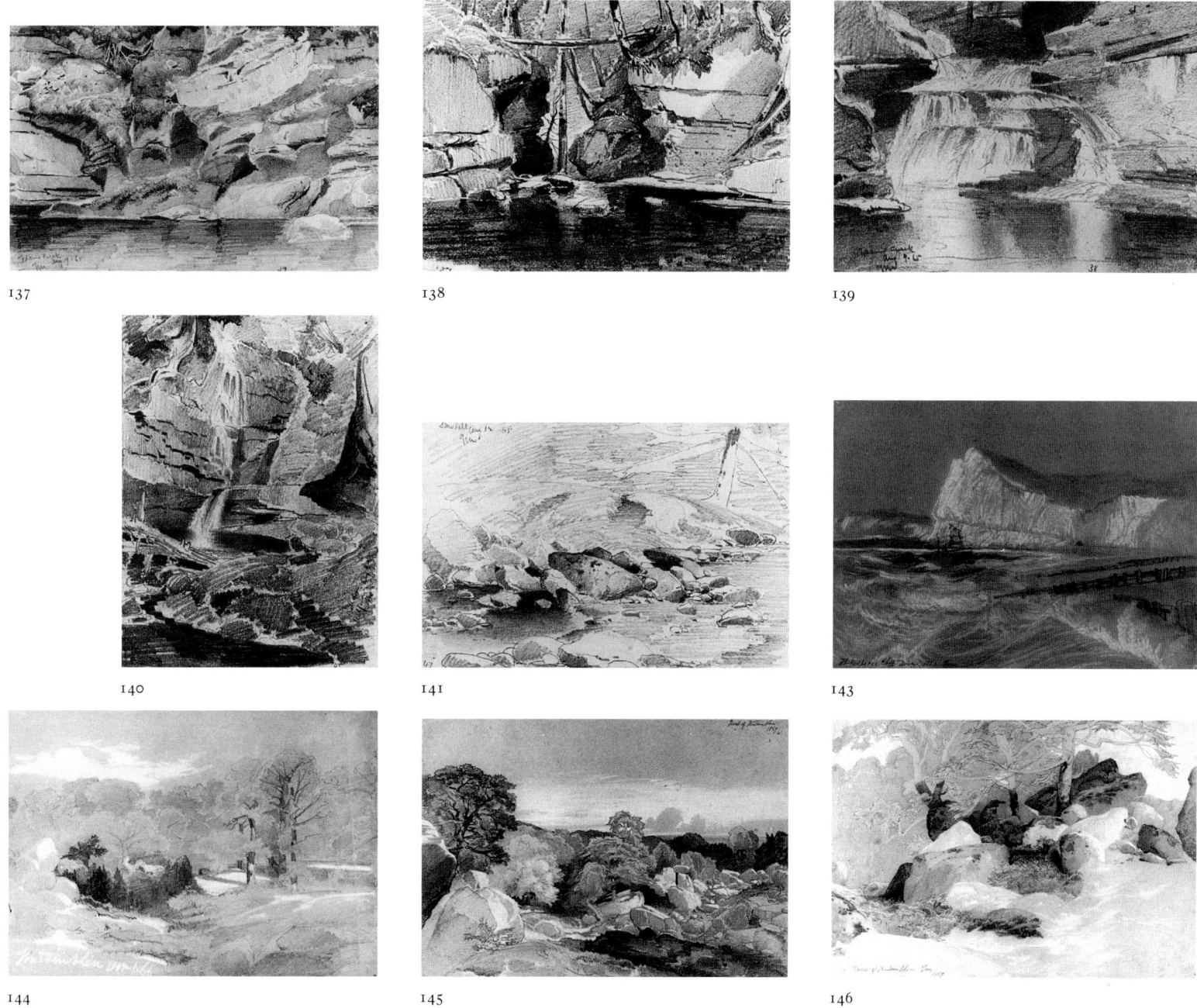

137

138

139

140

141

143

144

145

146

147
GORGE OF APPREMONT,
FONTAINEBLEAU
Graphite and white chalk on gray wove
9³/₄ by 13¹/₂
1376.933 Gilcrease
Dated: "1867" l.l.
Signed: "TM" l.l.
Inscribed: "Gorge of Appremont Fontainbleau"
l.l.
Provenance: TG
1916 ledger: 38

148
FONTAINEBLEAU [descriptive]
Graphite and white chalk on wove
9³/₄ by 13¹/₈
1376.675 Gilcrease
Provenance: TG

†149a
LEGHORN
Graphite on wove
Upper sketch 5 by 9¹/₂, sheet 10 by 14
1376.595 Gilcrease
Inscribed: "Leghorn" l.r.; color and miscella-
neous notes
Provenance: TG

†149b
LEGHORN
Graphite on wove
Lower sketch 5 by 14, sheet 10 by 14
1376.595 Gilcrease
Inscribed: "Leghorn" l.l.
Provenance: TG

†150a
CIVITAVECCHIA
Graphite on gray wove
Upper sketch 3⁷/₈ by 13⁵/₈, sheet 9³/₄ by 13⁵/₈
1376.935 Gilcrease
Dated: "Feb 23–1867" u.l.
Signed: "TM" u.l.
Inscribed: "Civita Vecchia" u.l.
Provenance: TG
1916 ledger: 309

†150b
CIVITAVECCHIA [descriptive]
Graphite on gray wove
Lower sketch 6¹/₈ by 13⁵/₈, sheet 9³/₄ by 13⁵/₈
1376.935 Gilcrease
Dated: "1867" l.l.
Signed: "TM" l.l.
Provenance: TG

151
PONTE SAN BARTOLOMEO, ROME
Graphite on wove
9⁵/₈ by 13⁵/₈
1376.922 Gilcrease
Dated: "1867" l.r.
Inscribed: "Ponto S Bartolomeo Rome" l.r.; mis-
cellaneous notes
Provenance: TG

152
PONTE SAN BARTOLOMEO
Graphite and wash on wove
2¹/₂ by 5¹/₄
35 East Hampton Library
Inscribed: "Ponto Bartolomo" l.r.
Provenance: EH

153
FROM THE PONTE ROTTO
Graphite on wove
2¹/₂ by 5¹/₄
34 East Hampton Library
Inscribed: "from the Ponto Rotto" u.l.
Provenance: EH

*154
COLOSSEUM, ROME
Graphite and watercolor on wove
3⁷/₈ by 6¹/₈
0276.863 Gilcrease
Dated: "1867" l.l.; "Feb 27. 1867" on verso
Signed: "TMoran" l.l.
Inscribed: "Coliseum. Rome" on verso
Provenance: TG
1916 ledger: 72

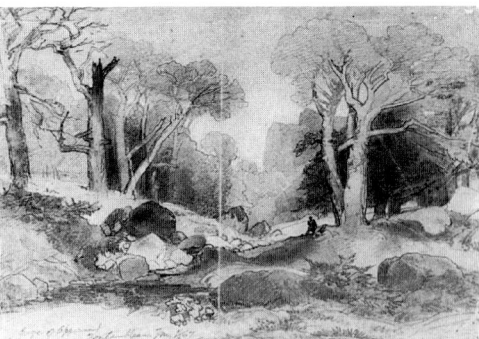

147

*155
RUINS OF THE PALACE OF THE
CAESARS, ROME
Graphite, watercolor, and white gouache on
wove
9³/₄ by 13¹/₂
0276.864 Gilcrease
Dated: "Feb 26th, 1867" u.l.
Inscribed: "Ruins of the Palace of the Cesars
Rome" u.l.; color notes
Provenance: TG
1916 ledger: 68

*156
PALACE OF THE CAESARS, ROME
Graphite, watercolor, and white gouache on gray
wove
9⁵/₈ by 13
0276.941 Gilcrease
Dated: "Feb 27. 1867" u.r.
Inscribed: "Palace of the Cesars. Rome" u.r.; "2"
u.l. in ink
Provenance: Ruth K. Henschel, New York; 1964
Thomas Gilcrease Foundation, Tulsa, Okla.;
1970 The Thomas Gilcrease Institute of American History and Art, Tulsa, Okla.

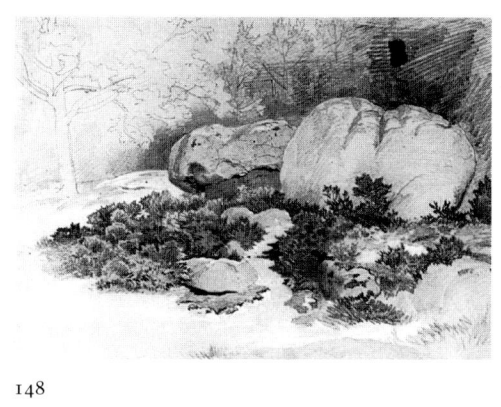

148

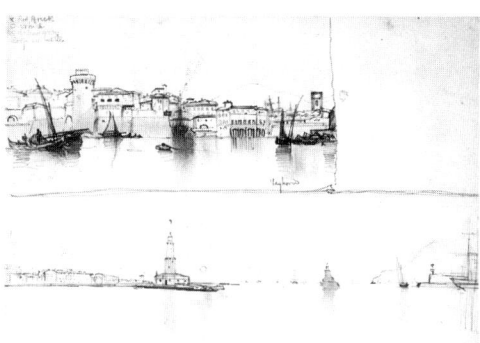

149 ab

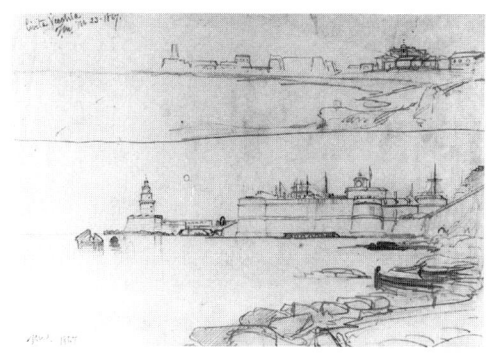

150 ab

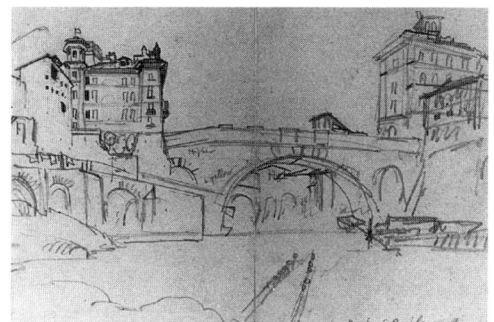

151

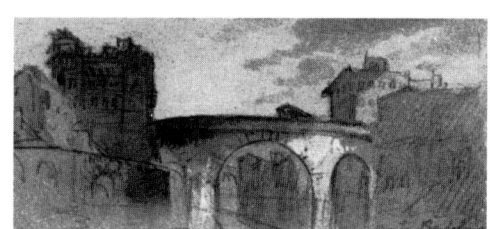

152

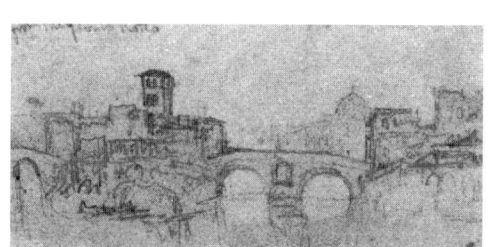

153

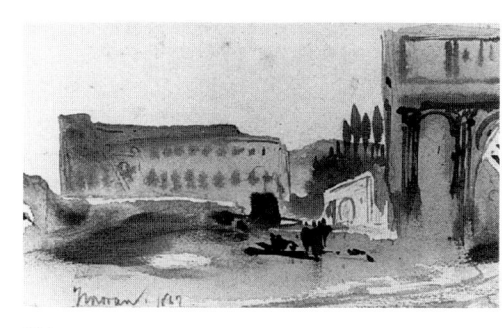

154

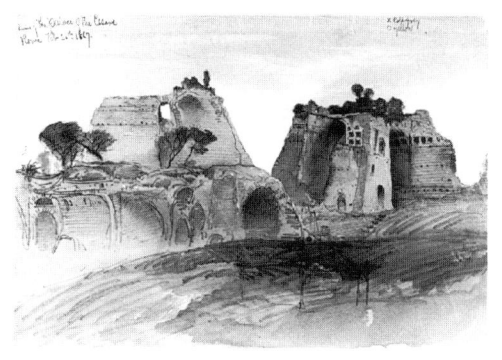

155

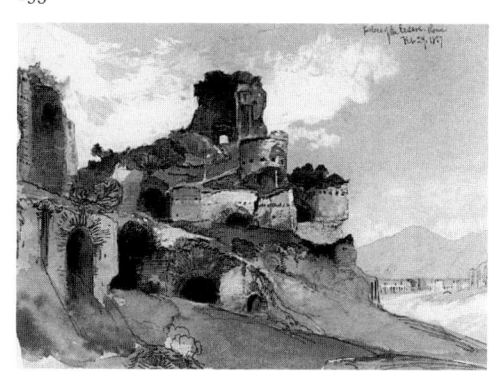

156

157
PALACE OF THE CAESARS, ROME
Graphite and watercolor on wove
9³/₄ by 13⁵/₈
0276.858 Gilcrease
Dated: "Feb 27. 1867" u.l.
Inscribed: "Palace of the Cesars" u.l.; miscella-
neous notes
Provenance: TG
1916 ledger: 78
Note: Sketch on verso; small sketch u.r. on recto

158a
PALACE OF THE CAESARS, ROME
[descriptive]
Graphite and watercolor on wove
Upper sketch 2¹/₈ by 3⁷/₈, sheet 5³/₄ by 4
0276.759 Gilcrease
Provenance: TG
Note: Sketch on verso

158b
PALACE OF THE CAESARS, ROME
[descriptive]
Graphite and watercolor on wove
Center sketch 1⁵/₈ by 3⁷/₈, sheet 5³/₄ by 4
0276.759 Gilcrease
Provenance: TG

158c
PALACE OF THE CAESARS, ROME
[descriptive]
Graphite on wove
Lower sketch 2 by 3⁷/₈, sheet 5³/₄ by 4
0276.759 Gilcrease
Provenance: TG

159
PALACE OF THE CAESARS, ROME
[descriptive]
Graphite and watercolor on wove
2¹/₂ by 4¹/₄
0276.769 Gilcrease
Provenance: TG
Note: Sketch on verso

160
BATHS OF CARACALLA, ROME
Graphite and wash on wove
9³/₄ by 7
12 East Hampton Library
Dated: "1867" lower edge on mount in ink
Signed: "TMoran" lower edge on mount in ink
Inscribed: "Baths of Caracalla, Rome" lower edge
on mount in ink; "8 Pencil" u.l. on mount in ink
Provenance: EH
1916 ledger: 150

161
THE CAMPAGNA NEAR ROME
Graphite, blue and gray washes, and white
gouache on wove
7³/₄ by 13⁵/₈
0276.861 Gilcrease
Dated: "March-1867" u.l.
Signed: "TM" u.l.
Inscribed: "The Campagna near Rome" u.l.
Provenance: TG
1916 ledger: 325

162
THE AQUEDUCT ON THE CAMPAGNA,
ROME
Graphite, blue and gray washes on wove
9³/₄ by 13⁵/₈
0276.862 Gilcrease
Dated: "March 1867" l.l.
Inscribed: "The Acqueduct on the Campagna
Rome" l.l.
Provenance: TG
1916 ledger: 360

163
CLAUDIAN AQUEDUCT
Graphite, gray wash, and white gouache on gray
wove
6 by 5
0276.857 Gilcrease
Dated: "1867" u.r.
Inscribed: "Claudian Acqueduct" u.r.
Provenance: TG

157

164
ROME FROM THE CLAUDIAN
AQUEDUCT
Graphite and wash on wove
4 by 8
Dated: "March 6th 1867" l.c.
20 East Hampton Library
Signed: "TM" l.c.
Inscribed: "Rome from the Claudian Acque-
duct" l.l.
Provenance: EH

165
TOMB OF ST. HELENA, CAMPAGNA,
ROME
Graphite, gray and blue washes on wove
9³/₄ by 13⁵/₈
0276.859 Gilcrease
Dated: "1867" l.r.
Inscribed: "Tomb of St. Helena. Campagna
Rome" l.r.
Provenance: TG
1916 ledger: 65
Note: Sketch on verso; small sketch across top
edge

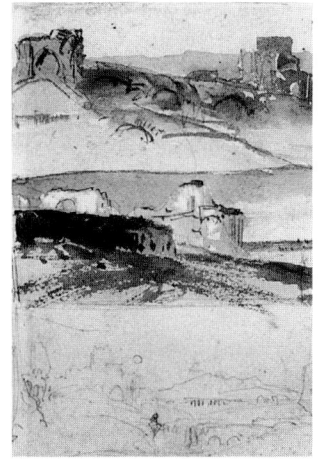

158 abc

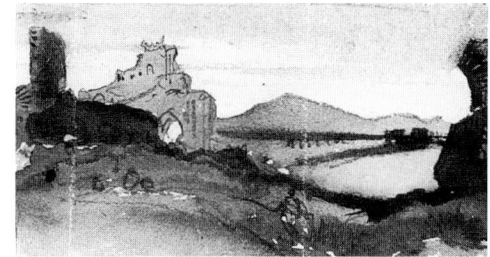

159

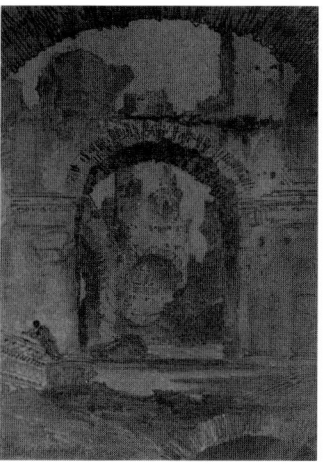

160

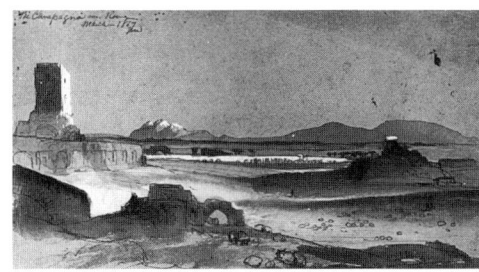

161

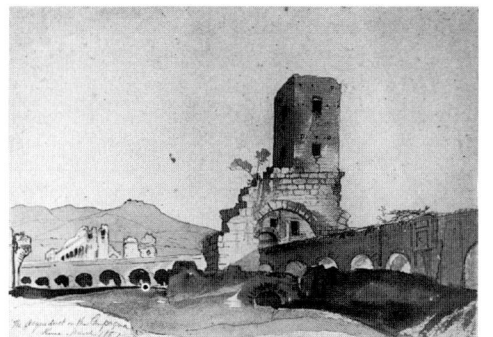

162

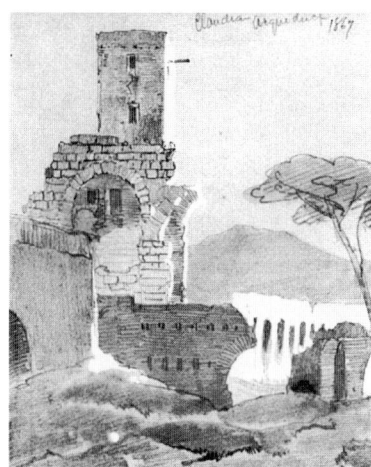

163

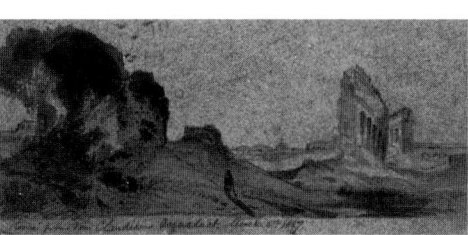

164

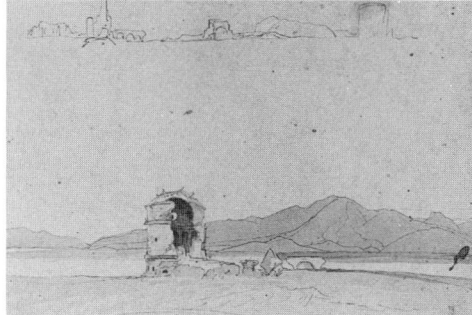

165

166
CAMPAGNA, ROME
Graphite, gray wash, and white gouache on gray wove
5 by 8¹/₂
0276.871 Gilcrease
Dated: "1867" u.l.
Inscribed: "Campagna. Rome" u.l.
Provenance: TG

167
CLAUDIAN AQUEDUCT, ROME
Graphite, gray wash, and white gouache on wove
6¹/₄ by 8¹/₈
0276.870 Gilcrease
Dated: "Mar. 1867" u.l.
Inscribed: "Claudian Acqueduct. Rome" u.l.
Provenance: TG

168
PART OF AQUEDUCT—ROME
Graphite, blue and gray washes, and white gouache on wove
3⁵/₈ by 13¹/₄
0276.867 Gilcrease
Dated: "1867" l.r.
Inscribed: "part of Acqueduct—Rome" l.r.
Provenance: TG
1916 ledger: 79

†169
THE GREAT AQUEDUCT OF THE CAMPAGNA, ROME
Graphite, blue and gray washes on wove
Sketch 7³/₄ by 13¹/₄, mount 8¹/₈ by 13³/₄
0276.860 Gilcrease
Dated: "1867" u.l.; "1867" l.l. in ink
Signed: "TMoran" l.l.
Inscribed: "The Great Acqueduct of the Campagna. Rome" u.l.; "The Claudian Acqueduct. Campagna Rome" l.l. in ink; "13 pencil & wash" u.l. of mount in ink
Provenance: TG
1916 ledger: 148
Note: Sketch and inscription on verso: "Castel Gandalfo"

170
ROME FROM THE AQUEDUCT
Graphite and wash on wove
6¹/₄ by 13⁵/₈

0276.856 Gilcrease
Dated: "March 1867" l.r.
Signed: "TMoran" l.r.
Inscribed: "Rome from the Acqueduct" l.r.
Provenance: TG
1916 ledger: 42
Note: Sketch on verso

171
ALBANO FROM THE ROAD TO THE LAKE
Graphite on wove
7¹/₄ by 9⁵/₈
1376.924 Gilcrease
Dated: "1867" u.c.
Signed: "TM" u.c.
Inscribed: "Albano from the Road to the Lake" u.l.
Provenance: TG
1916 ledger: 170
Note: Sketch and inscription on verso: "The edge of L. Albano"

172
LAKE ALBANO LOOKING TOWARD CASTEL GANDOLFO
Graphite on wove
6¹/₄ by 9³/₄
1376.888 Gilcrease
Dated: "1863" l.l. [see note]
Signed: "TMoran" l.l.; "TM" l.r.
Inscribed: "Lake Albano looking toward Castel Gandolfo" u.l.
Provenance: TG
Note: Moran was not traveling outside the United States in 1863. The date was added later, and may not even be Thomas Moran's writing. The sketch is stylistically similar to others made in 1867. There is a sketch on verso.

173
GENZANO [ledger title]
Graphite on tan ruled laid
5 by 7⁷/₈
1917–17–65 Cooper-Hewitt Museum
Provenance: TM
1916 ledger: 1
Note: Sketch and inscription on verso: "Tetons from the Plains Aug 28–79"

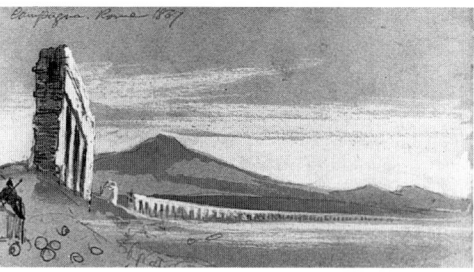
166

174
LAKE NEMI
Graphite and white chalk on gray wove
9⁵/₈ by 13¹/₂
1376.920 Gilcrease
Dated: "March 12–1867" u.l.
Inscribed: "L. Nemi" u.l.
Provenance: TG
1916 ledger: 276

175
NAPLES [ledger title]
Graphite on wove
5 by 7⁷/₈
78 East Hampton Library
Provenance: EH
1916 ledger: 4

176
ROME
Graphite and chalk on blue wove
8¹/₈ by 5¹/₂
1376.928 Gilcrease
Dated: "1867" l.r. in ink
Signed: "TMoran" l.r. in ink
Inscribed: "Rome" l.r. in ink; "Between Albano & Lariccia" on verso
Provenance: TG
1916 ledger: 428

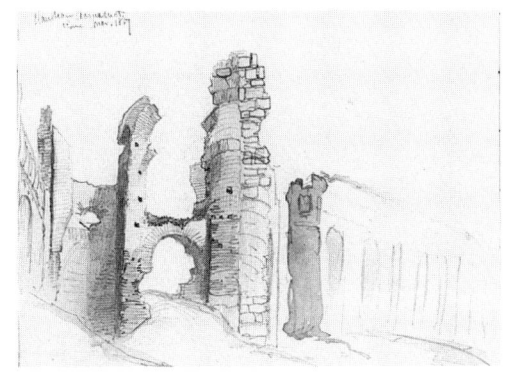

167

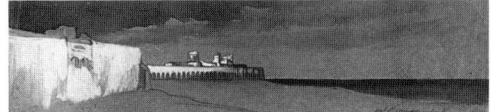

168

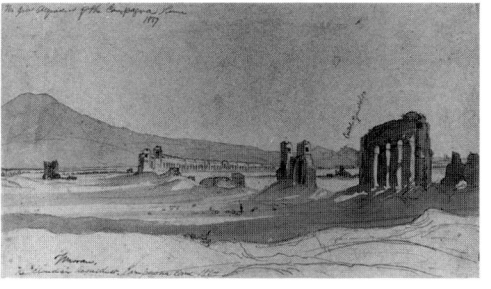

169

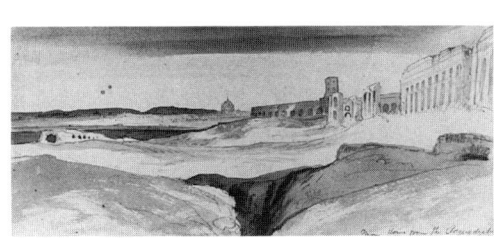

170

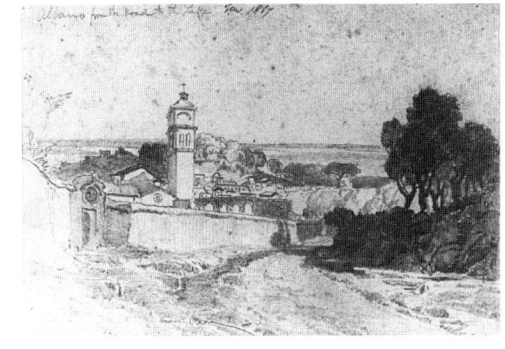

171

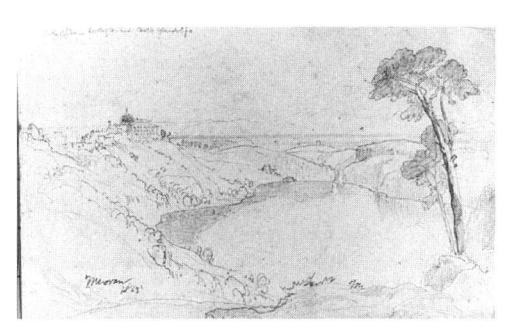

172

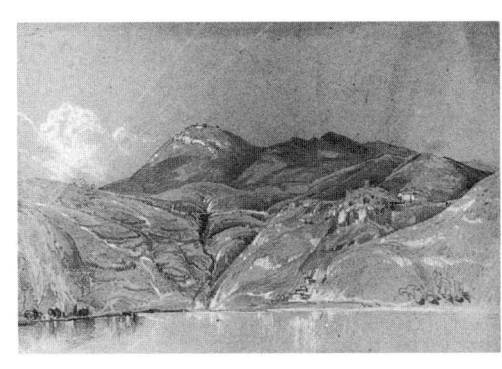

174

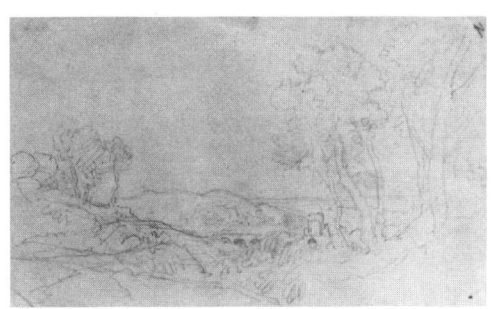

175

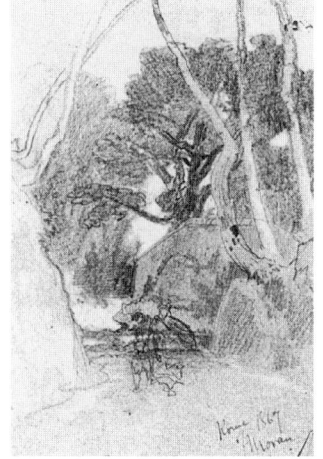

176

177
NEAR ROME
Graphite on wove
5¹/₈ by 6¹/₄
1376.921 Gilcrease
Dated: "1867" l.l.
Signed: "TM" l.c.
Inscribed: "near Rome" l.l.
Provenance: TG

178
NEAR ROME [descriptive]
Graphite on wove
7¹/₈ by 5⁷/₈
1376.604 Gilcrease
Provenance: TG
Note: Sketch on verso

179
ROME [descriptive]
Graphite on wove
3³/₄ by 3¹/₄
106 East Hampton Library
Provenance: EH

180
ROME
Graphite on wove
5³/₈ by 7¹/₂
31 East Hampton Library
Dated: "1867" l.l.
Signed: "TM" l.l.
Inscribed: "Rome" l.l.; "Villa Borghese, Rome
1867" on verso
Provenance: EH
1916 ledger: 395

181
ROME
Graphite on wove
5¹/₄ by 6¹/₈
91 East Hampton Library
Dated: "1867" l.r.
Signed: "TM" l.r.
Inscribed: "Rome" l.r.; Villa Borghese, Rome
1867" on verso
Provenance: EH
1916 ledger: 317

182
ALPINE PINE IN THE BORGHESE
VILLA, ROME
Graphite on watermarked wove
13⁵/₈ by 9¹/₄
1376.925 Gilcrease
Dated: "Mar. 1867" u.r.
Signed: "TM" l.l.
Inscribed: "Alpine Pine in the Borghese Villa
Rome" u.r.
Provenance: TG
1916 ledger: 419

†183
OAKS IN THE VILLA BORGHESE, ROME
Graphite and sepia wash on wove
15¹/₄ by 9¹/₄
0276.869 Gilcrease
Dated: "March-1867" l.r.
Inscribed: "Oaks in the Villa Borghese Rome"
l.r.
Provenance: TG
1916 ledger: 94
Note: Sketches on verso

184
PINES IN THE VILLA BORGHESE, ROME
Graphite and sepia wash on wove
Sketch 13¹/₂ by 8³/₄, mount 14³/₄ by 10³/₄
0276.868 Gilcrease
Dated: "March-1867" l.l.; "1867" on mount l.l. in
ink
Signed: "TM" l.l.; "TMoran" on mount l.l. in ink
Inscribed: "pines in the Villa Borghese Rome"
l.l.; "Study of An Italian Pine" on mount l.l. in
ink; "7. pencil & sepia" u.l. in ink on mount
Provenance: TG
1916 ledger: 149

185
BORGHESE GARDENS
Graphite on gray wove
4¹/₂ by 10¹/₈
1376.926 Gilcrease
Dated: "1867" u.r.
Signed: "TM" u.r.
Inscribed: "Borghese Gardens" u.r.; miscella-
neous notes
Provenance: TG
1916 ledger: 424

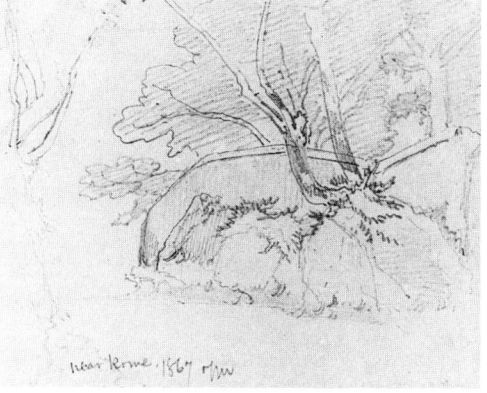

177

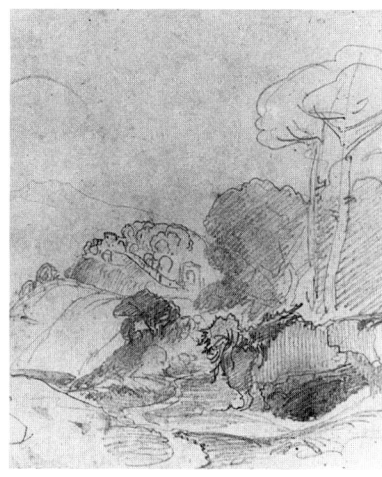

178

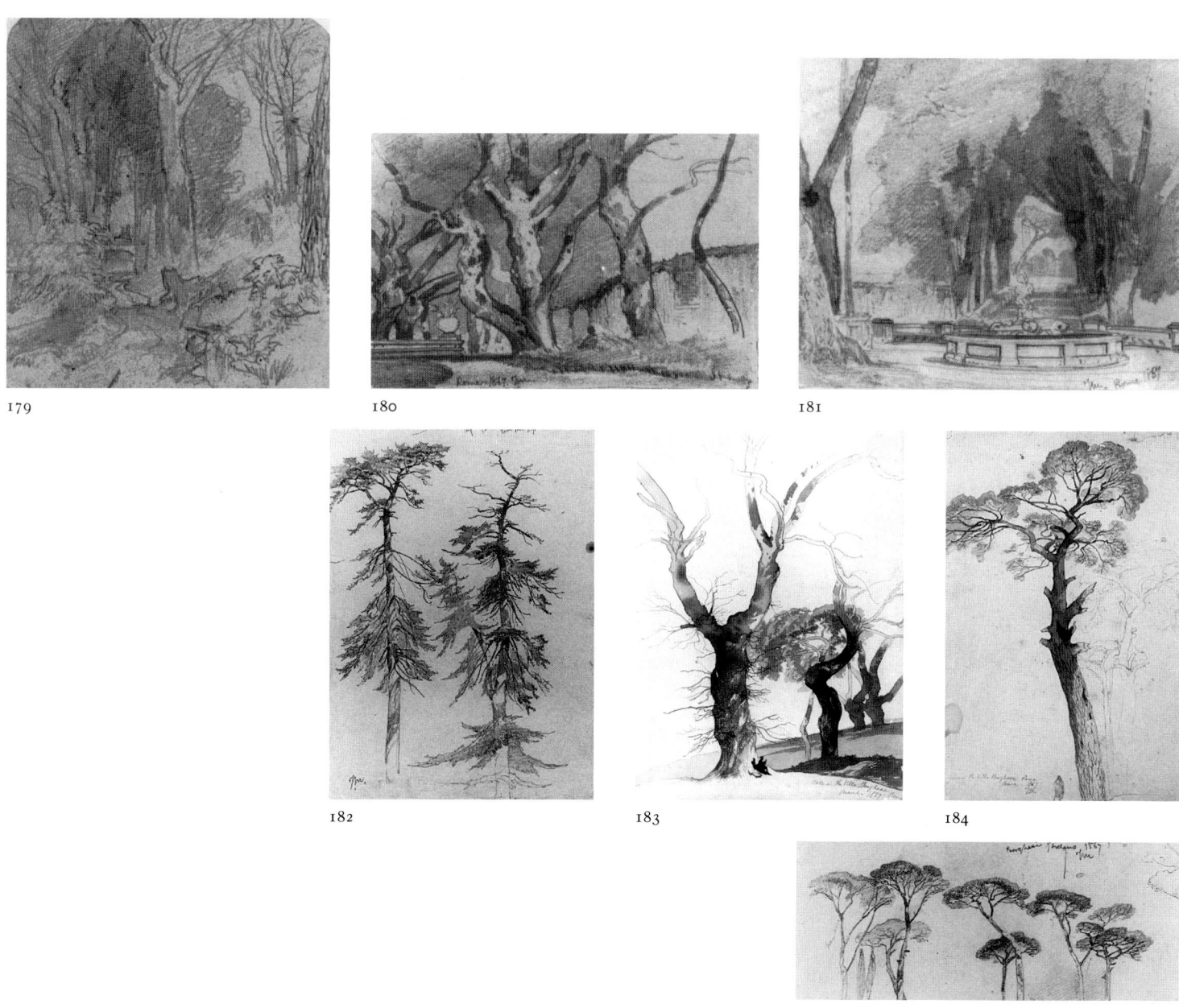

179

180

181

182

183

184

185

†186
BETWEEN FLORENCE AND BOLOGNA
Graphite and sepia wash on wove
10¹/8 by 7¹/2
0276.865 Gilcrease
Dated: "1867" u.l.
Inscribed: "Between Florence & Bologna" u.l.
Provenance: TG

187
ARGEGNO, LAKE OF COMO
Graphite and red conté crayon on watermarked
wove
11⁵/8 by 9¹/2
1376.919 Gilcrease
Dated: "April 1st 1867" l.l.
Inscribed: "Argegno. Lake of Como" l.l.
Provenance: TG
1916 ledger: 75

188
LAKE COMO
Graphite on wove
12¹/8 by 18³/4
1376.929 Gilcrease
Dated: "1867" l.r.
Signed: "TM" l.r.
Inscribed: "Lake Como" l.r.
Provenance: TG
Note: Sketch on verso

189
AIROLO
Graphite on brown wove
8⁵/8 by 10⁷/8
1376.889 Gilcrease
Dated: "1863" l.l.
Signed: "TMoran" l.l.
Inscribed: "Airolo Village in the [illegible] Alps" l.l.
Provenance: TG
Note: Moran was not traveling outside the
United States in 1863. The date was added later
and may not even be in Thomas Moran's writ-
ing. The sketch is stylistically similar to others
made in 1867. Sketch and inscription on verso:
"The high snow peak at Como."

190
PASS OF FAIDO
Graphite, wash, and white gouache on tan wove
22 by 28

1917–17–12 A Cooper-Hewitt Museum
Dated: "1867" l.l.
Signed: "TMoran" l.l.
Inscribed: "Pass of Faido" u.r.; "Near Pass of
Faido, Italy" l.l.
Provenance: TM

191
PASSAGE OF THE ST. GOTTHARD,
NEAR AMSTEAG
Graphite on wove
9³/8 by 13⁵/8
1376.927 Gilcrease
Dated: "March 1867" u.l.
Inscribed: "passage of the St. Gothard Near
Amsteag" u.l.
Provenance: TG
1916 ledger: 243
Note: Sketch on verso

192
WEST, TIME, ¹/2 PAST 6 O'CLOCK
Graphite and gray wash on newsprint
7³/4 by 12¹/8
0226.883 Gilcrease
Dated: "June 28th 1870" u.l.
Signed: "TM" u.c.
Inscribed: "West time ¹/2 6 Oclock" u.l.; "Dark
Clouds with Light gray edges" c.; color notes
Provenance: TG
1916 ledger: 432

†193
FALLS OF SCHUYLKILL
Graphite on newsprint
7³/4 by 12¹/8
1326.953 Gilcrease
Dated: "June 28th 1870" u.l.
Signed: "TM" u.l.
Inscribed: "Falls of Schuylkill" u.c.; "sunset" u.l.;
"Dark Blue gray with Warm edge Reflected
grays" center; color notes
Provenance: TG
1916 ledger: 433

†194
FALLS OF SCHUYLKILL
Graphite on newsprint
Sketch 7³/4 by 12¹/8, mount 10³/4 by 14³/4
1326.955 Gilcrease
Dated: "1870" u.l.; "1870" l.l. in ink on mount

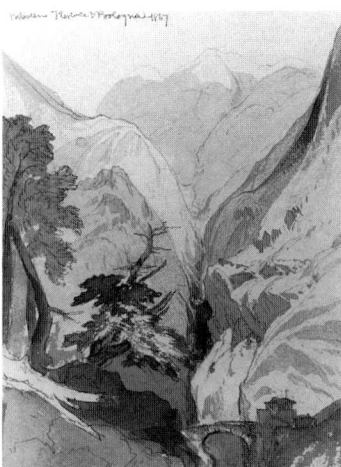
186

Signed: "TMoran" l.l. on mount
Inscribed: "Falls of Schuylkill" u.l.; "Looking
East evening" u.l.; "pencil sketch of a sky." l.l. in
ink on mount; "15 pencil" u.l. on mount; extensive color and atmospheric notes
Provenance: TG
1916 ledger: 104

195
STORM—EVENING LOOKING
SOUTHWEST
Graphite on newsprint
7³/4 by 12¹/2
1326.954 Gilcrease
Dated: "June 30th 1870" u.l.
Inscribed: "Storm—evening looking S.W." u.l.;
"very dark Blue gray clear Blue to a dull Red"
l.c.
Provenance: TG
1916 ledger: 302

196
STORM CLOUDS [descriptive]
Graphite on wove
11³/4 by 18¹/2
1326.657 Gilcrease
Signed: "TM" l.l.
Provenance: TG
1916 ledger: 331

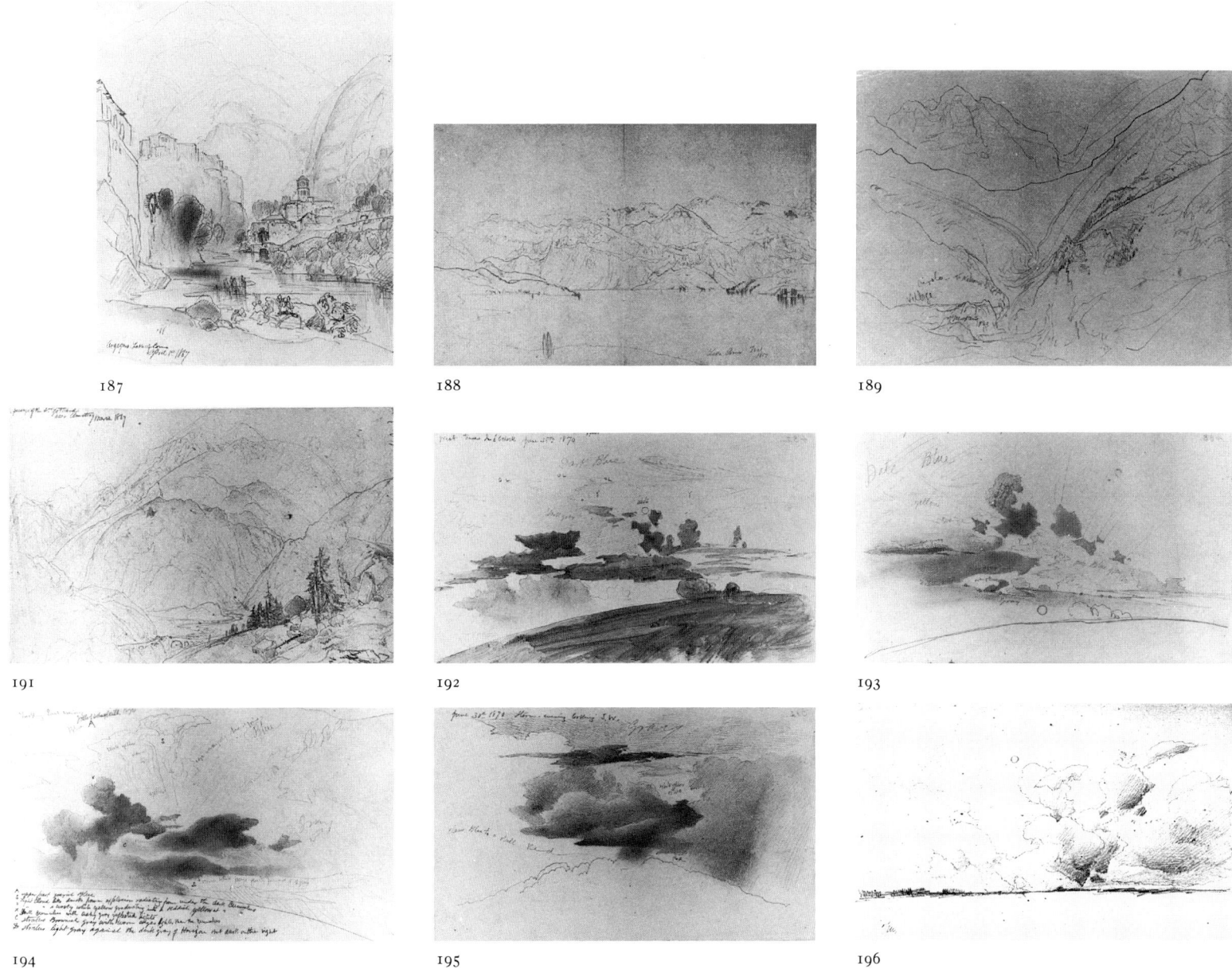

187

188

189

191

192

193

194

195

196

197
FALLS OF SCHUYLKILL
Graphite and erasures on white laid coated with gray paint
4³/₈ by 6¹/₂
1326.1036 Gilcrease
Dated: "Aug 8th 1870" l.l.
Signed: "TM" l.l.
Inscribed: "Falls of Schuylkill" l.l.
Provenance: Ruth K. Henschel, New York; 1964 Thomas Gilcrease Foundation, Tulsa, Okla.; 1970 The Thomas Gilcrease Institute of American History and Art, Tulsa, Okla.
1916 ledger: 36
Note: Moran used a technique reminiscent of that used by Turner in his *Temple of the Sibyl Seen from Below* (1819, British Museum, illustrated in Wilton, *J.M.W. Turner: His Art and Life,* p. 139).

198
SCHUYLKILL RIVER SCENE [descriptive]
Graphite and wash on tan wove
9⁵/₈ by 18¹/₄
0226.782 Gilcrease
Provenance: TG
Note: Sketches on verso

199a
FALLS OF SCHUYLKILL
Graphite on wove
Upper left sketch 3³/₈ by 4⁵/₈, sheet 6¹/₂ by 9⁷/₈
1326.956 Gilcrease
Dated: "Sep. 1870" l.r.
Signed: "TM" l.r.
Inscribed: "Falls of Schuylkill" l.r.
Provenance: TG

199b
FALLS OF SCHUYLKILL
Graphite on wove
Upper right sketch 3¹/₂ by 5¹/₈, sheet 6¹/₂ by 9⁷/₈
1326.956 Gilcrease
Dated: "Sep. 1870" u.l.
Signed: "TM" u.c.
Inscribed: "Falls of Schuylkill" u.l.
Provenance: TG

199c
FALLS OF SCHUYLKILL [descriptive]
Graphite on wove

Lower left sketch 3¹/₈ by 4⁵/₈, sheet 6¹/₂ by 9⁷/₈
1326.956 Gilcrease
Provenance: TG

199d
FALLS OF SCHUYLKILL [descriptive]
Graphite on wove
Lower right sketch 3 by 5, sheet 6¹/₂ by 9⁷/₈
1326.956 Gilcrease
Provenance: TG

200a
SCHUYLKILL FALLS
Graphite on wove
Upper sketch 2¹/₂ by 4¹/₄, sheet 6 by 4¹/₄
70 East Hampton Library
Dated: "Sep 22nd 1870" u.l.
Signed: "TM" u.l.
Inscribed: "alls" u.l.
Provenance: EH
Note: Sketch trimmed slightly along left edge

200b
WISSAHICKON
Graphite on wove
Lower sketch 4 by 4¹/₂, sheet 6 by 4³/₄
70 East Hampton Library
Dated: "Sep 1870" l.r.
Signed: "TM" l.r.
Inscribed: "Wissahickon" l.r.
Provenance: EH

201a
BELMONT [descriptive]
Graphite on wove
Upper left sketch 2¹/₈ by 4, sheet 6¹/₂ by 9⁷/₈
1326.613 Gilcrease
Provenance: TG
Note: Sketch on verso

201b
BELMONT
Graphite on wove
Upper center sketch 2¹/₈ by 3¹/₄, sheet 6¹/₂ by 9⁷/₈
1326.613 Gilcrease
Inscribed: "Belmont" l.l.
Provenance: TG

201c
BELMONT
Graphite on wove

Upper right sketch 2 by 1⁷/₈, sheet 6¹/₂ by 9⁷/₈
1326.613 Gilcrease
Inscribed: "Belmont" l.l.
Provenance: TG

201d
BELMONT
Graphite on wove
Lower left sketch 1⁷/₈ by 4, sheet 6¹/₂ by 9⁷/₈
1326.613 Gilcrease
Inscribed: "Belmont" l.l.
Provenance: TG

201e
BELMONT [descriptive]
Graphite on wove
Lower center sketch 2¹/₂ by 4¹/₄, sheet 6¹/₂ by 9⁷/₈
1326.613 Gilcrease
Inscribed with miscellaneous notes
Provenance: TG

201f
BELMONT [descriptive]
Graphite on wove
Lower right sketch 2¹/₂ by 4, sheet 6¹/₂ by 9⁷/₈
1326.613 Gilcrease
Provenance: TG

*202
FIRST SKETCH MADE IN THE WEST AT GREEN RIVER, WYOMING
Graphite, watercolor, and white gouache on wove
3³/₄ by 8¹/₈
0236.882 Gilcrease
Dated: "1871" l.l. and l.r. on mount
Signed: "TMoran" l.l.
Inscribed: "First sketch made in the West at Green River. Wyoming" lower edge on mount
Provenance: TG

203
GREEN RIVER
Graphite, ink, and wash on wove
4⁷/₈ by 7¹/₄
1917–17–7 Cooper-Hewitt Museum
Dated: "1871" l.l.
Inscribed: "Green River W" l.l.
Provenance: TM
1916 ledger: 121

204
CORINNE, UTAH
Graphite on wove
5 by 8
71 East Hampton Library
Dated: "1871" l.l.
Signed: "TM" l.l.
Inscribed: "Corinne, Utah" l.l.
Provenance: EH
1916 ledger: 130

205
BEAVERHEAD CANYON, MONTANA
Graphite, watercolor, and white gouache on wove
10³/₈ by 14¹/₈
60.427 Museum of Fine Arts, Boston
Dated: "July 4th 1871" u.c.
Signed: "TM" u.c.
Inscribed: "Beaver Head Canon, Montana" l.r.
Provenance: MK

206
WARM SPRINGS CREEK, IDAHO
Graphite, watercolor, and white gouache on wove
3³/₈ by 7¹/₈
8535 Yellowstone National Park, Wyoming
Dated: "July 8" u.l.; "1871" l.l. in ink
Signed: Colophon l.l. in ink; "TMoran" l.r.
Inscribed: "W Springs C, Idaho" u.l.
Provenance: GP
1916 ledger: 29

207
THE YELLOWSTONE RANGE FROM
NEAR FORT ELLIS
Graphite, watercolor, and white gouache on wove
10¹/₈ by 13³/₄
8531 Yellowstone National Park, Wyoming
Dated: "1871" l.l.
Signed: "TM" l.l.
Inscribed: "The Yellowstone Range from near Fort Ellis" u.l.; "Near Fort Ellis" l.l.
Provenance: GP

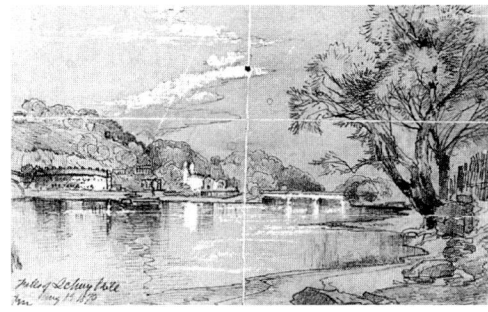

197

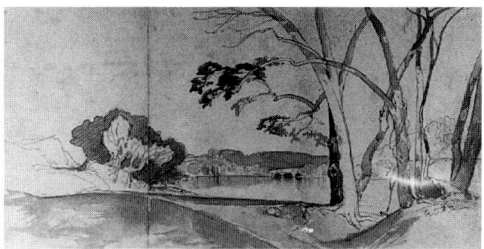

198

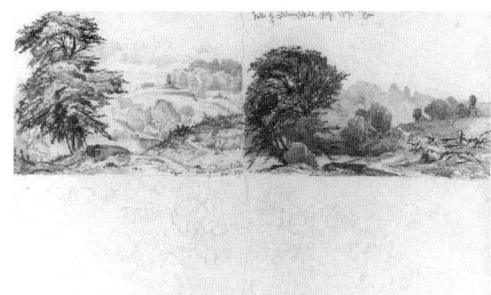

199 abcd

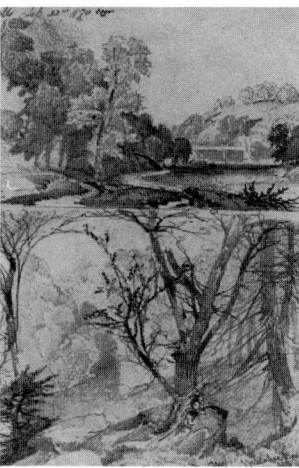

200 ab

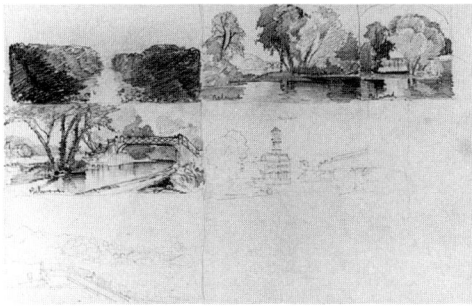

201 abcdef

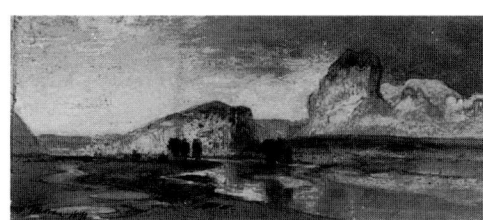

202

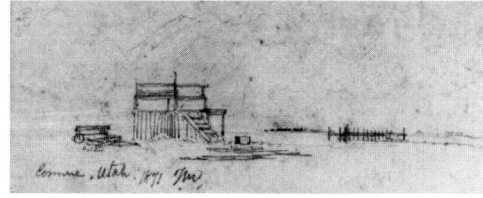

204

208
CINNABAR MOUNTAIN,
YELLOWSTONE RIVER
Graphite, watercolor, and white gouache on
wove
10³/8 by 14¹/8
8534 Yellowstone National Park, Wyoming
Dated: "July 20th 1871" u.l.
Signed: "TM" u.l.; "TMoran" l.l.
Inscribed: "Cinnabar Mt. Yellowstone River"
u.l.; color notes
Provenance: GP
1916 ledger: 19

209
THE DEVILS SLIDE, YELLOWSTONE
Graphite, watercolor, and white gouache on
wove
10¹/4 by 7
8533 Yellowstone National Park, Wyoming
Dated: "1871" l.l.
Signed: "TMoran" l.l.
Inscribed: "The Devils Slide Yellowstone" l.l.
Provenance: GP
1916 ledger: 11

210
LOWER YELLOWSTONE VALLEY
Graphite on gray wove
4 by 6¹/4
4218 Jefferson National Expansion Memorial
Dated: "1871" verso
Signed: "TMoran" l.r.
Inscribed: "Lower Yellowstone Valley" u.c.
Provenance: JNEM

211
YELLOWSTONE ABOVE BOETTLERS
RANCH
Graphite on wove
7 by 10
5845 Jefferson National Expansion Memorial
Dated: "July 21st 1871" u.c.
Inscribed: "Yellowstone Above Boettlers Ranch"
u.l.
Provenance: JNEM
Note: Sketch on verso

†212
BUNSEN PEAK
Graphite on blue wove

6¹/4 by 10
5847 Jefferson National Expansion Memorial
Signed: "TM" l.r.
Inscribed: "Bunsens Peak" u.r.; "Cleopatra" and
"Jupiter" l.l.
Provenance: JNEM
1916 ledger: 210

213
HOT SPRINGS OF GARDNER RIVER
YELLOWSTONE
Graphite on wove
6 by 12¹/2
4225 Jefferson National Expansion Memorial
Dated: "1871" u.c.
Signed: "TM" u.c.
Inscribed: "Hot Springs of Gardiners River Yel-
lowstone" upper edge
Provenance: JNEM
1916 ledger: 61

214
GARDNER RIVER
Graphite, watercolor, and gouache on wove
5 by 7³/4
8526 Yellowstone National Park, Wyoming
Dated: "July 1871" u.r.
Signed: "TMoran" l.l.
Inscribed: "Gardiners River" u.r.
Provenance: GP

215
LIBERTY CAP AND CLEMATIS GULCH
[descriptive]
Graphite, watercolor, and gouache on wove
10 by 6⁷/8
8524 Yellowstone National Park, Wyoming
Dated: "1871" l.l. in ink
Signed: colophon l.l. in ink
Provenance: GP

216
TOWER CREEK
Graphite and watercolor on wove
7³/4 by 9¹/2
8528 Yellowstone National Park, Wyoming
Signed: "TMoran" l.l.
Inscribed: "Tower Creek" l.l.
Provenance: GP
Note: Sketch and inscription on verso: "Above
the Yellowstone Falls"

217
TOWER FALL
Graphite on gray wove
5 by 8
4219 Jefferson National Expansion Memorial
Dated: "1871" u.c.
Inscribed: "Tower Falls" u.c.
Provenance: JNEM
1916 ledger: 159

218
TOWER FALL [descriptive]
Graphite, watercolor, and gouache on wove
7⁷/8 by 5
8523 Yellowstone National Park, Wyoming
Dated: "1871" l.r. in ink
Signed: Colophon l.r. in ink
Provenance: GP

219
NEAR MEADOW CREEK
Graphite, wash, and white gouache on wove
5 by 7⁷/8
1917–17–8 Cooper-Hewitt Museum
Dated: "July 25th 1871" u.r.
Signed: "TM" u.r.
Inscribed: "Near Meadow Creek" u.r.
Provenance: TM
1916 ledger: 311

220
IN THE GRAND CANYON
Graphite and white gouache on wove
7⁵/8 by 5
8540 Yellowstone National Park, Wyoming
Dated: "July 1871" u.l.
Signed: "TM" u.l.; "TMoran" twice l.r.
Inscribed: "In the Grand Canon" u.l.
Provenance: GP
Note: Sketch and inscription on verso: "Mea-
dow Creek"

221
IN THE CANYON
Graphite on wove
5¹/8 by 7³/4
4215 Jefferson National Expansion Memorial
Inscribed: "In the Canon" u.l.
Provenance: JNEM
Note: Sketch and inscription on verso: "Mud
Spring at Crater"

222
CANYON WALLS YELLOWSTONE
Graphite, watercolor, and white gouache on green wove
8¹/₈ by 5¹/₈
8538 Yellowstone National Park, Wyoming
Dated: "1871" l.l.
Inscribed: "Canon Walls Yellowstone" l.l.
Provenance: GP
1916 ledger: 330

223
SAND IN THE CANYON
Graphite, watercolor, and white gouache on wove
5³/₄ by 10
8542 Yellowstone National Park, Wyoming
Signed: "TMoran" l.c.
Inscribed: "Sand in the Canon" u.l.
Provenance: GP

224
CRYSTAL FALLS, CRYSTAL CREEK
Graphite, watercolor, and white gouache on wove
11 by 8¹/₈
8541 Yellowstone National Park, Wyoming
Dated: "1871" l.r.
Signed: "TM" l.l.
Inscribed: "Crystal Falls, Crystal Creek" lower edge
Provenance: GP

225
MUD VOLCANO
Graphite on laid
5 by 7¹/₂
4223 Jefferson National Expansion Memorial
Signed: "TMoran" l.r.
Inscribed: "Mud Volcano" l.l.
Provenance: JNEM
Note: Sketch and inscription on verso: "Lake back of Ellis 1871"

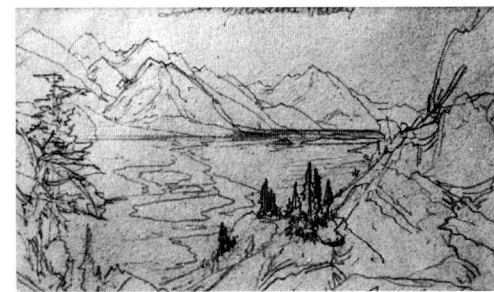

210

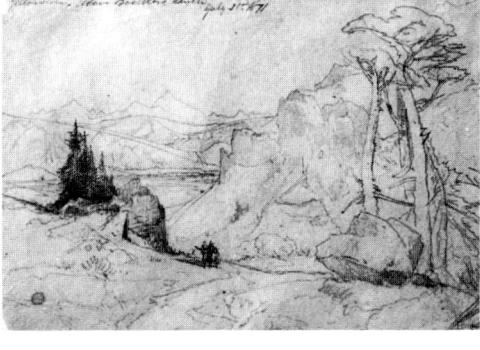

211

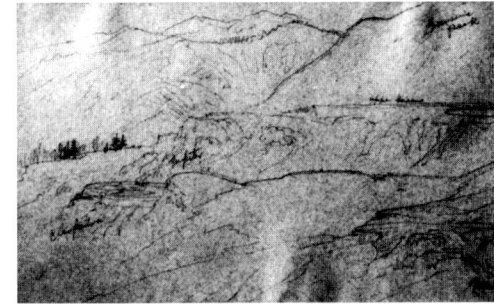

212

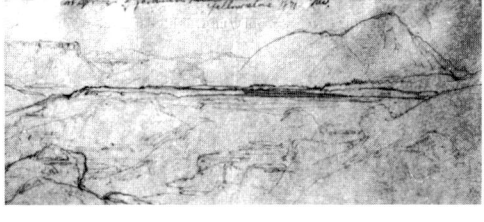

213

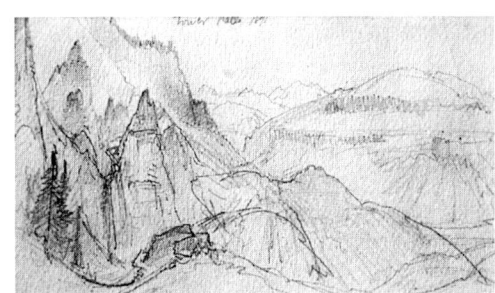

217

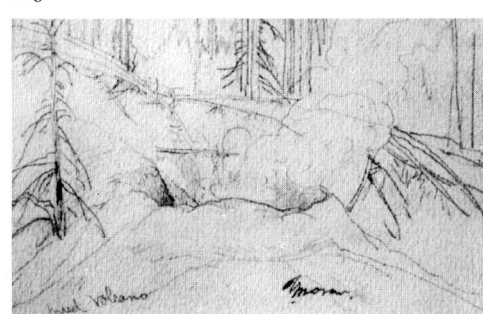

225

226
TREES NEAR MUD VOLCANO
[descriptive]
Graphite on gray wove
12 1/4 by 9 1/8
1376.674 Gilcrease
Provenance: TG

†227
YELLOWSTONE LAKE
Graphite on laid
5 by 7
4217 Jefferson National Expansion Memorial
Dated: "Aug 4th–1871" u.r.
Signed: "TMoran" l.c.
Inscribed: "Yellowstone Lake" u.r.
Provenance: JNEM
Note: Sketch and inscription on verso: "Upper Falls of the Yellowstone"

228
THE YELLOWSTONE LAKE
Graphite on wove
4 3/4 by 9 3/4
5846 Jefferson National Expansion Memorial
Dated: "Aug 6th 1871" u.l.
Inscribed: "The Yellowstone Lake" u.l.
Provenance: JNEM

229
LOWER ENTRANCE TO MADISON
CANYON
Graphite, watercolor, and white gouache on wove
5 1/4 by 8 1/4
4299 Jefferson National Expansion Memorial
Dated: "Aug 8" u.c.
Signed: "TMoran" u.c.
Inscribed: "Lower Entrance to Madison Canon" upper edge
Provenance: JNEM

*230
IN LOWER MADISON CANYON
Graphite, watercolor, and white gouache on wove
8 1/8 by 5 3/4
0236.1576 Gilcrease
Dated: "Aug 8" u.r.
Signed: colophon l.r.
Inscribed: "in Lower Madison Canon" u.c.

Provenance: Ruth K. Henschel, New York; 1964 Thomas Gilcrease Foundation, Tulsa, Okla.; 1974 The Thomas Gilcrease Institute of American History and Art, Tulsa, Okla.

231
RAVINE IN MADISON CANYON
Graphite on wove
10 1/4 by 14 1/2
5848 Jefferson National Expansion Memorial
Dated: "Aug 9th 1871" u.l.
Signed: "TM" u.l.
Inscribed: "Ravine in Madison Canon" u.l.
Provenance: JNEM
Note: Sketch and inscription on verso: "Green River"

232
YOSEMITE
Graphite on wove
7 3/4 by 9 5/8
57 787 Yosemite National Park, California
Dated: "1872" u.l.
Signed: "TM" u.l.
Inscribed: "Yosemite" u.l.
Provenance: YOS
1916 ledger: 86
Note: Sketch on verso

†233
YOSEMITE
Graphite on wove
10 3/4 by 14 7/8
57 778 Yosemite National Park, California
Dated: "1872" u.l.
Signed: "TMoran" u.l.
Inscribed: "Yosemite" u.l.; color notes
Provenance: YOS
1916 ledger: 93

234
YOSEMITE VALLEY
Graphite on green wove
10 3/4 by 14 7/8
57 786 Yosemite National Park, California
Dated: "1872" l.r.
Signed: "TM" l.r.
Inscribed: "Yosemite V." l.r.; miscellaneous and color notes
Provenance: YOS
1916 ledger: 104

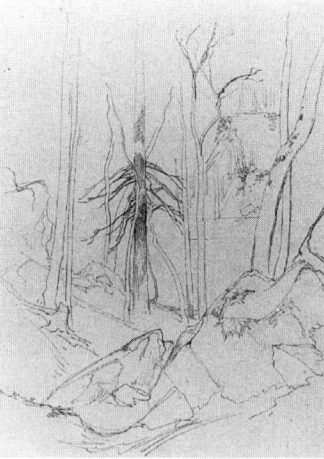

226

235
SOUTH DOME OF YOSEMITE
Graphite and wash on wove
7 3/8 by 5 3/8
1917–17-15 Cooper-Hewitt Museum
Dated: "1872" l.l. in ink
Signed: Colophon stamp and "oran" l.r. in ink
Inscribed: "South Dome of Yosemite" l.l. in ink
Provenance: TM
1916 ledger: 277

236
GORGE NEAR GENTRY'S, YOSEMITE
Graphite on wove
9 7/8 by 12 5/8
57 781 Yosemite National Park, California
Dated: "1872" u.l.
Signed: "TM" u.l.
Inscribed: "Gorge near Gentrys Yosemite" u.l.
Provenance: YOS
Note: Sketch on verso

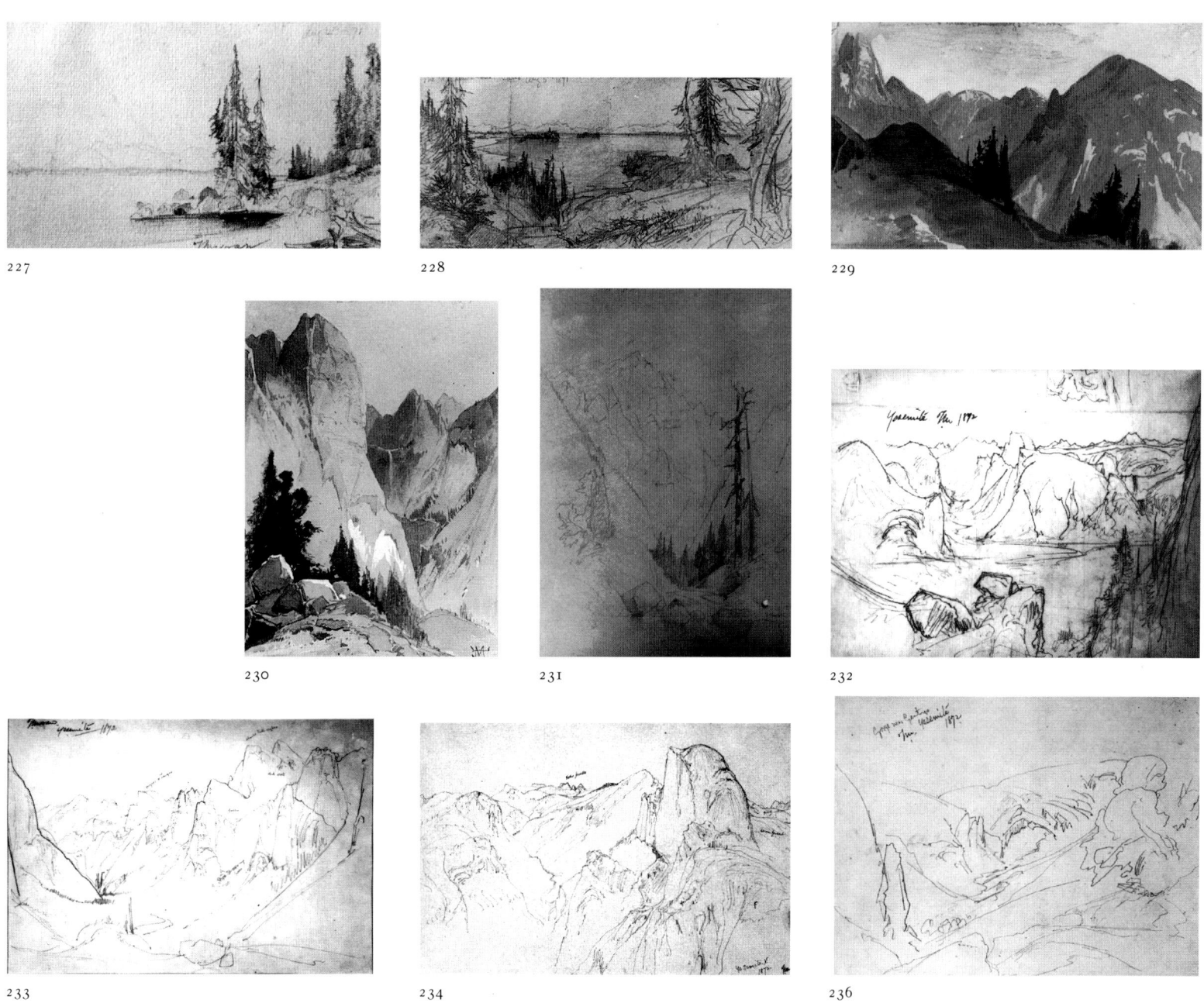

227

228

229

230

231

232

233

234

236

237
NEAR GENTRY'S, YOSEMITE
Graphite on wove
14⁷/₈ by 10⁵/₈
Dated: "1874" l.c. [see note]
57 785 Yosemite National Park, California
Signed: "TM" l.l.
Inscribed: "Near Gentrys. Yosemite" l.l.
Provenance: YOS
1916 ledger: 108
Note: This sketch is misdated. Moran is not
known to have been in Yosemite in 1874.

238
NEAR GENTRY'S, YOSEMITE
[descriptive]
Graphite, wash, and white gouache on wove
12³/₄ by 9¹/₂
0236.847 Gilcrease
Provenance: TG

239
LOOKING DOWN YOSEMITE VALLEY
Graphite, wash, and white gouache on wove
7⁷/₈ by 5¹/₂
1917–17–14 Cooper-Hewitt Museum
Dated: "1872" on verso
Signed: "TM" l.l.
Inscribed: "Looking Down Yosemite Valley" l.r.;
"The North Dome," Washington Column," and
"Royal Arch from the Vernal Fall Stream" on
verso
Provenance: TM
1916 ledger: 284
Note: This sketch is similar to Moran's pretrip
illustration, "North Dome and Royal Arches"
(*Scribner's Monthly* [January 1872]: 266).

240
NORTH DOME, YOSEMITE
Graphite, wash, and white gouache on wove
15 by 10³/₄
57 876 Yosemite National Park, California
Dated: "1872" l.l.
Signed: "TM" l.l.
Inscribed: "North Dome. Yosemite" l.l.
Provenance: YOS
1916 ledger: 27
Note: Sketch on verso

241
SENTINEL AND EL CAPITAN
Graphite and wash on wove
10⁵/₈ by 7¹/₂
57 872 Yosemite National Park, California
Dated: "1872" l.l.
Signed: Colophon stamp l.l.
Inscribed: "Sentinel & El Capitan" u.c.
Provenance: YOS
1916 ledger: 87

242
NEVADA FALL, YOSEMITE
Graphite and wash on gray wove
12⁷/₈ by 9⁵/₈
57 870 Yosemite National Park, California
Dated: "1872" l.c.
Signed: "TM" l.c.
Inscribed: "Nevada Falls. Yos." l.l.
Provenance: YOS
1916 ledger: 96

†243
GLACIER POINT FROM TRAIL TO
VERNAL FALL
Graphite, wash, and white gouache on gray
wove
12³/₄ by 9⁷/₈
0236.835 Gilcrease
Dated: "1904" u.r. [see note]
Signed: "TM" u.r.
Inscribed: "Glacier Point from trail to Vernal
fall" u.c.
Provenance: TG
Note: Stylistically, this drawing relates to the
work of 1872. The date was added later.

244
CASCADES OF VERNAL FALL
Graphite and wash on wove
10³/₄ by 7⁵/₈
57 873 Yosemite National Park, California
Dated: "1872" l.c.
Inscribed: "Cascades of Vernal Fall" l.l.
Provenance: YOS
Note: This sketch is similar to Moran's pretrip
illustration, "Vernal Falls; 350 Feet High" (*Scribner's Monthly* [January 1872]: 273).

245
VERNAL FALL, YOSEMITE
Graphite on wove
6³/₈ by 4³/₈
57 783 Yosemite National Park, California-
Dated: "1872" u.c.
Inscribed: "Vernal fall. Yo." u.l.
Provenance: YOS
1916 ledger: 95
Note: This sketch is similar to Moran's pretrip
illustration, "Vernal Falls; 350 Feet High" (*Scribner's Monthly* [January 1872]: 273). There is a
sketch on verso.

246
YOSEMITE FALL
Graphite on wove
15 by 10³/₄
57 779 Yosemite National Park, California
Dated: "1872" l.l.
Signed: "TM" l.l.
Inscribed: "Yosemite Fall" l.l.
Provenance: YOS
1916 ledger: 338
Note: Sketch on verso

247
FALLS OF YOSEMITE
Graphite and wash on wove
13¹/₂ by 9¹/₂
1917–17–17 Cooper-Hewitt Museum
Dated: "1872" l.r.
Signed: "TM" l.r.
Inscribed: "falls of Yosemite (2700 feet from the
Merced)" l.r.
Provenance: TM
1916 ledger: 97
Note: This sketch is similar to Moran's pretrip
illustration, "The Yosemite Falls" (*Scribner's
Monthly* [January 1872]: 271).

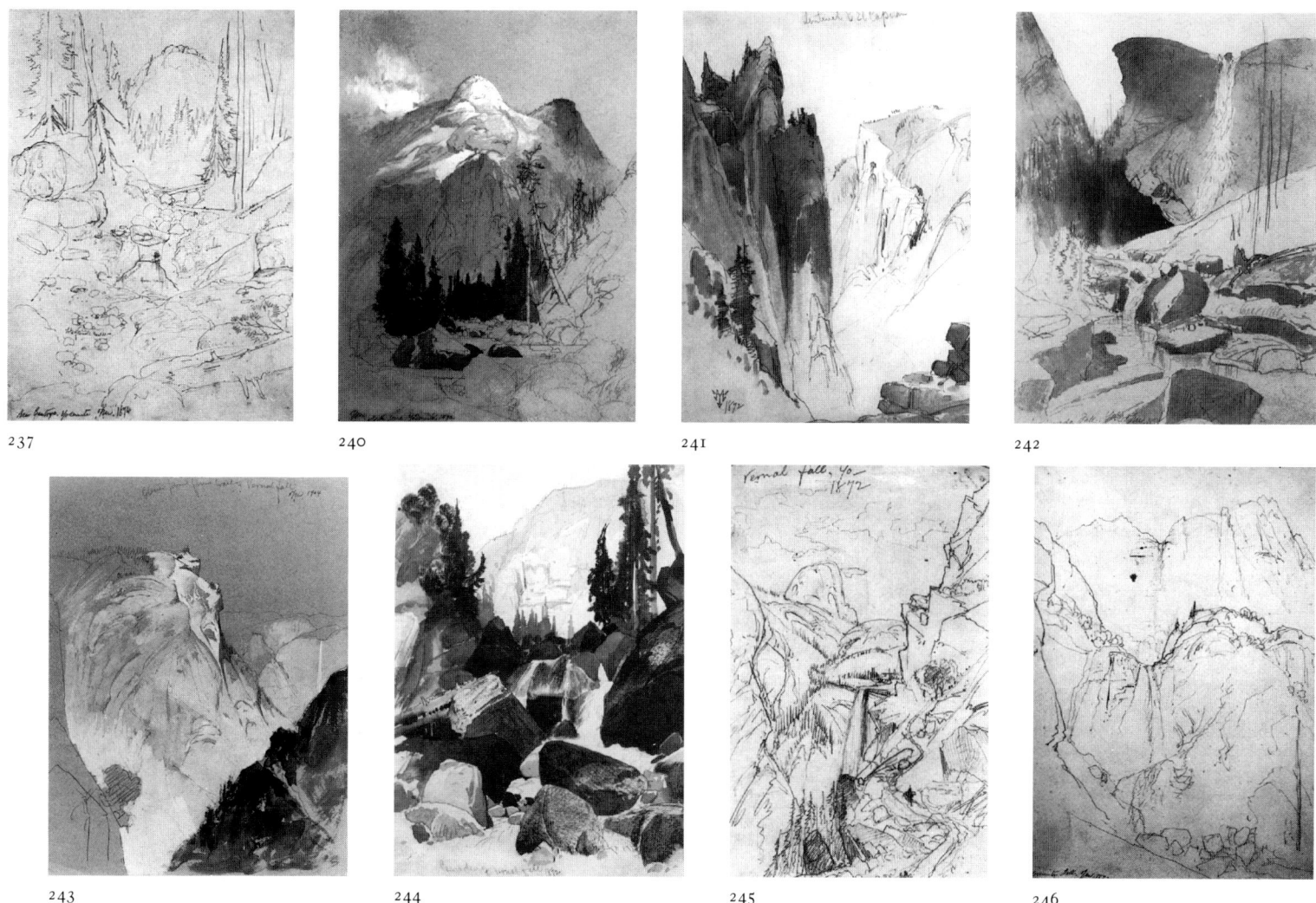

237

240

241

242

243

244

245

246

248
YOSEMITE—LOOKING DOWN FROM
MIRROR LAKE
Graphite and wash on laid
15 by 10⁵/₈
1917–17–84 Cooper-Hewitt Museum
Signed: "TMoran" l.c.
Inscribed: "Yosemite—looking down from Mir-
ror lake" l.c.; "Mirror Lake & North Dome" l.l.
Provenance: TM
1916 ledger: 340
Note: This sketch is similar to Moran's pretrip
illustration, "Mirror Lake; Watkins' and Clouds'
Rest" (*Scribner's Monthly* [January 1872]: 274).

249
YOSEMITE VALLEY [descriptive]
Graphite, wash, and white gouache on wove
10 by 4¹/₂
1917–17–16 Cooper-Hewitt Museum
Dated: "1872" l.l.
Signed: Colophon stamp l.l.
Provenance: TM

250
BRIDALVEIL FALL, YOSEMITE VALLEY
Graphite, wash, and white gouache on wove
14³/₄ by 10³/₄
0236.836 Gilcrease
Dated: "1904" l.l. [see note]
Signed: "TMoran" l.l.
Inscribed: "Bridal Veil fall Yosemite Valley" l.l.
in ink
and "900 feet" l.l. in ink
Provenance: TG
1916 ledger: 98
Note: Stylistically, this drawing relates to the
work of 1872. The date was added later.

†251
EDDY ON RANGELEY STREAM
Graphite and wash on gray wove
9³/₄ by 12⁵/₈
0226.877 Gilcrease
Dated: "1876" l.l. [see note]
Signed: "TMoran" l.l.
Inscribed: "Eddy on Rangely Stream" l.l.
Provenance: TG
Note: This sketch and the following three of
Rangeley were probably made in 1873, during
Moran's trip to Maine in the early summer be-

fore he left for the West. The date 1876 was
added later to Nos. 252 and 254.

252
LOOKING TOWARD THE LAKE FROM
THE CAMP, DOWN THE RANGELEY
STREAM
Graphite and wash on wove
5 by 8⁵/₈
0226.940 Gilcrease
Inscribed: "Looking toward the lake from the
Camp. Down the Rangely stream" upper edge;
"1¹/₂ col." u.l.; miscellaneous notes
Provenance: Ruth K. Henschel, New York; 1964
Thomas Gilcrease Foundation, Tulsa, Okla.;
1971 The Thomas Gilcrease Institute of American History and Art, Tulsa, Okla.
Note: This sketch was the basis of the illustration "Meeting of the Waters—Junction of Rangeley and Kennebago" in Seymour, "Trout-Fishing in the Rangeley Lakes," p. 438. For the date
of this sketch, see the note to No. 251.

†253
STONY BATTER ISLAND AND BALD
MOUNTAIN
Graphite and wash on gray wove
7 by 12⁵/₈
0226.876 Gilcrease
Dated: "1876" u.l. [see note to No. 251]
Signed: "TM" u.l.
Inscribed: "Stony Batter island & Bald Moun-
tain" u.l.; miscellaneous notes
Provenance: TG

254
STONY BATTER ISLE
Graphite on gray wove
9³/₄ by 12³/₄
1326.619 Gilcrease
Inscribed: "stony Batter isle" u.l.
Provenance: TG
Note: This sketch was the basis of the illustration "Stony Batter" in Seymour, "Trout-Fishing
in the Rangeley Lakes," p. 446. For the date of
this sketch, see the note to No. 251.

255
SUMMIT OF MT. NEBO
Graphite on gray wove
12³/₄ by 9⁵/₈

1917–17–74 Cooper-Hewitt Museum
Signed: "TM" u.r.
Inscribed: "Summit of Mt. Nebo" u.r.; color notes
Provenance: TM
1916 ledger: 80

256
A SPUR OF MT. NEBO
Graphite on wove
10 by 12¹/₂
4241 Jefferson National Expansion Memorial
Signed: "TM" u.l. and l.r.
Inscribed: "A Spur of Mt. Nebo" u.l.
Provenance: JNEM
1916 ledger: 182
Note: Sketch on verso

257a
CAMP COLBURN, MT. NEBO
Graphite on gray wove
Lower right sketch recto 6¹/₄ by 4³/₄, sheet 9³/₄
by 12³/₄
4228 Jefferson National Expansion Memorial
Signed: "TM" l.r.
Inscribed: "Camp Colburn/Mt. Nebo" l.r.
Provenance: JNEM
1916 ledger: 163
Note: The sheet was folded to make eight sur-
faces for drawings. Six were used, designated
here as 257a–f.

257b
SUMMIT OF NEBO
Graphite on gray wove
Lower left sketch recto 6¹/₄ by 4³/₄, sheet 9³/₄ by
12³/₄
4228 Jefferson National Expansion Memorial
Dated: "1873" upper edge
Signed: "TM" upper edge
Inscribed: "Summit of Nebo" upper edge
Provenance: JNEM

257c
FROM NEBO/UTAH LAKE
Graphite on gray wove
Upper left sketch recto 6¹/₄ by 4³/₄, sheet 9³/₄ by
12³/₄
4228 Jefferson National Expansion Memorial
Signed: "TM" u.r.
Inscribed: "from Nebo/Utah Lake" u.r.
Provenance: JNEM

257d
MT. NEBO [descriptive]
Graphite on gray wove
Upper right sketch recto $6^1/_4$ by $4^3/_4$, sheet $9^3/_4$
by $12^3/_4$
4228 Jefferson National Expansion Memorial
Signed: "TM" u.r.
Provenance: JNEM

257e
FROM NEBO
Graphite on gray wove
Upper left sketch verso $4^3/_4$ by $6^1/_4$, sheet $9^3/_4$
by $12^3/_4$
4228 Jefferson National Expansion Memorial
Inscribed: "from Nebo" u.r.
Provenance: JNEM

257f
NEBO
Graphite on gray wove
Upper right sketch verso $6^1/_4$ by $4^3/_4$, sheet $9^3/_4$
by $12^3/_4$
4228 Jefferson National Expansion Memorial
Inscribed: "Nebo" u.l.
Provenance: JNEM

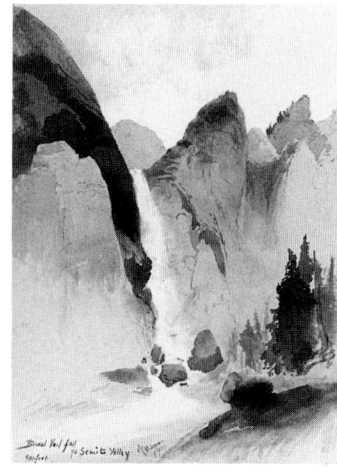

250

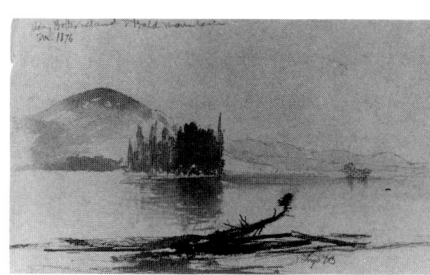

251

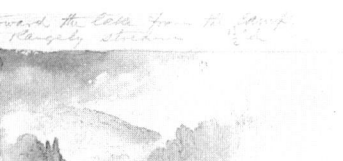

252

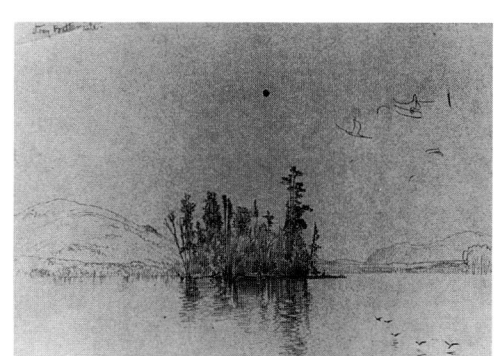

254

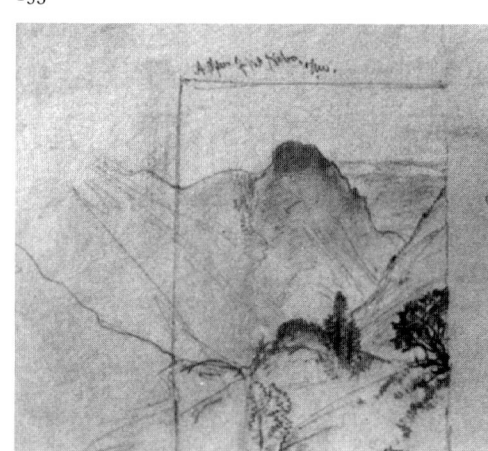

256

†258
SPANISH FORK CANYON
Graphite on gray wove
9⁷/₈ by 12³/₄
1336.952 Gilcrease
Dated: "1873" u.r.
Signed: "TM" u.r.
Inscribed: "spanish fork Canon" u.r.
Provenance: TG
1916 ledger: 179

†259
SPANISH FORK CANYON, UTAH
Graphite on wove
7¹/₂ by 10⁷/₈
1336.951 Gilcrease
Dated: "1873" u.l.
Signed: "TM" u.l.
Inscribed: "Spanish fork Canon Utah" u.l.; color notes
Provenance: TG
1916 ledger: 181

260
LOOKING UP THE EAGLE CLIFF, SPANISH FORK CANYON
Graphite on gray wove
7⁷/₈ by 6³/₈
1336.950 Gilcrease
Dated: "1873" u.r.
Signed: "TM" u.r.
Inscribed: "Looking Up the Eagle Cliff, Spanish fork Kanyon" upper edge
Provenance: TG
1916 ledger: 185

261
TOQUERVILLE, SOUTH UTAH
Graphite on wove
3⁷/₈ by 7³/₈
1930.12.26 National Museum of American Art
Dated: "1873" l.r.
Signed: "TM" l.r.
Inscribed: "Toquerville S Utah" l.r.; color notes
Provenance: WH
1916 ledger: 301

262
UTAH, RIO VIRGIN
Graphite on ruled wove
5¹/₄ by 8
1336.949 Gilcrease
Dated: "July 23–1873" l.l.
Signed: "TMoran" l.c.
Inscribed: "Utah Rio Virgin" l.l.
Provenance: TG

†263
VALLEY OF THE RIO VIRGIN, SOUTH UTAH
Graphite on blue wove
10³/₄ by 15
5852 Jefferson National Expansion Memorial
Dated: "1873" u.l.
Signed: "TM" l.r. and u.l.
Inscribed: "Valley of the Rio Virgen S. Utah No. 1" l.r.; color notes
Provenance: JNEM
1916 ledger: 177
Note: Nos. 263 and 264 are two parts of a larger drawing.

†264
VALLEY OF THE RIO VIRGIN
Graphite on blue wove
10³/₄ by 15
5850 Jefferson National Expansion Memorial
Dated: "1873" l.r.
Signed: "TM" l.r.
Inscribed: "Valley of the Rio Virgin No. 2" l.r.; color notes
Provenance: JNEM
1916 ledger: 128
Note: Sketch and inscription on verso: "Perfectly clear blue"

265
THE CATHEDRAL, RIO VIRGIN
Graphite on blue wove
10³/₄ by 15
4244 Jefferson National Expansion Memorial
Signed: "TM" u.l.
Inscribed: "The Cathedral/Rio Virgin" u.l.
Provenance: JNEM
1916 ledger: 158

266
RIO VIRGIN
Graphite on gray wove
10³/₄ by 14⁷/₈
1917-17-21 Cooper-Hewitt Museum
Dated: "1873" l.l.
Signed: "TM" l.l.
Inscribed: "Rio Virgin" l.l.; miscellaneous and color notes
Provenance: TM

267
RIO VIRGIN CANYON
Graphite on gray wove
10³/₄ by 15
1917-17-22 Cooper-Hewitt Museum
Dated: "1873" l.l.
Signed: "TM" l.l.
Inscribed: "Rio Virgin Canon" l.l.; miscellaneous and color notes
Provenance: TM
1916 ledger: 114

268
LOOKING DOWN THE CANYON, RIO VIRGIN
Graphite on wove
10³/₄ by 15
5851 Jefferson National Expansion Memorial
Dated: "1873" l.c.
Signed: "TM" l.c.
Inscribed: "Looking down the Canon Rio Virgin" l.l.; miscellaneous and color notes
Provenance: JNEM
1916 ledger: 79

269
RIO VIRGIN
Graphite on laid
8¹/₄ by 11³/₄
4235 Jefferson National Expansion Memorial
Dated: "1873" l.l.
Signed: "TM" l.l.
Inscribed: "Rio Virgin" l.l.; miscellaneous notes
Provenance: JNEM
1916 ledger: 304

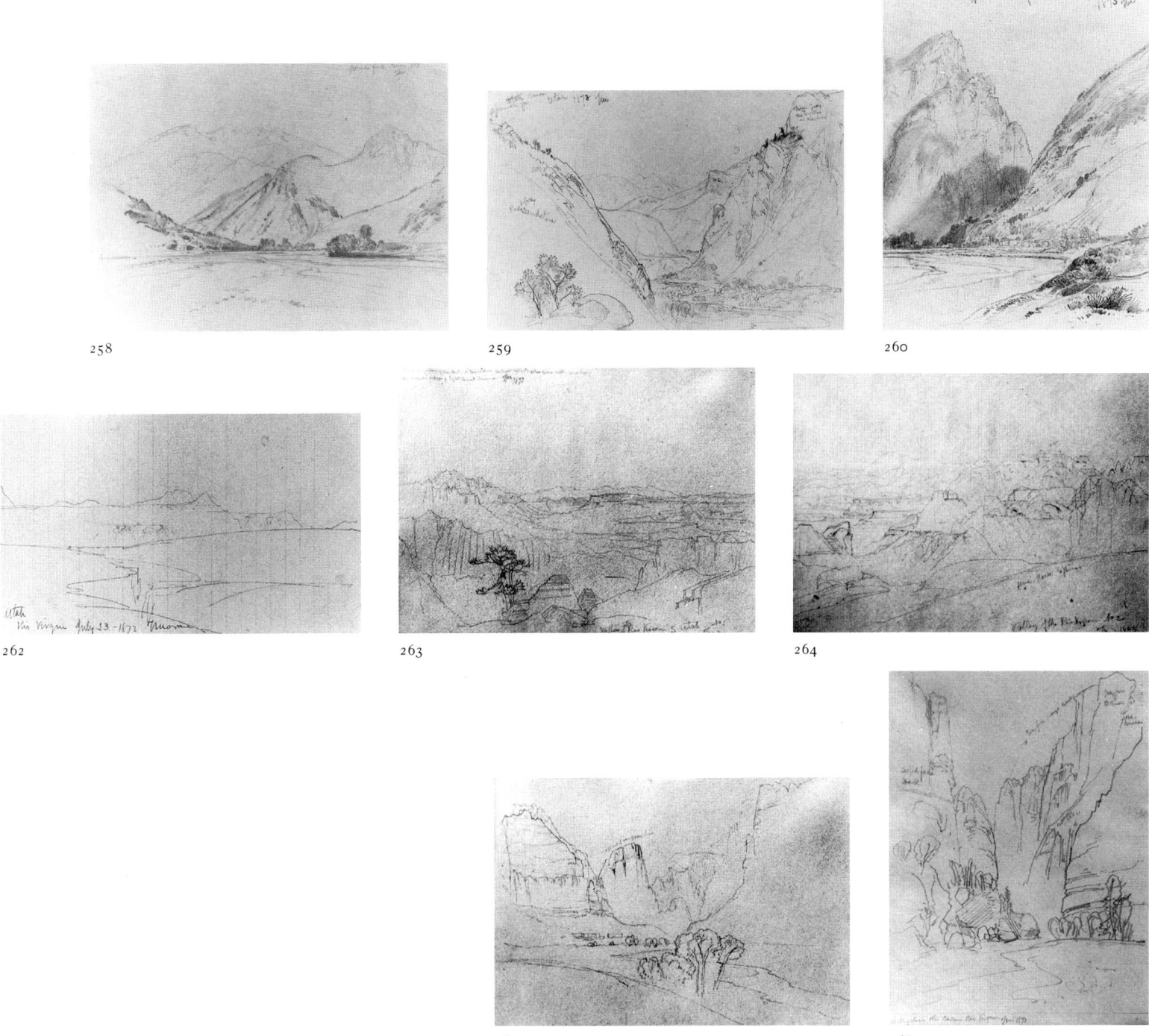

258

259

260

262

263

264

265

268

270
RIO VIRGIN [descriptive]
Graphite and wash on wove
8 by 5 1/2
4261 Jefferson National Expansion Memorial
Dated: "1873" l.r.
Provenance: JNEM
Note: Sketch and inscription on verso: "Great
White Throne"

271
RIO VIRGIN
Graphite on gray wove
9 3/4 by 12 3/4
5849 Jefferson National Expansion Memorial
Dated: "1873" l.l.
Signed: "TM" l.l.
Inscribed: "Rio Virgin" l.l.; miscellaneous notes
Provenance: JNEM
1916 ledger: 81

272
THE GATE OF LITTLE ZION VALLEY
Graphite on wove
10 3/4 by 15
5854 Jefferson National Expansion Memorial
Dated: "July 25–1873" u.l.
Signed: "TM" l.l.
Inscribed: "The Gate of Little Zion Valley" u.l.
Provenance: JNEM
1916 ledger: 180
Note: Sketch and inscription on verso: "Kanab
1873 TM"; miscellaneous and color notes

273
RIO VIRGIN, SOUTH UTAH
Graphite on green wove
15 by 21 1/2
4260 Jefferson National Expansion Memorial
Dated: "1873 u.l.
Signed: "TM" u.l.
Inscribed: "Rio Virgin S. Utah" u.l.
Provenance: JNEM
1916 ledger: 151

*274
IN THE NARROWS, ZION VALLEY, THE
GATE KEEPER
Graphite, watercolor, and white gouache on wove
Sketch 9 3/4 by 6 3/8, mount 15 1/2 by 11 3/8
0236.878 Gilcrease

Dated: "1873" u.l.
Inscribed: "In the Narrows Zion Valley The Gate
Keeper" u.l.; miscellaneous notes
Provenance: TG
1916 ledger: 38

275
FOOT OF TOROWEAP
Graphite on wove
10 3/4 by 15
4233 Jefferson National Expansion Memorial
Dated: "1873" u.l.
Signed: "TM" u.l.; "TMoran" l.r.
Inscribed: "Foot of Toro Weap" u.l.; lengthy color
notes
Provenance: JNEM

276
GRAND CANYON FROM MUAV CANYON
Graphite on wove
10 3/4 by 15
1917–17–28 Cooper-Hewitt Museum
Dated: "1873" l.l.
Signed: "TM" l.l.
Inscribed: "Grand Canon from Mu-Av Canon"
l.l.; color notes
Provenance: TM
1916 ledger: 74

277
ROCK TOWERS, GRAND CANYON OF
COLORADO
Graphite on wove
13 7/8 by 10 3/4
1917–17–23 Cooper-Hewitt Museum
Signed: "TM" l.r.
Inscribed: "Rock Towers Grand Canon of Col-
orado" l.r.; miscellaneous and color notes
Provenance: TM
1916 ledger: 302

†278
GRAND CANYON [ledger title]
Graphite on wove
10 7/8 by 14 1/2
1336.916 Gilcrease
Provenance: TG
1916 ledger: 253

279
GRAND CANYON [descriptive]
Graphite on wove
10 3/4 by 15
4238 Jefferson National Expansion Memorial
Provenance: JNEM
1916 ledger: 139

280
GRAND CANYON [descriptive]
Graphite on blue wove
10 3/4 by 15
4236 Jefferson National Expansion Memorial
Inscribed with lengthy notes
Provenance: JNEM
1916 ledger: 255

281
GRAND CANYON [descriptive]
Graphite on wove
7 7/8 by 5
1336.908 Gilcrease
Provenance: TG

282
ACROSS THE GRAND CANYON FROM
BASS
Graphite on ruled wove
8 by 10
4231 Jefferson National Expansion Memorial
Inscribed: "Across the Grand Canon from Bass"
u.l.; miscellaneous notes
Provenance: JNEM
1916 ledger: 252

283
SIDE GULCH, GRAND CANYON
Graphite on ruled wove
4 1/8 by 7 3/4
72 East Hampton Library
Dated: "Aug 10–73" u.l.
Inscribed: "side gulch Grand Canyon" u.l.; mis-
cellaneous notes
Provenance: EH
1916 ledger: 137

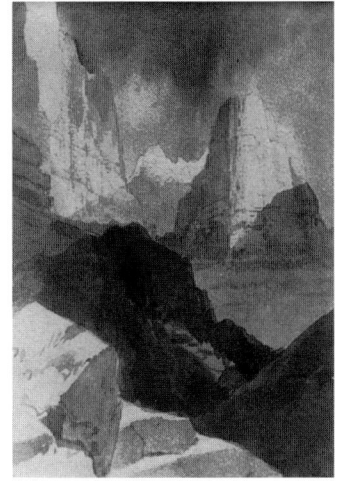

270

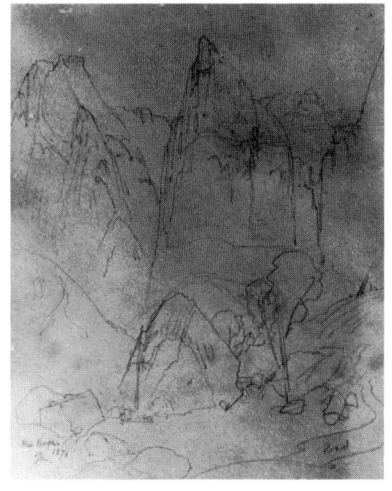

271

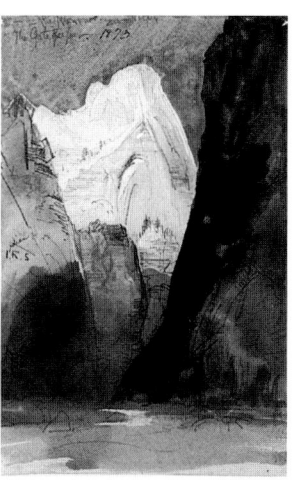

274

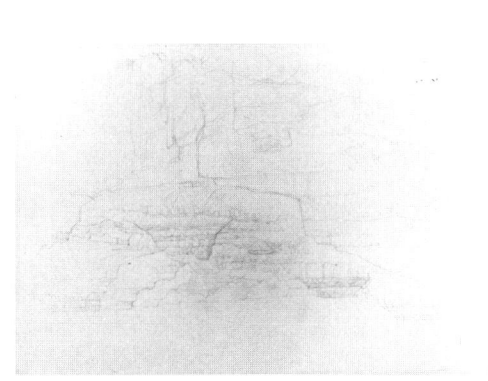

278

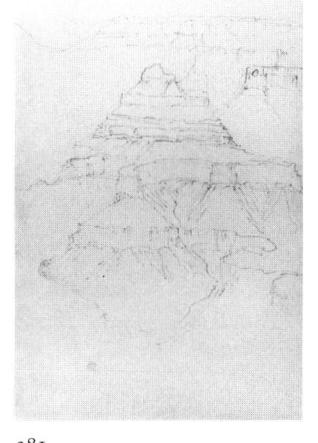

281

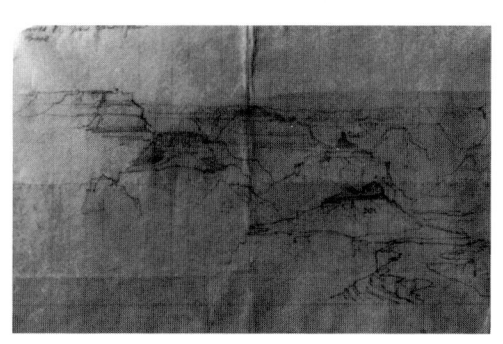

282

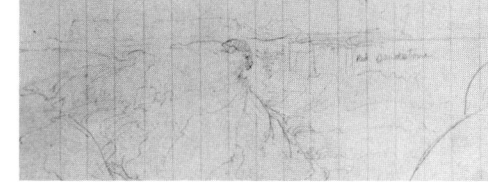

283

284
CANYON AT GRAND VIEW [ledger title]
Graphite on wove
10³/₄ by 15
4232 Jefferson National Expansion Memorial
Provenance: JNEM
1916 ledger: 171

285
GRAND CANYON [ledger title]
Graphite on blue wove
10³/₄ by 15
4251 Jefferson National Expansion Memorial
Provenance: JNEM
1916 ledger: 254

286
AYRES BUTTE
Graphite on wove
4¹/₂ by 7
1947.13.45 National Museum of American Art
Signed: "TM" l.r.
Inscribed: "Ayres Butte" l.r.
Provenance: WH
1916 ledger: 188

287
CAMP OF THE TWO PINES
Graphite on wove
7¹/₂ by 10³/₄
5856 Jefferson National Expansion Memorial
Dated: "Aug 9th 1874" l.l.
Signed: "TM" l.r.
Inscribed: "Camp of the Two Pines" l.l.; "Looking S.E. Holy Cross Trip" l.r.
Provenance: JNEM

†288
CAMP OF THE EVENING STAR,
ON THE PLATTE
Graphite on wove
7¹/₂ by 10³/₄
4249 Jefferson National Expansion Memorial
Dated: "Aug 10th 1874" u.r.
Signed: "TM" u.r.
Inscribed: "No. 2 Camp of the Evening Star on the Platte" u.r.
Provenance: JNEM
Note: Sketch and inscription on verso: "Pike's Peak from the road to Fairplay Aug 10th"

†289
HOLY CROSS TRIP, CAMP VEXATION
Graphite on wove
7¹/₄ by 10³/₄
4245 Jefferson National Expansion Memorial
Dated: "Aug 12th 1874" l.r.
Signed: "TM" l.r.
Inscribed: "Holy Cross Trip Camp Vexation S. Branch of the N. Platte" l.r.
Provenance: JNEM

290
IN THE CANYON BEYOND FAIRPLAY
Graphite on blue wove
5¹/₂ by 7¹/₂
4247 Jefferson National Expansion Memorial
Signed: "TMoran" l.r. in purple pencil
Inscribed: "Camp No. 5 in the Canon beyond Fairplay" lower edge
Provenance: JNEM

291
THE ARKANSAS DIVIDE
Graphite and wash on wove
6 by 9¹/₂
1917–17–36 Cooper-Hewitt Museum
Dated: "Aug. 1874" l.l.
Inscribed: "The Arkansas Divide" l.l.; "On the trip to the Mt. of the Holy Cross" l.c.
Provenance: TM
1916 ledger: 78

292
CAMP ON THE UPPER ARKANSAS, IN
TENNESSEE PASS
Graphite on wove
5¹/₂ by 8
4256 Jefferson National Expansion Memorial
Dated: Aug 18 1874" u.c.
Signed: "TM" l.r.
Inscribed: "Camp on the Upper Arkansas in Tennessee Pass" upper edge; "No. 7" u.l.; "H. C. Trip" l.r.
Provenance: JNEM

293
CAMP ON EAGLE RIVER
Graphite on blue laid
8³/₄ by 11
1336.917 Gilcrease
Inscribed: "Camp on Eagle River" l.l.; "No 91 Thursday 20th" l.c.
Provenance: TG
1916 ledger: 332
Note: Sketch and Inscription on verso: "Arundel Castle"

294
HOLY CROSS CREEK
Graphite on gray wove
9³/₄ by 15
5858 Jefferson National Expansion Memorial
Signed: "TMoran" l.r. in purple pencil
Inscribed: "Holy Cross Creek" l.r.; miscellaneous notes
Provenance: JNEM

†295
MOUNT HOLY CROSS
Graphite on blue wove
10³/₄ by 15
1917–17–30 Cooper-Hewitt Museum
Dated: "1874" l.l.
Signed: "TMoran" l.l.
Inscribed: "Mt. Holy Cross" u.l.; miscellaneous and color notes
Provenance: TM
1916 ledger: 75

296
DELANO VALLEY, EAGLE RIVER
Graphite on blue wove
9³/₄ by 15
5859 Jefferson National Expansion Memorial
Dated: "Aug 23rd–74" u.l.
Inscribed: "Delano Valley Eagle River" u.l.; miscellaneous and color notes
Provenance: JNEM

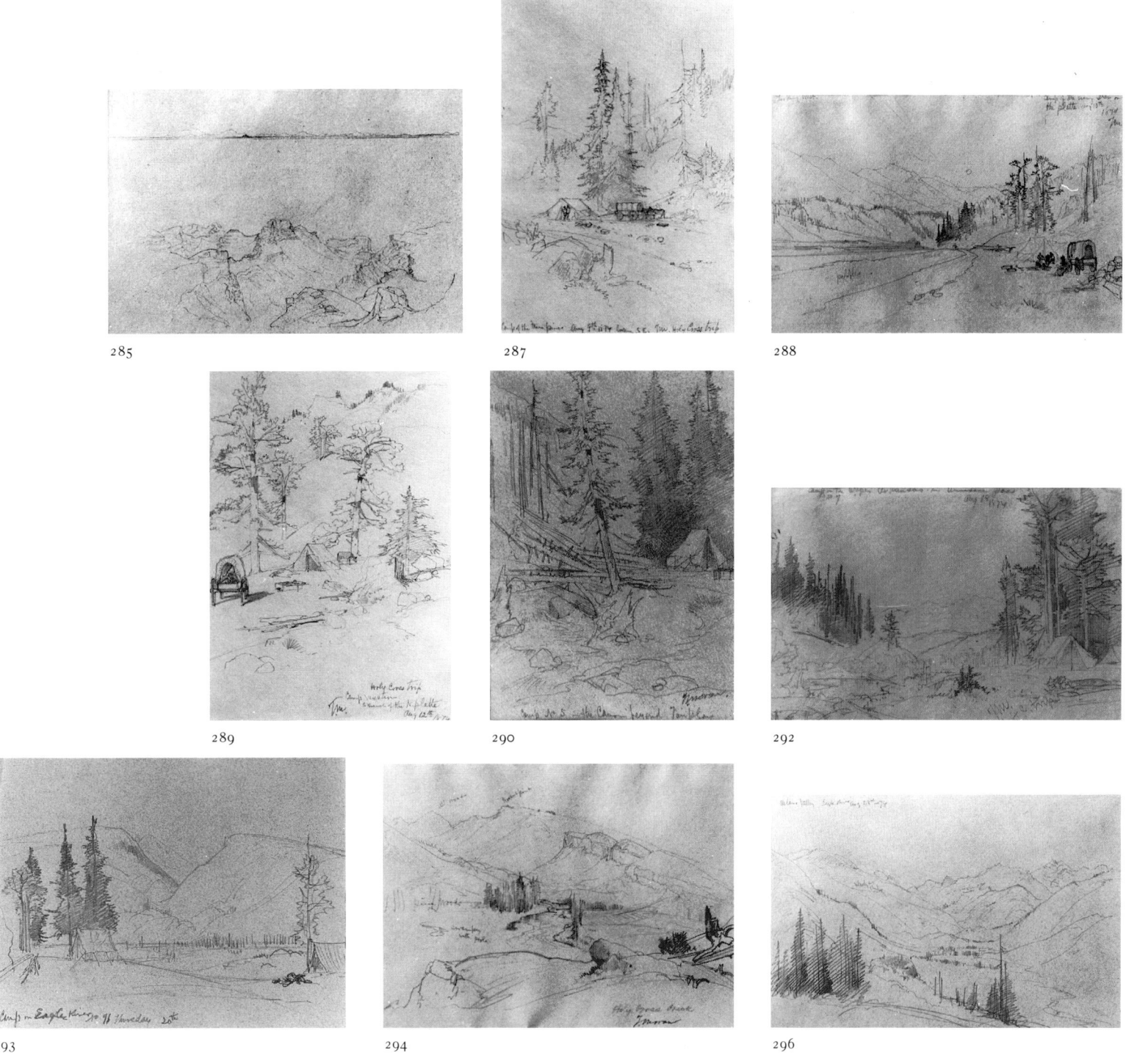

285

287

288

289

290

292

293

294

296

297
UPPER TWIN LAKE
Graphite on wove
10³/₄ by 15
4230 Jefferson National Expansion Memorial
Dated: "Aug 26th-74" l.r.
Inscribed: "Upper Twin Lake" l.r.; miscellaneous and color notes
Provenance: JNEM

298
HOLY CROSS TRIP [descriptive]
Graphite on wove
5¹/₂ by 8
5857 Jefferson National Expansion Memorial
Signed: "TM" l.l.
Inscribed: "Horizontal line a little lower" u.l.
Provenance: JNEM

299
HOLY CROSS TRIP [descriptive]
Graphite on blue wove
10³/₄ by 15
4252 Jefferson National Expansion Memorial
Inscribed with miscellaneous notes
Provenance: JNEM

300
ALPINE PASS AT CASCADE TWIN
LAKES COLORADO
Graphite, watercolor, and white gouache on gray wove
9¹/₂ by 12¹/₄
1917–17–71 Cooper-Hewitt Museum
Inscribed: "Alpine Pass at Cascade Twin Lakes Colorado" u.r.
Provenance: TM

301
MADISON, WISCONSIN
Graphite on watermarked laid
8¹/₈ by 12¹/₄
1326.944 Gilcrease
Dated: "1876" l.l.
Signed: "TMoran" l.r.; "TM" l.c.
Inscribed: "Madison Wis" l.l.
Provenance: TG

302
FIRST LAKE, MADISON, WISCONSIN
Graphite on watermarked laid
5³/₄ by 9¹/₄
1326.945 Gilcrease
Dated: "July 27 1876" u.r.
Inscribed: "1st Lake Madison Wis" u.r.
Provenance: Ruth K. Henschel, New York; 1964 Thomas Gilcrease Foundation, Tulsa, Okla.; 1971 The Thomas Gilcrease Institute of American History and Art, Tulsa, Okla.
Note: The three lakes around Madison are Mendota, Waubesa, and Kegonsa.

303
SECOND LAKE
Graphite on watermarked laid
6 by 9¹/₂
1326.683 Gilcrease
Inscribed: "2nd Lake" u.r.; miscellaneous notes
Provenance: TG
Note: The three lakes around Madison are Mendota, Waubesa, and Kegonsa.

*304
THIRD LAKE, MADISON, WISCONSIN
Graphite, watercolor, and white gouache on wove
9³/₄ by 13¹/₈
0226.939 Gilcrease
Dated: "1876" l.r.
Signed: "TMoran" l.r.
Inscribed: "3rd Lake Madison Wisconsin" l.r.; miscellaneous notes
Provenance: TG
Note: The three lakes around Madison are Mendota, Waubesa, and Kegonsa.

305
JACKSONVILLE
Graphite on wove
5¹/₄ by 2³/₄
64 East Hampton Library
Signed: "TM" u.l.
Inscribed: "Jacksonville" u.l.
Provenance: EH
1916 ledger: 391

297

306
ST. AUGUSTINE
Graphite on wove
6¹/₂ by 9⁷/₈
1326.938 Gilcrease
Dated: "Feb 22nd–1877" u.l. in ink
Inscribed: "St. Augustine" u.l. in ink
Provenance: TG

307
FORT GEORGE ISLAND, FLORIDA
Graphite on wove
Sketch 7⁷/₈ by 6³/₈, mount 10³/₄ by 7³/₄
1326.941 Gilcrease
Dated: "1877" l.l. on mount in ink; "March 1st-77" u.r.
Signed: "TMoran" l.l. on mount in ink; "TM" l.l.
Inscribed: "Fort George Island, Florida" u.r.; "Scrub palmetto in foreground" l.l.; "23 pencil" u.r. on mount in ink
Provenance: TG
1916 ledger: 144

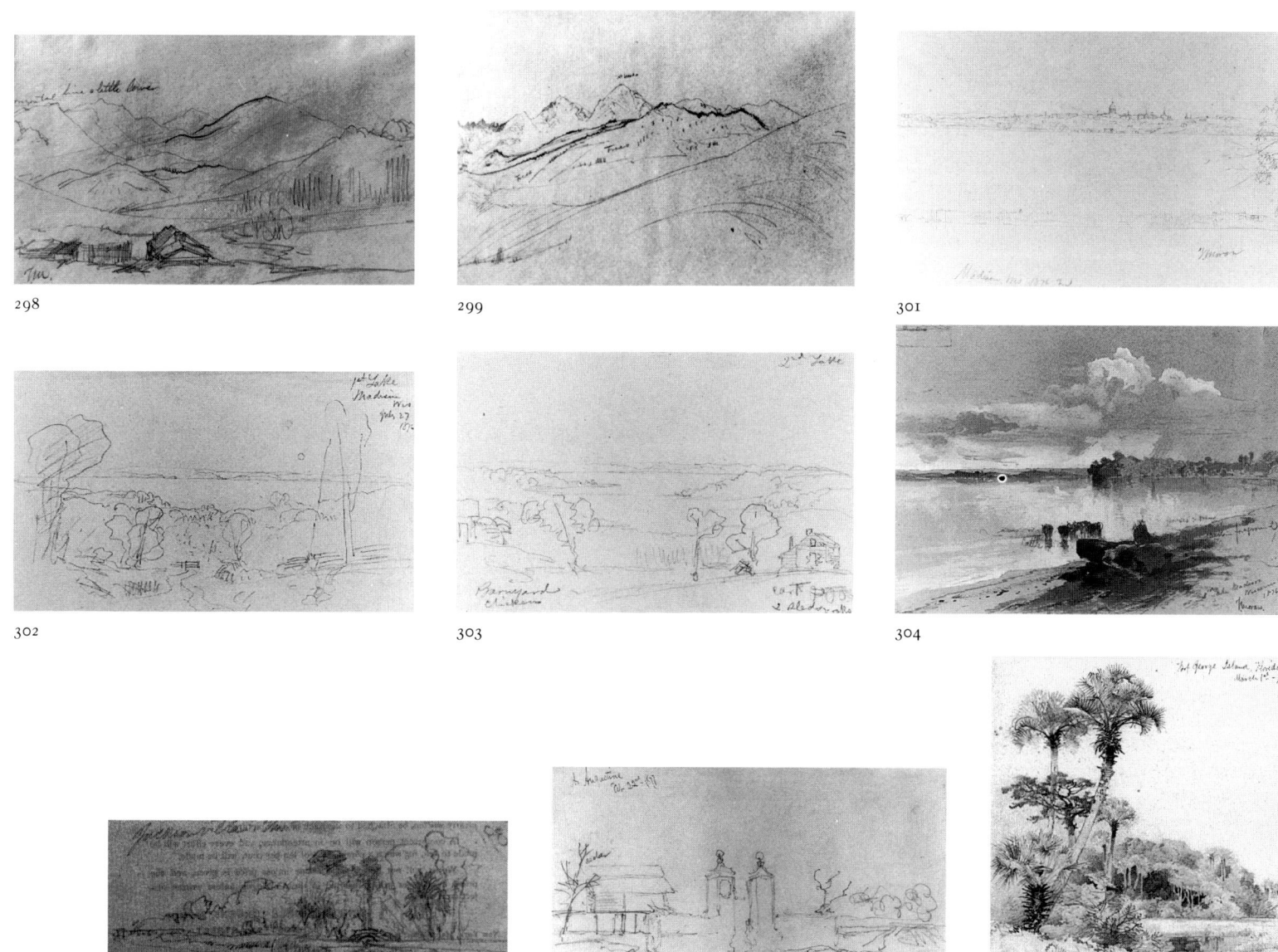

298

299

301

302

303

304

305

306

307

†308
FROM SHELL HUMMOCKS, FORT
GEORGE ISLAND
Graphite on wove
6⁷/₈ by 6³/₈
1326.1020 Gilcrease
Dated: "March 1" u.r. in ink
Inscribed: "From shell Hummocks. Fort George
Island" u.r. in ink
Provenance: Ruth K. Henschel, New York; 1964
Thomas Gilcrease Foundation, Tulsa, Okla.;
1971 The Thomas Gilcrease Institute of Ameri-
can History and Art, Tulsa, Okla.

309
FORT GEORGE ISLAND
Graphite on tan wove
6 by 9
10 East Hampton Library
Dated: "March 1st 1877" u.r.
Signed: "TM" u.r.
Inscribed: "Fort George Island" u.r.
Provenance: EH

310
FORT GEORGE ISLAND
Graphite on pink wove
2¹/₄ by 9
107 East Hampton Library
Dated: "March 1st 77" l.r.; "1877" l.l.
Signed: "TM" l.l.
Inscribed: Fort George Island" l.r.
Provenance: EH
1916 ledger: 214

311
FORT GEORGE ISLAND
Graphite on wove
4³/₈ by 9¹/₄
50.3959 Museum of Fine Arts, Boston
Dated: "March 1st-77" u.r.
Signed: "TM" u.r.
Inscribed: "Fort George Island" u.r.
Provenance: MK
1916 ledger: 220

†312
SAND AND PALMETTO
Graphite on wove
7³/₈ by 12³/₈
1326.659 Gilcrease

Signed: "TM" l.r.
Inscribed: "Sand & Palmetto" l.l.; miscellaneous
notes
Provenance: TG
1916 ledger: 358
Note: This sketch was the basis of the illustration "The Southern End of Fort George Island,"
in Dodge, "Island of the Sea," p. 652.

†313
LAKE ISABEL, FORT GEORGE ISLAND,
FLORIDA
Graphite on wove
10³/₄ by 7³/₈
1326.1015 Gilcrease
Dated: "March 5th 1877" u.c. in ink
Signed: "TM" u.c. in ink
Inscribed: "Lake Isabel. Fort George Island.
Florida" u.l. in ink
Provenance: Carmen H. Messmore, New York;
1964 Thomas Gilcrease Foundation, Tulsa,
Okla.; 1969 The Thomas Gilcrease Institute of
American History and Art, Tulsa, Okla.
1916 ledger: 377

†314
LAKE ISABEL, FORT GEORGE ISLAND,
FLORIDA
Graphite and wash on wove
11 by 7¹/₂
0226.873 Gilcrease
Dated: "March 5th 1877" l.c. in ink
Signed: "TM" l.c. in ink
Inscribed: "Lake Isabel. Fort George Island
Florida" l.l. in ink
Provenance: TG
1916 ledger: 165
Note: This sketch was the basis of the illustra-
tion "The Road, Fort George Island," in Dodge,
"Island of the Sea," p. 656.

315
PALMETTO TREES AT LAKE ISABEL,
FORT GEORGE ISLAND, FLORIDA
Graphite and wash on wove
10⁷/₈ by 7¹/₂
0226.874 Gilcrease
Dated: "March 5th 1877" l.l. in ink
Signed: "TM" l.l. in ink
Inscribed: "Palmetto trees at Lake Isabel Ft
George Island. Florida" l.l. in ink

Provenance: TG
1916 ledger: 91

316
FORT GEORGE ISLAND
Graphite on wove
7³/₈ by 10⁵/₈
1326.641 Gilcrease
Dated: "March" l.l. in ink
Inscribed: "Fort George Island" l.l. in ink
Provenance: TG

317
FORT GEORGE ISLAND
Graphite on wove
6¹/₄ by 9⁵/₈
1326.940 Gilcrease
Dated: "March 77" l.l.
Signed: "TMoran" l.r.
Inscribed: "Fort George Island" l.l.
Provenance: TG
Note: This sketch was the basis of the illustra-
tion "Edgewood Avenue, Fort George Island,"
in Dodge, "Island of the Sea," p. 653. There is a
sketch on verso.

318
FROM POINT ISABEL, FORT GEORGE
ISLAND, FLORIDA
Graphite on wove
8¹/₂ by 12¹/₂
1973.368 Museum of Fine Arts, Boston
Dated: "March 1877" u.l.
Signed: "TM" l.r.
Inscribed: "From Point Isabel Fort George Is-
land Florida" u.l.
Provenance: MK
1916 ledger: 89
Note: This sketch was the basis of the illustra-
tion "Point Isabel, Fort George Island," in
Dodge, "Island of the Sea," p. 655.

319
THE GHOST HOUSE, FORT GEORGE
ISLAND
Graphite on wove
3 by 6³/₈
1326.943 Gilcrease
Inscribed: "The Ghost House Fort George Is-
land" l.l. in ink
Provenance: TG

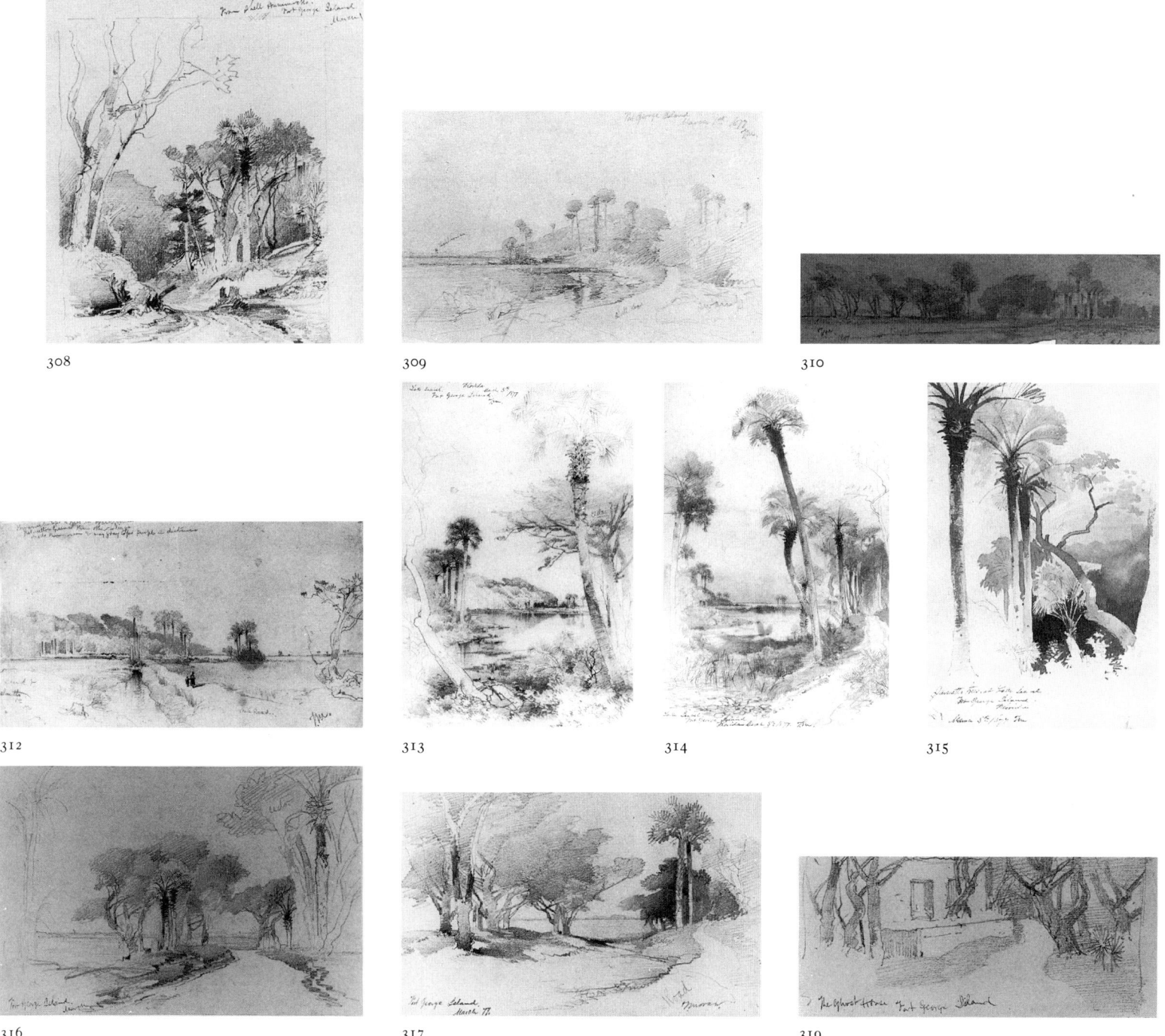

308

309

310

312

313

314

315

316

317

319

320
ALLIGATOR BEND
Graphite on wove
4³/₄ by 9
1326.688 Gilcrease
Inscribed: "Alligator Bend" u.r.; "Fort George
Island" u.r. in ink
Provenance: TG
Note: Sketch on verso

321
FORT GEORGE ISLAND
Graphite on wove
6¹/₂ by 9⁷/₈
1326.937 Gilcrease
Dated: "March 5th" l.l. in ink; "1877" l.c.
Inscribed: "Fort George Island" l.l. in ink; mis-
cellaneous notes
Provenance: TG
Note: This sketch anticipated Mary Nimmo
Moran's etching, *Point Isabel, Florida* (1887).
There is a sketch on verso.

322
FORT GEORGE ISLAND, FLORIDA
Graphite on wove
5³/₈ by 9⁵/₈
1326.1027 Gilcrease
Dated: "1877" u.r.
Inscribed: "Fort George Island Florida" u.r.
Provenance: TG

323
FORT GEORGE ISLAND, FLORIDA
[descriptive]
Graphite and white chalk on wove
7⁵/₈ by 11¹/₄
1326.640 Gilcrease
Provenance: TG
1916 ledger: 252

324
FORT GEORGE ISLAND, FLORIDA
[descriptive]
Graphite on wove
2⁵/₈ by 5¹/₄
77 East Hampton Library
Signed: "TM" l.r.
Provenance: EH
1916 ledger: 392.2

325
FLORIDA
Graphite on wove
4¹/₈ by 5¹/₈
59 East Hampton Library
Signed: "TM" l.r.
Inscribed: "Florida" l.r.
Provenance: EH
1916 ledger: 21

326
FORT GEORGE ISLAND
Graphite on wove
2¹/₄ by 3³/₄
49 East Hampton Library
Inscribed: "Fort George Island" l.l.
Provenance: EH

327
FORT GEORGE ISLAND, FLORIDA
Graphite on wove
4³/₈ by 7¹/₂
29 East Hampton Library
Dated: "1877" l.l.
Signed: "TM" l.c.
Inscribed: "Fort George Island. Florida" l.l.
Provenance: EH
1916 ledger: 176

†328
OLD SLAVE QUARTERS, FORT GEORGE
ISLAND
Graphite and ink on wove
3³/₄ by 9¹/₂
1326.646 Gilcrease
Inscribed: "Old Slave Quarters Fort George Is-
land" u.l.; miscellaneous notes
Provenance: TG

329
SPRING, FORT GEORGE ISLAND
Graphite, pen and ink on wove
7¹/₂ by 5¹/₂
1326.647 Gilcrease
Inscribed: "Spring Fort George Island" l.l. in ink
Provenance: TG

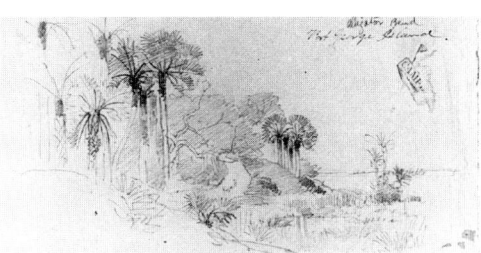

320

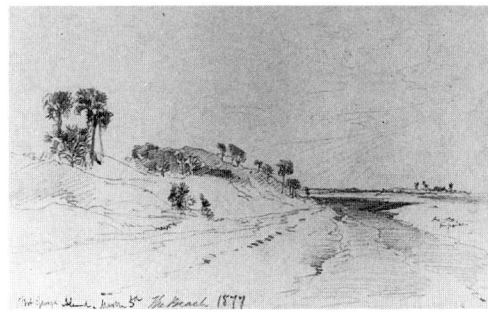

321

330
THE GHOST HOUSE
Graphite on wove
5¹/₂ by 7¹/₂
1326.942 Gilcrease
Dated: "March 1877" u.r. in ink
Signed: "TM" u.r. in ink
Inscribed: "The Ghost House" u.r.; "Fort George
Island" u.r. in ink
Provenance: TG

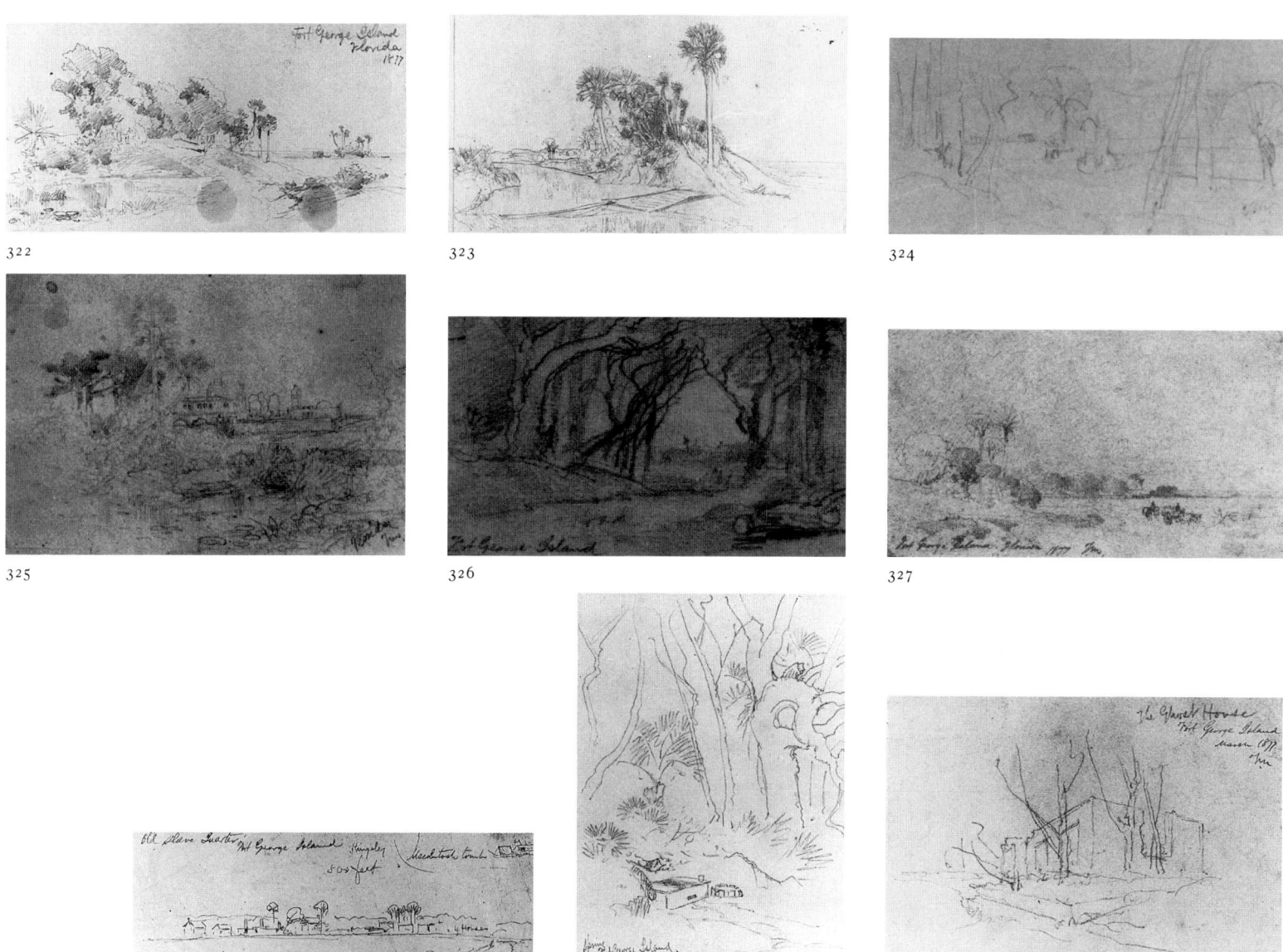

322

323

324

325

326

327

328

329

330

331
FORT GEORGE ISLAND
Graphite on wove
7 3/8 by 11
1326.936 Gilcrease
Dated: "March 5th" u.r. in ink
Inscribed: "Fort George Island" u.r. in ink; miscellaneous notes
Provenance: TG

332
GLEN NEAR HOTEL, FORT GEORGE ISLAND
Graphite on wove
4 5/8 by 4 3/8
1326.686 Gilcrease
Inscribed: "Glen near Hotel Fort George Island" l.l. in ink
Provenance: TG

333
FORT GEORGE ISLAND, FLORIDA [descriptive]
Graphite on wove
2 5/8 by 4 1/8
1326.687 Gilcrease
Provenance: TG
Note: This sketch was the basis for Moran's steel engraving, St. Johns River, Florida.

334
FORT GEORGE ISLAND
Graphite on wove
6 3/8 by 9 7/8
1326.939 Gilcrease
Dated: "March 5th" verso in ink; "1877" verso in chalk
Inscribed: "Fort George Island" u.r.; "Sand span Bayonet" l.c.; miscellaneous notes
Provenance: TG
Note: Sketch and inscription on verso: "Mouth of the St. Johns River from Fort George"

335
ON THE ST. JOHNS RIVER, FLORIDA
Graphite on wove
6 by 9
1326.684 Gilcrease
Signed: "TM" l.c.
Inscribed: "on the St Johns River Florida" l.l.
Provenance: TG
1916 ledger: 155
Note: Sketch on verso

*336
FORT GEORGE ISLAND
Graphite and watercolor on wove
10 1/2 by 18 5/8
0226.792 Gilcrease
Signed: "TMoran" l.l.
Inscribed: "Fort George Island" l.l. and on verso
Provenance: TG
1916 ledger: 115

337
FORT GEORGE ISLAND [descriptive]
Graphite and watercolor on wove
2 by 6
16 East Hampton Library
Provenance: EH

338
FELTVILLE DAM
Graphite on wove
4 7/8 by 8 1/8
1826.16.1 Gilcrease
Dated: "July 16. 78" u.l.; "July 1878" on verso
Inscribed: "Feltville Dam" u.l.
Provenance: TG
Note: Sketch on verso

339
FELTVILLE [descriptive]
Graphite on wove
4 7/8 by 8 1/8
1826.16.2 Gilcrease
Provenance: TG
Note: Sketch on verso

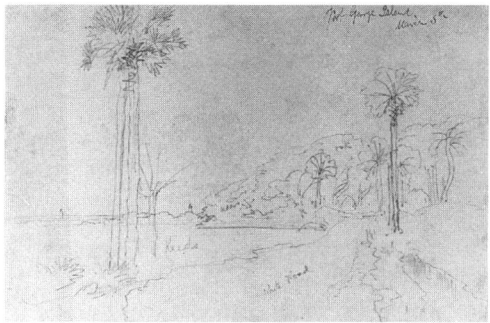

331

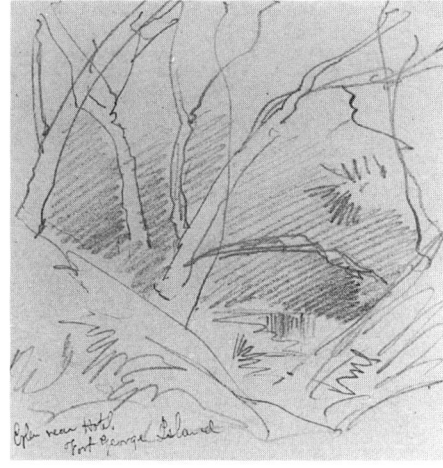

332

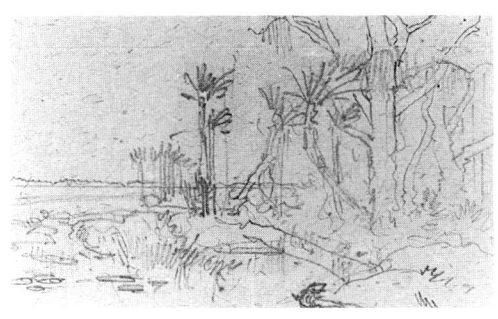

333

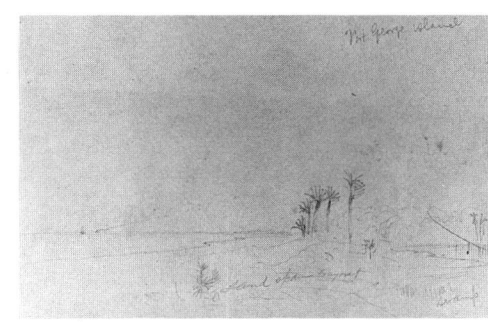

334

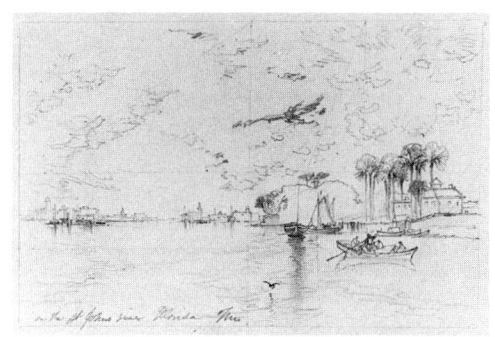

335

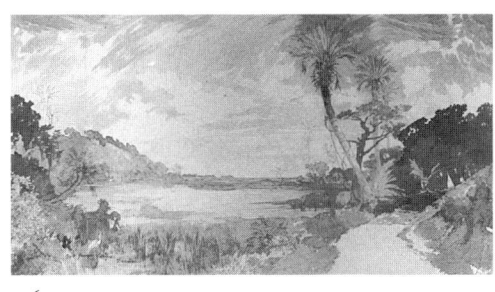

336

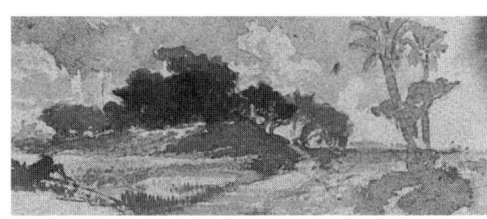

337

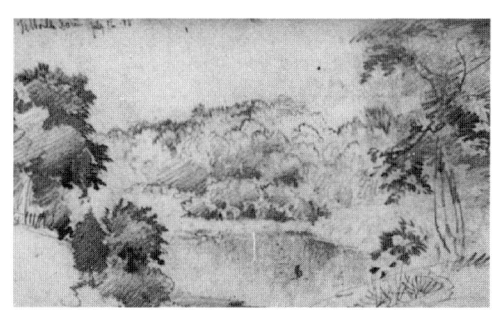

338

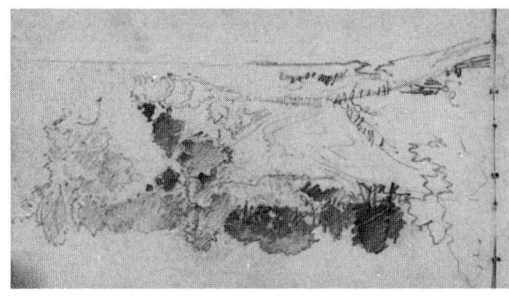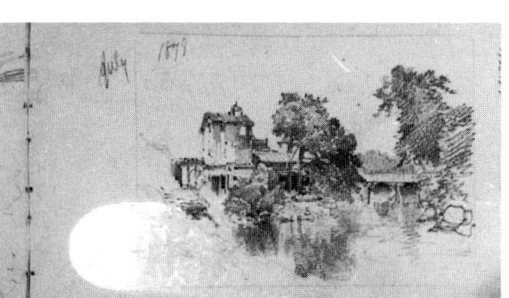

339

340
FELTVILLE [descriptive]
Graphite on wove
8¹/₈ by 4⁷/₈
1826.16.3 Gilcrease
Provenance: TG

341
FELTVILLE
Graphite and black conté crayon on wove
4⁷/₈ by 8¹/₈
1826.16.4 Gilcrease
Dated: "July 20th-78" l.l. in black conté crayon
Signed: "TM" l.r.
Inscribed: "Feltville" l.l. in black conté crayon
Provenance: TG
Note: Sketch on verso

†342
FELTVILLE [descriptive]
Graphite on wove
8¹/₈ by 4⁷/₈
1826.16.5 Gilcrease
Provenance: TG

†343
FELTVILLE
Graphite and black conté crayon on wove
8¹/₈ by 4⁷/₈
1826.16.6 Gilcrease
Dated: "July 30th-78" l.l.
Signed: "TM" l.l.
Inscribed: "F.Ville" l.l.
Provenance: TG
1916 ledger: 45

†344
FELTVILLE
Graphite and black conté crayon on wove
4⁷/₈ by 8¹/₈
1826.16.7 Gilcrease
Dated: "July 20th 1878" l.r.
Inscribed: "Feltville" l.r.
Provenance: TG

345
FELTVILLE [descriptive]
Graphite on wove
8¹/₈ by 4⁷/₈
1826.16.8 Gilcrease
Provenance: TG

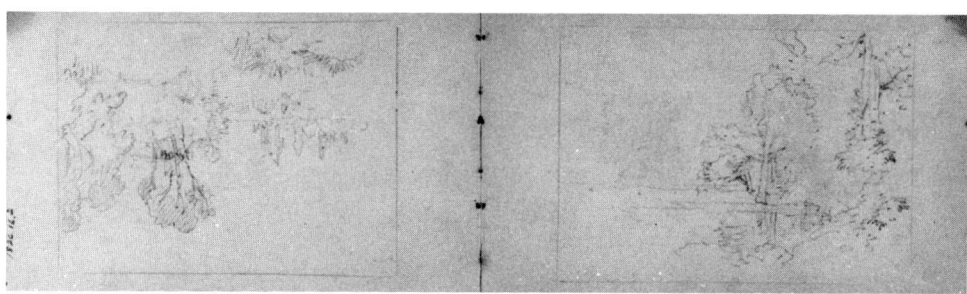

340

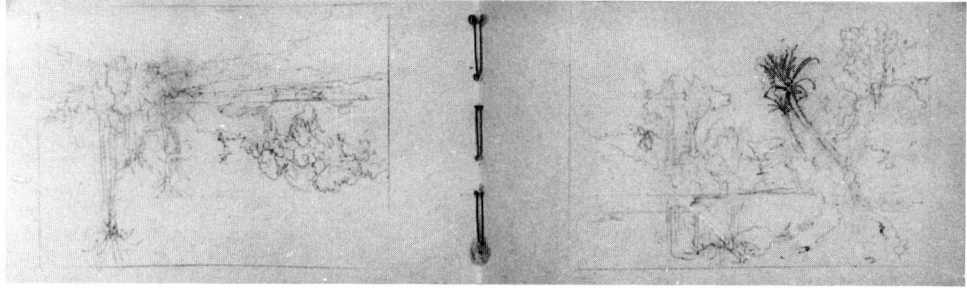

341

346
FELTVILLE
Graphite on wove
4⁷/₈ by 8¹/₈
1826.16.9 Gilcrease
Dated: "July 25th 78" l.l.
Inscribed: "Feltville" l.l.
Provenance: TG

347
FELTVILLE [descriptive]
Graphite on wove
8¹/₈ by 4⁷/₈
1826.16.10 Gilcrease
Provenance: TG

348
FELTVILLE
Graphite on wove

6¹/₄ by 4⁷/₈
1326.960 Gilcrease
Dated: "Aug 78" l.r.
Signed: Colophon l.l.
Inscribed: "Feltville: l.r.
Provenance: TG

*349
NEAR FELTVILLE, NEW JERSEY
Graphite, wash, and white gouache on blue wove
9⁵/₈ by 12⁵/₈
0226.789 Gilcrease
Signed: "TMoran" l.l.
Inscribed: "Near Feltville, N.J." l.l.
Provenance: TG
1916 ledger: 362
Note: Sketch and color notes on verso

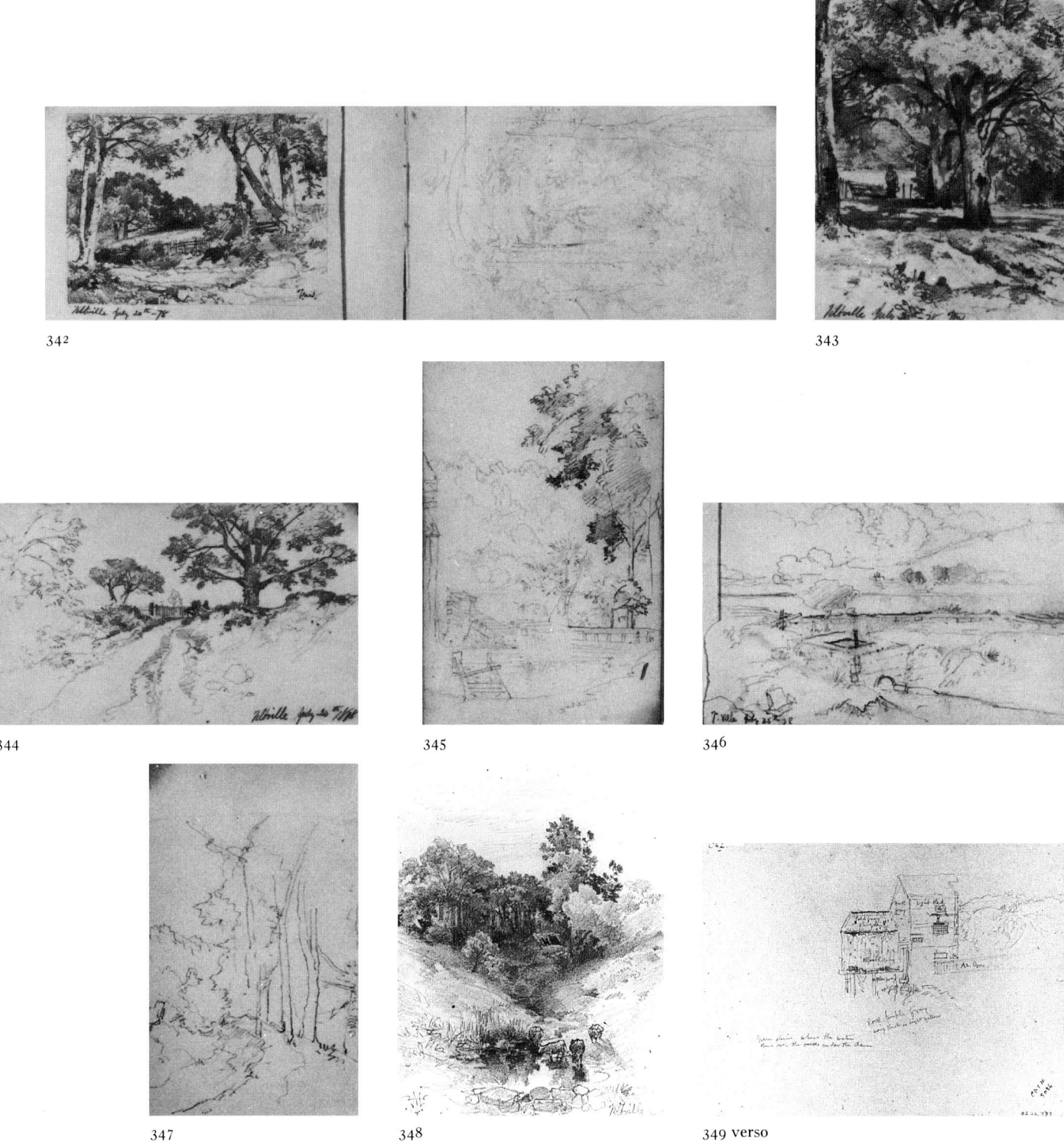

342

343

344

345

346

347

348

349 verso

†350
FELTVILLE [descriptive]
Graphite on blue wove
9³/₄ by 12⁵/₈
1326.528 Gilcrease
Provenance: TG

351
FELTVILLE [descriptive]
Graphite on wove
4⁷/₈ by 6¹/₄
1326.566 Gilcrease
Provenance: TG
Note: Sketch on verso

352
FELTVILLE
Graphite on wove
6¹/₄ by 9⁵/₈
1326.959 Gilcrease
Dated: "1878" u.r.
Inscribed: "Feltville" u.r.
Provenance: TG

353
FELTVILLE [descriptive]
Graphite on gray wove
9 by 12¹/₈
1326.536 Gilcrease
Provenance: TG

354
FELTVILLE [descriptive]
Graphite on gray wove
12¹/₈ by 9¹/₈
1326.561 Gilcrease
Provenance: TG

355
EAST HAMPTON
Graphite on wove
4⁷/₈ by 8¹/₂
1826.16.11 Gilcrease
Dated: "Sep 7–78" u.c.
Inscribed: "Easthampton" u.c.
Provenance: TG

†356
PIG-PEN, EAST HAMPTON
Graphite on wove
4⁷/₈ by 8¹/₈
1826.16.12 Gilcrease
Dated: "Sep 9th–78" l.l.
Inscribed: "Pig-Pen Easthampton" l.l.
Provenance: TG

†357
EAST HAMPTON
Graphite on wove
4⁷/₈ by 8¹/₈
1826.16.13 Gilcrease
Dated: "Sep 7th–78" u.c.
Inscribed: "Easthampton" u.c.
Provenance: TG
Note: Sketch on verso

358
EAST HAMPTON
Graphite and wash on wove
4⁷/₈ by 8¹/₈
1826.16.14 Gilcrease
Dated: "Sep 7–78" u.r.
Inscribed: "Easthampton" u.r.
Provenance: TG

359
EAST HAMPTON
Graphite on wove
4⁷/₈ by 8¹/₈
1826.16.15 Gilcrease
Dated: "Sep 7–78" u.r.
Inscribed: "Easthampton" u.r.; miscellaneous
notes
Provenance: TG

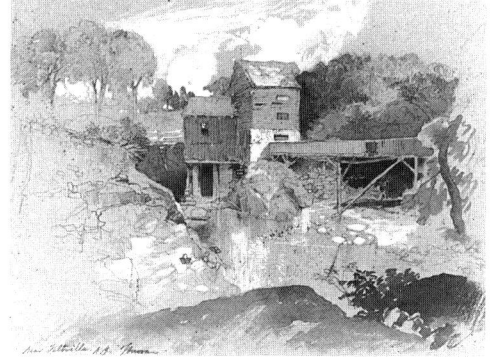

349 recto

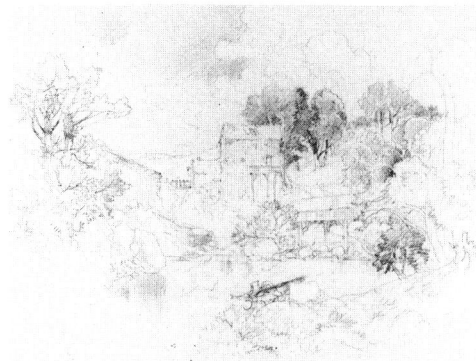

350

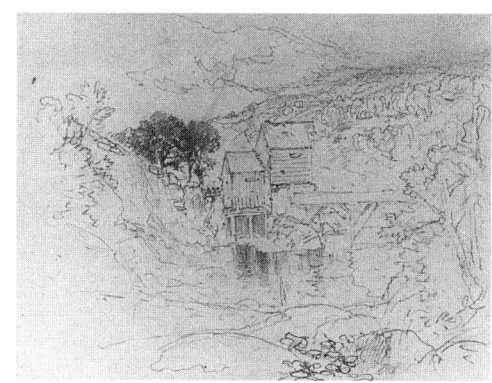

351

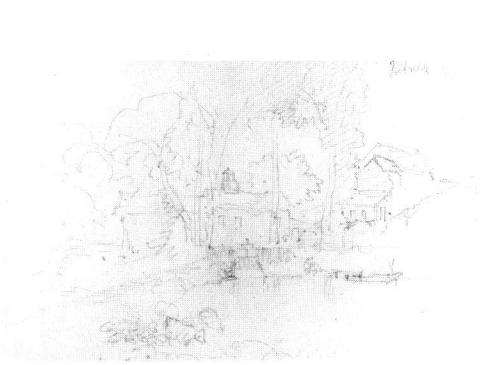

352

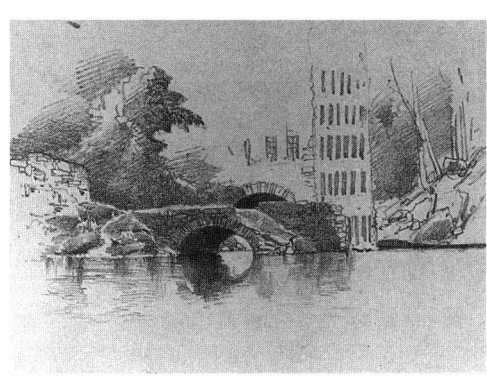

353

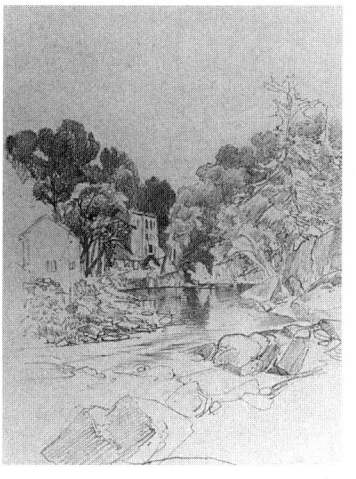

354

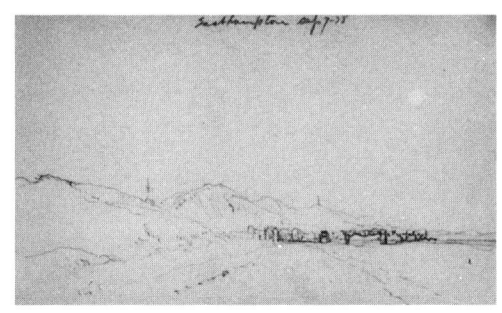

355

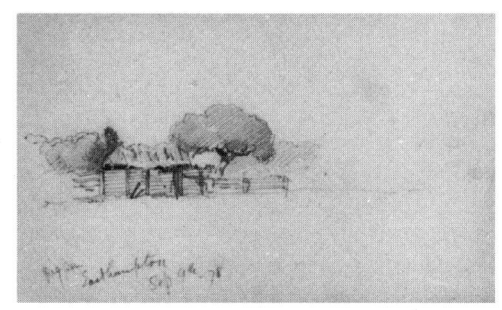

356

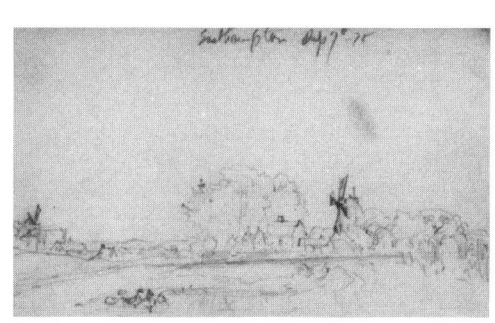

357

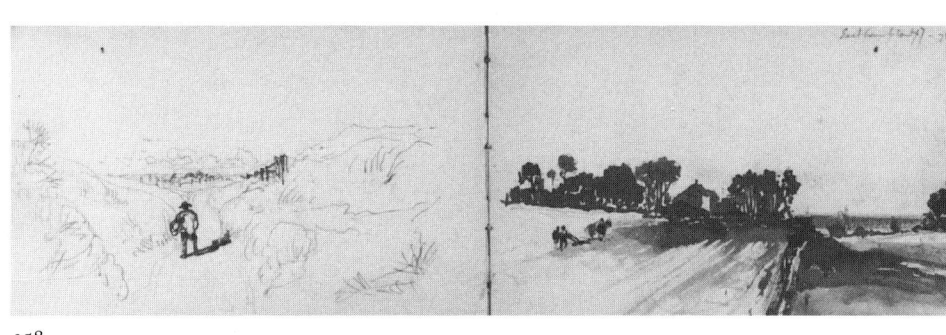

358

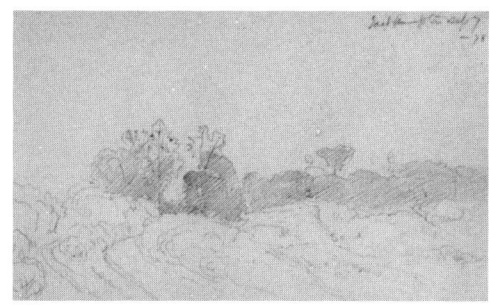

359

360
EAST HAMPTON
Graphite on wove
4⁷/8 by 8¹/8
1826.16.16 Gilcrease
Dated: "Sep 7–78" u.r.
Inscribed: "Easthampton" u.r.
Provenance: TG

361
EAST HAMPTON [descriptive]
Graphite on wove
4⁷/8 by 8¹/8
1826.16.17 Gilcrease
Provenance: TG

362
EAST HAMPTON
Graphite on wove
4⁷/8 by 8¹/8
1826.16.18 Gilcrease
Dated: "Sep 8–78" u.r.
Inscribed: "Easthampton" u.r.
Provenance: TG

†363
EAST HAMPTON [descriptive]
Graphite on wove
4⁷/8 by 8¹/8
1826.16.19 Gilcrease
Provenance: TG

364
EAST HAMPTON [descriptive]
Graphite on wove
4⁷/8 by 8¹/8
1826.16.20 Gilcrease
Provenance: TG

365
EAST HAMPTON
Graphite on wove
4⁷/8 by 8¹/8
1826.16.21 Gilcrease
Dated: "Sep 9–78" u.r.
Inscribed: "Easthampton" u.r.
Provenance: TG

†366
EAST HAMPTON
Graphite on wove
4⁷/8 by 8¹/8
1826.16.22 Gilcrease
Dated: "Sep 9th–78" u.r.
Inscribed: "Easthampton" u.r.
Provenance: TG

367
EAST HAMPTON [descriptive]
Graphite on wove
4⁷/8 by 8¹/8
1826.16.23 Gilcrease
Provenance: TG

368
MONTAUK LIGHT
Graphite on wove
4⁷/8 by 8¹/8
1826.16.24 Gilcrease
Dated: "Sep 14th-78" u.r.
Inscribed: "Montauk light" u.r.
Provenance: TG
Note: Sketch on verso

369
DEBRIS, MONTAUK [descriptive]
Graphite on wove
4⁷/8 by 8¹/8
1826.16.25 Gilcrease
Provenance: TG

370
DEBRIS, MONTAUK [descriptive]
Graphite on gray wove
5 by 10³/4
1326.543 Gilcrease
Provenance: TG
Note: Sketch on verso

371
MONTAUK [descriptive]
Graphite on wove
4⁷/8 by 8¹/8
1826.16.26 Gilcrease
Inscribed: "very dark blue sky" u.c.
Provenance: TG

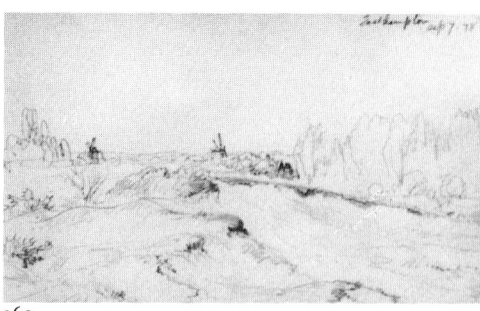
360

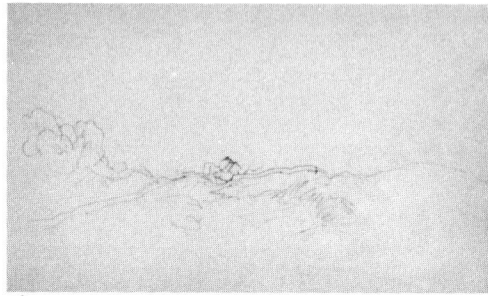
361

372
MONTAUK [descriptive]
Graphite and wash on wove
4⁷/8 by 8¹/8
1826.16.27 Gilcrease
Inscribed: "V.D.B.S." u.c.
Provenance: TG
Note: Sketch on verso

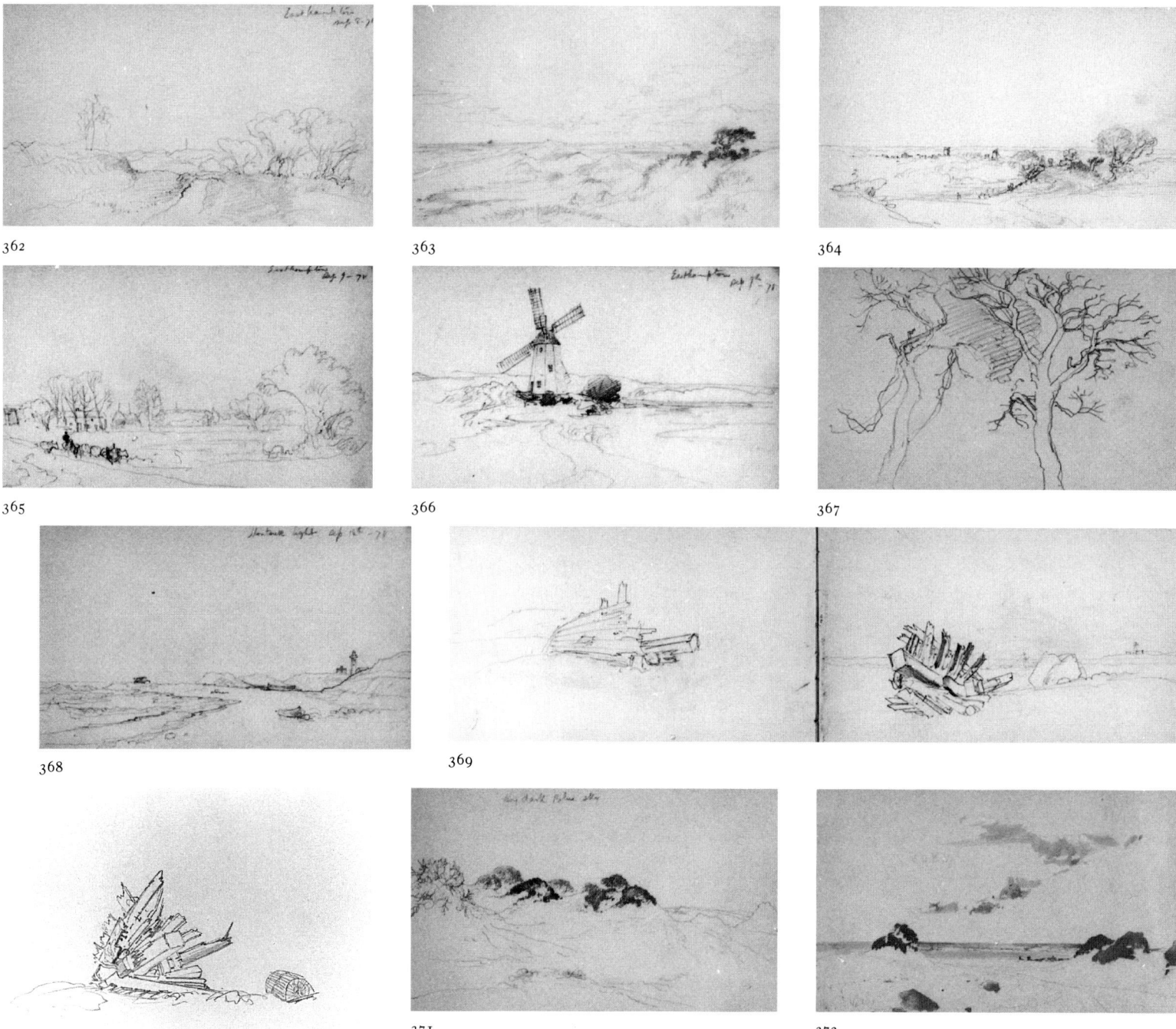

362

363

364

365

366

367

368

369

370

371

372

373
MONTAUK [descriptive]
Graphite on wove
4⁷/₈ by 16¹/₄
1826.16.28 Gilcrease
Inscribed with miscellaneous notes
Provenance: TG

374
MONTAUK [descriptive] Graphite on wove
4⁷/₈ by 8¹/₈
1826.16.29 Gilcrease
Inscribed: "D. Bluish" and "D. Greenish" u.c.
Provenance: TG
Note: Sketch on verso

375
MONTAUK
Graphite on wove
4⁷/₈ by 8¹/₈
1826.16.30 Gilcrease
Dated: "Sep 14–78" u.r.
Inscribed: "Montauk" u.r.; miscellaneous notes
Provenance: TG
Note: Sketch on verso

376
LOOKING SOUTH, MONTAUK
Graphite on wove
4⁷/₈ by 16¹/₄
1826.16.31 Gilcrease
Dated: "Sep 14–78" u.r.
Inscribed: "looking South. Montauk" u.r.; mis-
cellaneous notes
Provenance: TG
Note: Sketch on verso

†377
MONTAUK [descriptive]
Graphite on wove
4⁷/₈ by 16¹/₄
1826.16.32 Gilcrease
Inscribed with miscellaneous notes
Provenance: TG

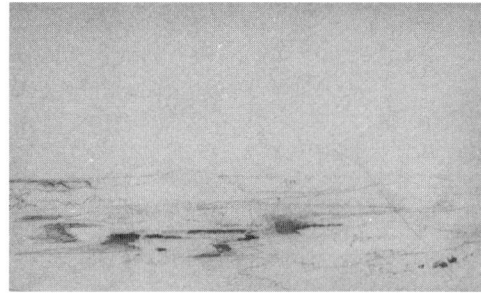

373

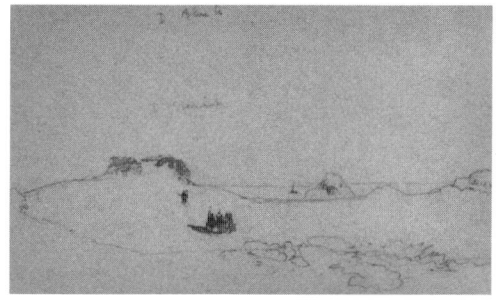

374

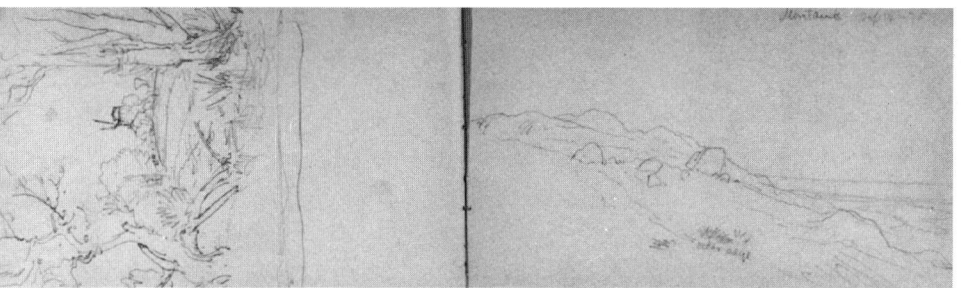

375

378
MONTAUK [descriptive]
Graphite on wove
4⁷/₈ by 8¹/₈
1826.16.33 Gilcrease
Inscribed with miscellaneous notes
Provenance: TG
Note: Sketch on verso

379
MONTAUK [descriptive]
Graphite on wove
4⁷/₈ by 16¹/₄
1826.16.34 Gilcrease
Inscribed with miscellaneous notes
Provenance: TG

380
MONTAUK [descriptive]
Graphite on wove
4⁷/₈ by 8¹/₈

1826.16.35 Gilcrease
Provenance: TG
Note: Sketch on verso

381
FARM BUILDINGS [descriptive]
Graphite on wove
4⁷/₈ by 16¹/₄
1826.16.36 Gilcrease
Provenance: TG

382
SOUTH ORANGE
Graphite on wove
4³/₄ by 12³/₄
1326.962 Gilcrease
Dated: "79" l.l.
Signed: "TM" l.l.
Inscribed: "South Orange" l.l.
Provenance: TG
1916 ledger: 398

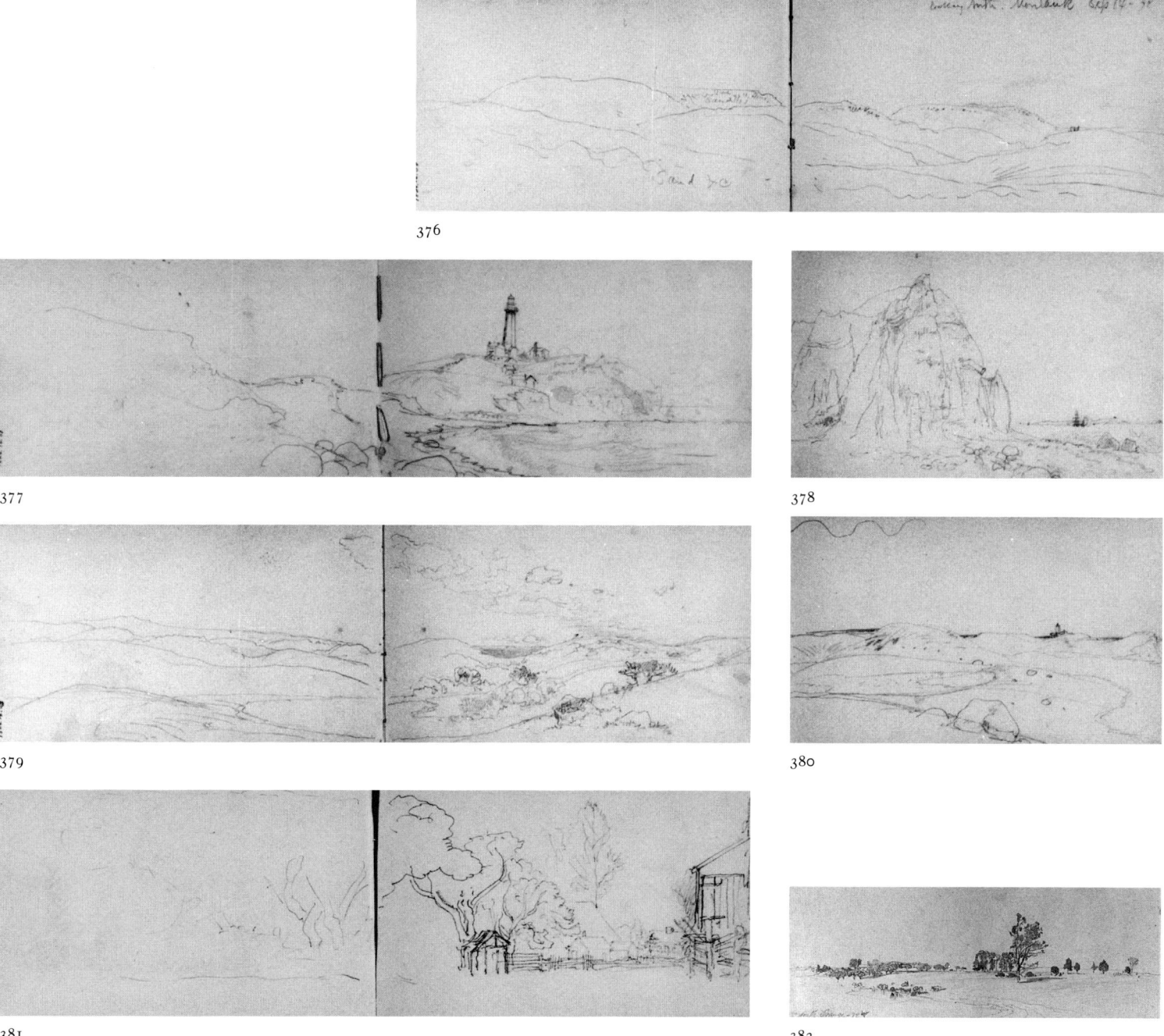

376

377

378

379

380

381

382

383
SOUTH ORANGE
Graphite on wove
5 1/4 by 8 1/4
92 East Hampton Library
Dated: "79" l.c.
Signed: "TM" l.c.
Inscribed: "South Orange" l.c.
Provenance: EH
1916 ledger: 217

384
NEWARK
Graphite on wove
4 3/4 by 12 7/8
1326.948 Gilcrease
Dated: "1873" u.l. [see note]
Signed: "TM" u.l.
Inscribed: "Newark" u.l.
Provenance: TG
1916 ledger: 348
Note: This sketch relates stylistically to sketches
from 1879. The date was added later.

385
AFTER THE THAW, NEAR
COMMUNIPAW FERRY
Graphite, wash, and white gouache on green wove
9 by 11 1/4
26 Guild Hall, East Hampton, New York
Dated: "Jan. 28–1879" u.l.
Signed: Colophon l.l. in ink
Inscribed: "After the Thaw near Communipaw
Ferry" u.l.
Provenance: GH

386
MONTAUK
Graphite and watercolor on laid
10 1/2 by 14
S-21 East Hampton Library
Dated: "July 11th 79" u.l.
Signed: Colophon l.l.
Inscribed: "Montauk" u.l.; miscellaneous notes
Provenance: EH
1916 ledger: 122

387
MURPHY'S CABIN FROM KESEBERG'S
CAMP, DONNER PARTY
Graphite on gray laid

4 by 10 1/2
1336.963 Gilcrease
Dated: "Aug 5th 79" l.r.
Signed: "TMoran" l.r.
Inscribed: "Murphys Cabin from Kiesbergs
camp, Donner party" l.r.
Provenance: TG

388
DONNER LAKE
Graphite, wash, and white gouache on tan wove
6 by 5 1/2
1917–17–44 Cooper-Hewitt Museum
Dated: "1879" l.r.
Inscribed: "Donner Lake" l.r.
Provenance: TM
1916 ledger: 352

389
DONNER LAKE
Graphite on wove
9 1/2 by 12 3/4
1336.664 Gilcrease
Signed: "TM" u.r.
Inscribed: "Donner Lake" u.r.
Provenance: TG

390
TAHOE
Graphite on gray laid
10 5/8 by 4 1/8
1336.971 Gilcrease
Dated: "Aug 5th 1879" u.r.
Signed: "TM" u.r.
Inscribed: "Tahoe" u.c.
Provenance: TG

391
TAHOE
Graphite on wove
11 by 15 1/4
1336.629 Gilcrease
Signed: "TMoran" l.l.
Inscribed: "Tahoe" u.c.
Provenance: TG
Note: Sketch on verso

*392
TAHOE
Graphite, watercolor, and white gouache on blue
wove

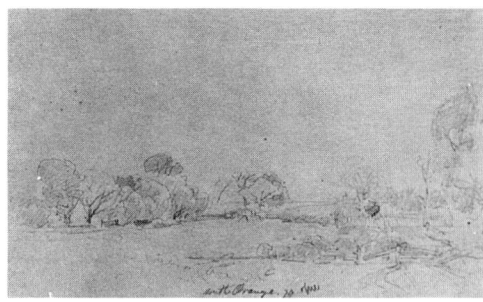

383

Sketch 10 7/8 by 14 3/4, mount 15 1/2 by 19 3/4
0236.886 Gilcrease
Dated: "Aug 8th–79" u.l.
Signed: "TM" and "TMoran" l.l.; "TM" u.l.
Inscribed: "Tahoe" u.l.
Provenance: TG
1916 ledger: 329

*393
LAKE TAHOE
Graphite and watercolor on watermarked laid
9 1/2 by 12 3/8
0236.881 Gilcrease
Dated: "1871" l.l. [see note]
Signed: "TM" l.l.
Inscribed: "Lake Tahoe" l.l.
Provenance: TG
1916 ledger: 71
Note: This sketch relates stylistically to the work
of 1879. The date was added. Moran did not
visit Lake Tahoe in 1871, although he may have
stopped there during his trip to California in
1872.

†394
CHINESE WHEEL FOR RAISING
WATER, ELKO
Graphite on pink wove
10 3/4 by 14 1/2
1336.965 Gilcrease
Dated: "Aug 8th–79" u.l.
Signed: "TMoran" u.c.
Inscribed: "Chinese Wheel for raising water.
Elko" u.l.
Provenance: TG
Note: Sketch on verso

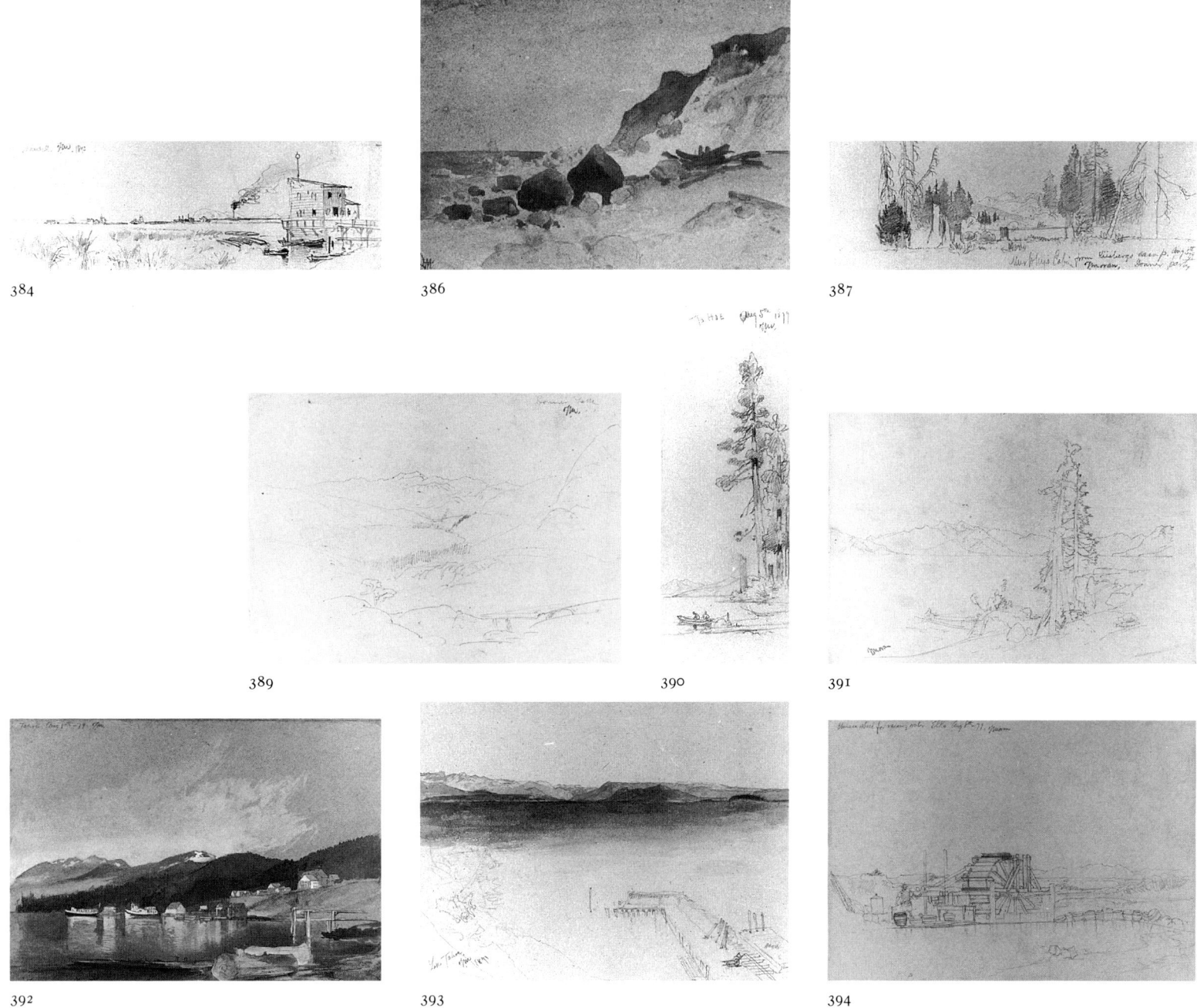

384

386

387

389

390

391

392

393

394

395
HOT SPRING ELKO
Graphite and watercolor on wove
5¹/₂ by 9⁷/₈
0236.842 Gilcrease
Inscribed: "Hot Spring Elko" u.l.
Provenance: TG

396
THE RUBY RANGE
Graphite and watercolor on wove
8¹/₂ by 14³/₈
38.67 Cleveland Museum of Art
Dated: "Aug. 8th–79" l.l.
Signed: "TM" and "TMoran" l.l.
Inscribed: "The Ruby Range" l.l.
Provenance: The artist; Ruth B. Moran, East Hampton, New York; Milch Galleries, New York; Biltmore Salon, Los Angeles, California; Mrs. Henry A. Everett; Bequest of Mrs. Henry A. Everett for the Dorothy Burnham Everett Memorial Collection
1916 ledger: 9

397
ON THE BORDER OF GREAT SALT LAKE, UTAH
Graphite on gray wove
8⁷/₈ by 14³/₄
1973.371 Museum of Fine Arts, Boston
Dated: "Aug 11–79" l.l.
Signed: "TM" l.c.
Inscribed: "On the Border of Great Salt Lake Utah" l.l.
Provenance: MK
1916 ledger: 187

398
UPPER END OF COTTONWOOD CANYON
Graphite on green laid
4 by 10¹/₂
113 East Hampton Library
Dated: "Aug 12–79" u.c.
Signed: "TM" l.l.
Inscribed: "Upper End of Cottonwood Canon" u.l.
Provenance: EH
1916 ledger: 178

399
AVALANCHE IN COTTONWOOD CANYON
Graphite on wove
6⁷/₈ by 4³/₈
69 East Hampton Library
Signed: "TM" l.r.
Inscribed: "Avalanche in Cottonwood Canon" upper edge
Provenance: EH
1916 ledger: 143

400
QUARRYING GRANITE IN COTTONWOOD CANYON
Graphite on blue wove
5⁷/₈ by 7³/₈
20 East Hampton Library
Signed: "TM" u.r.
Inscribed: "Quarrying Granite in Cottonwood Canon" upper edge
Provenance: EH
1916 ledger: 141
Note: This sketch and No. 401 resemble Charles R. Savage's photograph *Quarrying Granite for the Mormon Tabernacle, Cottonwood Cañon, Utah* (c. 1870–72, U.S. Geological Survey Collection, Denver, W. H. Jackson No. 146).

401
GRANITE QUARRY IN COTTONWOOD CANYON [descriptive]
Graphite on blue wove
10³/₄ by 9¹/₄
1336.570 Gilcrease
Signed: "TM" l.l.
Inscribed: "too large" u.r.
Provenance: TG
1916 ledger: 154
Note: Although Moran's ledger identifies this as Green River, this sketch stylistically resembles No. 400. See also note for No. 400.

402
DEVILS GATE, UTAH
Graphite on blue wove
5⁵/₈ by 7¹/₄
114 East Hampton Library
Signed: "TM" u.c.
Inscribed: "Devils Gate Utah" u.l.
Provenance: EH
1916 ledger: 262

*403
IN LITTLE COTTONWOOD CANYON
Graphite and watercolor on watermarked gray laid
10 by 14³/₄
0236.887 Gilcrease
Dated: "Aug 13–79" u.l.
Signed: "TM" u.l.
Inscribed: "In Little Cottonwood Canon" u.l.
Provenance: TG
1916 ledger: 328

404
UPPER END OF COTTONWOOD CANYON, WASATCH RANGE, UTAH
Graphite and white gouache on green wove
14 by 19¹/₂
4258 Jefferson National Expansion Memorial
Dated: "1879" l.l.
Signed: "TM" l.l.
Inscribed: "Upper End of Little Cottonwood Canon Wasatch Range Utah" l.l.
Provenance: JNEM
1916 ledger: 300

405
THE UPPER END OF LITTLE COTTONWOOD CANYON
Graphite, watercolor, and white gouache on gray wove
10 by 14⁵/₈
1917-17-79 Cooper-Hewitt Museum
Dated: "Aug 13th–79" u.l.
Inscribed: "The Upper End of Little Cottonwood Canon" u.l.; color notes
Provenance: TM
1916 ledger: 57

*406
UPPER END OF COTTONWOOD CANYON
Graphite, watercolor, and white gouache on watermarked gray laid
11 by 14⁵/₈
0236.884 Gilcrease
Dated: "Aug 13–79" u.l.
Signed: "TMoran" u.c.
Inscribed: "upper end of Cottonwood Canon" u.l.; "IV" l.l.
Provenance: TG

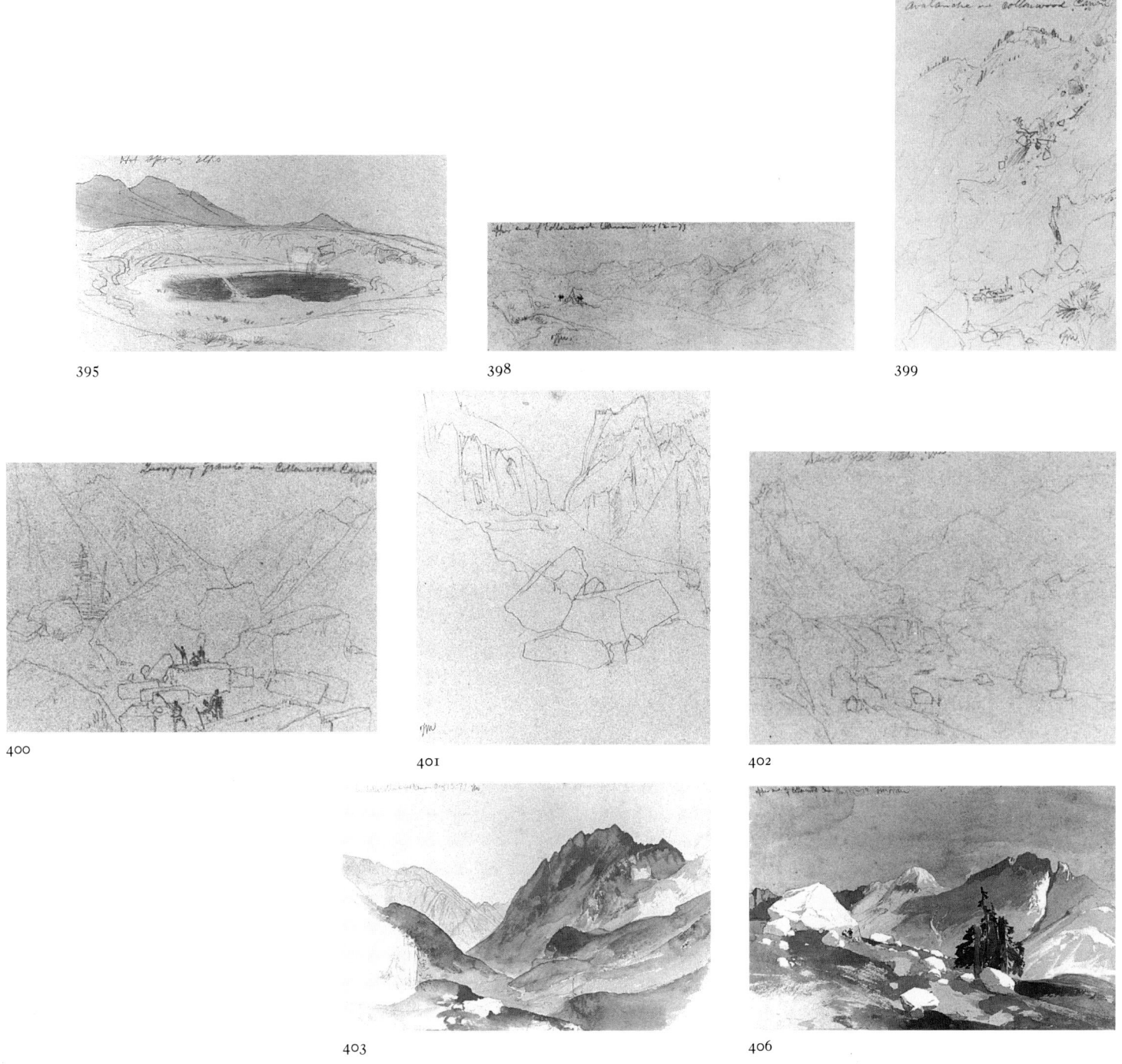

395

398

399

400

401

402

403

406

*407
NEAR THE SUMMIT OF COTTONWOOD
CANYON
Graphite, watercolor, and white gouache on
pink wove
10$^1/_2$ by 14$^1/_2$
0236.890 Gilcrease
Dated: "Aug 13th–79" u.l.
Signed: "TMoran" l.r.
Inscribed: "Near the summit of Cottonwood
Canon" u.l.
Provenance: TG
1916 ledger: 324

*408
TOLEDO MINE, COTTONWOOD
CANYON, UTAH
Graphite and watercolor on laid
8$^1/_2$ by 11$^3/_4$
0236.889 Gilcrease
Dated: "1879" u.r.
Signed: "TMoran" u.r.
Inscribed: "Toledo Mine Cottonwood Canon
Utah" u.r.; color notes
Provenance: TG
1916 ledger: 50

409
ALTA, UTAH
Graphite on watermarked gray laid
10$^1/_8$ by 14$^5/_8$
1336.968 Gilcrease
Dated: "Aug 14th–79" u.l.
Signed: "TM" u.l.
Inscribed: "Alta Utah" u.l.; color notes
Provenance: TG
1916 ledger: 169

410
ABOVE ALTA, UTAH
Graphite on laid
8$^1/_4$ by 12$^5/_8$
1336.969 Gilcrease
Dated: "1879" u.l.
Signed: "TM" u.l.
Inscribed: "Above Alta Utah" u.l.; color notes
Provenance: TG
1916 ledger: 170

*411
AMERICAN FORK CANYON
Graphite and watercolor on wove
10 by 13$^7/_8$
0236.888 Gilcrease
Dated: "1879" l.l.
Signed: "TMoran" l.l.
Inscribed: "American Fork Canon" l.l.; "Above
Alta" u.l.; color notes
Provenance: TG
1916 ledger: 322

*412
PORTNEUF CANYON, IDAHO
Graphite and watercolor on wove
12 by 19$^3/_4$
0236.855 Gilcrease
Signed: "TM" l.l.
Inscribed: "Port Neuf Canon Idaho" l.l.
Provenance: TG
1916 ledger: 332

413
PORTNEUF
Graphite and watercolor on wove
6$^3/_4$ by 5$^3/_8$
1917–17–25 Cooper-Hewitt Museum
Inscribed: "Port Neuf Between the [illegible]
Pass" u.r.
Provenance: TM

414
PORTNEUF CANYON [descriptive]
Graphite, watercolor, and white gouache on
wove
10$^3/_4$ by 14$^7/_8$
0236.851 Gilcrease
Provenance: TG
Note: Sketch on verso

*415
IOWA GULCH, IDAHO
Graphite, watercolor, and white gouache on
wove
11$^7/_8$ by 19$^3/_8$
0236.892 Gilcrease
Dated: "1879" l.r.
Signed: "TMoran" l.r.
Inscribed: "Idaho [altered to Iowa] Gulch, Col-
orado" l.r. in ink; color notes
Provenance: TG

Note: This is probably near the Tetons; a site on
an 1883 Northern Pacific Railroad map identifies an Iowa Bar (Modelski, *Railroad Maps of
North America*, p. 90), and there is a photograph
by W. H. Jackson (Gilcrease Archives 4336.
5489) identified as Iowa Gulch. Stylistically, the
sketch resembles works made in the Portneuf
Canyon region of Idaho.

416
SNAKE RIVER, ABOVE TAYLOR'S
BRIDGE
Graphite on blue laid
8$^1/_4$ by 12$^1/_2$
4253 Jefferson National Expansion Memorial
Dated: "Aug 22–79" u.r.
Signed: "TM" u.r.
Inscribed: "Snake River Above Taylors Bridge"
u.r.; miscellaneous and color notes
Provenance: JNEM

†417
RAILROAD AND TAYLOR'S BRIDGE,
SNAKE RIVER
Graphite on laid
6$^1/_4$ by 8$^1/_4$
1336.918 Gilcrease
Signed: "TM" u.r.
Inscribed: "R.R. & Taylors Bridge Snake River"
u.r.; "Andersons store" u.l.; miscellaneous notes
Provenance: TG

418
FORT HALL, IDAHO
Graphite, watercolor, and white gouache on
wove
7$^1/_2$ by 11$^1/_2$
Grand Teton National Park, Wyoming
Signed: "TMoran" l.l.
Inscribed: "Fort Hall, Idaho" l.l.
Provenance: GT

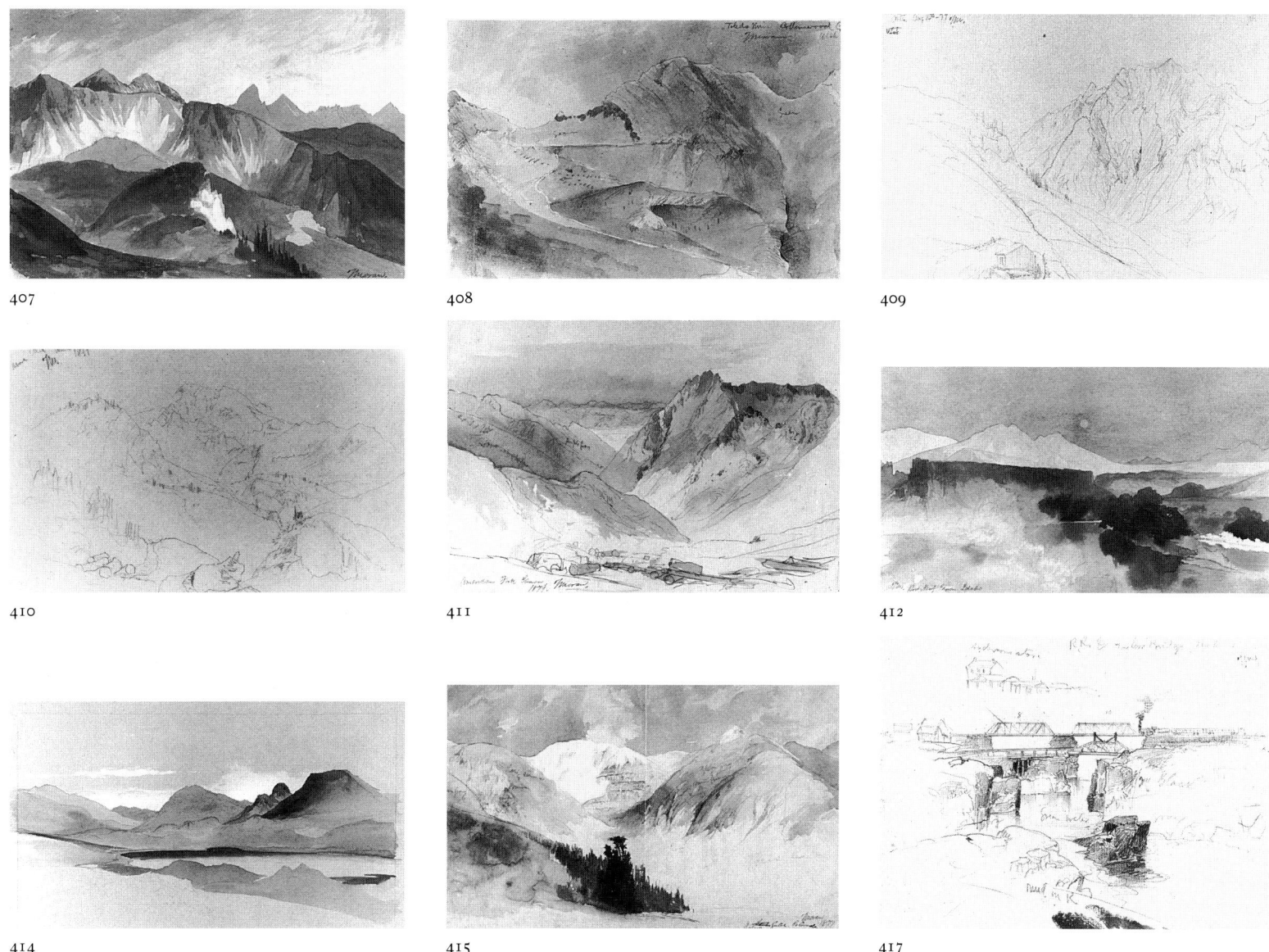

407

408

409

410

411

412

414

415

417

419
THE THREE TETONS
Graphite and watercolor on wove
12⁵/₈ by 9¹/₄
Grand Teton National Park, Wyoming
Dated: "Aug 26th 1879" l.r.
Signed: Colophon l.l. in ink
Inscribed: "The Three Tetons 18 Miles Distant"
l.r.
Provenance: GT
1916 ledger: 342

420
ENTRANCE TO THE TETON CANYON
Graphite on wove
10 by 13¹/₂
Grand Teton National Park, Wyoming
Dated: "Aug. 27th–79" u.l.
Signed: "TM" u.l. and l.l.
Inscribed: "Entrance to the Teton Canon" u.l.
Provenance: GT

421
THE TETONS, IDAHO
Graphite and watercolor on gray wove
8¹/₄ by 14³/₈
Inscribed: "The Tetons Idaho" u.l.
1917–17–33 Cooper-Hewitt Museum
Provenance: TM
1916 ledger: 56

†422
THE TETONS
Graphite and watercolor on wove
9³/₄ by 13⁷/₈
8530 Yellowstone National Park, Wyoming
Dated: "1879" u.l. and l.l.
Signed: Colophon l.l.
Inscribed: "The Tetons" u.l.
Provenance: GP

†423a
GREEN RIVER
Graphite on wove
Upper sketch 4⁷/₈ by 14⁵/₈, sheet 10³/₈ by 14⁵/₈
1336.907 Gilcrease
Dated: "Sep 1st" u.l.
Signed: "TM" u.l.
Inscribed: "Green River" u.l.; color notes
Provenance: TG
1916 ledger: 245

†423b
GREEN RIVER [descriptive]
Graphite on wove
Lower sketch 5¹/₂ by 14⁵/₈, sheet 10³/₈ by 14⁵/₈
1336.907 Gilcrease
Signed: "TM" l.l.
Inscribed with color notes
Provenance: TG

†424
BACK OF THE CASTLE ROCK, GREEN
RIVER, WYOMING
Graphite on wove
7¹/₂ by 10³/₄ [irregular]
1336.964 Gilcrease
Dated: "1879" u.r.
Signed: "TM" u.r.
Inscribed: "Back of the Castle Rock. Green
River, W" upper edge
Provenance: TG

425
GREEN RIVER, EROSION [ledger title]
Graphite on wove
10³/₄ by 7¹/₂
1336.913 Gilcrease
Inscribed: "Indian Red with yellow Cracks on
top graduating to a blue grey at Bottom sage in
water line" upper edge; color notes
Provenance: TG
1916 ledger: 239
Note: Sketch on verso

426
GREEN RIVER, WYOMING
Graphite on wove
4⁷/₈ by 6⁷/₈
1336.909 Gilcrease
Signed: "TM" u.r.
Inscribed: "Green River. Wyoming" u.r.; "North
Cliff from under the Castle Rock" u.c.; color
notes
Provenance: TG
1916 ledger: 357

427
GREEN RIVER
Graphite on blue wove
7¹/₂ by 10³/₄
1336.910 Gilcrease
Signed: "TM" l.r.
Inscribed: "Green River" l.r.
Provenance: TG
1916 ledger: 240
Note: Sketch and inscription on verso: "Green
River"

428
GREEN RIVER
Graphite on gray wove
4³/₄ by 10³/₄
1336.551 Gilcrease
Signed: "TM" l.l.
Inscribed: "Green River" l.l.
Provenance: TG
1916 ledger: 244

429
BETWEEN THE CLIFFS, GREEN RIVER
Graphite on wove
4¹/₂ by 11¹/₄
18 East Hampton Library
Inscribed: "Between the Cliffs Green River"
upper edge
Provenance: EH
1916 ledger: 237

430
GREEN RIVER
Graphite on gray wove
8¹/₂ by 14¹/₂
5860 Jefferson National Expansion Memorial
Dated: "1879" u.l.
Signed: "TM" u.l.
Inscribed: "Green River" u.l.
Provenance: JNEM
1916 ledger: 126

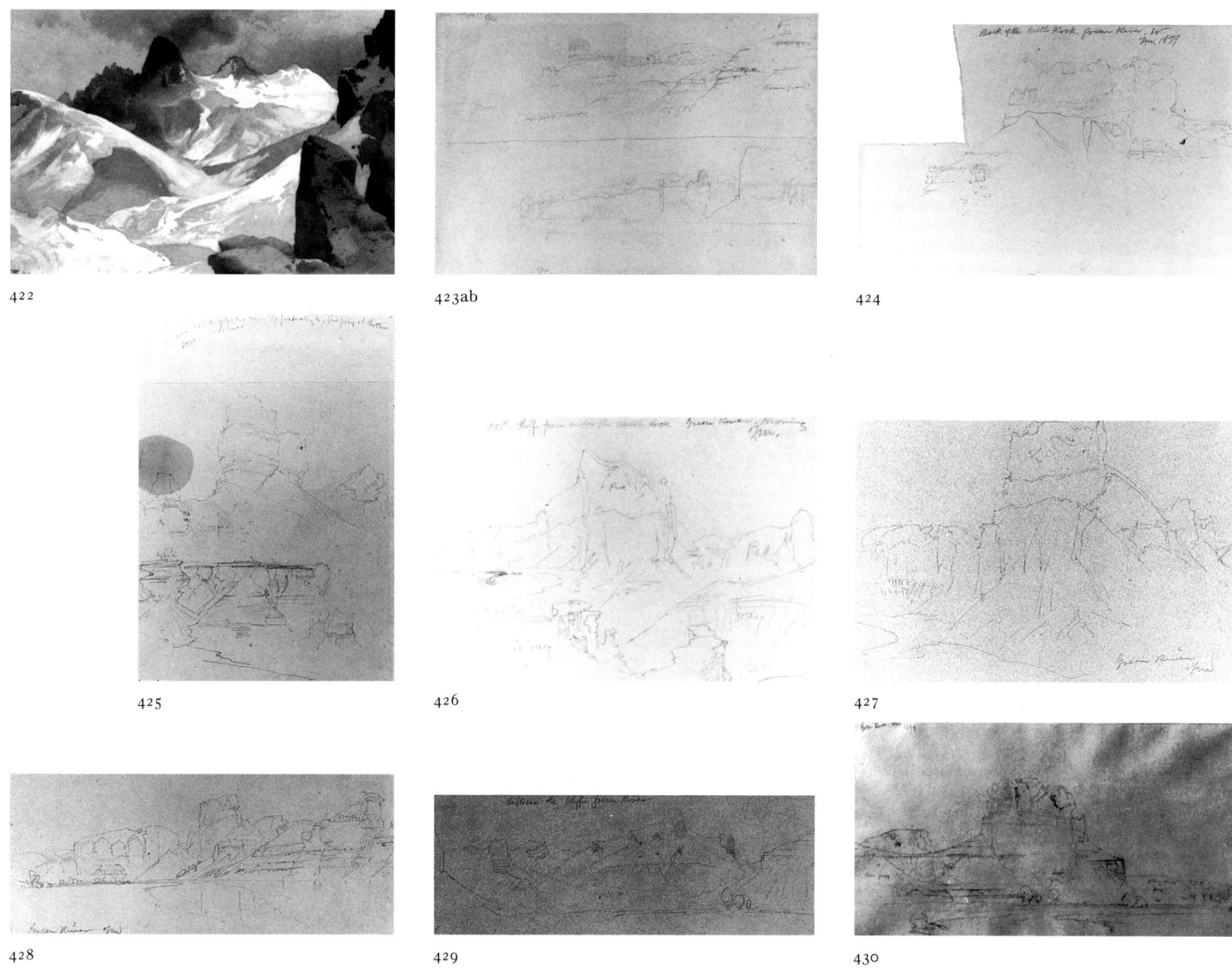

422

423ab

424

425

426

427

428

429

430

*431
GREEN RIVER
Graphite, watercolor, and white gouache on
gray wove
Sketch 9³/₈ by 12³/₄, mount 12¹/₈ by 15¹/₈
0236.891 Gilcrease
Dated: "1879" l.l. in ink, l.l. in ink on mount
Signed: Colophon l.l. in ink
Inscribed: "Green River" l.l. in ink
Provenance: TG
1916 ledger: 35

432
GREEN RIVER, WYOMING TERRITORY
Graphite, watercolor, and white gouache on blue
wove
10 by 14¹/₄
4297 Jefferson National Expansion Memorial
Dated: "Sept 10th 1879" l.r.; "1879 l.l. in ink
Signed: "TM" l.r. and colophon l.l. in ink
Inscribed: "Green River Wyoming Ter" l.r.
Provenance: JNEM

433
GREEN RIVER FROM THE FERRY
Graphite, watercolor, and white gouache on
gray wove
8¹/₂ by 14³/₈
1917–17–38 Cooper-Hewitt Museum
Dated: "Sept 11–79" u.r.; "1880" l.l. in ink
Signed: Colophon l.r. in ink
Inscribed: "Green River from the Ferry" u.r.
Provenance: TM
1916 ledger: 58

434
GREEN RIVER, WYOMING
Graphite, watercolor, and white gouache on wove
12⁵/₈ by 18
1917–17–39 Cooper-Hewitt Museum
Dated: "1879" l.l.
Inscribed: "Green River Wyoming" l.l.
Provenance: TM

435
GREEN RIVER
Graphite, watercolor, and white gouache on tan
wove
8 by 13
George F. McMurray Collection at Trinity College, Hartford

Dated: "Sep 12th–79" l.l.
Signed: "TMoran" l.l.
Inscribed: "Green River" l.l.

*436
GREEN RIVER BUTTES, WYOMING
Graphite, watercolor, and white gouache on
wove
10¹/₄ by 13⁷/₈
0236.885 Gilcrease
Dated: "1879" l.l.
Signed: "TMoran" l.l.
Inscribed: "Green River Buttes. Wyoming" l.l.;
color notes
Provenance: TG
1916 ledger: 323

†437
CLIFFS OF GREEN RIVER, WYOMING
Graphite on watermarked gray laid
10¹/₂ by 14³/₄
1336.849 Gilcrease
Dated: "1894" l.r. [see note]
Signed: "TMoran" l.r.
Inscribed: "Cliffs of Green River, Wyoming"
l.c.; "2" u.l. with registration arrow
Provenance: TG
1916 ledger: 124
Note: This sketch forms the right half of a panoramic image with No. 438. The inscribed date is
1894, but the date was added later. The paper is
the same laid Moran used extensively during the
1879 trip. Although Moran most probably made
this sketch in 1879, it is possible that he made
later, undocumented trips to or through Green
River in which he could have produced sketches
such as this. A studio watercolor, *Castle Buttes,
Green River, Wyoming* (Fenn Galleries, Santa
Fe, 14 by 21), is dated 1894, although composi-
tionally it does not resemble the two-part field
sketch. There is a sketch on the verso of No. 437.

†438
GREEN RIVER, WYOMING
Graphite on watermarked laid
10¹/₂ by 14³/₄
1336.911 Gilcrease
Inscribed: "Green River. W." l.r.; "1/2 Green
River" l.l.; "no. 2" l.r.; "1" u.r. with a registration
arrow
Provenance: TG

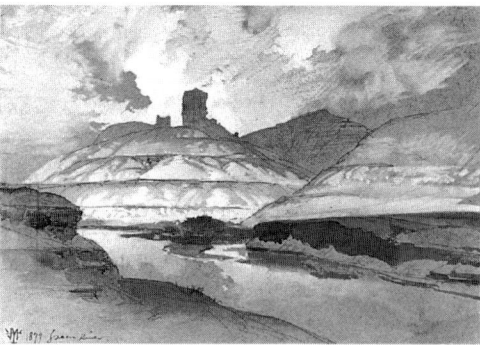

431

1916 ledger: 125
Note: This sketch forms the left half of a panoramic image with No. 437.

*439
THE CLIFFS OF GREEN RIVER,
WYOMING
Graphite, watercolor, and white gouache on laid
Sketch 9³/₄ by 23, mount 15¹/₂ by 25⁵/₈
0236.930 Gilcrease
Dated: "1879" l.l.
Signed: "TM" and "TMoran" l.l.
Inscribed: "The Cliffs of Green River. Wyo-
ming Tery." l.l.; miscellaneous notes
Provenance: TG
1916 ledger: 2

440
BALTIMORE FROM FEDERAL HILL
Graphite on wove
5 by 8
18 East Hampton Library
Dated: "June 12/80" l.l.
Inscribed: "Balt. from Fed. Hill" l.l.
Provenance: EH

†441
NEWARK MEADOWS
Graphite and gray wash on wove
5¹/₄ by 12¹/₈
0226.790 Gilcrease
Inscribed: "Newark, Meadows" l.l.; miscella-
neous notes
Signed: "TM" l.l.
Provenance: TG
1916 ledger: 171

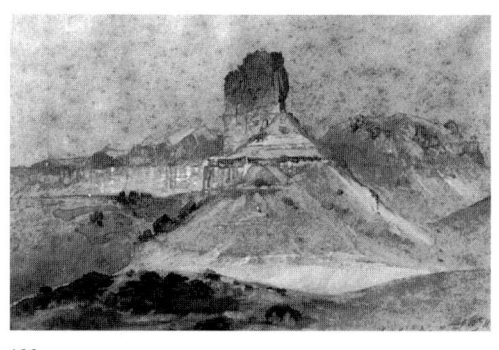

432

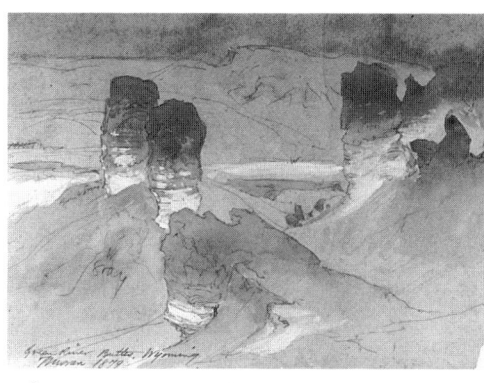

436

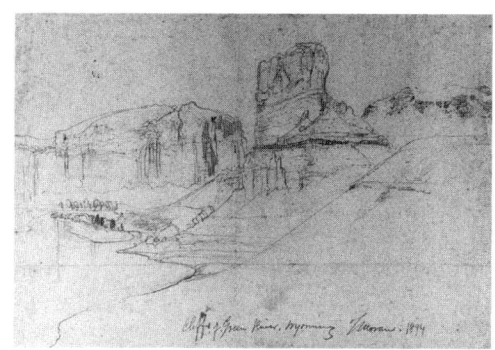

437

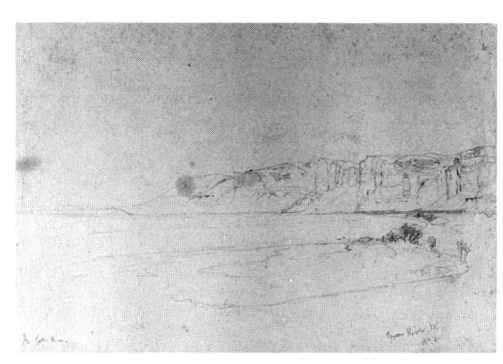

438

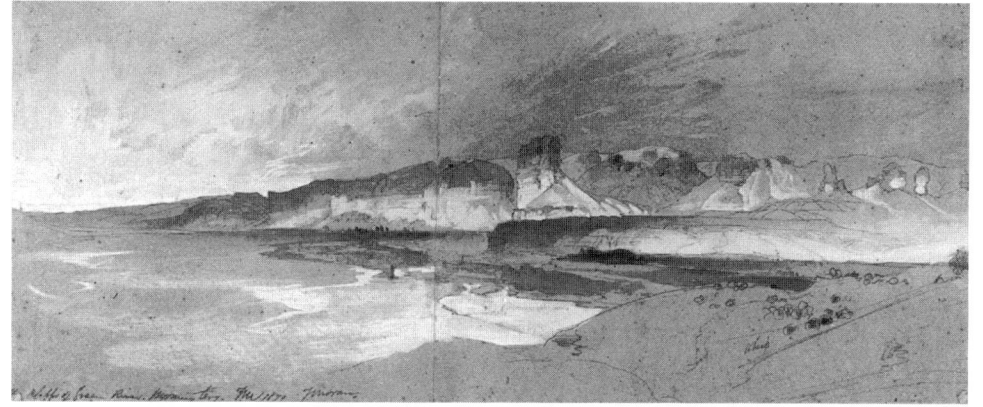

439

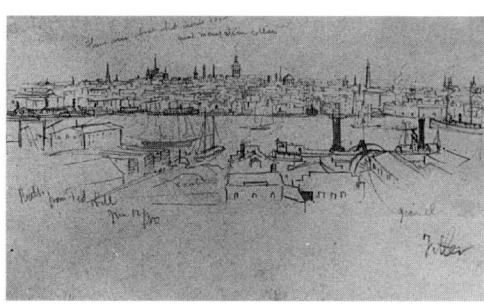

440

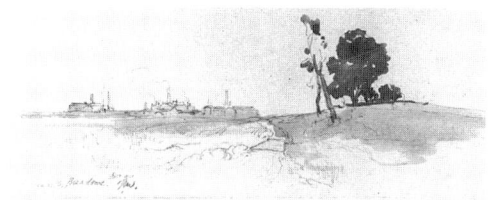

441

†442
NEWARK
Graphite on wove
9⁵/₈ by 12⁷/₈
1326.946 Gilcrease
Dated: "1875" u.l.
Signed: "TM" u.l.
Inscribed: "Newark" u.l.
Provenance: TG
1916 ledger: 195

443
NEWARK
Graphite on wove
9⁵/₈/ by 12⁷/₈
1326.991 Gilcrease
Dated: "1880" u.l.
Signed: "TM" u.l.
Inscribed: "Newark" u.l.
Provenance: TG
1916 ledger: 308
Note: Sketch on verso

444
COMMUNIPAW SUGAR REFINERIES
Graphite on laid
8¹/₄ by 13¹/₂
60.430 Museum of Fine Arts, Boston
Dated: "1876" l.l. [see note]
Signed: "TM" l.l.
Inscribed: "Communipaw Sugar Refineries" l.l.
Provenance: MK
1916 ledger: 157
Note: This sketch relates stylistically to those of 1880.

†445
NEWARK
Graphite on wove
9¹/₂ by 15
1326.680 Gilcrease
Signed: "TM" l.r.
Inscribed: "Newark" l.r.
Provenance: TG
1916 ledger: 168

†446
COMMUNIPAW [descriptive]
Graphite on wove
9 by 13⁵/₈
1326.981 Gilcrease

Dated: "1880" l.l.
Signed: "TM" l.l.
Provenance: TG
1916 ledger: 245

447
COMMUNIPAW [descriptive]
Graphite on wove
5 by 8
76 East Hampton Library
Signed: "TM" l.l.
Provenance: EH
1916 ledger: 303

448
MORRIS CANAL, COMMUNIPAW
Graphite on wove
4¹/₂ by 6
53 East Hampton Library
Signed: "TM" u.c.
Inscribed: "Morris Canal. Communipaw" u.l.
Provenance: EH
1916 ledger: 265

†449
COMMUNIPAW
Graphite, pen and ink, and gray wash on laid
embossed with AS conjoined
4¹/₂ by 6⁷/₈
1326.989 Gilcrease
Dated: "1880" u.l.
Signed: "TMoran" l.l.
Inscribed: "Communipaw" u.l.
Provenance: TG
1916 ledger: 29
Note: Sketch and inscription on verso: "Communipaw 1880"

450
COMMUNIPAW [descriptive]
Graphite and wash on ruled wove notepaper
4⁷/₈ by 8
S-10 East Hampton Library
Dated: "1880" l.l. in ink
Signed: Colophon l.l. in ink
Provenance: EH
1916 ledger: 12

451
COMMUNIPAW SUGAR REFINERIES
Pen and wash on ruled wove notepaper

442

6³/₄ by 8¹/₄
S-7 East Hampton Library
Dated: "1880" u.l. in ink and l.r. in ink on mat
Signed: "TMoran" l.r. on mat
Inscribed: "Communipaw" u.l. in ink; "Sugar Refineries" l.r. in ink on mat; "28. pen & wash" u.l. in ink on mat
Provenance: EH
1916 ledger: 430

452
COMMUNIPAW, NEW JERSEY
Graphite on wove
3¹/₄ by 10¹/₈
A 403 42.200 Washington County Museum of Fine Arts, Hagerstown, Md.
Dated: "1880" u.l.
Signed: "TMoran" u.l.
Inscribed: "Communipaw, N.J." l.r.

453
HACKENSACK MEADOWS, SNAKE HILLS
Graphite and watercolor on watermarked green laid
6 by 9
4248 Jefferson National Expansion Memorial
Inscribed: "Hackensack Meadows Snake Hills" u.l.
Provenance: JNEM
1916 ledger: 361
Note: Sketch of Liberty Cap geyser on verso

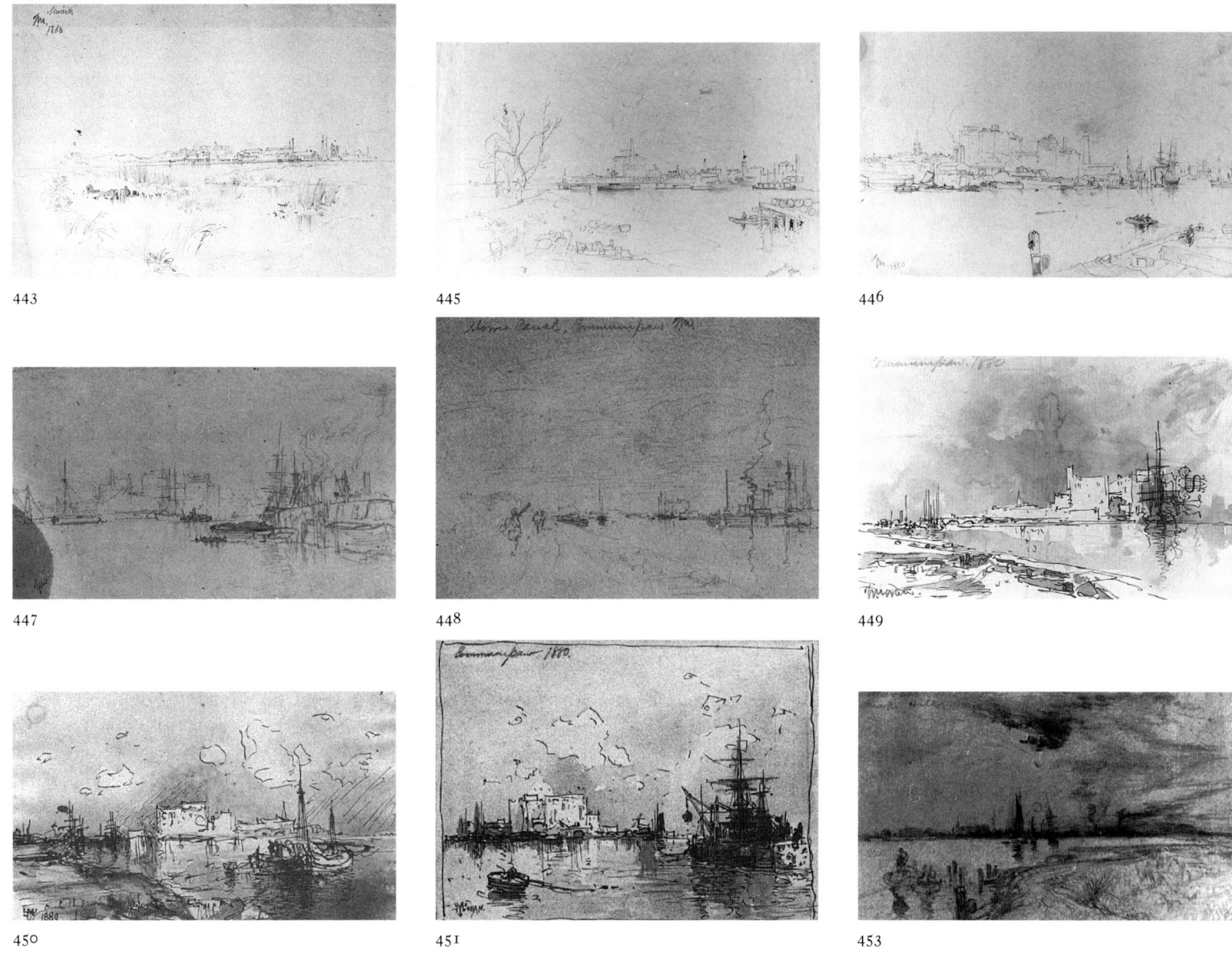

443

445

446

447

448

449

450

451

453

454
NEW YORK FROM HOBOKEN
Graphite on blue wove
12³/₄ by 19⁵/₈
1326.983 Gilcrease
Dated: "1880" l.l.
Signed: "TM" l.l.
Inscribed: "New York from Hoboken" l.l.
Provenance: TG
1916 ledger: 386

455
SKETCHES OF HOUSES [descriptive]
Graphite on wove
7¹/₈ by 4³/₈
Folder 1 East Hampton Library
Provenance: EH

456
EAST HAMPTON
Graphite on wove
4³/₈ by 7¹/₈
Folder 1 East Hampton Library
Dated: "June 29th 1880" u.r.
Inscribed: "East Hamp" u.r.
Provenance: EH

457
EAST HAMPTON BEACH
Graphite on wove
4³/₈ by 7¹/₈
Folder 1 East Hampton Library
Dated: "June 23. 1880" u.c.
Inscribed: "Easthampton Beach" u.l.
Provenance: EH

458
THE POND, EAST HAMPTON
Graphite on wove
4³/₈ by 7¹/₈
Folder 1 East Hampton Library
Dated: "1880" u.r.
Inscribed: "The Pond East Hamp" u.r.
Provenance: EH

459
THE POND FROM EGYPT ROAD
Graphite on wove
4³/₈ by 7¹/₈
Folder 1 East Hampton Library
Dated: "Sep 12 1880" u.r.
Inscribed: "The pond from Egypt Road" u.r.
Provenance: EH

460
BACK OF MULFORD'S, EAST HAMPTON
Graphite on wove
4³/₈ by 7¹/₈
Folder 1 East Hampton Library
Dated: "1880" u.r.
Inscribed: "Back of Mulfords East H." u.r.
Provenance: EH

461
FITHIAN'S YARD
Graphite on wove
7¹/₈ by 4³/₈
Folder 1 East Hampton Library
Dated: "1880" u.c.
Inscribed: "Fithians Yard" u.l.
Provenance: EH

462
EAST HAMPTON
Graphite on wove
4³/₈ by 7¹/₈
Folder 1 East Hampton Library
Dated: "1880" u.r.
Inscribed: "East H" u.r.
Provenance: EH

463
THE POND, EAST HAMPTON
Graphite on wove
4³/₈ by 7¹/₈
Folder 1 East Hampton Library
Dated: "1880" u.r.
Signed: "TM" u.r.
Inscribed: "The Pond. East Hamp" u.r.
Provenance: EH

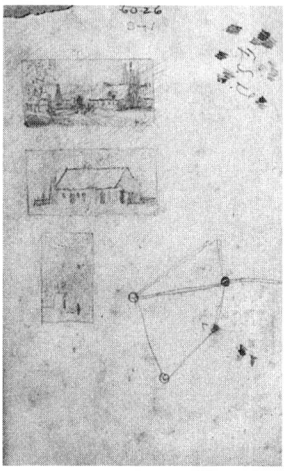

454

455

464
EAST HAMPTON [descriptive]
Graphite on wove
4³/₈ by 7¹/₈
Folder 1 East Hampton Library
Provenance: EH

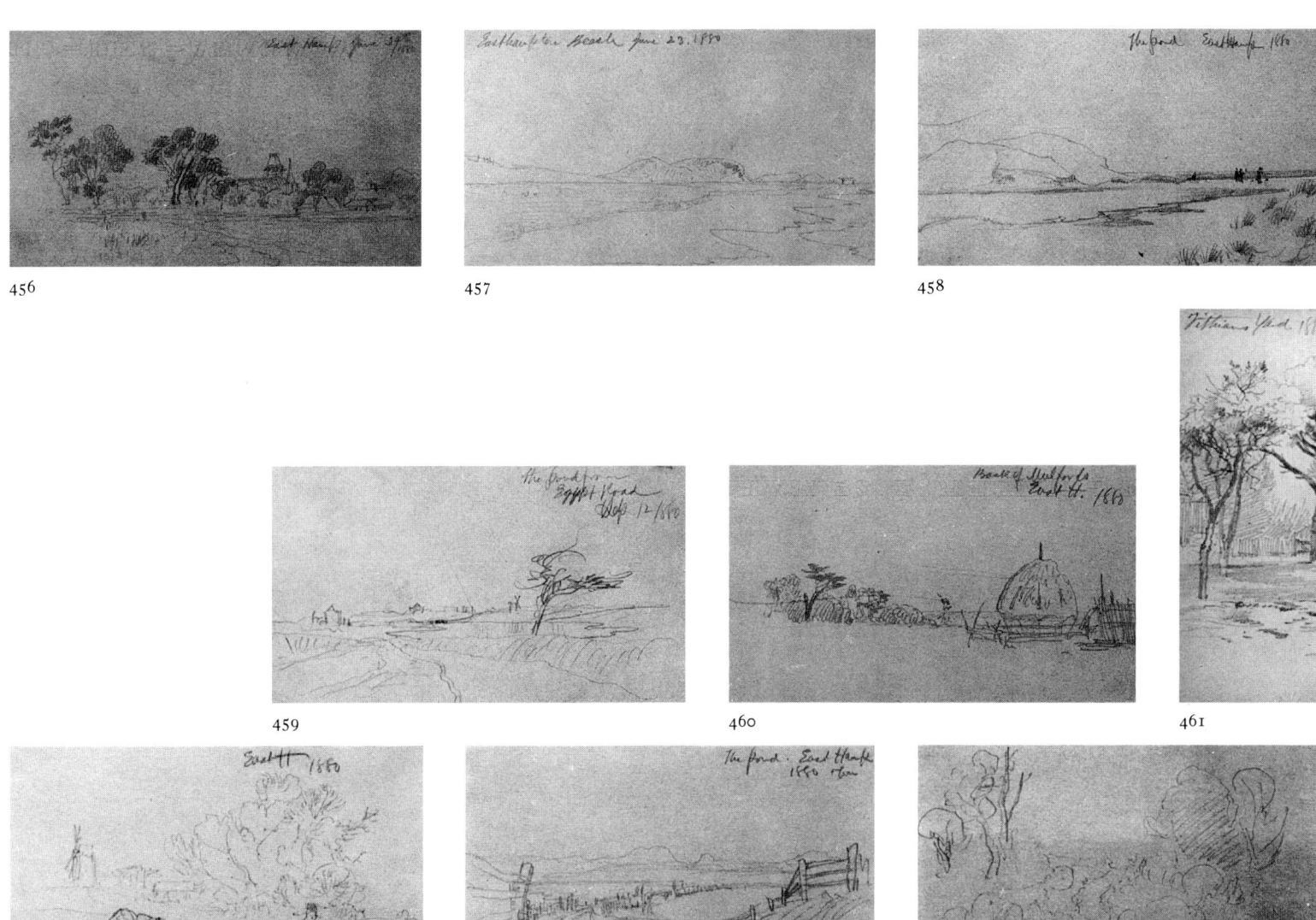

456

457

458

459

460

461

462

463

464

465
LOOKING TOWARD BRIDGEHAMPTON,
EAST HAMPTON
Graphite on wove
7 1/8 by 4 3/8
Folder 1 East Hampton Library
Dated: "1880" u. r.
Signed: "TM" u.r.
Inscribed: "Looking toward Bridgehampton
East H." upper edge
Provenance: EH

466
EAST HAMPTON
Graphite on wove
4 3/8 by 7 1/8
Folder 1 East Hampton Library
Dated: "July 1880" u.r.
Signed: "TM" u.r.
Inscribed: "East Hamp." u.r.
Provenance: EH

467
EAST HAMPTON
Graphite on wove
4 3/8 by 7 1/8
Folder 1 East Hampton Library
Dated: "1880" u.r.
Signed: "TM" u.r.
Inscribed: "East H" u.r.
Provenance: EH

468
EAST HAMPTON
Graphite on wove
4 3/8 by 7 1/8
Folder 1 East Hampton Library
Dated: "Aug 5–80" u.c.
Inscribed: "East Hamp" u.l.; "Sassafras Hill"
u.r.
Provenance: EH

469
EAST HAMPTON, SASSAFRAS GROVE
Graphite on wove
4 3/8 by 7 1/8
Folder 1 East Hampton Library
Dated: "1880" u.r.
Inscribed: "East H. Sassafras Grove" u.r.
Provenance: EH

470
NEAR BATHING PLACE, EAST
HAMPTON
Graphite on wove
4 3/8 by 7 1/8
Folder 1 East Hampton Library
Inscribed: "Near Bathing Place East Hamp" u.r.
Provenance: EH

471
EAST HAMPTON
Graphite on wove
4 3/8 by 7 1/8
Folder 1 East Hampton Library
Dated: "Aug 27th 1880" u.l.
Inscribed: "East H." u.l.
Provenance: EH

472
SASSAFRAS TREES, EAST HAMPTON
Graphite on wove
7 1/8 by 4 3/8
Folder 1 East Hampton Library
Dated: "Aug 15 1880" l.c.
Signed: "TM" l.c.
Inscribed: "Sassafras Trees East Hamp" l.l.
Provenance: EH

473
EAST HAMPTON [descriptive]
Graphite on wove
4 3/8 by 7 1/8
Folder 1 East Hampton Library
Provenance: EH

474
EAST HAMPTON [descriptive]
Graphite on wove
4 3/8 by 7 1/8
Folder 1 East Hampton Library
Dated: "Aug 28" u.r.
Provenance: EH

475
EAST HAMPTON [descriptive]
Graphite on wove
4 3/8 by 7 1/8
Folder 1 East Hampton Library
Provenance: EH

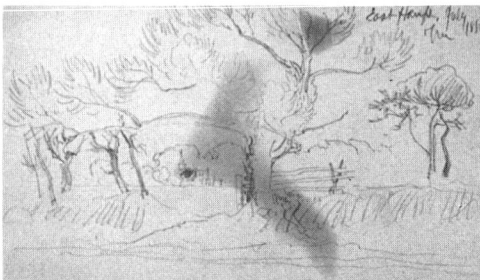

465

466

476
EGYPT ROAD
Graphite on wove
4 3/8 by 7 1/8
Folder 1 East Hampton Library
Dated: "Sep 10 1880" u.r.
Inscribed: "Egypt Road" u.r.
Provenance: EH

477
EAST HAMPTON [descriptive]
Graphite on wove
4 3/8 by 7 1/8
Folder 1 East Hampton Library
Provenance: EH

478
EAST HAMPTON [descriptive]
Graphite on wove
4 3/8 by 7 1/8
Folder 1 East Hampton Library
Provenance: EH

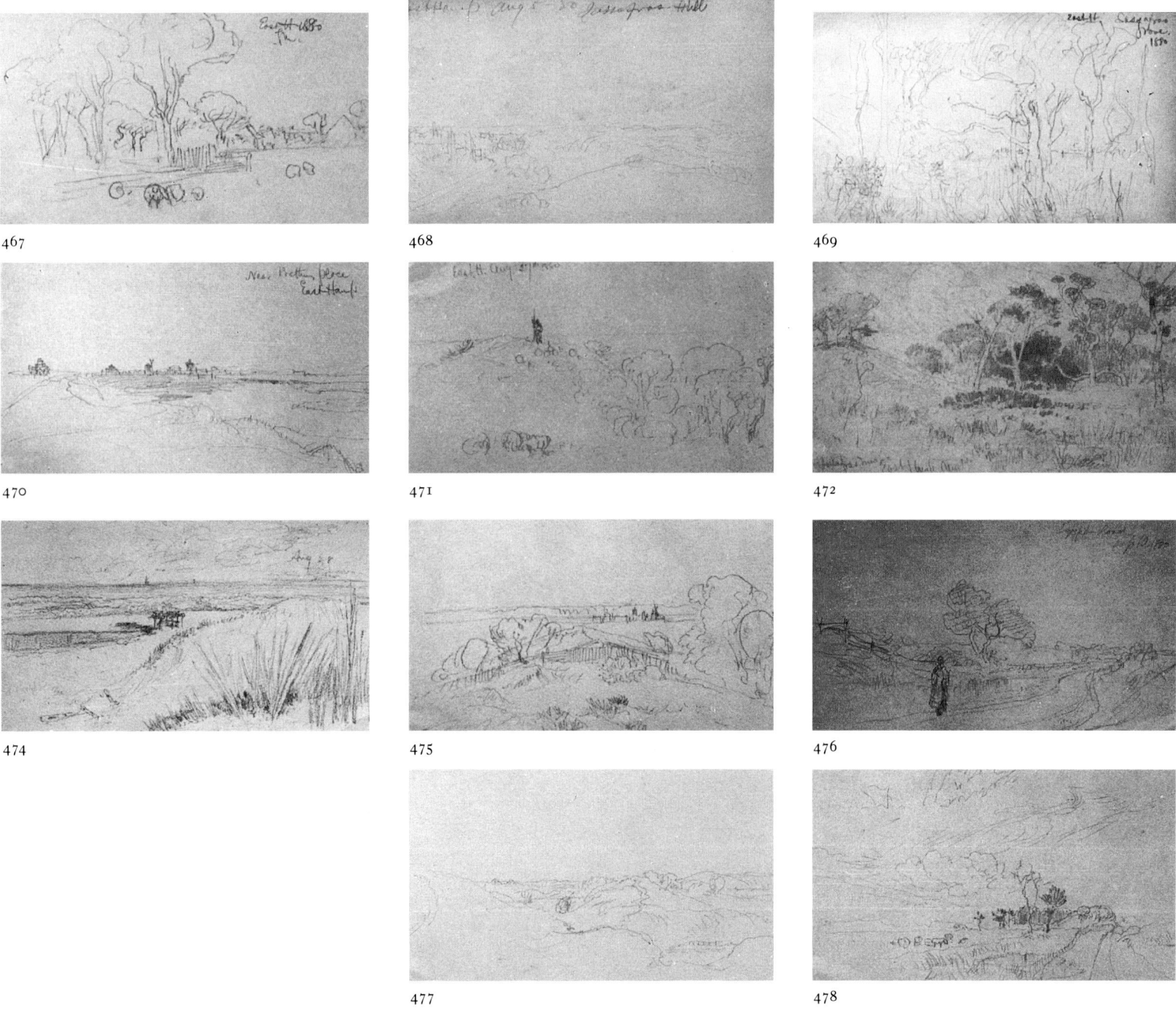

467

468

469

470

471

472

474

475

476

477

478

479
EAST HAMPTON [descriptive]
Graphite on wove
4³/₈ by 7¹/₈
Folder 1 East Hampton Library
Provenance: EH

480
EAST HAMPTON
Graphite on wove
4³/₈ by 7¹/₈
Folder 1 East Hampton Library
Dated: "Aug 2–80" u.r.
Inscribed: "E Hamp" u.r.
Provenance: EH

481
SAND HILL ROAD TO GEORGICA
POND, EAST HAMPTON
Graphite on wove
4³/₈ by 7¹/₈
Folder 1 East Hampton Library
Dated: "July 12–80" u.r.
Inscribed: "Sand Hill Road to Georgica Pond
E. Hamp" upper edge
Provenance: EH

482
EAST HAMPTON
Graphite on gray wove
8³/₄ by 11⁵/₈
1326.690 Gilcrease
Signed: "TM" l.r.
Inscribed: "E.H." l.r.
Provenance: TG
1916 ledger: 307

483
EAST HAMPTON [descriptive]
Graphite on wove
10 by 13
S-65 East Hampton Library
Provenance: EH

484
MONTAUK
Graphite on wove
5¹/₂ by 7¹/₂
S-77 East Hampton Library
Signed: "TM" l.r.
Inscribed: "Montauk" l.r.
Provenance: EH

485
EAST HAMPTON [descriptive]
Graphite on tracing paper
6 by 9¹/₂
1326.571 Gilcrease
Provenance: TG

486
EAST HAMPTON
Graphite on wove
7¹/₈ by 9¹/₄
1326.984 Gilcrease
Dated: "July 6 1880" l.l.
Signed: "TM" l.l.
Inscribed: "East Hampton" l.l.
Provenance: TG
1916 ledger: 73

487
GEORGICA
Graphite on wove
7¹/₄ by 11
1326.699 Gilcrease
Signed: "TM" u.r.
Inscribed: "Georgica" u.r.
Provenance: TG
1916 ledger: 239

488
WATERMILLS, LONG ISLAND
Graphite on wove
9¹/₈ by 10⁵/₈
1326.982 Gilcrease
Dated: "July 23rd 1880" u.l.
Signed: "TM" u.l.
Inscribed: "Watermills, L.I." u.l.
Provenance: TG
1916 ledger: 205

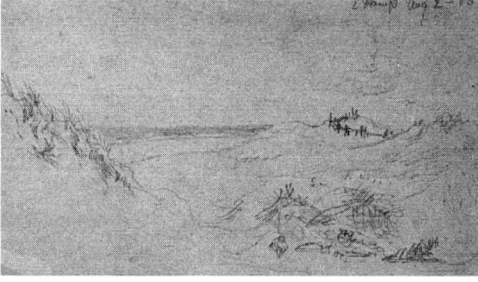

479

480

489
EAST HAMPTON, THE GOOSE POND
Graphite on wove
6 by 8³/₄
2 East Hampton Library
Dated: "1880" l.r.
Signed: "TM" l.r.
Inscribed: "E.H. The Goose Pond" l.r.
Provenance: EH

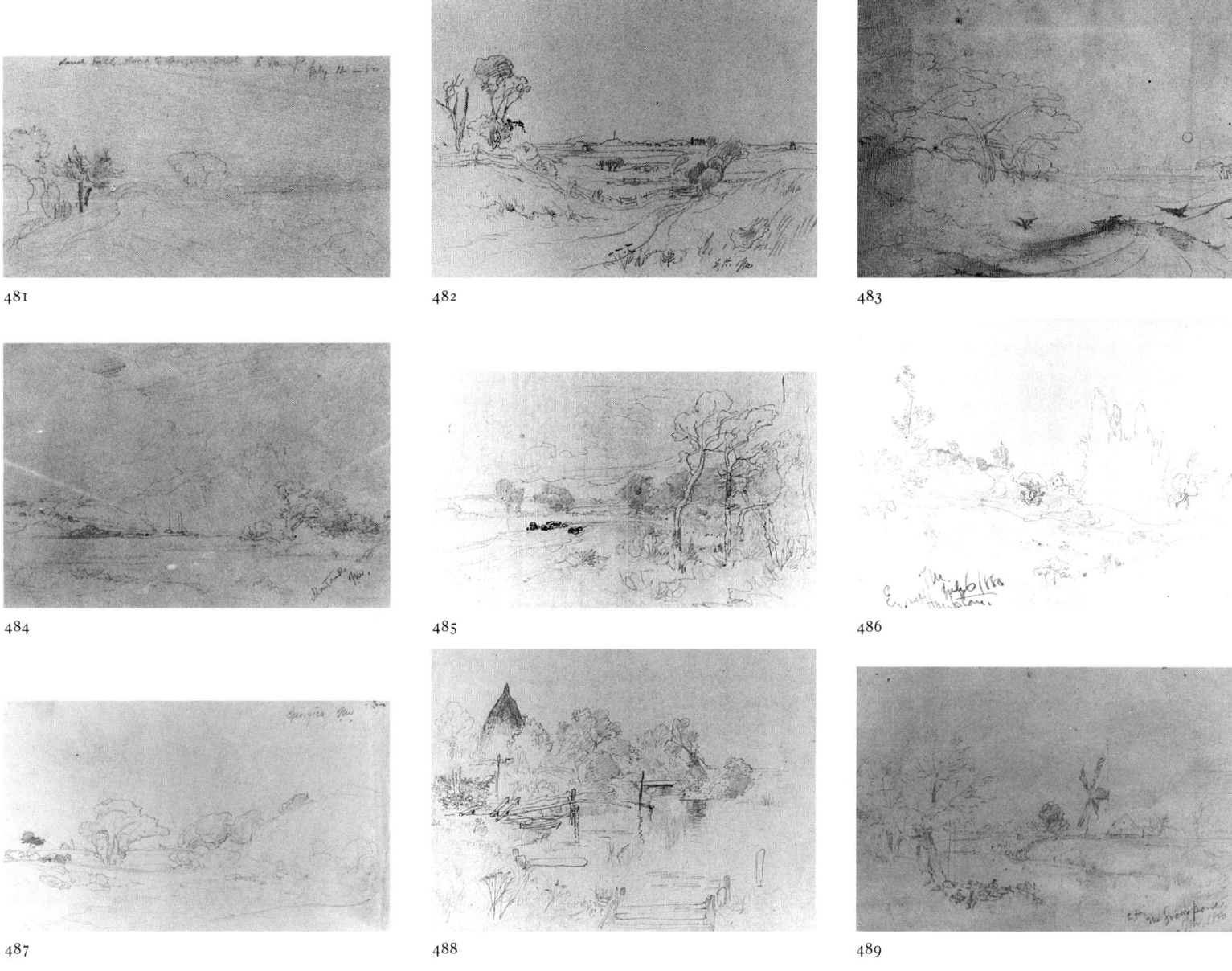

481

482

483

484

485

486

487

488

489

490
EAST HAMPTON [descriptive]
Graphite on wove
6³/₄ by 10
4 East Hampton Library
Provenance: EH

491
WATERMILLS [descriptive]
Graphite on wove
7 by 10¹/₈
1326.698 Gilcrease
Signed: "TM" u.l.
Provenance: TG
1916 ledger: 393

492
WATERMILLS [descriptive]
Graphite on wove
9⁵/₈ by 12⁵/₈
1326.639 Gilcrease
Provenance: TG

†493
GEORGICA POND, EAST HAMPTON
Graphite on green wove
8⁷/₈ by 11¹/₂
1326.700 Gilcrease
Signed: "TM" l.l.
Inscribed: "Georgica Pond. EH." l.l.
Provenance: TG
1916 ledger: 197

494
LONG ISLAND [descriptive]
Graphite on wove
5 by 12⁷/₈
1326.544 Gilcrease
Provenance: TG

†495
EVENING, EAST HAMPTON
Graphite on green wove
4¹/₂ by 10¹/₄
1326.987 Gilcrease
Dated: "Aug 12, 1880" l.l.
Signed: "TM" l.c.
Inscribed: "Evening" l.l.; "Easthamp" l.c.
Provenance: TG
1916 ledger: 274
Note: Sketch on verso

496
MONTAUK
Graphite on wove
7 by 10⁵/₈
1326.988 Gilcrease
Dated: "Sep 2nd 1880" u.r.
Inscribed: "Montauk" u.r.; miscellaneous notes
Provenance: TG
1916 ledger: 19

†497
EAST HAMPTON [descriptive]
Graphite on wove
6¹/₄ by 12¹/₂
1326.550 Gilcrease
Provenance: TG

†498
EAST HAMPTON [descriptive]
Graphite on wove
6¹/₂ by 12¹/₂
1326.564 Gilcrease
Provenance: TG

499
MONTAUK
Graphite on wove
4⁵/₈ by 15
1326.636 Gilcrease
Signed: "TMoran" l.c.; "TM" on verso
Inscribed: "Montauk" on verso
Provenance: TG
1916 ledger: 174

500
EAST HAMPTON [descriptive]
Graphite on wove
5 by 10¹/₈
1326.546 Gilcrease
Provenance: TG

501
MONTAUK [descriptive]
Graphite on wove
2⁷/₈ by 5¹/₂
1326.1023 Gilcrease
Provenance: W. F. Davidson at M. Knoedler &
Co., New York; 1964 Thomas Gilcrease Foundation, Tulsa, Okla.; 1971 The Thomas Gilcrease Institute of American History and Art, Tulsa, Okla.

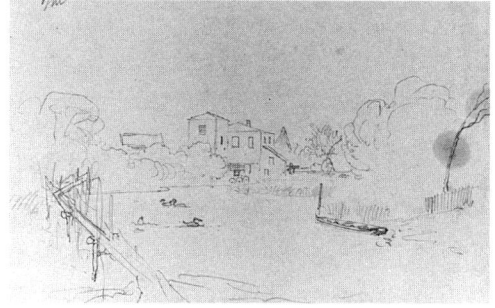

490

491

502
MONTAUK [descriptive]
Graphite on blue wove
4¹/₂ by 10³/₄
1326.527 Gilcrease
Provenance: TG

503
EAST HAMPTON
Graphite on wove
5¹/₄ by 9¹/₂
S-80 East Hampton Library
Signed: "TM" l.l.
Inscribed: "E.H." l.l.
Provenance: EH

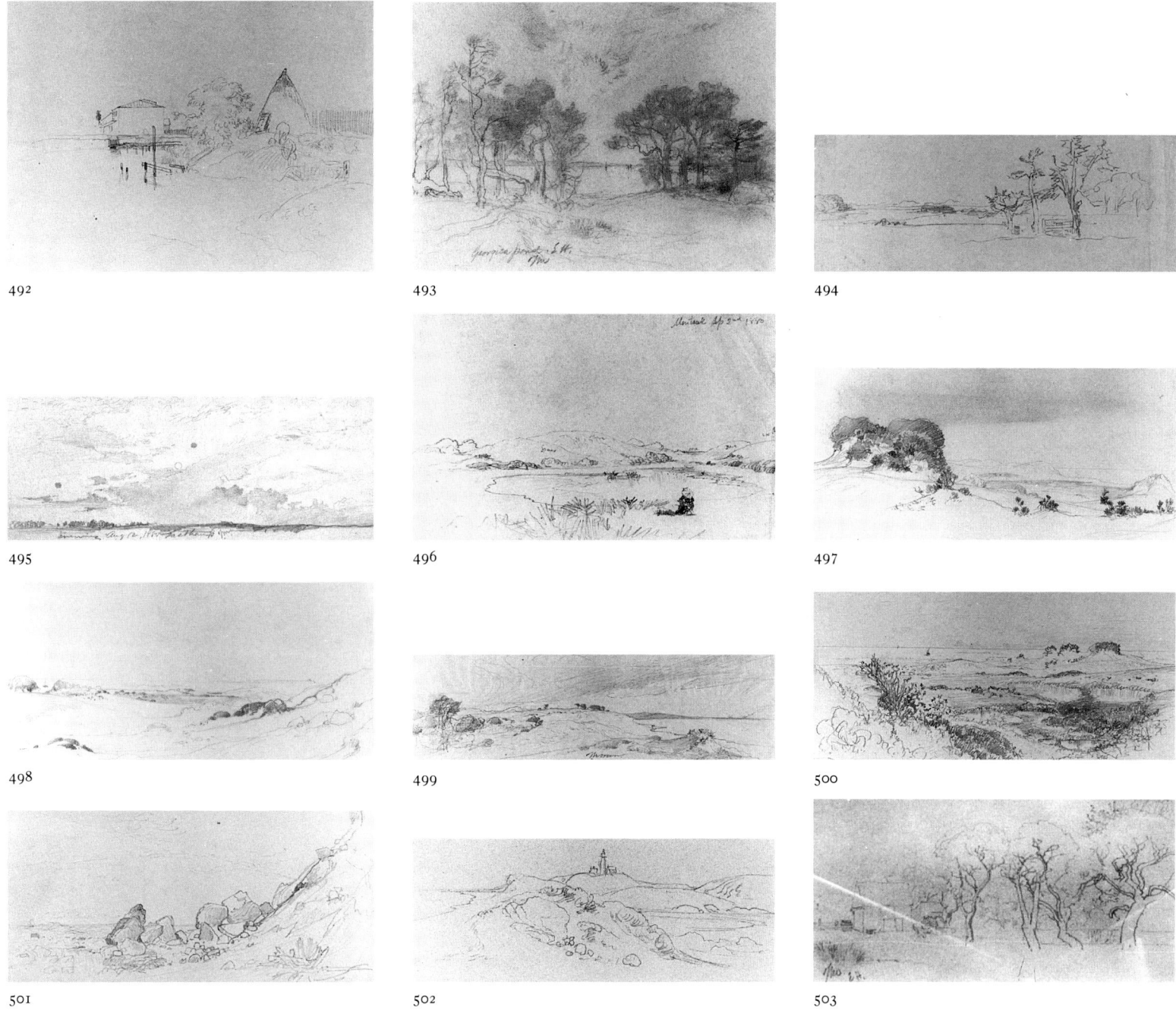

492

493

494

495

496

497

498

499

500

501

502

503

504
EAST HAMPTON [descriptive]
Graphite on wove
9³/₄ by 6
1 East Hampton Library
Signed: "TM" l.l.
Provenance: EH
1916 ledger: 26

505
EAST HAMPTON
Graphite on wove
5 by 10
S-75 East Hampton Library
Signed: "TM" l.l.
Inscribed: "E.H." l.l.
Provenance: EH

506
EAST HAMPTON
Graphite on wove
14¹/₄ by 10
S-64 East Hampton Library
Inscribed: "E.H." l.l.
Signed: "TM" l.l.
Provenance: EH
1916 ledger: 312

507
MONTAUK [descriptive]
Graphite on wove
4⁷/₈ by 8¹/₈
1826.16.37 Gilcrease
Provenance: TG

508
NAPEAGUE
Graphite on wove
4⁷/₈ by 8¹/₈
1826.16.38 Gilcrease
Dated: "Sep 5th 1880" u.r.
Inscribed: "Napeague" u.r.
Provenance: TG
Note: Sketch on verso

509
NAPEAGUE
Graphite on wove
4⁷/₈ by 8¹/₈
1826.16.39 Gilcrease
Inscribed: "Napeague" u.r.
Provenance: TG
Note: Sketch on verso

510
NAPEAGUE [descriptive]
Graphite on wove
4⁷/₈ by 16¹/₄
1826.16.40 Gilcrease
Provenance: TG

511
NAPEAGUE [descriptive]
Graphite on wove
4⁷/₈ by 8¹/₈
1826.16.41 Gilcrease
Provenance: TG

512
INDUSTRIAL HARBOR [descriptive]
Graphite on wove
4⁷/₈ by 8¹/₈
1826.16.42 Gilcrease
Provenance: TG

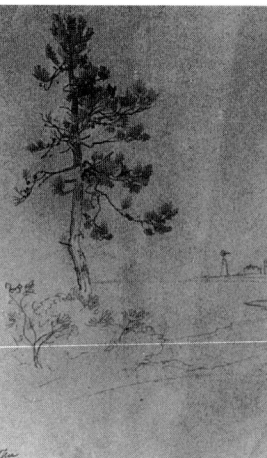

504

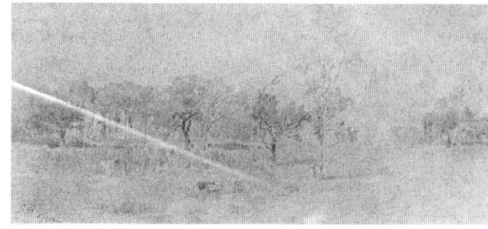

505

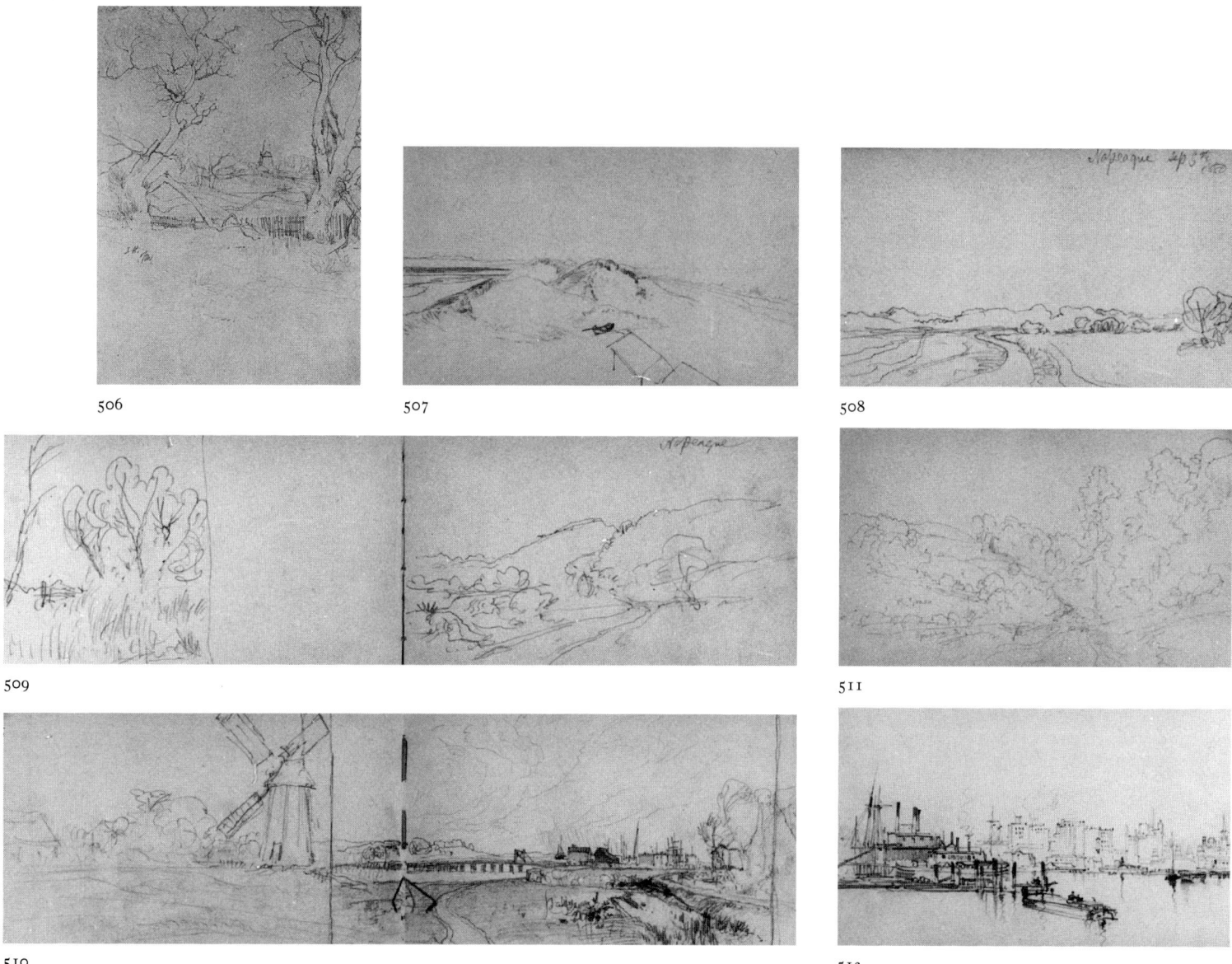

506

507

508

509

511

510

512

513
EAST HAMPTON [descriptive]
Graphite on wove
4⅞ by 8⅛
1826.16.43 Gilcrease
Provenance: TG

514
EAST HAMPTON [descriptive]
Graphite on wove
4⅞ by 8⅛
1826.16.44 Gilcrease
Inscribed with color notes
Provenance: TG

515
EAST HAMPTON [descriptive]
Graphite and white chalk on wove
4⅞ by 8⅛
1826.16.45 Gilcrease
Inscribed with color notes
Provenance: TG

516
EAST HAMPTON [descriptive]
Graphite on wove
4⅞ by 8⅛
1826.16.46 Gilcrease
Provenance: TG

517
AMAGANSETT
Graphite on wove
10⅛ by 8
1326.985 Gilcrease
Dated: "Sep 12th 1880" l.r.
Signed: "TM" l.r.
Inscribed: "Amagansett" l.r.
Provenance: TG
1916 ledger: 347
Note: Sketch on verso

518
AMAGANSETT
Graphite on wove
6¾ by 10
5 East Hampton Library
Inscribed: "Amagansett" l.r.
Provenance: EH

519
AMAGANSETT
Graphite on blue wove
9⅞ by 12¾
1326.990 Gilcrease
Dated: "Sep 12 1880" u.r.
Signed: "TM" u.r.
Inscribed: "Amagansett" u.r.
Provenance: TG
1916 ledger: 237
Note: Sketch on verso

520
GEORGICA
Graphite on yellow onionskin paper
4¾ by 3½
1326.696 Gilcrease
Signed: "TM" l.r.
Inscribed: "Georgica" l.r.
Provenance: TG
1916 ledger: 215

521
AMAGANSETT
Graphite on wove
4¾ by 8¼
1326.967 Gilcrease
Dated: "1879" l.l. [see note]
Signed: "TM" l.l.
Inscribed: "Amagansett" l.l.; color notes
Provenance: TG
1916 ledger: 161
Note: The date on this sketch was added later.
Stylistically, the sketch resembles the work from
1880.

522
WHITE FLOWERS
Graphite on blue wove
5⅜ by 12½
1326.627 Gilcrease
Signed: "TM" l.r.
Inscribed: "white flowers" u.r.
Provenance: TG
1916 ledger: 395

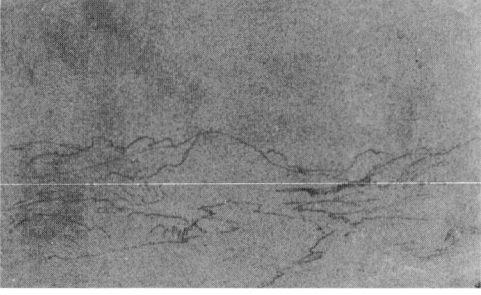

513

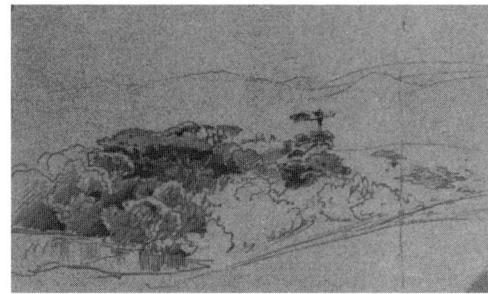

514

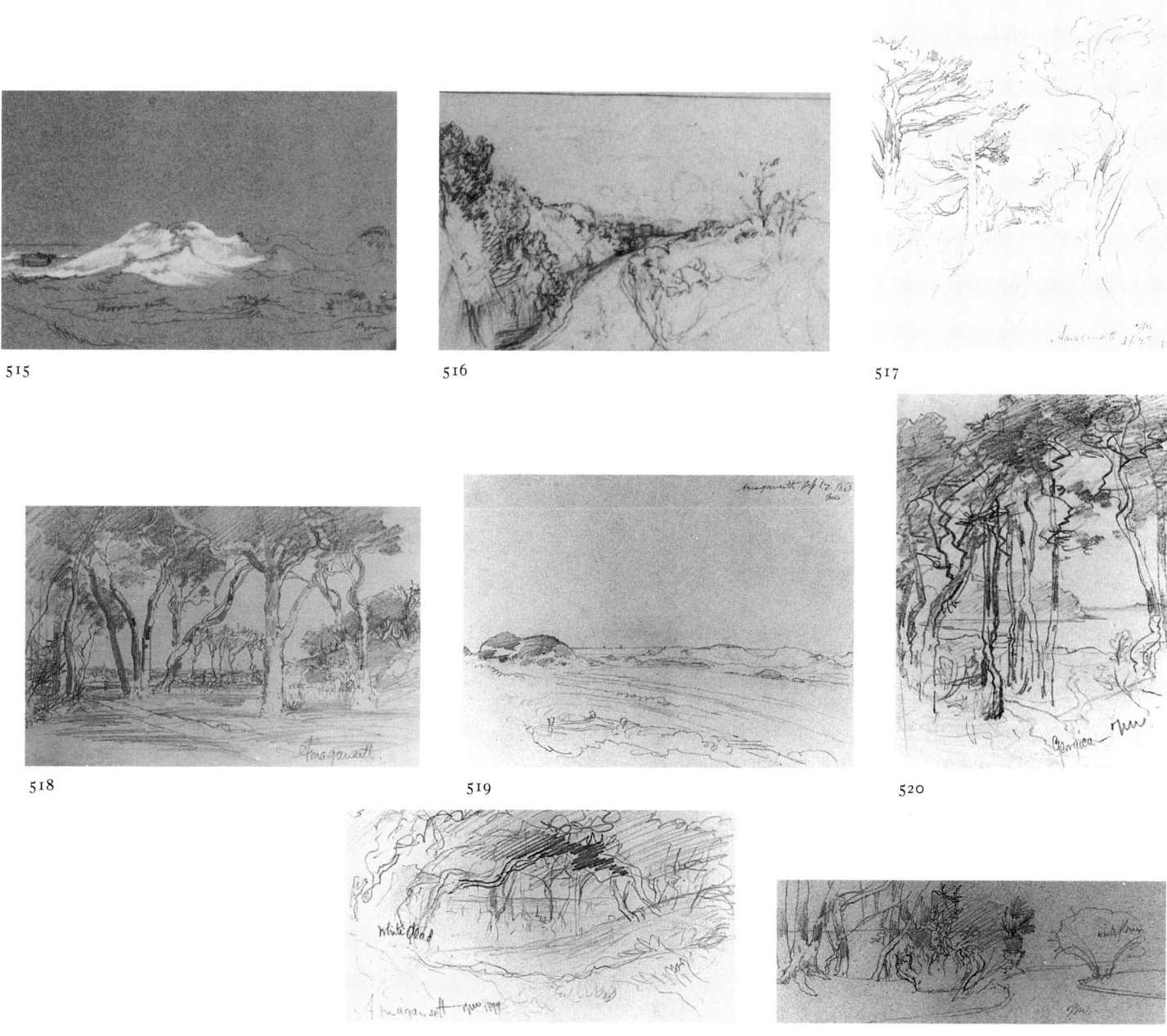

515

516

517

518

519

520

521

522

523
AT THREE MILE HARBOR
Graphite on wove
12³/8 by 8³/4
1326.689 Gilcrease
Signed: "TM" l.r.
Inscribed: "at 3 Mile Harbor" and "Easthamp" l.r.
Provenance: TG
1916 ledger: 271

524
THREE MILE HARBOR
Graphite on blue wove
13¹/2 by 18³/4
1326.701 Gilcrease
Signed: "TM" l.l.
Inscribed: "3 Mile Harbor" l.l.; miscellaneous
notes
Provenance: TG
1916 ledger: 154

†525
EAST HAMPTON
Graphite on wove
6³/4 by 9³/4
1326.691 Gilcrease·
Signed: "TM" l.l.
Inscribed: "E.H." l.l.
Provenance: TG
1916 ledger: 224
Note: This sketch anticipates the etching *Sassa-
fras Trees* (Morand and Friese, *Prints of Thomas
Moran*, p. 109). There is a sketch on verso.

†526
EAST HAMPTON
Graphite on gray wove
6¹/4 by 9³/4
1326.692 Gilcrease
Signed: "TM" l.l.
Inscribed: "E.H." l.l.
Provenance: TG
1916 ledger: 211

527
THREE MILE HARBOR
Graphite on blue wove
10 by 14¹/4
S-67 East Hampton Library
Dated: "1880" l.l.

Signed: "TM" l.l.
Inscribed: "3 Mile Harbor" l.l.
Provenance: EH
1916 ledger: 199

528
EAST HAMPTON
Graphite on wove
7¹/2 by 5
73 East Hampton Library
Signed: "TM" l.l.
Inscribed: "E.H." l.l.
Provenance: EH
1916 ledger: 320

529
EAST HAMPTON
Graphite on wove
6³/4 by 10
6 East Hampton Library
Signed: "TM" u.l.
Inscribed: "E.H." u.l.
Provenance: EH
1916 ledger: 306

530
EAST HAMPTON
Graphite on wove
5¹/8 by 7¹/2
68 East Hampton Library
Signed: "TM" l.l.
Inscribed: "E.H." l.l.
Provenance: EH
1916 ledger: 238

531
MONTAUK [descriptive]
Graphite on wove
5¹/2 by 2³/4
52 East Hampton Library
Provenance: EH

532
EAST HAMPTON
Graphite on wove
3¹/4 by 7¹/2
S-74 East Hampton Library
Signed: "TM" l.l.
Inscribed: "EH" l.l.
Provenance: EH

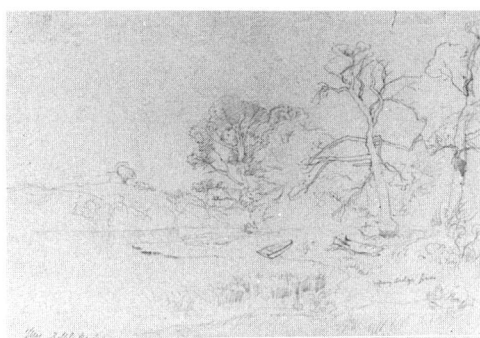

523

524

533
AMAGANSETT
Graphite on laid
4³/4 by 11¹/4
S-78 East Hampton Library
Signed: "TM" u.l.
Inscribed: "Amagansett" u.l.
Provenance: EH

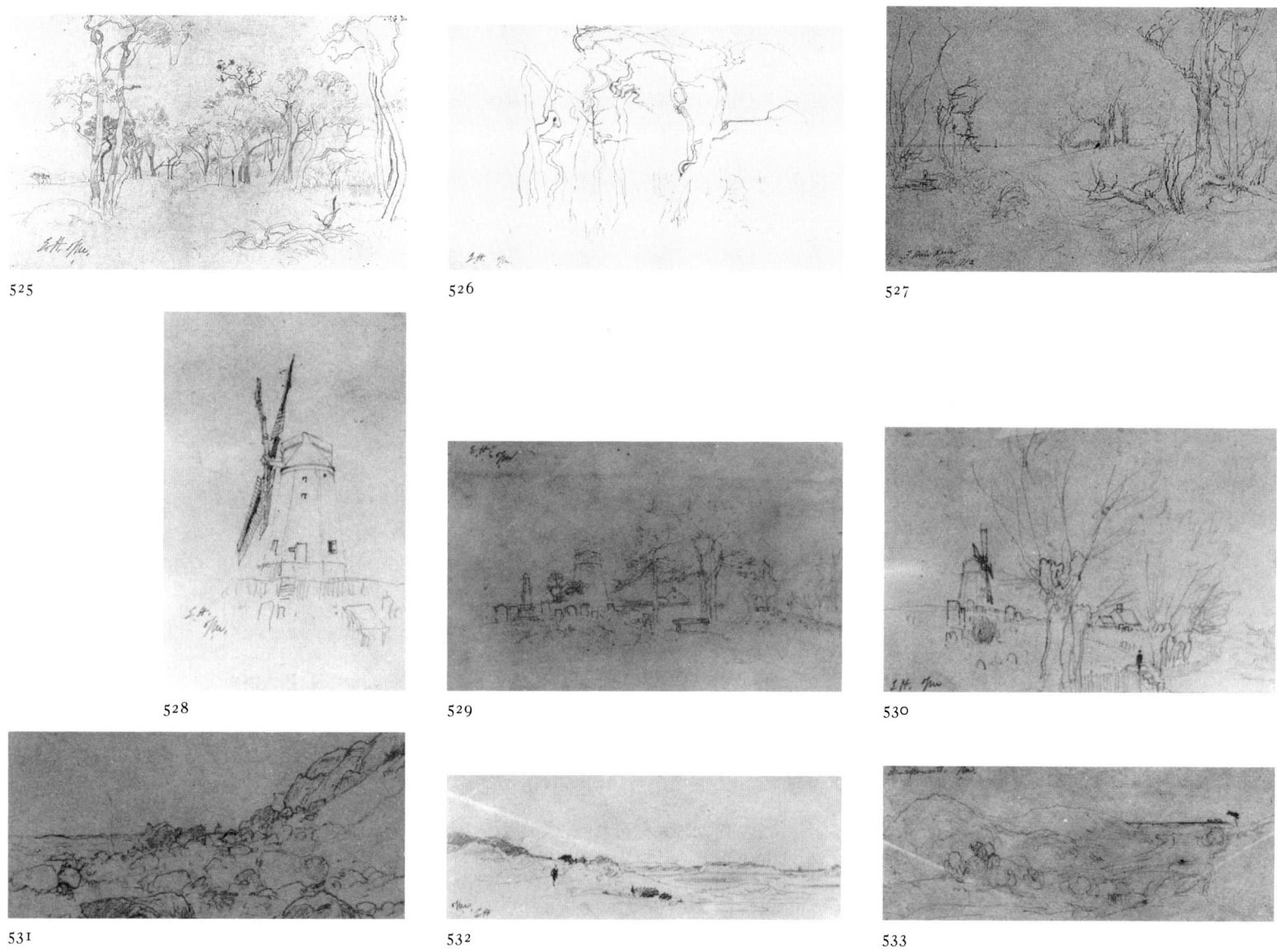

525

526

527

528

529

530

531

532

533

534
MONTAUK
Graphite on green wove
4¹/₄ by 10¹/₂
S-79 East Hampton Library
Inscribed: "Montauk" l.l.
Provenance: EH

535
EAST HAMPTON
Graphite on wove
14¹/₄ by 10¹/₈
1326.702 Gilcrease
Signed: "TM" l.l.
Inscribed: "E.H." l.l.
Provenance: TG
1916 ledger: 223

536
STUDY OF ROAD AND BANK [ledger title]
Graphite on wove
6³/₄ by 10¹/₈
1326.1029 Gilcrease
Provenance: Ruth K. Henschel, New York; 1964 Thomas Gilcrease Foundation, Tulsa, Okla.; 1970 The Thomas Gilcrease Institute of American History and Art, Tulsa, Okla.
1916 ledger: 233

†537
THE RAPIDS BELOW LOWER
SUSPENSION BRIDGE, NIAGARA
Graphite, gray wash, and white gouache on gray wove
10⁷/₈ by 14¹/₄
0226.901 Gilcrease
Dated: "June 29th 1881" l.r. in ink
Signed: "TMoran" l.r. in ink
Inscribed: "The Rapids below Lower Suspension Bridge Niagara" lower edge in ink; "Full page?" l.r.
Provenance: TG
1916 ledger: 121
Note: This sketch anticipates the wood engraving of the same title (Morand and Friese, *Prints of Thomas Moran,* p. 203).

†538
THE NIAGARA RIVER, FROM BROCK
MONUMENT

Graphite, gray wash, and white gouache on gray wove
11 by 14³/₈
0226.900 Gilcrease
Dated: "June 30th 1881" l.c. in ink
Signed: "TMoran" l.c. in ink
Inscribed: "The Niagara River. From Brock Monument" l.l. in ink; "Showing Lake Ontario & Toronto in distance" l.l. in ink; "Niagara River from Brocks" l.c.; "Leave out Toronto & opposite shore of lake. Cannot be seen from Brocks Monument" l.r.; "Full page?" l.l.; miscellaneous notes
Provenance: TG
1916 ledger: 405

†539
UNDER THE AMERICAN FALL FROM
GOAT ISLAND
Graphite, gray wash, and white gouache on gray wove
11 by 7¹/₈
0226.899 Gilcrease
Dated: "June 1881" l.r. in ink
Signed: "TM" l.r. in ink
Inscribed: "Under the American Fall From Goat Island" l.r. in ink; "Would not this look well full page size?" l.l.; "Cave of the Winds" l.c.; miscellaneous notes on verso
Provenance: TG
1916 ledger: 207
Note: This sketch anticipates the painting *Cave of the Winds, Niagara* (illustrated in Adamson, *Niagara: Two Centuries of Changing Attitudes,* fig. 66).

540
DAM AT RELAY, B & O
Graphite on gray wove
9³/₄ by 12¹/₂
1326.1007 Gilcrease
Dated: "1881" u.l.
Signed: "TM" u.l.
Inscribed: "Dam at Relay. B & O" u.l.
Provenance: TG
1916 ledger: 442

541
PATENT OFFICE
Graphite on wove
5¹/₂ by 8

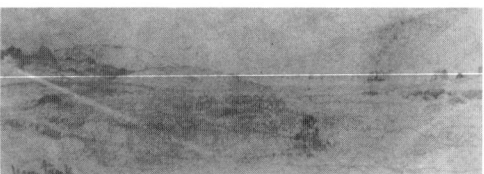

534

1326.620 Gilcrease
Inscribed: "patent office" l.l.; color notes
Provenance: TG
Note: Sketch and inscription on verso: "Arlington House"

542
POINT OF ROCKS
Graphite on wove
7¹/₄ by 10⁷/₈
1326.1005 Gilcrease
Dated: "1881" u.c.
Signed: "TM" u.c.
Inscribed: "Point of Rocks" and "No 2 quarter page" u.l.; "B. & O. R.R." u.c.; "Higher" and "All foliage" u.r.
Provenance: TG
1916 ledger: 439

543
BELOW HARPERS FERRY
Graphite on wove
7¹/₄ by 10⁷/₈
1326.704 Gilcrease
Signed: "TM" u.c.
Inscribed: "Below Harpers ferry" u.l.; "Combination No 3" u.c.; "No. 2 quarter page" u.l., then deleted by Moran
Provenance: TG
1916 ledger: 438

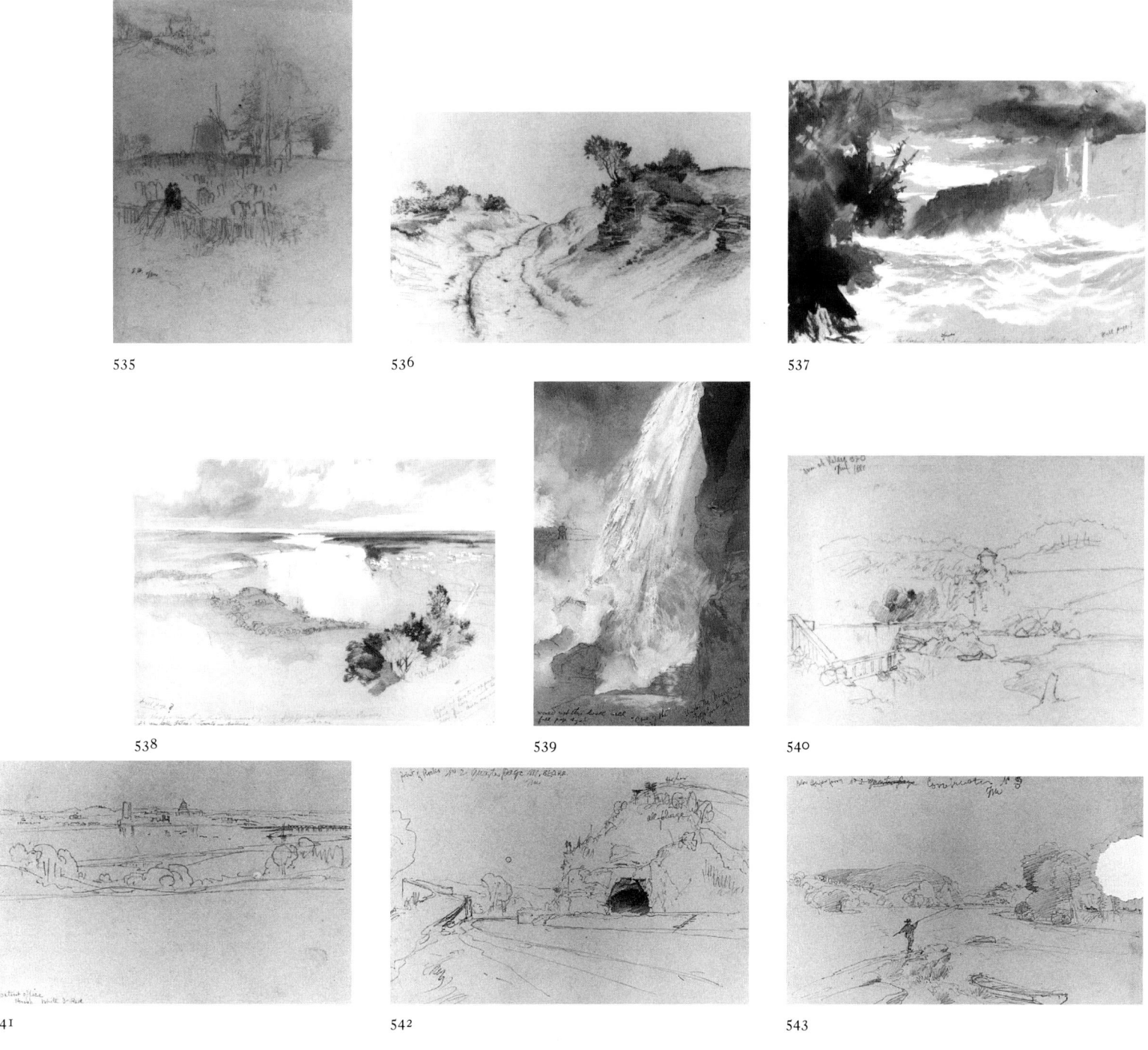

535

536

537

538

539

540

541

542

543

544
THE POTOMAC AT CATOCTIN
MOUNTAIN, BALD EAGLE ISLAND
Graphite on wove
7 1/4 by 10 7/8
1326.993 Gilcrease
Dated: "July 30 1881" u.r.
Signed: "TM" u.r.
Inscribed: "The Potomac at Catoctin Mt Bald
Eagle island" u.r.; "No 3" u.l.
Provenance: TG
1916 ledger: 443

545
HARPERS FERRY
Graphite and wash on gray wove
10 7/8 by 12 7/8
1326.1004 Gilcrease
Dated: "1881" u.r.
Signed: "TM" u.r.
Inscribed: "Harpers Ferry" and "B. & O." u.r.;
"No 6 1/2 page" u.l.; miscellaneous notes
Provenance: TG
1916 ledger: 441
Note: This sketch anticipates the wood engraving *Street in Harper's Ferry* (Morand and Friese, *Prints of Thomas Moran,* p. 210).

†546
HARPERS FERRY
Graphite on wove
4 1/4 by 6 7/8
1326.1002 Gilcrease
Dated: "1881" u.c.
Signed: "TM" u.c.
Inscribed: "Harpers ferry" u.l.
Provenance: TG
1916 ledger: 445

547
RAWLEY
Graphite on wove
7 1/4 by 10 7/8
1326.998 Gilcrease
Dated: "Aug 8th 1881" u.r.
Signed: "TM" u.r.
Inscribed: "Rawley" and "Combination 1/2 page"
u.r.; "Looking south" u.l.
Provenance: TG
1916 ledger: 440

548
THE IDIOTIC LEAP, RAWLEY
Graphite on wove
10 1/2 by 14
1326.1001 Gilcrease
Dated: "Aug 9th 1881" u.l.
Signed: "TM" u.l.
Inscribed: "The idiotic leap. Rawley" and "Looking east" u.l; "Com 1/2 page No 14" u.l., then deleted by Moran
Provenance: TG
1916 ledger: 435

549
DRIPPING SPRINGS, WEST VIRGINIA
Graphite on wove
8 7/8 by 11 7/8
1326.662 Gilcrease
Dated: "1881" center right, written vertically
Signed: "TM" l.l.
Inscribed: "Dripping S. W. Va" l.l.; "No 25, full page" u.l.
Provenance: TG
1916 ledger: 454

550
DRIPPING SPRINGS, WEST VIRGINIA
Graphite on wove
8 7/8 by 11 7/8
1326.661 Gilcrease
Dated: "1881" written vertically, center right
Signed: "TM" l.l.
Inscribed: "Dripping springs, W. Va" l.l.
Provenance: TG
1916 ledger: 450

551
DRIPPING SPRINGS, WEST VIRGINIA
Graphite on wove
12 by 8 7/8
1326.1003 Gilcrease
Dated: "1881" l.r.
Signed: "TM" l.l.
Inscribed: "Dripping S W. V." l.l.; miscellaneous notes
Provenance: TG
1916 ledger: 452

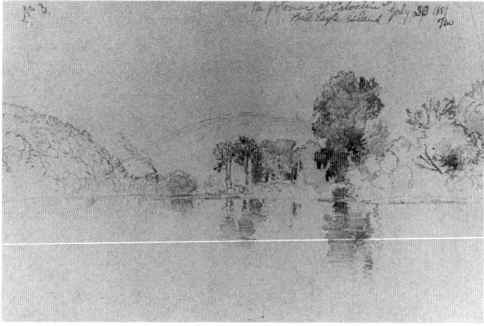

544

552
DRIPPING SPRINGS, WEST VIRGINIA
Graphite on wove
12 by 8 7/8
1326.1000 Gilcrease
Dated: "1881" l.l.
Signed: "TM" l.l.
Inscribed: "Dripping S. W. Va" l.l.; miscellaneous notes
Provenance: TG
1916 ledger: 453

553
DRIPPING SPRINGS, WEST VIRGINIA
Graphite on wove
11 3/4 by 8 3/4
1326.999 Gilcrease
Dated: "1881" l.r.
Signed: "TM" l.l.
Inscribed: "Dripping S.W. V." l.l.
Provenance: TG
1916 ledger: 451

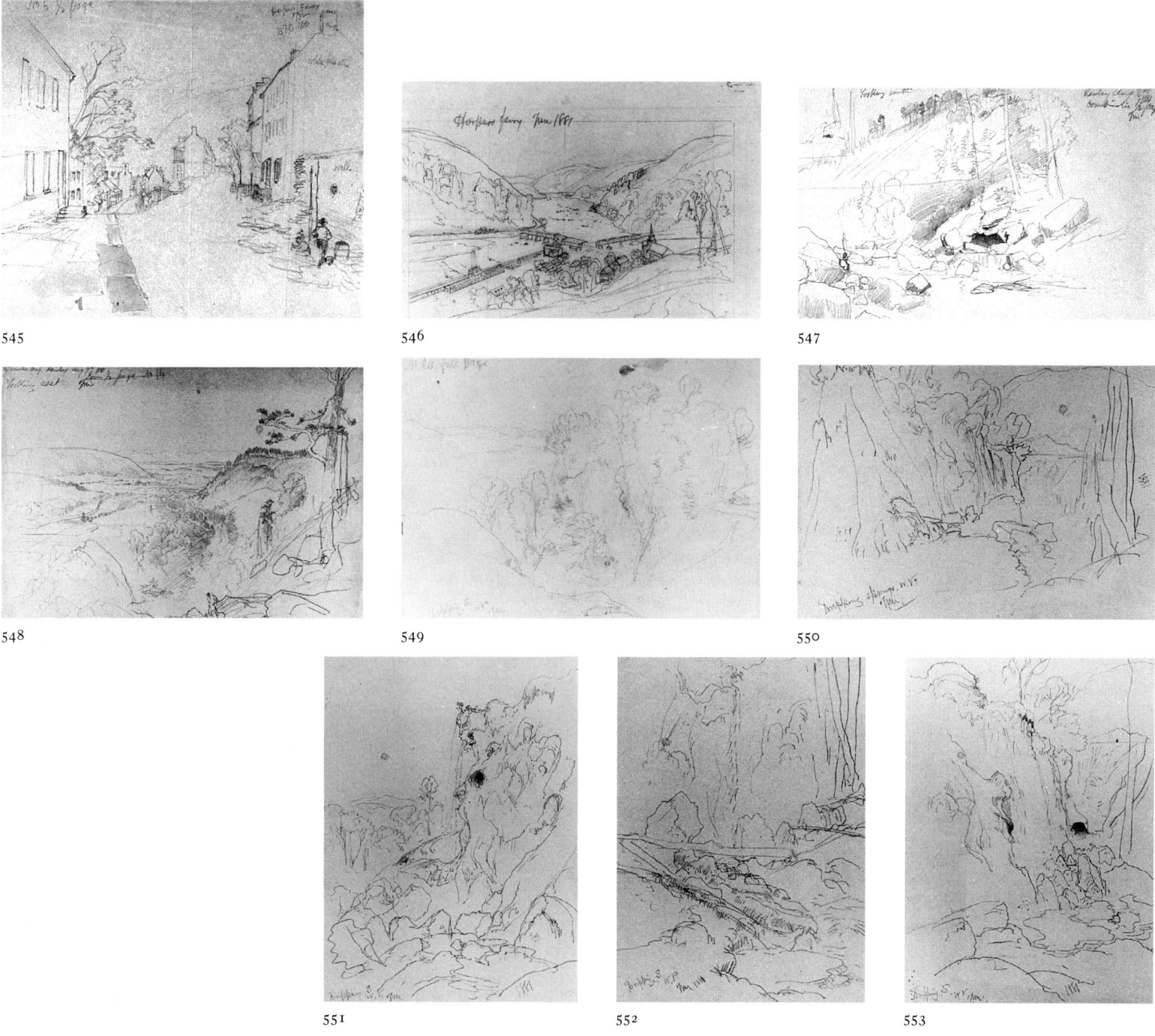

545

546

547

548

549

550

551

552

553

554
ENTRANCE, LURAY CAVE
Graphite on gray wove
6³/8 by 9⁷/8
1326.997 Gilcrease
Dated: "1881" l.r.
Signed: "TM" l.r.
Inscribed: "Entrance, Luray Cave" l.r.; miscellaneous notes
Provenance: TG
1916 ledger: 448

†555
ANGEL WING FALLEN COLUMN AND
SARACEN DEN, LURAY CAVE
Graphite, wash, and white gouache on gray wove
6¹/2 by 9⁷/8
0226.897 Gilcrease
Dated: "Aug 1881" l.r.
Signed: "TM" l.r.
Inscribed: "angel wing fallen Column & Saracen den Luray Cave" lower edge
Provenance: TG
1916 ledger: 449

†556
LURAY CAVE
Graphite on gray wove
11 by 14³/8
1326.995 Gilcrease
Dated: "Aug 1881" l.l.
Signed: "TM" l.l.
Inscribed: "Luray Cave" l.l.; "No 27 full page com." written vertically, l.l.; miscellaneous notes
Provenance: TG
1916 ledger: 417

†557
IN LURAY CAVE
Graphite on wove
10⁷/8 by 7¹/4
1326.1006 Gilcrease
Dated: "Aug 1881" l.l.
Signed: "TM" l.c.
Inscribed: "In Luray Cave" l.l.; miscellaneous notes
Provenance: TG
1916 ledger: 416

†558
ALLEGHENY MOUNTAINS, TUNNEL
NEAR THE SOURCE OF THE POTOMAC
Graphite and wash on wove
8⁵/8 by 11⁷/8
0226.791 Gilcrease
Signed: "TM" u.r.
Inscribed: "Allegheny Mts tunnel near the source of the Potomac" and "No 37 ¹/2 ¹/2 page" u.r.
Provenance: TG
1916 ledger: 434
Note: A grid pattern was inscribed on this sketch. The sketch anticipates the wood engraving *Near the Source of the Potomac* (Morand and Friese, *Prints of Thomas Moran,* p. 207).

†559
VIEW IN THE NARROWS,
CUMBERLAND, B & O
Graphite, gray and blue washes, and white gouache on green wove
9⁷/8 by 12⁷/8
0226.896 Gilcrease
Dated: "1881" u.r.
Signed: "TM" u.r.
Inscribed: "View in the Narrows, Cumberland B. & O." u.c.; "Above Cumberland" l.l.
Provenance: TG
1916 ledger: 421

†560
CUMBERLAND, FROM ROSE HILLS
CEMETERY
Graphite on wove
8⁵/8 by 8⁷/8
1326.709 Gilcrease
Dated: "Aug 2nd" u.c.
Signed: "TM" u.r.
Inscribed: "Cumberland from Rose Hills cem" and "No 31²/3 page Cumberland" u.c.; miscellaneous notes
Provenance: TG
1916 ledger: 444

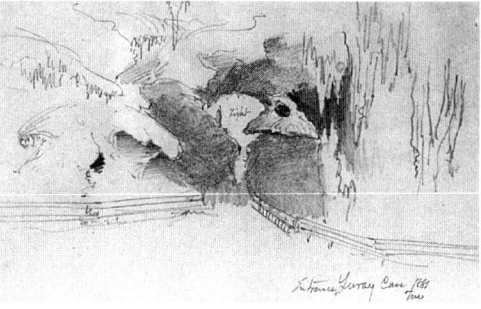

554

561
WILLS CREEK NEAR COOKS MILLS,
PITTSBURGH DIVISION, B & O
Graphite and wash on wove
10³/4 by 7¹/4
0226.895 Gilcrease
Dated: "Aug 2nd 1881" u.r.
Signed: "TM" u.r.
Inscribed: "Wills Creek Near Cooks Mills Pitts Div. B & O" and "No 32 Com.¹/2 page" u.r.
Provenance: TG
1916 ledger: 447

†562
OHIOPYLE
Graphite on blue wove
9³/4 by 12⁷/8
1326.656 Gilcrease
Inscribed: "Ohio pyle" l.l.; "34" u.r.; miscellaneous notes
Provenance: TG
1916 ledger: 437

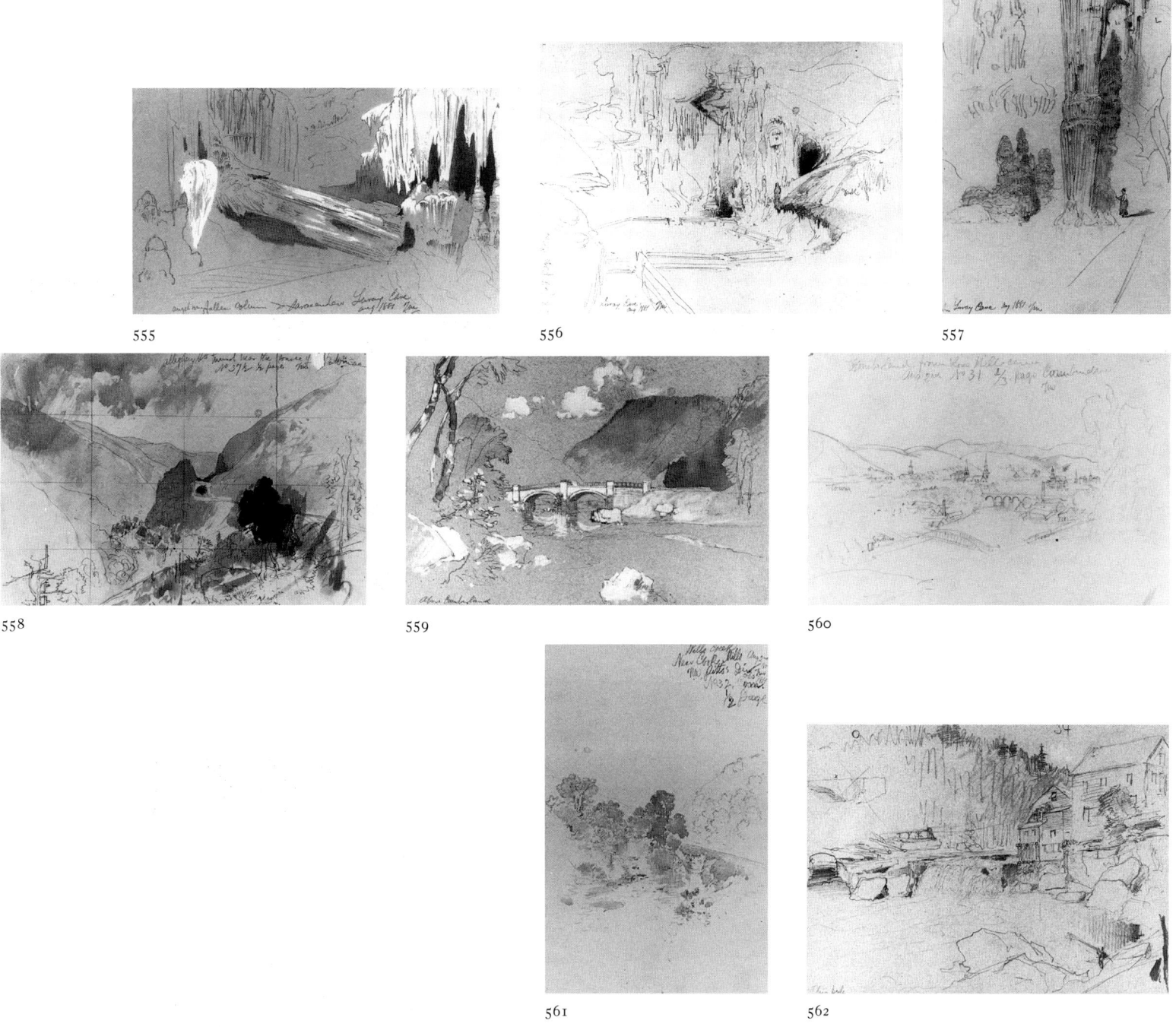

555

556

557

558

559

560

561

562

563
OHIOPYLE
Graphite on wove
7 1/4 by 10 7/8
1326.992 Gilcrease
Dated: "Aug 1881" u.c.
Signed: "TM" u.c.
Inscribed: "Ohio pyle" and "No 34" u.l.
Provenance: TG
1916 ledger: 446
Note: A grid pattern was inscribed on this sketch.

564
OHIOPYLE [descriptive]
Graphite on green laid
5 by 6 7/8
119 East Hampton Library
Provenance: EH

†565
HILLSIDE, PITTSBURGH
Graphite on wove
9 5/8 by 12 7/8
1326.642 Gilcrease
Inscribed: "Hillside. Pittsburgh" u.r.
Provenance: TG

566
ROCHESTER [descriptive]
Graphite on wove
6 1/2 by 9 5/8
1326.534 Gilcrease
Provenance: TG
Note: Sketches on verso

567
ROCHESTER
Graphite on wove
6 1/2 by 9 1/2
1326.626 Gilcrease
Inscribed: "Rochester" l.l.; color notes
Provenance: TG

*568
GARDEN OF THE GODS
Graphite and watercolor on wove
Sketch 10 by 13 7/8, mount 15 by 19
0236.844 Gilcrease
Signed: "TMoran" l.r.
Inscribed: "Garden of the Gods" l.l.

Provenance: TG
1916 ledger: 42

*569
GLEN EYRIE
Graphite and watercolor on wove
10 1/2 by 14 1/2
0236.781 Gilcrease
Signed: "TM" u.l.
Inscribed: "Glen Eyrie" u.l.; "No 68" written vertically u.r.; miscellaneous notes
Provenance: TG

*570
HEYWOOD HOT SPRINGS
Graphite, watercolor, and white gouache on gray wove
Sketch 9 1/2 by 12 1/2, mount 12 1/2 by 19
0236.846 Gilcrease
Signed: "TMoran" l.r.
Inscribed: "Heywood Hot springs" u.l.; "in Colorado" and "Magnificent [illegible]" lower edge; miscellaneous notes
Provenance: TG

571
VETA MOUNTAIN
Graphite on wove
8 6/8 by 23 1/4 [two sheets joined]
1336.912 Gilcrease
Signed: "TM" u.c. of second page
Inscribed: "Veta Mountain" u.l. of second page and "take good care of these sketches & return them when through. TMoran" on verso; miscellaneous notes
Provenance: TG
1916 ledger: 183

*572
OJO CALIENTE
Graphite and watercolor on wove
Sketch 7 1/4 by 10 7/8, mount 12 3/4 by 16
0236.845 Gilcrease
Signed: "TMoran" u.c.
Inscribed: "Ojo Caliente 3rd oldest city in US from The Springs Hotel" u.l.; "Burro train Crossing Creek" c.; miscellaneous notes
Provenance: TG
1916 ledger: 65

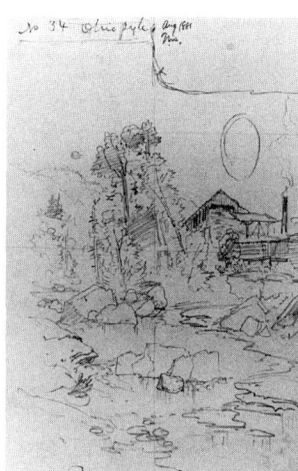

563

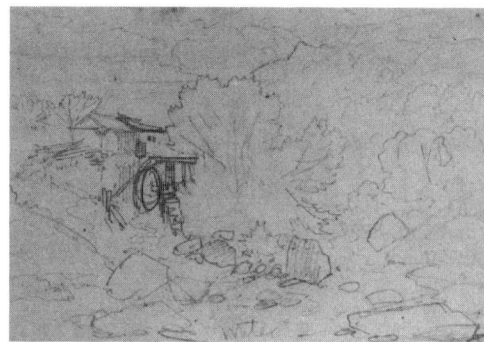

564

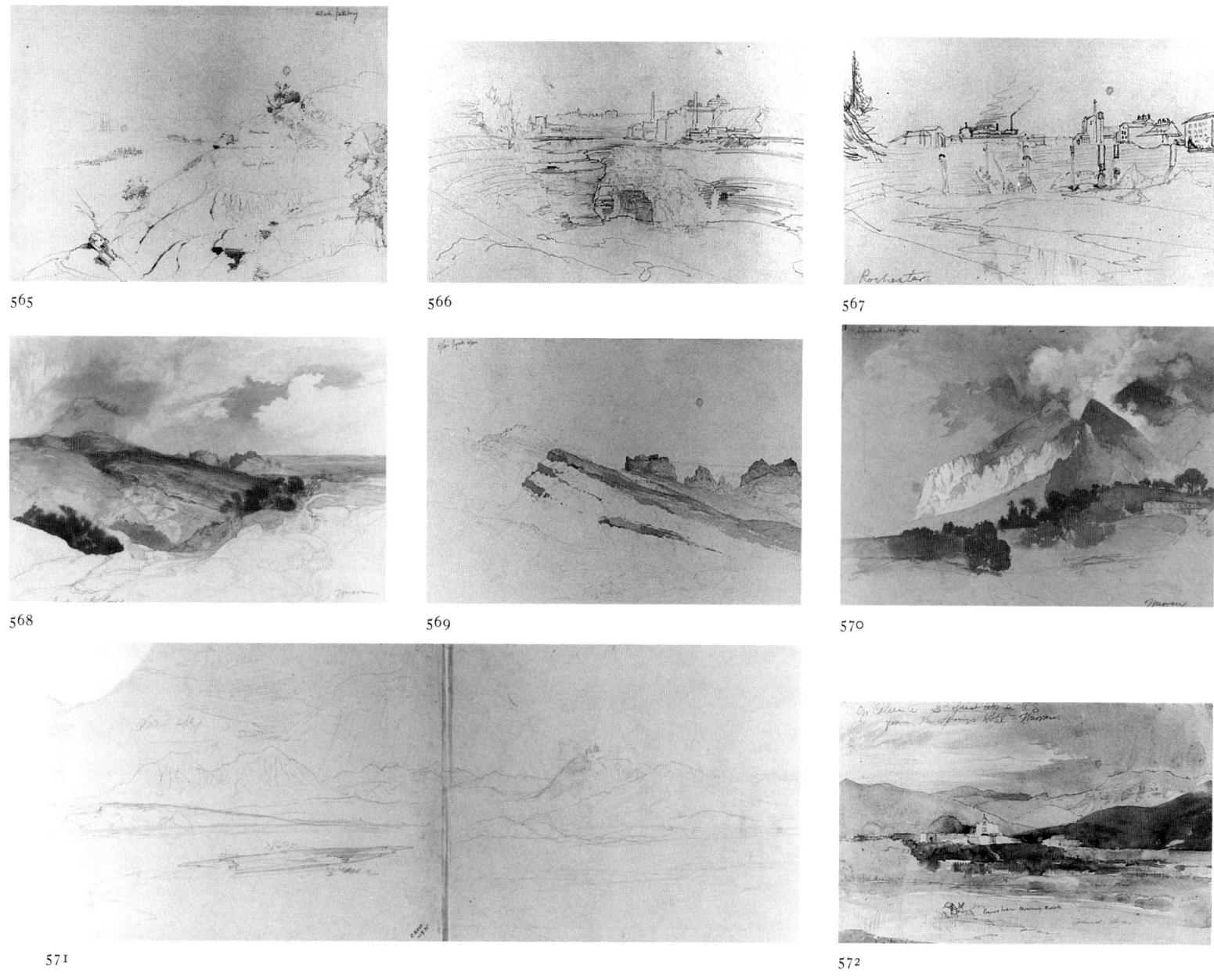

565

566

567

568

569

570

571

572

*573
SAN JUAN, NEW MEXICO
Graphite and watercolor on wove
Sketch 7 1/4 by 10 7/8, mount 11 3/4 by 16 1/4
0236.843 Gilcrease
Signed: "TMoran" u.l.
Inscribed: "San Juan New Mexico" u.l.
Provenance: TG
1916 ledger: 33
Note: This sketch anticipates Moran's etching
Church of San Juan—New Mexico (Morand and
Friese, *Prints of Thomas Moran*, p. 110).

574
ESPAÑOLA, NEW MEXICO
Graphite and watercolor on letterhead from
Baltimore & Ohio Railroad
5 3/4 by 8 7/8
0236.848 Gilcrease
Signed: "TMoran" l.l.
Inscribed: "Espanola New Mexico" u.l.; "Rio
Grande" c.; "Adobe Houses" l.c.
Provenance: TG
1916 ledger: 359

575
IN THE LOS PIÑOS VALLEY
Graphite on wove
8 5/8 by 11 7/8
1336.630 Gilcrease
Signed: "TM" l.l.
Inscribed: "In the Los Pinos Valley" u.l.; "The
San Juan Mountains from Twilight" u.l. in ink;
"Sage plain water washed" l.l.; miscellaneous
notes
Provenance: TG
1916 ledger: 156

576
LOOKING DOWN LOS PIÑOS
Graphite and watercolor on gray wove
9 7/8 by 12 3/4
0236.780 Gilcrease
Signed: "TM" u.l.
Inscribed: "Looking down Los Pinos" u.l.
Provenance: TG
1916 ledger: 166

577
NEAR TOLTEC TUNNEL
Graphite and ink on wove
10 by 6 3/4
1336.663 Gilcrease
Signed: "TM" u.r.
Inscribed: "Near Toltec Tunnel" u.c.; "Phan-
toms" u.r. in ink; miscellaneous notes
Provenance: TG
1916 ledger: 157

578
WORKMEN'S CABIN, TOLTEC TUNNEL
Graphite on wove
6 by 8 3/4
3 East Hampton Library
Signed: "TM" u.l.
Inscribed: "Wrkmens Cabin Toltec Tunnel" u.l.
Provenance: EH
1916 ledger: 148

579
TOLTEC GORGE, EVA CLIFFS FROM
THE WEST
Graphite, watercolor, and white gouache on tan
wove
9 5/8 by 15
1917-17-31 Cooper-Hewitt Museum
Signed: "TM" l.l. and colophon l.r. in ink
Inscribed: "Toltec Gorge Eva Cliffs from the
West" u.l.
Provenance: TM
1916 ledger: 341

580
ON THE SAN JUAN ABOVE ARBOLES
Graphite and wash on verso of newspaper illus-
tration
6 3/4 by 10 1/4
0236.894 Gilcrease
Signed: "TM" u.c.
Inscribed: "on the San Juan above Arbolles" u.l.
Provenance: TG
1916 ledger: 6
Note: The printed cartoon on the verso is dated
August 6, 1881.

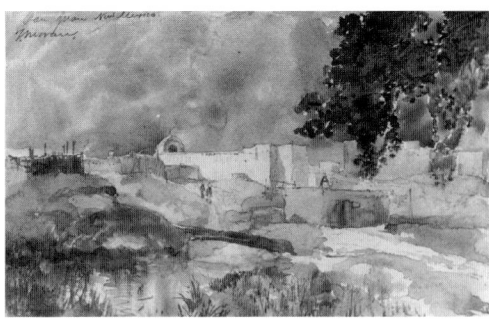
573

581
THE SAN JUAN RANGE FROM THE UTE
RESERVATION, LOS PIÑOS VALLEY
Graphite on wove
8 3/4 by 12
1336.878 Gilcrease
Signed: "TM" u.c.
Inscribed: "The San Juan Range from the Ute
Reservation Los Pinos Valley" u.l.
Provenance: TG
1916 ledger: 155

†582
UPPER TWIN LAKE, WASATCH
MOUNTAINS
Graphite on wove
10 1/2 by 14
1336.996 Gilcrease
Dated: "Sep 15th 1881" u.c.
Signed: "TM" u.c.
Inscribed: "Upper Twin Lake Wasatch Mts" u.l.;
miscellaneous notes
Provenance: TG
1916 ledger: 152

583
LAKE, WASATCH MOUNTAINS
Graphite on wove
10 1/2 by 14
1336.705 Gilcrease
Signed: "TM" u.r.
Inscribed: "Lake. Wasatch Mts" u.r.; color notes
Provenance: TG
1916 ledger: 164

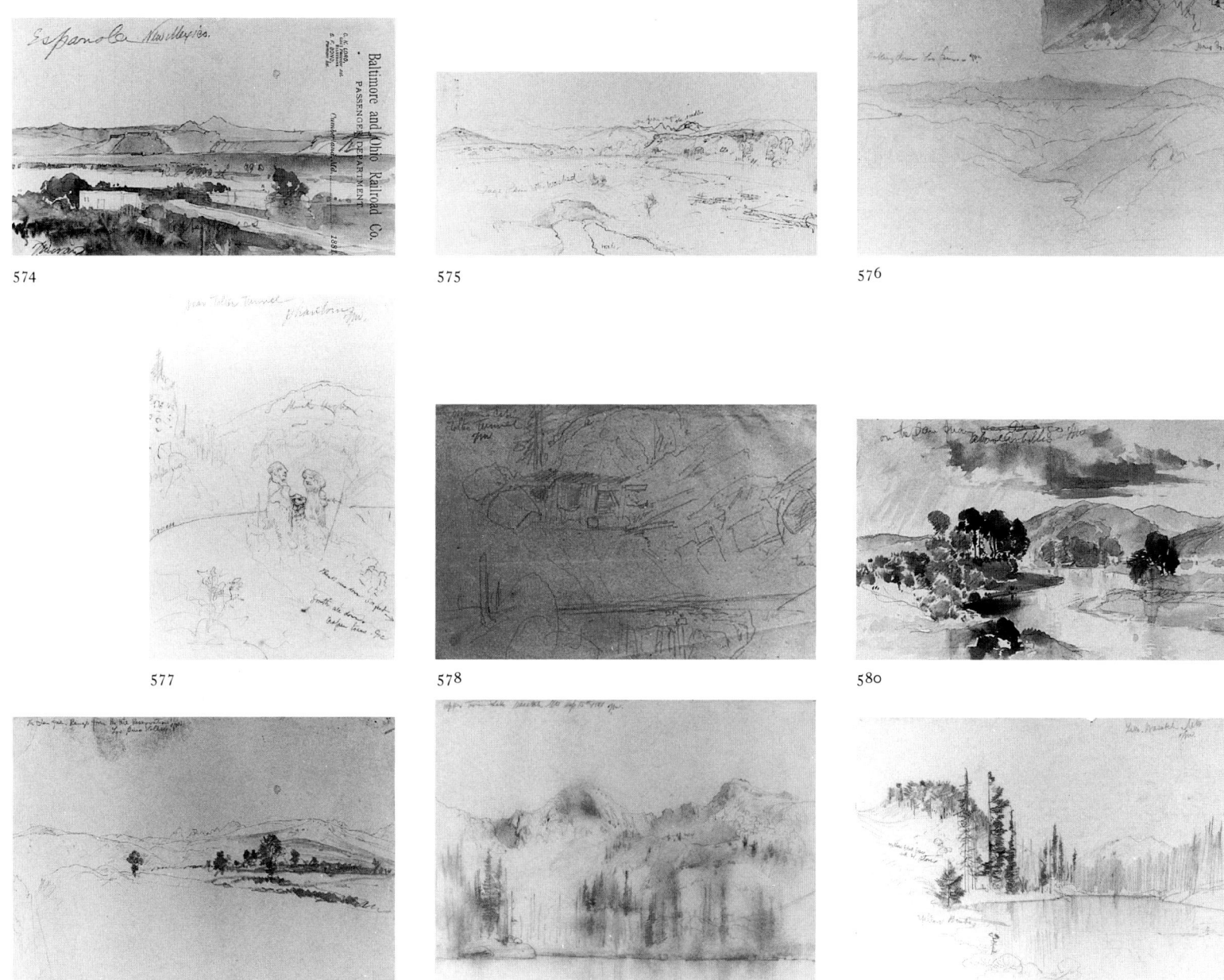

574

575

576

577

578

580

581

582

583

584
MARTHA LAKE
Graphite on gray wove
10 by 13³/₄
1336.994 Gilcrease
Dated: "Sep 16th 1881" u.l.
Signed: "TM" u.l.
Inscribed: "Martha Lake" u.l.
Provenance: TG
1916 ledger: 361

585
LAKE MARTHA
Graphite on wove
6⁷/₈ by 4³/₈
1336.648 Gilcrease
Signed: "TM" l.r.
Inscribed: "Lake Martha" l.c.
Provenance: TG
1916 ledger: 268

*586
GREEN RIVER
Graphite and watercolor on wove
9⁷/₈ by 13⁷/₈
0236.898 Gilcrease
Dated: "Sep 20th 1881" u.l.
Signed: "TMoran" u.l.
Inscribed: "Green River" u.l.; miscellaneous
notes
Provenance: TG
1916 ledger: 32
Note: Sketch on verso

587
GREEN RIVER BUTTES, WYOMING
TERRITORY
Graphite and watercolor on wove
10³/₈ by 19¹/₈
31.18/6 Stark Museum of Art, Orange, Texas
Dated: "Sep 20th 1881" l.l.
Signed: "TMoran" l.l.
Inscribed: "Green River Buttes Wyoming Tery"
l.l.
Provenance: Joseph Sartor Galleries, Dallas,
Texas; H. J. Lutcher Stark, Orange, Texas
1916 ledger: 36

†588
STRATHAVEN CASTLE
Graphite on wove
12³/₄ by 10
1376.774 Gilcrease
Dated: "June 1st 1882" u.l.
Signed: "TM" u.c.
Inscribed: "Strathaven Castle" u.l.; miscellane-
ous notes
Provenance: TG
1916 ledger: 177

†589
STRATHAVEN
Graphite on wove
6¹/₂ by 8⁷/₈
85 East Hampton Library
Dated: "1882" l.l.
Signed: "TM" l.l.
Inscribed: "Strathaven" l.l.
Provenance: EH
1916 ledger: 219
Note: This sketch is the study for Moran's etch-
ing *Strathaven Castle—Scotland, 1882* (Morand
and Friese, *Prints of Thomas Moran,* p. 114).

590
STRATHAVEN
Graphite on wove
6¹/₂ by 10
1376.777 Gilcrease
Dated: "June 1st 1882" u.r.
Inscribed: "Strathaven" u.r.; miscellaneous notes
Provenance: TG
1916 ledger: 346

591
SPECTACLE EYE, STRATHAVEN
Graphite on wove
10 by 12³/₄
1376.781 Gilcrease
Dated: "1882" u.r.
Signed: "TM" u.r.
Inscribed: "Spectacle Eye. Strathaven" u.r. on
left half of sheet
Provenance: TG
1916 ledger: 193

584

†592
PASS OF GLENCOE
Graphite on blue wove
10¹/₄ by 14⁵/₈
1376.783 Gilcrease
Dated: "1882" u.l.
Signed: "TMoran" u.l.
Inscribed: "Pass of Glencoe" u.l.
Provenance: TG
1916 ledger: 343
Note: This sketch anticipates the etching *The
Pass of Glencoe* (Morand and Friese, *Prints of
Thomas Moran,* p. 142). There is a sketch on
verso.

†593
PASS OF GLENCOE
Graphite on newsprint
12¹/₂ by 10
1376.782 Gilcrease
Dated: "1882" l.l.
Signed: "TM" l.l.
Inscribed: "Pass of Glencoe" l.l.
Provenance: TG
Note: Moran duplicated this sketch in his etch-
ing *Bridge in the Pass of Glencoe—Scotland*
(Morand and Friese, *Prints of Thomas Moran,*
p. 112).

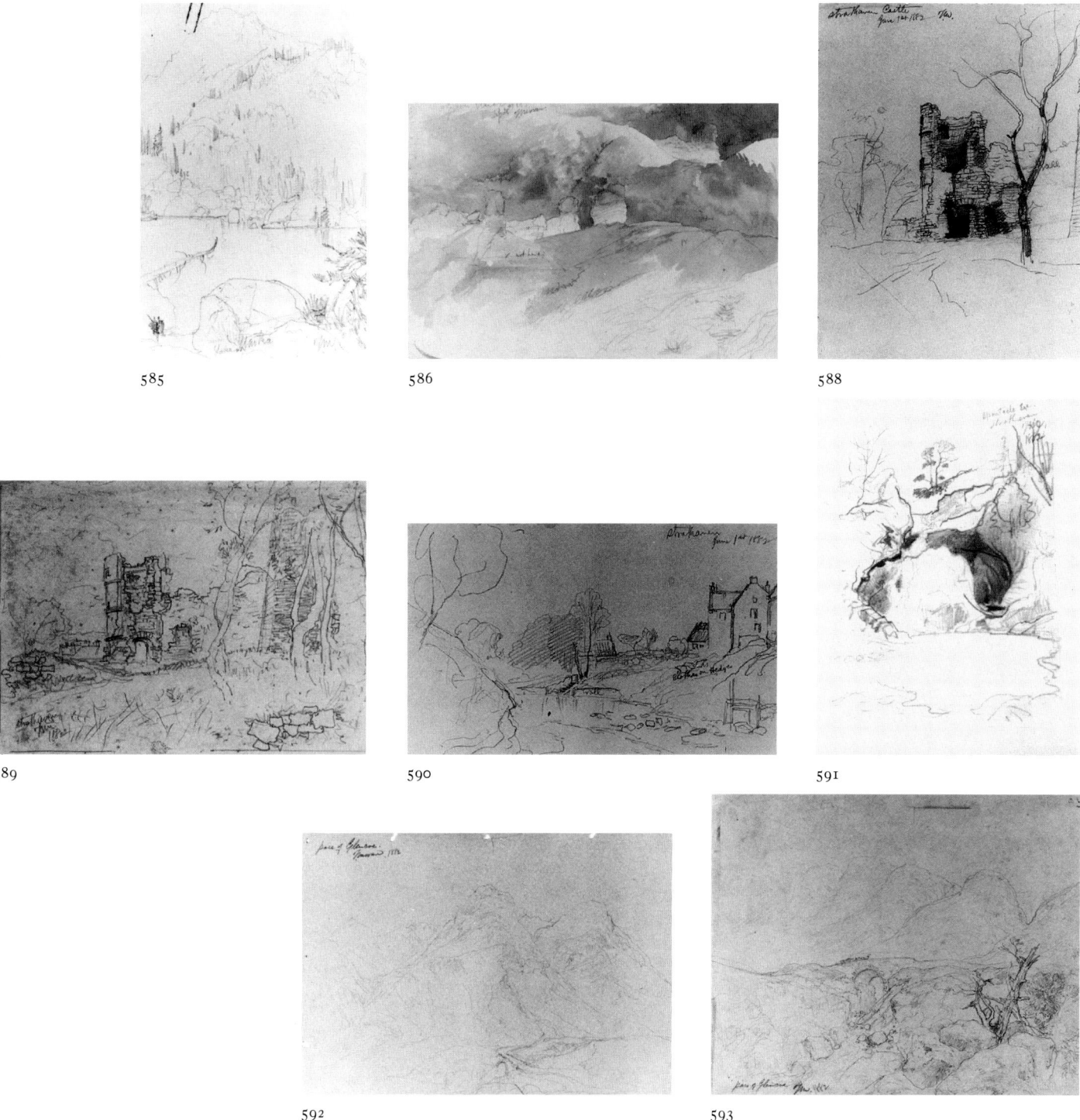

585

586

588

589

590

591

592

593

594
FINGAL'S CAVE, STAFFA
Graphite on blue wove
6 by 8³/₈
17 East Hampton Library
Dated: "1882" l.r.
Signed: "TM" l.r.
Inscribed: "Fingals Cave Staffa" l.r.
Provenance: EH
1916 ledger: 369
Note: This sketch anticipates Moran's painting
Fingal's Cave, Island of Staffa, 1884–85, The
High Museum.

595
CONWAY CASTLE
Graphite on newsprint
9³/₄ by 12¹/₄
1376.790 Gilcrease
Dated: "1882" l.l.
Signed: "TM" l.l.
Inscribed: "Conway Castle" c.r.
Provenance: TG
1916 ledger: 321

596
CONWAY
Graphite, wash, and watercolor on wove
4 by 7
39 East Hampton Library
Dated: "Sep 10th 1882" u.c.
Signed: "TM" u.r.
Inscribed: "Conway" u.c.
Provenance: EH
1916 ledger: 259

597
CONWAY
Graphite on newsprint
7⁷/₈ by 12¹/₂
1376.776 Gilcrease
Dated: "1882" l.l.
Signed: "TM" l.l.
Inscribed: "Conway." l.l.
Provenance: TG
1916 ledger: 340

598
CONWAY
Graphite on wove
10¹/₂ by 13
1376.773 Gilcrease
Dated: "1882" u.l.
Signed: "TM" u.l.
Inscribed: "Conway" u.l.
Provenance: TG
1916 ledger: 272

599
CONWAY CASTLE
Graphite on newsprint
10 by 12¹/₂
1376.771 Gilcrease
Dated: "1882" l.l.
Signed: "TM" l.l.
Inscribed: "Conway Castle" l.l.; miscellaneous
notes
Provenance: TG
1916 ledger: 179

600
CONWAY CASTLE
Graphite on wove
10⁵/₈ by 15
S-63 East Hampton Library
Dated: "1883" l.l.
Signed: "TM" l.l.
Inscribed: "Conway Castle" l.l.
Provenance: EH
1916 ledger: 153

601
CONWAY CASTLE
Graphite on newsprint
6 by 10
1376.785 Gilcrease
Dated: "1882" l.l.
Signed: "TM" l.l.
Inscribed: "Conway C." l.l.
Provenance: TG
1916 ledger: 158

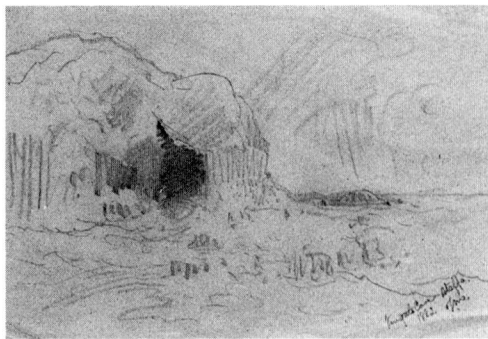

594

602
CONWAY WALLS
Graphite on wove
6¹/₂ by 10
1376.791 Gilcrease
Dated: "1882" l.l.
Signed: "TM" l.l.
Inscribed: "Conway Walls" l.l.
Provenance: TG
1916 ledger: 182

†603
CONWAY CASTLE FROM THE WALLS
Graphite on wove
11⁵/₈ by 20 [irregularly torn edges and two pieces
joined]
1376.788 Gilcrease
Dated: "1882" l.l.
Signed: "TMoran" l.l.
Inscribed: "Conway Castle from The Walls" l.l.;
miscellaneous notes
Provenance: TG
1916 ledger: 375

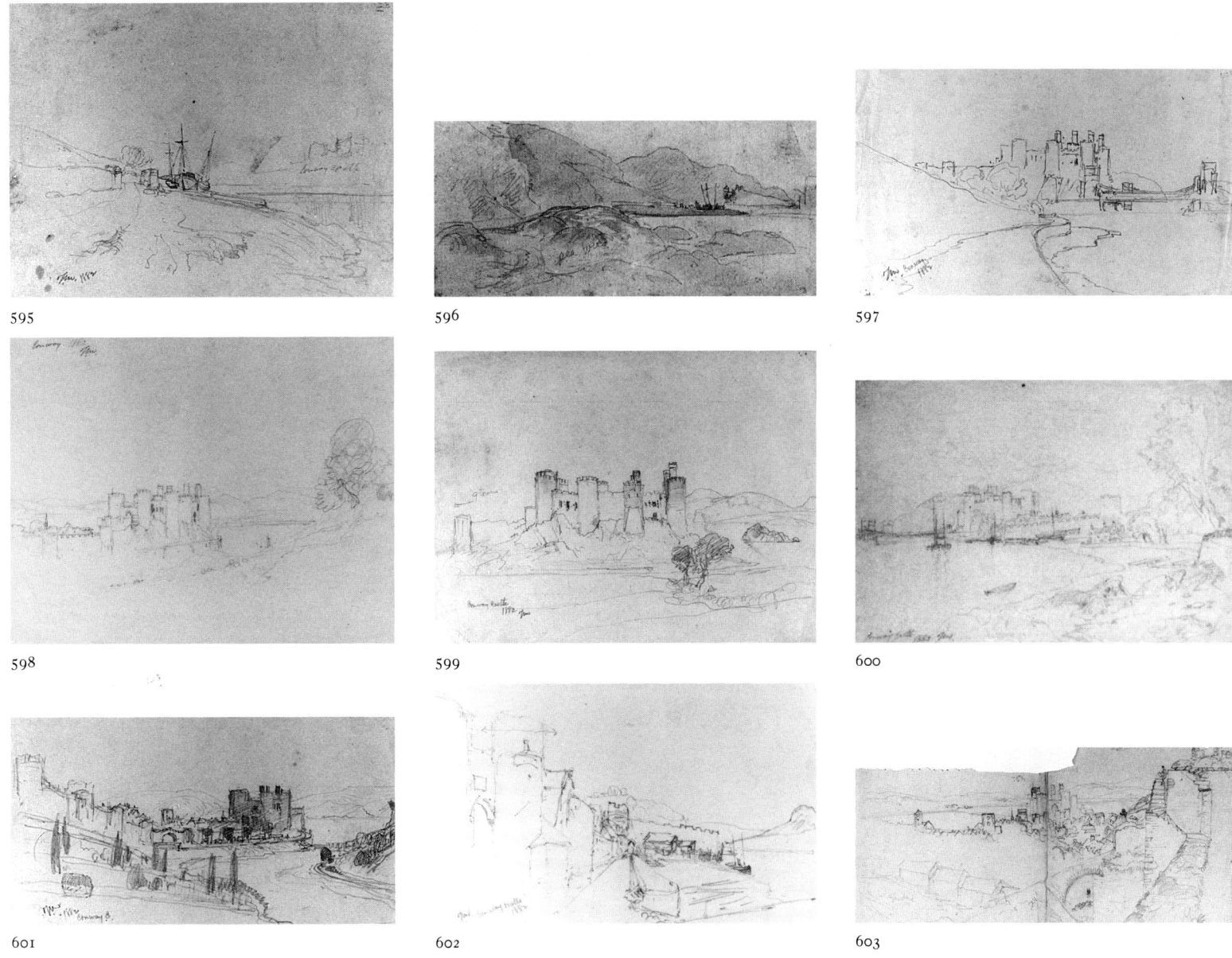

595

596

597

598

599

600

601

602

603

*604
CONWAY, NORTH WALES
Graphite and watercolor on wove
12 1/8 by 17 3/4
0276.803 Gilcrease
Dated: "1882" l.l.
Signed: "TMoran" l.l.
Inscribed: "Conway. N.W" l.l. in ink
Provenance: TG
1916 ledger: 152

†605
CONWAY FROM ACROSS THE RIVER,
NEAR TURNER'S POINT OF VIEW
Graphite on blue wove [two pieces joined]
15 by 21 1/2
1376.793 Gilcrease
Dated: "1882" l.l.
Signed: "TMoran" l.l.
Inscribed: "Conway from Across the River near
Turners Point of View" l.l.; "Conway. From
Turners Point of View. by TMoran. The original
picture now in my possession. 1882" on verso;
miscellaneous notes
Provenance: TG
1916 ledger: 225
Note: This sketch relates to the etching *Conway
Castle* (Morand and Friese, *Prints of Thomas
Moran*, p. 88).

*606
CONWAY CASTLE
Graphite and watercolor on wove
Sketch 12 by 18, mount 15 3/4 by 22
0276.804 Gilcrease
Dated: "1882" l.l.
Signed: "TMoran" l.l.
Inscribed: "Conway Castle" l.l.; "Conway Cas-
tle. N. Wales 1882" l.l. on mount; "not for sale"
l.r. on mount; "35. Conway" in ink on mount
Provenance: TG
1916 ledger: 154

607
SEA WEED AT THE BASE ON ROCK
Graphite on newsprint
10 by 12 5/8
1376.772 Gilcrease
Dated: "1882" l.l.
Signed: "TM" l.l.

Inscribed: "Sea Weed at the base on Rock"; miscellaneous notes
Provenance: TG
1916 ledger: 344

608
CONWAY
Graphite on wove
4 by 7
1376.779 Gilcrease
Dated: "Sep 14th 1882" l.r.
Signed: "TM" l.r.
Inscribed: "Conway" l.r.
Provenance: TG
1916 ledger: 371

†609
NEAR CONWAY
Graphite on wove
12 7/8 by 20
1376.787 Gilcrease
Dated: "1882" l.r.
Signed: "TMoran" l.r.
Inscribed: "Near Conway" l.r.
Provenance: TG
1916 ledger: 164

610
CHWILOG, WALES
Graphite on ruled wove
4 by 7
1376.780 Gilcrease
Dated: "Sep 15th 1882" u.c.
Signed: "TM" u.c.
Inscribed: "Chwilog Wales." u.l.
Provenance: TG
1916 ledger: 269

*611
AFON WEN, NORTH WALES,
CARDIGAN BAY
Graphite and watercolor on newsprint
6 1/8 by 10
0276.805 Gilcrease
Dated: "Sep 15th 1882" u.r.
Signed: "TMoran" l.r.
Inscribed: "Afonwen N. Wales Cardigan Bay"
u.r.
Provenance: TG
1916 ledger: 410

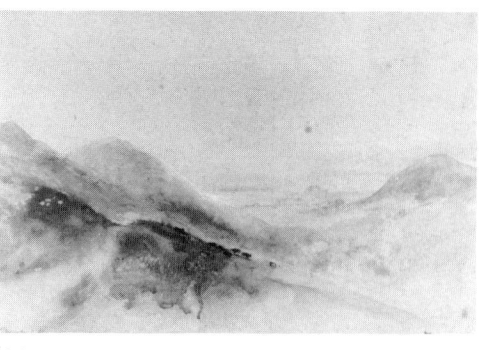

604

*612
CRICCIETH CASTLE, CARDIGAN BAY,
NORTH WALES
Graphite and watercolor on newsprint
5 1/2 by 10
0276.806 Gilcrease
Dated: "Sep 15th 1882" u.r.
Signed: "TM" u.r.
Inscribed: "Cricieth Castle. Cardigan Bay N.
Wales" u.r.
Provenance: TG
1916 ledger: 192

613
CRICCIETH CASTLE, NEAR
HARLECH, WALES
Graphite on wove
9 East Hampton Library
6 by 9 3/4
Dated: "1882" l.l.
Signed: "TM" l.l.
Inscribed: "Crickieth Castle near Harlech Wales"
l.l.
Provenance: EH
1916 ledger: 247

614
CRICCIETH CASTLE, NORTH WALES
Graphite on ruled wove
4 by 7
81 East Hampton Library
Dated: "1882" u.c.
Signed: "TM" u.c.
Inscribed: "Criccieth Castle N.W." u.l.
Provenance: EH
1916 ledger: 262

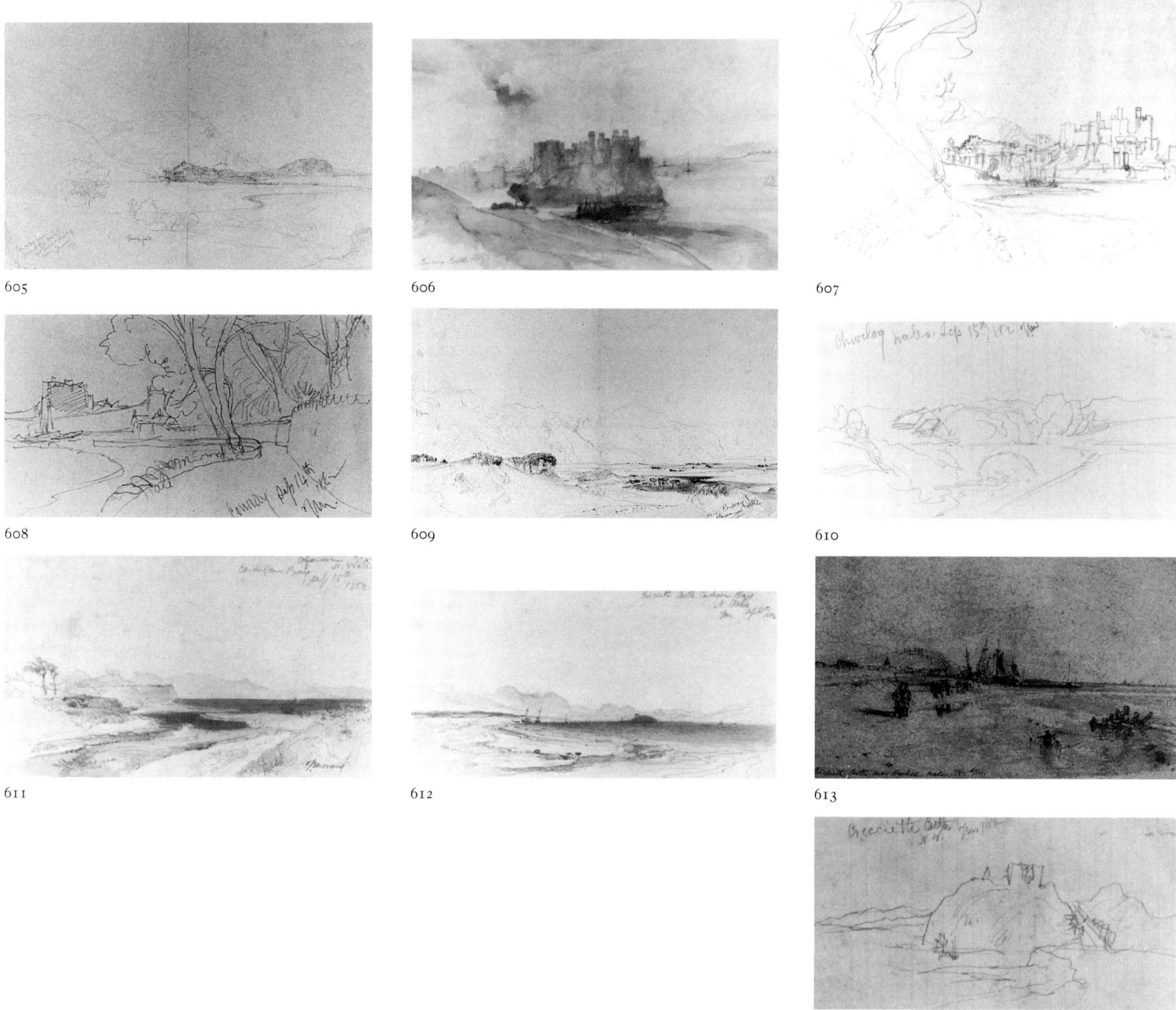

605

606

607

608

609

610

611

612

613

614

615
DOLLWYDELLAN TOWER, NORTH
WALES
Graphite on ruled wove
4 by 7
88 East Hampton Library
Signed: "TM" u.c.
Inscribed: "Dollwydellan Tower N. Wales" upper
edge
Provenance: EH

616
HARLECH
Graphite on tan ruled wove
4 by 7
58 East Hampton Library
Signed: "TM" l.l.
Inscribed: "Harlech" l.l.
Provenance: EH
1916 ledger: 260

617
HARLECH CASTLE AND SNOWDEN,
NORTH WALES
Graphite on wove
10 1/2 by 13
1376.786 Gilcrease
Dated: "Sep 15th 1882" u.r.
Signed: "TM" u.r.
Inscribed: "Harlech Castle & Snowden North
Wales" u.r.; miscellaneous notes
Provenance: TG
1916 ledger: 316

*618
HARLECH CASTLE, NORTH WALES
Graphite and watercolor on wove
5 3/4 by 9 1/4
0276.938 Gilcrease
Dated: "Xmas 1882" l.r.
Signed: "TMoran" l.r.
Inscribed: "Harlech Castle N. Wales." l.l.
Provenance: Ruth K. Henschel, New York; 1964
Thomas Gilcrease Foundation, Tulsa, Okla.;
1971 The Thomas Gilcrease Institute of Ameri-
can History and Art, Tulsa, Okla.

619
HARLECH CASTLE, WALES
Graphite on wove
7 3/8 by 10 3/4

1376.638 Gilcrease
Signed: "TM" l.r.
Inscribed: "Harlech Castle Wales" l.r.
Provenance: TG
1916 ledger: 209

†620
HARLECH
Graphite on wove
6 1/2 by 10
1376.775 Gilcrease
Dated: "1882" u.r.
Signed: "TM" u.r.
Inscribed: "Harlech" u.r.; miscellaneous notes
Provenance: TG
Note: This sketch anticipates the etching *Har-
lech Castle—Wales* (Morand and Friese, *Prints
of Thomas Moran,* p. 118).

621
FROM HOTEL WINDOW, HARLECH
Graphite on wove
10 1/2 by 13
1376.789 Gilcrease
Dated: "Sep 15th 1882" u.r.
Signed: "TM" u.r.
Inscribed: "from Hotel Window Harlech" u.r.;
miscellaneous notes
Provenance: TG
1916 ledger: 341

622
RINGWOOD, ENGLAND
Graphite on wove
6 1/2 by 10
1376.784 Gilcrease
Dated: "1882" l.l.
Signed: "TM" l.l.
Inscribed: "Ringwood. England" l.l.; miscella-
neous notes; small sketch u.l.
1916 ledger: 162
Provenance: TG
Note: There is one-half of a chessboard pattern
drawn on the verso of this sketch; it matches the
verso of No. 624. This sketch anticipates the
etching *An English River* (Morand and Friese,
Prints of Thomas Moran, p. 120).

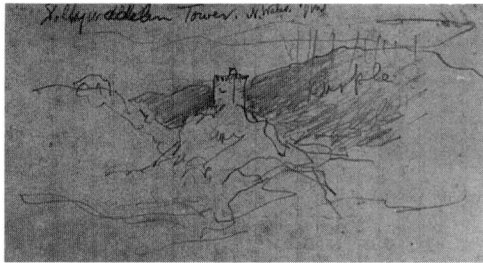

615

623
RINGWOOD NEAR THE NEW
FOREST, ENGLAND
Graphite on wove
6 1/2 by 10
1376.624 Gilcrease
Signed: "TM" l.l.
Inscribed: "Ringwood near the New Forest. En-
gland" l.l.; miscellaneous notes
Provenance: TG
1916 ledger: 203
Note: This sketch anticipates the etching *An
English River* (Morand and Friese, *Prints of
Thomas Moran,* p. 120).

624
RINGWOOD, NEW FOREST
Graphite on wove
6 1/2 by 10
1376.835 Gilcrease
Dated: "1890" l.l. [see note]
Signed: "TM" l.l.
Inscribed: "Ringwood. New Forest" l.l.; miscellaneous notes
Provenance: TG
1916 ledger: 184
Note: This sketch resembles the sketches from
1882. There is one-half of a chessboard pattern
drawn on the verso of this sketch; it matches the
verso of No. 622.

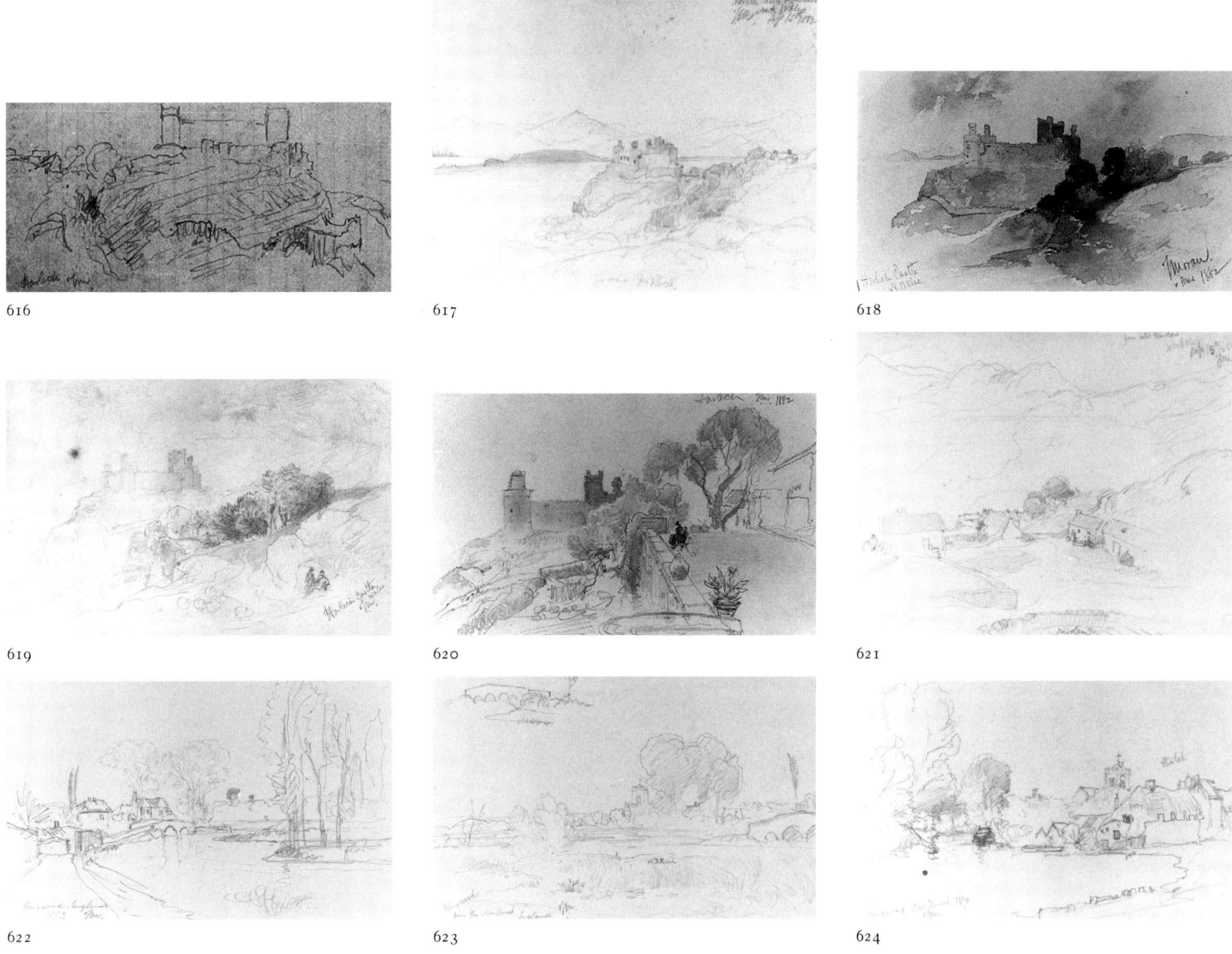

616

617

618

619

620

621

622

623

624

625
FOOT OF FITHIAN'S LOT
Graphite on wove
6$^{1}/_{2}$ by 10$^{1}/_{8}$
1326.792 Gilcrease
Dated: "Sep 26th 1882" l.l.
Signed: "TMoran" l.r.
Inscribed: "Foot of Fithians lot" l.l.; "East Hampton" l.r.
Provenance: TG
1916 ledger: 169

626
EAST HAMPTON
Graphite on wove
6$^{7}/_{8}$ by 7$^{1}/_{4}$
82 East Hampton Library
Dated: "1882" u.l.
Signed: "TM" u.l.
Inscribed: "E.H." u.l.
Provenance: EH

*627
HAVANA
Graphite and watercolor on wove
Sketch 9$^{1}/_{2}$ by 13$^{3}/_{4}$, mount 15 by 18$^{3}/_{4}$
0296.825 Gilcrease
Dated: "Jan 30th 1883" u.l.
Signed: "TM" u.l.
Inscribed: "Havanna" u.l.
Provenance: TG
1916 ledger: 414
Note: This sketch was mounted on cardboard sometime after 1916.

628
THE CABANO, HAVANA
Graphite, wash, and white gouache on wove
15 by 10$^{1}/_{2}$
East Hampton Library
Dated: "Feb 2nd 1883" l.l.
Signed: "TMoran" l.l.
Inscribed: "The Cabano Havana" l.l.
Provenance: EH

*629
HAVANA
Watercolor and white gouache on blue laid
8$^{5}/_{8}$ by 11$^{5}/_{8}$
0296.807 Gilcrease
Dated: "1883" l.l.
Signed: "TMoran" l.l.
Inscribed: "Havana" l.l.
Provenance: TG
1916 ledger: 409

*630
SUNSET, GULF OF MEXICO
Watercolor on wove
10 by 14$^{1}/_{4}$
0296.814 Gilcrease
Dated: "1883" l.l.
Signed: "TMoran" l.l.
Inscribed: "Sunst. Gulf of Mexico" l.l.
Provenance: TG
1916 ledger: 9

*631
VERA CRUZ
Graphite, watercolor, and white gouache on wove
Sketch 10 by 14$^{1}/_{4}$, mount 14 by 19$^{1}/_{2}$
0246.815 Gilcrease
Dated: "Feb 3rd 1883" l.l. [changed from "4^{t}" to "3rd" by Moran]
Signed: "TMoran" l.l.
Inscribed: "Vera Cruz" l.l.
Provenance: TG
1916 ledger: 89
Note: This sketch was mounted on cardboard sometime after 1916.

*632
SAN JUAN D'ULLOA, VERA CRUZ
Graphite, watercolor, white and yellow gouache on blue wove
10 by 14$^{1}/_{4}$
0246.826 Gilcrease
Dated: "Feb 4th 1883" u.r.
Signed: "TMoran" u.r.
Inscribed: "San Juan D'Ullua Vera Cruz" u.r.; miscellaneous notes
Provenance: TG
1916 ledger: 23

625

633
SAN JUAN D'ULLOA, VERA CRUZ, MEXICO
Graphite on wove
5$^{5}/_{8}$ by 8$^{7}/_{8}$
1346.669 Gilcrease
Inscribed: "San Juan D'Ulloa Vera Cruz. Mexico" l.l.
Provenance: TG
1916 ledger: 82

634
VERA CRUZ, MEXICO
Graphite on blue wove
10 by 14$^{1}/_{4}$
1346.807 Gilcrease
Dated: "Feb 1883" l.l.
Signed: "TM" l.l.
Inscribed: "Vera Cruz Mexico" l.l.
Provenance: TG
1916 ledger: 69
Note: Sketch and inscription on verso: "Santa Catarina near Monterey March 11th 1883 TM"

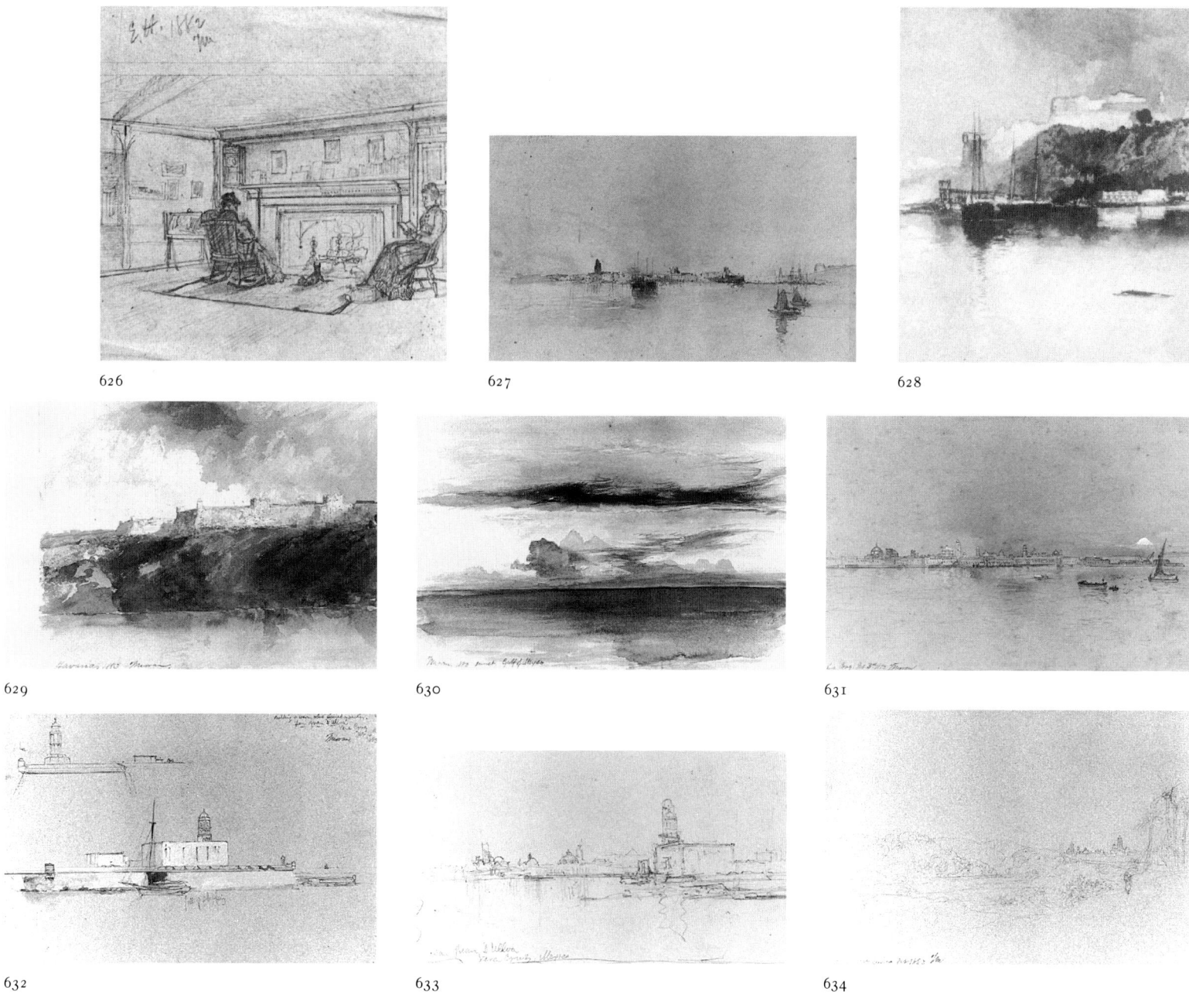

626

627

628

629

630

631

632

633

634

635
SPANISH FORT, PASO DEL MACHO
Graphite on newsprint
5⅞ by 8⅜
1346.827 Gilcrease
Dated: "Sunday Feb 4th 1883" u.c.
Signed: "TM" u.c.
Inscribed: "spanish fort paso del Macho" u.l.;
miscellaneous notes
Provenance: TG
1916 ledger: 75
Note: Sketch on verso

636
ON THE METLAC RIVER, MEXICO
Graphite on blue laid
8⅝ by 11⅝
1346.820 Gilcrease
Dated: "Sun. Feb 4th 1883" u.c.
Signed: "TM" u.c.
Inscribed: "on the Metlac River Mexico" u.l.;
"Orizaba" u.c.
Provenance: TG
1916 ledger: 74

637
CORDOVA
Graphite and wash on ruled wove
4 by 14
S-19 East Hampton Library
Dated: "Feb 4th" u.l.
Signed: "TM" l.l.
Inscribed: "Cordova" u.l.
Provenance: EH

638
ORIZABA
Graphite on blue laid
8⅝ by 11⅝
1346.819 Gilcrease
Dated: "Feb 5th 1883" u.l.
Signed: "TM" u.l.
Inscribed: "Orizaba" u.l.; color notes
Provenance: TG
1916 ledger: 72
Note: This sketch was used in preparation for
Orizaba, Mexico (Clark, *Thomas Moran: Water-
colors of the American West*, p. 150, no. 221). There
is graphite for tracing on the verso, and Moran
combined the use of soft graphite with hard line
for certain contours and lines used in tracing.

639
ORIZABA
Graphite on wove
5¾ by 8½
117 East Hampton Library
Dated: "Feb 5th 1883" u.l.
Signed: "TM" u.l.
Inscribed: "Orizaba" u.l.
Provenance: EH
1916 ledger: 40

†640
ORIZABA, MEXICO
Graphite on blue laid
8⅝ by 11⅝
1346.808 Gilcrease
Dated: "1883" l.l.
Signed: "TM" l.l.
Inscribed: "Orizaba, Mex." l.l.
Provenance: TG
1916 ledger: 63

641
ORIZABA
Graphite on newsprint
5⅞ by 8⅜
1346.804 Gilcrease
Dated: "1883" u.l.
Signed: "TM" u.l.
Inscribed: "Orizaba" u.l.; color notes
Provenance: TG
1916 ledger: 32

*642
NEAR VERA CRUZ
Graphite and watercolor on newsprint
5⅞ by 8⅜
0246.810 Gilcrease
Dated: "Feb 6th 1883" u.l.
Signed: "TM" u.c.
Inscribed: "near Vera Cruz" u.l.; color notes
Provenance: TG
1916 ledger: 411

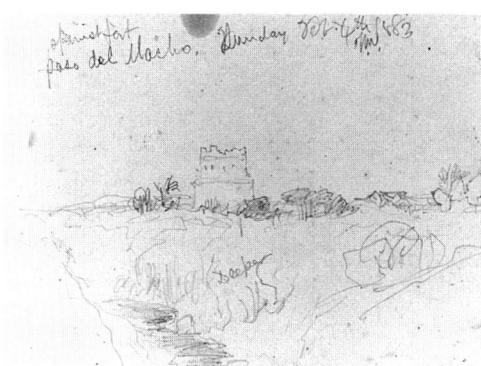

635

643
WATERFALL AT ATOYAC
Graphite on blue wove
5⅞ by 8⅜
26 East Hampton Library
Dated: "Feb 6th 1883" u.l.
Signed: "TMoran" u.c.
Inscribed: "Waterfall at Atoyac" u.l.
Provenance: EH

*644
THE PEAK OF ORIZABA FROM
ESPERANZA
Graphite, watercolor, and white gouache on blue
laid
Sketch 8⅝ by 11⅝, mount 9¼ by 12¼
0246.827 Gilcrease
Dated: "1883" l.l.
Signed: "TMoran" l.l.
Inscribed: "the Peak of Orizaba from Esper-
anza" u.l.; "Orizaba. Mexico 1883" l.l. on mount;
color notes
Provenance: TG
1916 ledger: 13
Note: This sketch was mounted on cardboard
sometime after 1916. There is a sketch on verso.

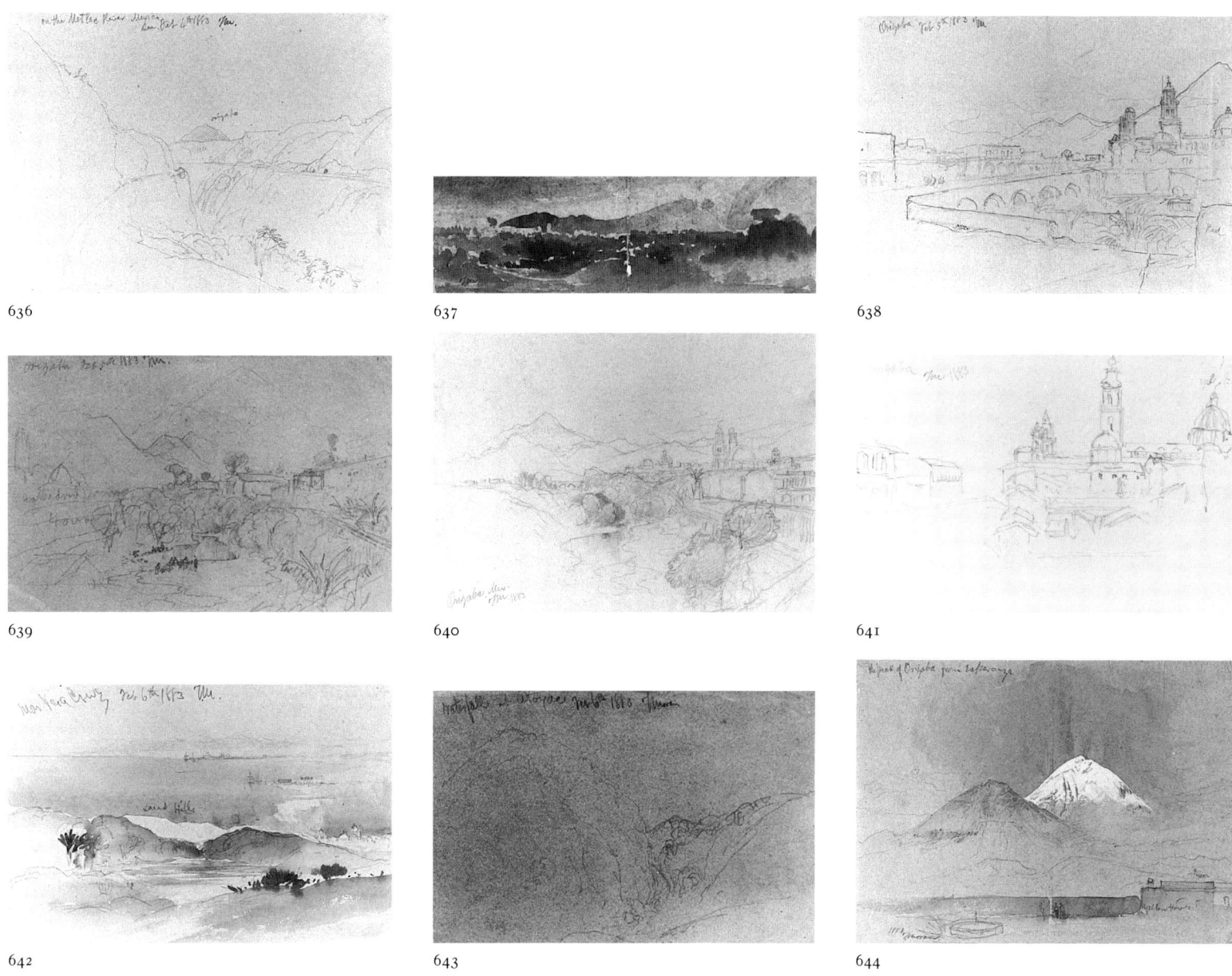

636

637

638

639

640

641

642

643

644

645
MEXICO FROM MONTEZUMA'S
PALACE, CHAPULTEPEC
Graphite on blue laid
8⅝ by 11⅝
1346.822 Gilcrease
Dated: "1883" l.c.
Signed: "TM" l.c.
Inscribed: "Mexico. from Montezumas Palace.
Chapultepec" l.l.
Provenance: TG
1916 ledger: 44

†646
CHAPULTEPEC
Graphite on blue laid
8⅝ by 11⅝
1346.799 Gilcrease
Dated: "1883" u.l.
Signed: "TM" u.l.
Inscribed: "Chapultepec" u.l.; "Ixtacihuatl" u.c.;
"Popo" u.r.
Provenance: TG
1916 ledger: 56

647
MEXICO
Graphite on blue laid
8⅝ by 11⅝
1346.797 Gilcrease
Dated: "Feb 7th 1883" u.c.
Signed: "TM" u.c.
Inscribed: "Mexico" u.c.
Provenance: TG
1916 ledger: 55

†648
IXTACIHUATL AND POPOCATÉPETL
Graphite and white gouache on blue laid
2⅞ by 11⅝
1346.628 Gilcrease
Signed: "TM" u.c.
Inscribed: "Ixtacihuatl" u.c.; "Popocataptl" u.r.
Provenance: TG
1916 ledger: 36

*649
MEXICO
Graphite, watercolor, and white gouache on blue
laid
6⅛ by 11⅝, mount 16⅝ by 11⅝

0246.813 Gilcrease
Dated: "Feb 8th 1883" l.r.
Signed: "TM" l.r.
Inscribed: "Mexico" l.r.
Provenance: TG
1916 ledger: 15
Note: This sketch was mounted on cardboard
sometime after 1916.

650
OUTSKIRTS OF MEXICO
Graphite on blue laid
11⅝ by 8⅝
1346.811 Gilcrease
Dated: "Feb 8th 1883" u.l.
Signed: "TMoran" u.c.
Inscribed: "outskirts of Mexico" u.l.; color notes
Provenance: TG
1916 ledger: 26

651a
MEXICO [descriptive]
Graphite on wove
Upper left sketch 2⅝ by 5, sheet 8½ by 10
1346.545 Gilcrease
Provenance: TG
1916 ledger: 3
Note: Sketch on verso

651b
MEXICO [descriptive]
Graphite on wove
Upper right sketch 2⅝ by 5, sheet 8½ by 10
1346.545 Gilcrease

651c
MEXICO
Graphite on wove
Lower sketch 5⅞ by 10, sheet 8½ by 10
1346.545 Gilcrease
Signed: "TM" u.c.
Inscribed: "Mexico" c.l. in Mexico

652
VOLCANO OF TOLUCA, MEXICO
Graphite on newsprint
5⅞ by 8⅜
1346.818 Gilcrease
Dated: "1883" u.c.
Signed: "TM" u.c.
Inscribed: "Volcan of Toluca Mex" u.l.

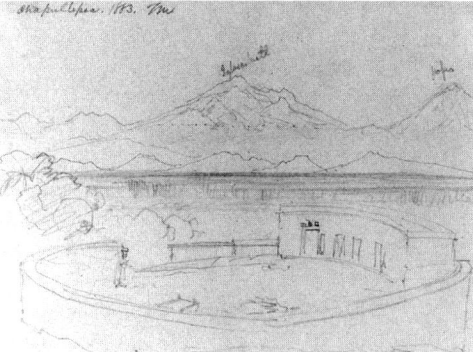

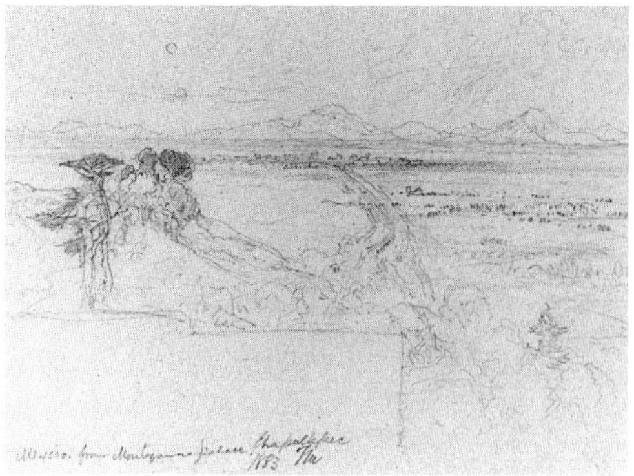

645

646

Provenance: TG
1916 ledger: 77

*653
MARAVATIO
Graphite and watercolor on wove
10 by 14¼
0246.809 Gilcrease
Dated: "Feb 9th 1883" u.r.
Signed: "TMoran" u.r.
Inscribed: "Maravatio" u.r.; miscellaneous notes
Provenance: TG

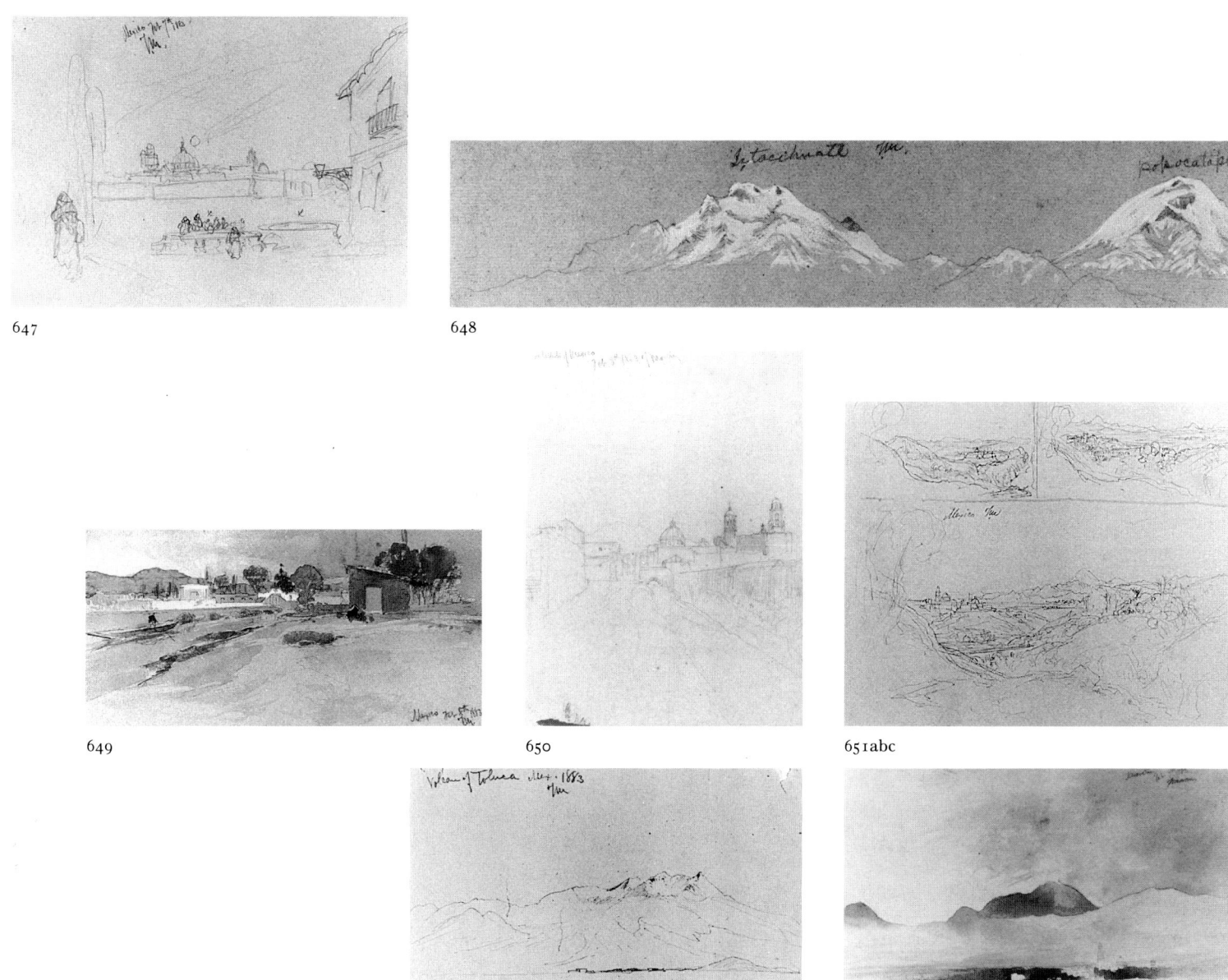

647

648

649

650

651abc

652

653

*654
SUNDAY MORNING, MARAVATIO
Graphite, watercolor, and white gouache on blue
wove
10 by 7 3/8
0246.812 Gilcrease
Dated: "Feb 11th 1883" u.l. and 1883 l.r. in ink
Signed: "TM" u.l. and colophon l.r. in ink
Inscribed: "Sunday Morning Maravatio" u.l.;
"Not for Sale" on verso
Provenance: TG
1916 ledger: 34

*655
FROM ACAMBARO, WEST
Graphite and watercolor on newsprint
5 3/8 by 8 7/8
0246.821 Gilcrease
Dated: "Feb 12 1883" u.r.
Signed: "TM" u.r.
Inscribed: "from Acambaro. West" u.r.; miscel-
laneous notes
Provenance: TG
1916 ledger: 4

656
LAKE CUITZEO, HACIENDA
ANDOCUTIN
Graphite on wove
10 by 14 1/4
1346.812 Gilcrease
Dated: "1883" u.l.
Signed: "TM" u.l.
Inscribed: "Lake? Cuitzeo Hacienda Andocutin"
u.l.
and "Andocutin" u.r.
Provenance: TG
1916 ledger: 68
Note: Sketch on verso

†657
PAYDAY, BEYOND MARAVATIO
Graphite and red watercolor on newsprint
5 7/8 by 8 3/8
1346.806 Gilcrease
Dated: "Monday 12 Feb. 1883" u.r.
Signed: "TM" u.r.
Inscribed: "Payday Beyon[d] Maravatio" u.r.;
miscellaneous notes
Provenance: TG
1916 ledger: 5

658
MARAVATIO
Graphite and watercolor on wove
10 by 14
Littlejohn Collection, Parrish Art Museum,
Southampton, New York
Dated: "Feb 12th 1883" u.r.
Inscribed: "Maravatio" u.r.

659
MARAVATIO
Graphite and watercolor on newsprint
5 7/8 by 7 1/4
0246.820 Gilcrease
Dated: "Feb 13–83" u.l.
Signed: "TMoran" u.l.
Inscribed: "Maravatio" u.l.; miscellaneous notes
Provenance: TG
1916 ledger: 28
Note: Sketch on verso

660
MARAVATIO
Graphite and watercolor on wove
5 3/4 by 8 3/8
S-20 East Hampton Library
Dated: "1883" l.l.
Signed: "TM" l.l.
Inscribed: "Maravatio" l.l.
Provenance: EH

661
MARAVATIO, MEXICO
Graphite on wove
5 by 8
89 East Hampton Library
Dated: "1883" l.c.
Inscribed: "Maravatio, Mex" l.c.
Provenance: EH

662
MARAVATIO, MEXICO
Graphite on newsprint
5 7/8 by 8 3/8
1346.667 Gilcrease
Signed: "TM" u.l.
Inscribed: "Maravatio Mex" u.l.
Provenance: TG
1916 ledger: 2

654

*663
MARAVATIO
Graphite and watercolor on newsprint
5 7/8 by 8 3/8
0246.811 Gilcrease
Dated: "Feb 13 1883" l.l.
Inscribed: "Maravatio" l.l.; miscellaneous notes
Provenance: TG
1916 ledger: 14
Note: Sketch and inscription on verso: "San Jose
Beyond Maravatio, Feb. 13th, 1883"

664
MOUNTAINS NEAR MARAVATIO
Graphite on blue laid
8 5/8 by 11 5/8
1346.798 Gilcrease
Dated: "1883" u.r.
Signed: "TM" u.r.
Inscribed: "Mountains Near Maravatio" u.r.
Provenance: TG
1916 ledger: 54

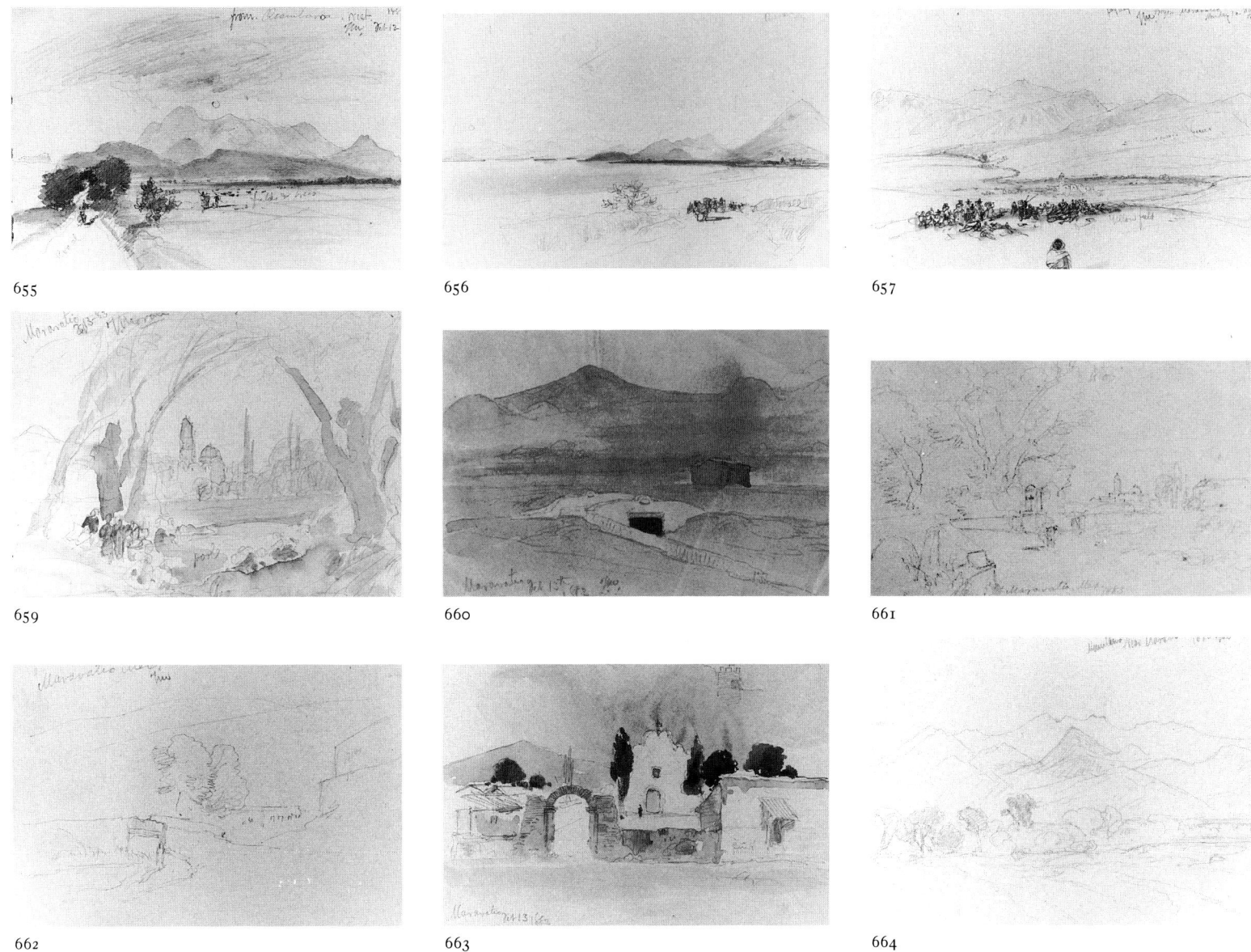

655

656

657

659

660

661

662

663

664

*665
SAN JOSÉ, BEYOND MARAVATIO
Graphite, watercolor, and white gouache on blue wove
Sketch 10 by 14¹/₄, mount 15 by 19¹/₈
0246.822 Gilcrease
Dated: "Feb 13th 1883" l.r.; "1883" l.l. ink
Signed: Colophon l.l. in ink; "TMoran" l.r.
Inscribed: "San Jose. beyond Maravatio" l.r.
Provenance: TG
1916 ledger: 88
Note: This sketch was mounted on cardboard sometime after 1916.

666
SAN JOSÉ, MEXICO
Graphite on wove
4 by 5¹/₄
103 East Hampton Library
Dated: "Feb 14 1883" u.c.
Signed: "TM" u.r.
Inscribed: "Mex. San Jose Sunday" u.l.
Provenance: EH

*667
MORELIA, MEXICO
Graphite, watercolor, and white gouache on blue wove
10 by 14¹/₄
0246.824 Gilcrease
Dated: "1883" u.l.
Signed: "TMoran" u.l.
Inscribed: "Morelia. Mexico" u.l.; miscellaneous notes
Provenance: TG
1916 ledger: 10

668
AQUEDUCT, MORELIA, MEXICO
Graphite on blue wove
10 by 14¹/₄
1346.803 Gilcrease
Dated: "1883" l.l.
Signed: "TM" l.l.
Inscribed: "Augeduct Morelia Mexico" l.l.; color notes
Provenance: TG
1916 ledger: 70

669
MORELIA, MEXICO
Graphite and watercolor on blue wove
10 by 14¹/₄
56.733 Museum of Fine Arts, Boston
Provenance: MK

670
MORELIA, MEXICO
Graphite on laid
5¹/₄ by 8¹/₂
1346.816 Gilcrease
Dated: "1883" u.r.
Signed: "TM" u.r.
Inscribed: "Morelia. Mexico" u.r.; "or any other Mexican town" l.l.; miscellaneous notes
Provenance: TG
1916 ledger: 64

671
MORELIA
Graphite on newsprint
5⁷/₈ by 8³/₈
1346.817 Gilcrease
Dated: "1883" u.l.
Signed: "TM" l.l.
Inscribed: "Morelia" u.l.
Provenance: TG
1916 ledger: 58

672
MORELIA, MEXICO
Graphite on newsprint
5⁷/₈ by 8³/₈
1346.805 Gilcrease
Dated: "1883" u.l.
Signed: "TM" u.l.
Inscribed: "Morelia Mex." u.l.; color notes
Provenance: TG
1916 ledger: 33

673
QUIRIO, MEXICO
Graphite on newsprint
5⁷/₈ by 8³/₈
1346.810 Gilcrease
Dated: "Feb 17th 1883" u.l. [changed from 14th to 17th by Moran]
Signed: "TM" u.l.
Inscribed: "Quirio Mex." u.l.; miscellaneous notes

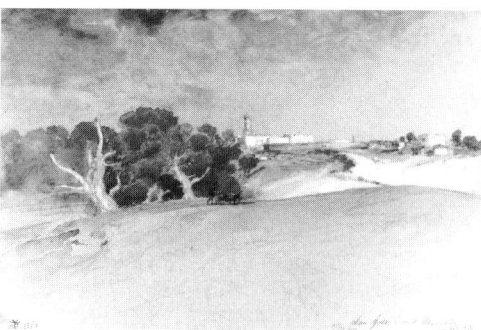

665

Provenance: TG
1916 ledger: 35
Note: Sketch and inscription on verso: "San Jose Beyond Maravatio, Feb 13 1883, TMoran"

*674
RAVINE NEAR THE TROJES MINE, MEXICO
Graphite, watercolor, and white gouache on blue wove
10 by 14¹/₄
0246.823 Gilcrease
Dated: "1883" u.l.
Signed: "TM" u.l.
Inscribed: "Ravine near the Trojes Mine Mexico" u.l.
Provenance: TG
1916 ledger: 48

†675
THE TROJES SILVER MINE, NEAR MARAVATIO
Graphite on wove
10 by 14¹/₄
1346.1033 Gilcrease
Dated: "1883" l.l.
Signed: "TM" l.l.
Inscribed: "The Trojes silver Mine. Near Maravatio" l.l.; "19" l.l. in ink; miscellaneous notes
Provenance: Ruth K. Henschel, New York; 1964 Thomas Gilcrease Foundation, Tulsa, Okla.; 1970 The Thomas Gilcrease Institute of American History and Art, Tulsa, Okla.
1916 ledger: 62

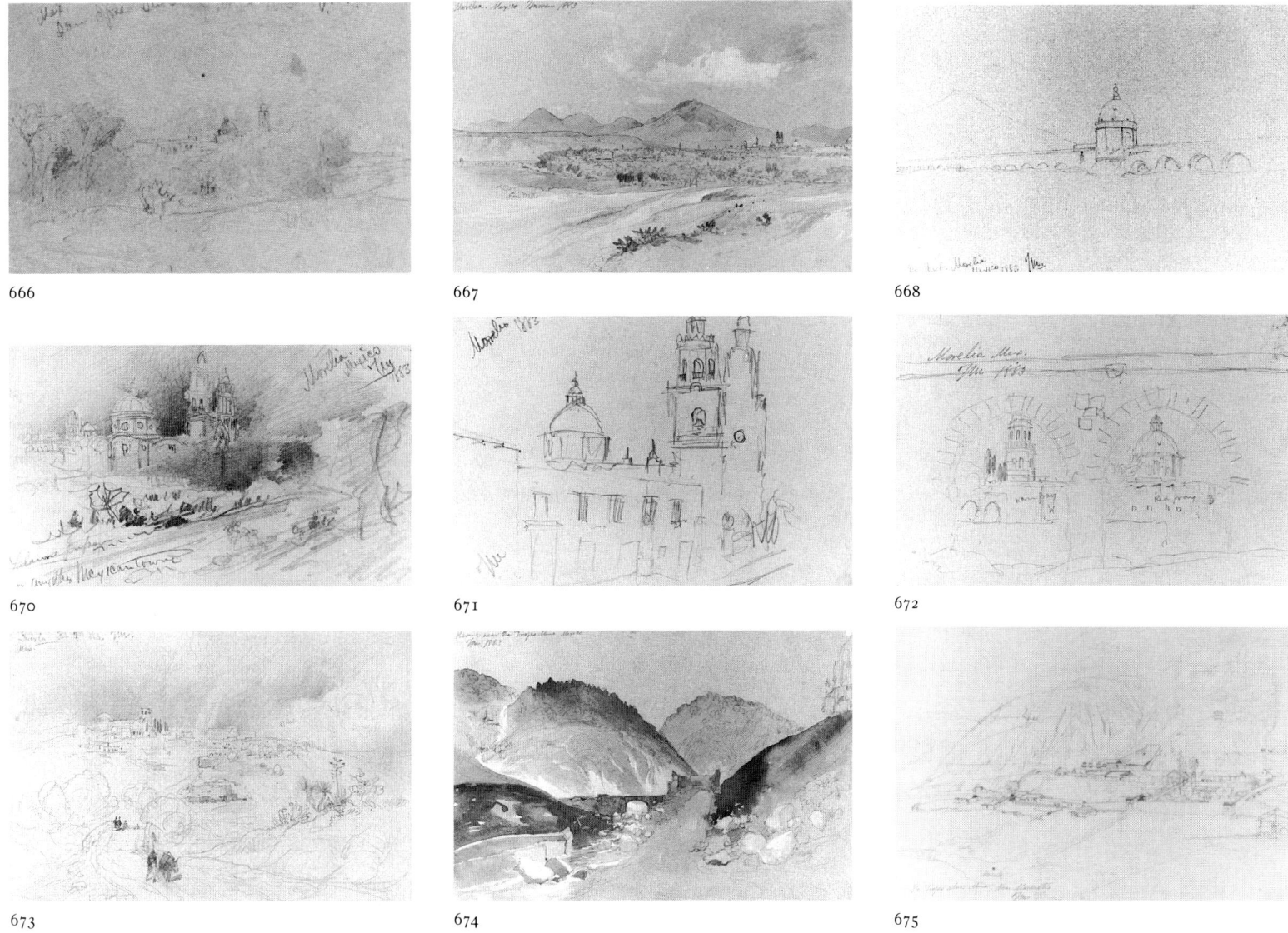

666

667

668

670

671

672

673

674

675

†676
THE TROJES MINE, MEXICO
Graphite on wove
10 by 14^1/$_4$
1346.830 Gilcrease
Dated: "1883" l.r.
Signed: "TM" l.r.
Inscribed: "The Trojes Mine Mexico" l.r.; miscellaneous notes
Provenance: TG
1916 ledger: 43

677
THE PEAK OF CULIACAN
Graphite on blue wove
10 by 14^1/$_4$
1346.802 Gilcrease
Dated: "1883" u.l.
Signed: "TM" u.l.
Inscribed: "The Peak of Juliacan" u.l.; miscellaneous notes
Provenance: TG
1916 ledger: 83

678
THE ALAMEDA, CELAYA, MEXICO
Graphite on wove
7 by 10
1346.825 Gilcrease
Dated: "1883" l.c.
Signed: "TM" l.c.
Inscribed: "The Alameda. Celaya Mexico" l.l."
and "Celaya" u.l.; miscellaneous notes
Provenance: TG
1916 ledger: 7

†679
FROM HOTEL WINDOW, CELAYA
Graphite on wove
10 by 14^1/$_4$
1346.778 Gilcrease
Dated: "Feb 25th 1883" u.r.
Signed: "TM" u.r.
Inscribed: "from Hotel Window Celaya" u.r.; miscellaneous notes
Provenance: TG
1916 ledger: 67

*680
CALDERON, MEXICO
Graphite, watercolor, and white gouache on wove
10 by 14^1/$_4$
0246.808 Gilcrease
Dated: "Feb 25th 1883" u.r.
Signed: "TM" u.r.
Inscribed: "Calderon Mex" u.r.; miscellaneous notes
Provenance: TG
1916 ledger: 51
Note: Sketch on verso

681
AQUEDUCT, NEAR SANTUARIO
Graphite on ruled wove
3646.144.3 Gilcrease
Inscribed: "Acquedu near Santuario" l.l.
Provenance: TG
Note: The sketch is included in Moran's brief diary of his Mexican journey.

682
DOLORES HIDALGO
Graphite on wove
9 by 13^7/$_8$
1346.801 Gilcrease
Dated: "Feb Tuesday Feb 27 1883" u.r.
Signed: "TM" u.r.
Inscribed: "Dolores Hidalgo" u.r.
Provenance: TG
1916 ledger: 71

*683
ON THE PLATEAU ABOVE DOLORES
Graphite, watercolor, and white gouache on blue wove
10 by 14^1/$_4$
0246.816 Gilcrease
Dated: "Feb 28th 1883" u.l.
Signed: "TM" u.l.
Inscribed: "on the plateau above Dolores" u.l.; miscellaneous notes
Provenance: TG
1916 ledger: 8

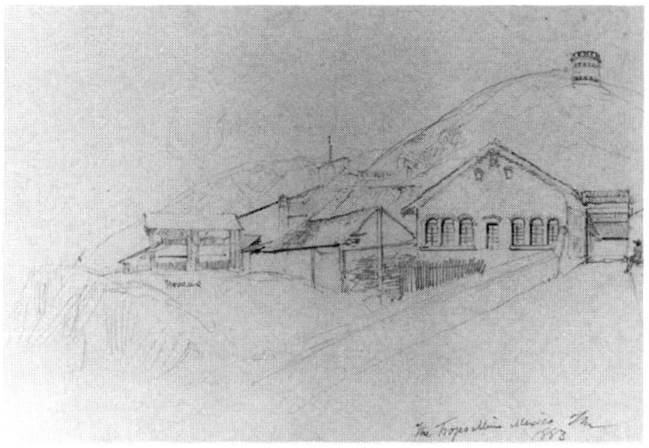

676

684
THE GATE OF CHIRIMOLLA
Graphite on wove
10 by 14^1/$_4$
1346.821 Gilcrease
Dated: "Feb 28th 1883" u.l.
Signed: "TMoran" u.l.
Inscribed: "The Gate of Chirimolla" u.l.; miscellaneous notes
Provenance: TG
1916 ledger: 65
Note: Sketch on verso

685
CONICAL GRANARIES, JARAL
Graphite on ruled wove
7 by 4^1/$_8$
3646.144.5 Gilcrease
Inscribed: "Conical Granaries" above image in text
Provenance: TG
Note: The sketch is included in Moran's brief diary of his Mexican journey.

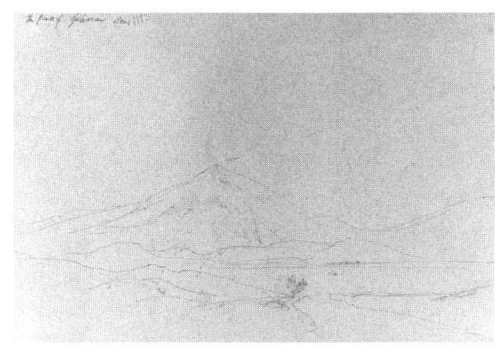

677

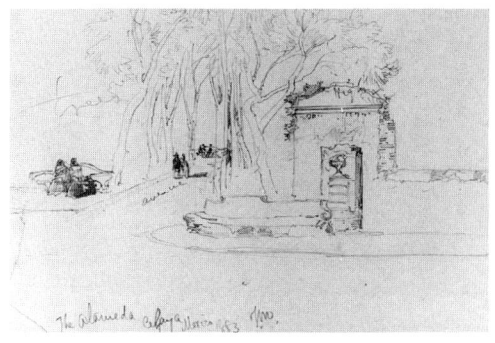

678

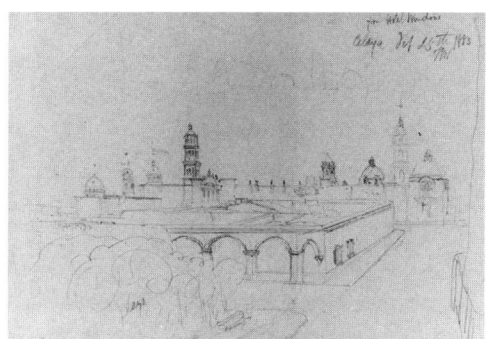

679

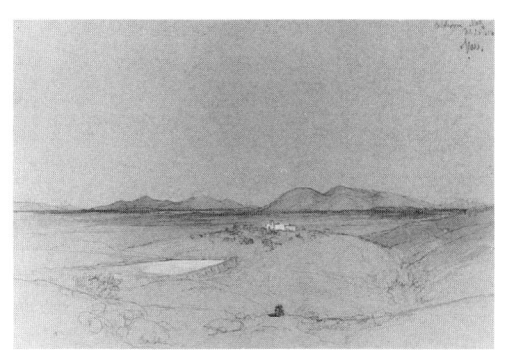

680

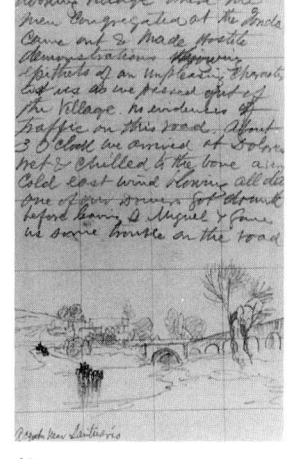

681

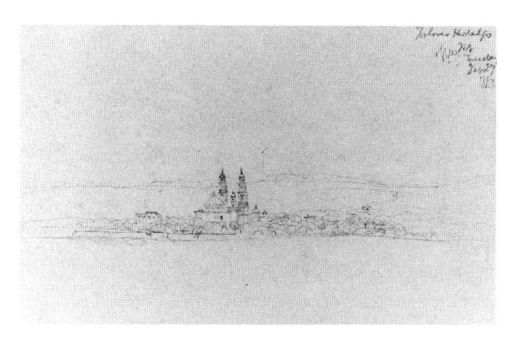

682

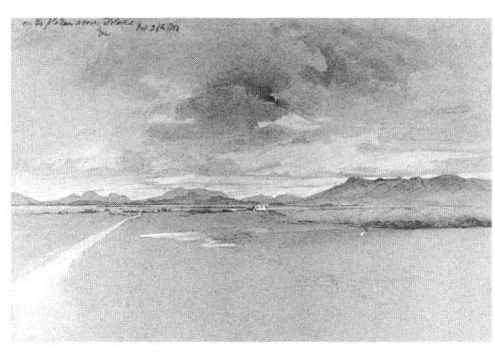

683

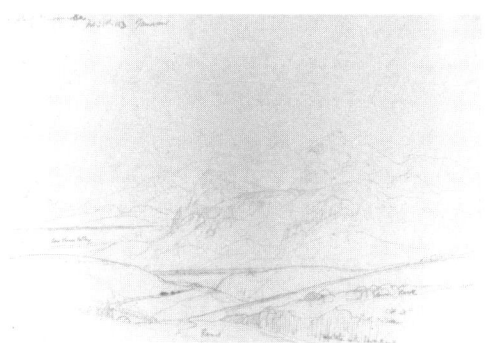

684

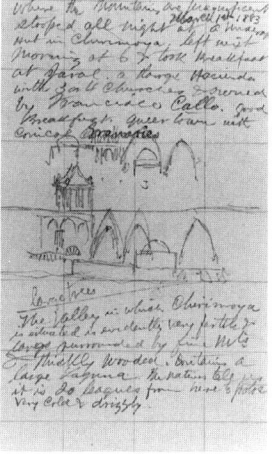

685

686
SLAG OF SILVER MINE, SAN
FRANCISCO, MEXICO
Graphite on ruled wove
4¹/₈ by 7
3646.144.5 Gilcrease
Signed: "TMoran" l.l.
Inscribed: "Slag of Silver Mine San Francisco
Mexico" upper edge
Provenance: TG
1916 ledger: 50
Note: The sketch is included in Moran's brief
diary of his Mexican journey.

687
NEAR SAN FRANCISCO
Graphite, watercolor, and white gouache on wove
10 by 13⁷/₈
1917–17–45 Cooper-Hewitt Museum
Dated: "March 1st 1883" u.r.; "1883" l.l. in ink
Signed: "TMoran" and colophon l.l in ink; "TM"
u.r.
Inscribed: "Near San Francisco" u.r.
Provenance: TM

688
EL FRAILE NEAR CATORCE
Graphite on newsprint
5⁷/₈ by 8³/₈
1346.795 Gilcrease
Dated: "March 7th 1883" u.c.
Signed: "TM" u.c.
Inscribed: "'El Fraile' near Catorce" u.l.
Provenance: TG
1916 ledger: 79

689
THE MOUNTAIN RANGE ON THE
WEST SIDE OF THE SAN LUIS VALLEY,
ABOVE SAN FRANCISCO
Graphite and watercolor on wove
9 by 13³/₄
Addison Gallery of American Art, Phillips
Academy, Andover, Mass.
Dated: "1883" l.r.
Signed: TM" l.r.
Inscribed: "The Mountain Range on the West
Side of the San Louis Valley above San Fran-
cisco" l.r.

Provenance: The artist; 1926 Ruth B. Moran,
East Hampton, New York; MacBeth Gallery,
New York

690
YUCCA GROVE BEYOND CEDRAL
Graphite on blue wove
6 by 8¹/₂
12 East Hampton Library
Dated: "Friday March 8th 1883" u.c.
Signed: "TM" u.c.
Inscribed: "Yucca Grove beyond Cedral" u.l.
Provenance: EH

*691
OJO DE AGUA, SALTILLO
Graphite, watercolor, and white gouache on blue
wove
10 by 14¹/₄
0246.818 Gilcrease
Dated: "March 8th 1883" u.l.
Signed: "TMoran" u.l.
Inscribed: "Ojo De Agua Saltillo" u.l.; miscella-
neous notes
Provenance: TG
1916 ledger: 11

†692
THE ARROYO AT SALTILLO
Graphite on blue wove
10 by 14¹/₄
1346.814 Gilcrease
Dated: "March 11th 1883" u.l.
Signed: "TM" u.l.
Inscribed: "The Arroyo at Saltillo" u.l.; miscel-
laneous notes
Provenance: TG
1916 ledger: 81

†693
SALTILLO, MEXICO
Graphite on blue wove
10 by 14¹/₄
1346.829 Gilcrease
Dated: "1883" u.l.
Signed: "TMoran" u.l.
Inscribed: "Saltillo Mexico" and "Arroyo fore-
ground" u.l.
Provenance: TG
1916 ledger: 47

†694
SALTILLO
Graphite on blue wove
10 by 14¹/₄
1346.823 Gilcrease
Dated: "Sunday March 11th 1883" u.l.
Signed: "TM" u.l.
Inscribed: "Saltillo" and "Fortin De los Ameri-
canos X Gen Taylor" u.l.; color notes
Provenance: TG
1916 ledger: 73

695
FORTIN DE LOS AMERICANOS,
SALTILLO
Graphite on wove
10 by 14¹/₄
1346.809 Gilcrease
Dated: "1883" u.c.
Signed: "TM" twice u.c.
Inscribed: "Fortin De los Americanos. Saltillo"
u.l.; "Yellow gray with spots of growth" l.r.
Provenance: TG
1916 ledger: 66

696
SANTA CATARINA, NEAR MONTERREY
Graphite on blue laid
8⁵/₈ by 11⁵/₈
1346.800 Gilcrease
Dated: "March 11th 1883" u.c.
Signed: "TMoran" u.c.
Inscribed: "Santa Catherina near Monterey" u.l.;
miscellaneous notes
Provenance: TG
1916 ledger: 78

697
SANTA CATARINA, NEAR MONTERREY
[descriptive]
Graphite on brown wove
12 by 17
1346.678 Gilcrease
Provenance: TG

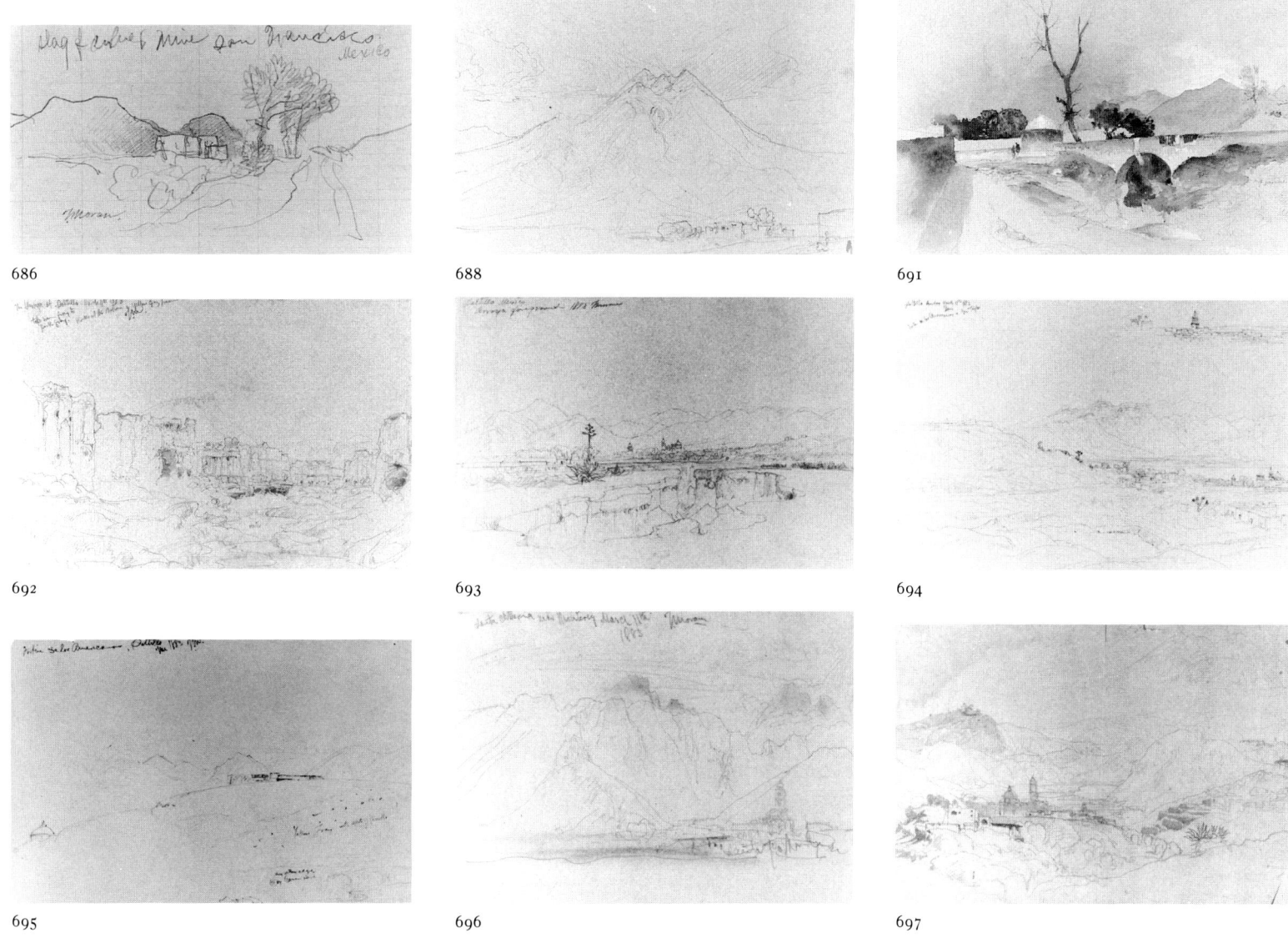

686

688

691

692

693

694

695

696

697

698
NEAR MONTERREY
Graphite on blue laid
8⁵/₈ by 11⁵/₈
1346.668 Gilcrease
Dated: "March 13th" u.l.
Signed: "TM" u.c.
Inscribed: "Near Monterey" u.l.; miscellaneous
notes
Provenance: TG
1916 ledger: 80

*699
MONTERREY, FROM THE HOTEL ROOF
Graphite, watercolor, and white gouache on blue
wove
10 by 14¹/₂
0246.819 Gilcrease
Dated: "1883" l.l.
Signed: "TMoran" l.l.; "TM" u.l.
Inscribed: "Monterey from the Hotel Roof" u.l.;
miscellaneous notes
Provenance: TG
1916 ledger: 17

700
MONTERREY
Graphite on blue wove
10 by 4⁷/₈
1347.858 Gilcrease
Dated: "1904" l.l.
Signed: "TM" l.r.
Inscribed: "Monterey" l.c.; miscellaneous notes
Provenance: TG
Note: This sketch relates to the work of 1883.
The date was added later.

701
AMAGANSETT
Graphite and white gouache on green wove
4 by 3¹/₂
33 East Hampton Library
Dated: "July 1883" l.r.
Signed: "TM" l.r.
Inscribed: "Amagansett" l.c.
Provenance: EH

702
AMAGANSETT
Graphite and white gouache on green wove
2¹/₈ by 3¹/₂

66 East Hampton Library
Dated: "1883" l.r.
Signed: Colophon l.l.
Inscribed: "Amagansett" l.r.
Provenance: EH

703
BETWEEN NAPEAGUE BEACH AND
AMAGANSETT
Graphite on wove
11 by 17¹/₈
1326.815 Gilcrease
Dated: "August 1883" l.l.
Signed: "TMoran" l.l.
Inscribed: "Between Napeague Beach & Ama-
gansett" l.l.
Provenance: TG
1916 ledger: 240

*704
GARDINER BAY
Graphite and white gouache on blue wove
4 by 10
0226.936 Gilcrease
Dated: "Aug 31st 83" u.l.
Signed: "TM" u.l.; "TMoran" l.r.
Inscribed: "Gardiner Bay" u.l.
1916 ledger: 327
Provenance: W. F. Davidson at M. Knoedler &
Co., New York; 1964 Thomas Gilcrease Founda-
tion, Tulsa, Okla.; 1969 The Thomas Gilcrease
Institute of American History and Art, Tulsa,
Okla.
Note: Moran began to write "Se" in the date,
then changed it to "Aug."

705
FRESH POND, GARDINER BAY
Graphite and white gouache on blue wove
7 by 14¹/₄
9 East Hampton Library
Dated: "Aug 31st 1883" l.c.
Signed: "TM" l.c.
Inscribed: "Fresh Pond. Gardiners Bay" l.l.
Provenance: EH

706
GARDINER BAY [descriptive]
Graphite and white gouache on blue wove
7 by 14¹/₄
East Hampton Library

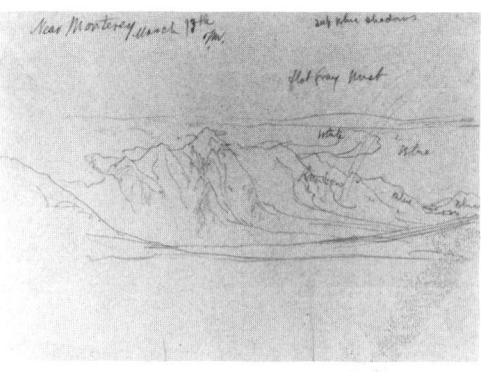

698

Dated: "1885" l.l.
Signed: "TMoran" l.l.
Provenance: EH
Note: This sketch is similar stylistically to the
work of 1883. The date was added later.

707
FRESH POND
Graphite and white gouache on blue wove
9⁷/₈ by 13
0226.943 Gilcrease
Dated: "Aug 31st–83" u.l.
Signed: "TMoran" l.l.
Inscribed: "Fresh Pond" u.l.
Provenance: TG

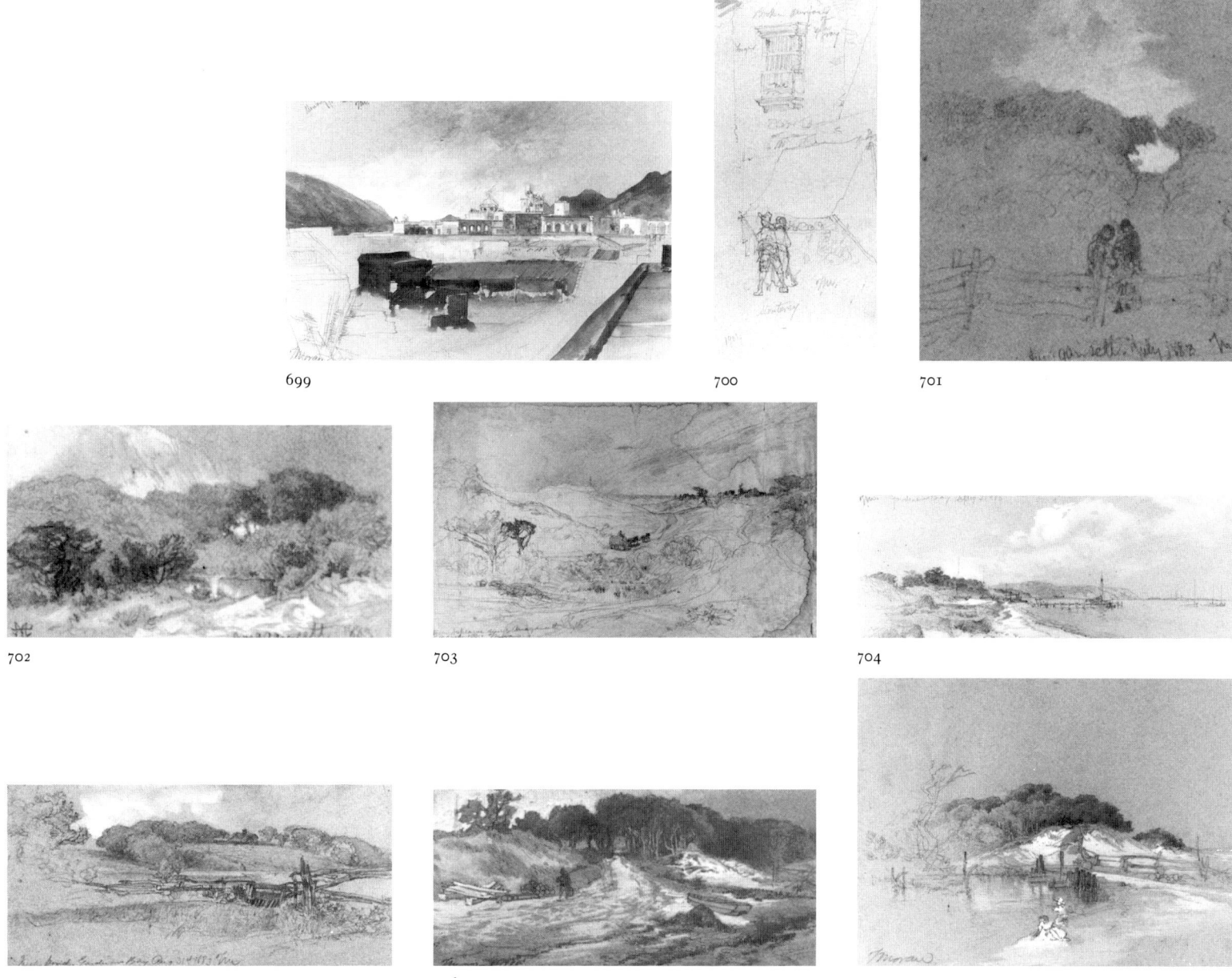

699

700

701

702

703

704

705

706

707

708
GARDINER BAY
Graphite, watercolor, and white gouache on blue
wove
7 by 14¹/₄
S-66 East Hampton Library
Signed: "TM" l.r.
Inscribed: "Gardiners Bay" l.r.
Provenance: EH
1916 ledger: 328

709
NEAR NAPEAGUE BEACH
Graphite and white gouache on wove
10¹/₈ by 14¹/₄
1326.794 a and b Gilcrease
Dated: "1883" u.l.
Signed: "TM" u.l.
Inscribed: "Near Napeague Beach" u.l.
Provenance: TG
1916 ledger: 342
Note: Sketch on verso

710
EAST HAMPTON
Graphite, watercolor, and white gouache on
wove
3 by 9³/₄
S-69 East Hampton Library
Dated: "Sep 26th 1883" u.l.
Signed: "TM" u.l.
Inscribed: "East Hampton" u.l.
Provenance: EH

711
AT FOOT OF FITHIAN'S LOT, EAST
HAMPTON
Graphite and white gouache on wove
10 by 7³/₄
11 East Hampton Library
Dated: "Sep 26th 1883" l.l. and u.l.
Signed: "TM" l.l.; "TMoran" u.l.
Inscribed: "at foot of Fithians lot. Easthamp-
ton" l.l.; "East Hamp" u.l.
Provenance: EH
1916 ledger: 196

712
EAST HAMPTON
Graphite on wove
5¹/₄ by 12

16 East Hampton Library
Dated: "Sep 27th 1883" u.l.
Signed: "TM" u.l.
Inscribed: "East Hamp." u.l.
Provenance: EH
1916 ledger: 319

713
EAST HAMPTON
Graphite on wove
10 by 13¹/₂
1326.828 Gilcrease
Dated: "Sep 1883" l.r.
Signed: "TM" l.r.
Inscribed: "Easthampton" l.r.
Provenance: TG
1916 ledger: 187

714
EAST HAMPTON [descriptive]
Graphite on wove
10 by 14¹/₄
1326.635 Gilcrease
Signed: "TM" l.r.
Provenance: TG
1916 ledger: 323

715
FRESH PONDS, EAST HAMPTON
Graphite on blue wove
9³/₈ by 12
1326.681 Gilcrease
Signed: "TM" l.l.
Inscribed: "Fresh Ponds. EH." l.l.
Provenance: TG
1916 ledger: 218

716
EAST HAMPTON, LONG ISLAND
[ledger title]
Graphite on green wove
10 by 13⁷/₈
1326.562 Gilcrease
Provenance: TG
1916 ledger: 404

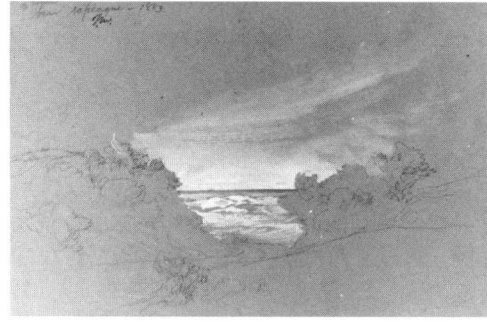

708

709

717
MONTAUK LIGHT
Graphite, watercolor, and white gouache on gray
wove
5¹/₂ by 10
S-76 East Hampton Library
Signed: "TMoran" l.l.
Inscribed: "Montauk Light" l.l.
Provenance: EH
1916 ledger: 124

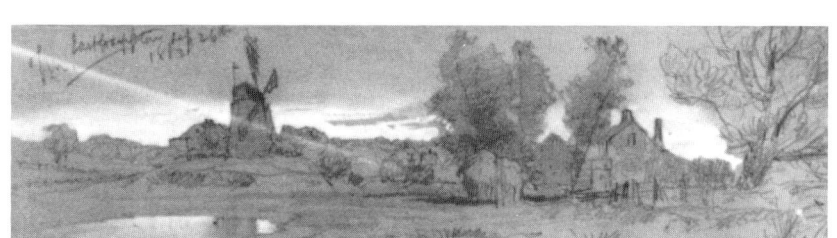

710

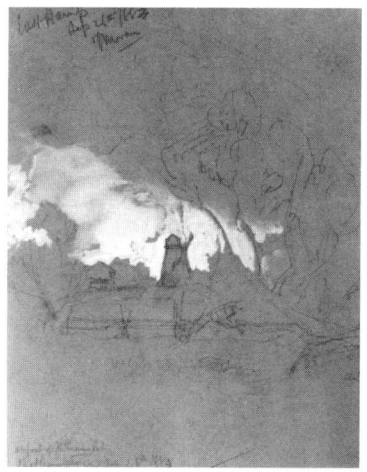

711

712

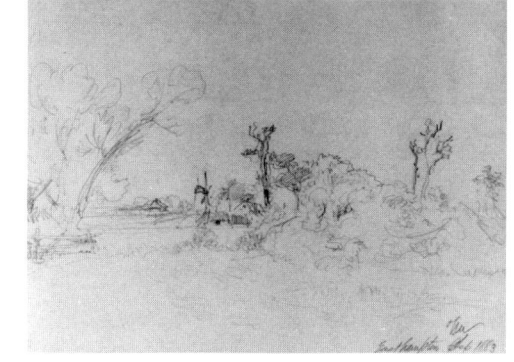

713

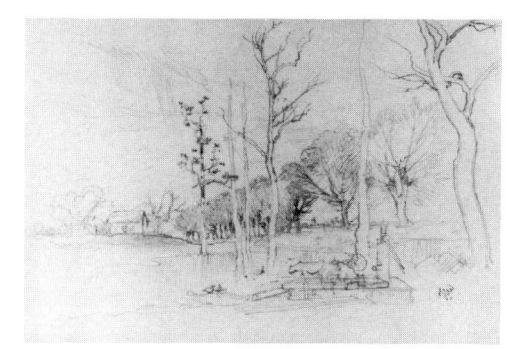

714

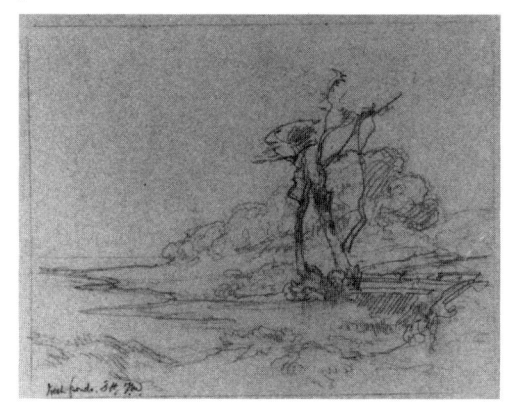

715

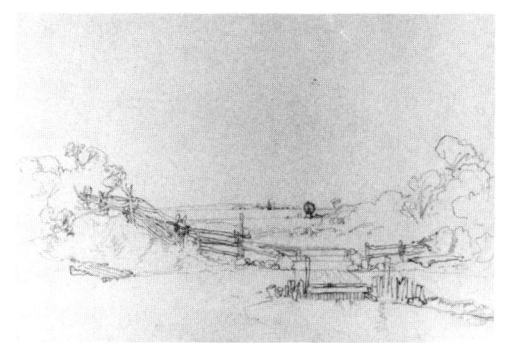

716

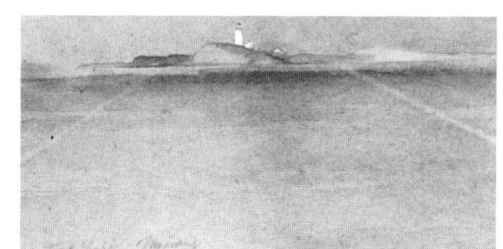

717

718
WINDMILL, EAST HAMPTON
[descriptive]
Graphite on wove
5 by 7
S-73 East Hampton Library
Provenance: EH

719
JEFFERSON MARKET
POLICE COURT
Graphite on wove
9¹/8 by 5³/4
1326.679 Gilcrease
Signed: "TM" u.r.
Inscribed: "Jefferson Market Police Court" u.r.
Provenance: TG
1916 ledger: 334
Note: Sketch on verso

720
EAST HAMPTON
Graphite on wove
3³/4 by 12¹/4
17 East Hampton Library
Dated: "1884" l.r.
Signed: "TM" l.r.
Inscribed: "E.H." l.r.
Provenance: EH
1916 ledger: 318

721
HOOK POND
Graphite on blue wove
5 by 9¹/2
111 East Hampton Library
Dated: "1884" l.r.
Signed: "TM" l.r.
Inscribed: "Hook Pond" l.r.
Provenance: EH
1916 ledger: 201

722
GEORGICA
Graphite on watermarked gray laid
10 by 7
1326.980 Gilcrease
Dated: "Oct 12 85" u.r.
Signed: "TM" u.r.
Inscribed: "Georgica" u.r.
Provenance: TG
1916 ledger: 305

723
SWAMP, GEORGICA
Graphite on watermarked gray laid
7 by 10
1326.979 Gilcrease
Dated: "Oct 12/85" u.r.
Inscribed: "Swamp. Georgica" u.r.; miscella-
neous notes
Provenance: TG
1916 ledger: 329

724
SWAMP, GEORGICA
Graphite on watermarked gray laid
7 by 10
1326.978 Gilcrease
Dated: "Oct 12 85" u.r.
Signed: "TM" u.r.
Inscribed: "Swamp Georgica" u.r.; miscellane-
ous notes
Provenance: TG
1916 ledger: 188

725
MONTAUK
Graphite on watermarked gray laid
7 by 10
1326.694 Gilcrease
Signed: "TM" l.r.
Inscribed: "Montauk" l.r.
Provenance: TG
1916 ledger: 315

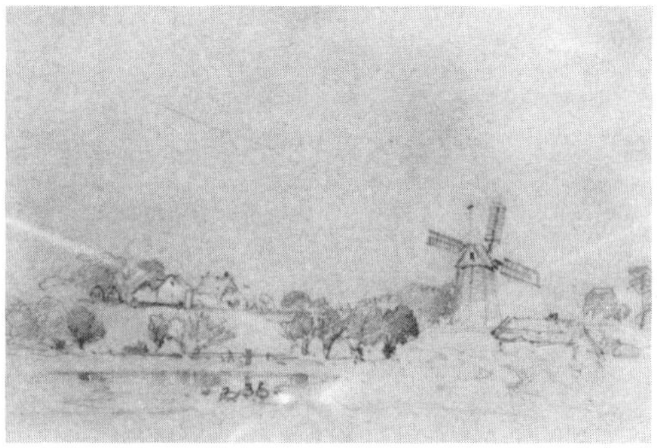

718

726
GEORGICA POND
Graphite on gray wove
7 by 10
1326.697 Gilcrease
Signed: "TM" l.l.
Inscribed: "Georgica Pond" l.l.
Provenance: TG
1916 ledger: 173

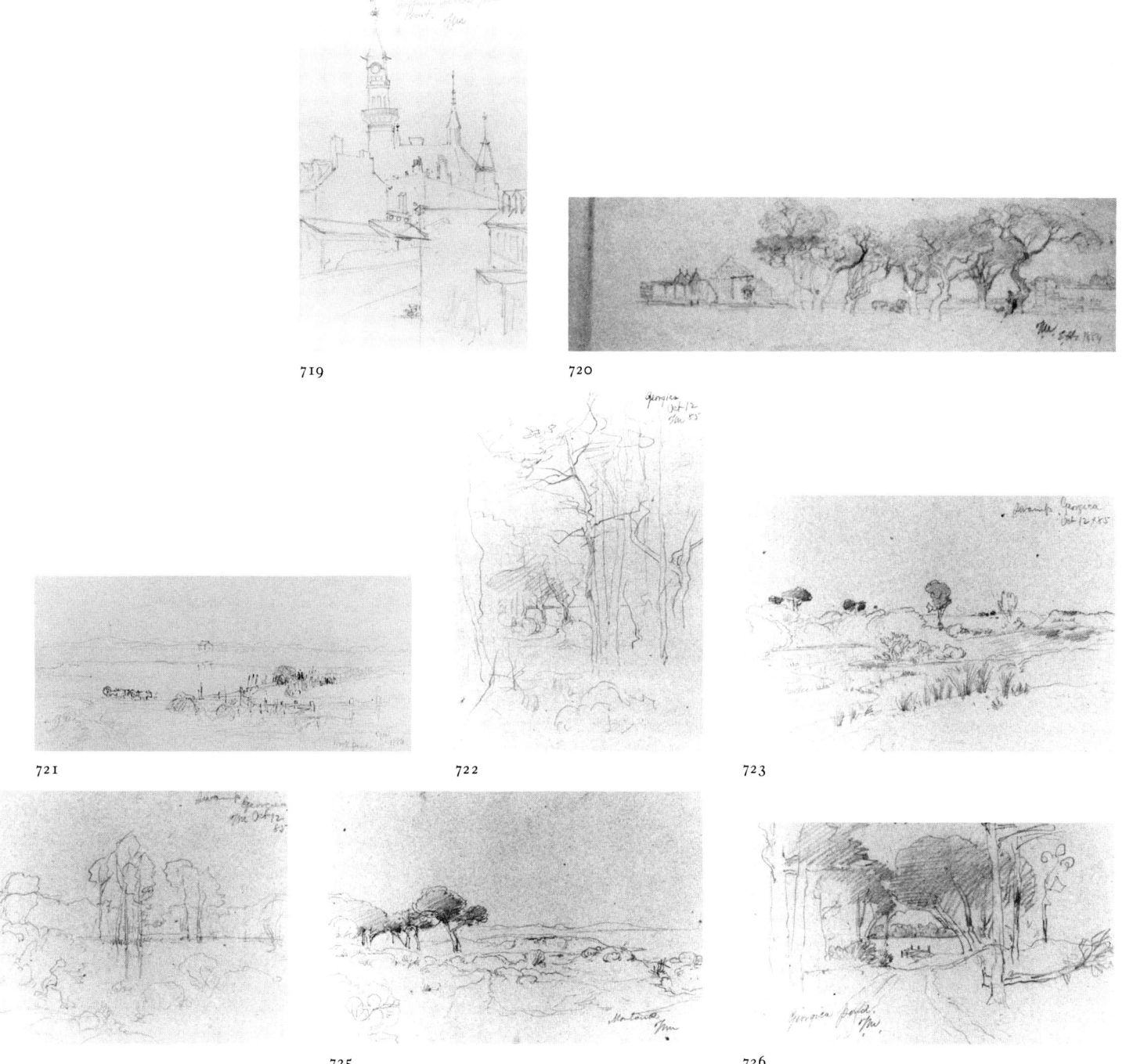

719

720

721

722

723

724

725

726

727
VENICE
Graphite and red conté crayon on wove
5¹/₂ by 9¹/₈
1876.17.1 Gilcrease
Dated: "May 6th 1886" u.c.
Signed: "Thomas Moran" u.c.
Inscribed: "Venice" u.c.
Provenance: TG
Note: Sketch on verso

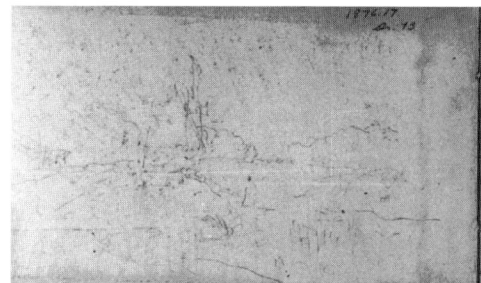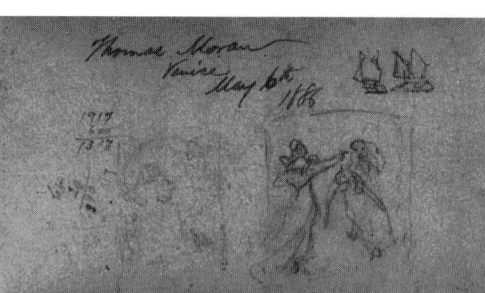

727

728
CEMETERY CHURCH
Graphite on wove
5¹/₂ by 9¹/₈
1876.17.2 Gilcrease
Inscribed: "Cemetery Church" u.r.; miscellane-
ous notes
Provenance: TG
Note: Sketch on verso

729
SALUTE
Graphite on wove
5¹/₂ by 9¹/₈
1876.17.3 Gilcrease
Inscribed: "Salute" u.c.; miscellaneous notes
Provenance: TG
Note: Sketch on verso

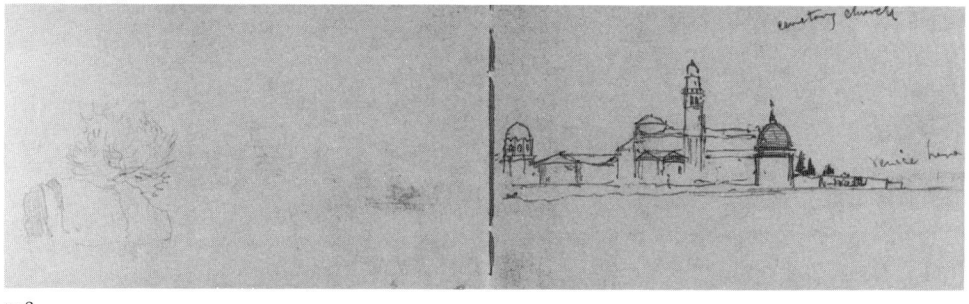

728

†730
CUSTOMS HOUSE
Graphite on wove
5¹/₂ by 9¹/₈
1876.17.4 Gilcrease
Signed: "TM" l.l.
Inscribed: "Custom House" u.c.; miscellaneous
notes
Provenance: TG
1916 ledger: 246

731
GREEN WINDOW SHUTTERS
Graphite on wove
9¹/₈ by 5¹/₂
1876.17.5 Gilcrease
Inscribed: "Green Window Shutters" u.r.; mis-
cellaneous notes
Provenance: TG
Note: Sketch of frame on verso

732
CAMPANILE
Graphite on wove
5¹/₂ by 9¹/₈
1876.17.6 Gilcrease
Inscribed: "Campanile" u.r.; "San Georgio" u.l.;
"Salut" c.
Provenance: TG

†733
ST. MICHAEL IN CAMPO SANTO
Graphite on wove
5¹/₂ by 9¹/₈
1876.17.7 Gilcrease
Dated: "May 7th 1886" u.r.

Inscribed: "St. Michael in Campo Santo" u.c.;
miscellaneous notes
Provenance: TG
1916 ledger: 248
Note: Sketch on verso

734
TILE ROOF
Graphite on wove
5¹/₂ by 9¹/₈
1876.17.8 Gilcrease
Signed: "TM" l.l.
Inscribed: "tile Roof" u.r.
Provenance: TG

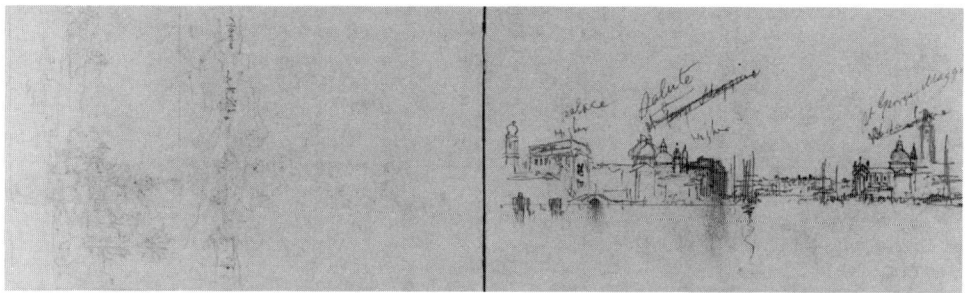

729

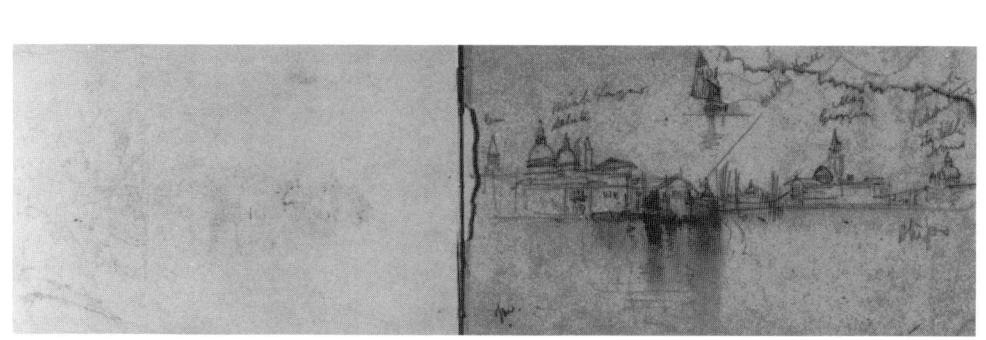

730

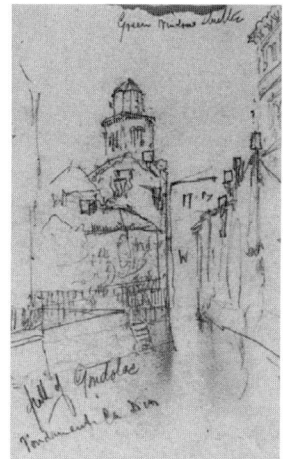

731

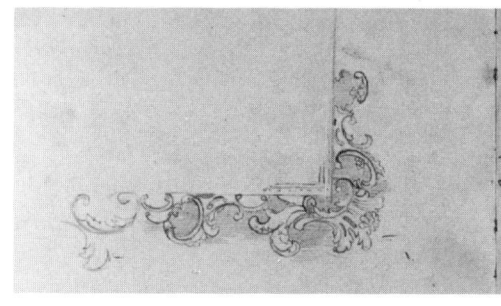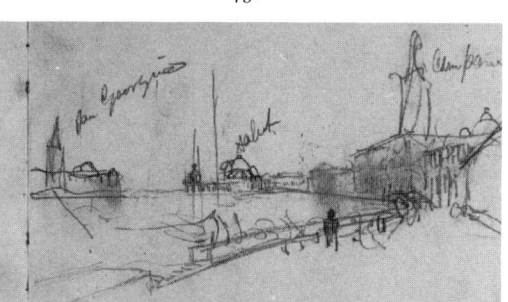

732

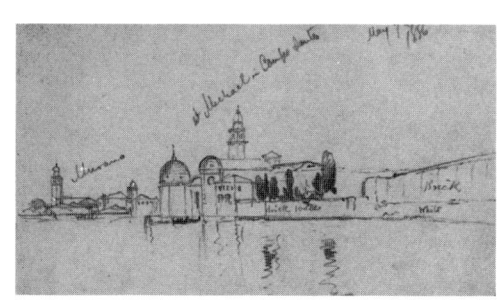

733

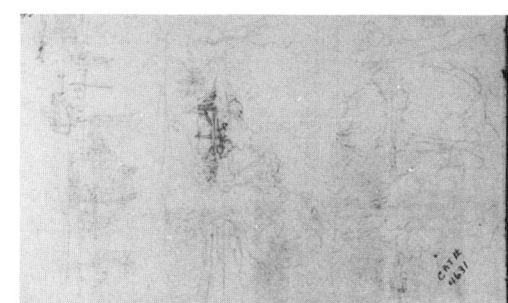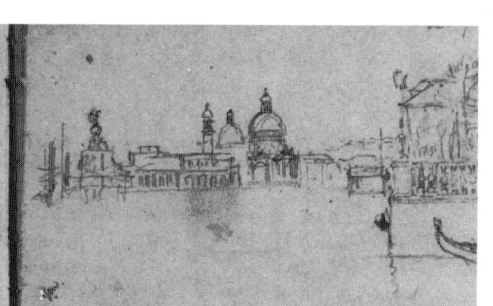

734

735
CUSTOMS HOUSE
Graphite on wove
5¹/₂ by 9¹/₈
1876.17.9 Gilcrease
Inscribed: "Customs House" u.r.
Provenance: TG

736
SAN GIORGIO MAGGIORE
Graphite on wove
5¹/₂ by 9¹/₈
1876.17.10 Gilcrease
Inscribed: "St. George Maggiore from same side
as The Salute" u.r.
Provenance: TG
Note: Sketch on verso

†737
THE TUTELLA
Graphite on wove
5¹/₂ by 9⁷/₈
1876.17.11 Gilcrease
Inscribed: "The Tutella from same side as Sa-
lute" u.c.
Provenance: TG

738
ENTRANCE TO GRAND CANAL,
VENICE
Graphite on wove
5¹/₂ by 9¹/₈
1876.17.12 Gilcrease
Dated: "1886" u.r.
Inscribed: "Entrance to Grand Canal. Venice"
upper edge
Provenance: TG
Note: Sketch of woman on verso

739
VENICE [descriptive]
Graphite on wove
5¹/₂ by 9¹/₈
1876.17.13 Gilcrease
Provenance: TG

740
VENICE [descriptive]
Graphite on wove
5¹/₂ by 9¹/₈
1876.17.14 Gilcrease
Provenance: TG

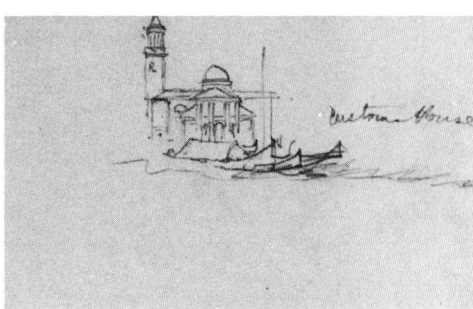

735

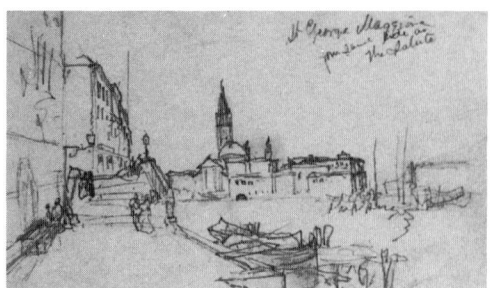

736

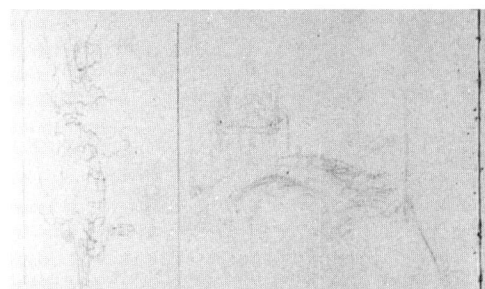

737

741
CASTLE [descriptive]
Graphite on wove
5¹/₂ by 9¹/₈
1876.17.15 Gilcrease
Provenance: TG

742
VENICE [ledger title]
Graphite on ruled wove
6³/₄ by 8¹/₄
1376.591 Gilcrease
Signed: "TM" l.l.
Inscribed: "Back at 2 o clock TMoran" on verso
Provenance: TG
1916 ledger: 25

743
VENICE
Graphite on laid
8 by 9³/₄
1376.582 Gilcrease
Signed: "TMoran" l.l.
Inscribed: "Venice" l.l.

Provenance: TG
1916 ledger: 23

744
VENICE [descriptive]
Graphite on wove
7⁷/₈ by 12¹/₂
1376.583 Gilcrease
Signed: "TM" l.l.
Provenance: TG
1916 ledger: 304

†745
VENICE [descriptive]
Graphite on wove
4¹/₂ by 7³/₄
1376.580 Gilcrease
Signed: "TMoran" l.l.
Provenance: TG
1916 ledger: 24
Note: This sketch anticipates the etching *The
Gate of Venice* (Morand and Friese, *Prints of
Thomas Moran*, p. 158).

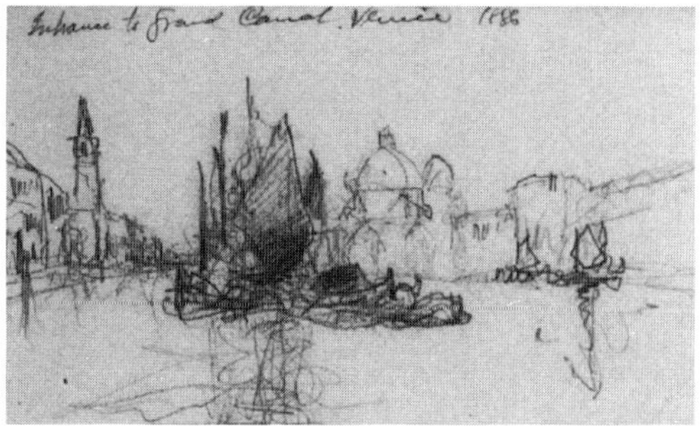

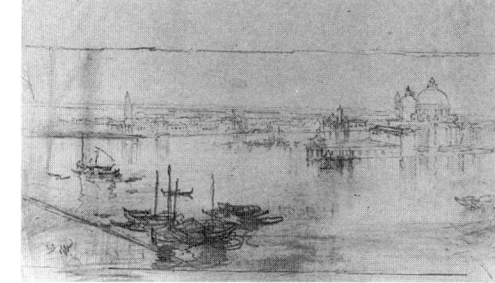

738

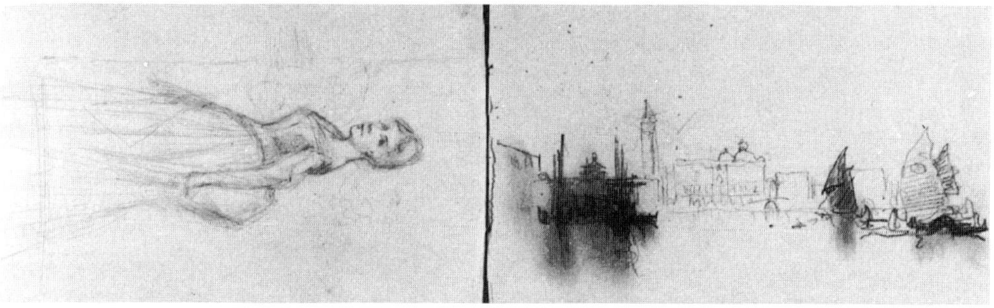

739

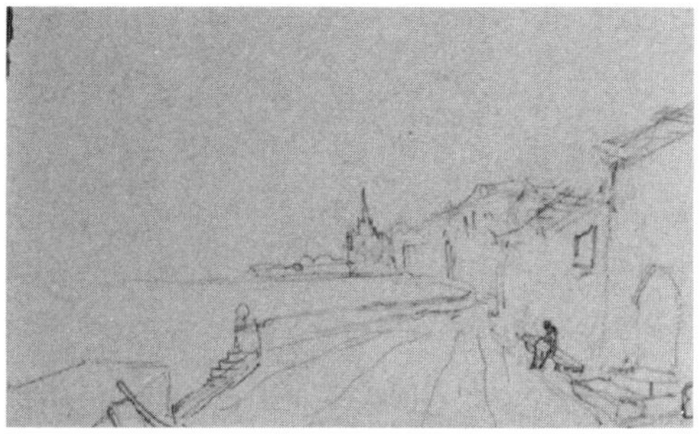

740

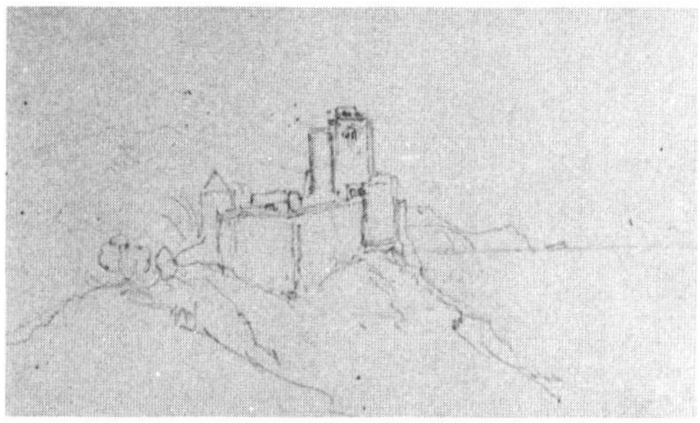

741

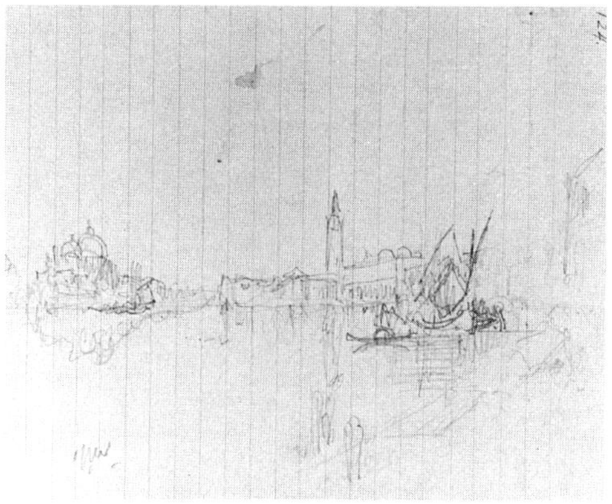

742

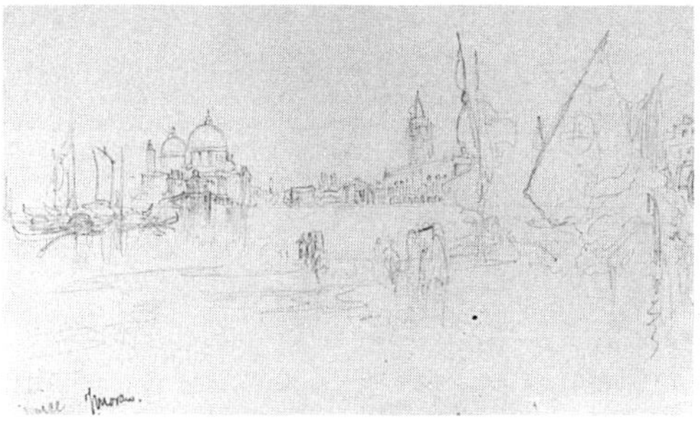

743

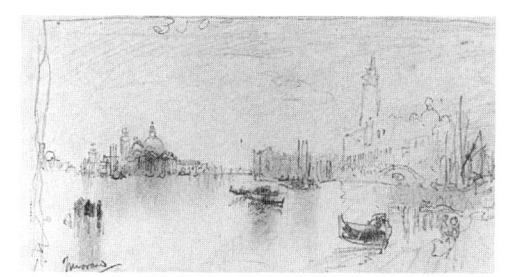

744

745

746
CEMETERY WALL, VENICE
Graphite on wove
3$^{1}/_{8}$ by 5$^{1}/_{4}$
1376.585 Gilcrease
Signed: "TM" l.l.
Inscribed: "Cemetery Wall. Venice" u.l.
Provenance: TG

747
VENICE [descriptive]
Graphite on wove
8 by 5
21 East Hampton Library
Signed: "TM" l.l.
Provenance: EH
1916 ledger: 256

748
VENICE [descriptive]
Graphite on wove
3$^{1}/_{4}$ by 5
9 East Hampton Library
Provenance: EH

749
CAMPO SANTO, VENICE
Graphite on wove
2$^{3}/_{8}$ by 4$^{1}/_{4}$
8 East Hampton Library
Signed: "TM" l.r.
Inscribed: "Campo Santo Venice" l.r.
Provenance: EH

750
LONG ISLAND [descriptive]
Graphite on wove
5$^{1}/_{2}$ by 9$^{1}/_{8}$
1826.17.16 Gilcrease
Inscribed with miscellaneous notes
Provenance: TG

751
LEATHERWOOD
Graphite on wove
5$^{1}/_{2}$ by 9$^{1}/_{8}$
1826.17.17 Gilcrease
Inscribed: "Leatherwood" u.r.
Provenance: TG

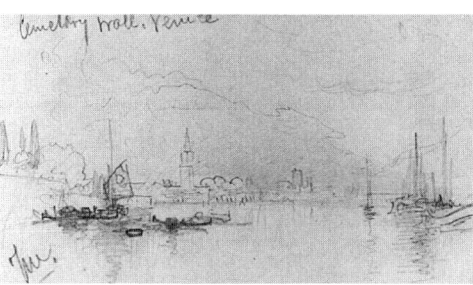

746

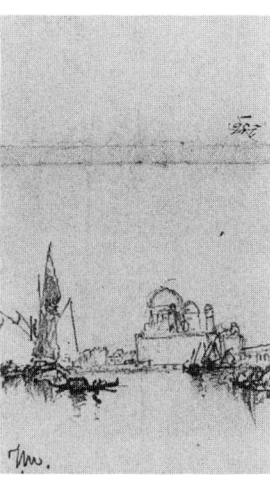

747

752
LONG ISLAND [descriptive]
Graphite on wove
5$^{1}/_{2}$ by 18$^{1}/_{4}$
1826.17.18 Gilcrease
Inscribed with miscellaneous notes
Provenance: TG
Note: Sketch and inscription on verso: "Linden"

753
THREE MILE HARBOR
Graphite on wove
5$^{1}/_{2}$ by 9$^{1}/_{8}$
1826.17.19 Gilcrease
Dated: "Sep 4th 1888" u.l.
Inscribed: "3 Mile Harbor" u.l.
Provenance: TG

754
LONG ISLAND [descriptive]
Graphite on wove
5$^{1}/_{2}$ by 9$^{1}/_{8}$
1826.17.20 Gilcrease
Provenance: TG

755
TABLE LEGS [descriptive]
Graphite on wove
5$^{1}/_{2}$ by 9$^{1}/_{8}$
1826.17.21 Gilcrease
Provenance: TG

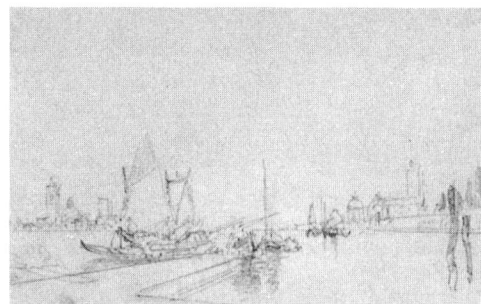

748

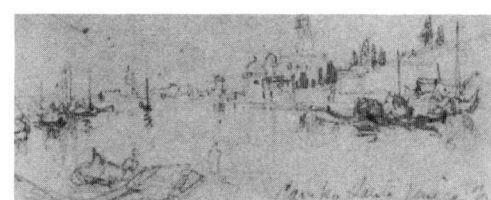

749

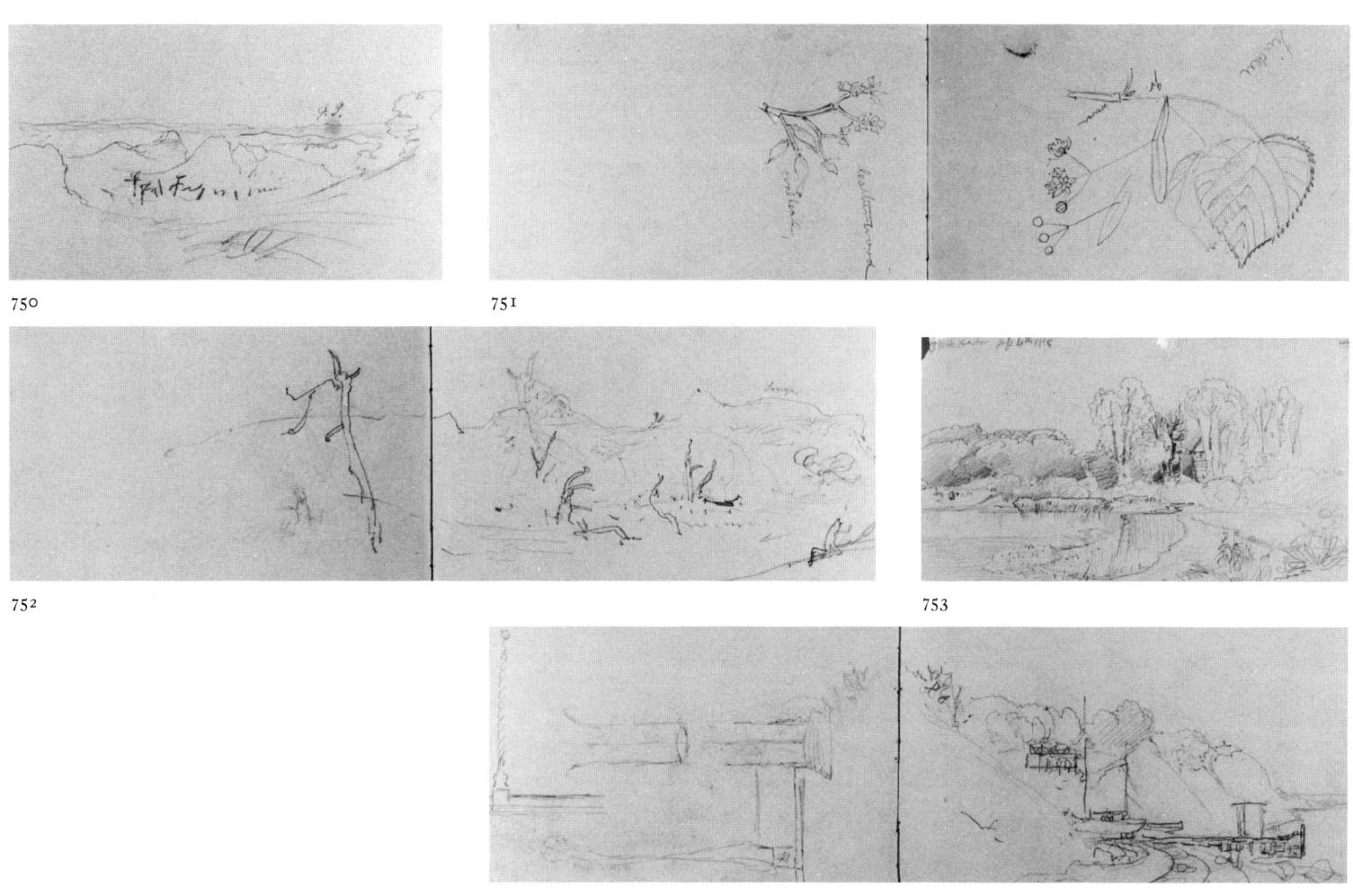

750

751

752

753

754, 755

756
MISERICORDIA
Graphite on wove
5 1/2 by 9 1/8
1826.17.22 Gilcrease
Inscribed: "Misericordia" u.c.; miscellaneous notes
Provenance: TG
Note: Sketch on verso

757
LONG ISLAND [descriptive]
Graphite on wove
5 1/2 by 9 1/8
1826.17.23 Gilcrease
Provenance: TG
Note: Sketch on verso

758
EAST HAMPTON BEACH
Graphite on wove
19 by 25
1326.977 Gilcrease
Dated: "Aug 1886" l.r.
Signed: "TM" l.r.
Inscribed: "Easthampton Beach" l.r.; color notes
Provenance: TG
1916 ledger: 212
Note: Sketch on verso

†759
ICEBERG
Graphite on wove
4 1/2 by 7
1396.1236 Gilcrease
Dated: "April 28 1890" u.l.
Signed: "TM" u.c.
Inscribed: "Iceberg" u.l.; "Lat. 44.59 Lon. 38.06" in a box u.r.; "1" u.r.; miscellaneous notes
Provenance: TG
1916 ledger: 270

760
ICEBERGS IN THE MIDDLE ATLANTIC
Graphite on wove
4 1/2 by 7
1396.1237 Gilcrease
Dated: "April 28 1890" u.l.
Signed: "TM" u.r.

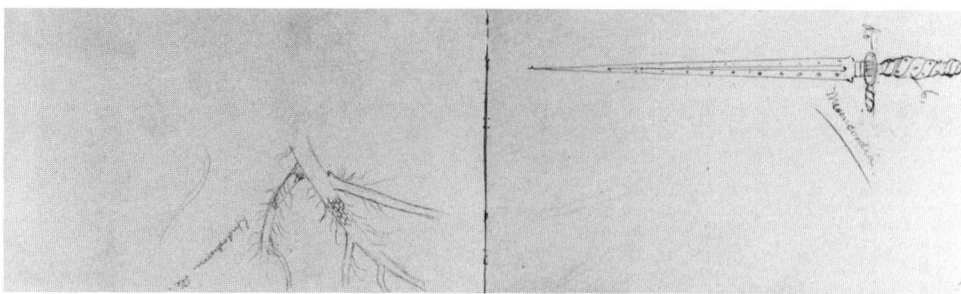

756

Inscribed: "Icebergs in the middle Atlantic" u.c. and "2" u.r.
Provenance: TG
1916 ledger: 393

†761
TOWER OF SPRAY
Graphite on wove
4 1/2 by 7
1396.1239 Gilcrease
Dated: "April 28th 1890" u.l.
Signed: "TM" u.l.
Inscribed: "Tower of Spray" u.c.; "water pouring over the sides of berg" and "polished dome" c.; "Deep Blue water with great rollers capped with foam" l.r.; "3" u.r.
Provenance: TG
1916 ledger: 388

†762
ICEBERG
Graphite on wove
4 1/2 by 7
1396.1240 Gilcrease
Dated: "April 28–1890" u.l.
Signed: "TM" u.c.
Inscribed: "Iceberg" l.l.; "spray shot out from here," "polished dome," "Spray 300 feet," and "4" u.r.
Provenance: TG
1916 ledger: 186

763
BERG TO THE NORTH OF US
Graphite on wove
4 1/2 by 7
1396.1238 Gilcrease
Dated: "April 28 1890 Monday" u.l.
Signed: "TM" u.r.
Inscribed: "Berg to the north of us" u.c.; "Green caverns & shadows" and "22" u.r.
Provenance: TG
1916 ledger: 396

764
BERG TO THE NORTH AFTER PASSING
Graphite on wove
4 1/2 by 7
1396.1241 Gilcrease
Dated: "April 28th 1890" u.l.
Signed: "TM" u.r.
Inscribed: "Berg to the north after Passing" u.edge; "5" u.r.; "Halt in shadow. Shadow pale green gray. Cave deep green Blue" across upper edge
Provenance: TG
1916 ledger: 390

765
RAINBOW [descriptive]
Graphite on wove
4 1/2 by 7
1396.881 Gilcrease
Signed: "TM" l.l.
Inscribed: "6" u.r.
Provenance: TG
1916 ledger: 382

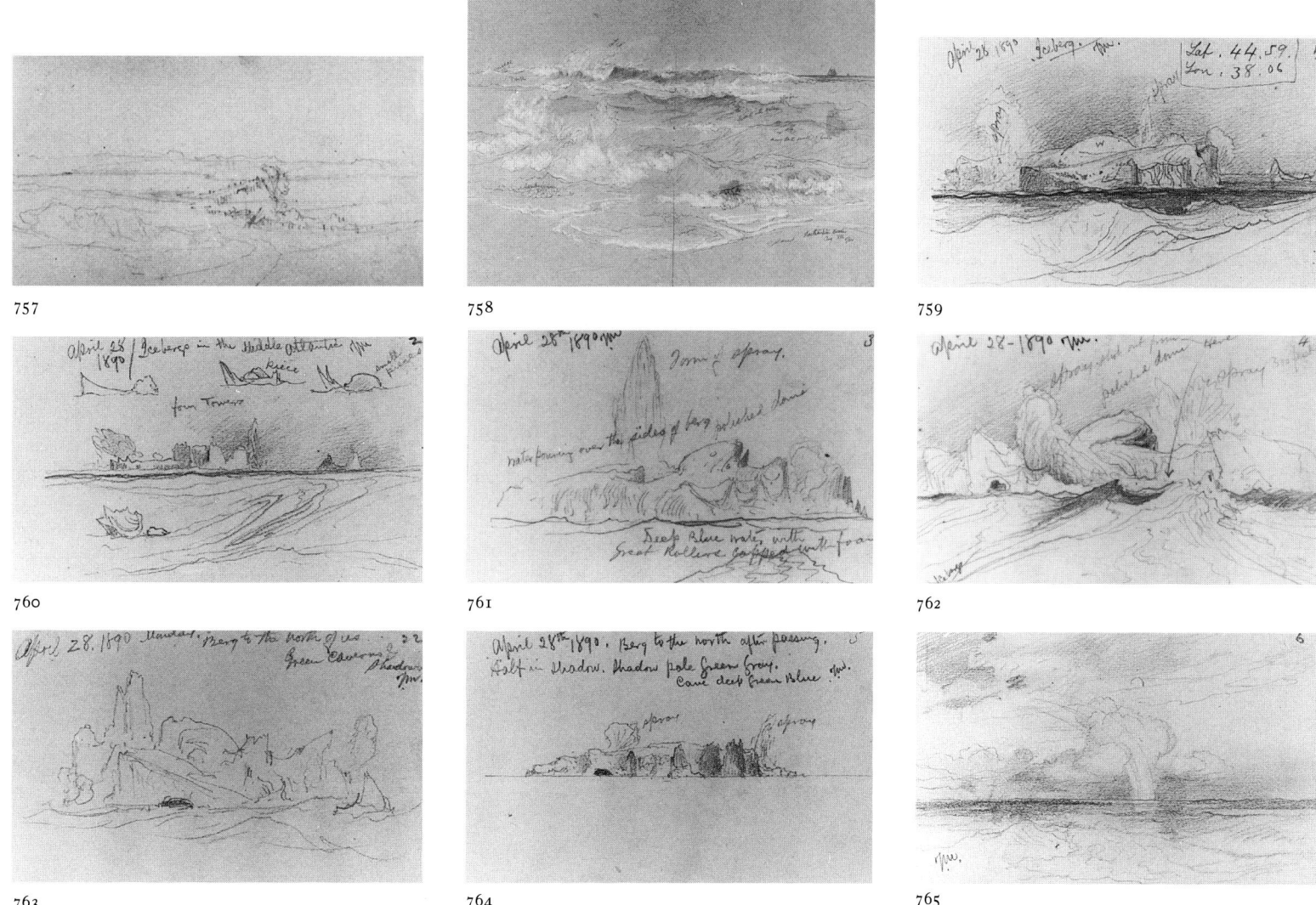

757

758

759

760

761

762

763

764

765

766
ICEBERGS [ledger title]
Graphite on watermarked laid
7⅞ by 9¾
1396.1242 Gilcrease
Dated: "Monday April 28th 1890" u.r.
Signed: "TM" u.r.
Inscribed: "Same" u.r.
Provenance: TG
1916 ledger: 403

767
AT SEA
Graphite on wove
4½ by 7
1396.1243 Gilcrease
Dated: "May 1st 1890" u.l.
Signed: "TM" u.l.
Inscribed: "at Sea" u.l.; "7" u.r.
Provenance: TG
1916 ledger: 401

768
COLOGNE
Graphite on wove
4½ by 7
1376.836 Gilcrease
Dated: "May 9th 1890" u.c.
Signed: "TM" u.l.
Inscribed: "Cologne" u.l.; "8" u.r.; miscellaneous
notes
Provenance: TG
1916 ledger: 264

†769
ST. MARK, COLOGNE
Graphite on wove
4½ by 7
1376.837 Gilcrease
Dated: "May 9th 1890" u.r.
Signed: "TM" l.l.
Inscribed: "St Mark Cologne" u.l.; "9" u.r.; mis-
cellaneous notes
Provenance: TG
1916 ledger: 389

†770
VERONA FROM THE BRIDGE OF
ST. PETER
Graphite and blue wash on yellow-brown wove
8⅝ by 11¾
1376.834 Gilcrease
Dated: "May 17th 1890" u.l.
Signed: TM" u.l.
Inscribed: "Verona from the Bridge of St Peter"
u.l.; "Tostolini packer of gondola" l.r.; "2" u.c.
Provenance: TG
1916 ledger: 329

771
CASTLE OF ST. PETER AND
BRIDGE, VERONA
Graphite on wove
4½ by 7
1376.831 Gilcrease
Dated: "May 17th 1890" u.r.
Signed: "TM" u.r.
Inscribed: "Castle of St Peter & Bridge Verona"
u.l.; "11" u.r.; miscellaneous notes
Provenance: TG
1916 ledger: 230

772
VERONA
Graphite and wash on wove
4 by 7
0276.834 Gilcrease
Dated: "May 17th 1890" u.c.
Signed: "TM" u.r.
Inscribed: "Verona" u.c.; "10" u.r.; miscellane-
ous notes
Provenance: TG
1916 ledger: 415

†773
VENICE
Graphite on wove
4½ by 7
1376.838 Gilcrease
Dated: "May 18th 1890" l.c.
Signed: "TM" l.c.
Inscribed: "Venice" l.l.; "12" u.r.; miscellaneous
and color notes
Provenance: TG
1916 ledger: 278

†774
SAN GIORGIO MAGGIORE
Graphite on wove
4½ by 7
1376.839 Gilcrease
Dated: "20 May 1890" u.r.
Signed: "TM" u.r.
Inscribed: "San Giorgio Maggiore" u.c.; "13" u.r.
Provenance: TG
Note: Sketch on verso

775
ISLAND FROM THE LIDO, LOOKING
SOUTH
Graphite on wove
4½ by 7
10 East Hampton Library
Dated: "May 20th 1890" u.r.
Signed: "TM" l.r.
Inscribed: "Island from the Lido Looking South"
u.l.; "14" u.r.; miscellaneous notes
Provenance: EH

†776
SAN GIORGIO MAGGIORE FROM
THE GIUDECCA
Graphite on wove
4½ by 7
1376.832 Gilcrease
Dated: "May 22nd 1890" u.r.
Signed: "TM" l.l.
Inscribed: "San Giorgio Maggiore from the Giu-
decca" u.c.; "16" u.r.
Provenance: TG
1916 ledger: 279
Note: Sketch on verso

*777
MURANO
Graphite and watercolor on wove
4⅜ by 6⅞
0276.766 Gilcrease
Dated: "May 23rd" u.r.
Inscribed: "Murano"; "18" u.r.; miscellaneous
notes
Provenance: TG
1916 ledger: 254

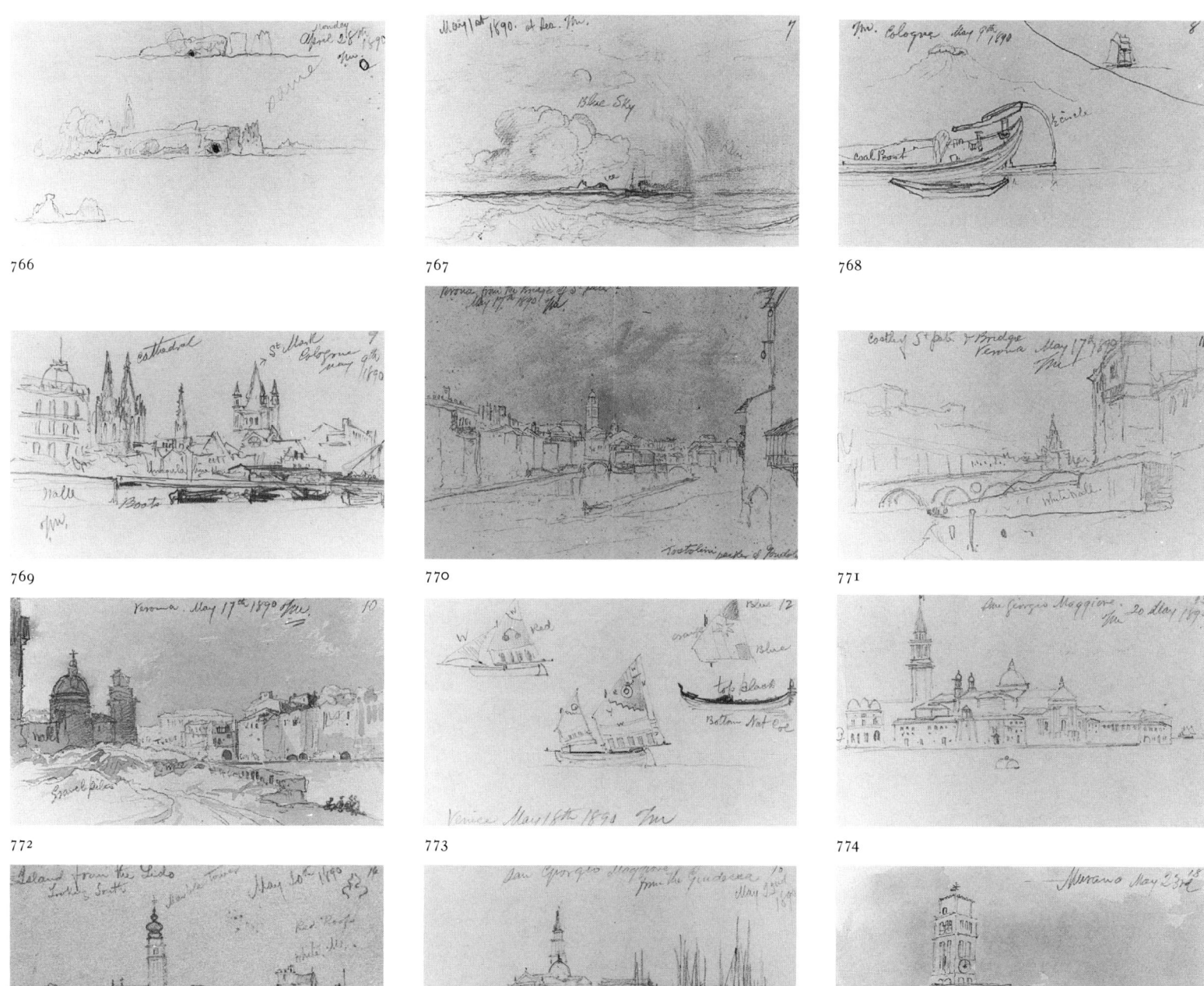

766

767

768

769

770

771

772

773

774

775

776

777

778
BURANO FROM MURANO
Graphite on wove
4 1/2 by 7
16 East Hampton Library
Dated: "May 23rd 1890" u.r.
Inscribed: "Burano from Murano" and "19" u.r.;
miscellaneous notes
Provenance: EH
1916 ledger: 286

779
MURANO
Graphite on wove
4 3/8 by 7
30 East Hampton Library
Signed: "TM" l.c.
Inscribed: "Murano" u.c.; "20" u.r.
Provenance: EH

780
MURANO
Graphite on wove
4 3/8 by 7
87 East Hampton Library
Dated: "May 23rd" l.r.
Inscribed: "Murano" l.r.; "21" u.r.; miscellane-
ous notes
Provenance: EH

781
THE GARIBALDE
Graphite on wove
4 1/2 by 7
1376.840 Gilcrease
Dated: "May 26th" u.r.
Inscribed: "The Garibalde" and "Lido" u.r.; mis-
cellaneous notes
Provenance: TG

782
CANAL BURANO
Graphite on wove
4 by 7
1376.592 Gilcrease
Dated: "29th" u.r.
Inscribed: "Canal Burano" u.r.; miscellaneous
notes
Provenance: TG
1916 ledger: 281

783
BURANO
Graphite on wove
4 3/8 by 7
86 East Hampton Library
Dated: "May 29th 1890" u.r.
Inscribed: "Burano" u.r.
Provenance: EH
1916 ledger: 285

784
MOONLIGHT FETE IN VENICE
Graphite and pen and ink on wove
4 3/8 by 7 3/4
1376.587 Gilcrease
Signed: "TM" l.c.
Inscribed: "Moonlight fete in Venice" l.r. in ink
Provenance: TG
1916 ledger: 137
Note: Sketch on verso with same inscription and
signature

785
VENICE [ledger title]
Pen and ink and wash on laid
4 1/2 by 8
1376.588 Gilcrease
Signed: "TMoran" l.l.
1916 ledger: 27
Provenance: TG
Note: Color notes on verso

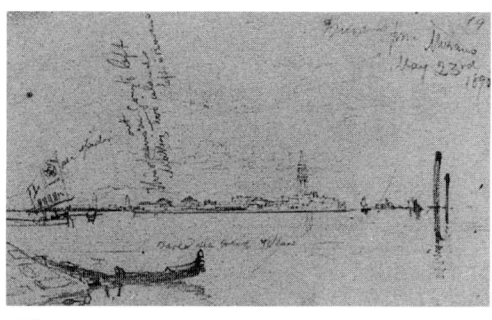

778

786
VENICE [descriptive]
Graphite and pen and ink on wove
4 1/2 by 6 3/4
S-12 East Hampton Library
Signed: "TMoran" l.l. in ink
Provenance: EH
1916 ledger: 28

787
IL BUGGIONE'S HOUSE
Graphite on wove
12 by 9 1/4
1376.612 Gilcrease
Inscribed: "il Buggione's House The Man who
Dwells in the wall & Keeps cheap beds (Buggy)
for travellers" upper edge
Provenance: TG

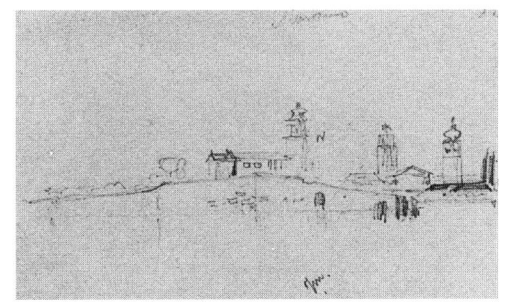

779

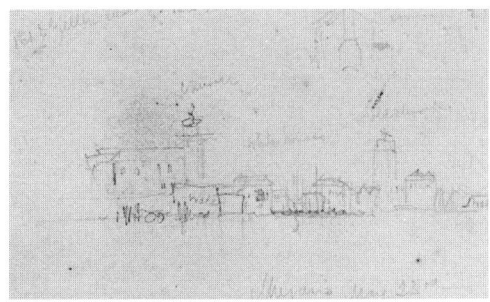

780

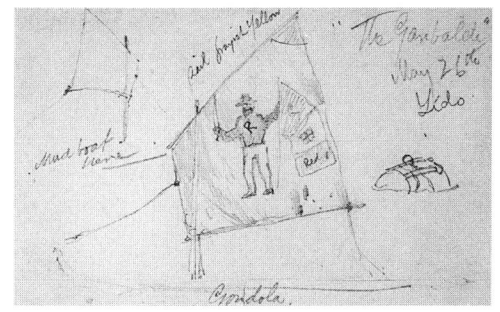

781

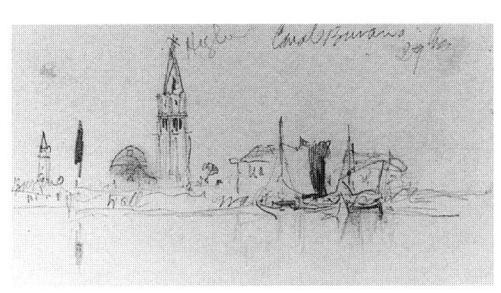

782

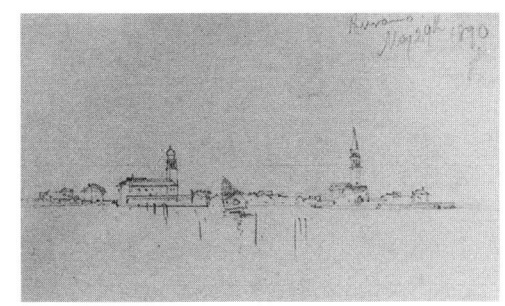

783

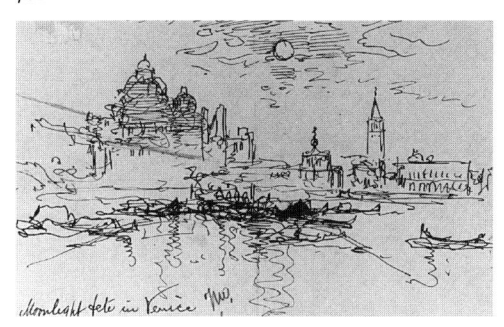

784

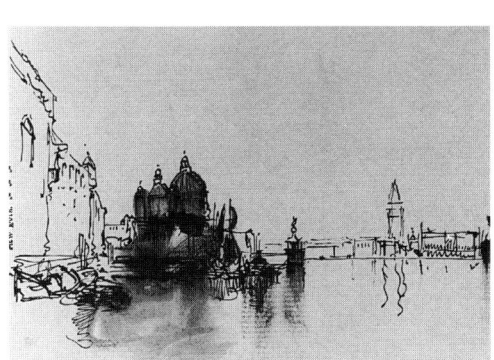

785

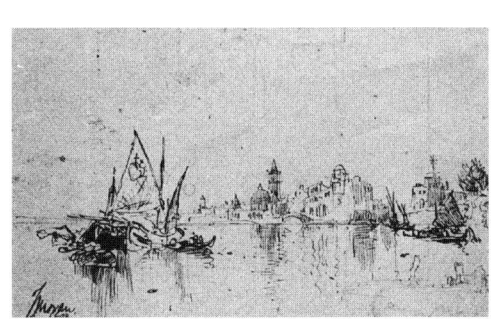

786

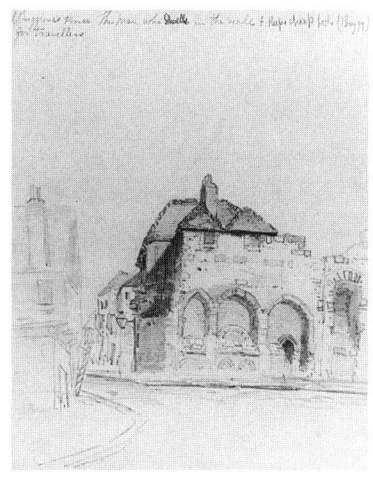

787

788
VENICE [ledger title]
Graphite on gray wove
14⁷/₈ by 21¹/₂
1376.593 Gilcrease
Signed: "TM" c.r.
Provenance: TG
1916 ledger: 393

789
VENICE [ledger title]
Graphite on green wove
12³/₄ by 19¹/₂
1376.598 Gilcrease
Signed: "TMoran" l.l.
Inscribed: "San Giorgio Here" c.l.
Provenance: TG
1916 ledger: 48

*790
VENICE
Graphite, watercolor, and white gouache on
green wove
12³/₄ by 19¹/₂
0276.765 Gilcrease
Signed: "TMoran" l.l.
Inscribed: "Venice" l.r.; miscellaneous notes
Provenance: TG
1916 ledger: 183

*791
VENICE FROM MALAMOCCO
Graphite and watercolor on green wove
8³/₄ by 12³/₄
0276.833 Gilcrease
Dated: "May 31st 1890" u.r.
Signed: Colophon l.l. in ink
Inscribed: "Venice from Malamocco" u.r.
Provenance: TG
1916 ledger: 97
Note: Sketch on verso

792
CHIOGGIA
Graphite and pastel on gray wove
10³/₄ by 15¹/₈
1376.597 Gilcrease
Signed: "TM" u.l.
Inscribed: "Chioggia" u.l.
Provenance: TG
1916 ledger: 385

*793
PICTURE OF SAILS FROM CHIOGGIA
Graphite, watercolor, and white gouache on
green wove
8³/₈ by 12³/₄
0276.832 Gilcrease
Dated: "May 31st 1890" u.r.
Signed: "TMoran" l.l.
Inscribed: "Picture of Sails from Chioggia" u.r.;
miscellaneous notes
Provenance: TG
1916 ledger: 413
Note: Sketch on verso

794
PELLESTRINA
Graphite on green wove
9 by 13³/₄
1376.833 Gilcrease
Dated: "May 31st 1890" u.r.
Inscribed: "Palestrina" u.r.; miscellaneous notes
Provenance: TG

795
VENICE
Graphite on green laid
9¹/₄ by 11¹/₄
1376.526 Gilcrease
Provenance: TG
Note: Sketch on verso

†796
VILLA ALEXANDRIA
Graphite on green wove
4¹/₂ by 7
40 East Hampton Library
Dated: "March 21st–91" l.l.
Signed: "TM" l.l.
Inscribed: "Villa Alex" l.l.
Provenance: EH
1916 ledger: 400

788

797
SHIPROCK, NEW MEXICO
[descriptive]
Graphite and watercolor on wove
9³/₈ by 16³/₄
31.18/7 Stark Museum of Art of Art, Orange,
Texas
Dated: "1892" l.l.
Signed: "TMoran" l.l.
Provenance: Joseph Sartor Galleries, Dallas,
Texas; H. J. Lutcher Stark, Orange, Texas

†798
OPPOSITE HANCE CAMP
Graphite on wove
5 by 7⁷/₈
1336.843 Gilcrease
Dated: "May 25th 1892" u.r.
Signed: "TM" l.r.
Inscribed: "opposite Hance camp" u.r.
Provenance: TG
1916 ledger: 251

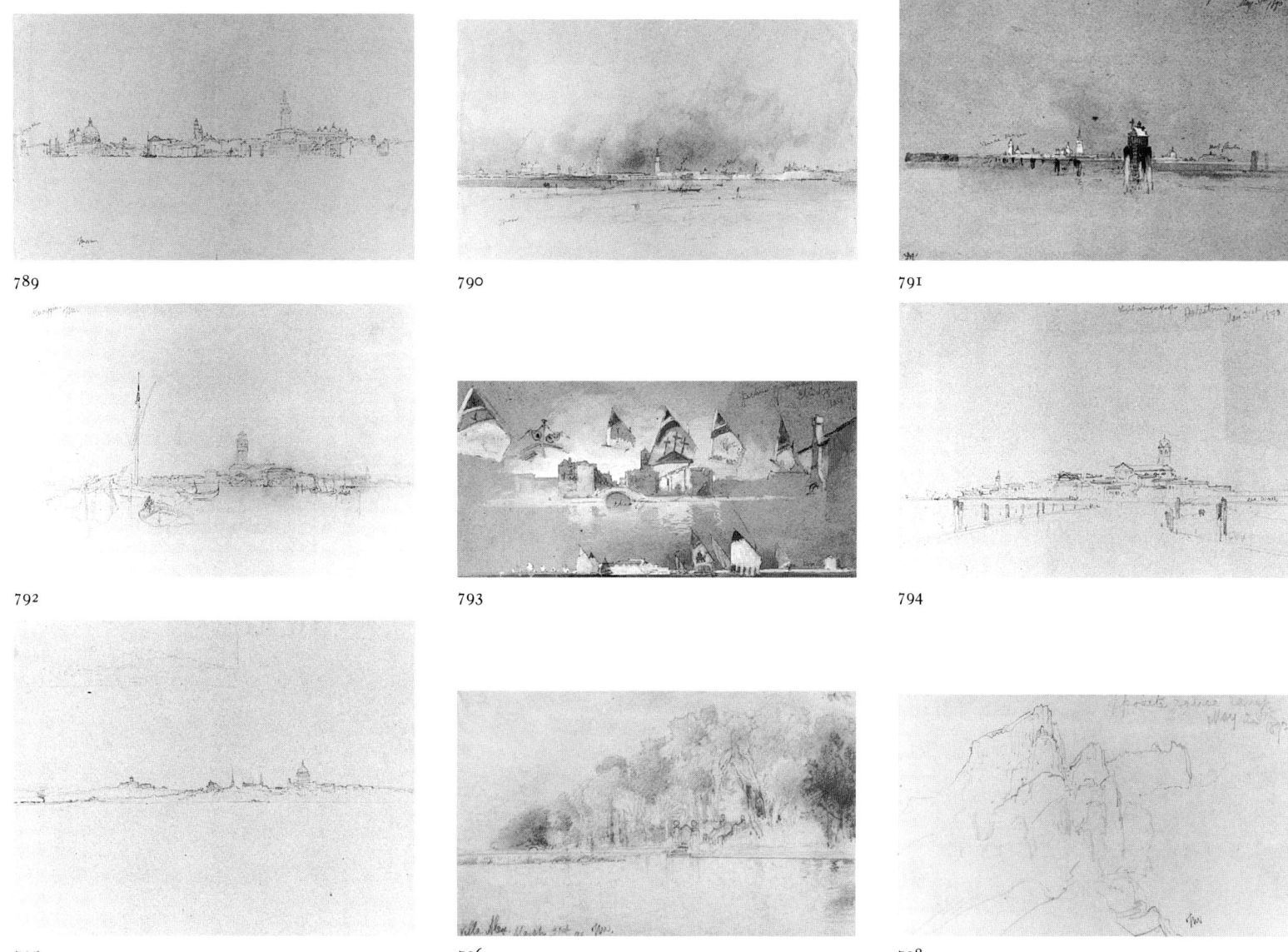

789

790

791

792

793

794

795

796

798

799
HANCE CANYON
Graphite on wove
5 by 7⁷/₈
41 East Hampton Library
Dated: "May 27 1892" l.r.
Signed: "TM" [twice] l.r.
Inscribed: "Hance Canon" l.r.; miscellaneous
notes
Provenance: EH
1916 ledger: 249

*800
THE GRAND CANYON OF
THE COLORADO
Graphite and watercolor on wove
Sketch 11¹/₂ by 24¹/₂, mount 15³/₄ by 25¹/₄
0236.931 Gilcrease
Dated: "May 29th 1892" u.r.; "1892 May" l.l. in
ink
Signed: "TMoran" u.r.
Inscribed: "The Grand Canon of The Colorado.
Looking West from Hances" l.l. in ink; "The
Grand Canon of the Colorado. Arizona. Look-
ing West" u.r.; "Canon of the Colorado. Looking
West from Hances Trail" u.l. of mount in ink;
"Grand Canon from Higgins Point" l.c.
Provenance: TG

801
LOOKING NORTH FROM MORAN
POINT, GRAND CANYON
Graphite on wove
5 by 7⁷/₈
54 East Hampton Library
Dated: "Sunday May 29th 1892" u.r.
Signed: "TM" l.r.
Inscribed: "Looking North from Morans Point
Grand Canon"
u.r.; miscellaneous notes
Provenance: EH
1916 ledger: 172

802
LOOKING WEST FROM MORAN POINT
Graphite on wove
5 by 7⁷/₈
5853 Jefferson National Expansion Memorial
Dated: "May 29 1892" u.r.
Signed: "TM" u.c.

Inscribed: "Looking West from Morans Point"
u.r.; "Ayres Butte" written vertically l.c.
Provenance: JNEM
1916 ledger: 224

803
LOOKING WEST FROM MORAN POINT
Graphite and watercolor on wove
5 by 7⁷/₈
S-15 East Hampton Library
Dated: "Sunday May 29 1892" u.r.
Signed: "TMoran" l.l.; "TM" l.r.
Inscribed: "Looking West from Morans Point"
u.r.; color notes and geographic location
Provenance: EH
1916 ledger: 15

804
GRAND CANYON FROM HANCES TRAIL
Graphite and watercolor on wove
4¹/₂ by 6³/₄
S-14 East Hampton Library
Signed: "TMoran" written vertically on right
edge
Inscribed: "Grand Canon from Hances Trail
Ayres Butte in foreground" written vertically
on right edge
Provenance: EH

805
SHADOWS, GRAND CANYON
Graphite on wove
5 by 7⁷/₈
19 East Hampton Library
Dated: "May 29th 1892" ["1892" altered to
"1893"] u.r.
Signed: "TM" u.r.
Inscribed: "Shadows Grand Canon" u.r.
Provenance: EH
1916 ledger: 248

†806
SHIVA TEMPLE
Graphite and watercolor on wove
4³/₈ by 6³/₈
S-16 East Hampton Library
Dated: "May 31st 1892" u.r.
Signed: "TMoran" l.l.
Inscribed: "Shivas Temple" u.r.
Provenance: EH
1916 ledger: 47

807
SHIVA TEMPLE
Graphite and watercolor on wove
5 by 7⁷/₈
4296 Jefferson National Expansion Memorial
Signed: "TMoran" l.l.
Inscribed: "Shivas Temple" u.r.
Provenance: EH
1916 ledger: 10

808
SAN FRANCISCO MOUNTAINS, FROM
BETWEEN FLAGSTAFF AND CEDAR
RANCH
Graphite on wove
4¹/₂ by 7
1336.844 Gilcrease
Dated: "June 1st 1892" u.r.
Signed: "TM" u.r.
Inscribed: "San Francisco Mts. from between
Flagstaff & Cedar Ranch" u.r.
Provenance: TG
1916 ledger: 247

809
THE NEEDLES
Graphite and watercolor on laid
5 by 7⁷/₈
1917–17–18 Cooper-Hewitt Museum
Dated: "June 2 1892" u.r.
Signed: "TM" l.r.
Inscribed: "The Needles" u.r.
Provenance: TM
1916 ledger: 82

810
ROCK TOWER NEAR MANUELITO
Graphite on wove
4¹/₂ by 7
1947.13.1 National Museum of American Art
Dated: "June 3rd 1892" u.r.
Signed: "TM" u.r.
Inscribed: "Rock Tower near Manuelito" u.r.
Provenance: WH
1916 ledger: 147

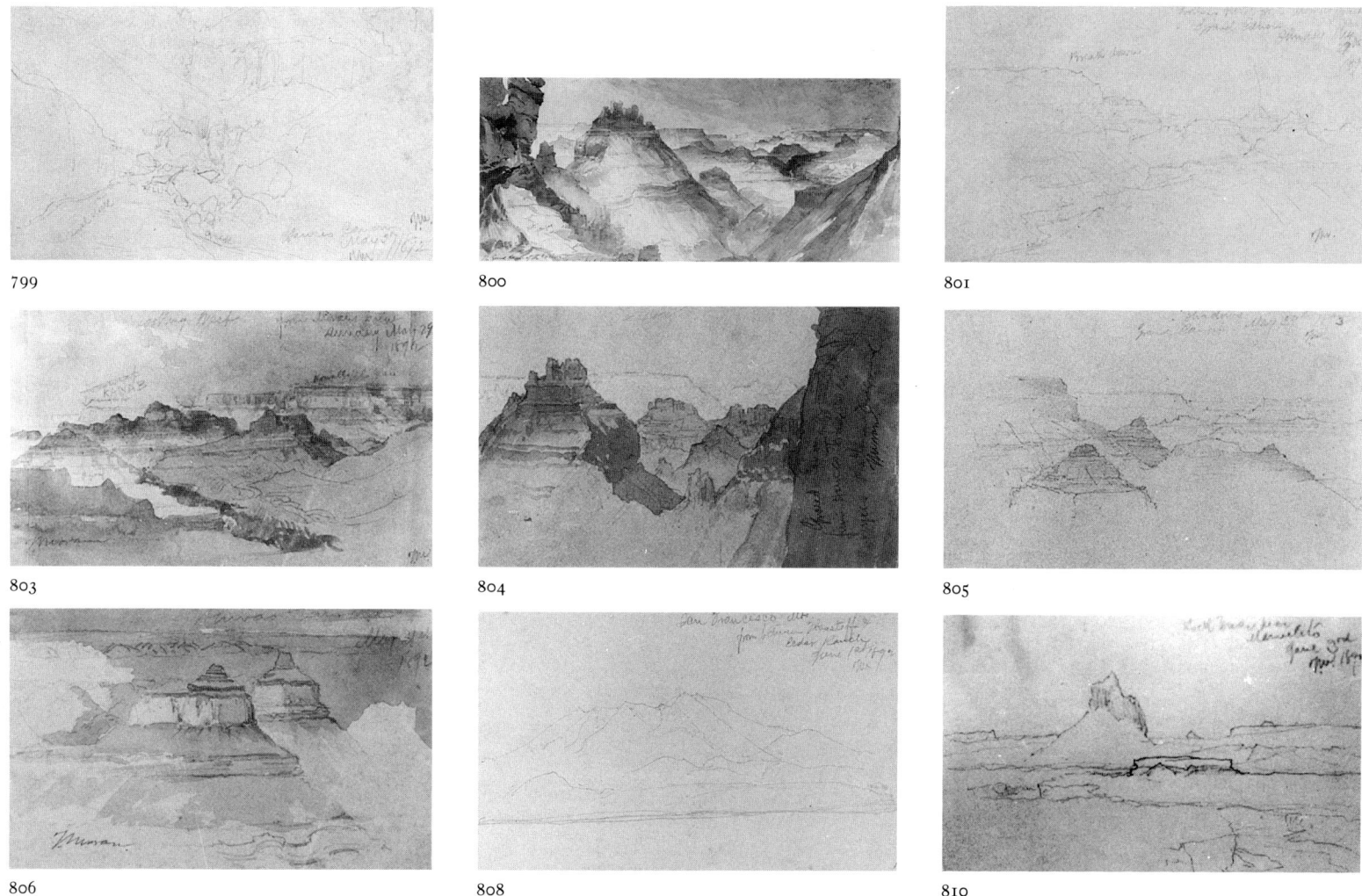

799

800

801

803

804

805

806

808

810

811
LAGUNA FROM EAST
Graphite and watercolor on wove
4¹/₂ by 7
S-6 East Hampton Library
Dated: "Saturday June 4th 1892" u.r.
Signed: "TM" l.l.
Inscribed: "Laguna from East" u.r.
Provenance: EH
1916 ledger: 308

812
IN THE VALLEY OF THE CHAMA,
NEW MEXICO
Graphite on gray wove
8⁷/₈ by 12⁵/₈
1917–17–49 Cooper-Hewitt Museum
Signed: "TM" u.l.
Inscribed: "in the Valley of the Chama. N. Mexico" u.l.
Provenance: TM
1916 ledger: 354

813
CHAMA BELOW THE SUMMIT
Graphite and watercolor on tan wove
8³/₄ by 11⁷/₈
1917–17–50 Cooper-Hewitt Museum
Dated: "1892" u.c.
Signed: "TM" u.c.
Inscribed: "Chama below the Summit" u.l.
Provenance: TM
1916 ledger: 306

814
SMELTING WORKS AT DENVER
Graphite and watercolor on wove
13³/₄ by 16⁵/₈
38.56 Cleveland Museum of Art, Ohio
Dated: "June 12th 1892" l.r.
Signed: "TMoran" l.l. and l.r. and colophon l.l.
Inscribed: "Smelting Works at Denver" l.r.
Provenance: Biltmore Salon, Los Angeles, California; Mrs. Henry A. Everett
1916 ledger: 339

815
WELLINGTON LAKE, NEAR DENVER
Graphite on wove
5 by 7⁷/₈
1336.842 Gilcrease

Dated: "June 18th 1892" u.r.
Signed: "TM" u.r.
Inscribed: "Wellington Lake. near Denver" u.r.
Provenance: TG
1916 ledger: 173

816
NESMITH FALL, WELLINGTON LAKE
Graphite on wove
7³/₄ by 10⁵/₈
1917–17–62 Cooper-Hewitt Museum
Dated: "June 18th 1892" u.r.
Signed: "TM" u.l.
Inscribed: "Nesmith fall. Wellington Lake" upper edge
Provenance: TM
1916 ledger: 309

817
HAIL STORM ON CABIN CREEK
Graphite on watermarked laid
7⁷/₈ by 9⁷/₈
1947.13.44 National Museum of American Art
Dated: "1892" l.c.
Signed: "TM" l.c.
Inscribed: "Hail Storm on Cabin Creek on the way to the Devils Tower" l.l.
Provenance: WH
1916 ledger: 127

818
THE CANYON OF THE BELLE
FOURCHE, WYOMING
Graphite, wash, and white gouache on gray wove
7 by 9⁵/₈
1930.12.23 National Museum of American Art
Dated: "1892" l.c.
Signed: "TM" l.l.
Inscribed: "The Canon of the Belle Fourche, Wyoming" l.l.
Provenance: WH
1916 ledger: 319

819
THE DEVILS TOWER
Graphite on wove
4¹/₂ by 7
4222 Jefferson National Expansion Memorial
Dated: "1892" u.c.
Signed: "TM" u.r.

Inscribed: "The Devils Tower" u.l.
Provenance: JNEM
1916 ledger: 202

820a
THE DEVILS TOWER TRIP
Graphite on wove
Upper sketch 2¹/₄ by 4¹/₂, sheet 7 by 4¹/₂
4224 Jefferson National Expansion Memorial
Dated: "1892" u.r.
Inscribed: "The Devils Tower Trip" upper edge
Provenance: JNEM
1916 ledger: 295

820b
THE TOWER FROM JOHNSTON'S
Graphite on wove
Lower sketch 4³/₄ by 4¹/₂, sheet 7 by 4¹/₂
4224 Jefferson National Expansion Memorial
Inscribed: "The Tower from Johnstons" upper edge; "The storm cloud" l.l.; color notes
Provenance: JNEM

821
GOOSE CREEK, SHERIDAN
Graphite on wove
4⁷/₈ by 7
1947.13.2 National Museum of American Art
Dated: "July 3" u.c.
Signed: "TM" u.r.
Inscribed: "Goose Creek, Sheridan" u.l.
Provenance: WH
1916 ledger: 258

822a
NEAR SHERIDAN
Graphite on green wove
Upper sketch 4⁷/₈ by 12⁵/₈, sheet 9⁷/₈ by 12⁵/₈
1930.12.19 National Museum of American Art
Dated: "July 3rd 1892" u.r.
Signed: "TM" u.r.
Inscribed: "near Sheridan" u.r.; miscellaneous notes
Provenance: WH
1916 ledger: 204

822b
NEAR SHERIDAN
Graphite on green wove
Lower sketch 5 by 12⁵/₈, sheet 9⁷/₈ by 12⁵/₈
1930.12.19 National Museum of American Art

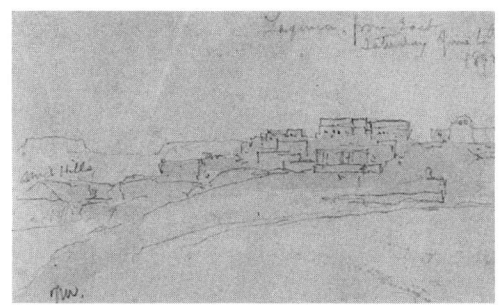

811

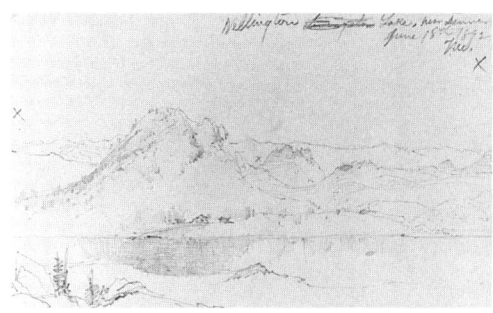

815

817

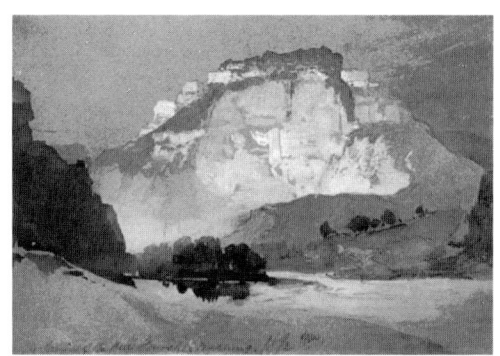

818

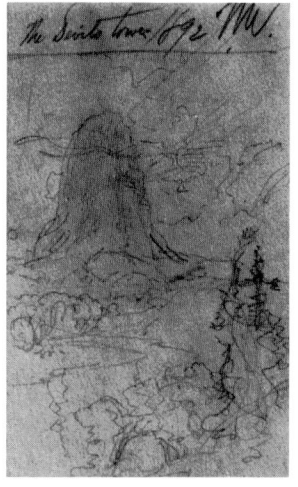

819

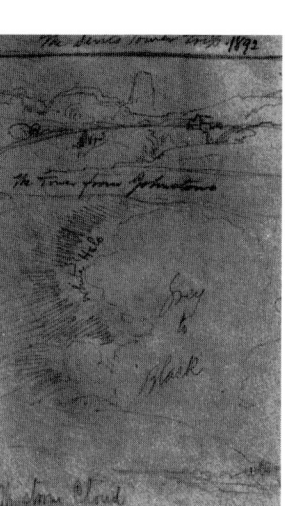

820ab

Dated: "July 3rd 1892 u.r.
Signed: "TM" u.r.
Inscribed: "Near Sheridan" u.r.
Provenance: WH

823
ON THE WAY FROM TONGUE RIVER
Graphite on wove
5 by 7⅞
1947.13.5 National Museum of American Art
Dated: "July 7th 92" l.c.
Signed: "TM" l.r.
Inscribed: "on the way from Tongue River" l.l.
and "Head of Little Big Horn?" l.r.
Provenance: WH
1916 ledger: 273

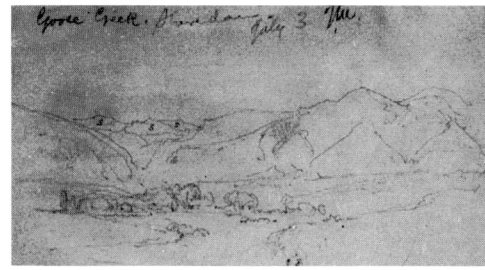

821

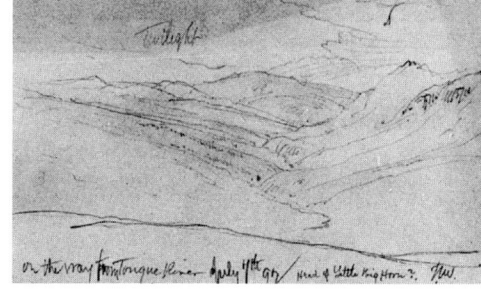

823

824
ON THE NORTH FORK OF TONGUE
RIVER, BIG HORN MOUNTAINS
Graphite on wove
5 by 7⁷/₈
1917–17–60 Cooper-Hewitt Museum
Dated: "July 7th 1892" u.c.
Signed: "TM" u.c. and l.r.
Inscribed: "on the North fork of the Tongue
River. Big Horn Mt." upper edge
Provenance: TM
1916 ledger: 223

825
BIG HORN MOUNTAINS,
TONGUE RIVER
Graphite on wove
5 by 7⁷/₈
1947.13.3 National Museum of American Art
Dated: "July 7th 1892" u.c.
Signed: "TM" u.c.
Inscribed: "Big Horn. Tongue River" u.l.; "fore-
ground blocks of limestone" l.l.
Provenance: WH
1916 ledger: 231

826
TONGUE RIVER CLIFFS
Graphite on wove
7⁷/₈ by 5
1947.13.4 National Museum of American Art
Dated: "July 7th 92" l.l.
Signed: "TM" l.l.
Inscribed: "Tongue River Cliffs" l.l.; miscella-
neous notes
Provenance: WH
1916 ledger: 228

827
ON SUNSHINE FORK OF CLARKS FORK
Graphite on green wove
8 by 9⁷/₈
1930.12.16 National Museum of American Art
Dated: "July 13 1892" l.r.
Signed: "TM" l.r.
Inscribed: "on Sunshine fork of Clarksfork" l.r.;
color notes
Provenance: WH
1916 ledger: 273

828
SUNSHINE FORK
Graphite on wove
5 by 7⁷/₈
1917–17–63 Cooper-Hewitt Museum
Signed: "TM" l.r.
Inscribed: "Sunshine fork" l.r.; "2" u.l.
Provenance: TM
1916 ledger: 219
Note: This may be one of Moran's two-part
sketches. The composition seems to be oddly
formatted, appearing cut off.

829
HEART MOUNTAIN, FROM CAMP
Graphite on green wove
9⁷/₈ by 12¹/₂
1930.12.17 National Museum of American Art
Dated: "July 14th 1892" l.l.
Signed: "TM" l.c.
Inscribed: "Heart Mountains from camp" l.l.;
"near Chapmans Branch" l.c.
Provenance: WH
1916 ledger: 205

830
SOUTH FORK OF CLARK'S FORK,
SUNSHINE RIVER
Graphite on wove
5 by 7⁷/₈
1917–17–64 Cooper-Hewitt Museum
Dated: "July 15th" l.c.
Signed: "TM" l.c.
Inscribed: "South fork of Clarks fork. Sunshine
River"
l.l.
Provenance: TM
1916 ledger: 200

831
THE YELLOWSTONE RANGE, FROM
DEAD INDIAN HILL
Graphite on wove
5 by 7⁷/₈
1947.13.6 Jefferson National Expansion Memorial
Dated: "July 15th 1892" u.r.
Signed: "TM" u.r.
Inscribed: "The Yellowstone Range from Dead
indian Hill" upper edge

Provenance: JNEM
1916 ledger: 220

832
PEAK ON THE SUNSHINE FORK
Graphite on wove
5 by 7⁷/₈
1917–17–59 Cooper-Hewitt Museum
Dated: "July 16th 1892" u.r.
Signed: "TM" u.r.
Inscribed: "Peak on the Sunshine Fork" u.r.;
miscellaneous notes
Provenance: TM
1916 ledger: 229

833
MOUNTAIN TOP NEAR CAMP,
COOKE CITY
Graphite on wove
7⁷/₈ by 5
1947.13.78 National Museum of American Art
Dated: "July 18th 1892" l.r.
Inscribed: "Mountain top near Camp Cook City"
lower edge
Provenance: WH
1916 ledger: 194

834
ON THE SODA BUTTE CREEK
Graphite on wove
5 by 7⁷/₈
1947.13.8 National Museum of American Art
Dated: "July 18th–92" u.r.
Signed: "TM" u.r.
Inscribed: "on The Soda Butte Creek" u.r.
Provenance: WH
1916 ledger: 212

835
INDEX
Graphite on wove
7⁷/₈ by 5
1917–17–61 Cooper-Hewitt Museum
Dated: "July 18th 1892" u.l.
Signed: "TM" u.c.
Inscribed: "Index" u.l.
Provenance: TM
1916 ledger: 296

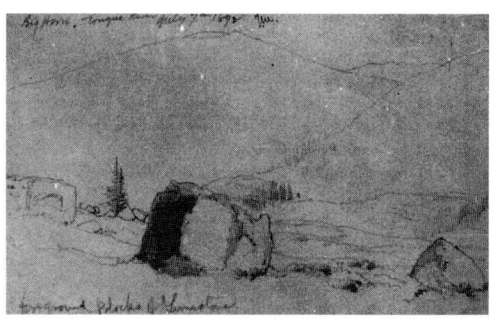

825

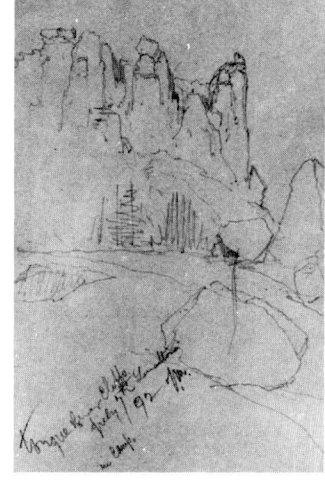

826

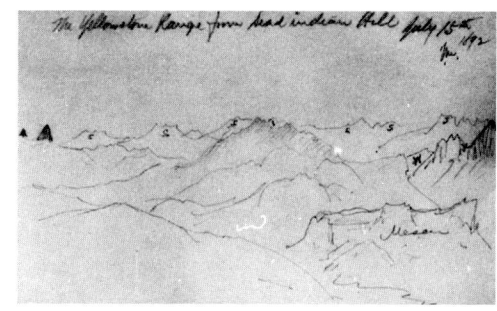

831

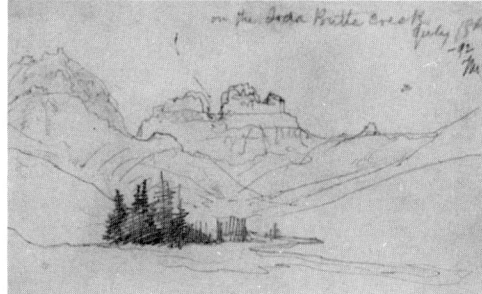

834

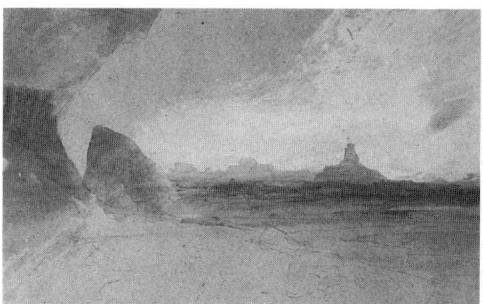

836

*836
INDEX PEAK [descriptive]
Graphite, watercolor, and white gouache on
wove
7 1/8 by 11 1/8
0236.850 Gilcrease
Provenance: TG
Note: Sketch on verso

*837
INDEX PEAK [descriptive]
Graphite, watercolor, and white gouache on
wove
5 1/8 by 11 1/4
0236.849 Gilcrease
Provenance: TG

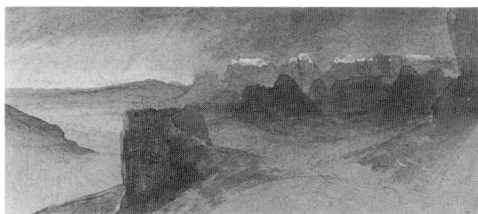

837

838
INDEX PEAK [descriptive]
Graphite, watercolor, and white gouache on
wove
5 by 8
S-18 East Hampton Library
Provenance: EH

839
INDEX PEAK, CLARKS FORK,
WYOMING
Graphite and watercolor on blue wove
9⁵/₈ by 12⁵/₈
1917–17–69 Cooper-Hewitt Museum
Dated: "1892" l.l. in ink and l.r.
Signed: "TM" l.r. and colophon l.l. in ink
Inscribed: "Index Peak. Clarks fork Wyoming"
l.l. in ink; "Index Peak. Wyoming Clarks fork" l.r.
Provenance: TM
1916 ledger: 110

840
LOWER FALLS OF SOUTH FORK OF
GARDNER RIVER
Graphite on green wove
6³/₈ by 5
1947.13.9 National Museum of American Art
Dated: "July 19th 1892" l.c.
Signed: "TM" l.c.
Inscribed: "Lower falls of S. fork R Gardners
River" l.l.
Provenance: WH
1916 ledger: 199

841
SULPHUR MOUNTAIN
Graphite on wove
5 by 7⁷/₈
1947.13.10 National Museum of American Art
Dated: "July 19" u.r.
Signed: "TM" u.r.
Inscribed: "Sulphur Mt" u.r.; miscellaneous and
color notes
Provenance: WH
1916 ledger: 230

842
SULPHUR MOUNTAIN
Graphite on wove
5 by 7⁷/₈
1947.13.11 National Museum of American Art
Dated: "July 1892" u.c.; "July 19th" u.l.
Signed: "TM" u.c.
Inscribed: "Sulp Mt." u.l.; "Yell" u.c.
Provenance: WH
1916 ledger: 225

843
YELLOWSTONE PARK
Graphite on laid
9⁵/₈ by 12⁵/₈
1930.12.21 National Museum of American Art
Dated: "July 1892" l.l.
Signed: "TM" l.l.
Inscribed: "Yellowstone Park" l.l.; "Mammoth
Hot Sp." l.c.; miscellaneous notes
Provenance: WH
1916 ledger: 206

844
DEAD SINCE FIRST VISIT IN 1871
Graphite, watercolor, and white gouache on
wove
12⁵/₈ by 9⁵/₈
1917–17–70 Cooper-Hewitt Museum
Dated: "July 21st 92" l.l.; "1892" l.r. in ink
Signed: "TM" l.l. and colophon l.r. in ink
Inscribed: "Dead since first visit in '71" l.c.
Provenance: TM
1916 ledger: 64

*845
UPPER BASINS
Graphite, watercolor, and white chalk on wove
Sketch 9¹/₂ by 12⁵/₈, mount 11 by 14¹/₂
0236.831 Gilcrease
Dated: "July 21st 1892" l.l.; "1892 l.r. in ink
Signed: "TM" l.r. in ink and l.l.
Inscribed: "Upper Basins" l.l. on mount; miscel-
laneous notes
Provenance: TG
1916 ledger: 62

846
EXTINCT CRATERS, GARDNER RIVER
Graphite, watercolor, and white gouache on
wove
5¹/₈ by 9¹/₂
8532 Yellowstone National Park, Wyoming
Dated: "1871" l.r. in ink [see note]
Signed: Colophon l.r. in ink
Inscribed: "Extinct Craters Gardiners River
Showing the Manner of formation" lower edge
Provenance: GP
1916 ledger: 325
Note: This sketch resembles stylistically the
work done in 1892. The date and colophon were
added later.

847
HOT SPRING, YELLOWSTONE
Graphite, watercolor, and white gouache on
wove
9⁷/₈ by 12³/₄
8527 Yellowstone National Park, Wyoming
Dated: "1892" l.r.
Signed: "TMoran" l.r.
Inscribed: "Hot Spring Yellowstone" l.r.
Provenance: GP
1916 ledger: 34

848
HOT SPRINGS OF GARDNER RIVER,
YELLOWSTONE PARK;
Graphite, watercolor, and white gouache on
wove
10¹/₂ by 14
8529 Yellowstone National Park, Wyoming
Dated: "1871" l.l. [see note]
Signed: Colophon l.l. in ink
Inscribed: "Hot Springs of Gardiners River Yel-
lowstone Park"
l.l.; "Gardiners river" l.r.
Provenance: GP
Note: This sketch resembles stylistically the
work done in 1892. The date and colophon were
added later.

849
HOT SPRINGS, YELLOWSTONE
Graphite and watercolor on green wove
9³/₄ by 12³/₄
1917–17–47 Cooper-Hewitt Museum
Dated: "1892" u.l.
Signed: "TM" u.l.
Inscribed: "Hot Springs Y" u.l.
Provenance: TM
1916 ledger: 214

850
GOLDEN GATE ROAD
Graphite on wove
4¹/₂ by 7
1947.13.12 National Museum of American Art
Dated: "1892" u.r.; "July 23rd" l.r.
Signed: "TM" u.r.
Inscribed: "Golden Gate Road" l.r.
Provenance: WH
1916 ledger: 222

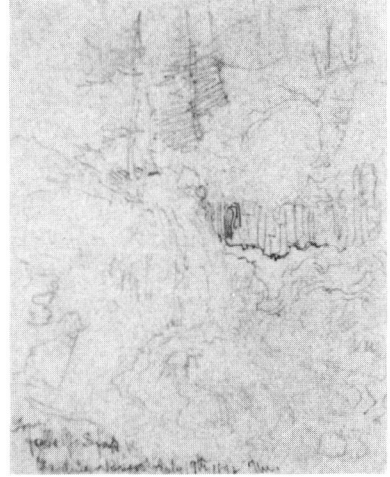

840

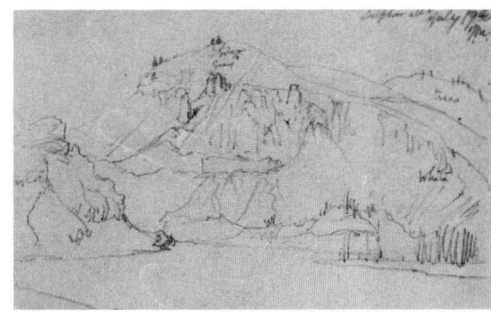

841

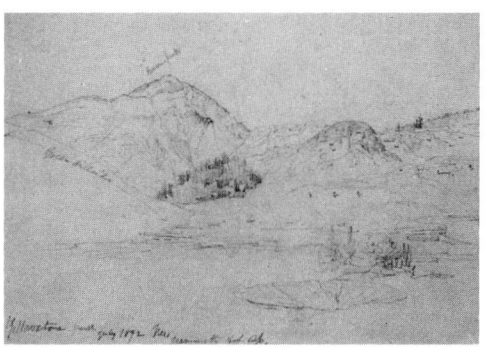

843

851
YELLOWSTONE PARK
Graphite on wove
4³/₈ by 6⁵/₈
1930.12.25 National Museum of American Art
Dated: "July 1892" l.r.
Signed: "TM" l.c.
Inscribed: "Yell Park" l.r.; miscellaneous notes
Provenance: WH
1916 ledger: 233

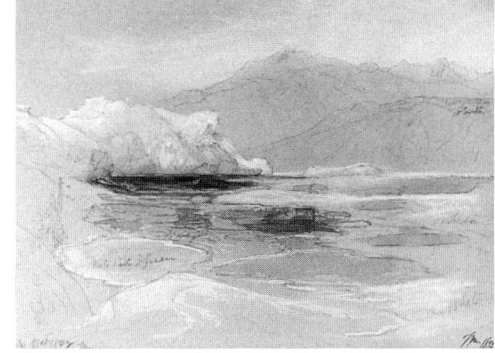

845

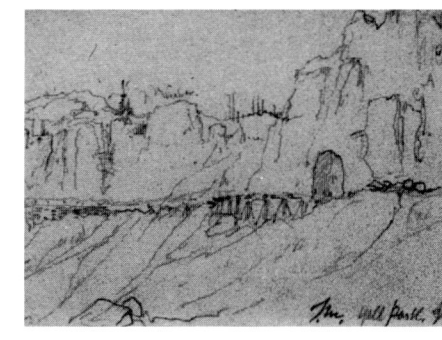

851

852
YELLOWSTONE PARK, GOLDEN GATE
Graphite on wove
4¹/₂ by 7
1947.13.13 National Museum of American Art
Dated: "July 23rd" l.r.
Signed: "TM" l.r.
Inscribed: "Yell Park golden Gate" l.r.
Provenance: WH
1916 ledger: 221

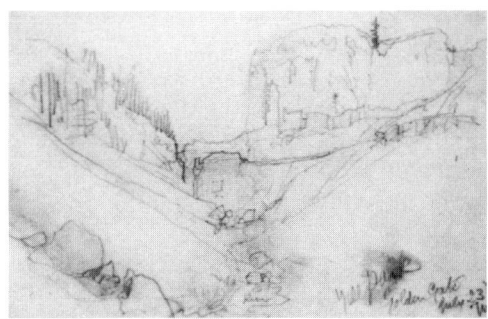

852

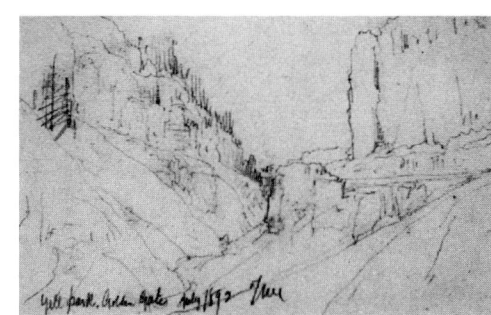

853

853
YELLOWSTONE PARK, GOLDEN GATE
Graphite on wove
4¹/₂ by 7
1947.13.15 National Museum of American Art
Dated: "July 1892" l.c.
Signed: "TM" l.c.
Inscribed: "Yell Park. Golden Gate" l.r.
Provenance: WH
1916 ledger: 273

854
GOLDEN GATE, YELLOWSTONE PARK
Graphite on wove
4$^{1}/_{2}$ by 7
1947.12.14 National Museum of American Art
Dated: "July 23rd 1892" l.l.
Signed: "TM" l.c.
Inscribed: "Yell Park Golden Gate" l.l.; miscellaneous notes
Provenance: WH
1916 ledger: 353

855
NEW GEYSER, NORRIS BASIN
Graphite on watermarked laid
7$^{7}/_{8}$ by 9$^{3}/_{4}$
1947.13.20 National Museum of American Art
Dated: "July 24th 1892" l.r.
Signed: "TM" l.r.
Inscribed: "New Geyser. Norris Basin" l.r.
Provenance: WH
1916 ledger: 297

856
THE BEEHIVE GEYSER
Graphite on wove
6$^{1}/_{2}$ by 11$^{1}/_{2}$
4234 Jefferson National Expansion Memorial
Dated: "1871" u.l. [see note]
Signed: "TM" u.l.
Inscribed: "The Beehive Geyser Yellowstone" u.l.
Provenance: JNEM
Note: This sketch resembles stylistically the work done in 1892. The date was added later.

857
THE DEVIL'S DEN, YELLOWSTONE
Graphite on gray wove
4$^{3}/_{4}$ by 7$^{7}/_{8}$
1917–17–10 Cooper-Hewitt Museum
Dated: "1871" l.r. [see note]
Signed: "TM" l.r.
Inscribed: "The Devils Den Yellowstone" l.r.
Provenance: TM
1916 ledger: 276
Note: This sketch resembles stylistically the work done in 1892. The date was added later.

858
NEW GEYSER, NORRIS
Graphite on watermarked laid
7$^{7}/_{8}$ by 9$^{3}/_{8}$
1947.13.21 National Museum of American Art
Dated: "July 24–92" l.l.
Signed: "TM" l.l.
Inscribed: "New Geyser Norris" l.l.; miscellaneous notes
Provenance: WH
1916 ledger: 203

859
NORRIS GEYSER BASIN,
YELLOWSTONE PARK
Graphite on watermarked laid
8 by 9$^{7}/_{8}$
1947.13.16 National Museum of American Art
Dated: "July 24th" u.l.; "1892" u.c.
Signed: "TM" u.l.
Inscribed: "Norris Geyser Basin Y.P." u.l.
Provenance: WH
1916 ledger: 211

860
THE HURRICANE VENT
Graphite on tan watermarked laid
4$^{7}/_{8}$ by 8$^{3}/_{4}$
1947.13.17 National Museum of American Art
Dated: "July 24" l.l.
Signed: "TM" l.l.
Inscribed: "Geyser in Hillside Norris The Hurricane" l.l.; miscellaneous notes
Provenance: WH
1916 ledger: 226

861
NORRIS
Graphite on watermarked laid
7$^{7}/_{8}$ by 9$^{7}/_{8}$
1947.13.18 National Museum of American Art
Dated: "July 24"
Signed: "TM" l.l.
Inscribed: "Norris" l.l.
Provenance: WH
1916 ledger: 265

862
NORRIS
Graphite on watermarked laid
7$^{7}/_{8}$ by 9$^{3}/_{8}$

1947.13.19 National Museum of American Art
Dated: "July 24th" u.l.
Signed: "TM" l.r.
Inscribed: "Norris" u.l.; miscellaneous notes
Provenance: WH
1916 ledger: 267

863
WEST WALL OF THE CANYON
Graphite on wove
9$^{3}/_{4}$ by 7$^{7}/_{8}$
1917–17–19 Cooper-Hewitt Museum
Dated: "July 26th 1892" l.l.
Signed: "TM" l.l.
Inscribed: "West Wall of the Canon from the edge of the Lower Fall of the Yellowstone" l.l.
Provenance: TM
1916 ledger: 235

864
EAST WALL OF THE CANYON,
FROM INSPIRATION POINT
Graphite, watercolor, and white gouache on wove
12$^{5}/_{8}$ by 19$^{5}/_{8}$
8537 Yellowstone National Park, Wyoming
Dated: "1892" l.l.
Signed: "TM" l.l.
Inscribed: "East Wall of the Canon from Inspiration Point" l.l.
Provenance: GP
1916 ledger: 366

865
FROM NEAR INSPIRATION POINT,
YELLOWSTONE CANYON
Graphite on blue wove
9$^{1}/_{2}$ by 12$^{1}/_{2}$
1930.12.20 National Museum of American Art
Dated: "July 1892" l.r.
Signed: "TM" l.r.
Inscribed: "From Near Inspiration Point Yell Canon" l.r.
Provenance: WH
1916 ledger: 299

866
YELLOWSTONE [descriptive]
Graphite on wove
7$^{7}/_{8}$ by 10
1947.23.46 National Museum of American Art

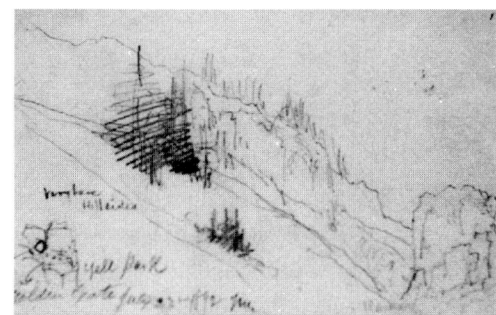

854

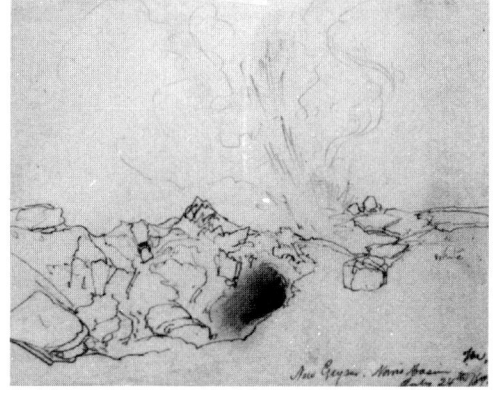

855

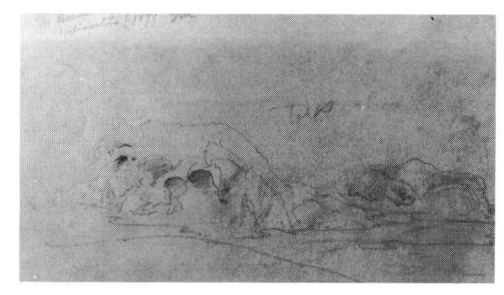

856

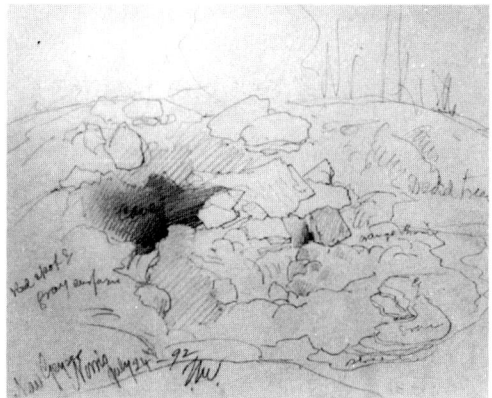

858

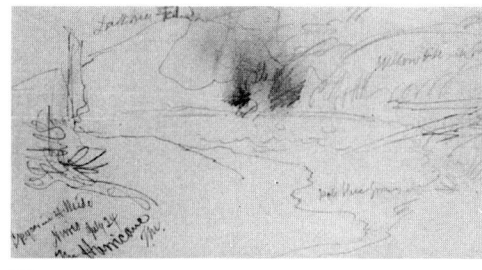

860

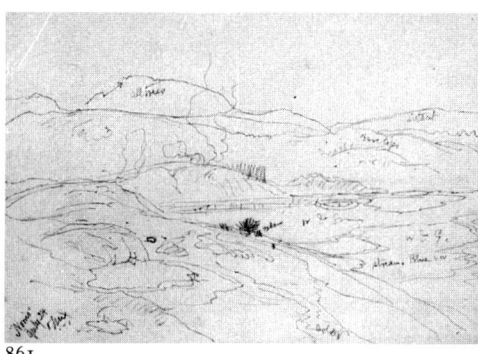

861

Signed: "TM" l.r.
Provenance: WH
1916 ledger: 271

867
SPRINGS ON THE BORDER OF
YELLOWSTONE LAKE
Graphite and watercolor on wove
5 by 10⅞
8525 Yellowstone National Park, Wyoming
Dated: "July 28th" l.l.; "1871" l.r. [see note]
Signed: "TMoran" l.c. and colophon l.r.
Inscribed: "Springs on the Border of Yellow-
stone Lake" l.l.
Provenance: GP
Note: This sketch resembles stylistically the
work done in 1892. The month and day refer to
the time of Moran's visit to Yellowstone Lake
in 1892. The year and colophon were added
later.

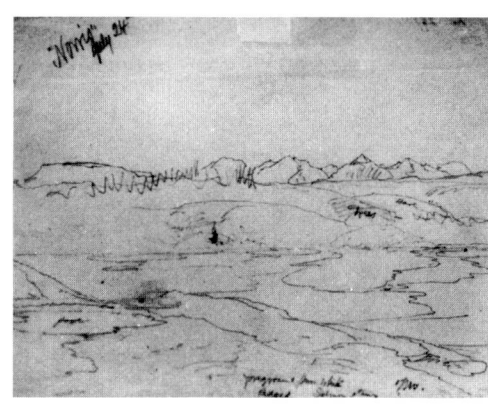

862

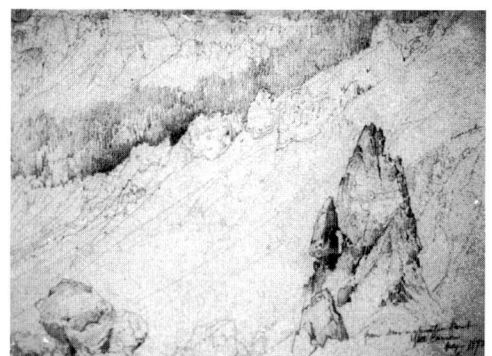

865

868
STEVENSON ISLAND,
YELLOWSTONE LAKE
Graphite on wove [two pieces joined]
4^1/$_2$ by 7
1947.13.23 National Museum of American Art
Dated: "July 28th 1892" u.c.
Signed: "TM" u.c.
Inscribed: "Stevenson Island Y. Lake" and
"Stevenson Island" u.c.; miscellaneous and color
notes
Provenance: WH
1916 ledger:s 232 and 197

869
YELLOWSTONE LAKE
Graphite and watercolor on watermarked laid
9^1/$_4$ by 12
4295 Jefferson National Expansion Memorial
Dated: "1871" l.l. [see note]
Signed: "TM" l.l.
Inscribed: "Yellowstone Lake" l.l.; miscellane-
ous notes
Provenance: JNEM
1916 ledger: 70
Note: This sketch resembles stylistically the
work done in 1892. The date was added later.

870
FROM OLD FAITHFUL
Graphite on wove
4^3/$_4$ by 6^7/$_8$
1917–17–54 Cooper-Hewitt Museum
Dated: "July 28th 1892" u.c.
Signed: "TM" u.c.
Inscribed: "from old faithful" u.c.; miscellane-
ous notes
Provenance: TM
1916 ledger: 131

†871
STREAM FROM FAITHFUL
Graphite on wove
4^1/$_2$ by 7
1336.1016 Gilcrease
Signed: "TM" l.r.
Inscribed: "stream from Faithful" l.l.; color notes
Provenance: W. F. Davidson at M. Knoedler &
Co., New York; 1964 Thomas Gilcrease Founda-
tion, Tulsa, Okla.; 1969 The Thomas Gilcrease

Institute of American History and Art, Tulsa,
Okla.
1916 ledger: 193

872
THE CASTLE FROM OLD FAITHFUL
Graphite on wove
4^3/$_4$ by 6^7/$_8$
1917–17–56 Cooper-Hewitt Museum
Dated: "1892" l.r.
Signed: "TM" l.r.
Inscribed: "The Castle from old Faithful. Sun-
set Glow After Rain" upper edge; extensive notes
on upper edge
Provenance: TM
1916 ledger: 290

873
CASTLE
Graphite on wove
4^3/$_4$ by 6^7/$_8$
1917–17–55 Cooper-Hewitt Museum
Dated: "July 29th 1892" u.c.
Signed: "TM" u.c.
Inscribed: "Castle" c.; miscellaneous notes
Provenance: TM

874
LOWER GEYSER BASIN
Graphite on wove
4^1/$_2$ by 7
1947.13.27 National Museum of American Art
Dated: "July 29th 1892" u.l.
Signed: "TM" l.r.
Inscribed: "Lower Geyser B" u.l.
Provenance: WH
1916 ledger: 209

875
LOWER GEYSER BASIN
Graphite on wove
4^1/$_2$ by 7
1947.13.28 National Museum of American Art
Dated: "July 29, 1892" u.l.
Signed: "TM" u.l. and l.r.
Inscribed: "Lower Geyser B" l.l.; miscellaneous
notes
Provenance: WH
1916 ledger: 196

876
LOWER FIRE HOLE GEYSER BASIN
Graphite on wove
9^1/$_4$ by 12
1917–17–52 Cooper-Hewitt Museum
Dated: "1892" ["71" marked through] u.l.
Signed: "TM" u.l.
Inscribed: "Lower fire Hole Geyser Basin" u.l.
Provenance: TM
1916 ledger: 288

*877
LOWER GEYSER BASIN
Graphite and watercolor on laid
Sketch 7^7/$_8$ by 9^7/$_8$, mount 9^5/$_8$ by 11^3/$_4$
0236.829 Gilcrease
Dated: "July 29th 1892" u.l.
Signed: "TMoran" u.l.
Inscribed: "Lower Geyser Basin" u.l.; color notes
Provenance: TG
1916 ledger: 21

878
GREAT SPRINGS OF THE
FIREHOLE RIVER
Graphite and watercolor on wove
8^1/$_8$ by 11^1/$_8$
8536 Yellowstone National Park, Wyoming
Signed: "TMoran" l.r.
Inscribed: "Great Springs of the Firehole River"
u.l.; miscellaneous notes
Provenance: GP
1916 ledger: 18

879
LIONESS AND CUBS, UPPER
GEYSER BASIN
Graphite on wove
4^1/$_2$ by 7
1947–13-26 National Museum of American Art
Dated: "July 29th 1892" u.c.
Signed: "TM" u.r.
Inscribed: "Lioness & Cubs Upper Geyser Ba-
sin" u.l.; miscellaneous notes
Provenance: WH
1916 ledger: 201

880
THE FAN GEYSER
Graphite on wove
7 1/2 by 7
1947.13.24 National Museum of American Art
Dated: "July 29 1892" u.r.
Signed: "TM" u.r.
Inscribed: "The Fan" u.r.; color notes
Provenance: WH
1916 ledger: 259

881
EXCELSIOR GEYSER
Graphite on wove
4 3/4 by 6 7/8
1917–17–57 Cooper-Hewitt Museum
Dated: "July 29" u.r.
Signed: "TM" u.r.
Inscribed: "Excelsior Geyser" u.r.
Provenance: TM
1916 ledger: 218

882
EXCELSIOR GEYSER
Graphite on wove
12 1/2 by 9 7/8
1947.13.25 National Museum of American Art
Dated: "July 29" u.r.
Signed: "TM" u.r.
Inscribed: "Excelsior Geyser" u.r.
Provenance: WH
1916 ledger: 356

883
THE BERYL SPRING
Graphite on watermarked laid
7 7/8 by 10
1947.13.31 National Museum of American Art
Dated: "July 30th 1892" l.r.
Signed: "TM" l.r.
Inscribed: "The Beryl Spring on the Road from
the Lower Basin to Norris" u.r.; "on the road
from Lower Basin to Norris" lower edge; color
notes
Provenance: WH
1916 ledger: 289

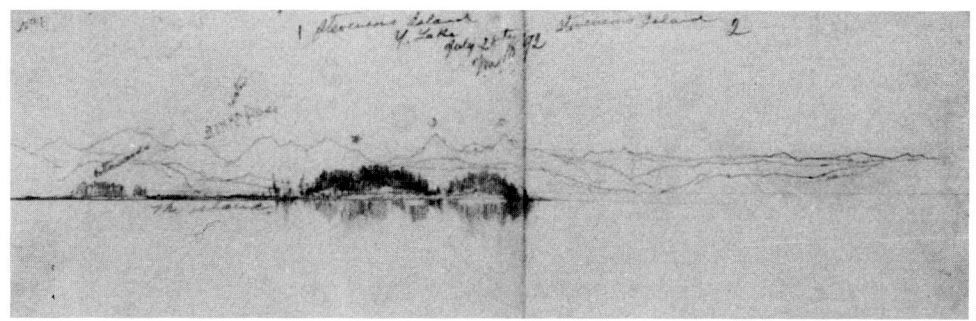

868

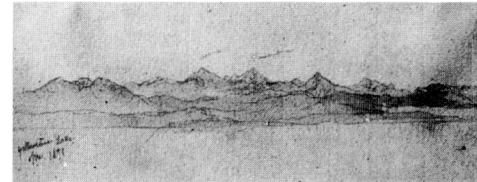

869

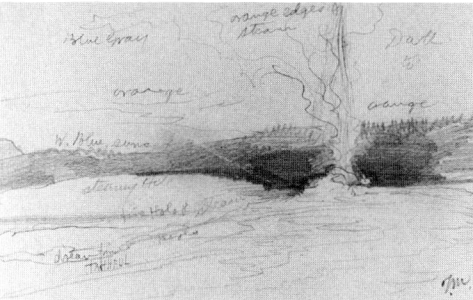

871

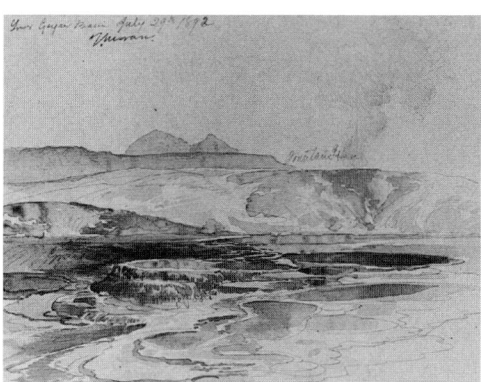

877

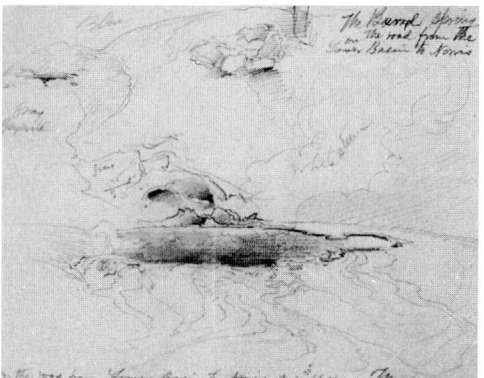

883

884
THE GREAT FOUNTAIN GEYSER,
LOWER GEYSER BASIN
Graphite on watermarked laid
9⁷/₈ by 7⁷/₈
1847.13.29 National Museum of American Art
Signed: "TM" l.r.
Inscribed: "The Fountain Lower G. Basin" u.l.;
color notes
Provenance: WH
1916 ledger: 275

885
BERYL GEYSER ON GIBBON RIVER,
YELLOWSTONE PARK
Graphite on wove
4¹/₂ by 7
1947.13.30 National Museum of American Art
Dated: "1892" u.c.
Signed: "TM" u.c.
Inscribed: "Beryl Geyser on Gibbon River Y.P."
u.l.
Provenance: WH
1916 ledger: 216

886
TURRETED PEAKS IN
YELLOWSTONE CANYON
Graphite on laid
9¹/₄ by 6
1947.13.32 National Museum of American Art
Dated: "July 31st 1892" l.r.
Signed: "TM" l.r.
Inscribed: "Turreted Peaks in Yellowstone
Canon" lower edge
Provenance: WH
1916 ledger: 272

887
THE UPPER FALL
Graphite on watermarked laid
7⁷/₈ by 9⁷/₈
1947.13.35 National Museum of American Art
Dated: "July 31st 1892"
Signed: "TM" l.r. and u.r.
Inscribed: "The Upper Fall" l.r.
Provenance: WH
1916 ledger: 274

888
UPPER FALL OF THE YELLOWSTONE
Graphite on watercolor on wove
12³/₄ by 9³/₄
31.18/3 Stark Museum of Art, Orange, Texas
Dated: "1892" l.r.
Signed: "TMoran" l.r.
Inscribed: "upper Fall of the Yellowstone" l.r.
Provenance: Joseph Sartor Galleries, Dallas,
Texas; H. J. Lutcher Stark, Orange, Texas

889
LOOKING OVER THE LOWER FALLS
Graphite on watermarked laid
9⁷/₈ by 7⁷/₈
1947.13.37 National Museum of American Art
Dated: "July 31st" l.l.
Signed: "TM" l.r.
Inscribed: "looking over the Lower fall" ["Up-
per" deleted by Moran] l.l.; miscellaneous and
color notes
Provenance: WH
1916 ledger: 268

890
MORAN POINT, YELLOWSTONE
CANYON
Graphite on wove
9⁷/₈ by 12⁷/₈
1917–17–51 Cooper-Hewitt Museum
Dated: "July 31st 1892" l.l.
Signed: "TM" l.l.
Inscribed: "Moran's Point, Yellowstone Cañon"
l.l.
Provenance: TM
1916 ledger: 278

891
CLIFF IN YELLOWSTONE CANYON,
MORAN POINT
Graphite on verso of printed card
3¹/₂ by 4¹/₂
4216 Jefferson National Expansion Memorial
Dated: "1892" u.r.
Signed: "TM" u.r.
Inscribed: "Cliff in Y Canon. Morans point"
upper edge
Provenance: JNEM
1916 ledger: 234

Note: The card on which this sketch was made
reads "College of the Sacred Heart Denver Colo.
Graduating exercises, Wednesday June 22nd in
the College Hall 8 o'clock p.m. Admit one."

892
UPPER FALL YELLOWSTONE
Graphite on watermarked laid
14 by 10
1947.13.34 National Museum of American Art
Dated: "1892" u.r.
Signed: "TM" u.r.
Inscribed: "Upper Fall Yell." u.r.
Provenance: WH
1916 ledger: 257

893
LOOKING AT INSPIRATION POINT
FROM THE WHITE AMPHITHEATER
Graphite on laid
12¹/₄ by 9¹/₄
1930.12.18 National Museum of American Art
Signed: "TM" l.l.
Inscribed: "Looking at Insp. Point From the
White Amphitheatre" l.l.; color notes
Provenance: WH
1916 ledger: 270

894
LOOKING UP FROM INSPIRATION
POINT
Graphite on laid
9³/₈ by 12¹/₄
1930.12.22 National Museum of American Art
Signed: "TM" l.r.
Inscribed: "Look. Up from I. point" l.r.; color
notes
Provenance: WH
1916 ledger: 263

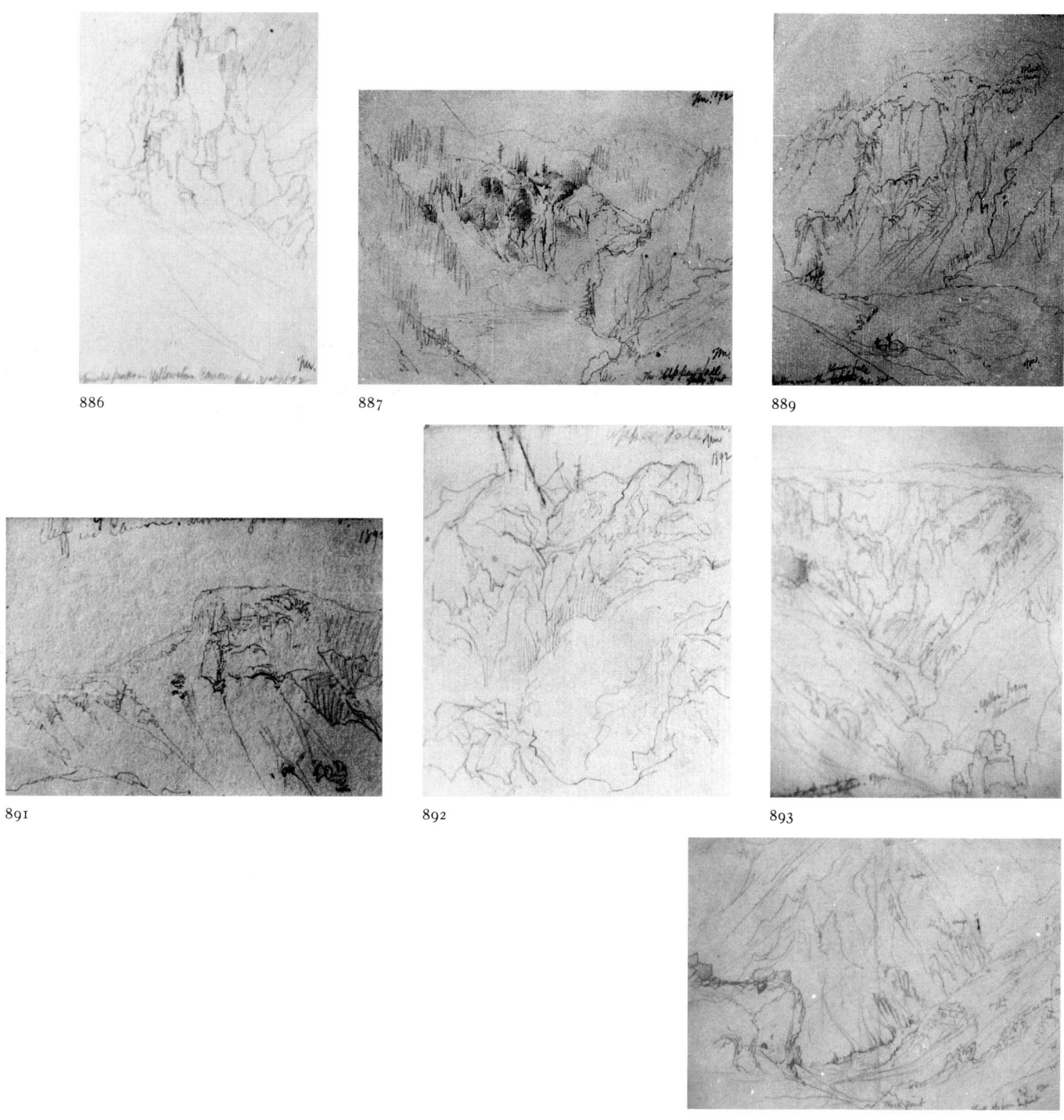

886

887

889

891

892

893

894

895
ABOVE THE LOWER FALLS,
YELLOWSTONE
Graphite on wove
9¹/₈ by 7⁷/₈
1947.13.38 National Museum of American Art
Dated: "July 1892" u.c.
Signed: "TM" u.c.
Inscribed: "above the Lower fall. Yell." u.l.; color
notes
Provenance: WH
1916 ledger: 275

896
FROM THE BRINK OF THE
UPPER FALLS
Graphite on watermarked laid
9⁷/₈ by 7⁷/₈
1947.13.36 National Museum of American Art
Dated: "1892" l.c.
Signed: "TM" l.c.
Inscribed: "from the Brink of the Upper falls
Y.C." lower edge; color notes
Provenance: WH
1916 ledger:.264

897
FALLS OF YELLOWSTONE
Graphite on wove
7 by 10⁵/₈
1947.13.33 National Museum of American Art
Signed: "TM" u.l.
Inscribed: "Falls of Y" u.l.
Provenance: WH
1916 ledger: 133

*898
MORAN POINT, YELLOWSTONE
CANYON
Graphite, watercolor, and white gouache on
green wove
Sketch 9¹/₂ by 12¹/₂, mount 10¹/₂ by 13
0236.830 Gilcrease
Dated: "July 31st 1892" u.l.; "1892" l.l. on mount
in ink
Signed: "TM" u.l.; "TMoran" l.l.
Inscribed: "Morans Point Yellowstone Cañon"
u.l.; color notes
Provenance: TG
1916 ledger: 22

899
RED ROCK [descriptive]
Graphite, watercolor, and white gouache on wove
8¹/₈ by 10⁵/₈
8543 Yellowstone National Park, Wyoming
Signed: "TMoran" l.l.; colophon l.l. in ink
Provenance: GP

900
YELLOWSTONE CANYON
Graphite, watercolor, and white gouache on
wove
10¹/₈ by 14
8544 Yellowstone National Park, Wyoming
Dated: "Aug 3 1871" u.r. [see note]
Signed: Colophon l.l.
Inscribed: "Yellowstone Canon" l.l.; "part of the
Great Canon of the Yellowstone looking east"
u.r.
Provenance: GP
Note: This sketch resembles stylistically the
work done in 1892. The month and day refer to
the time of Moran's visit to Yellowstone Canyon in 1892. The year and colophon were added
later.

901
YELLOWSTONE CANYON
Graphite, watercolor, and white gouache on
wove
8¹/₈ by 11¹/₈
8539 Yellowstone National Park, Wyoming
Dated: "1871" u.l. [see note]
Signed: "TMoran" u.l.
Inscribed: "Yellowstone Canon" u.l.
Provenance: GP
1916 ledger: 17
Note: This sketch resembles stylistically the
work done in 1892. The date was added later.
There is a sketch on verso.

902
CINNABAR MOUNTAIN
Graphite on laid
4 by 5
1947.13.39 National Museum of American Art
Dated: "Aug 3" u.l.
Inscribed: "Cinnabar Mt" u.l.
Provenance: WH
1916 ledger: 195

903a
YELLOWSTONE BADLANDS
Graphite on laid
Upper sketch 1³/₄ by 5, sheet 4 by 5
1947.13.40 National Museum of American Art
Dated: "Aug 4th" u.r.
Signed: "TM" u.r.
Inscribed: "Yellowstone Badlands" u.r.; color
notes
Provenance: WH
1916 ledger 72

903b
YELLOWSTONE BUTTES
Graphite on laid
Lower sketch 2¹/₄ by 5, sheet 4 by 5
1947.13.40 National Museum of American Art
Signed: "TM" u.r.
Inscribed: "Yellowstone Buttes" u.r.; color notes
Provenance: WH

904
BADLANDS OF THE YELLOWSTONE
Graphite on laid
4 by 5
1947.13.41 National Museum of American Art
Dated: "Aug 4" l.c.
Inscribed: "Badlands of the Yellowstone" lower
edge
Provenance: WH
1916 ledger: 198
Note: Sketch on verso

905
YELLOWSTONE RIVER NEAR
ROSEBUD
Graphite on verso of printed card
2⁵/₈ by 4⁵/₈
1930.12.24 National Museum of American Art
Dated: "Aug 4th 1892" l.r.
Signed: "TM" l.r.
Inscribed: "Yellowstone River near Rosebud"
lower edge; color notes
Provenance: WH
Note: The card on which this sketch was made
was the business card of photographer and pub-
lisher, F. Jay Haynes, St. Paul, Minn.

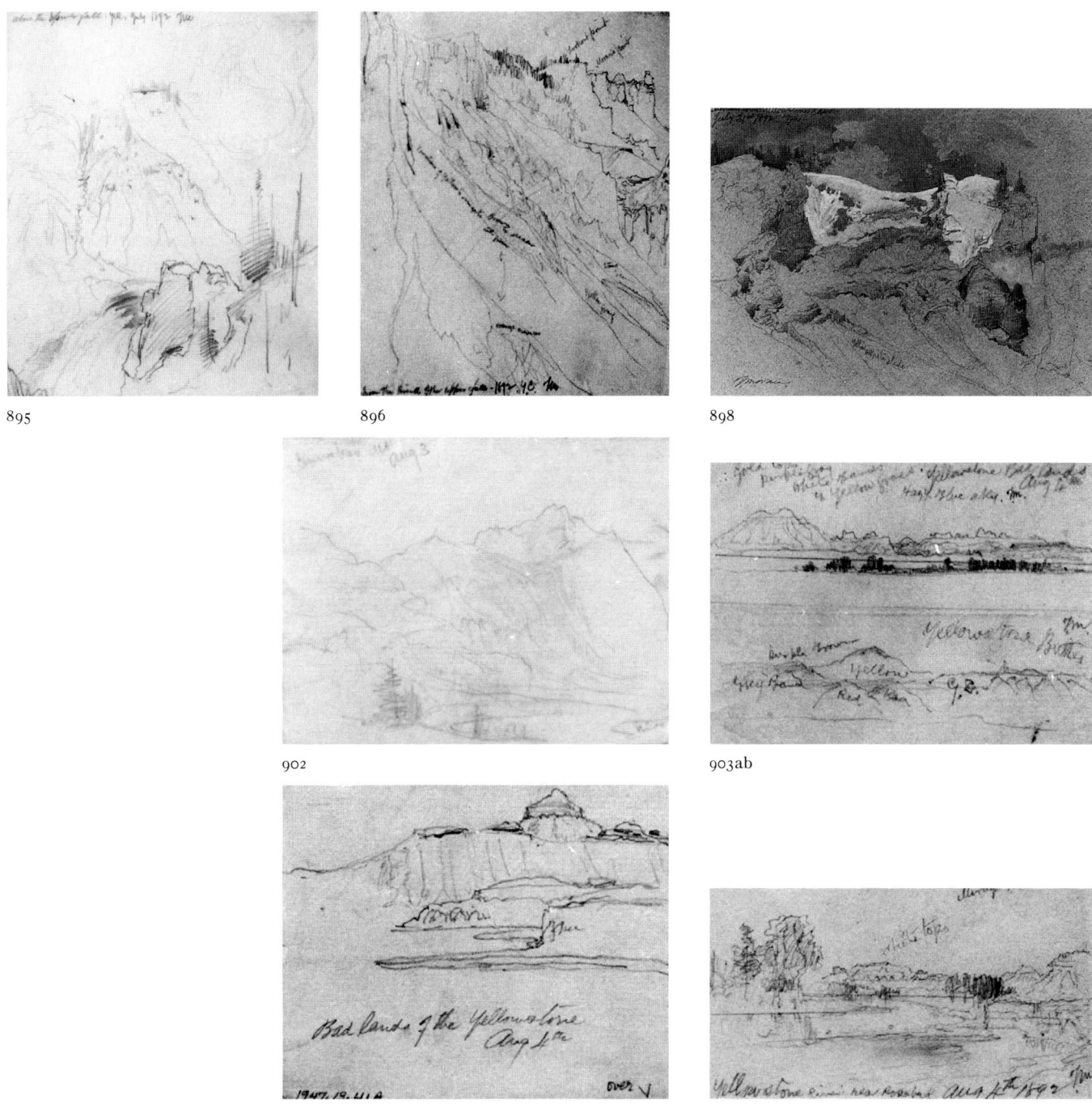

895

896

898

902

903ab

904

905

906
BADLAND NEAR BOICE
Graphite on laid
3⁷/₈ by 9³/₄
1947.13.42 National Museum of American Art
Dated: "Aug 4th 1892" u.c.; "Aug 4" u.r.
Signed: "TM" u.r.
Inscribed: "Bad land near Boice N.P.R.R." u.l.;
miscellaneous and color notes
Provenance: WH
1916 ledger: 190

907
THE BADLANDS OF DAKOTA
Graphite on laid
7³/₄ by 9⁷/₈
1917–17–66 Cooper-Hewitt Museum
Dated: "Aug 4th 1892" l.r.
Signed: "TM" u.l.
Inscribed: "The Bad Lands of Dacota" u.l.;
"Distance elongated by mirage pools. Trees on
edge of pool" u.l.
Provenance: TM
1916 ledger: 291

908
FIRE IN THE BAD LANDS OF DAKOTA
Graphite on wove
4¹/₂ by 7
1947.13.43 National Museum of American Art
Dated: "1892" l.c.
Signed: "TM" l.c.
Inscribed: "fire in the bad Lands of Dakota"; ex-
tensive color notes
Provenance: WH
1916 ledger: 293

909
IN THE YELLOWSTONE VALLEY
Graphite and wash on wove
8 by 5¹/₄
4290 Jefferson National Expansion Memorial
Signed: "TM" u.l.
Inscribed: "in the Yellowstone Valley" u.l.
Provenance: JNEM
1916 ledger: 269

910
THE RISING STORM CLOUD
Graphite and wash on wove

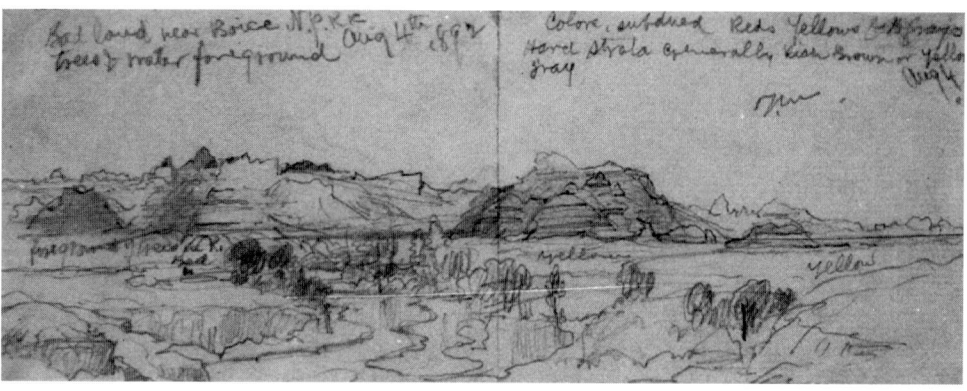

906

8¹/₂ by 10¹/₄
4284 Jefferson National Expansion Memorial
Dated: "1892" l.l. in ink
Inscribed: "The Rising Storm Cloud" l.l. in ink
Provenance: JNEM
1916 ledger: 30

911
LIZARD HEAD
Graphite on tan laid Denver and Rio Grande
Railroad letterhead
8¹/₂ by 11
1917–17–72 Cooper-Hewitt Museum
Dated: "Jan 8th–93" u.l.
Signed: "TM" u.l.
Inscribed: "Lizard Head" u.l.
Provenance: TM
1916 ledger: 175

912
LIZARD HEAD
Graphite on tan laid Denver & Rio Grande
Railroad letterhead
11 by 8¹/₂
1917–17–73 Cooper-Hewitt Museum
Dated: "Jan 8th 1893" u.l.
Signed: "TM" u.l.
Inscribed: "Lizard Head" u.l.
Provenance: TM
1916 ledger: 189

913
GLEN EYRIE
Graphite on wove
9⁷/₈ by 14⁷/₈
1336.652 Gilcrease
Signed: "TM" l.l.
Inscribed: "Glen Eyrie" l.l.; miscellaneous notes
Provenance: TG
1916 ledger: 138

914
GLEN EYRIE
Graphite on wove
10¹/₂ by 13⁷/₈
1336.653 Gilcrease
Signed: "TM" l.l.
Inscribed: "Glen Eyrie" l.l.; miscellaneous notes
Provenance: TG
1916 ledger: 140

915
GENERAL PALMER'S HOUSE, GLEN
EYRIE, COLORADO
Graphite on wove
10¹/₂ by 14
1917–17–58 Cooper-Hewitt Museum
Signed: "TMoran" l.l.
Inscribed: "Gen. Palmer's Glen Eyrie, Col." l.l.;
miscellaneous notes
Provenance: TM
1916 ledger: 160

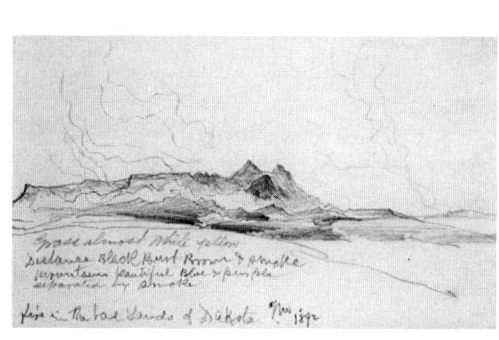

908

909

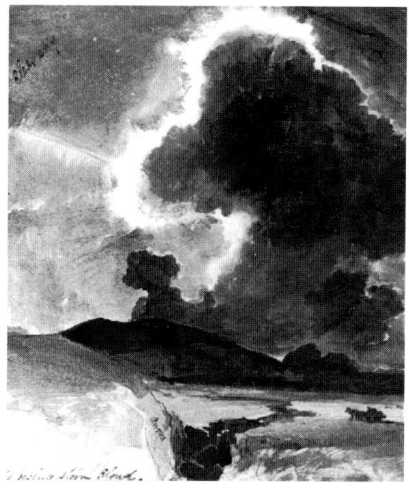

910

†916

GLEN EYRIE, COLORADO
Graphite on wove
10¹/₂ by 13⁷/₈
1336.666 Gilcrease
Signed: "TM" l.l.
Inscribed: "Glen Eyrie. Col." l.l.
Provenance: TG
1916 ledger: 161

917

GLEN EYRIE, COLORADO
Graphite and watercolor on wove
10¹/₂ by 14
1917–17–67 Cooper-Hewitt Museum
Signed: "TM" u.l.
Inscribed: "Glen Eyrie, Col." u.l.; miscellaneous
and color notes
Provenance: TM
1916 ledger: 84

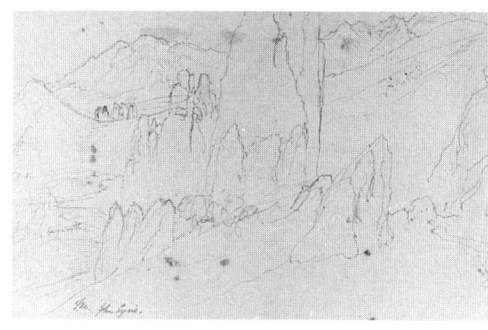

913

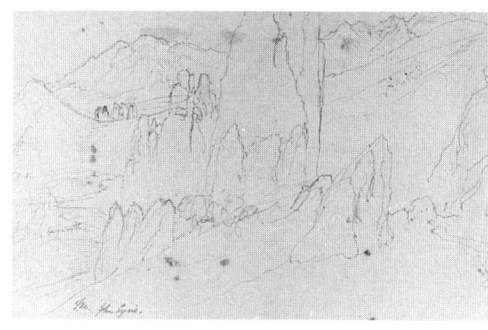

914

918

GLEN EYRIE, COLORADO
Graphite on wove
13⁷/₈ by 10¹/₂
1336.855 Gilcrease
Dated: "1902" l.l.
Signed: "TM" l.l.
Inscribed: "Glen Eyrie. Col" l.l.; color notes
Provenance: TG
1916 ledger: 307

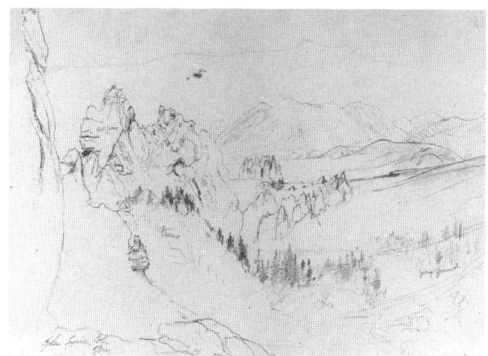

916

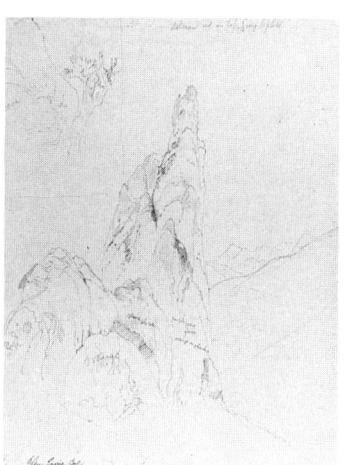

918

919
GLEN EYRIE, COLORADO
Graphite and wash on wove
13⁷/₈ by 10
1336.853 Gilcrease
Dated: "1900" u.l.
Signed: "TM" u.l.
Inscribed: "Glen Eyrie. Colorado" u.l.; miscellaneous notes
Provenance: TG
1916 ledger: 176

†920
PIKES PEAK FROM THE BLUFFS EAST OF COLORADO SPRINGS
Graphite on wove
8 by 10
1336.848 Gilcrease
Dated: "Jan 3rd 1893" u.r.
Signed: "TM" u.r.
Inscribed: "Pikes Peak from the Bluffs East C. Springs" u.r.; miscellaneous notes
Provenance: TG
1916 ledger: 150

921
PIKES PEAK NEAR COLORADO SPRINGS
Graphite on wove
6³/₄ by 9
1336.625 Gilcrease
Signed: "TM" l.r.
Inscribed: "Pikes Peak near Colorado Springs" l.l.
Provenance: TG
Note: On the verso of this sketch is a photographic illustration, "Panorama view of Grand Cañon from Hance's. Via Flagstaff, Arizona."

922
THE SAND HILLS BACK OF EAST HAMPTON
Graphite on gray wove
5¹/₈ by 9⁷/₈
1326.846 Gilcrease
Dated: "June 1st 1893" l.c.
Signed: "TM" l.c.
Inscribed: "The Sand Hills. Back of Easthampton" l.l.; color notes
Provenance: TG
1916 ledger: 292

923
SAG HARBOR
Graphite on gray wove
10 by 13³/₄
1326.695 Gilcrease
Signed: "TM" l.r.
Inscribed: "Sag Harbor" l.r.; miscellaneous notes
Provenance: TG
1916 ledger: 208

924
EAST HAMPTON
Graphite on wove
7¹/₂ by 11
1326.847 Gilcrease
Dated: "Sep 20. 93" l.r.
Signed: "TM" l.r.
Inscribed: "E.H." l.r.
Provenance: TG
1916 ledger: 383
Note: Sketch on verso

925
EAST HAMPTON [ledger title]
Graphite on wove
6⁷/₈ by 10
1326.600 Gilcrease
Provenance: TG
1916 ledger: 330

926
EAST HAMPTON POND
Graphite on wove
7¹/₂ by 11
1326.693 Gilcrease
Signed: "TM" l.r.
Inscribed: "E.H. Pond" l.r.
Provenance: TG
1916 ledger: 204

927
MONTAUK
Graphite on wove
8 by 10
1326.850 Gilcrease
Dated: "June 29 1896" u.r.
Signed: "TM" u.r.
Inscribed: "Montauk" u.r.; color notes
Provenance: TG
1916 ledger: 379

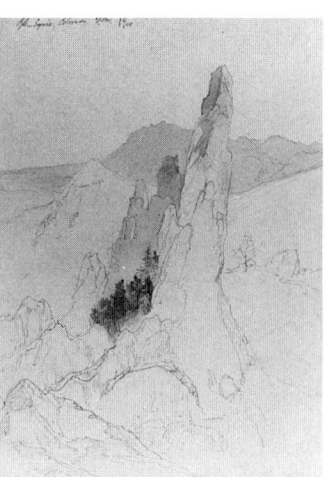

919

*928
BLUE LAKES, IDAHO
Graphite and watercolor on blue wove
10³/₄ by 15
0237.1578 Gilcrease
Dated: "1900" l.l.
Signed: "TMoran" l.l.
Inscribed: "Blue Lakes, Idaho" l.l.; "12" l.l. in ink; miscellaneous notes
Provenance: Ruth K. Henschel, New York; 1964 Thomas Gilcrease Foundation, Tulsa, Okla.; 1974 The Thomas Gilcrease Institute of American History and Art, Tulsa, Okla.
1916 ledger: 241

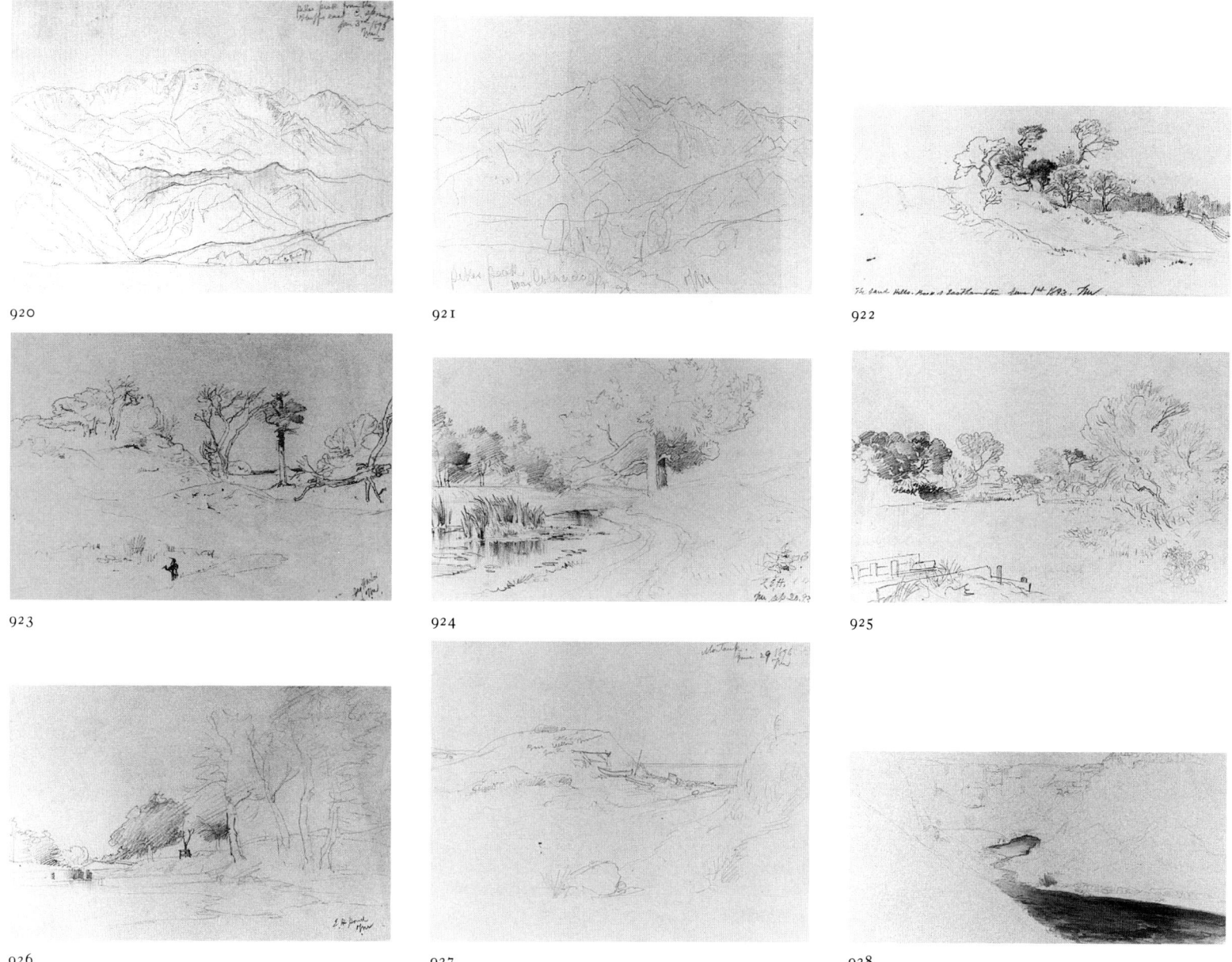

920

921

922

923

924

925

926

927

928

929
BLUE LAKES, SNAKE RIVER
Graphite on blue wove
10³/₄ by 15
1337.665 Gilcrease
Dated: "1900" verso
Signed: "TMoran" l.l.
Inscribed: "Blue Lakes. Snake River" l.l.
Provenance: TG
1916 ledger: 242

†930
SHOSHONE FALLS
Graphite on blue wove
10³/₄ by 15
1337.851 Gilcrease
Dated: "1900" u.l. verso
Inscribed: "Shoshone Falls" u.l. verso
Provenance: TG
1916 ledger: 243
Note: Sketch on verso

931
SHOSHONE FALLS,
SNAKE RIVER, IDAHO
Graphite on blue wove
10⁷/₈ by 15
1917–17–29 Cooper-Hewitt Museum
Signed: "TMoran" l.l.
Inscribed: "Shoshone Falls Snake River Idaho"
l.l.
Provenance: TM
1916 ledger: 83

932
ROCKY MOUNTAINS, CRIPPLE CREEK
RAILROAD, COLORADO
Graphite on manila envelope
9⁷/₈ by 11³/₄
1337.852 Gilcrease
Dated: "1900" u.l.
Signed: "TM" u.l.
Inscribed: "Rocky Mts. Cripple Creek R.R. Col."
u.l.
Provenance: TG
1916 ledger: 269

933
FROM ROWE POINT, LOOKING WEST
Graphite on gray wove

10³/₄ by 15
4243 Jefferson National Expansion Memorial
Dated: "May 24 1901" u.l.
Signed: "TM" u.l.
Inscribed: "from Rowe's Point looking West" u.l.;
miscellaneous notes
Provenance: JNEM
1916 ledger: 191

934
FROM HAVASUPAI POINT,
LOOKING EAST
Graphite on blue wove
15 by 19⁷/₈
1917–17–81 Cooper-Hewitt Museum
Dated: "May 25 1901" l.l.
Inscribed: "From Hava Supai Point Looking
East" l.l.
Provenance: TM

935
LOOKING UP THE TRAIL AT BRIGHT
ANGEL, GRAND CANYON, ARIZONA
Graphite, watercolor, white gouache, and pastel on gray wove
10³/₈ by 14⁷/₈
1917–17–83 Cooper-Hewitt Museum
Dated: "1901" l.c.
Signed: "TMoran" l.l.
Inscribed: "Looking up the trail at Bright Angel
Grand Canyon Arizona" l.l.
Provenance: TM
1916 ledger: 282

936
ON THE BRIGHT ANGEL TRAIL
Graphite on gray wove
10³/₄ by 15
5855 Jefferson National Expansion Memorial
Dated: "1901" u.l.
Signed: "TM" u.l.
Inscribed: "on the Bright Angel Trail" u.l.; color
notes
Provenance: JNEM
1916 ledger: 162

937
A SANDSTORM AT ACOMA
Graphite and watercolor on wove
8 by 10

31.18/2 Stark Museum of Art, Orange, Texas
Dated: "May 31st 1901" u.l.
Signed: "TMoran" u.l.
Inscribed: "A sandstorm at Acoma" u.l.
Provenance: Joseph Sartor Galleries, Dallas,
Texas; H. J. Lutcher Stark, Orange, Texas
1916 ledger: 44

938
ACOMA, NEW MEXICO
Graphite on laid [Moran Gallery letterhead]
5¹/₂ by 9¹/₄
4246 Jefferson National Expansion Memorial
Signed:" TM" l.r.
Inscribed: "Acoma, N.M." l.r.
Provenance: JNEM
1916 ledger: 145

939
MESA ENCANTADA, FROM ACOMA
Graphite on watermarked laid
8 by 10
4255 Jefferson National Expansion Memorial
Signed: "TM" u.l.
Inscribed: "Mesa Encantada from Acoma" u.l.
Provenance: JNEM
1916 ledger: 144

940
A BIT OF LAGUNA
Graphite and wash on wove
10 by 13⁷/₈
1917–17–78 Cooper-Hewitt Museum
Dated: "June 18 1901" l.c.; "1901" l.r.
Inscribed: "A Bit of Laguna" l.r.; "Laguna N.M."
l.c.; miscellaneous notes
Provenance: TM
1916 ledger: 303

941
SPANISH PEAKS, COLORADO
Graphite on laid
8 by 10
1337.854 Gilcrease
Dated: "June 2nd 1901" l.l.
Signed: "TMoran" l.c.
Inscribed: "Spanish Peaks. Colorado" l.l.; "Near
La Junta" l.l.
Provenance: TG
1916 ledger: 316

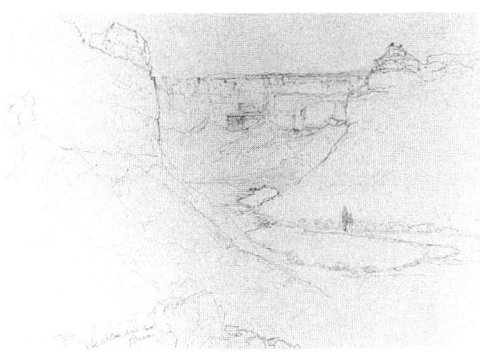

929

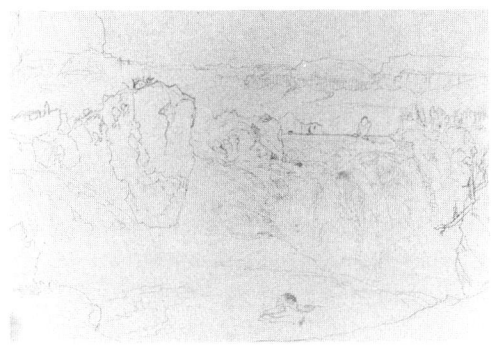

930

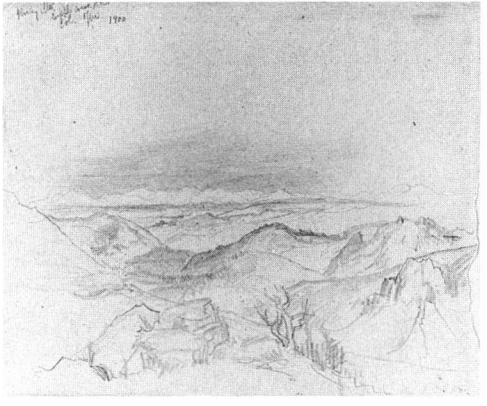

932

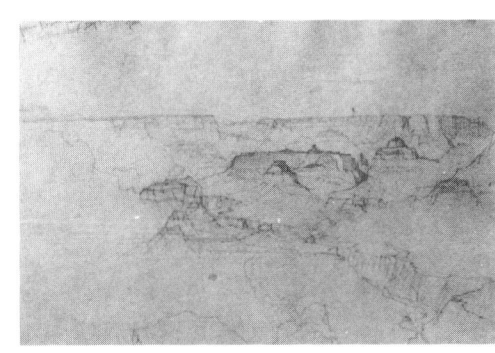

933

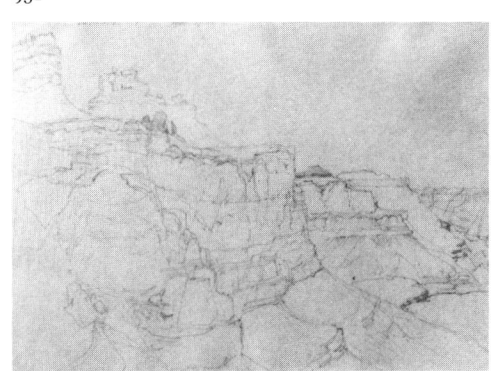

936

942
SPANISH PEAKS, COLORADO
Graphite and ink wash on wove
10 by 14
1917–17–77 Cooper-Hewitt Museum
Dated: "June 2nd 1901" u.l.
Signed: "TM" u.l.
Inscribed: "Spanish Peak Colorado" u.l.; color
notes
Provenance: TM
1916 ledger: 54

943
PIKES PEAK AND CAMERON'S COVE
AND MANITOU CANYON
Graphite and watercolor on wove
10⁷/₈ by 15¹/₈
66.73 Amon Carter Museum, Fort Worth, Texas
Dated: "June 7, 1901" l.l.
Signed: "TMoran" l.l.
Inscribed: "Pikes Peak & Camerons Cove &
Manitou Canon" l.l.
Provenance: Milch Galleries, New York; Charles
Moran 1973; J. N. Bartfield Art Galleries, Inc.,
New York; Amon Carter Museum
1916 ledger: 28

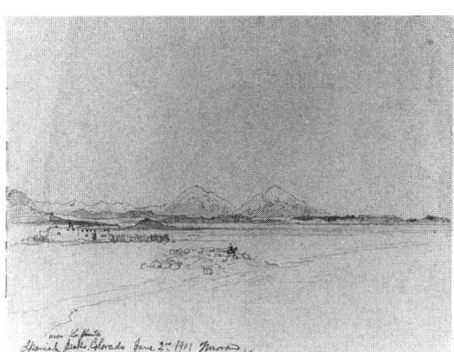

938

941

944
RUXTON, COLORADO AT MANITOU,
FROM THE COG RAILROAD
Graphite, watercolor, and white gouache on wove
10 by 14
1917–17–82 Cooper-Hewitt Museum
Dated: "June 7th 1901" l.l.
Signed: "TM" l.l.
Inscribed: "Ruxton Col at Manitou From the Cog R.R." l.l.
Provenance: TM

945
NAVAJO CHURCH NEAR WINGATE,
NEW MEXICO
Graphite on wove
4¹/₄ by 8³/₈
93 East Hampton Library
Dated: "June 8 1902" u.r.
Inscribed: "Navajo Church Near Wingate, N.M." u.r.; miscellaneous and color notes
Provenance: EH
1916 ledger: 135

946
HUEHUETOCA, MEXICO
Graphite on wove
3¹/₄ by 5
7 East Hampton Library
Dated: "May 7th 1903" u.r.
Signed: "TM" u.r.
Inscribed: "Huehuetoca, Mexico" u.r.; miscellaneous notes
Provenance: EH

947
TEOLOYUCAN CHURCH, MEXICO
Graphite on wove
3¹/₄ by 4⁷/₈
109 East Hampton Library
Signed: "TM" u.r.
Inscribed: "Teoloyucan Church Mex." upper edge
Provenance: EH
1916 ledger: 49

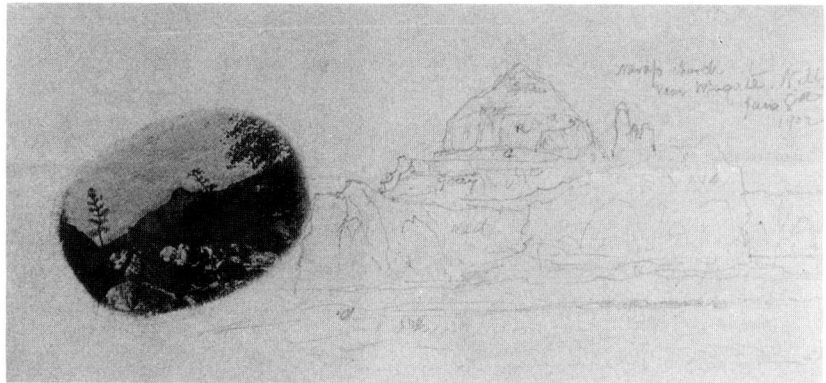

945

948
MEXICO
Graphite on wove
5 by 4¹/₈
108 East Hampton Library
Signed: "TMoran" l.r.
Inscribed: "Mexico" l.c.
Provenance: EH
1916 ledger: 50.6

949
MEXICO
Graphite on wove
5 by 7⁷/₈
74 East Hampton Library
Signed: "TMoran" l.r. and l.l.
Inscribed: "Mexico" l.l.
Provenance: EH
1916 ledger: 19

950
CUERNAVACA FROM THE WEST
BARANCA
Graphite on laid [Moran Gallery letterhead]
5¹/₂ by 8¹/₄
67 East Hampton Library
Dated: "1904" u.c.
Signed: "TMoran" l.l.; "TM" u.c.
Inscribed: "Cuernavaca from the W. Baranca" u.l.
Provenance: EH
1916 ledger: 61

951
LA RITA
Graphite on wove
1⁷/₈ by 3¹/₈
32 East Hampton Library
Signed: "TM" l.r.
Inscribed: "La Rita" u.c.
Provenance: EH
1916 ledger: 200
Note: This sketch is the field study for *La Rita, New Mexico* (oil on canvas, 14 by 23, Fenn Galleries, Santa Fe).

952
ALBUQUERQUE
Graphite on newsprint
4³/₈ by 7¹/₄
1837.18.1 Gilcrease
Dated: "Ap. 16 1903" u.l.
Inscribed: "Albuquerque" u.l.
Provenance: TG

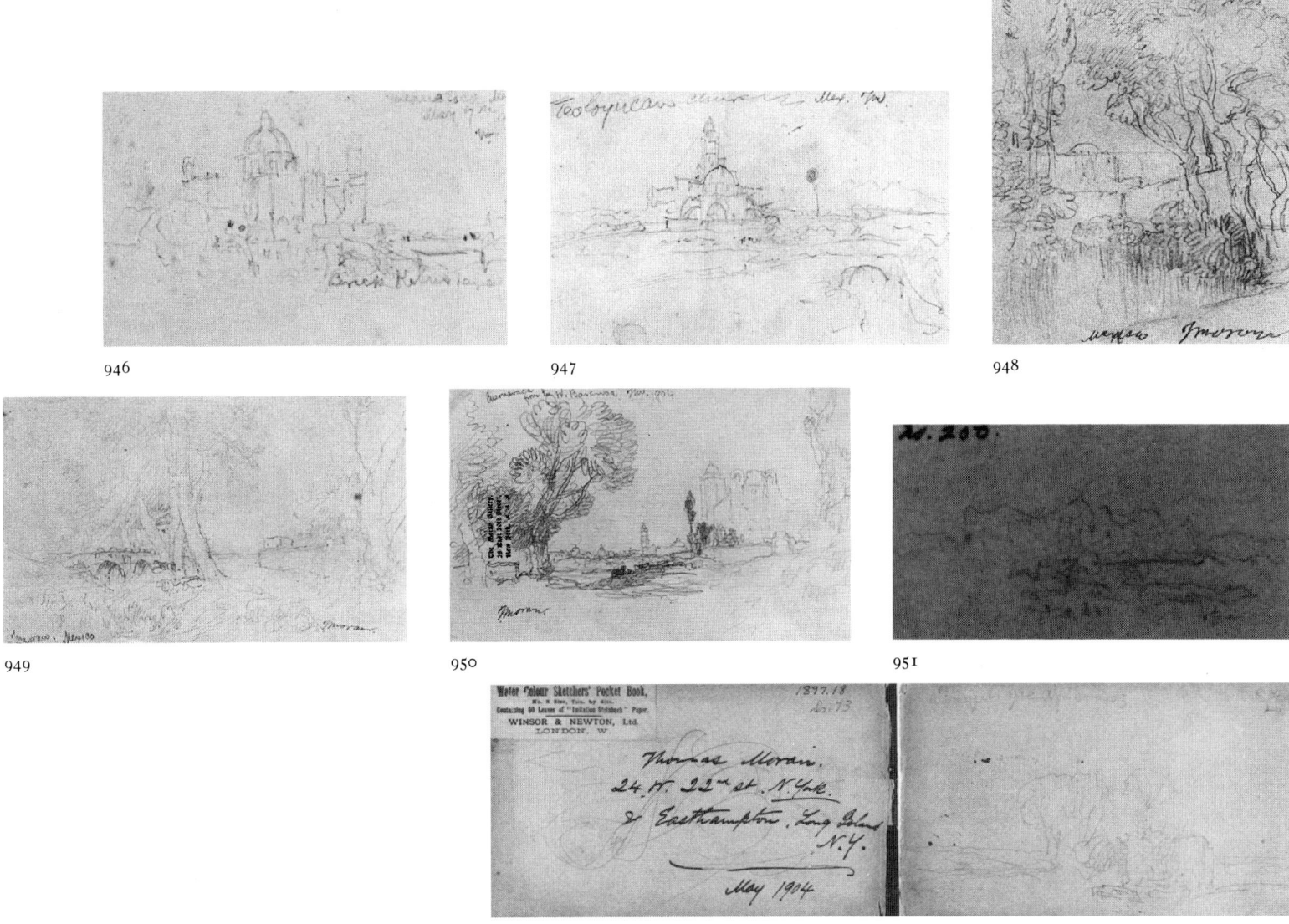

946

947

948

949

950

951

952

953
CUERNAVACA, BRIDGE OVER THE
BARANCA
Graphite on wove
4³/₈ by 7¹/₄
1847.18.2 Gilcrease
Dated: "May 1903" u.r. in ink
Inscribed: "Cuernavaca Bridge over the Bar-
anca Mexico" u.l.; miscellaneous notes
Provenance: TG

954
RUINED CHURCH AT
CUERNAVACA, MEXICO
Graphite on wove
4³/₈ by 14¹/₂
1847.18.3 Gilcrease
Dated: "1903" u.c. in ink
Inscribed: "Ruined Church at Cuernavaca.
Mex." u.c. in ink; miscellaneous notes
Provenance: TG

955
EAST BARANCA, CUERNAVACA
Graphite on wove
4³/₈ by 7¹/₄
1847.18.4 Gilcrease
Dated: "1903" u.l. in ink
Inscribed: "E. Baranca Cuernavaca" u.l.; mis-
cellaneous notes
Provenance: TG

956
CORTÉS PALACE
Graphite on wove
4³/₈ by 7¹/₄
1847.18.5 Gilcrease
Dated: "Ap 28" u.l.
Inscribed: "Cortez Palace" u.l.; miscellaneous
notes
Provenance: TG

†957
RUIN AT CUERNAVACA, MEXICO
Graphite on wove
4³/₈ by 7¹/₄
1847.18.6 Gilcrease
Dated: "Ap 28" u.l.; "1903" u.l. in ink
Inscribed: "Ruin at Cuernavaca Mexico" u.l.;
miscellaneous notes
Provenance: TG

953

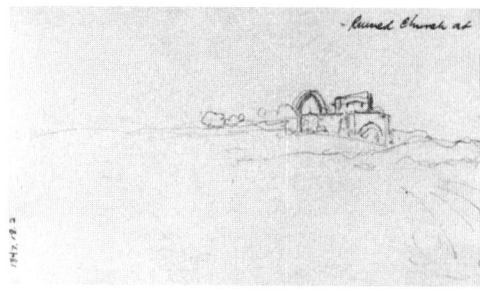

954

958
CUERNAVACA [descriptive]
Graphite on wove
7¹/₄ by 4³/₈
1847.18.7 Gilcrease
Provenance: TG

959
BARANCA, CUERNAVACA
Graphite on wove
4³/₈ by 7¹/₄
1847.18.8 Gilcrease
Inscribed: "Baranca & Cuernavaca" u.l.
Provenance: TG

960
WEST BARANCA, CUERNAVACA
Graphite on wove
4³/₈ by 14¹/₂
1847.18.9 Gilcrease
Dated: "1903" u.l. in ink
Inscribed: "West Baranca. Cuernavaca" u.l.;
miscellaneous notes
Provenance: TG

961
EAST HAMPTON
Graphite on wove
4³/₈ by 7¹/₄
1827.18.10 Gilcrease
Dated: "1903" u.l. in ink
Inscribed: "E. Hamp." u.l. in ink
Provenance: TG

962
CORTÉS PALACE, CUERNAVACA,
MEXICO
Graphite on wove
4³/₈ by 14¹/₂
1847.18.11 Gilcrease
Dated: "1903" u.c. in ink
Inscribed: "Corte's Palace. Cuernavaca. Mex."
u.c.
in ink
Provenance: TG

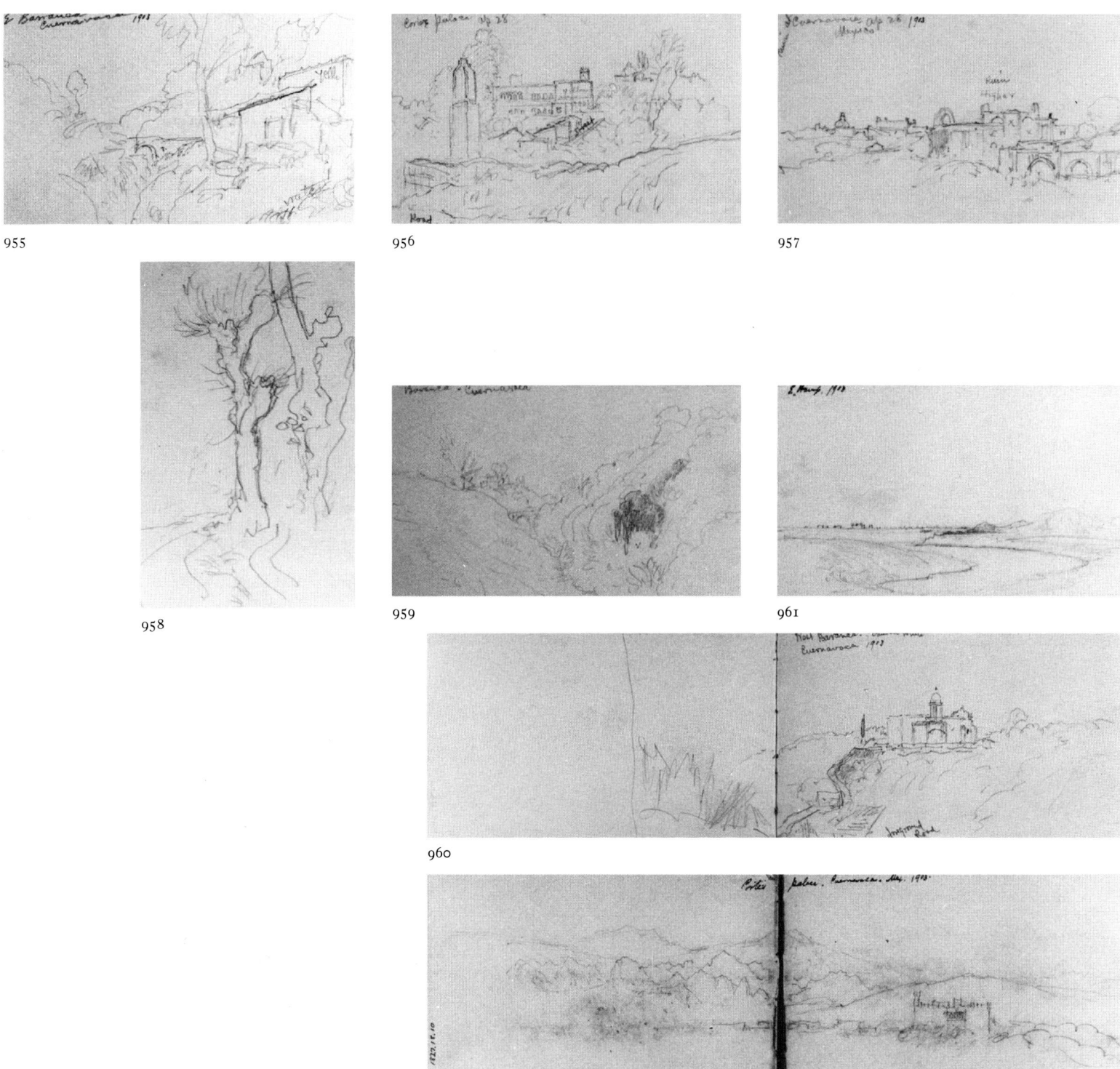

955

956

957

958

959

961

960

962

963
LIME KILNS AT TULA
Graphite on wove
4³/₈ by 7¹/₄
1847.18.12 Gilcrease
Dated: "May 7 1903" u.r.
Inscribed: "Lime Kilns at Tula" u.r.
Provenance: TG

964
CLOUD CROFT, GRAND VIEW
Graphite on wove
4³/₈ by 14¹/₂
1837.18.13 Gilcrease
Dated: "1903" u.l. in ink
Inscribed: "Cloud Croft. Grand View" u.l.; miscellaneous notes
Provenance: TG

965
GRAND CANYON [descriptive]
Graphite on wove
4³/₈ by 7¹/₄
1837.18.14 Gilcrease
Provenance: TG

966
GRAND CANYON
Graphite on wove
4³/₈ by 7¹/₄
1837.18.15 Gilcrease
Dated: "June 17th 1904" u.l.
Inscribed: "Gran Canon" u.l.
Provenance: TG

967
GRAND CANYON
Graphite on wove
4³/₈ by 7¹/₄
1837.18.16 Gilcrease
Dated: "May 17" u.r.
Inscribed: "Gran C." u.r.
Provenance: TG

968
GRAND CANYON [descriptive]
Graphite on wove
4³/₈ by 7¹/₄
1837.18.17 Gilcrease
Provenance: TG

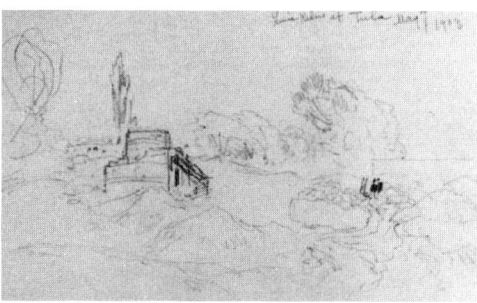

963

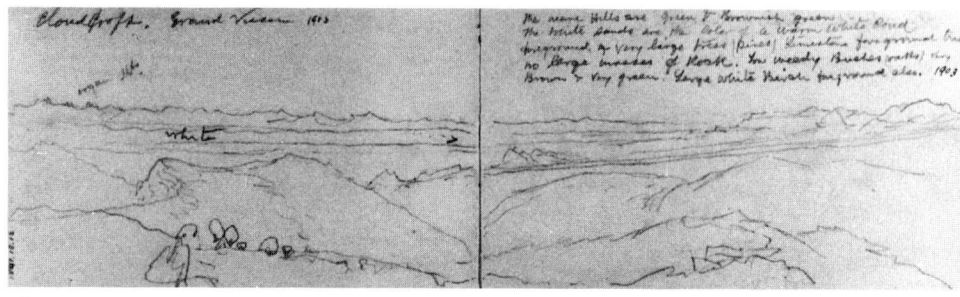

964

969
GRAND CANYON [descriptive]
Graphite on wove
4³/₈ by 7¹/₄
1837.18.18 Gilcrease
Provenance: TG

970
GRAND CANYON [descriptive]
Graphite on wove
4³/₈ by 7¹/₄
1837.18.19 Gilcrease
Provenance: TG

971
GRAND CANYON [descriptive]
Graphite on wove
4³/₈ by 7¹/₄
1837.18.20 Gilcrease
Provenance: TG

972
GRAND CANYON [descriptive]
Graphite on wove
4³/₈ by 7¹/₄
1837.18.21 Gilcrease
Provenance: TG

973
MOONLIGHT, GRAND CANYON
Graphite on wove
4³/₈ by 7¹/₄
1837.18.22 Gilcrease
Dated: "May 22nd" u.r.
Inscribed: "Moonlight G. Canon" u.c.
Provenance: TG

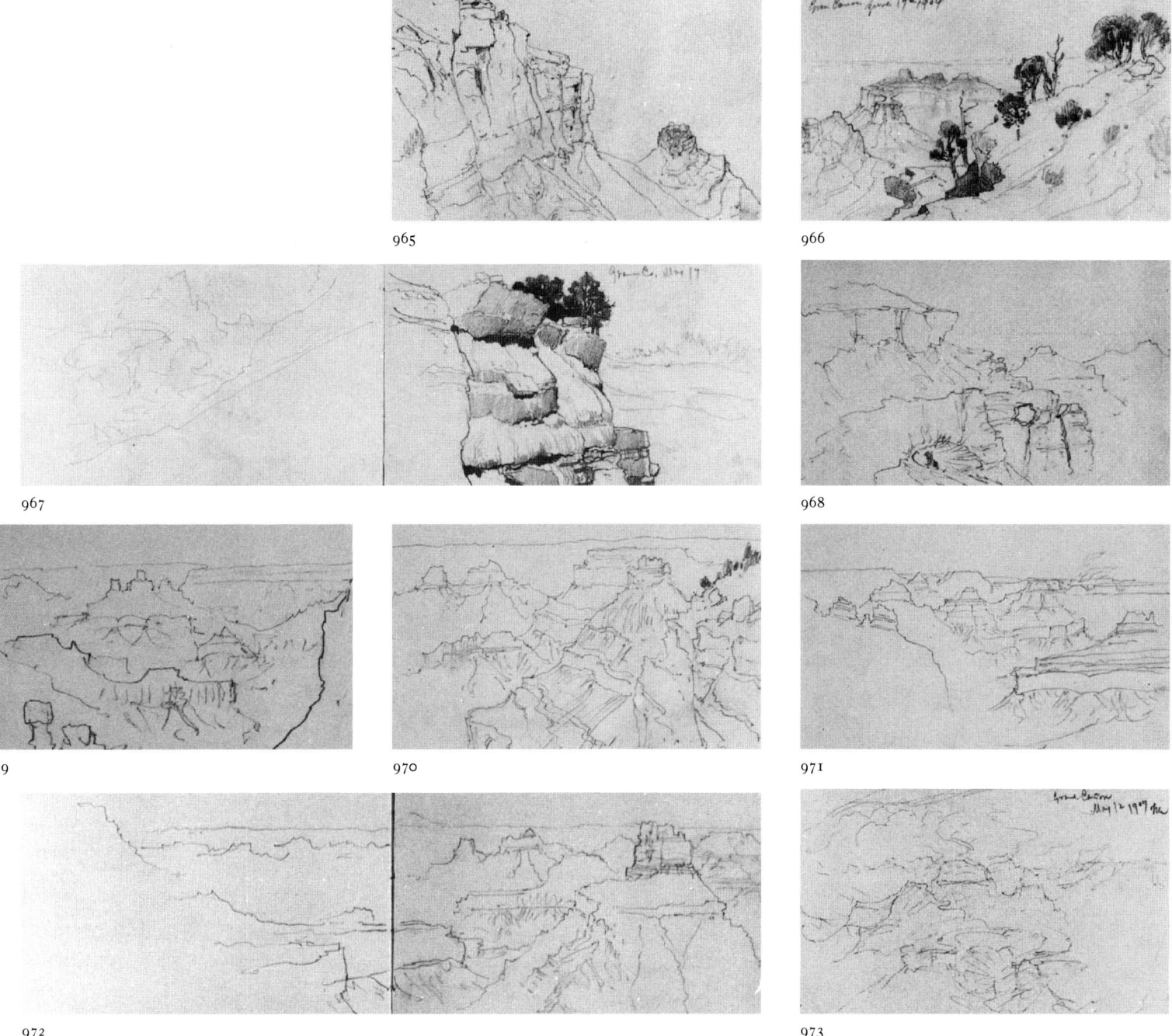

965

966

967

968

969

970

971

972

973

974
GRAND CANYON [descriptive]
Graphite on wove
4³/₈ by 7¹/₄
1837.18.23 Gilcrease
Inscribed with color notes
Provenance: TG

975
GRAND CANYON [descriptive]
Graphite on wove
4³/₈ by 7¹/₄
1837.18.24 Gilcrease
Inscribed with color notes
Provenance: TG

976
GRAND CANYON [descriptive]
Graphite on wove
4³/₈ by 7¹/₄
1837.18.25 Gilcrease
Provenance: TG

977
EAST HAMPTON
Graphite on wove
1827.18.26 Gilcrease
4³/₈ by 7¹/₄
Dated: "1903" u.l. in ink
Inscribed: "E.H." u.l. in ink
Provenance: TG

978
COYOACAN
Graphite on wove
4³/₈ by 7¹/₄
1847.18.27 Gilcrease
Dated: "1903" u.l. in ink
Inscribed: "Coyoacan" u.l.; "Mex." u.l. in ink;
miscellaneous notes
Provenance: TG

979
COYOACAN STREET
Graphite on wove
4³/₈ by 7¹/₄
1847.18.28 Gilcrease
Inscribed: "Coayacan Street" u.l.
Provenance: TG

980
COYOACAN, COURTYARD OF CHURCH
Graphite on wove
4³/₈ by 7¹/₄
1847.18.29 Gilcrease
Dated: "1903" u.l. in ink
Inscribed: "Coyoacan Courtyard of Church"
u.l.; miscellaneous notes
Provenance: TG

981
WALL OF LA BORDA
Graphite on wove
4³/₈ by 7¹/₄
1847.18.30 Gilcrease
Dated: "1903" u.c. in ink
Inscribed: "Wall of La Borda" u.l.; "Mex." u.l. in
ink
Provenance: TG

982
YOSEMITE
Graphite and white gouache on wove
10³/₄ by 15
7 East Hampton Library
Dated: "1904" l.r.
Signed: Colophon l.r.
Inscribed: "Yosemite" l.l.; miscellaneous notes
Provenance: EH

983
FROM GLACIER POINT, YOSEMITE
VALLEY
Graphite on gray wove
10³/₄ by 14⁷/₈
57 782 Yosemite National Park, California
Dated: "1904" l.r.
Signed: "TM" l.r.
Inscribed: "From Glacier Point Yosemite V."
l.r.; miscellaneous notes
Provenance: YOS
1916 ledger: 100

984
THE SOUTH DOME FROM GLACIER
POINT, YOSEMITE VALLEY
Graphite and white gouache on wove
15 by 21¹/₂
1917–17–86 Cooper-Hewitt Museum
Signed: "TM" l.r.

Inscribed: "The South Dome from Glacier Point
Yosemite V." l.r.
Provenance: TM
1916 ledger: 106

985
FROM MORAN POINT
Graphite on blue wove
10³/₄ by 15
57 780 Yosemite National Park, California
Signed: "TM" l.l.
Inscribed: "From Point Moran (near Glacier
Point Yosemite)" l.l.
Provenance: YOS
1916 ledger: 91

986
SOUTH DOME, YOSEMITE
Graphite and white gouache on blue wove
10³/₄ by 15
1917–17–76 Cooper-Hewitt Museum
Signed: "TM" l.l. and u.l.
Inscribed: "South Dome Yosemite" l.l.; "South
Dome Yosemite—from ravine back of Hard-
ings" u.l.
Provenance: TM
1916 ledger: 90

987
BACK OF SOUTH DOME, VERNAL
FALLS, YOSEMITE
Graphite, watercolor, and white gouache on
gray wove
12³/₄ by 9³/₄
1917–17–85 Cooper-Hewitt Museum
Dated: "1904" l.r.
Signed: "TMoran" l.r.
Inscribed: "Back of South dome Vernal Falls
Yosemite" l.r.
Provenance: TM
1916 ledger: 88
Note: This may be a composite drawing, not
South Dome but Liberty Cap or Cap of Liberty.

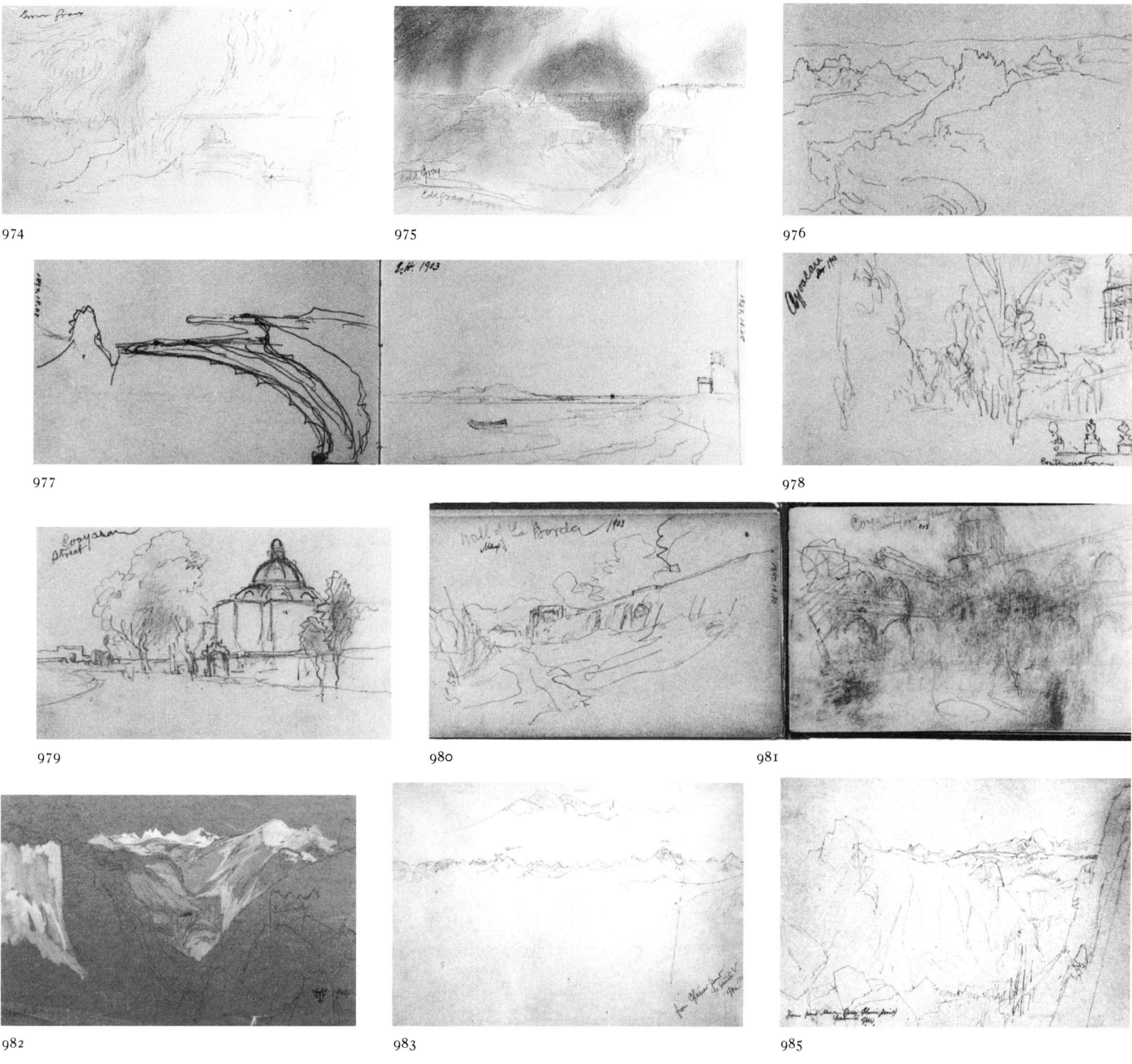

974

975

976

977

978

979

980

981

982

983

985

988
SOUTH DOME FROM THE NEVADA
FALL TRAIL
Graphite, wash, and white gouache on gray
wove
12³/₄ by 9⁷/₈
1917–17–47 Cooper-Hewitt Museum
Inscribed: "South Dome from the Nevada falls
Trail" l.r. in white gouache; "Back of S. Dome" u.l.
Provenance: TM

989
NORTH DOME, YOSEMITE
Graphite and wash on wove
12⁷/₈ by 9¹/₄
57 874 Yosemite National Park, California
Dated: "1874" l.l. [see note]
Signed: "TM" l.l.
Inscribed: "North Dome. Yo." l.l.
Provenance: YOS
1916 ledger: 94
Note: This sketch is similar stylistically to the
work of 1904. Moran is not known to have been
in Yosemite in 1874, even though several sketches
bear this date. There is a sketch on verso.

990a
CATHEDRAL ROCK, YOSEMITE
Graphite, wash, and white gouache on gray wove
Recto sketch 9¹/₂ by 6¹/₂
57 871 Yosemite National Park, California
Dated: "1904" l.c.
Signed: "TM" l.c.
Inscribed: "Cathedral Rocks. Yosemite" l.l.
Provenance: YOS
1916 ledger: 99

990b
SENTINEL
Graphite and white gouache on gray wove
Verso sketch 9¹/₂ by 6¹/₂
57 871 Yosemite National Park, California
Signed: "TM" u.c. and colophon stamp u.r.
Inscribed: "Sentinel" u.c.
Provenance: YOS

991
NEVADA FALL, YOSEMITE
Graphite and wash on wove
10³/₄ by 15
57 877 Yosemite National Park, California
Dated: "1904" l.r.
Signed: Colophon stamp three times vertically
u.r.
Inscribed: "Nevada Falls. Yos" l.r.; "Emerald
pools" l. c.
Provenance: YOS
1916 ledger: 72

992
YOSEMITE, NORTH AND SOUTH
DOMES
Graphite on wove
4³/₈ by 7¹/₈
57 784 Yosemite National Park, California
Dated: "May 27 1904" u.c.
Inscribed: "Yos." u.l.; "N. & S. Dome" u.c.
Provenance: YOS

993
BRIGHT ANGEL
Graphite on wove
4⁷/₈ by 8¹/₈
1337.860 Gilcrease
Dated: "May 18th 1905" l.l.
Signed: "TM" l.l.
Inscribed: "Bright Angel" l.l.
Provenance: TG

994
GRAND CANYON [descriptive]
Graphite on wove
4⁷/₈ by 8¹/₈
1337.2010 Gilcrease
Provenance: TG

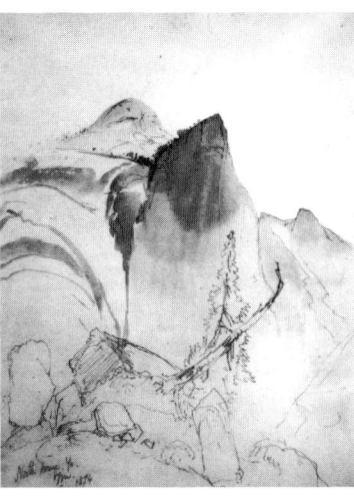

989

995
CONWAY
Purple pencil and graphite on wove
5 by 7
1877.20.1 Gilcrease
Dated: "Sep 6th 1906" l.l. in purple pencil
Inscribed: "Conway" and "The Smithy." l.l. in
purple pencil
Provenance: TG

996
CONWAY
Purple pencil on wove
5 by 7
1877.20.2 Gilcrease
Dated: "Sept 1906" u.l.
Inscribed: "Conway" u.l. in purple pencil
Provenance: TG

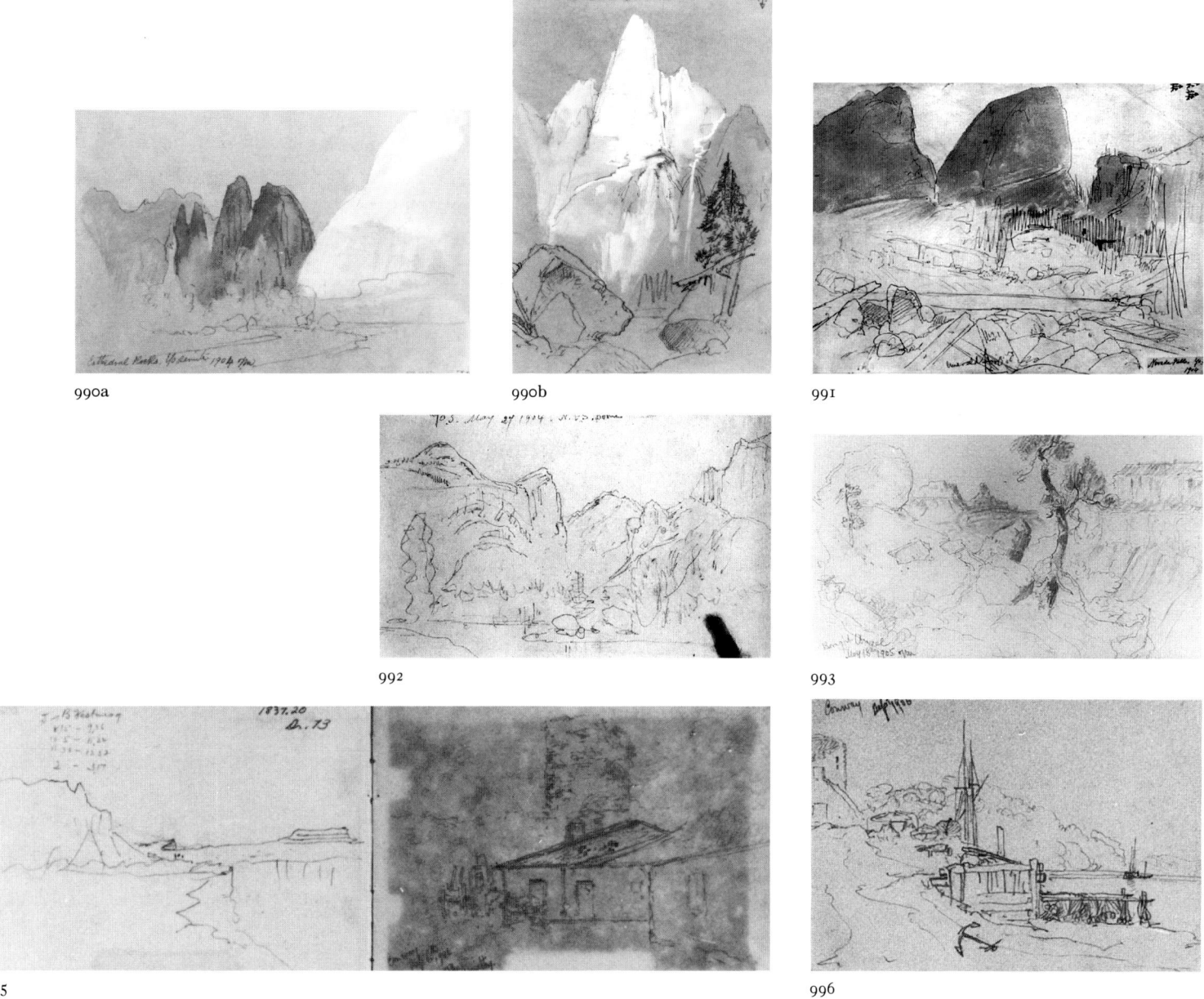

990a

990b

991

992

993

995

996

997
CONWAY
Purple pencil on wove
5 by 7
1877.20.3 Gilcrease
Dated: "Sep 8th 1906" l.r. in purple pencil;
"1906" u.r. in graphite
Signed: "TM" l.r. in purple pencil
Inscribed: "Conway" u.r. in black graphite and
l.r. in
purple pencil
Provenance: TG

998
THE QUEEN'S TOWER, CONWAY
CASTLE
Purple pencil on wove
7 by 5
1877.20.4 Gilcrease
Dated: "Sep 8th 1906" l.l. in purple pencil
Signed: "TM" l.l. in purple pencil
Inscribed: "The Queens Tower Conway Castle"
l.l. in purple pencil
Provenance: TG

999
CONWAY
Graphite on wove
5 by 7
104 East Hampton Library
Dated: "Sept 8 1906" l.l.
Signed: "TM" l.l.
Inscribed: "Conway" l.l.
Provenance: EH
1916 ledger: 289

1000
ROMAN LOOKOUT AT SWALLOW FALLS
Purple pencil on wove
5 by 7
1877.20.5 Gilcrease
Dated: "1906" l.r. in purple pencil
Inscribed: "Roman Lookout at Swallow Falls"
u.l. in purple pencil; "swallow falls on the lledr."
l.r. in purple pencil
Provenance: TG

†1001
CONWAY FROM THE MOUNTAIN
Purple pencil on wove
5 by 7
1877.20.6 Gilcrease
Dated: "Sep 11th 1906" u.l. in purple pencil
Signed: "TM" u.l. in purple pencil
Inscribed: "Conway from the Mt." u.l. in purple
pencil
Provenance: TG

1002
THE GATEWAY, CONWAY, NORTH
WALES
Purple pencil on wove
7 by 5
1877.20.7 Gilcrease
Dated: "Sep 11th 1906" u.r. in graphite
Signed: "TM" u.r. in graphite
Inscribed: "The Gateway. Conway. N. Wales"
u.r. in graphite
Provenance: TG

†1003
A LIGHTER AT CONWAY
Purple pencil on wove
5 by 7
1877.20.8 Gilcrease
Dated: "Sep 12th 1906" l.l. in purple pencil
Inscribed: "a lighter at Conway" l.l. in purple
pencil
Provenance: TG

1004
CONWAY
Purple pencil on wove
5 by 7
18773.20.9 Gilcrease
Dated: "Sep 1906" l.l. in graphite
Signed: "TM" l.l. in graphite
Inscribed: "Conway" l.l. in graphite
Provenance: TG

1005
CONWAY MOUNTAIN
Purple pencil on wove
5 by 14
1877.20.10 Gilcrease
Inscribed: "Conway Mountain" u.l. of second
leaf in purple pencil; "looks very high" u.r. in
purple pencil
Provenance: TG

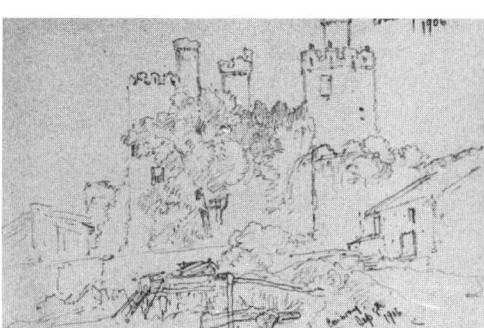

997

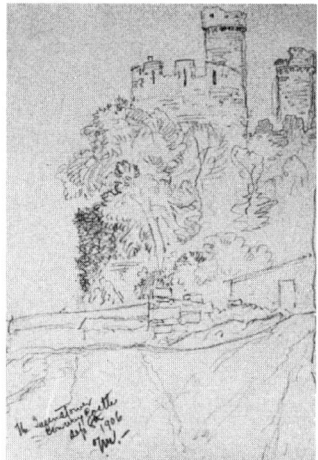

998

†1006
DOLLWYDELLAN TOWER
Graphite on wove
5 by 7
1877.20.11 Gilcrease
Dated: "Sep 1906" u.c.
Signed: "TM" u.c.
Inscribed: "Dollwydellon Tower. The Birth-
place of Llewellan the Great" u.l.; "Snowden"
c. Provenance: TG

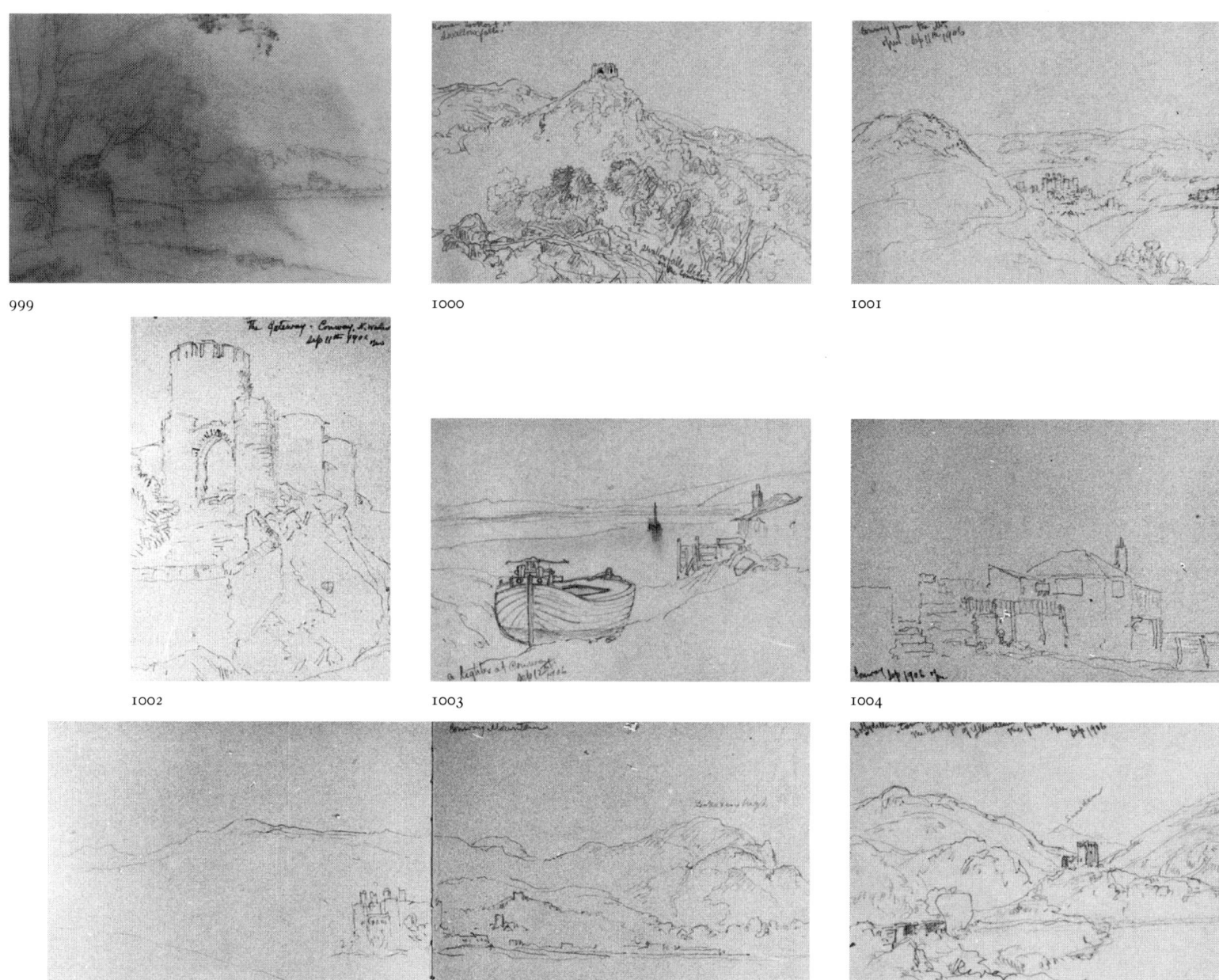

999

1000

1001

1002

1003

1004

1005

1006

†1007
HARLECH CASTLE FROM THE NORTH
Graphite on wove
5 by 7
1877.20.12 Gilcrease
Dated: "Sep 1906" u.l.
Signed: "TM" u.l.
Inscribed: "Harlech Castle from the North" u.l.
Provenance: TG

1008
HARLECH CASTLE, SOUTH SIDE
Graphite on wove
5 by 7
1877.20.13 Gilcrease
Dated: "Sep 1906" l.r.
Signed: "TM" l.r.
Inscribed: "Harlech Castle S. Side" l.r.; "plain"
l.l.
Provenance: TG

1009
HARLECH FROM THE ROAD,
NORTH SIDE
Graphite on wove·
5 by 7
1877.20. 14 Gilcrease
Inscribed: "Harlech from the Road. North Side"
u.l.
Provenance: TG

1010
HARLECH
Graphite on wove
5 by 7
1877.20.15 Gilcrease
Dated: "Sep 15 1906" u.l.
Inscribed: "Harlech" u.l.; "Snowdon" l.c.
Provenance: TG

†1011
DOLLWYDELLAN TOWER
Graphite on ruled wove
8 by 10¼
1377.862 Gilcrease
Dated: "Sep 15th 1906" u.r.
Inscribed: "Dolwydellan Tower where Llewellan
the Great was Born" u.r.
Provenance: TG

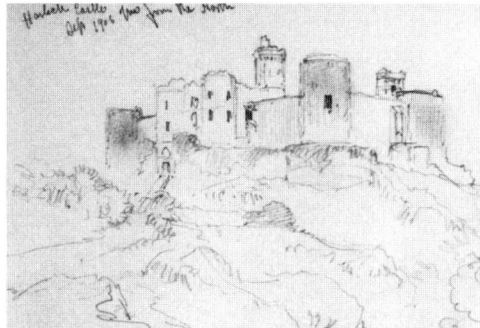

1007

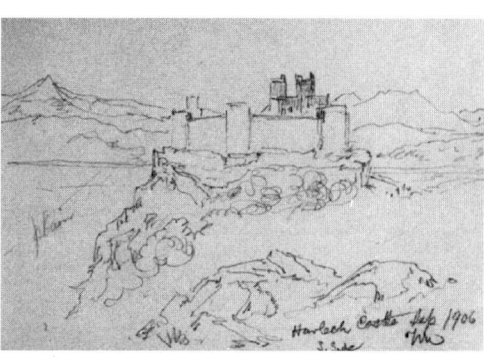

1008

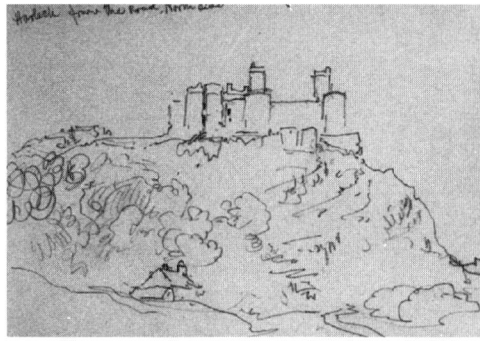

1009

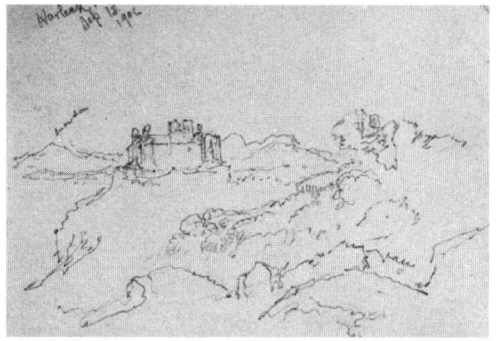

1010

†1012
GRAND CANYON [descriptive]
Graphite on wove
5 by 14
1837.20.16 Gilcrease
Provenance: TG

1013
SENTINEL POINT, LOOKING EAST
Graphite on wove
5 by 14
1837.20.17 Gilcrease
Dated: "1908" l.c.
Inscribed: "Sentinel Point Looking East" l.c.
Provenance: TG

1014
GRAND CANYON [descriptive]
Graphite on wove
5 by 7
1837.20.18 Gilcrease
Provenance: TG

†1015
GRAND CANYON
Graphite on wove
5 by 7
1837.20.19 Gilcrease
Dated: "May 25th 1907" u.l.
Inscribed: "Grand Canyon" and "dropping
clouds" u.l.
Provenance: TG

1016
GRAND VIEW
Graphite on wove
5 by 14
1837.20.20 Gilcrease
Dated: "May 21st 1907" u.r.
Inscribed: "Grand View" u.r.
Provenance: TG

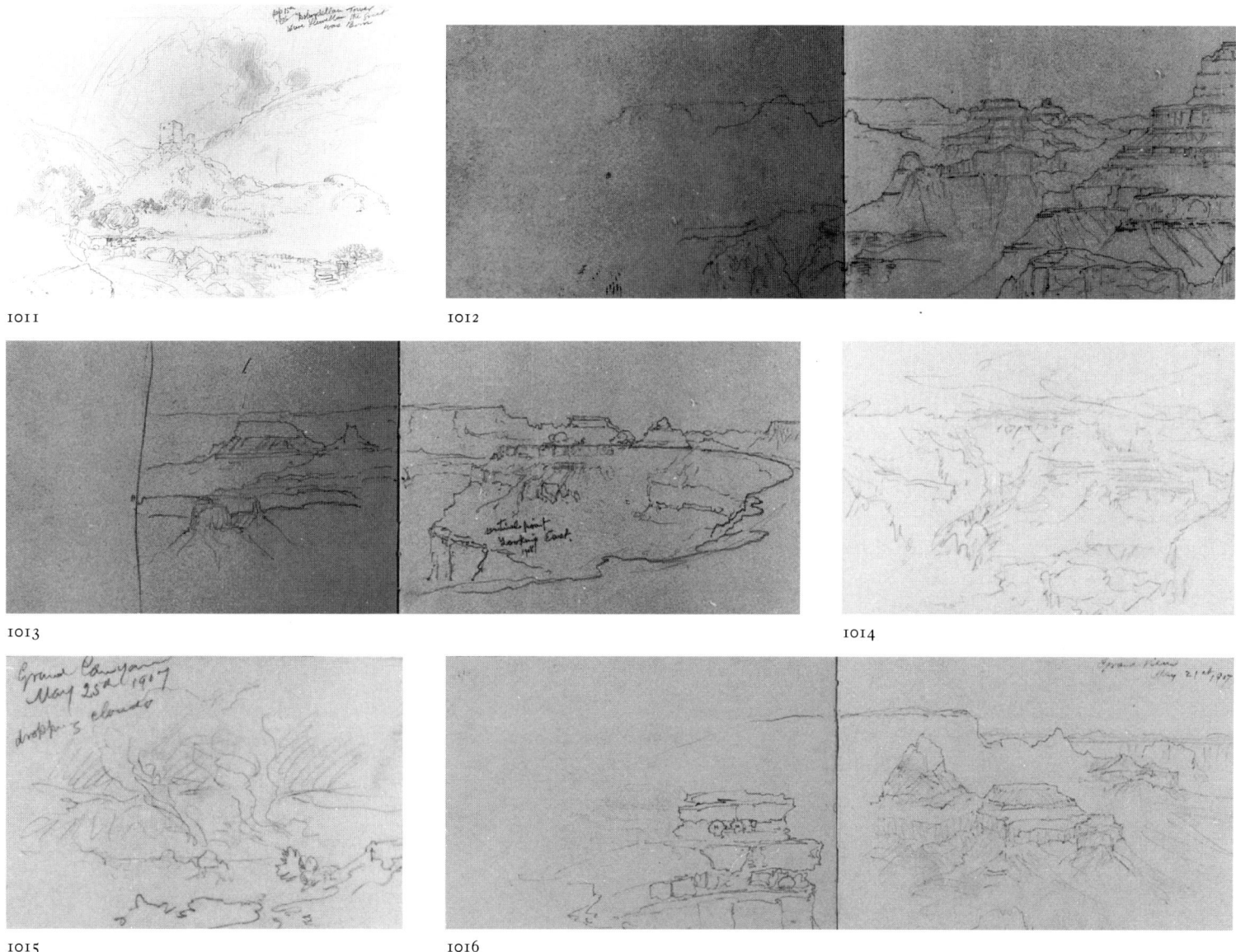

1011

1012

1013

1014

1015

1016

1017
GRAND VIEW
Graphite on wove
5 by 7
1837.20.21 Gilcrease
Dated: "May 21 1907" u.r.
Inscribed: "Grand View" u.r.
Provenance: TG

1018
GRAND CANYON
Graphite on wove
5 by 7
1837.20.22 Gilcrease
Dated: "May 12 1907" u.r.
Signed: "TM" u.r.
Inscribed: "Grand Cañon" u.r.
Provenance: TG

1019
CLOUDS AND MIST IN THE CANYON
Graphite on wove
5 by 7
1837.20.23 Gilcrease
Dated: "May 12 1907" u.r.
Signed: "TM" u.r.
Inscribed: "Clouds & Mist in the Canon" u.r.
Provenance: TG

1020
FROM O'NEILL POINT
Graphite on wove
4⁷/₈ by 8¹/₈
1337.622 Gilcrease
Inscribed: "from ONeils Point" u.r.; miscella-
neous notes
Provenance: TG

†1021
HERMIT CHASM, GRAND CANYON
Graphite on wove
8¹/₈ by 4⁷/₈
1337.864 Gilcrease
Dated: "June 1908" u.r.
Inscribed: "Hermit Chasm. Grand Canyon" u.c.
Provenance: TG

†1022
LOOKING WEST, BRIGHT ANGEL
Graphite on wove
8¹/₈ by 4⁷/₈
1337.861 Gilcrease
Inscribed: "Looking West. B Angel" u.l.
Provenance: TG

†1023
GRAND CANYON [descriptive]
Graphite on wove
4⁷/₈ by 8¹/₈
1337.623 Gilcrease
Provenance: TG

1024
RAIN IN CANYON
Ink on wove
6 by 9¹/₂
1917–17–88 Cooper-Hewitt Museum
Dated: "July 12th 1908" l.l. in ink
Signed: "TM" l.l. in ink
Inscribed: "Rain in Canon" l.l. in ink
Provenance: TM
1916 ledger: 312

1025
GRAND CANYON, ARIZONA
Ink on wove
6 by 9¹/₂
1917–17–87 Cooper-Hewitt Museum
Dated: "July 12 1908" u.r. in ink; "1908" in ink
on mat
Signed: "TM" u.r.; "TMoran" l.l. on mat
Inscribed: "Grand Canon Arizona" u.r. in ink;
miscellaneous notes
Provenance: TM
1916 ledger: 36

1026
BACK OF LAGUNA
Graphite on wove
4⁷/₈ by 8¹/₈
1337.867 Gilcrease
Inscribed: "Back of Laguna" u.r.; color notes
Provenance: TG

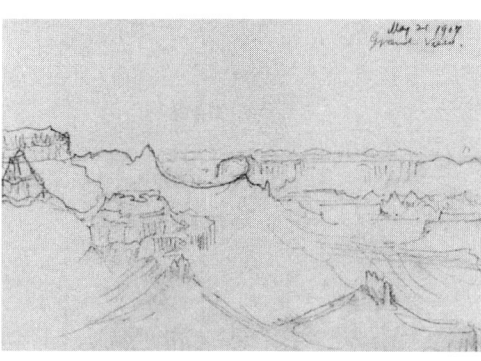

1017

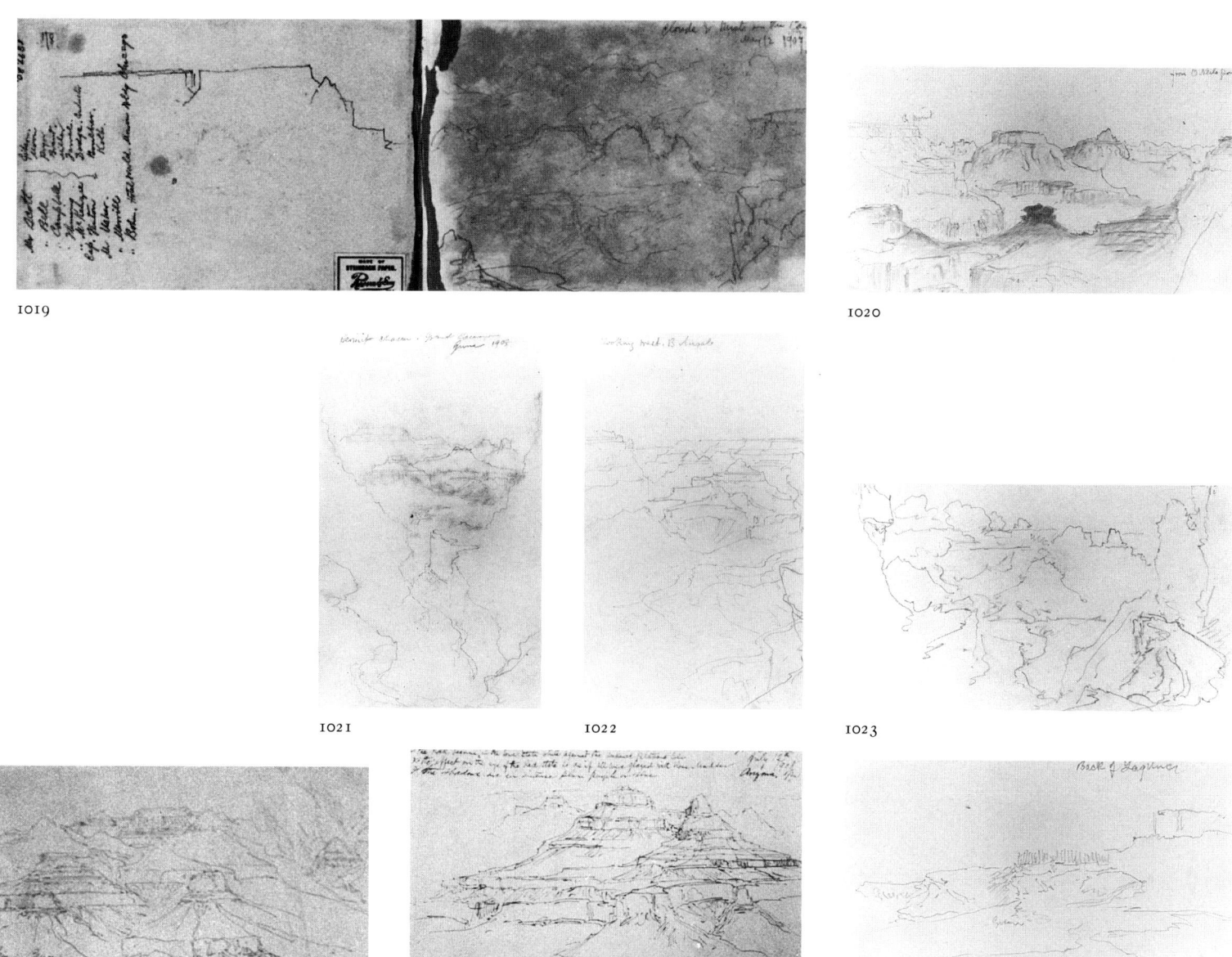

1019

1020

1021

1022

1023

1024

1025

1026

†1027
RAIN POOL IN ROCKS, LAGUNA
Graphite on wove
4⁷/₈ by 8¹/₈
1337.866 Gilcrease
Inscribed: "Rain Pool in Rocks Laguna" u.c.
Provenance: TG

1028
LAGUNA [descriptive]
Graphite on wove
4⁷/₈ by 8¹/₈
1337.1998 Gilcrease
Provenance: TG

1029
STEPS IN LAGUNA, AT SIDE OF
THE CHURCH
Graphite on wove
4⁷/₈ by 8¹/₈
1337.590 Gilcrease
Inscribed: "Steps in Laguna. at Side of the
Church" u.r.; miscellaneous notes
Provenance: TG
1916 ledger: 136

1030
A STREET IN LAGUNA, NEW MEXICO
Graphite on wove
4⁷/₈ by 8¹/₈
1337.865 Gilcrease
Dated: "July 28th. 1908" u.c.
Inscribed: "A Street in Laguna, N.M." u.l. and
"sand in distance" u.r.
Provenance: Ruth K. Henschel, New York; 1964
Thomas Gilcrease Foundation, Tulsa, Okla.;
1969 The Thomas Gilcrease Institute of Ameri-
can History and Art, Tulsa, Okla.

1031
LAGUNA [descriptive]
Graphite on wove
4⁷/₈ by 8¹/₈
1337.2009 Gilcrease
Provenance: TG

1032
A STREET IN LAGUNA
Graphite on wove
4¹/₈ by 7
1337.1012 Gilcrease

Inscribed: "A Street in Laguna" u.l.
Provenance: TG
1916 ledger: 360

1033
LAGUNA
Graphite on wove
7 by 8¹/₂
1337.655 Gilcrease
Signed: "TM" u.r.
Inscribed: "Laguna" u.c.; "Zuni one of the seven
cities of [illegible] The return from the Chase"
u.r.
Provenance: TG
1916 ledger: 165

†1034
BRIDGE AT WARWICK
Graphite on wove
5 by 6³/₄
1877.19.1 Gilcrease
Dated: "May 25th 1910" u.r.
Signed: "TM" u.r.
Inscribed: "Bridge at Warwick" u.r.
Provenance: TG

1035
TORQUAY
Graphite on wove
5 by 6³/₄
1877.19.2 Gilcrease
Dated: "May 31 1910" u.l.
Signed: "TM" u.l.
Inscribed: "Torquay" u.l.
Provenance: TG

†1036
ANSTEY COVE
Graphite on wove
5 by 6³/₄
1877.19.3 Gilcrease
Dated: "June 1st 1910" u.l.
Signed: "TM" u.l.
Inscribed: "Ansteys Cove" u.l.; color notes
Provenance: TG

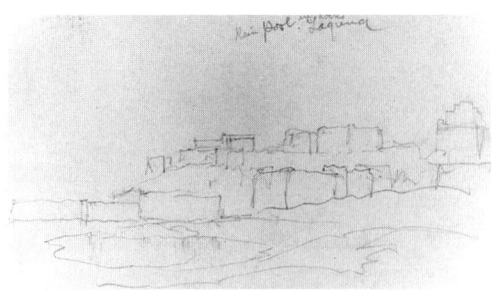

1027

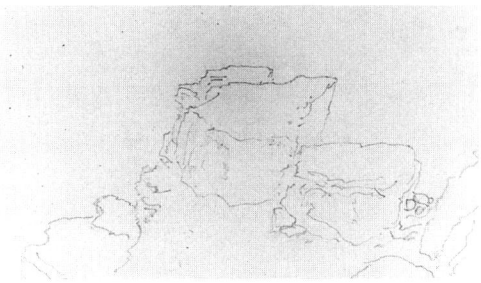

1028

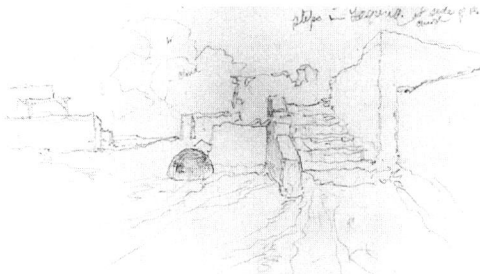

1029

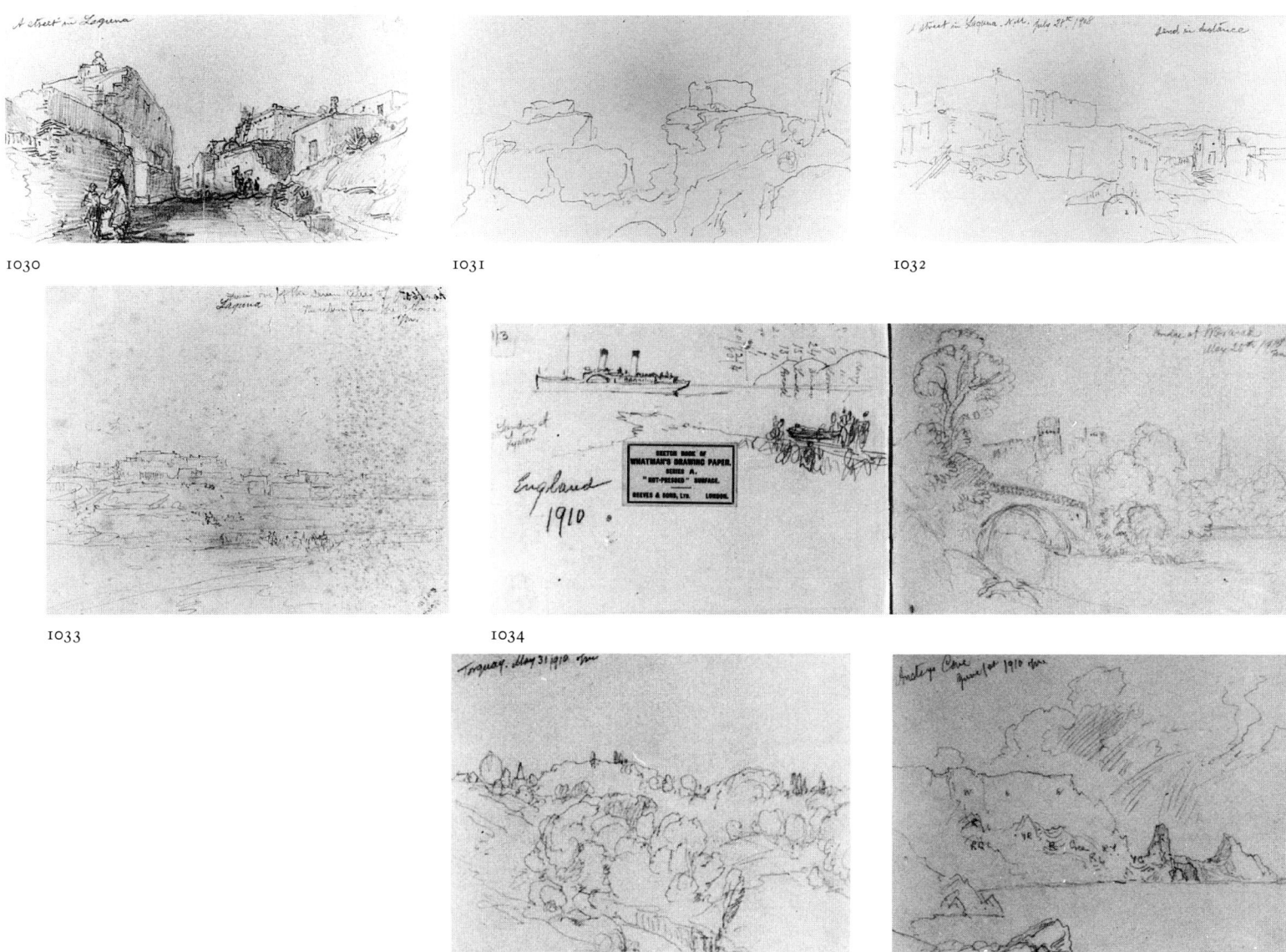

1030

1031

1032

1033

1034

1035

1036

1037
ANSTEY COVE
Graphite on wove
5 by 6³/₄
1877.19.4 Gilcrease
Dated: "June 1st 1910" u.l.
Signed: "TM" u.l.
Inscribed: "Ansteys Cove" u.l.; color notes
Provenance: TG

†1038
COCKINGTON QUARRY
Graphite on wove
5 by 6³/₄
1877.19.5 Gilcrease
Dated: "June 2nd 1910" l.r.
Signed: "TM" l.r.
Inscribed: "Cockington Quarry" l.r.
Provenance: TG

1039
COCKINGTON LANE
Graphite on wove
6³/₄ by 5
1877.19.6 Gilcrease
Dated: "June 2nd 1910" l.l.
Signed: "TM" l.l.
Inscribed: "Cockington Lane" l.l.; color notes
Provenance: TG

1040
BRIXHAM
Graphite on wove
5 by 6³/₄
1877.19.7 Gilcrease
Dated: "June 3rd 1910" u.l.
Inscribed: "Brixham" u.l.; miscellaneous notes
Provenance: TG

1041
BRIXHAM
Graphite on Ivorine tissue
4⁷/₈ by 6³/₄
1377.581 Gilcrease
Dated: "June 3rd 1910" u.l.
Inscribed: "Brixham" u.l.; miscellaneous notes
Provenance: TG

1042
AT NEWLYN
Graphite on wove
7¹/₄ by 5
28 East Hampton Library
Inscribed: "at Newlyn" u.c.
Provenance: EH
1916 ledger: 288

1043
LAND'S END
Graphite on wove
7⁵/₈ by 5
22 East Hampton Library
Dated: "July 1906" u.r.
Signed: "TM" u.r.
Inscribed: "Lands End" u.r.
Provenance: EH
1916 ledger: 423

1044
VALLEY OF ROCK, TINTAGEL
Graphite on wove
5 by 6³/₄
1877.19.8 Gilcrease
Dated: "June 7th 1910" u.l.
Inscribed: "Valley of Rock Tintagel" u.l.; miscellaneous notes
Provenance: TG

†1045
TINTAGEL
Graphite on wove
5 by 13¹/₂
1877.19.9 Gilcrease
Dated: "June 9th 1910" u.c.
Inscribed: "Tintagel" u.l. and u.c.
Provenance: TG

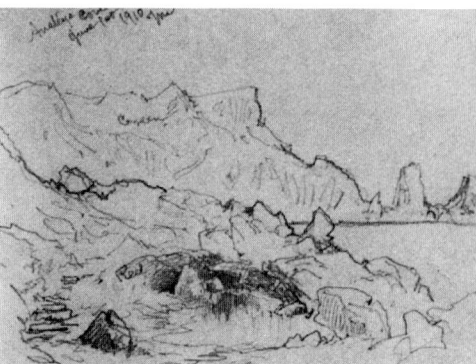

1037

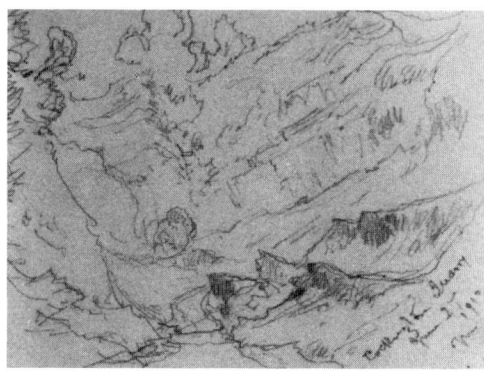

1038

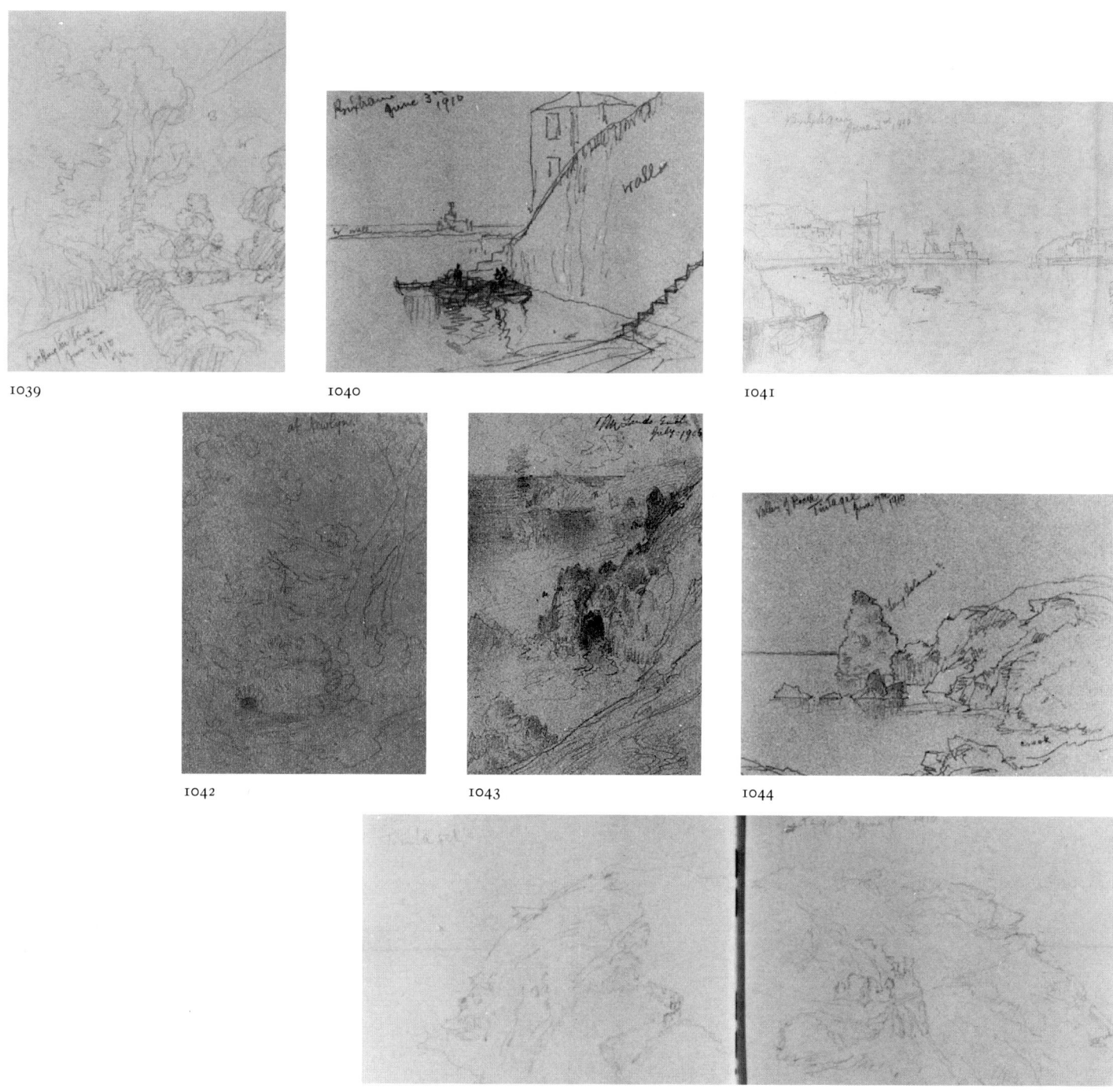

1039

1040

1041

1042

1043

1044

1045

1046
TINTAGEL, FROM OLD CHURCH
Graphite on wove
5 by 13¹/₂
1877.19.10 Gilcrease
Signed: "TM" l.r.
Inscribed: "Tintagel from old Church" l.r.
Provenance: TG

1047
NEAR TINTAGEL
Graphite on wove
5 by 13¹/₂
1877.19.11 Gilcrease
Inscribed: "near Tintagel" u.c.; miscellaneous
notes
Provenance: TG

1048
TINTAGEL, CORNWALL
Graphite on brown wrapping paper
3 by 4¹/₄
1377.841 Gilcrease
Inscribed: "Tintagel Cornwall" l.r.
Provenance: TG

1049
CLOVELLY
Graphite on wove
5 by 6³/₄
1877.19.12 Gilcrease
Dated: "June 11 1910" u.l.
Signed: "TM" u.l.
Inscribed: "Clovelly" u.l.; miscellaneous notes
Provenance: TG
Note: Sketch and inscription on verso: "Clovelly
June 12 1910"

†1050
CLOVELLY
Graphite on wove
5 by 6³/₄
1877.19.13 Gilcrease
Dated: "J 12 1910" u.l.
Inscribed: "Clovelly" u.l.
Provenance: TG

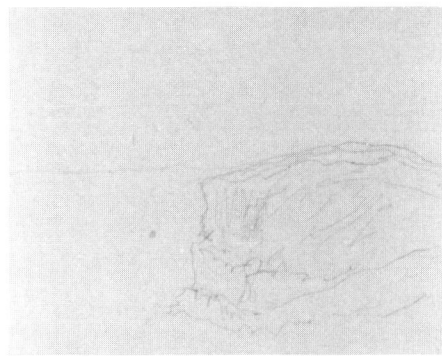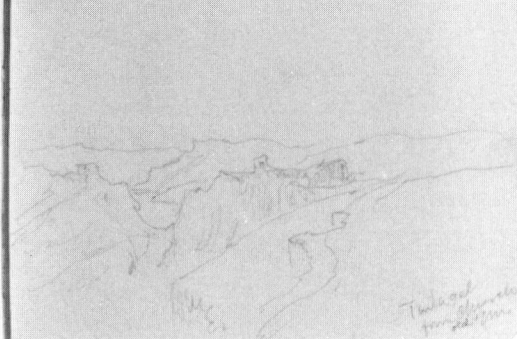

1046

1051
CLOVELLY
Graphite on wove
5 by 6³/₄
1877.19.14 Gilcrease
Dated: "June 13th 1910" l.r.
Inscribed: "Clovelly" and "2" l.r.; "Clovelly" l.l.
Provenance: TG

†1052
ILFRACOMBE
Graphite on wove
6³/₄ by 5
1877.19.15 Gilcrease
Dated: "June 15th 1910" l.l.
Inscribed: "Ilfracombe" l.l.; miscellaneous notes
Provenance: TG

1053
LYNMOUTH LIGHT TOWER AND BAY
Graphite on brown wrapping paper
5¹/₄ by 12³/₄
1377.870 Gilcrease
Dated: "June 17th 1910" l.l.
Inscribed: "Lynmouth light tower and Bay" l.l.;
miscellaneous notes
Provenance: TG

1054
LYNTON
Graphite on Ivorine tissue
4⁷/₈ by 6¹/₄
1377.975 Gilcrease
Dated: "1910" u.l.
Inscribed: "Lynton" u.l.
Provenance: TG

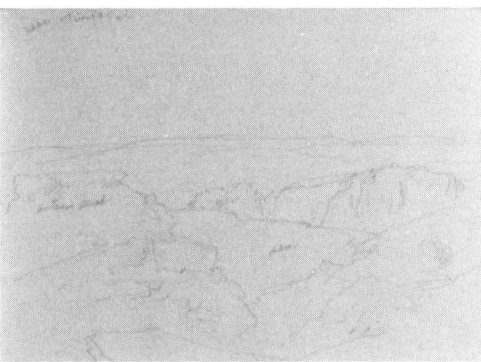

1047

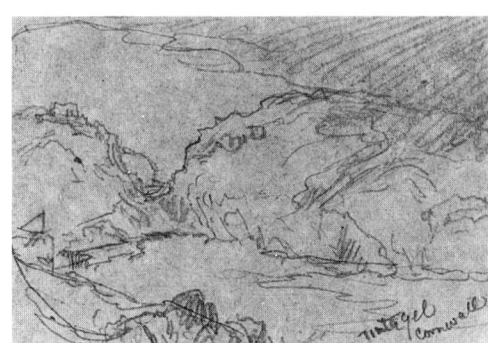

1048

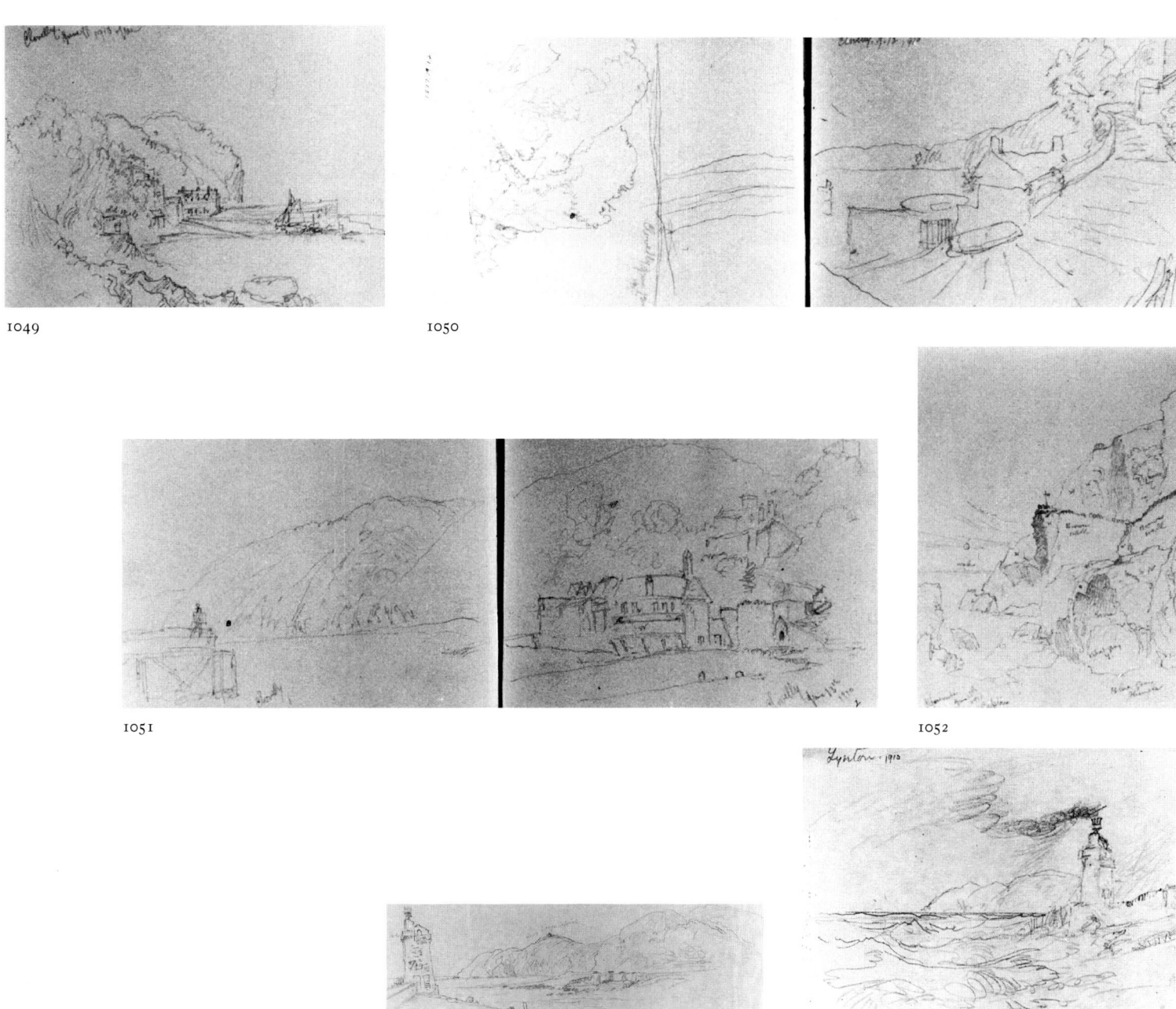

1049

1050

1051

1052

1053

1054

1055
LYNTON
Graphite on Ivorine tissue
4⁷/₈ by 6¹/₂
1377.599 Gilcrease
Inscribed: "Lynton" u.l.
Provenance: TG
Note: Sketch and inscription on verso: "Lynmouth"

1056
LYNTON
Graphite on brown wrapping paper
3 by 4¹/₂
1377.644 Gilcrease
Signed: "TM" l.l.
Inscribed: "Lynton" u.l.; "Lynton Lynmouth
Light." l.l.; miscellaneous notes
Provenance: TG

1057
VALLEY OF ROCKS, LYN
Graphite on wove
5 by 6³/₄
1877.19.16 Gilcrease
Dated: "19–10" l.l.
Inscribed: "V. of Rocks Lyn" l.l.; miscellaneous
notes
Provenance: TG

1058
THE CASTLE, VALLEY OF ROCKS,
LYNMOUTH
Graphite on wove
5 by 6³/₄
1877.19.17 Gilcrease
Dated: "18–10" l.r.
Inscribed: "The Castle. V of Rocks Lynmouth"
l.r.
Provenance: TG

1059
THE LYN
Graphite on wove
6³/₄ by 5
1877.19.18 Gilcrease
Dated: "1910" l.l.
Inscribed: "The Lyn" l.l.; miscellaneous notes
Provenance: TG

1060
LYNMOUTH [descriptive]
Graphite on wove
5 by 13¹/₂
1877.19.19 Gilcrease
Provenance: TG

1061
LYNMOUTH
Graphite on wove
5 by 6³/₄
1877.19.20 Gilcrease
Dated: "June 23–10" l.l.
Inscribed: "Lynmouth" l.l.
Provenance: TG

1062
MONNOW BRIDGE, MONMOUTH
Graphite on wove
4¹/₂ by 7
1377.869 Gilcrease
Dated: "J. 26th–10" l.c.
Inscribed: "Monnow Bridge. Monmouth" l.l.
Provenance: TG
Note: Sketches and inscriptions on verso: "Ludlow J. 28–10" and "Ludlow Castle J. 28–10"

1063
MONNOW MILL, MONMOUTH
Graphite on wove
4⁷/₈ by 6
1377.871 Gilcrease
Dated: "10" l.c.
Inscribed: "Monnow Mill Monmouth" l.c.
Provenance: TG

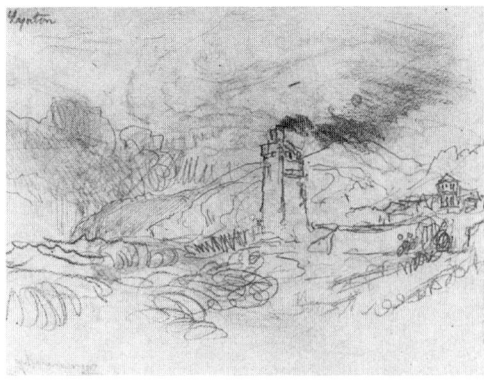

1055

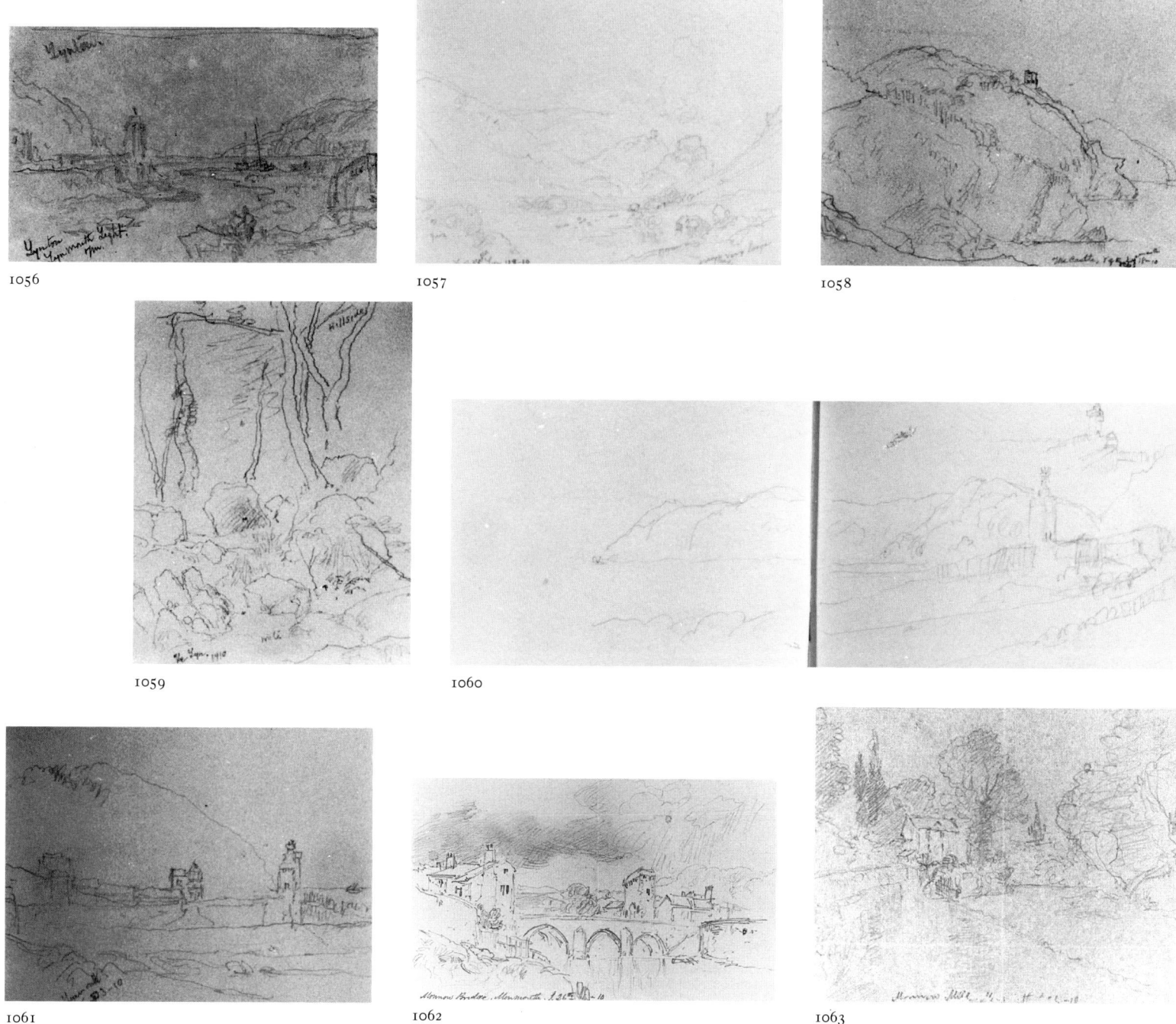

1056

1057

1058

1059

1060

1061

1062

1063

1064
CHEPSTOW
Graphite on wove
5 by 13¹/₂
1877.19.21 Gilcrease
Dated: "1910" l.l.
Inscribed: "Chepstow" l.l.
Provenance: TG

1065
CUMBERLAND
Graphite on brown wrapping paper
3 by 4¹/₂
1377.1068 Gilcrease
Inscribed: "Cumberland" and "Kirkstone Pass
& Brother Water" l.l.
Provenance: TG

1066
TROSSACHS
Graphite on wove
5 by 6³/₄
1877.19.22 Gilcrease
Dated: "July 13th–10" l.r.
Inscribed: "Trossachs" l.r.; "Ben. Venue" u.r.
Provenance: TG

1067
NEAR SILVER STRAND, KATRINE,
SCOTLAND
Graphite on wove
6³/₄ by 5
1877.19.23 Gilcrease
Dated: "J. 13–10" l.l.
Inscribed: "near Silver Strand Katrine Scot" l.l.;
miscellaneous notes
Provenance: TG
Note: Sketch and inscription on verso: "Bass
Rock. N. Berwick. I. July 20th 1910"

1068
BASS ROCK
Graphite on wove
5 by 6³/₄
1877.19.24 Gilcrease
Inscribed: "Bass Rock" u.l.
Provenance: TG

1069
CYPRUS POINT [descriptive]
Graphite on wove
5 by 6³/₄
1877.19.26 Gilcrease
Provenance: TG

1070
CYPRUS POINT
Graphite on wove
5 by 6³/₄
1877.19.27 Gilcrease
Dated: "Feb. 16th 1912" u.l.
Inscribed: "Cyprus Point" u.l.; miscellaneous
notes
Provenance: TG

1071
THE LYN
Graphite on wove
5 by 6³/₄
1877.19.28 Gilcrease
Dated: "1910" u.r.
Inscribed: "The Lyn" u.r.
Provenance: TG

1072
CYPRUS POINT [descriptive]
Graphite on wove
9 by 12¹/₂
1337.525 Gilcrease
Provenance: TG

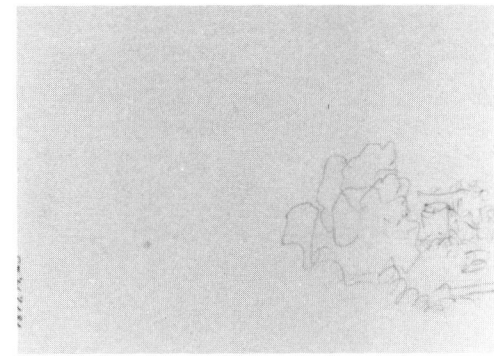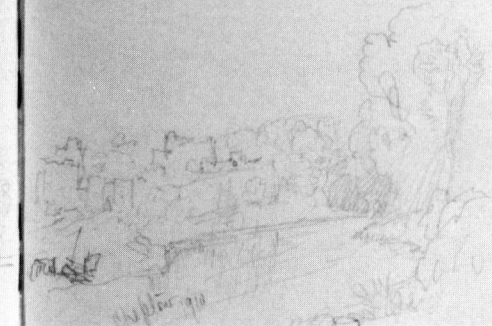

1064

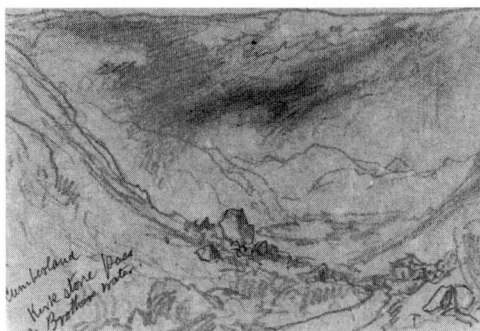

1065

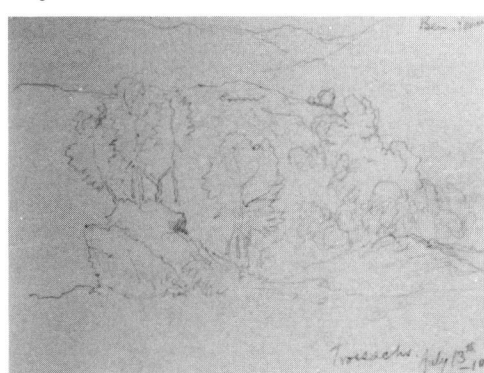

1066

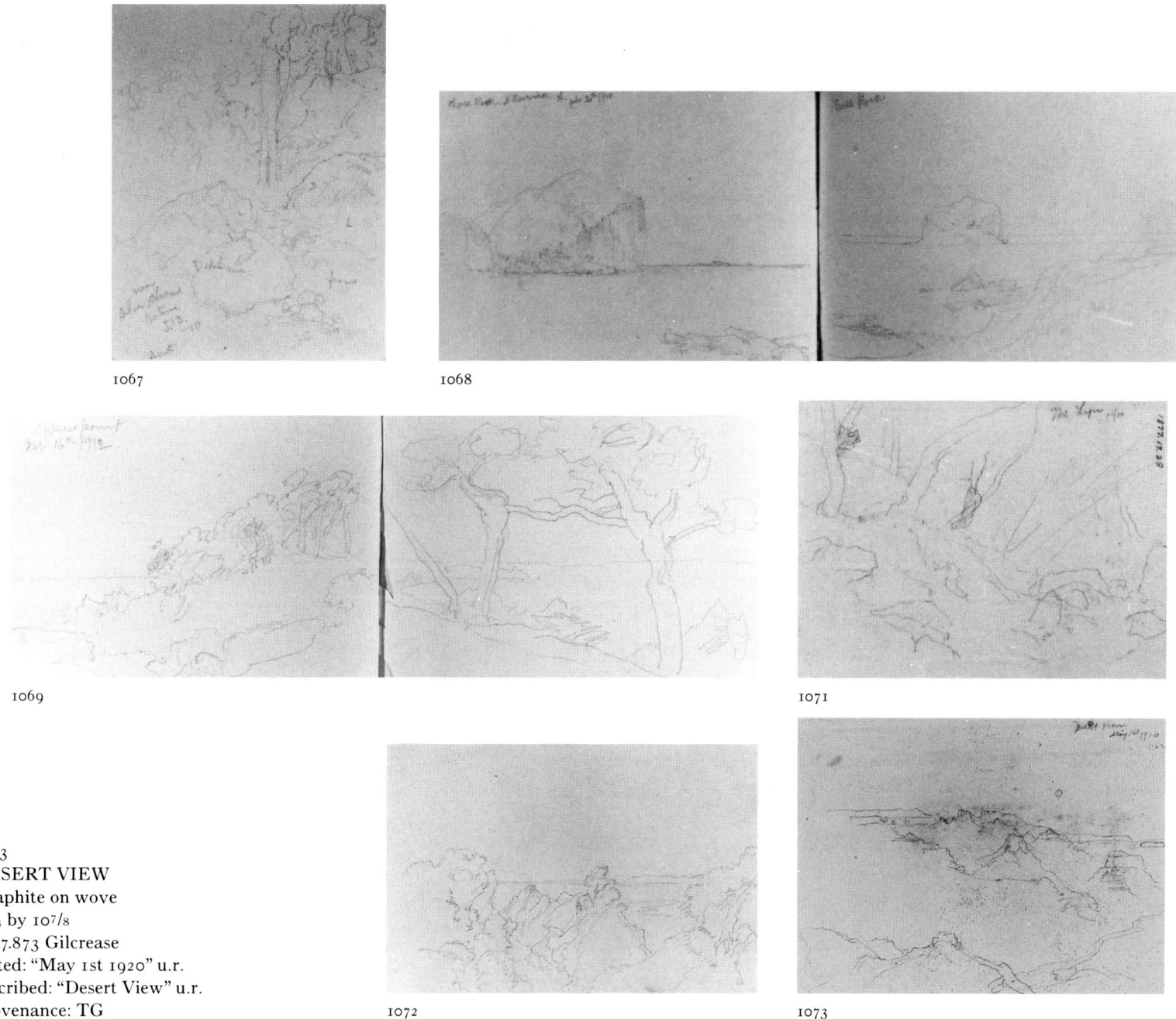

1067

1068

1069

1071

†1073
DESERT VIEW
Graphite on wove
8¹/₄ by 10⁷/₈
1337.873 Gilcrease
Dated: "May 1st 1920" u.r.
Inscribed: "Desert View" u.r.
Provenance: TG

1072

1073

1074
DESERT VIEW
Graphite on wove
8¹/₄ by 10⁷/₈
1337.872 Gilcrease
Dated: "May 15th 1920" u.r.
Inscribed: "Desert View" u.r.; color notes
Provenance: TG

†1075
CHILNUALNA, BELOW THE FALL
Graphite on green wove
18 by 9¹/₂
1337.649 Gilcrease
Dated: "June Saturday" u.r.
Signed: "TM" u.r.
Inscribed: "Chilnualpa below the fall" u.r.
Provenance: TG

†1076
CHILNUALNA FALL [descriptive]
Graphite on green wove
17 by 9³/₈
1337.539 Gilcrease
Provenance: TG

†1077
YOSEMITE [ledger title]
Graphite on blue wove
10³/₄ by 15
1337.859 Gilcrease
Dated: "1904" u.l.
Signed: "TM" u.l.
Provenance: TG
1916 ledger: 85

†1078
NEAR LOS OLIVOS
Graphite on wove
10³/₄ by 15
1337.874 Gilcrease
Dated: "March 29th 1923" u.r.
Signed: "TMoran" u.r.
Inscribed: "Near Los Olivos" u.r.; color notes
Provenance: TG

†1079
NEAR LOS OLIVOS, CALIFORNIA
Graphite on blue wove
10³/₄ by 15
1337.875 Gilcrease
Dated: "March 29th 1923" l.c.
Signed: "TMoran" l.c.
Inscribed: "Near Los Olivos Cal" l.l.
Provenance: TG

†1080
NEAR LOS OLIVOS, CALIFORNIA
Graphite on blue wove
10³/₄ by 15
1337.876 Gilcrease
Dated: "March 29 1923" l.l.
Signed: "TMoran" l.c.
Inscribed: "Near Los Olivos Cal." l.l.; "the last
out of door sketch made by Mr. Moran.—
R.B.M." l.r. edge
Provenance: TG

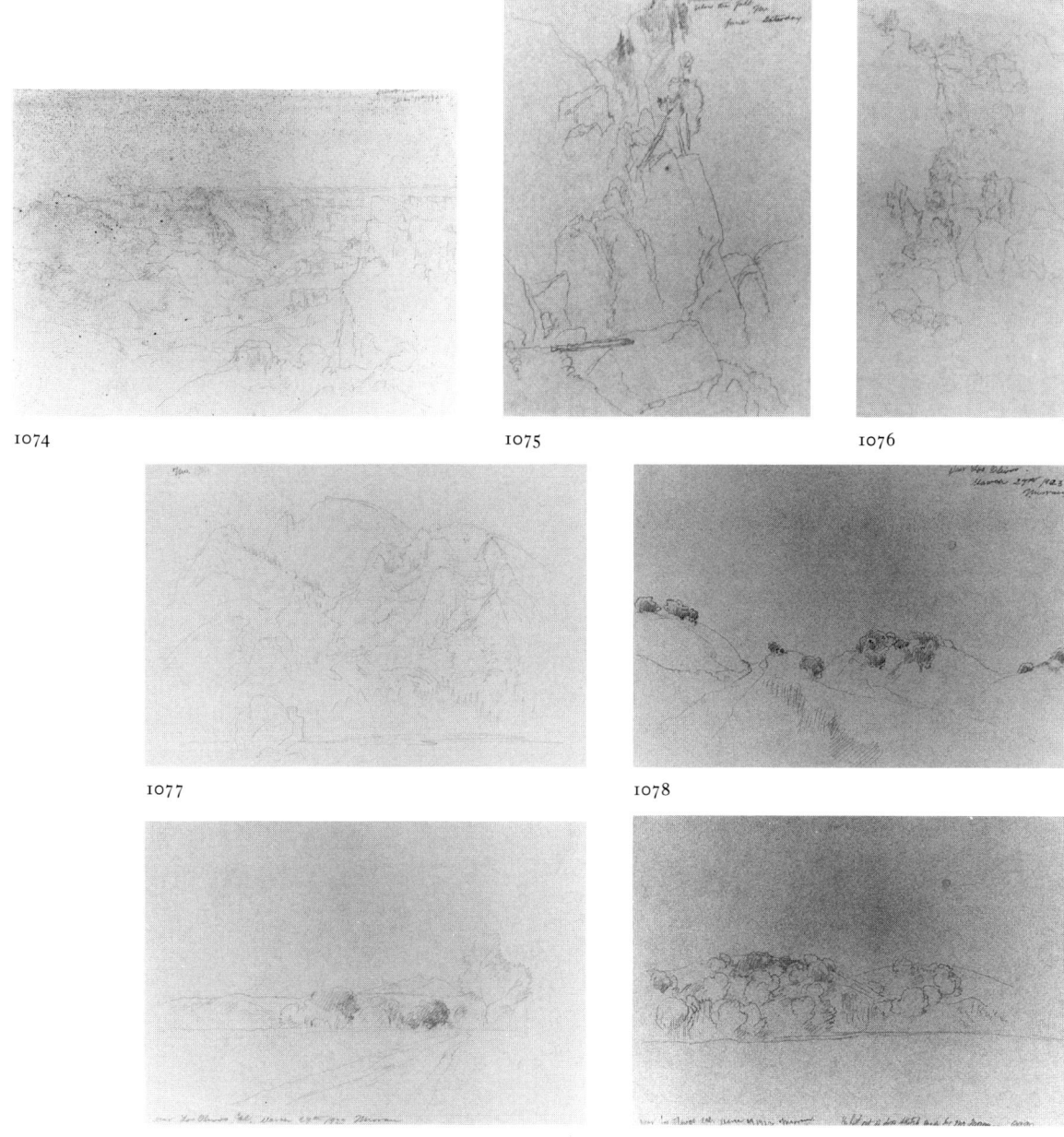

1074

1075

1076

1077

1078

1079

1080

Bibliography

Adamson, Jeremy E., et al. *Niagara: Two Centuries of Changing Attitudes, 1697–1901.* Washington, D.C.: The Corcoran Gallery of Art, 1985.

Anderson, Nancy K. "'The Kiss of Enterprise': The Western Landscape as Symbol and Resource." In *The West as America: Reinterpreting Images of the Frontier,* ed. William H. Truettner, pp. 237–83. Washington, D.C.: Smithsonian Institution Press, 1991.

Anderson, Nancy K., and Linda S. Ferber. *Albert Bierstadt: Art and Enterprise.* New York: Brooklyn Museum, 1991.

Anderson, Ralph H. "Carleton E. Watkins, Pioneer Photographer of the Pacific Coast." *Yosemite Nature Notes* 32 (April 1953): 33–37.

Bassford, Amy O., and Fritiof Fryxell, eds. *Home Thoughts from Afar: Letters of Thomas Moran to Mary Nimmo Moran.* East Hampton, N.Y.: East Hampton Free Library, 1967.

Boehme, Sarah E. *Rendezvous to Roundup: The First 100 Years of Art in Wyoming.* Cody, Wyoming: Buffalo Bill Historical Center, 1990.

Brocklehurst, Thomas U. *Mexico To-Day: A Country with a Great Future.* London: John Murray, 1883.

Bromley, Isaac H. "Wonders of the West: The Big Trees and Yosemite." *Scribner's Monthly* 3 (January 1872): 261–77.

Bryant, William Cullen, ed. *Picturesque America, or the Land We Live In.* New York: Appleton, 1874.

Buek, Gustave. "Thomas Moran, N.A., 'The Grand Old Man of American Art.'" *The Mentor* (August 1924): 29–37. Reprinted in Fritiof Fryxell, *Thomas Moran: Explorer in Search of Beauty,* pp. 63–71. East Hampton, N.Y.: East Hampton Free Library, 1958.

Carr, Gerald L. *The Icebergs.* Dallas: Dallas Museum of Fine Arts, 1980.

Clark, Carol. "Thomas Moran's Watercolors of the American West." Ph.D. dissertation, Case Western Reserve University, 1981.

———. *Thomas Moran: Watercolors of the American West.* Austin: University of Texas Press, 1980.

Claude Lorrain: Dessins du British Museum. Paris: Musée du Louvre, 1979.

Cole, Thomas. "Essay on American Scenery." Originally published 1836. In *American Art 1700–1960, Sources and Documents in the History of Art,* ed. John W. McCoubrey. Englewood Cliffs, N.J.: Prentice-Hall, 1965.

Crane, Newton. "Fairmount Park." *Scribner's Monthly* 1 (January 1871): 225–38.

Cumberland, Charles C. *Mexico: The Struggle for Modernity.* London: Oxford University Press, 1968.

Cunningham, Elizabeth. *Masterpieces of the American West: Selections from the Anschutz Collection.* Denver: Anschutz Collection, 1983.

Current, Karen. *Photography and the Old West.* New York: Abradale Press, 1978.

De Janosi, Carlette Engel. "The Forest of Fontainebleau in Painting and Writing." *The Journal of Aesthetics and Art Criticism* (June 1953): 390–96.

Dodge, Julia E. "Island of the Sea." *Scribner's Monthly* 14 (September 1877): 652–61.

Drawings and Watercolors of the West: Thomas Moran from the Collection of the Cooper-Hewitt Museum of Design. New York: Washburn Gallery, 1974.

Eldredge, Charles C. *The Arcadian Landscape: Nineteenth-Century American Painters in Italy.* Lawrence: University of Kansas, 1972.

Ferber, Linda S., and William H. Gerdts, eds. *The New Path: Ruskin and the American Pre-Raphaelites.* New York: Brooklyn Museum, 1985.

Fern, Thomas S. *The Drawings and Watercolors of Thomas Moran, 1837–1926.* Notre Dame, Ind.: Art Gallery of the University of Notre Dame, 1976.

Fink, Lois. "American Artists in France, 1850–70." *The American Art Journal* (November 1973): 32–49.

Foote, Mary Hallock. "A Diligence Journey in Mexico." *Century* 23 (November 1881): 1–14.

———. "From Morelia to Mexico City on Horseback." *Century* 23 (March 1882): 643–55.

———. "A Provincial Capital of Mexico." *Century* 23 (January 1882): 321–33.

Fowler, Don D. *The Western Photographs of John K. Hillers: Myself in the Water.* Washington, D.C.: Smithsonian Institution Press, 1989.

Fryxell, Fritiof. "Thomas Moran's Journey to the Tetons in 1879." *Augustana Historical Society Publications* 2 (1932): 3–12.

Gaunt, William. *A Concise History of English Painting.* New York: Frederick Praeger, 1964.

Goetzmann, William H. *Exploration and Empire.* New York: Alfred A. Knopf, 1966.

Goetzmann, William H., and William N. Goetzmann. *The West of the Imagination.* New York: W. W. Norton, 1986.

Hales, Peter B. *William Henry Jackson and the Transformation of the American Landscape.* Philadelphia: Temple University Press, 1988.

Hayden, F. V. *Preliminary Report of the United States Geological Survey of Montana and Portions of Adjacent Territories; Being a Fifth Annual Report of Progress.* Washington, D.C.: U.S. Government Printing Office, 1872.

———. "The Wonders of the West—II: More About the Yellowstone." *Scribner's Monthly* 3 (February 1872): 388–96.

Headley, J. T. "Philadelphia." *Scribner's Monthly* 2 (July 1871): 225–40.

Herbert, Robert L., ed. *The Art Criticism of John Ruskin.* Gloucester, Mass.: Peter Smith, 1969.

Hults, Linda C. "Thomas Moran's *Shoshone Falls:* A Western Niagara." *Smithsonian Studies in American Art* 3 (Winter 1989): 89–102.

Ingersoll, Ernest. "The Caverns of Luray." *Century* 23 (January 1882): 377–88.

———. *The Crest of the Continent: A Record of a Summer's Ramble in the Rocky Mountains and Beyond.* Chicago: R. R. Donnelley, 1885.

———. "Silver San Juan." *Harper's Monthly Magazine* 64 (April 1882): 689–704.

Jackson, Clarence. *Picture Maker of the Old West: William Henry Jackson.* New York: Charles Scribner's Sons, 1947.

Jackson, William H. *Time Exposure.* New York: G. P. Putnam's Sons, 1940.

———. "With Moran in the Yellowstone." *Appalachia* (September 1938). Reprinted in Fritiof Fryxell, *Thomas Moran: Explorer in Search of Beauty,* pp. 49–61. East Hampton, N.Y.: East Hampton Free Library, 1958.

Jones, William C. "William Henry Jackson in Mexico." *American West* 14 (July–August 1977): 10–19.

Kelly, Franklin. *The Early Landscapes of Frederic Edwin Church, 1845–54.* Fort Worth, Texas: Amon Carter Museum, 1987.

———. *Frederic Edwin Church.* Washington, D.C.: Smithsonian Institution Press, 1989.

———. *Frederic Edwin Church and the National Landscape.* Washington, D.C.: Smithsonian Institution Press, 1988.

Kinsey, Joni L. "Creating a Sense of Place: Thomas Moran and the Surveying of the American West." 2 vols. Ph.D. dissertation, Washington University, St. Louis, 1989.

———. *Thomas Moran and the Surveying of the American West.* Washington, D.C.: Smithsonian Institution Press, 1992.

Ladegast, Richard. "Thomas Moran, N.A." *Truth* 19 (September 1900): 209–12.

Langford, Nathaniel P. "The Ascent of Mount Hayden: A New Chapter in Western Discovery." *Scribner's Monthly* 4 (June 1873): 129–57.

———. "The Wonders of Yellowstone." *Scribner's Monthly* 2 (May 1871): 1–17; 3 (June 1871): 113–28.

Lurie, Ann Tzeutschler. "Corot: *The Roman Campagna.*" *Bulletin of the Cleveland Museum of Art* (February 1966): 51–57.

Modelski, Andrew M. *Railroad Maps of North America: The First Hundred Years.* Washington, D.C.: Library of Congress, 1984.

Monteith, James. *Barne's Complete Geography.* New York: American Book Co., 1885.

Moran, Thomas. "Knowledge a Prime Requisite in Art." *Brush and Pencil* (April 1903): 14–16.

Morand, Anne, and Nancy Friese. *The Prints of Thomas Moran.* Tulsa, Okla.: Thomas Gilcrease Institute, 1986.

The Moran Family. Huntington, N.Y.: Heckscher Museum, 1965.

Newhall, Beaumont, and Diana E. Edkins. *William Henry Jackson.* Forth Worth, Texas: Amon Carter Museum, 1974.

Ostroff, Eugene. *Western Views and Eastern Visions.* Washington, D.C.: Smithsonian Institution Traveling Exhibition Service, 1981.

Pangborn, J. G. *Picturesque B & O.* Chicago: Knight and Leonard, 1882.

Parry, Ellwood C., III. *The Art of Thomas Cole: Ambition and Imagination.* Newark, Del.: University of Delaware Press, 1988.

Philadelphia: Three Centuries of American Art. Philadelphia: Philadelphia Museum of Art, 1976.

Pomeroy, Earl. *In Search of the Golden West: The Tourist in Western America.* Lincoln: University of Nebraska Press, 1957, 1990.

Powell, John Wesley. *Report of Explorations in 1873 of the Colorado of the West and Its Tributaries.* Washington, D.C.: U.S. Government Printing Office, 1874.

Reilly, Bernard F., Jr. "The Early Work of John Moran, Landscape Photographer." *American Art Journal* 79 (Winter 1979): 65–75.

Ruskin, John. *The Elements of Drawing.* Originally published 1872. Reprint, New York: Dover, 1971.

Savage, Charles R. "A Photographic Tour of Near 9,000 Miles." *Philadelphia Photographer* (September 1867): 287–89 and (October 1867): 313–16.

Sears, John F. *Sacred Places: American Tourist Attractions in the Nineteenth Century.* New York: Oxford University Press, 1989.

Seymour, Edward. "Trout-Fishing in the Rangeley Lakes." *Scribner's Monthly* 13 (February 1877): 433–51.

Scharf, Aaron. "Camille Corot and Landscape Photography." *Gazette des Beaux Arts* (February 1962): 99–102.

Schimmel, Julia. *The Western Collection: Stark Museum of Art.* Orange, Texas: Stark Museum of Art, 1978.

Scranton, Philip, and Walter Licht. *Worksights: Industrial Philadelphia, 1890–1950.* Philadelphia: Temple University Press, 1986.

Sheldon, George W. *American Painters.* New York: D. Appleton, 1879.

Sloan, Kim. *Alexander and John Robert Cozens: The Poetry of Landscape.* New Haven: Yale University Press, 1986.

Sweeney, J. Gray. *Artists of Michigan from the Nineteenth Century.* Muskegon, Mich.: Muskegon Museum of Art, 1987.

———. *Themes in American Painting.* Grand Rapids, Mich.: Grand Rapids Art Museum, 1977.

Taft, Robert. *Photography and the American Scene: A Social History, 1839–89.* New York: Dover, 1938, 1964.

Troyen, Carol. "Innocents Abroad: American Painters at the 1867 Exposition Universelle, Paris." *American Art Journal* 16 (Autumn 1984): 2–29.

Truettner, William. "Scenes of Majesty and Enduring Interest: Thomas Moran Goes West." *Art Bulletin* 58 (June 1976): 241–59.

Tyler, Ron. *Visions of America: Pioneer Artists in a New Land.* London: Thames and Hudson, 1983.

Wilkins, Thurman. *Thomas Moran: Artist of the Mountains.* Norman: University of Oklahoma Press, 1966.

Wilson, E. L. "Views in the Yosemite Valley." *Philadelphia Photographer* 3 (1866).

Wilton, Andrew. *J.M.W. Turner: His Art and Life.* Secaucus, N.J.: Poplar Books, 1979.

Index

Illustrations are indicated by italic page numbers.

Acambaro, Mex., 69, 224, *225*, *pl. 57*
Acoma, N. Mex., 81, 272, *273*
Adams Creek, Pa., 27, 29, *31*, 128, *129*, 130, *131*
Adirondack Mountains, 8
Afon Wen, Cardigan Bay, Wales, 65, 214, *215*, *pl. 45*
Airolo, Switz., 140, *141*
Albano, It., 136, *137*
Albuquerque, N. Mex., 274, *275*
Aldine, The, 14, 28, 42, 81
Alfius Creek, Idaho, 8
Allegheny Mountains, 23, 56, 60, 122, *123*, 204, *205*
Alta, Utah, 178, *179*
Amagansett, N. Mex., 53, 196, *197*, 198, *199*, 230, 232, *233*
American Fork Canyon, Utah, 51, 178, *179*, *pl. 27*
Amsteag, Switz., 140, *141*
Angangueo, Mex., 70
Anstey Cove, Eng., 85, *86*, 290, *291*, *292*
Antonito, Colo., 58
Antwerp, Belg., 73
Arboles, San Juan River, Colo., 208, *209*
Argegno, Italy, 140, *141*
Ariccia, Italy, 34
Arizona, 8, 41–44, 77–80, 87–91, 154–56, 250–53, 272–73, 278–82, 286–89, 299–301

Arundel, Eng., 20–21, *23*, 112, *113*, 116, *117*, 156
Atlantic Ocean, 75–76, 244–46
Atoyac, Mex., 220, *221*

Bahama Islands, 98 n. 105
Baltimore, Md., 56, 182, *183*
Baltimore and Ohio Railroad, 56
Baranca River, Cuernavaca, Mex., 274, *275*, *276*, *277*
Bass Rock, North Berwick, Scot., 87, 298, *299*
Beaman, E. O., 43
Beaverhead Canyon, Mont., 143
Belgium, 73
Bell, William A., 67
Belle Fourche Canyon, Wyo., 254, *255*
Belmont, Pa., 142, *143*
Bexhill, Eng., 114, *115*, *pl. 5*
Bierstadt, Albert, 9, 35; *The Rocky Mountains, Lander's Peak,* 35
Big Horn Mountains, Wyo., 256, *257*
Birch, Thomas, 4
Blackmore, William, 38, 67
Blue Lakes, Idaho, 8, 81, 270, *271*, 272, *273*, *pl. 80*
Boettlers Ranch, Wyo., 37, 144, *145*
Boice, S. Dak., 268
Bolivar, Pa., 25, 118, *119*, *pl. 11*

Bologna, Italy, 34, *35*, *140*
Bolton, Eng., *20*, 63, 110, *111*
Bozeman, Mont., 37
Bridgehampton, N.Y., 188
British artists' exhibition in America, 12–13
Brixham, Eng., 292, *293*
Bucks County, Pa., 16
Bull Run, Pa., 130, *131*
Bunner, A. F., 73
Burano, Italy, 75, *248*

Cabin Creek, Wyo., 254, *255*
Cadorus Creek, York, Pa, 108, *109*
Calderon, Mex., 71, 228, *229*
California 6, 38–41, 90–92, 148–51, 174–75, 252, 280–83,
     298–301
Cameron's Cove, Colo., *273*
Cardigan Bay, Wales, 65, 214, *215*
Carisbrooke, Eng., 116, *117*
Castel Gandolfo, Italy, 34, 136, *137*
Catawissa, Pa., 16, 18, *19*, 104, 110, *111*
Catoctin Mountain, W. Va., *202*
Catorce, Mex., 230, *231*
Cedar Ranch, Ariz., 252, *253*
Cedral, Mex., 230, *231*
Celaya, Mex., *84*, 85, 228, *229*
Central Pacific Railroad, 38
Chama, valley, N. Mex., 254
Chapultepec, Mex., *68*, 222
Chase, William M., portrait of Thomas Moran, *pl. 1*
Chepstow, Wales, *298*
Chioggia, Italy, 9, 75, 250, *251*, *pl. 70*
Chirimolla, Mex., 228, *229*
Church, Frederic, 34, 46, 56, 75, 82; *Icebergs,* 75; *Nia-*
     gara, 34, 56, 82
Chwilog, Wales, 214, *215*
Citlalte'petl, Mex., 68–69
Civitavecchia, Italy, 32, *33*, 132, *133*
Clovelly, Eng., *86*, 294, *295*
Cockington, Eng., *87*, 292, *293*
Cole, Thomas, 5, 9; "Essay on American Scenery," 5;
     Roman Campagna, 33
Cologne, Ger., 75, *76*, 246, *247*
Colorado, 43, *45*, 56, 58, 78–79, 81, 156–58, 206–9,
     254–55, *268–74*
Colorado Springs, Colo., 79, *81*, 270, *271*
Colorado Tourist, The, 58
Communipaw, N.J., 18, 53, *55*, 174, 184, *185*; Morris
     Canal, 184, *185*; sugar refineries 53, *55*, 184, *185*
Conemaugh River (Pa.), 4, 23, 25, *26*, 118, *119*, *pl. 11*
Constable, John, 5, 7, 18, 34

Conway, Wales, 64, *65*, *66*, 82, *83*, 212, *213*, *214*, *215*,
     282, *283*, *284*
Cooke, Jay, 36, 38
Cooke City, Mont., *256*
Cooks Mills, Md., 204, *205*
Cordova, Mex., 220, *221*
Corinne, Utah, 37, *143*
Cornwall, Eng., *85*, *294*
Corot, Jean-Baptiste Camille, 5, 7, 31–32, 34, 72
Cottonwood Canyon, Utah, 51, 176, *177*, 178, *179*, *pls.*
     25, 26, 28, 29
Coyoacan, Mex., 280, *281*
Cozens, Alexander, 9, 34
Crayon, The, 13
Crescentville, Pa., 4, 11, *12*, 16, 104, 108, *109*
Criccieth Castle, Wales, 214, *215*, *pl. 46*
Cripple Creek Railroad, 272, *273*
Cuba, 67, 77, 218
Cuernavaca, Mex., *82*, 274, *275*, *276*, *277*; Baranca
     River, *274, 275, 276, 277*; Cortez Tower, *276, 277*
Culiacan Mountain, Mex., 228, *229*
Cumberland, Md., 56, 58, *61*, 204, *205*
Cumberland, Scot., *298*
Cyprus Point, Calif., 298, *299*

Deal, Eng., 20, 112, *113*; Sandown Castle, 112, *113*
Delacroix, Eugene, 8
Delaware, 104, 130
Delaware River (Pa.), 23, 27, 29
Delaware Valley Resort Cataract Region, Pa., 27
Delaware Water Gap, Pa., 16, *18*, 23, 106, *107*
Denver, Colo., 48, 58, 78, 79, 254; Nesmith Fall, Wel-
     lington Lake, 254, *255*; Smelting Works, 254
Denver Art League, Thomas Moran's Retrospective
     Exhibition, 79
Denver and Rio Grande Railroad, 58, 67
Detroit, Mich., 16
Devils Gate, Utah, 176, *177*
Devils Tower, Wyo., 254, *255*
Devon, Eng., 85
De Wint, Peter, 18
Dodge, Julia E., 44–45
Dollwydellan Tower, Wales, *83*, *84*, 85, *216*, 284, *285*,
     286, *287*
Dolores Hidalgo, Mex., 71, 228, *229*, *pl. 62*
Donner Lake, Calif., 174, *175*
Doughty, Thomas, 4
Dover, Eng., 20, 112, *113*, 130, *131*
Dripping Springs, W. Va., 202, *203*
Durand, Asher Brown, 4, 12, 29; "Letters on Land-
     scape Painting," 12, 29

East Hampton, N.Y., 46, *49*, *50*, 53, 56, *57*, *59*, 72, 79, 85, 91, 168, *169*, *170*, *171*, 186, *187*, *188*, *190*, *191*, *192*, *193*, *194*, *195*, *196*, *197*, *198*, *199*, 200, *201*, 218, *219*, 234, *235*, *236*, *237*, 244, *245*, 270, *271*, 276, *277*, 280, *281*; Egypt Road, 186, *187*, 188, *189*; Fithian's, 186, *187*, *218*, 234, *235*; Fresh Ponds, 234, *235*; Georgica Pond, 56, 57, *187*, 190, *191*, 192, *193*, 196, *197*, 236, *237*; Goose Pond, 190, *191*; Hook Pond, 236, *237*; Mulford's, 186, *187*; Sassafras, 188, *189*

Ecclesborne, Eng., 114

Elko, Nev., *50*, 51, 174, *175*, 176, *177*

England, 5, 7, 11, 13, 18–23, 29, 31, 63, 82, 84–87, 110–17, 130, 216–17, 290–99

Española, N. Mex., 58, 208, *209*

Esperanza, Mex., 68, 220, *221*, *pl. 52*

Faido Pass, Italy, 140

Fairplay, Colo., 156, *157*

Feltville, N.J., 18, 46, 47, *48*, 49, 53, 58, 164, *165*, *166*, *167*, *168*, *169*, *pl. 22*

Flagstaff, Ariz., 77, 252, *253*

Florence, Italy, 34–35, *140*

Florida, 44–47, 49, 77–78, 158–65, 250–51

Fontainebleau, France, 7, 31, *32*, 45, 130, *131*, *132*, *133*

Fort Ellis, Wyo., 37, 143

Fort George Island, Fla., 44–45, *46*, 47, 73, 77, 158, *159*, 160, *161*, *162*, *163*, *164*, *165*, *pl. 21*; Alligator Bend, *162*; Ghost House, 160, *161*, 162, *163*; Lake Isabel, *4–5*, *46*, 47, 160, *161*; Old Slave Quarters, 46, 162, *163*; St. Johns River, 164, *165*

Fort Hall, Idaho, 51, 178

Foster, J. W., 14

France, 7, 29, 31–32, 34, 130–33

Frémont, John C., 35

Gallitzin, Pa., 23, 25, *26*, 120, *121*

Garden of the Gods, Colo., 58, 206, *207*, *pl. 35*

Gardiner Bay, N.Y., 72, 232, *233*, 234, *pl. 68*

Gellée, Claude, 13, 18, 32; *Liber veritatis*, 13

Genzano di Roma, Italy, 136

Germany, 75–76, 246–47

Gillette, Wyo., 78

Glencoe Pass, Scot., *63*, *64*, 210, *211*

Glen Eyrie, Colo., 63, 79, *81*, 206, *207*, 268, *269*, 270, *pl. 39*

Grand Canyon, Ariz., 8, 27, 38, 41–42, *44*, 71, 77–78, 85, 87, *89*, 91, 156, 252, 278, 282, 286, 288, *pl. 74*; Ayres Butte, 156; Bass, 154, *155*; Bright Angel Trail, 272, *273*, 282, *283*, 288, *289*; Desert View, 87, *90*, *299*, 300, *301*; Grand View, *278*, 286, *287*, 288, 300;

Hance Camp, *78*, 250, *251*; Hance Canyon, 252, *253*; Hance Trail, 252, *253*; Havasupai Point, 272, *273*; Hermit Chasm, 81, 288, *289*; Higgins Point, 252, *253*; Kaibab Plateau, 42; Moran Point, 252, *253*; Muav Canyon, 154; O'Neill Point, 288, *289*; Rowe Point, 272, *273*; Sentinel Point, 286, *287*; Shiva Temple, 78, *80*, 252, *253*; Toroweap, 154

Grand Canyon of the Yellowstone, Wyo. *See* Yellowstone, Wyo.

Great Britain, 53, 82. *See also* England *and other place-names*

Green River (Utah), 63

Green River (Wyo.), 3, 6, 8–9, 36–37, 51–52, *53*, *54*, 63, 142, *143*, 180, *181*, 182, *183*, 210, *211*, *pls. 17, 32, 33, 34, 40*

Greenwich Park, Eng., 20, 21, *22*, 110, *111*

Hackensack Meadows, N.J., 184, *185*

Haden, Francis Seymour, 63

Hamilton, James, 13, 32, 35

Harlech, Wales, 64–65, *66*, 82, *83*, 85, 214, *215*, 216, *217*, 286, *pl. 44*

Harpers Ferry, W. Va., 58, *60*, 200, *201*, 202, *203*

Harper's Monthly, 18, 58

Harper's Weekly, 38

Hastings, Eng., 7, 20, 82, 112, *113*, *114*, *115*, *pls. 4, 6, 7, 8*

Havana, Cuba, 67, 77, 218, *219*, *pls. 47, 48*

Hayden, Ferdinand V., 36–38, 41, 81; *Yellowstone National Park and the Mountain Ranges of Portions of Idaho, Nevada, Colorado and Utah*, 81

Heart Mountain, Wyo., 256, *257*

Heywood Hot Springs, Colo., 58, 206, *207*, *pl. 38*

Hillers, John K., 7, 27, 41–43; *Virgin River Valley, below Zion Canyon, Utah*, 41

Hoboken, N.J., *186*

Holmes, William Henry, 43

Homer, Winslow, 8, 9

Huehuetoca, Mex., 274, *275*

Huntingdon, Pa., 23, *24*, *25*, 104, 116, *117*, 118, *119*

Huntington Mills, Pa., 104

Icebergs, Atlantic Ocean, *75*, *76*, 244, *245*, 246, *247*

Idaho, 8, 51–53, 81–82, 143, 178–81, 270–73

Ilfracombe, Eng., *85*, 87, 294

Index Peak, Wyo., 78, 256, *257*, *pl. 75, 76*

Ingersoll, Ernest, *The Crest of the Continent* (1885), 58

Inness, George, 9

Iowa Gulch, Idaho, 178, *179*, *pl. 31*

Italy, 5–6, 9, 32–35, 72–77, 132–41, 238–42, 246–51

Ixtacihuatl, Mex., 68, *69*, 222, *223*

Jackson, William Henry, 27, 36–38, 41, 43, 58, 78, 79; *Iowa Gulch, 178; Mammoth Hot Springs, 37; Minerva Terrace, 79, 80; Yellowstone Lake, 37, 38*
Jacksonville, Fla., 44, 158, *159*
Jaral, Mex., 228, *229*
Johnstown, Pa., 23–24, 118, *119, pl. 10*
Juniata River (Pa.), 4, 23–24, *25, 28,* 118, *119,* 122, *123*

Kanab, Utah, 41
Karst, John, 56, 58
Kensett, John Frederick, 54

La Borda, Mex., 280, *281*
La Rita, N. Mex., 274, *275*
Laguna, N. Mex., 81, 87, *89,* 254, *255,* 272, *273,* 288, *289,* 290, *291*
Lake Albano, Italy, 34
Lake Como, Italy, 34, 140, *141*
Lake Cuitzeo, Mex., 224, *225*
Lake Katrine, Scot., 87, 298, *299*
Lake Nemi, Italy, 34, 136, *137*
Lake Superior, Mich., 4, 6–8, 14, *15, 16, 17,* 104, *105,* 106, *107;* Pictured Rocks, Miners River, 4, *15, 16, 17,* 24, *105,* 106, *107*
Lake Tahoe, Calif., 51
Land's End, Eng., 292, *293*
Langford, Nathaniel P., 6, 35–36
Laredo, Mex., 67, 70
Lear, Edward, 8
Leghorn, Italy, 32, *33,* 132, *133*
Lehi, Utah, 41
Lewes, Eng., 20, 114, *115*
Liverpool, Eng., 20, 110, *111*
Lizard Head, Colo., 268, *269*
Lockport, Pa., 4, 23, 25–26, 118, *119*
London, Eng., 63, 67; Houses of Parliament, from Hungerford Bridge, 20–21, *22,* 110, *111;* St. Paul's Cathedral, from Waterloo Bridge, 20, 110, *111*
Longfellow, Henry Wadsworth, *Song of Hiawatha,* 15
Long Island, N.Y., 5, 46, 49, 53, 56, 64, 79, 192, *193,* 234, 242, *243,* 244, *245*
Lorrain, Claude. *See* Gellée, Claude
Los Olivos, Calif., *91, 92,* 300, *301*
Los Piños Valley, Colo., 208, *209*
Luray Cave, Va., 58, *62, 204, 205*
Lyn, Eng., 296, *297,* 298, *299*
Lynmouth, Eng., 294, *295,* 296, *297*
Lynton, Eng., 294, *295,* 296, *297*

Madison, Wis., 43–44, 158, *159, pl. 20*
Maine, 6, 8, *40,* 41, 46, 150

Malamocco., Italy, 75, 77, 250, *pl. 73*
Manayunk, Pa., 18, *19,* 23, 53, 108, *109,* 198
Manitou, Colo., *273,* 274
Manuelito, Ariz., 252, *253*
Mapleton, Pa., 122, *123*
Maravatio, Mex., 69, *70,* 222, *223, 224, 225,* 226, *227, pls. 54, 55, 56*
Margate, Eng., 5, 20, *21,* 112, *113*
Marquette, Mich., 105
Martha Lake, Utah, *210, 211*
Maryland, 56, 58, 61, 200–201, 204–5
Mesa Encantada, N. Mex., 272, *273*
Metlac River, Mex., 220, *221*
Mexican National Railroad, 67, 70
Mexico, 5–6, 8, 67–72, 82, 84–85, 218–33, 274–78, 280–81; Gulf of, *67,* 218, *219, pl. 49*
Mexico City, Mex., 68–69, 82, 222, *223, pl. 53*
Michigan, 4, 6–8, 14–17, 104–6
Milford, Pa., 27, 29, *30,* 122, *123,* 126, *127,* 130, *131*
Mill Creek, Pa., 4, 25, *27, 28,* 122, *123*
Monmouth, Eng., Monnow bridge and mill, 296, *297*
Montana, 37, 143, 256
Montauk, N.Y., 49, *50,* 53, 170, *171, 172, 173, 175,* 190, *191,* 192, *193,* 194, *195,* 198, *199,* 200, 234, *235, 236, 237,* 270
Monterrey, Mex., 71–72, 230, *231, 232, 233, pl. 65*
Moore, Charles, 36
Moran, Edward, 13, 16, 18, 23
Moran, John, 7, 16, 18, 25, 27, 37; photograph of Thomas Moran's *The Wissahickon, 18*
Moran, Mary Nimmo, 16, 29, 34, 39, 41, 46, 63, 65, 72, 77, 81
Moran, Paul Nimmo, 29, 77–78
Moran, Peter, 13, 49, 51
Moran, Thomas: *Autumn on the Conemaugh* (painting), 34; *Bridge in the Pass of Glencoe—Scotland* (etching), 210; *Castle Buttes, Green River, Wyoming* (watercolor), 182; *Cave of the Winds, Niagara* (painting), 200; *Chasm of the Colorado* (painting), 43; *Children of the Mountain* (painting), 34; *Church of San Juan—New Mexico* (etching), 208; *Cockington Lane* (painting), 87; *Conway Castle* (etching), 65, 214; *Death of Pan-Puk-Keewis* (watercolor), *14; English River* (etching), 216; *Fiercely the Red Sun Descending* (painting), 15; *Fiesta at Cuernavaca* (painting), 72, *pl. 67; Fingal's Cave, Island of Staffa* (painting), 212; *Gate of Venice* (etching), 73, 240; *Gate of Venice* (painting), 73; *Grand Canyon of the Yellowstone* (painting), 37, 43; *The Great Falls of the Snake River* (chromolithograph), *pl. 81; Harlech Castle—Wales*

(etching), 65, 216; *Hiawatha and the Serpents of Kenabeek* (painting), 15; *Hot Springs of Gardiner's River* (watercolor), 67; *Indian Pueblo, Laguna, New Mexico* (painting), 87; *La Rita, New Mexico* (painting), 274; *Lower Manhattan from Communipaw* (painting), 53; *Mountain of the Holy Cross* (painting), 43, 67, 82; *Mud Volcano* (watercolor), *36*; *Near the Source of the Potomac* (wood engraving), 56, 204; *Orizaba, Mexico* (watercolor), 220; *Pass at Glencoe, Scotland* (watercolor), 64, *pl. 41*; *Pass of Glencoe* (etching), 64, 210; *Rainbow over Niagara Falls* (painting), 56; *Rapids below Lower Suspension Bridge, Niagara* (wood engraving), 200; *St. John's River, Florida* (steel engraving), 164; *San Pablo Beach Florida* (painting), 77; *Sassafras Trees* (etching), 98; *Scene on Tohickon Creek, Autumn* (painting), 16; *Shoshone Falls of the Snake River* (painting), 81–82, *pl. 82*; *Spectres from the North* (painting), 75, *pl. 69*; *Strathaven Castle—Scotland* (etching), 64, 210; *Street in Harper's Ferry* (wood engraving), 202; *Summer on the Susquehanna at Catawissa* (painting), 18, *pl. 3*; *Upper Falls of the Yellowstone* (watercolor), 27, *pl. 13*; *Vera Cruz* (painting), 72, *pl. 66*; *Wissahickon* (painting), 16; *Yellowstone Range from Near Ft. Ellis* (watercolor), 24, *pl. 9*

Morelia, Mex., 8, 70, 226, *227*, *pl. 60*

Mountain of the Holy Cross, Colo., 41, 43, 45, 158; Alpine Pass at Cascade, Twin Lakes, 158; Arkansas Divide, 156; Camp of the Evening Star on the Platte, 43, *45*, 156, *157*; Camp of the Two Pines, 156, *157*; Camp on Eagle River, 156, *157*; Camp on the Upper Arkansas in Tennessee Pass, 156, *157*; Camp Vexation, 43, *45*, 156, *157*; Canyon beyond Fairplay, 156, *157*; Delano Valley, Eagle River, 156, *157*; Holy Cross Creek, 156, 157; Twin Lake, *158*

Mount Desert, Me., 46

Mount Nebo, Utah, *150*, *151*

Munising, Mich., *16*, 17, 106, *107*

Murano, Italy, 75, 77, 246, *247*, *248*, *249*, *pl. 71*

Napeague, N.Y., 194, *195*, 232, *233*, *234*

Naples, Italy, 32, 34, 136, *137*

Needles, Calif., 252, *253*

Nevada, 50–51, 174–77

Newark, N.J., 5, 42, 46, 53, *55*,'57, 174, *175*, 182, *183*, *184*, *185*

New Forest, Eng., 216, *217*

New Jersey, 5, 46–49, 164–69, 172–75, 182–86

Newlyn, Eng., 292, *293*

New Mexico, 9, 56, 58, 81, 87–89, 206–9, 250, 252–55, 272–75, 288–91

Newport River, St. Clair, Mich., 106

New York, state of, 5, 46, 49–50, 53, 56–57, 59–60, 72–73, 77–79, 106, 168–74, 186–201, 218–19, 232–37, 242–44, 270–71, 276–77, 280–81

Niagara Falls, N.Y., 56, *59*, *60*, 81, 200; American Falls, from Goat Island, 60, 200, *201*; Niagara River, from Brock Monument, 56, 59, 200, *201*; Rapids below Lower Suspension Bridge, *59*, 200, *201*

Northern Pacific Railroad, 36

Ohiopyle, Pa., 58, *62*, 204, *205*, *206*

Ojo Caliente, N. Mex., 58, 206, *207*, *pl. 37*

Olmsted, Frederick Law, 39

Orizaba, Mex., 68, 220, *221*, *pl. 52*

O'Sullivan, Timothy, 7, 81

Palestrina, Italy, 34

Palmer, William J., 67; sketch of home, *268*

Pangborn, J. G., 56, 58; *Picturesque B. & O. Historical and Descriptive* (1882), 56

Paris, France, 29, 31, 34

Paso del Macho, Mex., *220*

Passaic Falls, Pa., *108*, *109*

Pellestrina, Italy, 250, *251*

Pennsylvania, 4–7, 11–14, 16–19, 23–32, 34–35, 56, 58, 61, 62, 104–11, 116–30, 140–43, 204–7

Pennsylvania Central Railroad, 23

Philadelphia, Pa., 4, 11–14, 16, 18, 104; Fairmount Park, 4, 14, 34, 105; Fairmount Water Works, 13, *14*, 104, *105*

Pike County, Pa., 23, 27, 31–32

Pikes Peak, Colo., 43, 79, *81*, 270, *271*, *273*

Pittsburgh, Pa., 56, 58, *61*, 204, *205*, 206, *207*

Platte River (Colo.), 43

Point of Rocks, Md., 200, *201*

Popocatépetl, Mex., 68, *69*, *222*, *223*

Portchester, Eng., 114, *115*

Port Clinton, Pa., 18, *19*, 110, *111*

Portneuf Canyon, Idaho, 8, 51, 178, *179*, *pl. 30*

Potomac River (W. Va.), 56, *60*, *202*, 204, *205*

Powell, John Wesley, 27, 38, 41–42, 49

Pozzuoli, Italy, 34

Prang, Louis, 79, 81; after Thomas Moran's *Great Falls of the Snake River*, *pl. 81*

Quirio, Mex., 226, *227*

Ramsgate, Eng., 20, 112, *113*

Rangeley Lakes, Me., 6, 8, *40*, 41, 150, *151*

Rawley, W. Va., 202, *203*

Raymondskill, Pa., 27, 122, *123*, 124, *125*, 130, *131*

Reading Railroad, 104

Relay, Md., 200, *201*

Rembrandt, 31

Renshaw, Arthur G., 67–68

Richmond, Eng., 5, *20*, 21, *112*

Ringwood, Eng., 216, *217*

Rio Virgin, Utah, 41, *42*, 44, 152, *153*, 154, *155*

Rochester, Pa., 206, *207*

Rocky Mountains, Colo., 43, 91, 272, *273*

Roman Campagna, Italy, 50–56, 24, 32–33, *34*, 134, *135*, 136; Claudian Aqueduct, 134, *135*, 136, *137*; Great Aqueduct, 33, *34*, 134, *135*, 136, *137*; tomb of St. Helena, 134, *135*

Rome, Italy, 5–6, 32, 132, 136, *137*, 138, *139*; Baths of Caracalla, 134, *135*; Colosseum, 6, 32, 132, *133*, *pl. 14*; Palace of the Caesars, 6, 33, 132, *133*, 134, *135*, *pl. 15, 16*; Ponte San Bartolomeo, 132, *133*; Ponte Rotto, 132, *133*; Villa Borghese, 33, *34*, 138, *139*

Rosebud, Wyo., 266, *267*

Ruskin, John, 4, 7, 9–10, 12–13, 18, 63; *Elements of Drawing*, 12; *Elements of Perspective*, 12; *Fragment of the Alps*, 13

Russell, Andrew J., 36

Ruxton, Colo., 274

Sag Harbor, N.Y., 53, 270, *271*

St. Augustine, Fla., 158, *159*

St. Clair, Mich., 16, *17*, 106, *107*

St. Gotthard Pass, Switz., 5, 34, 140, *141*

Saltillo, Mex., 70, *71*, 72, 230, *231*, *pl. 64*

Salt Lake City, Utah, 41, 51

San Francisco, Calif., 38

San Francisco, Mex., 230, *231*

San Francisco Mountains, Ariz., 252

San José, Mex., 70, *226*, *227*, *pl. 59*

San Juan, N. Mex., 9, 58, *208*, *pl. 36*

San Juan Mountains, Colo., 58, 208, *209*

San Juan River (Colo.), 208, *209*

San Luis Valley, Mex., 230, *231*

Santa Barbara, Calif., 91

Santa Catarina, Mex., 230, *231*

Santa Fe Railroad, 77, 87

Santuario, Mex., 228, *229*

Sarony, Napoleon, portrait of Thomas Moran, *12*

Savage, Charles R., *Quarrying Granite for the Mormon Tabernacle, Cottonwood Cañon, Utah*, 176

Sawatch Range, Colo., 43

Sawkill, Pa., 5, 27, *28*, *29*, *31*, 124, *125*, *126*, *127*, *128*, *129*, 130

Schell and Hogan, 56

Schuylkill River (Pa.), 4, 13, 18, 104, *105*; *pl. 2*; falls, 34, *35*, *36*, 104, 140, *141*, 142, *143*

Scotland, 63–65, 85, 87, 210–13, 298

Scribner's Monthly Magazine, 34–36, 38–39, 42, 44–45, 148, 150, 160

Seneca Lake, N.Y., 106, *107*

Shaw, Joshua, 12

Sheridan, Wyo., 254, *255*

Shiprock, N. Mex., 250, *251*

Singleton, Edith, 31

Smith, Roswell, 36

Snake River (Idaho), 51, 81, 178, *179*; Shoshone Falls, 81, *82*, 272, *273*; Taylor's Bridge, 51, *52*, 178, *179*

Somerset, Eng., 85

Southampton, Eng., 116, *117*

South Dakota, 268–69

South Orange, N.J., 172, *173*, *174*

Spanish Fork Canyon, Utah, *40*, 41, *42*, 71, 152, *153*

Spanish Peaks, Colo., 272, *273*

Springville, Utah, 41

Spruce Creek, Pa., 23, 25, *26*, 27, 118, *119*, 120, *121*, *122*, *pl. 12*

Staffa, Fingal's Cave, Scot., *212*

Stevenson, James, 43

Stour Valley, Eng., 5

Strathaven, Scot., *64*, *65*, 210, *211*

Sulphur Mountain, Wyo., 258, *259*

Sunshine River (Wyo.), 256; Clarks Fork, 256, 258

Susquehanna River (Pa.), 110, *pl. 3*

Swallow Falls on the Lledr, Wales, 284, *285*

Swanevelt, Herman, 31

Switzerland, 5, 32, 34, 140

Tahoe, Calif., 174, *175*, *pls. 23, 24*

Teoloyucan, Mex., 274, *275*

Teton Mountains, Idaho, 51, *52*, 53, 79, 180

Three Mile Harbor, N.Y., 53, *198*, *199*, 242, *243*

Tintagel, Eng., *85*, 292, *293*, *294*

Tohickon Creek, Pa., 16, *19*, 108, *109*

Toltec Gorge, Eva Cliffs, Colo., 208; Toltec Tunnel, 208, *209*

Toluca, Mex., 222, *223*

Tongue River (Wyo.), *255*, 256, *257*

Toquerville, Utah, 152

Torquay, Eng., 290, *291*

Trojes Silver Mine, Mex., 70, *71*, 226, *227*, *228*, *pl. 61*

Trossachs, Scot., 87, *298*

Trumbull, Walter, 35

Tula, Mex., *278*

Turner, Joseph Mallord William, 5, 7, 13, 18, 20–21, 23, 32, 34, 64–65, 72–73, 77; *Liber studiorum*, 13;

Richmond Hill and Bridge, Surrey, 21; *Rivers of England,* 20, 23; *Rivers of France,* 13, 32; *Temple of the Sibyl Seen from Below,* 142
Tussey Mountain, Pa., 23, 25, *27,* 120, *121*
Twin Lake, Wasatch Mountains, Utah, *63,* 208, *209*

U.S. Geological and Geographical Survey of the Territories, 35–36
Union Pacific Railroad, 36, 49, 51
Universal Exposition, Paris, France, 29, 34–35, 56
Utah, 37, 40–42, 44, 51, 58, 63, 71, 143, 150–55, 176–78, 208–11

Valley of the Chama, N. Mex., 254
Vandermark, Pa., 27, 29, *30,* 126, *127,* 128, *129*
Varley, John, 18, 64
Venice, Italy, 5, 53, 72–73, *74,* 75, *76,* 77, *238, 241, 242,* 246, *247,* 248, *250, 251, pl. 72, 73;* Campanile, *238, 239;* Campo Santo, *242;* cemetery, *238, 242;* Customs House, *73,* 238, *239, 240;* Garibalde, *248, 249;* Grand Canal, *240, 241;* Lido, *246, 247;* Salute, *238, 239;* San Giorgio Maggiore, 75, 77, *240, 246, 247;* St. Michael in Campo Santo, *73, 74,* 238, *239;* Tutella, *73, 74, 240*
Vera Cruz, Mex., 5, 67–68, 70, 77, 218, *219,* 220, *221, pls. 50, 51, 58*
Verona, Italy, 75–76, 246, *247*
Veta Mountain, Colo., 206, *207*
Villa Alexandria, Fla., 77, *78,* 250, *251*
Virginia, 58, 62, 204
Virginia City, Mont., 37

Wales, 63–66, 82–85, 212–17, 282–87, 298
Warm Springs Creek, Idaho, 143
Warriors Ridge, Pa., 23, *24, 25,* 118, *119*
Warwick, Eng., *84,* 85, 290, *291*
Wasatch Mountains, Utah, 58, *63,* 176, 208, *209*
Washington, D.C., Patent Office, 200, *201*
Watermills, Long Island, N.Y., 190, *191, 192, 193*
Water Street, Pa., 122, *123*
Watkins, Carleton E., 39
Watkins Glen, N.Y., 106, *107*
West Virginia, 56, 58, 60, 200–205
Whitney, J. D., 14
Wight, Isle of, 116, *117*
Williams, Isaac, 14
Wilmington, Del., 104, 130, *131*
Wilmore, Pa., 23–25, *26,* 118, *119,* 120
Wingate, N. Mex., *274*
Windsor, Eng., 20, *21, 22,* 110, *111*
Wisconsin 43, 44, 158

Wissahickon Creek (Pa.), 14, 16, 18, *23, 110, 111,* 116, *117,* 142, *143*
Women's Centennial Committee of Wisconsin, 44
World's Columbian Exposition, Chicago, Ill., 78
Wyoming, 3, 4, 6–9, 24, 27, 35–39, 41, 51–54, 63, 77–80, 142–47, 180–83, 210–11, 254–69

Yellowstone, Wyo., 4, 6–7, 14, 24, 27, 35–38, 39, 73, 77–79, *145,* 258, *259,* 268, *269;* Badlands, 266, *267;* Beehive Geyser, 260, *261;* Beryl Spring, *263;* Bunsen Peak, 37, *38,* 144, *145;* Castle Geyser, 262; Cinnabar Mountain, *144,* 266, *267;* Clematis Gulch, 144; Crystal Falls of Crystal Creek, 145; Devil's Den, 260, *261;* Devils Slide, 144; Excelsior Geyser, 263; Fan Geyser, 263; Gibbon River, Beryl Geyser, 264; Golden Gate, 258, *259,* 260, *261;* Grand Canyon, 37, 79, 144, 260, *261,* 266; Hurricane Vent, 260, *261;* Inspiration Point, 260, *261;* Liberty Cap, 144, 184; Lower Falls, 37, 264, *265,* 266, *267;* Lower Geyser Basin of Firehole River, 37, 79, 262, *pl. 78;* Great Fountain Geyser, 264; Great Springs, 262; Lioness and Cubs, 262; Madison Canyon 6, 38, 146, *147, pl. 18;* Mammoth Hot Springs of Gardner River, 78–79, 144, *145,* 258, *259, pl. 77;* Meadow Creek, 144; Moran Point, 264, *265,* 266, *267;* Mud Volcano, *145, 146;* Norris Geyser Basin, 260, *261, pl. 79;* Old Faithful, 79, 80, 262, *263;* Soda Butte Creek, 256, *257;* Tower Creek, 144; Tower Fall, 37, *144;* Turreted Peaks, 264, *265;* Upper Falls, 37, 264, *265,* 266, *267;* Upper Geyser Basin of Firehole River, 37, 79; White Amphitheater, 264, *265;* Yellowstone Lake, 37, *39,* 41, 146, *147, 261;* Yellowstone River, 37, 144, 266, *267*
Yosemite, Calif., 6, 38, *39,* 41, *91,* 146, *147,* 148, 280, *281,* 300, *301;* Bridalveil Fall, 150, *151;* Cathedral Rock, 282, *283;* Chilnualna Fall, *90,* 91, 300, *301;* El Capitan, 39, 148, *149;* Gentry's, 146, *147,* 148, *149;* Glacier Point, 39, *40,* 41, 148, *149,* 280, *281;* Merced River, 148; Mirror Lake, 150; Moran Point, 280, *281;* Nevada Fall, 39, 148, *149,* 282, *283;* North Dome, 148, *149,* 282, *283;* Royal Arches, 148; Sentinel, 39, 148, *149,* 282, *283;* South Dome, 39, 146, 280, 282, *283;* Vernal Fall, 39, *40,* 41, 148, *149,* 280, *281;* Washington Column, 149; Yosemite Fall, 148, *149*
York, Pa., 108, *109*
Youghiogheny River (Pa.), 58

Zion, Utah, 41, 42, 154, *155, pl. 19*
Zola, Emile, 7, 13